PSYCHOLOGY
ENCYCLOPEDIA

The Dushkin Publishing Group, Inc.
Guilford, Connecticut

Library of Congress Catalog Card Number: 72-90092

Manufactured in the United States of America
Third Printing

PSYCHOLOGY ENCYCLOPEDIA

CONTRIBUTORS

Nina Adams, Yale University

Mona G. Affinito, Southern Connecticut State College

Constance R. Ahrons, Mental Health Associates, Madison, Wisconsin

Jerome G. Alpiner, University of Denver

Richard D. Ashmore, Rutgers University

Frank Auld, University of Windsor, Ontario

Brenda B. Bankart, Wabash College

C. Peter Bankart, Wabash College

W. T. Blackstone, University of Georgia

R. Gary Bridge, Columbia University

Barbara B. Brown, Veterans Administration Hospital, Sepulveda, California

Gordon M. Burghardt, University of Tennessee

Dennis P. Cantwell, University of California, Los Angeles

Morris E. Chafetz, National Institute on Alcohol Abuse and Alcoholism

Alphonse Chapanis, Johns Hopkins University

Walter Cheetham, Southern Connecticut State College

Roger Christenfeld, College of Physicians and Surgeons of Columbia University

Howard M. Cohen, State University College, New Paltz

Kay Deaux, Purdue University

Richard E. Dimond, Sangamon State University

T. L. Engle, Indiana University

David Feldman, Yale University

Mark Fineman, Southern Connecticut State College

James N. Fordham, National Institute of Mental Health

Frank A. Geldard, Princeton University

Austin E. Grigg, University of Richmond

Calvin S. Hall, Author, *A Primer of Freudian Psychology*

Duane Harmon, Southern Connecticut State College

Thom Herrmann, University of Tennessee

Douglas L. Hintzman, University of Oregon

Michael Hirt, Kent State University

Robert B. Innes, George Peabody College for Teachers

Robert M. Julien, University of California, Irvine

Daniel Kirk, Marist College

Walter G. Klopfer, Portland State University

Randolph S. Kraft, Federation of the Handicapped

Igor Kusyszyn, York University, Ontario

M. Powell Lawton, Philadelphia Geriatric Center

Jacob Levine, Veterans Administration Hospital, West Haven

Eugene E. Levitt, Indiana University School of Medicine

Louis G. Lippman, Western Washington State College

Joel F. Lubar, University of Tennessee

Cynthia MacRitchie, Southern Connecticut State College

Bruce L. Maliver, Author, *The Encounter Game*

Ragaa Mazen, Southern Connecticut State College

Irv J. Meitus, Purdue University

Emanuel Messinger, U.S. Veterans Hospital, Northport, N.Y.

Bruce Muller, Southern Connecticut State College

J. R. Newbrough, George Peabody College for Teachers

R. E. Paschke, William James College

Morton S. Perlmutter, University of Wisconsin

Robert Perloff, University of Pittsburgh

Dean G. Pruitt, State University of New York, Buffalo

Earl Rodney Rees, Western Washington State College

Edwin Robbins, New York University Medical Center

Gary Robertson, Test Department, Harcourt Brace Jovanovich, Inc.

Irvin Rock, Rutgers University

Harold Rosen, Johns Hopkins University

Michael Rothenberg, City College of the City University of New York

Joseph Rubinstein, Purdue University

James H. Satterfield, Gateways Hospital, Los Angeles

Gertrude R. Schmeidler, City College of the City University of New York

A. Ronald Seifert, University of Tennessee

Carl E. Sherrick, Princeton University

Edwin S. Shneidman, University of California, Los Angeles

Roland Siiter, Montclair State College

Louis Snellgrove, Lambuth College

Samuel Snyder, Yale University

Aletha Huston Stein, Pennsylvania State University

Harold Stevens, M.D.

Gerald Tolchin, Southern Connecticut State College

Frank T. Vitro, University of Maine

Wilse B. Webb, University of Florida

Alden E. Wessman, City College of the City University of New York

PUBLISHER'S PREFACE

An understanding of the tools of a science is essential to understanding the science—its development, accomplishments, and problems. Modern psychology is a science in all senses of the term, having developed an extensive methodology for generating theories as well as a language that is frequently as technical as that of any of the physical sciences.

The Language of Psychology

Nonprofessional readers are often surprised—and sometimes annoyed—to discover that discourse in psychology—lectures, books, even popular press articles—not only relies on technical terms but also uses ordinary language in special ways. In the language of psychology, even familiar words—"reinforcement," "extinction," "shaping," "meaningfulness," "repression," "savings"—have specific and, for the layman, unfamiliar meanings. It is natural that groups of people with a shared interest, be they sailors or psychologists, usually develop a common vocabulary in which particular words take on precise meanings and connotations. In each case, the jargon may initially appear formidable to outsiders, but there are good reasons for its existence, and its elements are soon mastered. The way in which scientific theories and findings lose or change their meaning when they are translated into simple language for the layman alerts us to the dangers of imprecise vocabulary. Psychologists use a particular terminology in the interests of precision—a vague and varying vocabulary does not help one experimenter explain his work to another.

Simple words often become more complicated because the psychologist's viewpoint is naturally influenced by his own experimental requirements. For example, the psychologist frequently finds it useful to classify everyday experiences into categories that also include the more artificial experiences he creates in the laboratory; and so he uses terms that become a kind of shorthand, conveying more information than the common word. Thus "cheating" becomes "deception"—a concept that includes a number of related behaviors performed under varied circumstances and investigated with similar techniques. For the same reason "eating" becomes "food intake"—a concept that includes forced feeding, intravenous feeding, and the use of surgical techniques that permit food to be ingested without entering the stomach.

Another way in which specialized vocabulary is substituted for common terms derives from the psychologist's need to define phenomena "operationally" (that is, in terms of the operations needed to measure them), so that "hunger" will be referred to as "food deprivation." Hunger cannot be pointed to or measured directly. When we have not eaten for a time, we experience a sensation that we call hunger, and we infer that under similar circumstances others have the same experience. But such words are merely abstractions that derive from consistently observed relationships—they are hypothetical constructs. In order to conduct research on hypothetical constructs, we have to define them in terms of observable behavior: that is, in terms of the operations and techniques used to influence or measure them. In laboratory practice, it is common to manipulate hunger by varying the period of food deprivation, so "food deprivation" is an operational definition for the hypothetical construct "hunger."

In this encyclopedia we have attempted to provide a comprehensive treatment of the language of psychology and of the full range of its theories, practices, and institutions. Our goal has been to fill specific informational needs as clearly and as concisely as possible.

Organization of the Encyclopedia

For maximum utility—because the editors insisted that you should be able to find the information you want in the first place you look it up—we adopted the short-entry, alphabetical form. More than 1,000 relatively short articles—arranged alphabetically and tied together by a system of direct cross references and item guides—form the book's web of easily accessed information. Because of this interweaving structure, almost any article in the encyclopedia can serve as the point of entry for a systematic study of the entire field.

The encyclopedia is fully comprehensive. It was constructed topically first and then arranged alphabetically for ease of access. Because of this organization, we have been able to build a number of guidance functions into it as integrated parts of its information system.

Cross references are of two kinds. *See* references, which appear as individual entries in the alphabetical sequence, take the place of a separate index and send you directly to the location of the information you want. *See also* references at the end of an article direct you to carefully selected supplementary articles.

Subject maps show in a single display the interrelationships among hundreds of articles for each of twelve major areas of psychological study. These subject maps allow you to see at once the encyclopedia's full coverage of the area you're exploring. The maps appear in the book under the following headings:

Abnormal and Clinical Psychology	Personality and Individual Difference
Developmental Psychology	Physiological Psychology
Emotion and Motivation	Psychology: Divisions and Schools
Intelligence	Sensation and Perception
Learning and Memory	Social Psychology
Measurement	Thinking and Language

Item guides point out specific relationships between individual articles in the book and lead in a meaningful sequence from one article to another. They accompany dozens of key articles in this edition.

Consult references at the end of an article or within articles are numerically keyed to a classified bibliography at the back of the volume. All of the bibliography titles have been selected by the authors of the encyclopedia articles as suggestions for further reading. Except for classic works, the bibliography includes mainly recent publications especially useful to nonprofessional readers in the field. A special feature of the encyclopedia is an article on the uses of *Psychological Abstracts,* a monthly publication of the American Psychological Association. With summaries of technical reports, journal articles, and books, it is a major reference tool for finding out more about psychology.

Illustrations are used functionally in the encyclopedia. The computer-composed format permits the inclusion of the original artwork, tables, graphs, charts, and photographs wherever the editors considered them valuable.

Authority

All of the articles in the encyclopedia were prepared by authorities working in their own specialties. Articles of fifteen or more lines in length bear the signature and affiliation of the contributor. The shorter, unsigned pieces were prepared by the same authorities who wrote the longer pieces. The decision not to sign these shorter articles was made for space reasons only. A few articles, primarily of a defining nature, were prepared by the staff as part of the effort to relate topics to each other.

Making an encyclopedia of this length is as much a problem of deciding what to leave out as of what to include. The advisers and authors were involved in a process of assembling an enormous body of information and, at the same time, of paring it down to essentials. We have sought to be of most value to nonprofessional readers, and this purpose guided our decisions about how best to present the information. Thus, all of the authorities listed on the contributor's page were chosen for their long experience in helping people with no training in psychology to understand the field. An examination of the bibliography at the end of this volume will show that many of our authors have made important professional contributions in their own areas of specialization, but for this book each was asked, first, to approach our articles from the viewpoint of the nonprofessional's information needs. Next, each writer was asked to give careful consideration to those points that his experience has shown to be problem areas for nonprofessionals. Finally, each contributor was asked to ensure that every article would be as complete as possible within the limitations of the space available. Thus, we sought to provide the best presentation of information possible within the limits of our chosen length.

Reader's Response

For psychologists, the type, accuracy, and measurability of the information available to them are critical considerations. The editors of this encyclopedia have faced the same problems in trying to meet your needs. Evaluating the quality and usefulness of information and deciding what to include are always demanding tasks. For the editors of this book these tasks are never completed. The revision for the next edition is already under way. Now, however, we hope to add a new level of information to the book: your opinion of it—for now it is possible for you to become involved in the life of this encyclopedia. I urge you to contribute your experience with it through the self-addressed, prepaid Reader's Response Form bound into the book. Please fill the form out. Let us know what you missed in the book, what you think could be done better, what was done well, and what more might be done. I'm looking forward to hearing from you.

Stanley Schindler
Publisher

ABILITY, the knowledge or skill necessary to perform some particular task. Abilities are measured by a variety of different types of tests, such as aptitude, intelligence, and achievement. Most psychologists believe that there is a general overall ability, because skills correlate with each other fairly consistently, although some correlations are very low. Others stress the importance of measuring more specific abilities, such as auditory or visual memory, arithmetic and verbal skills, and reasoning.

—Louis Snellgrove, *Lambuth College*
See also Intelligence and Intelligence Measurement.
Consult (12) Cronbach, 1970.

ABLATION, removing part of the brain of an experimental animal as a way of studying brain function. *See* Brain.

ABNORMAL, a term that is sometimes defined statistically as meaning away from the norm or average. In this sense "abnormal" can mean above or below the average. As usually employed, however, the word connotes disorder or sickness. *See* Abnormal Psychology.

ABNORMAL PSYCHOLOGY, the specialized field of psychology that studies behavior disorders such as mental retardation and mental illness. *(See Subject Map, page 2.)*

Abnormal psychology is closely related to clinical psychology and psychiatry. The difference is that clinical psychologists and psychiatrists focus more on the diagnosis and treatment of cases of psychopathology while abnormal psychologists search for causes and try to develop theories that will explain behavior disorders and provide principles to guide prevention and treatment. The distinction is hard to draw, however, because many clinicians both carry on treatment and make important contributions to theory.

It should also be noted that there is no clear line dividing abnormal psychology and clinical work from the rest of psychology. The distinction between normal and abnormal behavior can be hard to make as, for example, when experts disagree on whether an accused person is to be called "sane" or "insane" or whether he must be sent to a mental hospital. Another instance of the links between abnormal psychology and other fields is the fact that students of the abnormal get many insights from research in the normal areas. Psychologists working with mental illness, for example, now draw on learning theory to explain some problems and to change behavior.
Consult (13) Coleman, 1964.

ABREACTION, a process used in psychotherapy, in which a patient is encouraged to "relive" a painful experience. The assumption is that a conflict or complex involves painful feelings about this experience. The patient has repressed these emotions and is not aware of them, but they continue to cause trouble in his unconscious. The reliving will help him to get rid of the pent-up emotions and may also give him insight into his problems.

Abreaction may be induced by hypnosis. Josef Breuer, an associate of Sigmund Freud, found that he could relieve hysteria by using hypnotic suggestion to enable patients to "get at" repressed experiences. Freud developed the free-association technique as a means to recovering awareness of traumatic episodes. The term "catharsis" is sometimes used for this recovery and release of emotions.

In current practice drugs such as sodium pentothal may be used to speed up abreaction, as in treating soldiers suffering from combat neurosis.
See also Free Association.
Consult (13) Hall, 1954.

ACCIDENT PRONENESS. Attempts have been made to describe a personality type who would be likely to have repeated accidents. However, a study of 35,000 accidents showed that repeaters accounted for only a small proportion of all cases. People described as irresponsible and maladjusted had more accidents than normal people during youth but not in the years past thirty. It seems likely that there is a temporary "accident syndrome"—worry, anger, tiredness, or intoxication can make a person a dangerous driver, for example.

In psychoanalytic theory, some accidents are seen as the results of a person's unconscious wishes to punish himself. An unresolved conflict can make the individual at least temporarily accident prone. Studies of suicide suggest that many so-called accidents are in fact cases of self-destruction.
See also Suicide.
Consult (13) Menninger, 1938. (14) Schulzinger, 1954.

ACETYLCHOLINE (ACh), a chemical transmitter in the nerves. *See* Chemical Stimulation of the Brain.

ACHIEVEMENT DRIVE, the need to attain success and status in society and the development of self-esteem. The study of achievement motivation gained impetus from the work of David McClelland. His primary contribution was in developing a system for scoring its strength and devising testing situations for examining this attribute. He has shown that high achievement motivation is correlated with strong desire to affiliate with other individuals. The study of achievement motivation is of particular concern to industrial psychologists, who have attempted to assess the drive in prospective employees and developing executives.

ABNORMAL AND CLINICAL PSYCHOLOGY

Classifications of Mental and Emotional Disorders

Treatment and Prevention of Mental and Emotional Disorders

BRAIN DISORDERS
    ORGANIC BRAIN DISORDERS
    ACUTE BRAIN DISORDERS
    CHRONIC BRAIN DISORDERS
    APHASIA

PSYCHOTIC DISORDERS (Psychoses)
    FUNCTIONAL DISORDERS
    SCHIZOPHRENIA
    MANIC-DEPRESSIVE PSYCHOSIS
    PARANOIA

PSYCHONEUROTIC DISORDERS (Neuroses)
    AMNESIA
    ANXIETY
    ASTHENIC REACTION (Neurasthenia)
    DEFENSE MECHANISMS
    DEPRESSION
    DISSOCIATION
    DISPLACEMENT
    KLEPTOMANIA
    MULTIPLE PERSONALITY
    NERVOUS BREAKDOWN
    OBSESSIVE-COMPULSIVE REACTION
    PHOBIA
    SCHOOL PHOBIA

PSYCHOSOMATIC DISORDERS
    anorexia nervosa
    asthma
    colitis
    FRIGIDITY
    gastritis
    HYPERTENSION
    hyperventilation syndrome
    HYPOCHONDRIA
    IMPOTENCE
    migraine
    skin disorders
    ulcers

PERSONALITY DISORDERS (Character Disorders)
    addiction
    ALCOHOLISM
    antisocial personality
    COMPULSIVE PERSONALITY
    CYCLOTHYMIC PERSONALITY
    DRUGS AND BEHAVIOR
    EMOTIONALLY UNSTABLE PERSONALITY
    EXHIBITIONISM
    FETISHISM
    HOMOSEXUALITY
    HYPOMANIC PERSONALITY
    HYSTERICAL PERSONALITY
    INADEQUATE PERSONALITY
    MASOCHISM
    NECROPHILIA
    NEUROTIC PERSONALITY
    OBSESSIVE-COMPULSIVE REACTION
    PARANOID PERSONALITY
    PASSIVE-AGGRESSIVE PERSONALITY
    PEDOPHILIA
    SADISM
    SATYRIASIS
    SCHIZOID PERSONALITY
    SOCIOPATHIC PERSONALITY DISTURBANCE
    SUICIDE
    TRANS-SEXUALISM
    TRANSVESTISM
    VOYEURISM

TRANSIENT SITUATIONAL PERSONALITY DISORDERS
    AGING
    BREATH-HOLDING
    CIVILIAN CATASTROPHE REACTION
    COMBAT NEUROSIS
    ENURESIS
    NAIL BITING
    READING DISABILITY
    SPEECH DISORDERS
    TEMPER TANTRUMS
    THUMB SUCKING

MENTAL RETARDATION
    galactosemia
    mongolism
    phenylketonuria (PKU)
    RH factor
    rubella
    INTRA-UTERINE ENVIRONMENT
    borderline retardation
    mild retardation
    moderate retardation
    severe retardation
    profound retardation
    educable mentally retarded
    trainable mentally retarded

MENTAL HEALTH
CLINICAL PSYCHOLOGY
COMMUNITY PSYCHOLOGY
PSYCHOTHERAPY
    GROUP THERAPY
PSYCHOANALYSIS
BEHAVIOR THERAPY
HUMAN POTENTIAL MOVEMENT
PSYCHIATRY
    CHILD PSYCHIATRY
    CHEMOTHERAPY
    ELECTROCONVULSIVE THERAPY
    HYPNOTHERAPY
    PSYCHOSURGERY
MENTAL HOSPITALS
PSYCHOLOGY AND THE LAW

The Subject Maps in the Encyclopedia illustrate the coverage of particular aspects of psychology, showing the interrelationships among the articles in twelve major areas of study. Entries in capital letters are subjects for which there are separate articles in the Encyclopedia. Entries in small letters are cross references.

The Subject Maps appear in the Encyclopedia under the following titles:

Abnormal and Clinical Psychology
Developmental Psychology
Emotion and Motivation
Intelligence
Learning and Memory
Measurement
Personality and Individual Difference
Physiological and Comparative Psychology
Psychology: Divisions and Schools
Sensation and Perception
Social Psychology
Thinking and Language

ACHIEVEMENT TESTS, measures of the amount of information or skill an individual has acquired from past learning. Although such tests are used primarily in educational settings, they are also important to civil service examination procedures and in situations where individuals are tested for knowledge of specialized areas. A test may cover one area, such as history, or a battery of tests may cover several areas. The exams given by teachers in ordinary classrooms are achievement tests in specific subject matter areas.

—Louis Snellgrove, *Lambuth College*
See also Measurement.
Consult (12) Cronbach, 1970.

ACROPHOBIA, excessive fear of heights. *See* Phobia.

ACT PSYCHOLOGY. A German theologian-philosopher named Franz Brentano attempted, during the latter years of the nineteenth century, to broaden the concept of mental phenomena. Helmholtz, Wundt, and members of the British empiricist school of psychology held the popular view that consciousness could be analyzed (as in psychic science) into contents (sensations, images, and feelings) that were the basic elements of experience. Brentano argued that mental acts (hence the name) were the basic elements of experience.

The basic acts of seeing colors, shapes, or objects, hearing sounds, and feeling movements are fundamental to this view. Because the mind is seen as creative and interpretative, any "act" is viewed as intentional. Thus the activity of the mind in judging, sensing, imagining, or hating is regarded as the proper object of psychological studies.

Brentano's argument paved the way for what emerged years later as the Gestalt school of psychology.

—Thom Herrmann, *University of Tennessee*
See also Gestalt Psychology.
Consult (1) Murphy, 1949.

ACTH, adrenocorticotropic hormone. *See* Pituitary Gland.

ACTING OUT, a term that can mean a form of defense mechanism or a procedure in psychotherapy.

Defense mechanisms are ways of dealing with situations in which the ego feels threatened, as by anxiety or guilt. One way to deal with, for example, hostile feelings is simply to "let out" aggression on someone or something. Juvenile delinquents and members of minority groups are sometimes said to act out their frustrations by turning to violence.

In psychotherapy, children may be encouraged to release pent-up emotions by playing with dolls. Adults may take roles in psycho-dramas. The therapist directs and the patient goes on an actual stage and acts out a situation that has troubled him.

ACTIVITY DRIVE, a fundamental need of organisms to expend physical energy, as expressed in restlessness or in general movement. Restricting the movement of organisms has been shown to be one of the severest forms of punishment. Stocks, chains, and small cells adequately demonstrate this form of punishment through confinement. In the laboratory, activity drive forms the rationale for the use of mazes, escape and avoidance procedures, as well as activity wheels. Both descriptive and experimental evidence indicates that there exists a need for activity, which is basic for the survival and well-being of the organism.

—Thom Herrmann, *University of Tennessee*

ACUTE BRAIN DISORDERS, conditions resulting from temporary and reversible impairment of the function of brain tissue. Symptoms may include disorientation, disturbances of memory, judgment, and reasoning, mood changes, delirium, hallucinations, or delusions. In the Standard Nomenclature of the American Psychiatric Association, conditions producing acute disorders are classified as follows: (1) infection within the brain, as in encephalitis or meningitis; (2) infection of the whole system, as in pneumonia or typhoid; (3) intoxication by drugs such as barbiturates or opiate narcotics or by poisons such as lead or gas; (4) intoxication by alcohol; (5) head injury; (6) circulatory disturbances such as arteriosclerosis and cardiac disease; (7) convulsive disorders—epilepsy; (8) disturbances of metabolism such as diabetes, hyperthyroidism, and vitamin deficiency; (9) brain tumors; (10) unknown causes.

Acute disorders are distinguished from *chronic* in that the acute symptoms can usually be cleared up by time and treatment. The distinction is not always easy to make, however, because drugs, poisons, and head injuries can produce either temporary or permanent damage.

See also Brain Disorders; Chronic Brain Disorders.
Consult (13) American Psychiatric Association, 1952; Coleman, 1964.

ADAPTATION, the process whereby an individual responds to changes in his environment by altering his responses to keep his behavior appropriate to new environmental demands. Successful adaptation has been prerequisite to the survival and evolution of all species.

Adaptation is usually thought to require a high level of behavioral integration; the organism must be capable of combining and eliminating responses to meet changing re-

Activity drive. An activity wheel for small mammals serves their need to expend physical energy.

Psychodrama is a technique in psychotherapy in which a small group of people act out a variety of interpersonal roles.

Alfred Adler. Adler's differences with Freud led to the development of "individual psychology."

ADJUSTMENT

Adjustment can mean changing one's activities in response to changing demands from the environment. As the article ADAPTATION points out, such change can be essential for survival. For discussion of adaptation, using insights from biology, see BEHAVIORAL ECOLOGY. Adjustment can also imply merely "going along with the crowd," that is, CONFORMITY. More positive approaches of human adjustment are presented in MATURITY and SELF-ACTUALIZATION. Psychologists' efforts to point out ways to improve the environment are noted in BEHAVIORAL ECOLOGY.

The idea of desirable or effective adjustment has to be defined by contrast with maladjustment. Problems of adjustment (which some handle better than others) are described in PERSONALITY DISORDERS, PSYCHONEUROTIC DISORDERS, MENTAL HEALTH, and related articles.

sponse requirements. While adaptation of reflexive and innate behavior is usually evident only over a number of generations, there is some evidence that even such built-in behavior as nest building in birds will show evidence of adaptation to meet changing environmental requirements.

Most individual adaptation, however, can be explained in terms of the process of operant conditioning. The acquisition of new behaviors and new combinations of behaviors in order to acquire reinforcements and avoid or escape punishments can be viewed as the normal sequence of adaptive responding. In addition to changes in the form of behavior, changes in its rate, force, and sequence can also be seen as adaptive responses. Responses of this kind are evidenced almost immediately at birth: infants, for example, will adapt the rate and the occurrence of sucking in order to make a visual stimulus appear on a wall. Exposure to a variety of environmental stimuli in infancy has also been shown to increase an individual's adaptive abilities, suggesting that adaptation depends as much on experience as on genetically determined factors.

The term "adaptation" is used in a more limited sense to describe such bits of behavior as the adjustment of the eye to varying amounts of light.
—Brenda B. Bankart and C. Peter Bankart, *Wabash College*

See also Ethology; Operant Conditioning; Sensory Adaptation.

Consult (3) Darwin, 1859. (4) Gibson, 1970. (7) Lashley, 1949.

ADAPTATION, SENSORY. *See* Sensory Adaptation.

ADDICTION. *See* Alcoholism; Drugs and Behavior.

ADJUSTMENT, frequently understood as synonymous with "normality" or "health," was an early expression of the concern with living well in one's environment so as to fulfill one's needs and find happiness. Because it too often implied "adaptation," that is, conformity with environmental demands, the term encountered some opprobrium. Although adjustment may also be accomplished by acting on the environment so as to change it, this extension, in softening the "conformity" charge, fails to recognize conflict *within* the individual.

Adjustment must encompass techniques for resolving internal conflict while dealing adequately with the environment. In the light of recent emphasis on self-actualization, the term should be extended to apply to the development of an individual's potentials, which is an ongoing process, not an end state. The well-adjusted individual is not free of conflict but flexible in developing his poten-

tials; in making internal choices, he both adapts to and changes the environment. Many authors prefer such terms as "health," "maturity," or "self-actualization."
—M. G. Affinito, *Southern Connecticut State College*

See also Adaptation; Conformity; Maturity; Mental Health; Self-Actualization.

ADLER, ALFRED (1870–1937), Austrian psychiatrist. After receiving his M.D. from the University of Vienna in 1895, Adler specialized in psychiatry. He worked with Sigmund Freud from 1902 to 1911 as one of the charter members of the Vienna Psychoanalytic Society and later served as its president.

Disagreements with Freud, particularly over his theory of compensation for inferiority feelings, and greater emphasis on the social aspects of neurosis led Adler to develop his own rival approach, called *individual psychology*. During the 1920s he became internationally famous and was active in establishing child guidance clinics. In 1934 he moved to the United States, where he taught at Columbia University and Long Island College of Medicine. He died in Aberdeen, Scotland.

Theories. Adler's theories of personality emphasized the significance of social influences and goal striving. His early work mainly focused on psychological compensation for felt inferiority as basic to neurosis, but his later formulations broadened the conception of motivation, particularly emphasizing positive *social interest*.

Adler held that each individual from his early capacities, limitations, and experiences develops a unique style of life that is predominantly social in orientation. While every person has the same ultimate goal of *superiority*, or positive self-esteem, there are innumerable individual ways of striving for this goal. Maladjustment occurs when one has drawn false conclusions about the world and himself and consequently adopted a faulty style of life that is primarily self-centered and defensive. An understanding of the origins of inferiority feelings, often revealed through recollection of earliest childhood memories and analysis of the early *family constellation* due to birth order, can help free the individual to develop a more satisfying life style.

Adler's doctrine of the *creative self* emphasized the active role of the individual in shaping his personality toward a unified self-realization and fulfillment through a meaningful and socially useful life.
—Alden E. Wessman, *The City College of The City University of New York*
Consult (13) Ansbacher and Rowena, 1956.

ADOLESCENCE is a transitional stage in human development from the beginning of puberty to the attainment of the physical, emotional, and social maturity of adulthood. It has been viewed by most psychologists as a stressful period since the adolescent must adjust to the vast changes occurring within him after a long peaceful period of relatively slow growth.

Physiological and Physical Changes. The increase of hormonal activity during puberty seems to be responsible for these changes. The pituitary gland, which is located at the base of the brain, controls growth and stimulates the hormonal activities of the sex glands that bring the reproductive systems to maturity. This implies that a person becomes potentially capable of reproduction at that stage.

There is no specific time when puberty begins, although physical growth is usually most rapid a year or so before puberty. Wide variations in height, weight, and levels of sexual maturity have been observed within the same age group among different ethnic groups and between sexes. Physical growth may be hastened or retarded by many variables, such as environmental conditions, type of diet, or hereditary factors.

The different parts of the body may or may not mature uniformly, as growth often comes in spurts. Specific parts of the body may develop at different rates and at different times with no special regard to the overall body proportions. Organ systems such as the digestive, glandular, skeletal, cardiovascular, muscular, nervous, and reproductive systems also undergo considerable growth. The stomach, for example, increases in size and capacity, which in part accounts for the marked increase in appetite during this period. Skin glands become more active, leading to body odor and skin conditions.

Males and females both show changes in weight, height, size, and body proportions, in addition to changes in coordination, strength, and muscular development. Both sexes show growth in pubic and axillary hair and increase in perspiration. However, changes in size of ovaries and uterus and the beginning of the menstrual cycle are pertinent and unique in females, while growth of penis and testicles and involuntary ejaculations are characteristic of males.

Other secondary sex characteristics are also distinguishing features of femininity and masculinity—the widening of the hips and the development of the breasts in females versus the broadening of the shoulders and the slimness of the hips in males, for example.

Psychological Responses to Physical Changes. Although these changes are basically physiological and physical, they have great psychological impact on the adolescent. As a result of the rapid physical change, an adjustment has to be made to accept the new image of the physical self. An adolescent is forced to handle a body whose dimensions and structure are strange and unfamiliar. The legs take longer steps, the arms become long and not in harmony with the rest of the body, and frequently feelings of physical awkwardness occur. A part of this awkwardness stems from the unpredictability of the new body since it changes so rapidly that the adolescent is no longer sure of its capacities or limitations. Adjustment to this new body involves discovering its limitations by testing its strength, tolerance, and resistance, by exploring it, and by comparing it with others.

An adolescent is usually conscious of the different bodily sensations: his heart beats more rapidly, his pulse increases, he gets out of breath when he runs, his muscles become more tensed, and he perspires more than earlier. Being unaware of the internal changes and more sensitive to bodily sensations, he may perceive these symptoms as signs of illness or manifestations of abnormality.

In general, there is a compelling preoccupation with the body in the adolescent period. A male adolescent becomes concerned with his motor coordination, the size of his muscles, and his body build. Sexual feelings also stem from the new body and seem to be difficult to handle. Given the urgency of his sexual desires and the unacceptability of expressing them, he is torn between the urge to gratify them and the will to control them. The erection of the penis as a result of visual stimulation, or nocturnal emission, may lead to feelings of anxiety, guilt, and general psychological discomfort.

A female adolescent will become preoccupied with her appearance, height, and weight—especially when perceived as too great or too little—or with other feminine characteristics, such as the size of her breasts or hips. The type of psychological reaction that will be elicited in relation to becoming sexually mature will depend on the personality characteristics of the adolescent. She may relate menstruation to being dirty, or she may cope with it by denying her femininity and acting in a tomboyish fashion, or she may accept it with pride as a sign of becoming a mature female. Generally, the adolescent, whether a male or a female, comes to terms with his or her body by accepting its limitations and imperfections and enhancing its attributes. The acceptance of one's own body definitely contributes to the general acceptance of self.

Social and Emotional Adjustment. In the early stages of development a child learns to seek security and gratification from the external world, specifically from the parents. As he becomes older and through socialization he learns certain patterns of behavior and becomes equipped with certain sets of responses that allow him to deal effectively and comfortably with the world around him. In adolescence the need to be independent becomes so

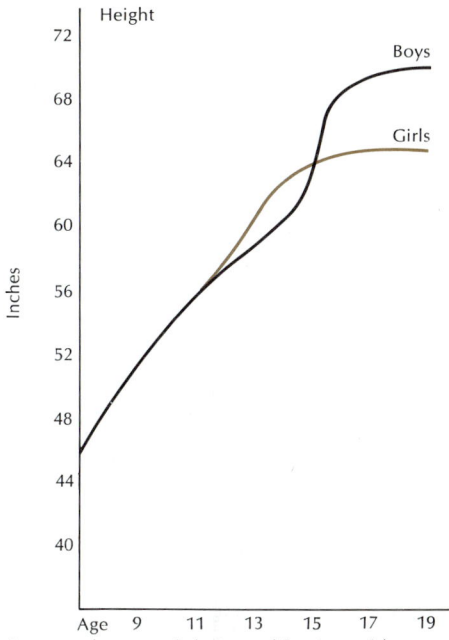

Between the ages of eleven and fourteen girls exceed boys in height and weight, reflecting the earlier onset of puberty.

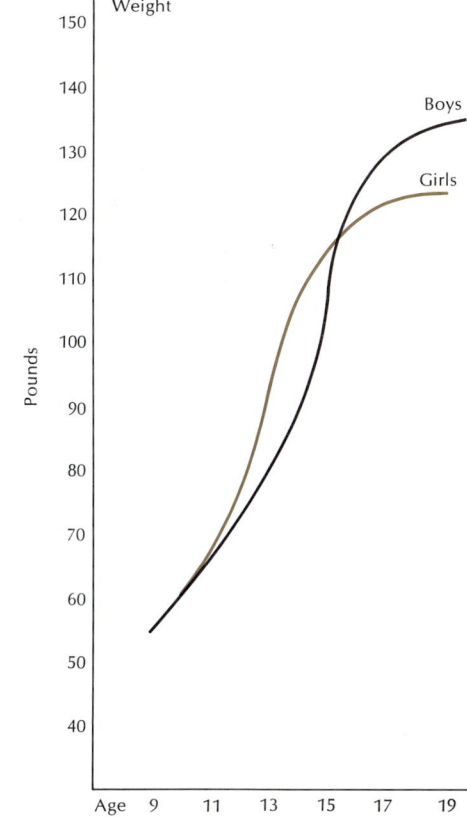

Membership in a peer group fulfills some of the adolescent's dependency needs and provides a feeling of belonging. The group will also influence his attitudes and values.

The psychological adjustment to sexual maturity depends in large measure on individual personality characteristics. Social adjustments are least difficult for those who have had normal relations with others of the opposite sex from an early age.

great that it is necessary for him to develop new views, values, and forms of behavior, abandoning the part of self that reflects the original identification with the parent. In his fight for independence and the establishment of an identity, he may deny the virtues of his parents in order to achieve feelings of worthiness and self-respect. However, while he is stripping them of their virtues and powers and resenting their values, he is also divesting himself of the security and support they provided him.

The world around him was determined to a great extent by the stability of his relationship to his parents, who provided him with fairly successful and adequate forms of behavior with which to deal with reality situations. Now the world is less defined, and the adolescent must redefine it in his own way by exploring, experimenting, and exposing himself to new experiences and situations. In this "soul search" he may discover that the world is sometimes thrilling and exciting, sometimes depressing and frightening. In his search for independence and identity, he will experience episodes of depression, loneliness, and isolation, where the need for support and guidance becomes vital. His peer group will serve as a substitute family, fulfilling his dependency needs and providing him with new values, beliefs, attitudes, and morality.

Membership in a peer group facilitates the process of individuation, which implies the development of personal, sexual, and social identity. The peer group also serves other functions, assisting the adolescent to learn new social roles, providing him with a feeling of belonging, and helping him to understand himself and others.

Dating also is an important aspect of the adolescent's social development, providing him with a smooth transition from unisexual to heterosexual relationships.

Intellectual Development. According to Jean Piaget, the final stage of intellectual development begins at early adolescence. This is the stage of formal operations, where the mode of cognitive representation is abstract symbolism. In this stage the adolescent engages in abstract logic, both verbal and mathematical. He can reason deductively and is capable of forming hypotheses and systematically testing them either overtly or in thought. The development of abstract thinking also affects the way the adolescent evaluates the quality of his own thinking. He becomes more analytical and introspective.

Theories of Adolescence. Many conflicting theoretical positions have been formulated to explain the phenomenon of adolescence, for example, biogenetic, psychoanalytic, and anthropological.

One of the early theoretical formulations was presented by G. Stanley Hall in his recapitulation theory, which postulated that as a child develops from birth to maturity he reenacts the social evolution of the human race. An infant, for instance, relives the animal stage, a youth recapitulates the life of savagery, and so on. The general orientation of this theory is biogenetic, since Hall assumed that the history of mankind has become a part of the genetic structure of the human being, where development is controlled by genetically determined physiological factors. Hall also perceived adolescence as a period of "storm and stress" characterized by instability and fluctuation.

Freud related the effects of early childhood experiences to the adolescent period, and Erik Erikson expanded and developed the psychoanalytic thought in this area. Erikson noted that an individual passes through stages of development where he gradually acquires a sense of self-worth, or an ego identity. The acquisition of ego identity can be achieved in different ways depending on the culture. During the early phases of his search for identity the adolescent may experience "role diffusion," identifying with a hero or a leader to the extent of appearing to lose his own identity. According to this theory, an ego identity involves achieving sexual and vocational identity in addition to forming values independent from parents.

Margaret Mead's anthropological approach provides an example of a third theoretical orientation. Her studies of primitive cultures suggest that adolescence may be neither stormy nor stressful. She contends the nature of the adolescent period is determined to a great extent by cultural factors rather than by the internal maturational processes that were considered so central by both Freud and Hall.

—Ragaa Mazen, *Southern Connecticut State College*

See also Child Development; Maturity. Consult (11) Blos, 1967; Erikson, 1950; Lambert, *et al.*, 1972; Muss, 1968; Skipper and Nass, 1966; Inhelder and Piaget, 1958; Winter and Nuss, 1969.

ADRENAL GLANDS, endocrine glands each located on top of a kidney. They are approximately 1 ¼ inch in length and ¼ inch in diameter in man and weigh approximately 4 grams in the adult.

The adrenal comprises two divisions, the cortex and the medulla. The adrenal *cortex* is responsible for the production of three important substances: mineralocorticoids, such as aldosterone, which are important for sodium balance; the glucocorticoids, which are responsible for the metabolism of glucose; and the androgens, which are responsible for male sexual characteristics. The adrenal *medulla* contains specialized secretory cells that release epinephrine or adrenalin into the bloodstream. Adrenalin increases the level of blood sugar and acts upon carbohydrate metabolism.

In a time of strong emotion or stress, adrenalin is involved in the process that alerts the body for action. This process is called the *adrenergic reaction.*

—Joel F. Lubar, *University of Tennessee*
See also Emotion.
Consult (13) Black, 1970.

ADVERTISING RESEARCH. *See* Consumer Psychology.

AFFECT, in psychology, a synonym for feeling or emotion. The term covers the whole range of moods or "feeling tones." If a person is apathetic, he may be said to be showing loss of affect. The label *affective psychosis* is applied to mental illness marked by disorders of mood—manic-depressive psychosis, for example. *See* Emotions; Psychotic Disorders.

AFFECTIONAL DRIVE, the urge or need to be close to or in contact with another living being either physically or emotionally through some form of tie or bond. The role of the affectional drive has been postulated by psychoanalysts and psychologists (Sigmund Freud, Erich Fromm, H. F. Harlow, and others) as more than a sexual relationship. Rather, it is the force behind the maturation-determined series of relationships a person passes through during his psychological development—relationships popularly called "love."

See also Interpersonal Attraction.

AFFILIATIVE DRIVE, the urge or need to associate with other living beings in order to form social attachments. The associations developed in a social context serve to support, guide, and protect the individuals involved. Studies indicate that the need or urge for affiliation is especially intense when an individual is undergoing an anxiety-producing experience. There is also evidence that the expression of this drive differs greatly from individual to individual, with a large portion of this difference dependent on early experience. The affiliative drive serves as a defense mechanism to protect individuals through the principle of "strength in numbers."

—Thom Herrmann, *University of Tennessee*

AFTERIMAGE, a visual impression that outlasts the stimulation that produced it. If you stare at the sun and then close your eyes, you will see a bright image. This is a *positive afterimage.* If you stare at a black triangle and then at the white page, you will see a light gray triangle on a darker gray page. If you stare at a colored square and then at a white page you will see a square of the complementary color (red/green,

blue/yellow). These *negative afterimages* are important indicators of black-white and color processes occurring within the retina.

—Nina Adams, *Yale University*

AGGRESSION. We live in a culture that has come to accept aggression and violence in almost all aspects of life, and we live in a world in which war seems almost inevitable. Therefore, the study of aggression is one of the most pressing concerns for modern psychology.

For all of its pervasiveness, aggression remains one of the most challenging areas of study because of the elusiveness of an adequate definition of the term. Some researchers have applied it to any act that inflicts pain or suffering on another individual; others feel that a proper definition must include some notion of intent to do harm. Still others use a situational definition, so that what might be described as aggression in one context might not be considered such in others. There is also controversy over whether aggression should be regarded as an intraspecies behavior or whether it includes interspecies behavior. This conflict over how aggression should be conceptualized has been partly responsible for the development of a number of competing notions of its origins and nature.

Animal Aggression. One of the most important contributions to the study of aggression has been made by the ethologists. The subject has been of particular interest to them because aggression occurs frequently in natural settings and seems to appear in almost all species, from insects to primates.

Konrad Lorenz, perhaps the best-known of the ethologists concerned with aggression, particularly within species, has proposed that aggressive behavior is largely instinctual in all social species, including man. His view is put forth in his controversial book *On Aggression,* l966. One of the most interesting aspects of Lorenz's position is the suggestion that as a way of coping with powerful aggressive instincts, most species have developed highly symbolic or ritualized behaviors to avoid or terminate aggression. Most animals can evade attack or stop a battle before any serious harm is done by signaling submission. Lorenz has suggested that man may be unique in the ferociousness of his aggressive behavior because he alone among all of the aggressive species does not have any built-in signals for limiting or preventing aggression. Although the smile may have developed for this purpose originally, it has apparently lost much of its symbolic meaning.

Another ethologist, Robert Ardrey, has contributed a second instinctual view of aggression in man and other animals. His book *The Territorial Imperative,* l966, argued that aggression is the natural result of territorial invasion. Ardrey noted that most wars are

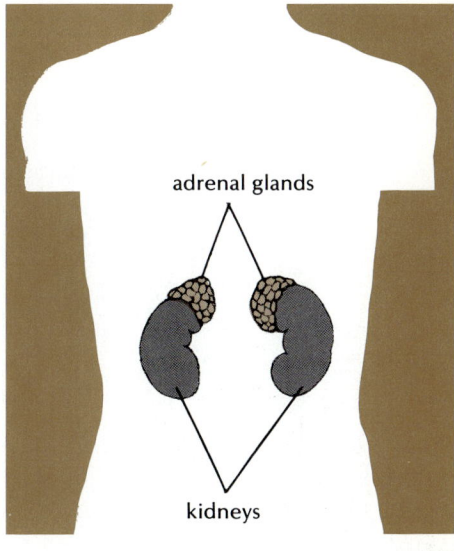

adrenal glands

kidneys

Aggressive behavior, according to ethologists, is instinctual in all social species. With one notable exception, most species have developed ritualized or symbolic behaviors to limit or prevent aggression.

Afterimage demonstration. Look fixedly at the triangle then transfer your gaze to the white area; a light gray triangle will be seen.

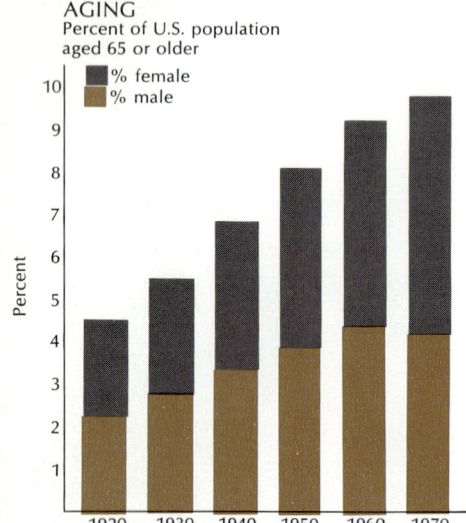

AGING
Percent of U.S. population
aged 65 or older

■ % female
■ % male

The percentage of people age sixty-five or over more than doubled in the period 1920–1960.

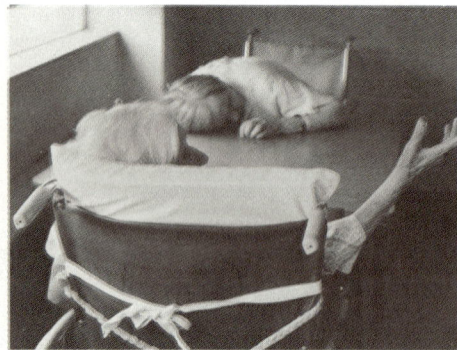

Of the 800,000 nursing-home patients in the United States, half or more have some form of mental illness. Most institutions provide minimal psychiatric treatment.

fought over territorial rights and that the defender of a territory is usually more successful than the invader, regardless of the size and experience of the combatants.

Psychoanalytic Theory. The psychoanalytic movement has also largely accepted the view that aggression is instinctual. Freud postulated that there are two instincts: *eros,* the life instinct, and *thanatos,* the death instinct. Thanatos represents the universal drive to return to the earth; suicide is the ultimate expression of thanatos, but its usual expression is only indirect.

When the death wish is directed toward other individuals, it is called *displacement.* This concept is often used to explain various social phenomena, such as scapegoating and the behavior of the Nazis before and during World War II. Displacement refers to the direct channeling of aggressive energies toward a specific group of persons or objects.

When aggressive impulses are not directly channeled, the result is described as *catharsis.* This indirect expression of the aggressive instinct is said to explain why people engage in athletics, watch aggressive movies and television, and kick doors, dogs, and car tires rather than other people or themselves. Catharsis provides a safe, socially acceptable, and tension-reducing means of dealing with thanatos.

Frustration-Aggression Theory. Closely allied with the psychoanalytic concept of aggression is the hypothesis proposed by John Dollard, Neal Miller, and their colleagues in the late 1930s. This view suggests that aggression is more than mere instinct; it is the instinctual response to frustration, and the presence of aggression inevitably indicates the presence of frustration somewhere in the individual's environment. Dollard and Miller conducted a number of experiments demonstrating aggression as an unlearned response to a wide variety of frustrating situations.

The frustration-aggression hypothesis was modified in the 1960s by Leonard Berkowitz, who found that aggression occurs even in the absence of observable frustration and that the form it takes depends upon previous experience. While this hypothesis still states that frustration is a primary determinant of aggression, frustration is no longer considered a necessary or sufficient precursor for aggression.

The data generated from the research on the frustration-aggression hypothesis eventually led to the view that aggression need not be regarded as entirely instinctual. Because some cultures have succeeded in remaining virtually free from violence, and because some individuals seem to be able to lead relatively nonaggressive lives, it would appear that if aggression is instinctual, man is capable of keeping that instinct under relatively tight control.

Social Learning Theory. In response to these challenges to the instinctual view, social learning theory, particularly as propounded by Richard Walters and Albert Bandura, has concentrated on how aggressive behaviors are learned and under what conditions aggression is exhibited and inhibited. The main point here is that no single set of variables, such as territoriality, thanatos, or frustration, can adequately explain all aggressive behavior. Bandura and Walters have maintained that it is more instructive to study an individual's learning history than it is to speculate on the nature of instinctive drives. They pose such questions as: Has the individual been rewarded for aggressive behavior in the past? Has a parent used primarily physically aggressive punishments in training a child? Does aggression attract attention from a child's parents or teachers?

The basic contribution of social learning theory to the study of aggression has been its focus on noninstinctual, environmental factors. By concentrating on the differences between the learning and the performance of aggressive acts, experimenters found that while performance usually occurs in the presence of frustration, learning of aggressive behavior usually does not involve any frustration. Perhaps more importantly, however, the social learning theorists have shown how important imitation is to both the acquisition and the performance of aggressive behavior.

—Brenda B. Bankart and C. Peter Bankart, *Wabash College*

See also Anger; Death Instinct; Ethology; Imitation; Life Instinct; Overcrowding.

Consult (3) Ardrey, 1966; Beach, 1948; Lorenz, 1966. (10) Bandura, 1969; Bandura and Walters, 1959; Bandura and Walters, 1963; Berkowitz, 1969; Dollard and Miller, 1939; Geen, 1968.

AGING. Although many employers say that old age begins at sixty-five, behavioral and biomedical research indicates that aging is a continuous process. Developmental psychologists study aging as the final stage of a process that starts in youth and continues through maturity and later years to end at death.

Biological Changes. Some human functions begin to decline during adolescence, others during middle age, while still others remain unimpaired through old age in the absence of physical illness. Although many of the processes of biological aging appear to be genetically programmed and orderly, there is also evidence that length of lifespan is at least partially dependent on the accumulated effects of disease, radiation damage, and possibly psychosocial stress. Aging does bring a decline in such qualities as recuperative capacity, resistance to infection, and muscular endurance, along with greater susceptibility to the major chronic diseases, such as cardiovascular conditions, cancer, arteriosclerosis, hypertension, and arthritis. The great majority of people sixty-five and over live functionally independent lives, but 40 percent of them have one or more chronic diseases. About 5 percent are institutionalized, and 12 to 15 percent of those living in the community have some major limitation on their functioning imposed by poor health.

Psychological Aging. Psychological changes during the latter part of the lifespan are most evident in processes closely related to biological functions. Dark adaptation, visual acuity, and almost all other sensory-perceptual functions show an apparent age-related decline. Psychomotor functions, such as speed of response, muscular coordination, and such complex skills as athletic performance, also decline with age.

A substantial amount of data also shows an apparent decline in higher cognitive skills with age. For example, there is a consistent decline in mean weighted full-scale scores on the Wechsler Adult Intelligence Scale (WAIS) as chronological age increases. In recent years, however, new research has shown that much of the supposed "age decline" is explainable on the basis of factors unrelated to the mere passage of time. This elderly generation completed an average of eight years of school; understandably, they will perform less well on tests than younger people with more years of education, acquired more recently.

Age is confounded with poor physical health in many studies. Older people frequently live in socially deprived environments and thus get no opportunity to practice intellectual skills. Each of these factors will lower test performance and give the appearance of age decline. Some "crystallized" abilities—vocabulary and the fund of useful information, for example—actually continue to improve at least through the seventh decade of life. "Fluid" abilities—those that depend upon speed, quick learning, or complex decision making—do appear to parallel the biological decline even when extraneous factors are controlled, though to a lesser degree than had formerly been supposed.

One may see how greatly human performance depends on both the person and the task by looking at the ages at which major creative achievements usually occur. The peak age for producing lyric poetry and mathematical breakthroughs is in the twenties, while production in philosophy, politics, and law moves far toward the end of the lifespan. The mere fact that masterpieces such as Goethe's *Faust*, Verdi's *Falstaff*, and Michelangelo's Sistine Chapel paintings were products of artists in very "old age" attests to the fact that aging *per se* is no bar to creativity.

Careful studies of personality changes related to age show that younger people do tend to have a somewhat greater sense of "active mastery" over themselves and their environments. Older people feel less in control, perhaps because of the role losses brought about by forced retirement, the loss of a spouse, the death of friends and family, or the increasing neglect of a society that actually deprives them of mastery.

Although most older people maintain close relationships with family and remain relatively independent, poor health and social deprivations shrink the behavioral worlds of increasingly more people as age increases. This fact led some observers to formulate the very influential "disengagement" theory of aging. This theory asserts that the final optimal developmental stage in life is the mutual disengagement of the aging individual and society, in preparation for the death of the individual. The individual invests less emotion in objects of the outer world and becomes increasingly involved with the self, while society in turn relinquishes its demands on him. However, empirical research consistently supports the opposing "activity" theory of optimal aging. That is, those who remain engaged both in inner life and in behavior appear to be happier, more satisfied, and better adjusted. Nevertheless, the disengagement theory has been verified to the extent that an identifiable minority of individuals do actively withdraw from society and yet maintain high morale.

While psychiatric disability is by no means an inevitable result of old age, rates of alcoholism, suicide, depression, and chronic and acute brain disorders increase with age. Many of these conditions can be treated effectively in outpatient or short-term hospital situations, yet few people over sixty-five are given such services. Too frequently, they end up in mental hospitals and nursing homes. Of the 800,000 nursing home patients in the United States, half or more have some form of mental condition, but these institutions provide minimal psychiatric treatment. In the 1970s a major effort was undertaken to provide health, personal, social, and psychiatric assistance to elderly people in the community in the hope of forestalling institutionalization.

Social Stereotypes. Society's negative attitude toward aging is seen in its concepts of dirty old men and complaining old women. These views are mirrored in older people's attitudes toward themselves. Negative age stereotypes may be seen psychodynamically as a wish to deny our own mortality—as if rejecting older people might magically avert aging and death for ourselves. Our readiness to "retire" older people from positions of power and influence may reflect unresolved childhood hostility and ambivalence toward our parents. Although this negative social attitude is uncon-

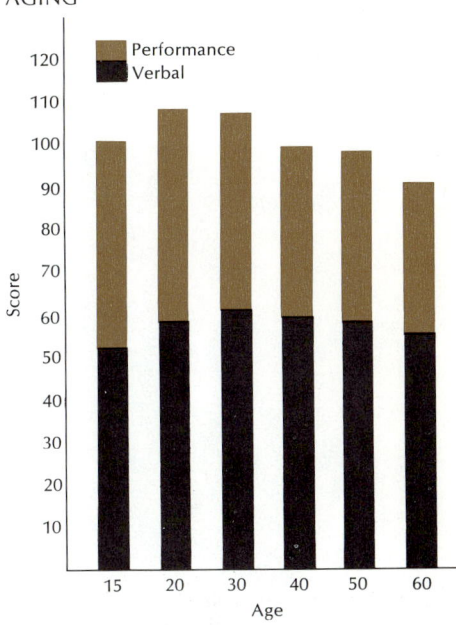

AGING

Typical scores at different ages for the performance and verbal parts of the Wechsler Adult Intelligence Scale.

Society's unconscious negative attitude toward aging is reflected in its readiness to "retire" older people from positions of responsibility.

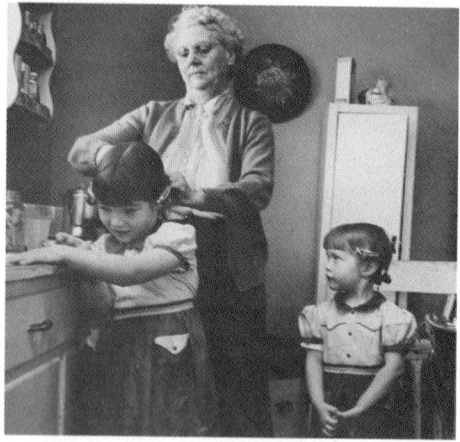

Those aged people who remain actively engaged with society seem to be happier and better adjusted to aging. Above, an older woman at work as an employment counselor; below, a grandmother in a multigeneration family.

scious and inevitable, we can, through education and intergenerational contact, become aware of it; and such awareness may counteract some of the gross social inequities our attitudes have caused. The science of psychology has a direct contribution to make to the social engineering required to change these attitudes as well as to the effort to treat the psychological disorders of old age.

—M. Powell Lawton, *Philadelphia Geriatric Center*

See also Middle Age.

Consult (11) Birren, 1964; Cumming and Henry, 1961; Eisdorfer and Lawton, 1972; Neugarten, 1964; Riley and Foner, 1968.

AGNOSIA. *See* Aphasia.

AGORAPHOBIA, excessive fear of open spaces. *See* Phobia.

ALCOHOL ADDICTION. *See* Alcoholism.

ALCOHOLICS ANONYMOUS (AA), a voluntary fellowship founded in 1935 and concerned solely with the personal recovery and continued sobriety of the alcoholic members who turn to the organization for help. AA does not engage in research or medical or psychiatric treatment, nor does it endorse causes or affiliate with other groups. AA is self-supporting through its own membership and declines contributions from all outside sources. Although AA may cooperate with other organizations concerned with problems of alcohol abuse and its members often take part in outside endeavors related to alcoholism research or treatment, members preserve personal anonymity in the press, films, broadcast, and other public information media.

For the past few decades, AA has been the major influence in gaining acceptance of the disease concept of alcoholism. The aim of AA members is to help each other maintain their sobriety and to share their recovery experience freely with anyone who may have an alcohol problem. The AA program consists basically of "Twelve Suggested Steps" designed for personal recovery from alcoholism. Several hundred thousand alcoholic people have achieved sobriety in this way, but members recognize that their program is not always effective with all alcoholic persons and that some individuals may require professional counseling or treatment.

The General Service Board of Alcoholics Anonymous publishes the monthly *AA Grapevine* and other materials.

See also Alcoholism.

Consult (13) Alcoholics Anonymous, 1957; Mann, 1970.

ALCOHOLISM. A person is classed as an alco-

holic if he or she experiences repeated episodes of intoxication or heavy drinking that impair health or consistently uses alcohol as a coping mechanism to deal with life's problems to a degree seriously interfering with effectiveness on the job, at home, in the community, or behind the wheel of a car. Although the most visible victims of alcoholism are on skid rows, they represent only from 3 to 5 percent of the alcoholic population in the United States. Most alcoholic individuals are in the working and homemaking populations. It has been estimated that as many as 10 percent of the United States work force are alcoholic individuals.

Effects. Prolonged heavy alcohol abuse can lead to disorders of the central and peripheral nervous systems, the liver, heart, muscles, gastrointestinal tract, and other organs and tissues. Alcoholism is often associated with nutritional disorders, which may be partially responsible for diseases of the neurological, digestive, and other systems. Alcoholic persons whose dependency is not successfully treated are subject to an exceptionally high rate of morbidity and mortality; their lifespans are reduced by as much as ten to twelve years.

The Search for Causes. The causal factors of alcoholism are unknown. Social, cultural, psychological, and physiological factors all play a part. Theorists have attempted to explain alcoholism on the bases of psychoanalysis, learning theory, and personality trait theory. Psychodynamic explanations include the Freudian view that alcoholism results from unconscious mechanisms of excessive orality or masochism; the Adlerian view that alcoholism represents a struggle for power; and the view that alcoholism develops as a response to an inner conflict between dependency drives and aggressive impulses. Learning theory explains alcoholism by considering drinking as a reflex response to some stimulus in the effort to reduce such feelings as fear or anxiety. Although some evidence indicates that alcohol reduces such emotions in an approach-avoidance situation, learning theory—like the other explanations—has not yet thoroughly explained alcoholism.

Similarly, researchers have been unsuccessful in delineating an "alcoholic personality." Some alcoholic people exhibit unusual responses to drinking. They may experience intense relief through the use of alcohol. Alcoholic persons tend to have difficulty dealing with depression, frustration, and anxiety, and they seem to be people who have been exposed to culturally determined ambivalence regarding the nature of appropriate drinking behavior.

Treatment. Treatment of alcoholism usually begins with cessation of drinking, nutritional rehabilitation, and management of medical needs. Anticonvulsant drugs and sedative compounds to prevent symptoms of withdrawal are often employed. Longer-range treatment of alcoholism may involve individual psychotherapy, group therapy, aversion therapy, or disulfiram (Antabuse) therapy.

Group therapies may involve videotape confrontation, including analysis of adaptive consequences of drinking behaviors, psychodrama, sensitivity training, or the pioneering and widely used program of Alcoholics Anonymous. Halfway houses fill a therapeutic gap for alcoholic people with no place to go between hospital and outpatient services.

At present about one-third of alcoholic patients improve greatly with treatment; one-third show some lesser benefits; and one-third remain unchanged. There is reason to expect this success rate to improve in the future as more resources are directed into treatment of this long-neglected illness.

To promote research and to spread information, the United States government has established two agencies, the National Institute on Alcohol Abuse and Alcoholism and the National Clearinghouse for Alcohol Information. Both institutes are associated with the National Institute of Mental Health.

—Morris E. Chafetz, *Director, National Institute on Alcohol Abuse and Alcoholism*

See also Alcoholics Anonymous.

Consult (13) Bier, 1962; Cahn, 1970; Chafetz and Denmore, 1962; Chafetz, 1965; Clinebell, 1968; McClelland, 1972.

ALEXIA, a language disorder often called word blindness or visual aphasia. *See* Aphasia.

ALIENATION. To be alienated means to be estranged from one's society. In past eras, those who were alienated often came from the ranks of the poor, unemployed, and minority groups. They were estranged because obstacles, usually economic, did not permit them to live a life that had any purpose. Today, these same groups feel left out. Even those who enjoy economic advantages find that affluence does not provide the assurance it once did that life will be meaningful.

One of the main causes of alienation is rapid social change, which, in turn, accounts for at least three different types of alienated behavior. The first type is man's inability to adapt to rapid change. The second is related to it, in that social change has produced a trend toward urban living and this has resulted in depersonalized living relationships. Third, social upheaval has introduced doubts and finally disagreements about all types of behavioral standards. The result has been widespread uncertainty about traditional values.

Indirectly, social change has an alienating affect on man's relationship to the world around him. Vocationally, the worker has become so specialized that there is very little perceivable connection between his work and the final product. Morally, man may be no better or worse than he used to be, but he has cut himself off from a traditional source of comfort because he is less likely to believe in God. Within the family the emotional ties have become weaker as trends toward mobility have allowed the family to lose contact with close relatives. With the responsibilities within the family becoming more specialized the mother is more exclusively entrusted with the upbringing of the children. Compared to earlier times she makes a bigger emotional investment in each child and he, in turn, becomes more dependent on her. This sets the stage for a common cause of male alienation, a close-binding mother and a detached father.

—Duane Harmon, *Southern Connecticut State College*

ALIENIST, a legal term sometimes used for a physician who can testify as to the competence of persons appearing in court as parties in a case or as witnesses. To qualify for this role, a physician does not have to be a psychiatrist. For a discussion of the legal responsibilities of psychiatrists and psychologists, see Psychology and the Law.

ALL-OR-NONE LAW, the property of neurons that forms the basis for their ability to code information. Neurons are analogous to digital converters. The analog inputs consist of many varying types of information dealing with the intensity of the stimuli and the quality and pattern of stimulation. This information is summated by the neuron and, once it reaches threshold, results in the production of the action potential, or nerve response.

The all-or-none property of the action potential is embodied in the fact that its amplitude is always the same; the neural code is determined by frequency rather than size of the nerve response. Stronger stimuli result in more impulses being generated per second, but each of them is of the same amplitude.

—Joel F. Lubar, *University of Tennessee*
Consult (3) Isaacson, *et al.,* 1971.

ALLELE, one of a pair of genes located at corresponding positions on a pair of chromosomes. Each pair of alleles controls or influences the formation of a specific trait (such as eye color). One allele is usually dominant, the other recessive. The trait ultimately displayed results from the dominance relationship between the alleles.

ALLPORT, GORDON WILLARD (1897–1967), American psychologist. Born in Montezuma, Indiana he received a Ph.D. from Harvard and

The visible victims of alcoholism represent only 3 to 5 percent of the U.S. alcoholic population. The total is estimated as being as high as 10 percent of the total work force.

Gordon W. Allport, an authority on prejudice and personality.

was chairman of the psychology department there after 1937.

Starting with his Ph.D. thesis, Allport conducted many and increasingly renowned studies of personality. He also published works on prejudice, and from 1937 to 1949 he was editor of the *Journal of Abnormal and Social Psychology*. He was one of the authors of the *Allport-Vernon-Lindzey Study of Values*. In 1939 he served as president of the American Psychological Association. Major publications include *Personality* (1937); *The Nature of Prejudice* (1954); *Becoming* (1955); *Personality and Social Encounter* (1960); and *Pattern and Growth in Personality* (1961).

ALLPORT-VERNON-LINDZEY STUDY OF VALUES

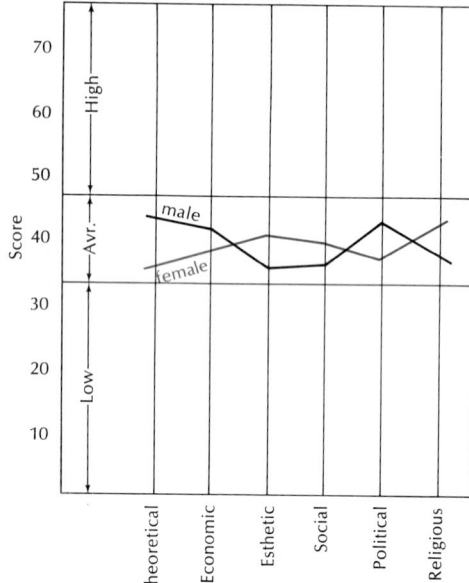

Showing average male and female profiles for the six types of values studied.

ALLPORT-VERNON-LINDZEY STUDY OF VALUES, a paper-and-pencil test of interests and attitudes. Easily administered and scored, it is used primarily in vocational counseling and personnel selection. It correlates well with other vocational-interest and attitude scales (Strong and Thurstone tests, for example). Subjects are rated on six basic "values"—theoretical, economic, aesthetic, social, political, and religious.

In the test, subjects are required to rate different statements "in order of personal preference." Alternatives are keyed on the various value categories, so that the ratings generate a raw score easily convertible into a graph depicting a "profile of values." This profile reflects the individual's relative interest or motivation in the six value categories.

—Randolph S. Kraft, *Federation of the Handicapped*
Consult (13) Allport, et al., 1960.

ALPHA WAVES (or alpha rhythm). *See* Brain Waves.

ALTRUISM, helping behavior that occurs at some cost to the helper. Altruism is usually motivated intrinsically, not by observable rewards or threats of punishment, and is therefore characterized by an unselfish motive.

It has been argued that it is difficult to determine the existence of truly altruistic behavior in humans because one can never really be sure what motivates helping behavior. Even when there are no observable material rewards, selfish internal motives, such as reduction of guilt or improving one's self-image, may be behind an altruistic act. However, several experiments demonstrating sharing in young chimpanzees in the absence of external rewards suggest that altruism does occur as intrinsically motivated behavior.

More recent experiments with humans have demonstrated that altruistic behavior is facilitated by empathy (the ability to understand the feelings of others) and offered some insight into possible motives behind altruism. Other variables that have been shown to

affect helping behavior include the finding that if someone has been helped in the past or has just experienced success on some task, he is more likely to help. If the recipient of the help is dependent on or evokes empathy from the helper, helping behavior is also facilitated. Finally, if an individual observes someone (a model) engaged in helping behavior, the probability of his engaging in subsequent altruism increases.

—Brenda B. Bankart and C. Peter Bankart, *Wabash College*
See also Empathy; Imitation.
Consult (10) Bandura and Walters, 1963; (13) Rogers, 1961.

AMBIGUOUS FIGURES. *See* Figure-Ground Perception.

AMBIVALENCE, being "of two minds" about a person or an issue. Conflicting feelings may be conscious or unconscious. Psychologists often apply the term "ambivalence" to love-hate feelings. According to Freudian theory, children develop contradictory attitudes toward the parents who both feed and frustrate them, and similar feelings may persist in adult life. Conflicts can, for example, be involved in neurotic problems and even in suicide—some suicide notes could be summed up as "Dear Mary: I hate you. Love, John."

See also Oral Character.

AMBIVERSION, a term used to describe personality. An ambivert would show a balance between introverted and extraverted tendencies. *See* Introversion-Extraversion.

AMERICAN PSYCHOLOGICAL ASSOCIATION (APA), a scientific and professional society of psychologists and educators. "The purpose of the APA is to advance psychology as a science, as a profession, and as a means of promoting human welfare. It attempts to further these objectives by holding annual meetings, publishing psychological journals, and working toward improved standards for psychological training and service." (APA *Directory*) Founded in 1892, the association is now the major psychological organization in the United States. The members (about 32,000) include most of the professionally qualified psychologists in this country. There are 52 affiliated state associations.

Members may apply to join one or more of thirty divisions according to their specialized interests:
1. Division of General Psychology
2. Division of the Teaching of Psychology
3. Division of Experimental Psychology
5. Division of Evaluation and Measurement
6. Division of Physiological and Comparative Psychology
7. Division of Developmental Psychology

8. Division of Personality and Social Psychology
9. The Society for the Psychological Study of Social Issues—A Division of the APA
10. Division of Psychology and the Arts
12. Division of Clinical Psychology
13. Division of Consulting Psychology
14. Division of Industrial Psychology
15. Division of Educational Psychology
16. Division of School Psychology
17. Division of Counseling Psychology
18. Division of Psychologists in Public Service
19. Division of Military Psychology
20. Division of Maturity and Old Age
21. Society of Engineering Psychologists—A Division of the APA
22. Division of Psychological Aspects of Disability
23. Division of Consumer Psychology
24. Division of Philosophical Psychology
25. Division for the Experimental Analysis of Behavior
26. Division of the History of Psychology
27. Division of Community Psychology
28. Division of Psychopharmacology
29. Division of Psychotherapy
30. Division of Psychological Hypnosis
31. Division of State Psychological Association Affairs
32. Division on Mental Retardation

The association publishes a number of periodicals: *American Psychologist, Contemporary Psychology* (containing critical book reviews), *Psychological Review, Psychological Abstracts* (giving summaries of books and articles from around the world), *Journal of Comparative and Physiological Psychology, Journal of Abnormal Psychology, Journal of Applied Psychology, Journal of Consulting Psychology, Journal of Educational Psychology, Journal of Counseling Psychology, Developmental Psychology.*

National headquarters of the APA is at 1200 17th Street, N.W., Washington, D.C. 20036.

See also explanation of how to use psychological journals in Psychological Abstracts.

AMES ROOM, an apparatus designed by psychologists to test visual perception. Careful matching and checking of the different images in the two eyes lead to appropriate depth and perceptual judgments. In this small, distorted room, the walls are trapezoidal, and the ceiling, floor, and back wall slope away from the observer but are shaded to appear rectangular.

When an observer looks into the room through a peephole with one eye, the usual depth cues are absent, and the room seems perfectly rectangular to him. Even illogical events—a man in the near corner (where the ceiling is low) seems enormous and a man in the far corner (where the ceiling is high) seems tiny—do not shake the belief that the surfaces

are horizontal and rectangular. Thus the Ames room actually demonstrates both the importance of visual cues and the crucial influence of past experience on perception.

—Nina Adams, *Yale University*
See also Illusion.
Consult (4) Ames, 1946.

AMNESIA, a general psychological term for "loss of memory." There are many different types and degrees of amnesia, just as there are diverse causes for this failure of mental function. The causes of memory loss can best be divided into two major classes: functional and organic.

Functional Causes. Functional disorders are those in which the disturbances of function are due to psychological, usually emotional, factors and are typically seen as manifestations of such neurotic states as hysteria or severe anxiety. In functional disorders no characteristic objective abnormalities can be found by any anatomical, pathological, physiological, biochemical, X-ray, EEG, or other clinical laboratory tests. In functional disorders there is no measurable persistent change in the form or function of the brain, and consequently recovery or marked improvement can be expected in amnesias due to such causes.

An actor forgetting his lines due to "stage fright" is a good example of temporary amnesia resulting from anxiety. The usually well-publicized cases of "lost identity" are predominantly hysterical in origin. These cases usually respond readily in a few days or couple of weeks to strong suggestive types of therapy, including hypnosis or "truth serum" injections (narcoanalysis) when administered by experienced psychiatrists in the metropolitan centers where such patients are apt to show up. In fact many "cases" are solved by knowledgeable police personnel in the course of their routine investigations.

A typical amnesia case would be a late adolescent or young adult female who has shown up at a police station saying she doesn't know who she is or where she's from. In the typical "hysterical" case she would look perplexed but not overtly distressed. If examination of her purse and clothing and referral to the records of the Missing Persons Bureau do not identify her, she is brought to the local psychopathic hospital. While the routine physical laboratory and psychiatric examinations are going on, photographs are taken to be disseminated to the news media. In most cases the patient is soon recognized and identified by family or friends. By then it is apparent that she has been "subconsciously" escaping or evading an unpleasant home or life situation, whose reality she reluctantly again begins to accept. Often in the blank interval between the time she left home and was taken to the hospital, she had become involved with shady

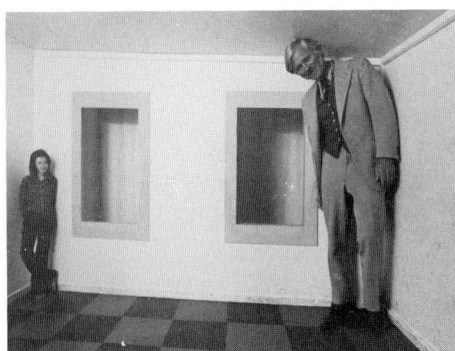

When viewed through a peephole, the distorted Ames room is perceived as rectangular and its inhabitants as distorted.

or unsavory characters and probably engaged in activities she understandably is ashamed to disclose.

The "chronic amnesias" described in romantic novels, in which the handsome stranger appears in town and builds a successful "new life" for many years, while remaining completely oblivious of his family origins, wife, and children, do not correspond to any actual clinical cases. While the novelists usually predicate that these "amnesias" follow serious head injuries, "shell shock," or terrifying war experiences, the psychiatrist's experience tells him that such events cannot completely "wipe out" the past, unless there also exists an underlying, unstable, hysterical personality. And such characters do not possess the positive, persistent personality strengths to maintain subsequent high-level adjustments to life's stresses.

Organic Causes. Organic disorders are those resulting from a physical disease, injury, or dysfunction of the brain due to anatomical, pathological, toxic, chemical, electrical, or circulatory abnormalities. Some examples are: arteriosclerosis (hardening of arteries) of the brain; senile deterioration of the brain; alcoholic addiction with associated dietary deficiencies; bacterial poisons (such as syphilis of the brain); chemical poisons (lead, mercury); and epileptic disorders. In all organic disorders doctors can expect to find physical, chemical, circulatory, X-ray, or electrical abnormalities that are characteristic of the underlying disease.

Amnesias due to organic causes are too numerous and varied to permit any extended descriptions here. However, a few clinical truisms are worth noting. Organic amnesias tend to be spotty, that is, not characterized by prolonged completely "blank memory" periods. Exceptions are seen in amnesias due to semicomatose states; epileptic confusional states; after severe head injuries or concussions, resulting in extended periods of unconsciousness. In these instances, the amnesia may be *retrograde* (involving the time period subsequent to the brain injury) or *anterograde* (involving the time period preceding the brain injury); toxic-delirious states, including gas poisoning; hypoglycemic states; episodes of pathological alcoholic intoxication.

Amnesias due to senility, senile dementia, or hardening of the arteries in the brain tend to show a relatively severe loss of memory for recent events with often fairly good preservation of memory for remote events. Thus, the oldster cannot recall what he had for breakfast this morning or dinner last night but can still describe in great detail certain significant episodes of his youth.

A particularly dramatic type of organic amnesia is not infrequently seen in inveterate chronic alcoholics who also are suffering from severe vitamin deficiencies. This is called the Korsakoff syndrome and is typically seen in a jocular, ruddy-faced individual who will greet every stranger as a friend or acquaintance. He will recall virtually nothing of his recent or remote past but will try to fill in the memory gaps by *confabulating*—recalling (usually on prompting by his interrogator) events that never happened. Thus although he has not been out of the hospital for months, he will readily recall having spent last night with the examiner at "Paddy's Bar" and "what a great time was had by all." Invariably, in such cases there is associated a rather severe degenerative peripheral neuritis, which causes generalized weakness and paralysis. However, when such cases are treated early enough and vigorously enough with adequate diet and vitamins, substantial improvement sometimes is obtained.

—Emanuel Messinger, M.D., *U.S. Veterans Hospital, Northport, N.Y.*

Consult (13) Arieti, 1966; Freedman and Kaplan, 1967.

AMPHETAMINES, stimulant drugs known by such popular terms as "speed" and "pep pills." Benzedrine, Dexedrine, and Methedrine are trade names. *See* Drugs and Behavior.

AMYGDALA. *See* Limbic Region.

ANAL CHARACTER. According to Sigmund Freud and Karl Abraham's psychoanalytic theory of personality development, the second psychosexual stage following the initial oral one is the anal. During this period, roughly about the second year of life, the child's major emotional concerns and psychodynamic conflicts are held to revolve around feelings connected with the anus and with the process of defecation. Both the expulsion and retention of feces are sources of erotic pleasure and satisfaction to the child and of potential conflict with the parents attempting to institute toilet training. The resulting feelings can become generalized ways of relating to important external objects. Thus some of the symbolic meanings of expulsion may signify giving or losing or rejecting and defiling, while retention may signify possessing or controlling.

Psychoanalysts have generally postulated two main character types as developing from conflicts and fixations at this period. The *anal-expulsive character* is held to be defiant, cruel, wantonly destructive, messy, and disorderly. The *anal-retentive character* is seen as meticulous, stingy, greedy, orderly, prudish, and obstinate.

—Alden E. Wessman, *The City College of The City University of New York*
See also Oedipus Complex; Oral Character.

Consult (13) Erikson, 1959; Fenichel, 1945.

ANAL STAGE. *See* Anal Character.

ANALYSIS, in the sense of treatment, the procedure used in psychoanalysis. The term *analyst* can mean any professional who practices psychoanalysis, but it may refer more strictly to a follower of the Freudian school or to a follower of the Jungian school of analytical psychology. *See* Psychoanalysis.

ANALYTIC PSYCHOLOGY (sometimes analytical psychology), the system developed by Carl Jung. Because of disagreements about the nature of personality dynamics, Jung broke away from Sigmund Freud and established his own school of psychology. Among Jung's distinctive ideas were his concept of psychological types (introverted and extraverted) and his belief that people have a collective unconscious (racial memories) in addition to the individual unconscious.
　　See also Introversion-Extraversion; Jung. *Consult* (13) Jacobi, 1962.

ANASTASI, ANNE (1908–), American psychologist. Born in New York City, she earned her Ph.D. at Columbia (1930) and has been a professor of psychology at Fordham University since 1951. Anastasi has been concerned with measurement, intelligence testing, and individual differences. Her major works include *Differential Psychology*, 1937; *Psychological Testing*, 1954 (rev. ed., 1968); *Human Relations and the Foreman*, 1951; and *Fields of Applied Psychology*, 1964. She is also the editor of *Individual Differences*, 1965, and *Testing Problems in Perspective*, 1966.

ANESTHETICS. *See* Drugs and Behavior.

ANGER. One of the most common human emotions, anger is considered to be one of the primary affects, along with the emotions of fear, grief, pain, and joy. In its mildest form, it is usually termed *annoyance*; very strong anger is termed *rage*.
　　Some attempts have been made to differentiate between various emotions in terms of the physiological responses that characterize them. This research has shown that the emotions of fear and anger are physiologically very similar. In general, however, fear is characterized by secretion of the hormone adrenalin; anger is characterized by the secretion of both adrenalin and noradrenalin. Fear and anger differ from each other in terms of seven basic autonomic nervous system responses. Anger is characterized by greater galvanic skin responses (GSRs), greater muscle tension, higher blood pressure, and lower heart rate than fear. In fear there is more muscle-tension peaking, higher skin conductance, and higher respiration than in anger.
　　The usual cause of anger is the thwarting of some goal-directed behavior or a threat from a nonfeared source. Thus anger can occur when a vending machine jams or when a salesclerk is rude. Insults, scoldings, and unjust accusations often result in anger also. On many occasions anger leads to aggressive or retaliatory behavior, and it is therefore often spoken of as a basic motive.
　　Severe anger (rage) responses can be observed when an animal is exposed to highly painful and inescapable stimulation such as shock.
　　　　—Brenda B. Bankart and C. Peter Bankart, *Wabash College*
　　See also Aggression; Psychosomatic Disorders.
　　Consult (8) Arnol 1960; Ax, 1953; Gates, 1926; Geen, 1968.

ANIMAL, EXPERIMENTAL. *See* Experimental Animals.

ANIMAL MAGNETISM. *See* Hypnosis.

ANIMAL PSYCHOLOGY, *See* Comparative Psychology.

ANONYMITY. Many nonnormative and antisocial impulses are normally held in check by fear of embarrassment or punishment. Two factors that can free an individual from these usual restraints, however, and provide him with the opportunity to engage in nontypical behavior are anonymity and deindividuation.
　　Anonymity refers to the conditions that occur when an individual is masked or not highly visible. Thus many burglars work at night, bank robbers wear masks, and members of the Ku Klux Klan wear white sheets that completely mask their identities. In an experiment testing the effects of anonymity on aggression, it was found that girls whose identities were masked with hoods delivered more than twice as much shock to a "victim" than did girls whose identities were not masked. Individuals are thought to seek anonymity as a defense against a hostile or threatening environment, where the individual fears punishment or retribution.
　　Deindividuation occurs when individuals are part of a large group and their identities are lost in a crowd. It is stressed by military establishments, for example, where recruits are required to dress, behave, and as much as possible look identical to one another. In *Mein Kampf* Adolf Hitler evidenced a clear understanding of the importance of deindividuation through identical dress and mass meetings to assure the blind following of authority.
　　　　—Brenda B. Bankart and C. Peter Bankart, *Wabash College*
　　See also Apathy-Indifference.
　　Consult (10) Ziller, 1964; Zimbardo, 1969.

American psychologist Anne Anastasi has focused on intelligence testing and individual differences.

Anonymity. Hitler understood very well that it is easier to assure the blind following of authority when individual identity is submerged in a crowd.

ANOREXIA NERVOSA, a psychoneurotic disorder marked by severe loss of appetite. Some patients develop such a distaste for food that they are in danger of starving to death. *See* Psychosomatic Disorders.

ANTABUSE THERAPY. Disulfiram (Antabuse) is a relatively inert chemical compound that has come to be a popular means of treating alcoholism, although some physicians are reluctant to use it. The drug has the effect of interfering with the metabolism of alcohol, resulting in a build-up of the toxin acetaldehyde in the blood. If alcohol is consumed, this condition leads to severe symptoms such as increased blood pressure, flushing of the skin, rapid breathing, and accelerated heart rate. If drinking continues, dizziness, nausea, and vomiting occur, eventually followed by a rapid fall in blood pressure, unconsciousness, and possibly death. Giving disulfiram is not itself a sufficient therapeutic program. However, many physicians regard the drug as a useful tool to help patients overcome the urge to drink while pursuing psychological rehabilitative techniques, such as group therapy.

See also Alcoholism.

ANTIDEPRESSANT DRUGS, amphetamines and other stimulants. *See* Drugs and Behavior.

ANTI-SEMITISM. *See* Prejudice.

ANTISOCIAL PERSONALITY, sometimes called psychopathic personality. *See* Personality Disorders; Sociopathic Personality Disturbance.

ANXIETY. One of the most frequently used terms in clinical psychology, anxiety usually refers to a feeling state very similar to fear but without any specific referent. Because fears tend to be directed toward specific situations or objects, such as height or snakes, while anxiety tends to be a diffuse feeling of uneasiness and tension not associated with any specific stimulus, anxiety has often been termed *vague fear* that may be associated with no object at all. Such a general and diffuse feeling without specific object is generally termed *free-floating anxiety.*

Anxiety is an unpleasant tension state, and the individual is highly motivated to rid himself of it. Most people manage to avoid many anxiety-producing situations and thus escape it. Often, however, anxiety results from mild threat, lack of appropriate social skills, and inner conflicts, and these situations cannot be easily avoided. In many of these cases conformity is seen as a means of relieving anxiety; if being or appearing different causes an individual to feel anxious, he may conform to reduce his anxiety. When anxiety becomes severe, the individual may attempt to relieve it through professional counseling.

Acute anxiety over a prolonged period or severe anxiety occurring in frequent episodes may be symptomatic of neurosis, specifically of a kind of neurosis known as *anxiety reactions.* Individuals suffering from acute anxiety and/or anxiety attacks should seek professional help.

—Brenda B. Bankart and C. Peter Bankart, *Wabash College*

See also Psychoneurotic Disorders; Psychosomatic Disorders.

Consult (8) Arnold, 1960. (13) Goldstein and Palmer, 1963; Spielberger, 1966.

APATHY-INDIFFERENCE. In an increasingly urban and impersonal society, apathy has become a problem of growing concern to social scientists. In 1964 at least thirty-eight individuals watched the stabbing murder of a girl in New York City; not one of them called for help during or after the stabbing. Two factors are known to contribute to the origins of this remarkable indifference.

Anonymity and deindividuation play a large role in creating a climate of indifference. Studies of helping behavior, for example, show that as the number of witnesses to a help-requiring situation increases, the amount of helping that occurs decreases and the time that passes before anyone offers help increases. Because the presence of others serves to increase the anonymity of the observers, it leads to diffusion of responsibility; no individual feels personally involved.

The second factor contributing to indifference is perceived loss of control. As individuals become convinced that they are less and less in charge of their own lives, their willingness to try to change things decreases. An analogous situation arises when dogs are exposed to a few trials of inescapable shock; they become apathetic and will not try to avoid shock in the future, even when it is possible to do so.

—Brenda B. Bankart and C. Peter Bankart, *Wabash College*

See also Anonymity; Bystander Apathy.

Consult (10) Altman, *et al.,* 1970; Darley and Latané, 1968; Latané and Darley, 1970; Ziller, 1964; Zimbardo, 1969.

APHASIA, impairment of the ability to use language. One of the many possible consequences of brain injury, it cuts across all language modalities—reading, writing, speaking, and listening. Aphasia refers specifically to the loss of the ability to use the linguistic rules regarding speech sounds, vocabulary, grammar, and meaning, once such rules have been learned. It is thus differentiated from those neurological disabilities that impair sensory and motor pathways at lower levels of mental function: *agnosia,* which refers to sensory impairment in the recognition of stimuli, and

Several frames from an 1885 series in the collection of the Museum of Modern Art, N.Y. When viewed in rapid sequence, the figures appear to move.

apraxia, which refers to motor impairment in formulating speech or manual responses.

Early study of aphasic disturbances led to the use of broad descriptive terminology—such as *receptive* impairment (difficulty understanding language), *expressive* impairment (difficulty producing language), or *receptive-expressive* impairment—to describe the behavior of the affected patient. Most recently, psycholinguistic approaches have led to more detailed categorization of aphasic errors. *Syntactic errors* reflect the inability to use the previously acquired grammatical structure of language. *Semantic errors* are seen in persons who maintain grammatical form in language but have difficulty recalling once-familiar proper names and substantive words (*anomia*). *Pragmatic errors* are revealed in the reduction of meaningful speech in which no context can be found. *Jargon* (nonsense speech) is often seen in severely impaired persons whose speech is unintelligible. *Global impairment* refers to the condition where little or no speech is available. Aphasic persons generally demonstrate various combinations of these difficulties rather than any one of the impairments.

Glossary of Aphasia

Auditory aphasia—difficulty in comprehension of spoken language; used to indicate receptive impairment of language.

Dysgraphia—disturbance of the ability to express thoughts in writing as a consequence of brain injury.

Dyslexia—disturbance of the ability to read as a consequence of brain injury. Also seen in children with multiple learning problems.

Dysphasia—partial loss of the ability to use language; used interchangeably with *aphasia.*

Motor aphasia—impairment in formulating and executing the movement patterns necessary for speaking; often used interchangeably with *apraxia.*

Stroke—a cerebral vascular accident (CVA), often resulting in brain injury. Aphasia frequently results when the dominant cerebral hemisphere is affected.

—Irv J. Meitus, *Purdue University*
See also Speech Disorders.
Consult (7) Halpern, 1972; Perkins, 1971; Schuell, *et al.,* 1964.

APPARENT MOVEMENT (also known as *stroboscopic movement* and the *phi phenomenon*), the experience of a moving object when the eye is stimulated by a succession of flashing stationary stimuli in different locations. Since no actual movement of the retinal image corresponds to the movement perceived, this illusory sensory experience has been of great importance in the history of psychology. It is a good example of a percep-

tion that differs from what the sensation would have to be presumed to be and yet is obviously not the result of a judgment. Therefore this phenomenon played an important role in the emergence of the Gestalt school of psychology.

It has been demonstrated that many species of animals, including newly hatched insects and fish, perceive movement under such conditions. The phenomenon depends upon such factors as brightness, the separation between the successive stimulus objects, the duration or "on" time of each, and the time interval between each. If the time interval is too short, both objects (or more if more are used) are perceived simultaneously; if it is too long, they are perceived successively; and in neither case is movement perceived. But, apart from these relevant factors, the explanation of the phenomenon is still not known.

Examples of movement perception based on this principle are moving pictures, television, and light displays used in advertising signs.

—Irvin Rock, *Rutgers University*
See also Perception.
Consult (4) Kolers, 1964; Rock, *et al.,* 1965.

APPLIED PSYCHOLOGY, a term that once meant a specialized field of psychology but now covers the whole range of ways in which the findings of psychologists are put to use in the world. In the nineteenth century and the first decades of the twentieth, most psychologists were researchers and theory builders. Applied psychology developed as a special effort to use theory as a guide to practice in such fields as advertising, personnel selection, and efficiency in industrial work. The *Journal of Applied Psychology,* founded in 1917, focused on applications of psychological theory of business and industry. Since that time, industrial psychology, personnel psychology, and consumer psychology have developed as important fields of specialization.

Currently, about two-thirds of American psychologists are working in what are primarily applied fields; the other third concentrates on research and teaching. The applications are made in clinical work, ecology, counseling, education, law, military affairs, and a long list of social problems in addition to fields such as consumer and engineering psychology (which contributes to space flights). It should be noted that it is often unprofitable to try to make distinctions between applied and research psychology. For example, one man or woman may both construct and use intelligence tests and contribute to the theoretical discussion about intelligence and its measurement. Encyclopedia articles that cover some major applications of psychology include Behavioral Ecology, Clinical Psychology, Consumer Psychology,

APPLIED PSYCHOLOGY

Psychology is put to use in many ways. The range of applications can be shown by a selection of articles. Studies of advertising and of consumer needs and attitudes are reported in CONSUMER PSYCHOLOGY. Contributions to the design of tools, machines, and working or living environments are covered in ENGINEERING PSYCHOLOGY, with special applications to space travel in SPACE PSYCHOLOGY.

Psychologists are taking a lead in efforts to help man live with, and improve, the earth's environment, as noted in BEHAVIORAL ECOLOGY. Also relevant are MENTAL HEALTH and MENTAL HOSPITALS (for evidence on how building design affects behavior). PSYCHOLOGY AND THE LAW reports how psychologists apply their findings to the work of courts and lawyers facing such problems as who should be put in a mental institution. A case of theory-into-action in clinical psychology is found in BEHAVIOR THERAPY.

For contributions to education, see EDUCATIONAL PSYCHOLOGY, SCHOOL PSYCHOLOGY, INTELLIGENCE AND INTELLIGENCE TESTING, and PROGRAMMED INSTRUCTION.

Educational Psychology, Engineering Psychology, Measurement, Military Psychology, Psychology and the Law, School Psychology, Space Psychology.

APRAXIA. *See* Aphasia.

APTITUDE TESTS. *See* Scholastic Aptitude Tests; Vocational Aptitude Tests.

AROUSAL, a measure of responsiveness or activity in organisms. Psychologically, arousal is related to activation in the brainstem reticular formation and can range from deep sleep or coma to intense excitement.

Arousal forms the basis for attention and, in particular, for the *orientation reflex,* or orienting response. The latter entails turning toward a source of stimulation, dilation of pupils, changes in the skeletal muscles and internal organs, and EEG activation (increase in the electrical activity of the brain). These adjustments prepare the organism to respond to a stimulus. The orientation reflex is believed to form the basis for learning.

—Joel F. Lubar, *University of Tennessee*
See also Attention.

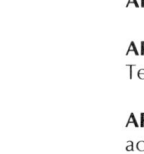

ASCH, SOLOMON (1907–), American psychologist. He received his Ph.D. from Columbia (1932) and is now professor of psychology at Rutgers University.

Asch is well known for his studies on the influence of the group on individual judgments. He generally found a high level of conformity to a majority opinion, even when it violated "objective" reality, in the perceptual task. In questioning subjects, Asch found that some people merely conform to majority opinion without rejecting their original judgment. He has continued to study group behavior attitude change and perceptual organization in learning. His textbook *Social Psychology* (1952) is widely used.

—Nina Adams, *Yale University*

ASPIRATION, LEVELS OF. Levels of aspiration designate ranges of goal-seeking behavior affected by cognitive influences. The term can also refer to forms of "felt urges" and drives.

Aspiration levels are determined by the individual's estimate of his own capabilities and his knowledge of the attainability of the goal. Individuals tend to raise or lower their levels of aspiration by attainment or nonattainment of goals rather than through their assessment of the absolute quality of their performance. The relationship between the level of aspiration and past as well as expected performance influences the risk the individual is willing to take in obtaining his goal.

—A. Ronald Seifert, *University of Tennessee*
See also Drive; Motivation.

ASSESSMENT, a term sometimes used for psychological testing or measurement. *See* Intelligence and Intelligence Testing; Measurement.

ASSIMILATION, in social psychology, "taking in" an attitude from another person or a group. *See* Attitudes and Attitude Change. In learning theory, the term *assimilation* refers to an aspect of Jean Piaget's view of intellectual growth. *See* Cognitive Development Theory.

ASSOCIATIONISM, the traditional theory that explains thinking and the contents of consciousness as the product of associative links between ideas. According to this doctrine, when one idea occurs in thinking, its occurrence is likely to evoke other associated ideas to which it is linked.

An idea may be thought of as a memory of an original sensory impression. Thus, a thoroughgoing associationistic doctrine posits ideas as coming from sensory experiences, and all thinking is considered to be chains of ideas that evoke each other by means of associative principles.

History. Associationism arose largely in opposition to other, older theories of the mind as composed of "innate" ideas that order rather than derive from sensory experience. Plato and Descartes advocated innate ideas. The seeds of associationism were sown by Aristotle, but it was not until Thomas Hobbes (1588–1679) that associations were proposed as a distinct alternative to innate ideas. Finally, the doctrine of associationism began to receive real impetus with the writings of John Locke (1632–1704), the first of the British empiricist philosophers who continued to develop associationism in considerable detail. Locke was followed by Bishop Berkeley (1685–1753), David Hume (1711–1776), and David Hartley (1705–1757), all of whom stated significant arguments in support of association principles.

In many respects, it was Hartley who combined his own and his predecessors' ideas into a comprehensive theory and consequently contributed more to the doctrine of associationism than other philosophers. Hartley was also the first thinker to postulate that associations could occur not only between ideas and sensations, but also between bodily movements and actions. This idea was a notable anticipation of modern doctrines of conditioning. Hartley's theory was truly comprehensive, since it contended that associations are the fundamental relationships and processes underlying all thinking, memory, meaning, imagination, dreams, and even morality.

At the beginning of the nineteenth century another philosopher, Thomas Brown (1778–1820), a Scotsman, made several suggestions about associations that were both original and eventually influential in psychology. He proposed that several "secondary" laws of

Group influence on individual judgment is the subject of major research by Solomon Asch.

association be added to the usual primary laws, and he recognized the importance of both individual differences in mental processes as well as the influence of emotional and constitutional factors on thinking. Unfortunately, many of Brown's ideas were ignored in his own time and did not receive their due until many years later.

Brown was ignored partly because of the popularity of a very mechanistic view of associations advocated by James Mill (1773–1836) and his son John Stuart Mill (1806–1873), the nineteenth-century popularizers of associationism. James Mill attributed all thinking to associative "compounds" of ideas and sensations, and he emphasized how events in experience determine mental events in a very mechanical fashion. He stressed the principle of *contiguity*: an association comes about merely because two items (ideas, sensations) occur together in space and time.

J. S. Mill did much to popularize associationistic principles and elaborated on his father's ideas. The ways in which he described how ideas could be combined came to be known as "mental chemistry," stressing the analogy of mental events with chemical compounding. In this context Mill suggested that in some cases the final "whole" idea might have a meaning or essence greater than the sum of its constituent parts—an idea that Gestalt psychology was to advocate in the twentieth century. Unlike his father, J. S. Mill held that associations were formed actively by the mind, not passively by experiences that determined the mind's working. This contrast between active vs. passive mind anticipated the modern contrast between cognitive psychology and S–R psychology.

Finally, near the end of the nineteenth century, Alexander Bain (1818–1903) presented the last comprehensive attempt to explain all psychological functions with associations. While such comprehensive explanations of behavior are no longer considered feasible, many of the basic ideas of associationism are still important in modern-day psychology.

Associative Laws. Many associative laws were formulated during the history of the doctrine, and these principles have often been used as hypotheses or as explanatory concepts in psychology. Perhaps the principle cited most often is *temporal contiguity*: Sensations, ideas, or movements that occur close together in time, or at nearly the same time, tend to become associated with each other. Temporal contiguity has been studied most thoroughly in conjunction with classical or Pavlovian conditioning situations, where it is of primary importance.

Other associative laws include:

Repetition (frequency)—Ideas that repeatedly occur together tend to become associated with each other.

Similarity—Ideas whose referents are similar tend to become associated with each other.

Recency—Associations that were formed recently are easiest to remember.

Vividness—The more vivid the associative experience, the stronger the associative bond.

The problem with such "laws" is not that they are invalid, but that all too often they have been expected to assume an explanatory burden far beyond their capacity. For example, temporal contiguity is a useful principle in learning theory, but contiguity of associations cannot account for all mental events and experiences. The philosophers who advocated a comprehensive associationism did not have to perform experiments to verify their claims, and they ignored differences between individuals, along with emotional and motivational factors.

On the other hand, many of the basic principles of associationism have profoundly influenced several areas of psychology. For example, free association became a preferred tool in psychoanalysis as therapy and influenced the thinking of both Freud and Jung.

—Roland Siiter, *Montclair State College*
See also Behaviorism; Free Association; Paired-Associate Learning; Pavlovian Conditioning; Serial Learning; Verbal Learning.

Consult (1) Murphy, 1949.

ASTHENIC REACTION, a psychoneurotic syndrome marked by chronic tiredness. The asthenic person finds it hard to concentrate and lacks the energy to complete mental or physical work. He may say that he needs extra sleep, but he wakes up feeling worse than when he went to bed. He often complains of headache, indigestion, or other bodily ailments. He tends to be listless and unable to cope with routine problems, though he may occasionally "wake up" and enjoy a card game or other specially interesting activity.

At one time the condition was labeled *neurasthenia* (literally, "nerve weakness") and was attributed to exhaustion of the nerves from prolonged overwork. The treatment of choice was rest and relaxation. Psychologists now believe that the problem is not fatigue from too much work but is a reaction to prolonged stress and frustration. Temporary feelings of fatigue or listlessness are normal in the face of conflict and stress. But where others get over these problems, the neurotic man or woman makes tiredness a way of life. Neurasthenic symptoms have a certain value in that they serve as an excuse for failure and a means to get attention. Psychotherapy can help the asthenic patient change his pattern.

See also Hypochondria.
Consult (13) Coleman, 1964.

ASTHMA, BRONCHIAL, a respiratory disorder

that is often related to anxiety and conflict (though allergies are also involved). *See* Psychosomatic Disorders.

ASTRAPHOBIA, excessive fear of electrical storms. *See* Phobia.

ASYLUM, an old term for an institution to contain those adjudged insane. Now called a hospital for the mentally ill. *See* Mental Hospital.

ATTENTION, the ability to focus on particular aspects of the environment. Attention allows an organism to select certain stimuli and to resist the distracting influence of all others. Most of the time this selectivity is useful: for example, it enables one to read in a noisy room or converse at a crowded party. At times, however, selective attention can prove dangerous, as when one reads billboards while driving.

Internal and external needs, past experience, or qualities of the stimulus itself, such as its intensity, size, contrast, or movement, determine which stimulus is selected for attention. For example, a mother will always hear her baby crying, an artist will notice variations in color, and an automobile backfire will usually disturb sleep. Even while attending to something, we are usually aware of other events occurring simultaneously and can ordinarily switch our attention to a new, previously nonattended stimulus. Experiments testing recognition and memory show that these nonattended stimuli are in our awareness but only their most gross features are remembered (for example, male or female voice, any strange sounds). The content, the style, and the language spoken are not subject to recall.

When a stimulus attracts our attention, we usually respond with a series of physiological reactions. These include movements of the head and body toward the stimulus, dilation of blood vessels in the head and constriction of blood vessels in the periphery, variations in the electrical activity of the brain, and changes in muscle tone, heart rate, and respiration. This overall response, called the *orienting reflex*, facilitates the reception of the stimulus and prepares us to react more specifically to the stimulus—quickly if necessary.

The evoked responses have been recorded during the different levels of attention, from sleep to alertness. There is always a reduction or disappearance of evoked responses to one stimulus while an animal orients or shifts attention to a novel stimulus. The evoked response to clicks is large while the animal is paying attention, but if a visual, olfactory, or tactile stimulus is presented, the evoked potential to the clicks decreases. The fluctuations of brain electrical activity recorded by the electroencephalogram vary in a systematic way with the behavioral state of attention. The changes in the evoked potential during attention occur only when the EEG activity is in an aroused state.

Most evidence indicates that the reticular formation, the region of the brain where all the sense modalities converge, is responsible for sending the impulses producing general arousal and changes in evoked potentials. The cortex is *not* crucial in controlling attention, since the changes in brain activity occur even when the cortex is removed. The reticular formation may prove to be the mechanism by which pertinent or important information is selected for attention.

—Nina Adams, *Yale University*
Consult (4) Bartley, 1969.

ATTENTION SPAN. In its usual meaning, this term refers to the length of time a person can attend to one stimulus. That span has been shown to vary as a function of age, task, and motivation. The term can also refer to the number of distinct objects that can be perceived in a single momentary presentation.

ATTITUDES AND ATTITUDE CHANGE. The notion of attitude has long been a central theme of American social psychology, but there is little agreement about how attitudes should be conceptualized. Most social psychologists agree that an attitude is a predisposition to respond to a focal object (attitude object), that these predispositions or *sets* are learned through experience, and that the existence of an attitude is inferred from consistencies in an individual's behavior. The important thing that different definitions of attitude have in common is that they are all trying to account for the simple fact that an individual exhibits consistent and predictable behavior in different situations and at different times.

Components of Attitudes. One popular view is that attitudes consist of *evaluative, affective* (feeling), and *conative* (action) components. To completely describe an individual's attitude toward something, we must know the *direction* and the *magnitude* (extremity) of his evaluation of the object (whether he believes it is good or bad and how much so), the *intensity* of the affect or emotion attached to this evaluation, and what action is implied by this evaluation and emotion. In general, the magnitude of an evaluation and the emotional intensity with which this evaluation is held are related by a U-shaped curve; the more extreme the opinion, the more intensely it is held. By far the most important component is the evaluative dimension. In fact, most attitude measures tap only this dimension, and most persuasion attempts are aimed at changing the evaluative component of attitudes. [*Consult* (10) Krech, *et al.*, 1962; Secord and Backman, 1964.]

Attitude Change: Components of Persuasion

Obviously, many people believe that behavior can be changed by changing attitudes. The American advertising industry spends more than $20 billion annually to influence attitudes, principally evaluations, that mediate consumer behavior. Modern political campaigns also revolve around sophisticated attempts to "sell" candidates. In military conflicts, particularly in so-called limited warfare, both sides use psychological operations to change enemy attitudes and behavior and to maintain the morale of partisans. [*Consult* (10) U. S. Army, 1962.]

One efficient way of analyzing any persuasion attempt is to ask: *Who* said *what to whom, how* and with *what effect?* In more formal terms, attitude change involves a *source, message, receiver* or target audience, *media* or mode by which the message is communicated, and the *effect* of the message. [*Consult* (10) Lasswell, 1948.]

Source. The source is the entity who communicates the message to the target audience, or at least the entity that the target audience believes is responsible for the message. In psychological warfare a distinction is made between three types of source: If the source is accurately identified, the propaganda is called "white"; if the message is falsely attributed to the enemy (as in rumors) it is labeled "black"; and if the source is left undefined the propaganda is "gray." [*Consult* (10) U.S. Army, 1962.]

The ability of the source to affect attitude change depends on how the audience feels about him. The more positive the evaluation, the more attitude change he can elicit. An audience will accept a source's argument if he has a great deal of *power* and they must *conform* in order to receive awards or avoid punishments, if he is *attractive* and they wish to *identify* with the source, or if he is very *credible* and they *internalize* his arguments and accept his information. [*Consult* (10) Kelman, 1958.]

Message. Message variables include the material that is communicated and the way it is presented. More research has been done on message factors in attitude change than any other, but it appears that what one says is less important than was once imagined. Some of the questions that have been asked include the following: Do arguments that provoke much fear elicit more attitude change than low-fear arguments? Is it better to put your strongest arguments at the beginning or the end of a presentation or should they be scattered throughout the presentation? When debating, is it better to speak first or last, and should one refute or ignore an opponent's charges? Should conclusions be made explicitly, or should they be left implicit in the argument? [*Consult* (10) Hovland, *et al.,* 1953; Janis, 1967.]

Receiver. The receiver is the target of the persuasion attempt, and much research has been conducted to determine what characteristics of the receiver facilitate persuasion. Emotional states, needs, and specific personality traits increase susceptibility in specific situations, but there is no evidence that there is a general gullibility factor. However, some evidence does suggest that susceptibility in different situations is correlated with a combination of various individual differences such as sex, age, and intelligence. [*Consult* (10) Janis, *et al.,* 1959.]

In study after study, females seem to be more generally suggestible than males. It has been suggested that this is because females generally have better verbal skills and are more likely than males to attend to and comprehend verbal arguments. Cultural training may be another reason females are more easily influenced than males; in our society, females are subject to stronger conformity pressures than are males, and this may lead to a general tendency to yield to persuasion attempts. The finding that females are more persuasible than males may also be an artifact of the experimental situations, which are dominated by male authorities. Hilgard, for example, argues that the predominate use of male hypnotists leads to the false conclusion that females are more hypnotizable than males. Evidence shows that, when both male and female hypnotists are used, the sex differences in hypnotic susceptibility disappear. [*Consult* (14) Hilgard, 1965; McGuire, 1954.]

Persuasibility seems to increase with age up until eight or nine and then drops off and finally stabilizes during adolescence.

There is no clear relationship between intelligence and susceptibility, although IQ is sometimes important in particular situations—that is, it interacts with other variables in the attitude-change situation. For example, high-IQ soldiers in one study responded more to two-sided arguments than to one-sided arguments, and low-IQ soldiers showed more attitude change when the conclusions were explicit rather than implicit in the argument. [*Consult* (10) Hovland, *et al.,* 1949.]

Media. The media include all of the channels (modes) of communication that the source uses to transmit his message to the target audience. Some people such as Marshall McLuhan argue that the "medium is the message," that how something is communicated is more important than what is communicated or who communicates it. However, it appears that media effectiveness is determined not by intrinsic qualities of the media but by the combined characteristics of the source, message, and receiver. In general, face-to-face communications have more impact on the individual receiver than mass communications, but again the effect depends upon what is being communicated. [*Consult* (10) McLuhan and Fiore, 1967.]

Effects. The effects of a persuasive communication may be seen immediately or they may be delayed. The delayed acceptance of a persuasive message, the so-called *sleeper effect,* probably occurs when the receiver forgets details that made him initially reject the message (for example, it came from a negative source). [*Consult* (10) Hovland, *et al.,* 1949.]

A more common finding is that opinion change immediately follows the persuasion attempt but that over time the individual reverts to his original opinion. This reversion probably occurs because the individual lives in an environment that strongly supports the original opinion.

Theories of Attitude Change

Most social psychologists subscribe to one of four basic theories of attitude change. They are, in the order of their popularity, cognitive-consistency theories, the information-processing model, the functional approach, and the perceptual approach.

Cognitive-Consistency Theories. Balance theory, congruity theory, dissonance theory, and "probabilogic" theory are collectively known as *cognitive-consistency* theories because they all assume that the individual has an acquired (learned) drive to maintain the maximum possible consistency between beliefs and that the presence of inconsistency between salient beliefs elicits a noxious tension state that the individual will attempt to reduce or avoid. This tension state operates as a psychological signal that the individual is not coping adequately. For example, to smoke (belief 1) is inconsistent with the knowledge that smoking causes lung cancer and heart disease (belief 2), and hence tension is provoked. Consistency can be achieved and tension reduced in several ways: by not smoking, by discounting the evidence that smoking is dangerous (altering belief 2), or by adding additional information (belief 3, smoking has great emotional benefits, which make it worth the cost). [*Consult* (10) Festinger, 1957; Heider, 1958; Kelman and Baron, 1968; McGuire, 1968; Osgood and Tannenbaum, 1955.]

The best-articulated and most-influential cognitive-consistency theory is Festinger's theory of cognitive dissonance. [*Consult* (10) Festinger, 1957.]

Postdecisional dissonance. Choosing between two attractive alternatives is difficult, and after the choice is made the individual will attempt to rationalize the decision by enhancing the characteristics of the chosen alternative and depreciating the rejected alternative. In general, the more difficult and irrevocable the decision, the more postdecisional dissonance that will occur. [*Consult* (10) Brehm and Cohen, 1962.]

Selective exposure to information. Seeking information that supports one's beliefs and avoiding information that challenges them are ways of avoiding or reducing dissonance, but this common-sense notion has proven to be a complex issue. [*Consult* (10) Freedman and Sears, 1965; Rhine, 1967.]

Forced compliance. Dissonance theory suggests the novel hypothesis that the *less* a person is paid to do a distasteful task, the *more* he will enjoy doing it. [*Consult* (10) Carlsmith *et al.,* 1966; Festinger and Carlsmith, 1959.]

The Information-Processing Model. Yale University psychologist William McGuire suggests that successful persuasion attempts involve five sequential processes: *attention, comprehension, yielding, retention,* and *action.* If the persuader cannot get the target's attention, he certainly cannot modify attitudes; moreover, if the target does not understand the arguments he hears or comprehend what is expected of him, he cannot change his attitudes and behavior as the persuader desires. But even if the individual attends to the argument and understands its implications, no attitude change will occur unless he yields to the argument and accepts its implications as a guide for his behavior and retains this decision until it is appropriate to act upon it. And finally, the individual must be motivated to act in accordance with the new attitude. If the sequence of processes is interrupted at any point, attitude change will not occur. [*Consult* (10) McGuire, 1954; McGuire, 1972.]

Functional Theories. The functional approach to attitudes assumes that people hold a particular attitude because it serves some basic need, and thus to change attitudes one must consider more than simply the individual's apparent attitude toward a particular focal object. [*Consult* (10) Katz, 1960; Smith, 1969.]

For example, ethnic prejudice, an indiscriminately negative attitude toward members of other ethnic groups, may be a result of a particular pattern of childhood socialization rather than a product of some experience with the other ethnic group. This approach to attitudes is favored by psychoanalytically inclined theorists and has been applied in the study of the authoritarian personality.

The Perceptual Approach. Proponents of this theory argue that the individual changes his perception of attitudes to suit his needs. For example, experiments show that a political slogan ("I hold that a little rebellion, now and then, is a good thing and is as necessary in the political world as storms are in the physical") has a very different meaning when it is attributed to Lenin than when it is attributed to Thomas Jefferson, its true author. The "meaning" of the motto is determined by a larger frame of reference. The perceptual approach to attitude change focuses on the categories, frames of reference, or labels that people use to organize their social environment. [*Consult* (10) Asch, 1952; Sherif and Sherif, 1969.]

—R. Gary Bridge, *Columbia University*
See also Attitude Measures; Internal-External Control; Prejudice.

Consult (10) Fishbein and Ajzen, 1972; McGuire, 1968; Sears and Abeles, 1969; Smith, 1969.

ATTRIBUTES OF CONCEPTS. *See* Concept Learning.

AUDITION. *See* Hearing.

AUTHORITARIANISM. *See* Authoritarian Personality.

AUTHORITARIAN PERSONALITY, or authoritarian character, personality pattern marked by a desire for obedience from all who are lower in power or influence. Associated with this central trait are others such as dependence on authority and rigid rules, insistence on conformity to group values, admiration for power figures, and hostility to those perceived as minorities or "outgroups." At all these points, the authoritarian personality is at odds with the democratic personality.

The authoritarian personality was first defined at length as a result of a study of anti-Semitism, and the pattern has been found to match that of Nazi party members. The authors of the study concluded that anti-Semitic prejudice was part of a general personality structure. They believed that this pattern represents a way of venting buried hostility: the syndrome develops in persons who are overly controlled and obedient in childhood. Hostile feelings are eventually turned against "safe" targets such as ethnic minorities.

See also Prejudice.

AUTISM, INFANTILE, a behavioral syndrome first described in 1943. [*Consult* (13) Kanner, 1944.] The diagnosis should be restricted to children who have the onset, before 30 months of age, of a disorder involving failure to develop interpersonal relationships, a delay in speech and language development, and ritualistic behavior. It is much more common in boys, and population prevalence rates are 4 to 5 per 10,000.

The cause of autism is unknown, but there is now good evidence that it is not a form of schizophrenia, a form of brain damage, a form of mental retardation, a form of social withdrawal, a disorder of arousal, a genetic disorder, or a psychogenic disorder. The best evidence is that autism is most likely the result of some form of central cognitive disorder, probably a central disorder of language that involves both the comprehension of language and the utilization of language and conceptual skills in thinking.

Four factors are related to long-term prognosis of autistic children: (1) IQ—the single most important factor, (2) development of useful language, (3) overall severity of the disorder, (4) educational treatment. Overall, only one autistic child in six makes a good social adjustment as an adult, with another one in six making a fair adjustment. The other two-thirds are severely handicapped and unable to lead an independent life. More than 25 percent develop epileptic fits in adolescence or early adult life. Very few autistic children with a normal IQ develop fits, while most autistic children with an IQ below 50 do, suggesting that autistic children with severe intellectual retardation have a form of brain damage (as do most nonautistic children with that level of intellectual retardation).

Systematic studies of treatment results are sparse, but the available evidence suggests that psychodynamic psychotherapy has little value. Behavioral techniques have been effective, but recent evidence suggests that developmental approaches that involve the parents in the treatment may be of greater benefit. The only controlled study of educational therapy indicates that a structured approach that involves training in perceptual and linguistic skills offers the most promise.

—Dennis P. Cantwell, M.D., *University of California, Los Angeles*
Consult (13) Rutter, 1971; Wing, 1966.

AUTISTIC THINKING, a tendency to turn to wish-fulfilling fantasies as an escape from objective reality. Autism covers a wide range of imaginative, wish-fulfilling thinking. For example, "conquering hero" daydreams are common in childhood and adolescence—a boy imagines he has been drafted by a pro football team, or a girl casts herself as homecoming queen. Such fantasies are not necessarily abnormal and may even provide motivation. On the other hand, spending too much time in an unreal world can be a sign of a psychotic problem.

The term *infantile autism* is applied to a severe disorder observed in young children.

See also Autism, Infantile; Daydreaming; Psychotic Disorders.

AUTOEROTICISM, in general, sexual self-stimulation. This may take the form of conscious fantasy, looking at pictures or reading books, listening to music, or stimulating erogenous areas of the body by hand or with implements. When the penis, clitoris, or vagina are directly stimulated, the autoerotic behavior is called masturbation, especially if it results in orgasm. Autoerotic behavior is common among people of all ages. Among adults, how-

An autistic child. Autism is believed to be the result of a central disorder of language.

ever, the practice of autoeroticism to the exclusion of other sexual outlets is rare.

—Eugene E. Levitt, *Indiana University School of Medicine*
See also Masturbation.
Consult (13) Dearborn, 1967; Katchadourian and Lunde, 1972.

AUTONOMIC NERVOUS SYSTEM. As opposed to the somatic nervous system, the autonomic nervous system is involved in the regulation of the visceral organs and their secretions and in the control of smooth muscles. It consists of two main divisions: the sympathetic and the parasympathetic. Within each of these divisions there are both afferent (sensory) and efferent (motor) components. The sympathetic branch of the autonomic system arises from the thoracic and lumbar portions of the spinal cord. The parasympathetic division originates in the sacral division of the cord and in the brainstem. Thus, the term "parasympathetic" literally means next to or surrounding the sympathetic nervous system.

The Sympathetic System. Specifically arising from cell bodies located in the lateral horn of the gray matter of the spinal cord in the thoracic and lumbar regions, the sympathetic system is primarily an efferent or output system. Axons leave the cell bodies and exit through the ventral root of the spinal cord along with somatic fibers destined for striated muscles. The main difference between autonomic and somatic outflow is that in the case of the autonomic outflow there is a ganglion and ganglionic synapse. Thus, fibers exiting in the autonomic nervous system leave the ventral root a short distance from the cord via the *white ramus* and there enter a ganglionic chain known as the sympathetic *paravertebral ganglionic chain*. Once these fibers enter the chain they may ascend or descend in the chain and then exit at a different level; synapse in the chain; or pass directly through the ganglionic chain at the same level without synapse. If they choose the third route, they then travel toward their target organ and synapse in a ganglion near it. In some cases a sympathetic fiber, after synapsing in the ganglionic chain, can reenter the main spinal nerve by means of the *gray ramus*.

The portion of the sympathetic outflow lying between the spinal cord and the ganglionic synapse is termed the *preganglionic fiber*. The portion beginning at the synapse and traveling toward the target organ is called the *postganglionic fiber*. All preganglionic fibers utilize acetylcholine as a neurotransmitter and hence are called *cholinergic fibers*. Almost all postganglionic fibers that enter visceral organs utilize norepinephrine (noradrenalin) as the neurotransmitter at their terminals and are called *adrenergic fibers*. Postganglionic sympathetic fibers that innervate blood vessels and the sweat glands, however, are cholinergic.

The Parasympathetic Nervous System. In the parasympathetic nervous system, fibers from the sacral portion of the spinal cord exit through the ventral roots but do not pass through a specific chain of ganglia. Instead they head directly toward the target organ in the sacral spinal nerves and synapse in parasympathetic ganglia located in its vicinity. Parasympathetic fibers exit from the brainstem within cranial nerves. So, for example, the *vagus nerve* (the tenth cranial nerve) carries parasympathetic fibers to internal organs located in the thoracic and abdominal regions of the body. The entire parasympathetic division is cholinergic.

Generally the two divisions of the autonomic nervous system, sympathetic and parasympathetic, act in opposition to one another. The sympathetic division is primarily active during periods of stress or emergency. The parasympathetic system predominates during quiet, restful periods. The latter is involved in homeostatic mechanisms—that is, the normal regulation of organ systems.

Both the sympathetic and parasympathetic divisions of the autonomic nervous system are represented in the *hypothalamus*. The anterior portion of the hypothalamus is primarily parasympathetic, whereas the posterior portion of the hypothalamus is primarily sympathetic. Stimulation of the posterior portions of the hypothalamus often results in increased metabolism, pupillary dilation, rage, and other sympathetic activities. Stimulation of the anterior portion of the hypothalamus may induce sleep, increase digestion, and lower metabolic rate.

—Joel F. Lubar, *University of Tennessee*
See also Nervous System.
Consult (3) Isaacson, *et al.,* 1971; Leukel, 1972.

AUTOSUGGESTION. *See* Suggestion.

AVERAGE, in statistics, a figure that provides some estimate of central tendencies or typical characteristics of a group. The three most common averages are the mean, the median, and the mode. *See* Mean; Median; Mode.

AVERSIVE COUNTERCONDITIONING. *See* Behavior Therapy.

AVOIDANCE LEARNING. *See* Escape Learning.

AXON. *See* Neuron.

BACKWARD CONDITIONING, a procedure used in learning experiments. In the standard conditioning procedure, a conditioned stimulus (CS—a tone, for example) is presented to

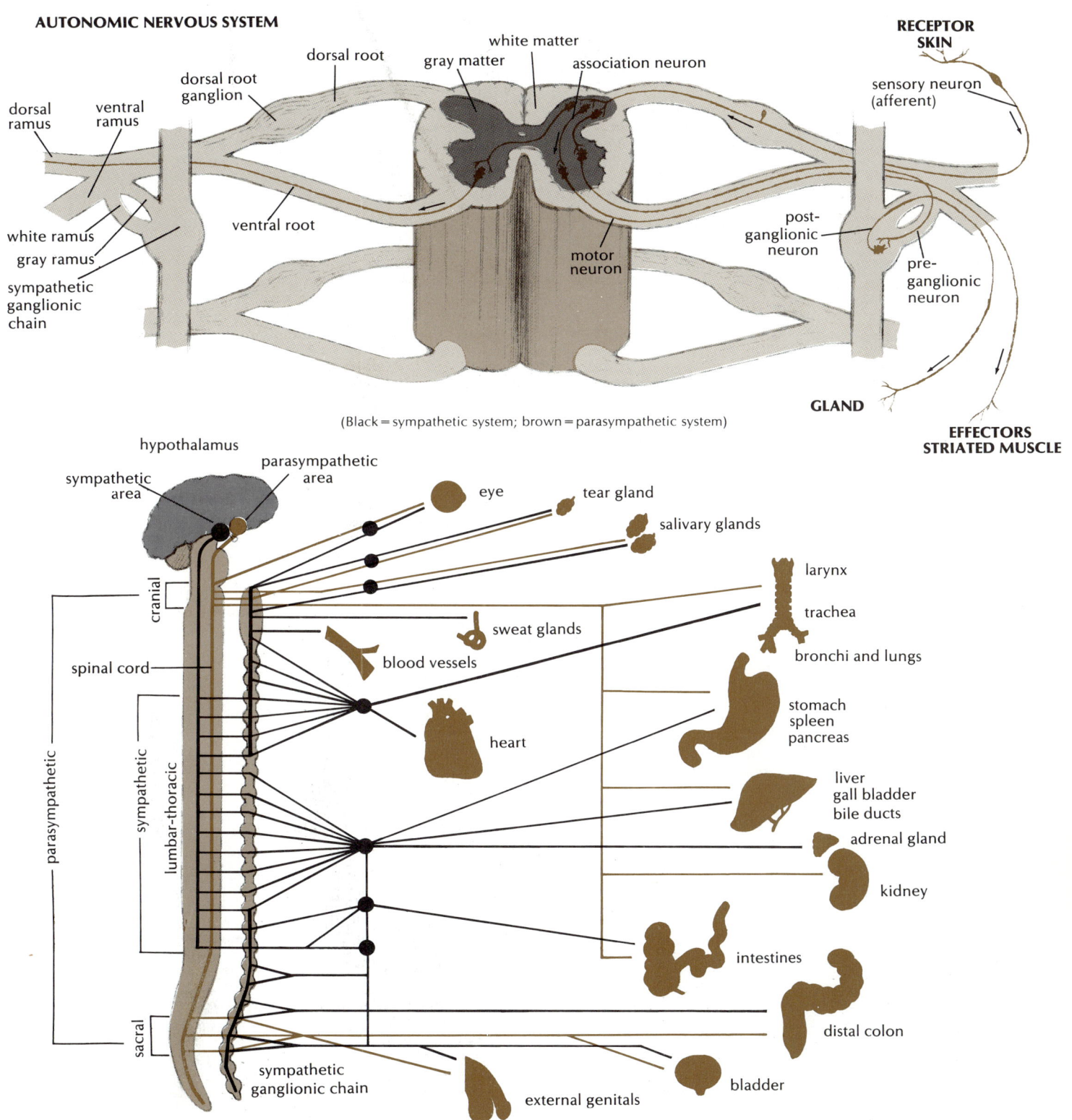

AUTONOMIC NERVOUS SYSTEM

dorsal root

dorsal root ganglion

white matter

gray matter

association neuron

RECEPTOR SKIN

sensory neuron (afferent)

dorsal ramus

ventral ramus

dorsal ramus

white ramus

gray ramus

sympathetic ganglionic chain

ventral root

motor neuron

post-ganglionic neuron

pre-ganglionic neuron

GLAND

(Black = sympathetic system; brown = parasympathetic system)

EFFECTORS STRIATED MUSCLE

hypothalamus

parasympathetic area

sympathetic area

eye

tear gland

salivary glands

cranial

larynx

trachea

sweat glands

bronchi and lungs

spinal cord

blood vessels

stomach spleen pancreas

parasympathetic

sympathetic

lumbar-thoracic

heart

liver gall bladder bile ducts

adrenal gland

kidney

intestines

sacral

distal colon

sympathetic ganglionic chain

external genitals

bladder

25

Albert Bandura, noted for his work on the role of modeling in learning.

The chief target of Theodore Barber's exploration has been the psychophysiology of hypnotic phenomena.

the subject first, followed at a short interval by an unconditioned stimulus (UCS—a shock, for example). The UCS produces a response, such as withdrawing from the shock. After a number of pairings of CS and UCS, the CS alone produces the response.

Experimenters have tried reversing the order and presenting the UCS first, followed by the CS. In most cases, little conditioning occurred, and the small effects observed are attributed to pseudoconditioning.

See also Pavlovian Conditioning; Pseudoconditioning.

Consult (6) Kimble, 1961.

BAD TRIP, a common term for a frightening and dangerous state sometimes produced by hallucinogenic drugs. LSD (lysergic acid), mescaline, and other mind-expanding drugs can bring on states described as transcendent and ecstatic. On the other hand, these drugs can cause terrifying hallucinations and have produced symptoms mimicking those of paranoid schizophrenia. One man described an LSD trip as "my twelve hours as a madman." Persons on "bad trips" may end up in hospitals because they are suffering from overwhelming panic or try murder or suicide.

See also Drugs and Behavior.

Consult (13) Katz, 1953; Louria, 1967.

BANDURA, ALBERT (1925–   ), American psychologist. He received a Ph.D. from the State University of Iowa in 1952, and was professor of psychology at Stanford University from 1964. He was president of the American Psychological Association in 1972.

Bandura is well-known for his work demonstrating the role of imitation or modeling in learning. According to Bandura, a person learns new responses by imitating another's behavior. Reinforcement does not play a major role in the initial learning of the behavior, since the learner may merely observe the behavior with no apparent response and no reinforcement and still successfully imitate the behavior at another time. Reinforcement comes into play in strengthening and maintaining the new behavioral pattern.

His work has particular application to child psychology. Since the child learns by imitation, the parents should be aware that they serve as models in the development of the child's personality.

Among Bandura's publications are *Adolescent Aggression* (with R. H. Walters, 1959) and *Social Learning and Personality* (with Walters, 1963).

BARBER, THEODORE XENOPHON, (1927–   ), American psychologist. Born in Martins Ferry, Ohio, he received a Ph.D. in psychology from American University (1956). At present, he is research associate in psychi-

atry at the School of Medicine, Boston University.

Barber has been active in the scientific analysis of hypnosis and hypnotic behavior, including the psychophysiology of pain under hypnosis, hallucinations, and amnesia. He is the author of the Barber Suggestibility Scale. He is outspoken in his skepticism about hypnotic phenomena being "a separate state." He is the author of *Hypnosis: A Scientific Approach* (1969) and numerous articles on hypnosis.

BARBITURATES, sedative-hypnotic drugs such as phenobarbital, widely used to reduce tension and induce sleep. Excessive use can lead to addiction and to barbiturate intoxication—poisoning that can cause brain damage. Overdoses can cause coma and death. *See* Drugs and Behavior.

BARGAINING, the process by which at least two (parties) with initially different preferences engage in a series of exchanges and compromises in search of a solution that is mutually satisfactory. This process can take the form either of *negotiation,* which involves verbal interchange, or of *tacit bargaining,* which involves communication by means of strategic moves. Psychologists interested in this topic have mostly studied bilateral negotiation, using experimental gaming methods.

Two kinds of behavior are typically found in bargaining: *distributive behavior* is aimed at eliciting concessions from the other party, and *conciliatory behavior* is aimed at finding a mutually acceptable solution. Distributive behavior often takes the form of extreme demands, commitments to specific positions, threats, and arguments about why the other party should yield. When one party engages in distributive behavior, the other typically follows suit. Conciliatory behavior entails concessions, proposals for the exchange of concessions, joint problem solving, and various informal communication moves that facilitate the exchange of *concession.* The latter include sending signals, employing intermediaries to transmit messages, and arranging for private conferences between the bargainers. In situations that are labeled *negotiation,* conciliatory behavior often follows distributive behavior.

Laboratory findings support several generalizations about negotiation: If agreement is reached, the party with the higher level of aspiration will gain more. The more extreme the aspirations of the two bargainers, the fewer agreements will be reached and the longer it will take to reach agreement. When the constraints governing the other party's behavior are unknown, a negotiator will become more conciliatory as the other's demands become more extreme; but the opposite is true if the constraints governing his behavior are known. New options that provide greater benefit to both parties than those currently available are most likely to be discovered when both parties maintain high levels of aspiration and engage in problem solving.

—Dean G. Pruitt, *State University of New York at Buffalo*

Consult (10) Kelley, *et al.,* 1967; Lewis and Pruitt, 1971; Nemeth, 1972; Pruitt, 1971; Schelling, 1960; White, 1970.

BARTLETT, SIR FREDERIC CHARLES (1886–), British psychologist. Born in Stow-on-the-Wold, England, he received an M.A. at London University and honorary doctorates at Athens, 1937, Princeton, 1947, Louvain, 1949, Edinburgh, 1961, and Oxford, 1962.

Bartlett is a leader in the field of experimental psychology in Great Britain and the author of many books and articles. His major works include: *Textbook of Experimental Psychology,* Part II, 1925 (with Myers); *Psychology and the Soldier,* 1927; *Remembering: An Experimental and Social Study,* 1932; *The Problem of Noise,* 1934; *Political Propaganda,* 1941; *The Mind at Work and Play,* 1951; *Thinking: An Experimental and Social Study,* 1958.

BAYLEY, NANCY (1899–), American psychologist. Born in The Dalles, Oregon, she took her Ph.D. in psychology at the University of Iowa in 1926. She is now consulting psychologist, Institute of Human Development, University of California at Berkeley.

Bayley has been concerned with growth and development of the human child, physically, psychologically, and intellectually. Her studies have often concerned infant behavior, how it changes with growth, and its use as a predictor of later behavior. In 1940, Bayley showed that intelligence scales for infants do not adequately predict later IQ scores. The best predictor of what the IQ will be at age six, according to her findings, is the educational level of the parents of the two-year-old.

Bayley is coauthor of *Growth Diagnosis,* 1959, and author of *Child Development,* 1950; *Correlations of Maternal and Child Behaviors with the Development of Mental Abilities,* 1964.

BEDLAM, a popular name for an asylum for the mentally ill. The word originated as a contraction of St. Mary of Bethlehem, which was the name of a hospital in London. Used for mental patients as early as 1402, the institution was formally designated a "lunatic asylum" by King Henry VIII in 1547. Conditions in Bedlam were so terrible that "bedlam" became a general term for confusion and uproar. *See also* Mental Hospital.

BEDWETTING. *See* Enuresis.

BEERS, CLIFFORD WHITTINGHAM (1876–1943), American mental hygienist. Born, New Haven, Conn. Regarded as the founder of the mental-hygiene movement in the United States, Beers began his work to reform mental institutions while himself a mental patient. After trying unsuccessfully to have hospital administrators improve conditions at his hospital, Beers smuggled letters out to state officials and in this way managed to instigate some improvements. Upon his release, Beers wrote *A Mind That Found Itself* (1908) to show that mental patients could recover and to detail the need for humane treatment of mental patients. He portrayed the mentally ill as sick people who could be treated and cured. The book, which drew praise from William James, set into motion Beers' plan for a national crusade for reform.

In 1908 Beers founded the Connecticut Society for Mental Hygiene, the first organization of its type. The purpose of the society was to eliminate restraint and punishment methods of treatment in mental hospitals and to provide information on mental disease to the public. Beers served as secretary of the National Committee for Mental Hygiene (1909–1939). He organized the American Foundation for Mental Hygiene in 1928, and in 1930 he helped organize the International Congress on Mental Health.

BEHAVIOR DISORDER. Roughly synonymous with "mental illness," this category includes psychoneurotic disorders (neuroses), functional and organic psychoses, personality (character) disorders, psychosomatic disorders, mental retardation, and temporary reactions to catastrophe and stress. The term focuses on the inadequate behavior rather than the "illness" producing it. The concept of behavior disorder depends in large part on comparison with some societal "norm." That is, a person is judged to be suffering from a disorder when his behavior deviates from what his society calls normal.

BEHAVIOR MODIFICATION. *See* Behavior Therapy; Psychotherapy.

BEHAVIOR SETTING. *See* Behavioral Ecology.

BEHAVIOR THERAPY, the treatment of behavior disorders through the application of learning principles. Proponents of behavior therapy believe that all abnormal behavior, except that which is organically based, is learned in the same way that normal behaviors are, through reinforcement and conditioning. The fact that such therapists direct their treatment toward the modification of behavior distinguishes them from the various kinds of psychotherapists who attempt to modify unconscious conflicts.

Clifford Beers pioneered the U.S. mental hygiene movement, stressing the need for change in the attitude toward and treatment of the mentally ill.

BEHAVIORAL ECOLOGY

Examples of the ecological approach in psychology can be found in COMMUNITY PSYCHOLOGY and MENTAL HEALTH. ANXIETY, STRESS, NOISE, and OVERCROWDING are areas of study for psychologists and psychiatrists in their examination of the ways in which environmental pollution causes or triggers mental disorders. An example of a specialized study of environmental effects—how architecture can harm or help behavior—is given in MENTAL HOSPITALS.

Environmental psychologists share a basic approach with ethologists, who specialize in studying animal behavior. Both stress studying behavior in its natural or actual setting rather than in a laboratory. See ETHOLOGY.

Methods. A number of different techniques employing learning principles can be used to modify behavior. The simplest of these is *extinction*, which involves removal of reinforcement. Many behaviors are strengthened through attention. A mother may respond to her child's tantrums with scolding, for example, but if this means that the child has gained attention, the scolding may actually strengthen the tantrum behavior. If it is ignored, and thereby not reinforced, it will eventually weaken and disappear.

Counterconditioning is a therapy in which maladaptive responses, including anxiety, are weakened or eliminated by strengthening incompatible responses. In *desensitization,* a form of positive counterconditioning, relaxation, which is incompatible with anxiety, is learned as a new response. Desensitization is used with considerable success in the treatment of phobias. In the case of snake phobias, for example, an *anxiety hierarchy* is constructed, in which the patient orders snake-related stimuli according to their degree of intensity, and the patient is then presented with the least-feared stimulus and instructed to relax. When he can successfully relax to the first stimulus without feeling any anxiety, the next stimulus is presented. In this way, relaxation gradually replaces the old fear response.

Aversive counterconditioning is employed in situations involving maladaptive sexual or drug-related responses. In one treatment for alcoholism, a drug administered to the patient makes him extremely nauseated when he consumes any alcohol. Thus, nausea becomes associated with drinking, and avoidance of alcohol is strengthened.

Positive reinforcement is a technique used to teach new behavior, such as speech in mute children or adults. In this procedure, any vocalization is reinforced at first, with candy, cigarettes, praise, or anything else the patient will work for. Once the patient is vocalizing reliably, he is required to make sounds that more closely approximate words. The procedure is continued until the patient eventually learns to speak normally.

The teaching of new behavior can be laborious and time-consuming, and it is often helpful to make use of imitation. The presence of a model who is rewarded for engaging in the desired behavior will help the patient learn more quickly.

Positive reinforcement has been applied in educational and institutional settings with considerable success. Since the administration of material rewards can be cumbersome, however, token-economy systems are often used. Patients are given tokens with an assigned value, which can be exchanged for material rewards or privileges. Tokens can be administered efficiently and have the advantage that the patient can choose his own reward. By using tokens, it is possible to modify several behaviors in group settings.

—Brenda B. Bankart and C. Peter Bankart, *Wabash College*

See also Operant Conditioning; Psychotherapy.

Consult (13) Bandura, 1969; Ullmann and Krasner, 1969; Wolpe, 1958; Wolpe and Lazarus, 1966.

BEHAVIORAL ECOLOGY, an area of psychology that focuses on the transaction between the ecological environment and behavior. The "transaction" implies that the interaction between an environment and the behavior within it is reciprocal. The term "ecological" indicates that behavioral ecology concerns itself with an organism's interaction with its entire environment rather than a piece of the environment such as a single stimulus.

Relations to Biology. Because ecological theory has its roots in biology, several researchers have employed concepts from biological ecology to explain psychological phenomena. The principle of *interdependence* is the cornerstone of ecological theory. This principle states that the parts of any system—whether they are groups of people inhabiting the same area, species in an ecosystem, divisions of an organization, or individuals in a small discussion group—are in a dynamic relationship and that a change in any part of the system affects the other parts. [*Consult* (14) Barker, 1969; Kelly, 1970; Sells, 1966; Trickett and Todd, 1972.]

The biological concepts of adaptation and the ecological niche also have important implications for psychology. An *ecological niche* is a "place" that can be defined in terms of its requirements for a unique set of survival skills (for example, a desert, a rain forest, a cocktail party). *Adaptation* is the sum of the change processes that allow an organism to "fit into" an ecological niche. The phrase "fit into" can mean anything from survive to "become self-actualized in," depending on the operational definition of success being used. A major concern of behavioral ecology is to define the skills needed to make successful adaptations in various types of settings. One study, for example, examined the skills needed to enter different types of high schools. [*Consult* (14) Trickett, *et al.,* 1970.]

Behavior Settings. Another major concern of behavioral ecology is the discovery of typical behavior patterns and the distribution of psychological phenomena in behavior settings. Barker defines a *behavior setting* as a setting characterized by a standing pattern of behavior. The most obvious examples of behavior settings are those such as libraries, football games, and churches. It is easy to predict, for example, that football game behavior would be unwelcome in a church. Behavioral ecologists have examined such questions as the amount of aggression and compliance in the behavior streams of children, the effects of seating arrangements on group interaction, and the behavior of the same child in different milieus. [*Consult* (14) Barker, 1968; Barker and Wright, 1955; Gump, *et al.,* 1963; Sommer, 1967; Willems, 1969.]

Research Philosophy. Behavioral ecology holds a research philosophy that reflects its basic viewpoint. The naturalistic research methods used by behavioral ecologists employ observational techniques to examine the environment without interfering with its natural functioning. The reason for this lies in the belief that the traditional laboratory method of breaking the whole into its parts and examining the parts destroys the essential structure of the environment. The naturalistic approach, however, is not seen as antagonistic to the laboratory method. The laboratory investigation allows the experimenter to make precise statements. Naturalistic observations outside the laboratory give the experimenter knowledge about the importance of his statements in everyday life. [*Consult* (14) Raush, 1969; Willems, 1969.]

—Robert B. Innes, *George Peabody College for Teachers*

See also Community Psychology; Ethology; Mental Health; Mental Hospital; Overcrowding; Stress.

Consult (14) Barker, 1963; Barker and Gump, 1964; Dubos, 1965; Faris and Dunmah, 1939; Gump and Kounin, 1960; Proshansky, *et al.,* 1970; Raush, *et al.,* 1959; Rhodes, 1970; Thomas, *et al.,* 1968; Willems and Raush, 1969.

BEHAVIORISM, a school of psychology that stresses the study of observable actions and reactions of organisms. Nineteenth-century psychologists gave a great deal of time to the study of consciousness through such means as introspection. Behaviorists charged that using your own or others' reports of mental experiences was unscientific. They proposed to concentrate on observable and quantifiable phenomena such as actions of glands and muscles. Behaviorists, influenced by British biological psychologists such as Charles Darwin and Lloyd Morgan, tended to view behavior as a process of adjusting to the environment. They also drew ideas from Ivan P. Pavlov's experiments and made conditioning the central process in learning. Concepts such as thinking, feeling, and willing were considered outside the proper focus of scientific psychology.

The emergence of behaviorism as a major school in American psychology can be dated from 1912, when John B. Watson began a series of lectures and articles setting forth his views. The school has had great influence in the United States—for example, in promoting rigorous standards for laboratory experiments and refinements of laboratory animals, particularly in learning experiments. The tradition of behaviorism is carried on by B. F. Skinner, who maintains that behavior can be predicted and controlled through studies of applications of conditioning.

On the other hand, critics of behaviorism maintain the role of emotions, cognitive processes, and social influences in learning and all kinds of behavior.

See also Cognitive Psychology; Learning Theory; Mind.

Consult (1) Dashiell, 1949; Wann, 1964; Watson, 1924; Woodworth and Sheehan, 1948. (2) Boring, 1950.

BENDER-GESTALT TEST. According to Lametta Bender, her Visual Motor Gestalt Test "has been used as a maturational test in visual motor gestalt function in children, to explore retardation, regression, loss of function and organic brain defects in both adults and children, and to explore personality deviations, especially where there are regressive phenomena." Although administration procedures vary, the subject is usually shown nine designs, each on a separate card, and asked to copy them. Some examiners then request that additional reproductions be made from memory. Bender's selection of the designs and theoretical orientation toward the task are based on principles of Gestalt psychology and psychomotor differentiation developed in her 1938 monograph.

Interpretation of the test results is based on the quality of the reproductions themselves, intratest observations and comments, method of organization, and projective implications of salient features or deviations. Maturational norms are provided by Bender, and attempts to standardize and quantify scoring methods have been undertaken for adult administration and for use with children.

—Randolph S. Kraft, *Federation of the Handicapped, N.Y.*

Consult (12) Bender, 1938; Bender, 1946; Koppitz, 1964; Pascal and Suttell, 1951.

BERKOWITZ, LEONARD (1926–   ), American social psychologist, born in New York City. He has been professor, department of psychology, University of Wisconsin from 1962.

Berkowitz is an experimental social psychologist. He has been particularly concerned with aggressive behavior and has studied the effects of violence in the mass media on rates of crime. He has also studied the psychology of altruism. His works include *Aggression: A Social Psychological Analysis,* 1962; *Development of Motives and Values in Children,* 1964; *Roots*

Experimental social psychologist Leonard Berkowitz has devoted special study to aggressive behavior.

of Aggression, 1969. He is also the editor (with J. Macaulay) of Altruism and Helping Behavior, 1970.

BESTIALITY, sexual contact by a human with an infrahuman animal, usually a domestic mammal or chicken in the case of the human male and a dog or cat by the human female. Sometimes termed zoophilia, this is one of the rarest sexual outlets. About 8 percent of American males—6 percent of city dwellers and 17 percent of those raised on farms—have had animal contact, mostly before age twenty. Animal contact is seldom an important source of orgastic gratification at any age.

Approximately 5 percent of American women have had animal contact, about 65 percent of them prior to age twenty-one. There is no tendency for animal contacts to occur more often among girls raised on a farm. The nature of the contact is very different for males and females. Among the males, coitus with the animal is the commonest form of contact. Among females, the most frequent behavior is simply general body contact with the animal or sometimes masturbating the animal. Coitus is very rare. Every state has a law declaring bestiality a crime. It is often incorrectly labeled as a form of sodomy in the law.

—Eugene E. Levitt, Indiana University
School of Medicine
Consult (13) Allen, 1962; Kinsey, et al., 1948.

BETTELHEIM, BRUNO (1903–), American psychologist. Born in Vienna, he received his Ph.D. from the University of Vienna in 1938 and was professor of educational psychology at the University of Chicago after 1950.

Bettelheim's work at the University of Chicago Orthogenic School is detailed in his book Love Is Not Enough—The Treatment of Emotionally Disturbed Children (1950). Using a psychoanalytic approach, Bettelheim contends that because of the complexities of modern living, parental love alone is not enough to provide an environment that supplies the needs of both the parents and the child; the parents must make a deliberate effort to provide such a setting. Permissiveness or rigidity in training does not affect a child's normal development so much as does the child's interpretation of the adult's actions. Thus the adult must react to the child's problems and conflicts in terms of the child's needs, and an adult free of conflict over a particular situation—like cleanliness versus dirtiness—will be better able to handle an anxious child in a way that will not threaten him. In the treatment of disturbed children, Bettelheim's approach offers the child simple personal relationships at the beginning of his treatment. When he is ready, the child will then select a parent figure.

Among Bettelheim's many publications

are Symbolic Wounds (1954), The Informed Heart (1960), Dialogues with Mothers (1962), The Empty Fortress (1967), and The Children of the Dream (1960).

BIAS. In research, see Experimenter Bias. In the sense of social attitude, see Prejudice.

BINET, ALFRED (1857–1911), French psychologist and educator born in Nice. Binet founded the first French psychological laboratory at the Sorbonne in 1889 and also founded L'année psychologique, the first French psychological journal, in 1895.

Binet was a pioneer in the study of individual differences in abilities and introduced intelligence tests that became widely used in Europe and the United States. He was asked by the French government to develop an objective method for distinguishing between retarded and normal children so that they could be given special instruction. In collaboration with Theodore Simon, he developed the first scales for measuring intelligence. He made use of simple materials, such as pictures and small objects, in devising these tests. Binet claimed that he was measuring "general mental ability" rather than specific achievement or learning. Items on the scale were placed according to the particular age group for which they were best suited (from three-year-old to adult). Binet also developed the concept of "mental age," which relates to a person's level of intellectual functioning, regardless of his actual age. Binet's efforts influenced Lewis M. Terman, an American psychologist who published the Stanford Revision of the Binet-Simon Scale (1916). This was for many years the most popular intelligence test in the United States.

—Michael Rothenberg, The City College
of The City University of New York
See also Intelligence and Intelligence Testing.

BINET-SIMON SCALE. See Stanford-Binet Intelligence Test.

BIOFEEDBACK, an important frontier area in psychology, dealing with the control of one's internal processes through conditioning procedures. Successful conditioning of heart rate, blood pressure, galvanic skin response, and several brain wave frequencies has already been demonstrated. Such conditioning is often called visceral learning.

Brain Rhythm. There is considerable current interest in the conditioning of alpha rhythm, a dominant rhythm recorded from the human brain. This consists of rhythmic waves that wax and wane in amplitude and range from 8 to 13 hertz. Alpha is most easily recorded from the occipital portions of the scalp and is most prominent when the eyes are

French psychologist Alfred Binet developed the first standardized test to measure school children's intelligence, as distinct from acquired knowledge.

closed. There are numerous claims that experimental control of alpha rhythm is beneficial in that it produces a state of relaxed alertness. If this is true, perhaps alpha wave conditioning might be a useful adjunct to psychotherapy or simply for achieving an intense state of relaxation.

Alpha conditioning essentially involves giving the subject feedback whenever he is producing the proper rhythm. The subject may then be asked to increase the amount of feedback available, which in turn results in increasing his alpha-rhythm density. Typically a light or a tone is presented to the subject when alpha is being produced. He is simply told to increase the amount of such feedback stimulation. Generally subjects can learn to do this in three or four sessions of approximately thirty minutes each; but not all subjects are equally adept at learning to control their alpha rhythm. Success seems to depend strongly on desire to learn and also on expectations that achieving alpha control will lead to a desirable mental state.

Other brain rhythms have also been studied. One is the somatomotor rhythm of 12 to 14 hertz recorded from the central portions of the scalp. Recent work at the University of California has shown that control of this rhythm could play a role in the suppression of epileptic seizures.

The Heart. A second area of biofeedback research deals with the control of the heart rate and blood pressure. The methodology is similar to that used in brain wave control. The subject is given a feedback signal to tell him that his heart rate has decreased by a certain amount, or that his blood pressure has either increased or decreased. With appropriate instructions, either a human subject or an experimental animal can learn to increase or decrease its heart rate or blood pressure. The changes produced are not great, but they are significant.

For hypertense individuals suffering from high blood pressure, such training might be a great help. Lowering blood pressure at critical times could forestall a heart attack. Many psychologists believe that biofeedback will play a significant role in the medicine of the future.

—Joel F. Lubar, *University of Tennessee*
See also Autonomic Nervous System; Brain Waves; Operant Conditioning.
Consult (6) Black, 1971; Miller, 1968; Part, 1969.

BIOLOGY. Relations with psychology, *see* Ethology; Psychobiology.

BIOPSYCHOLOGY. *See* Psychobiology.

BIRTH ADJUSTMENT. When a child moves from the prenatal to the postnatal environment, he or she has to adjust to sudden, vast, and radical changes. Four major critical adjustments have to be made: breathing and adapting to changes in temperature, nourishment, and elimination. The newborn has to obtain the oxygen by inhaling. He must adjust to a room temperature of 70 degrees, take his nourishment through the mouth, and eliminate waste products through the proper organs.

Children show a great range in difficulty of adjusting to the postnatal environment. Some die immediately after birth or a few days later, while most show some loss of weight or mild disorganization of behavior.
—Ragaa Mazen, *Southern Connecticut State College*
See also Birth Trauma.

BIRTH ORDER. Psychologists as well as parents have observed that order of birth in a family often affects the personality of the developing child. There is no biological factor at work; the effects depend on the relations of children with parents and siblings. The first-born usually gets more attention (often more anxious overprotection) than later children and is likely to be more oriented to adults than to children. For a time he has the status of only child and may be upset by the birth of a rival. The youngest child may be pampered because he or she is the baby of the family. Second or middle children may feel left out, as having the status of neither eldest nor "baby." On the other hand, they may have a warmer relation with the mother than a first-born because the mother is less anxious and tense. Obviously, the parents' behavior toward their children can make the birth-order problem anything from minor to traumatic.

One study of personality patterns in large families found that the first-born is often considered a responsible child, the second seems more sociable and well-liked, and the youngest tends to be spoiled. Other studies have reported that first-borns are often more dependent, anxious, and conservative than later children. Younger children tend to be happier and more aggressive and outgoing.
See also Family Size.
Consult (11) Bossard and Ball, 1955; Weiner and Elkind, 1972.

BIRTH TRAUMA. Freud suggested that the infant, separated suddenly at birth from a comfortable uterine environment, powerlessly faces the "danger" of nongratification of its needs as well as overwhelming stimulation from external sources. This he saw as the prototype of anxiety. Several of his disciples, including Otto Rank, argued that neurotic anxiety is created by the very early and primitive stress of acute birth trauma.

Rarely supported in its original form today, the basic theory was refined into Rank's

Eugen Bleuler's analysis of psychotic symptoms helped identify causes of schizophrenia (his word) and indicated that treatment was possible.

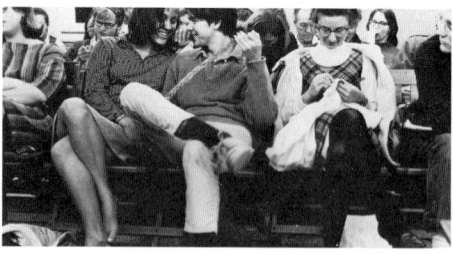

Body language is a means of communicating unconscious as well as conscious feelings through postures and gestures.

American "psychologist-at-large" Edwin Boring made contributions to the field in experimental work, education, and perhaps most as writer, editor, historian.

"fear of life." This is manifested in the wish not to be separated from people and leads to social conformity and failure to express individuality.
—M. G. Affinito, *Southern Connecticut State College*

BLEULER, EUGEN (1857–1939), Swiss psychiatrist, born in Zurich. He was director, Psychiatric Clinic, University of Zurich and Burgholzi Hospital.

Bleuler, in cooperation with his assistant C. G. Jung, developed a dynamic, or interpretive, approach to psychiatry. Using the results of Freud's work on neurotic behavior, Bleuler applied them to psychotic behavior in an attempt to understand the cause of the psychotic symptoms. Up until this time, psychotic symptoms were only described and classified, and they were attributed to brain damage rather than psychological causes.

Bleuler applied his dynamic approach to what was then called dementia praecox, a disorder believed incurable as the result of brain damage. He described the disorder as a group of psychiatric reactions that did not result in brain deterioration; he coined the term *schizophrenia* to name this disease. Bleuler showed that schizophrenics retreated from the unmanageable outside world to an inner world that they could handle, and he described this retreat as the reason for the delusions and fantasies of the schizophrenic. Among Bleuler's publications are *Dementia Praecox, or the Group of Schizophrenics* (1911).

BLOOD PRESSURE. The pressure exerted by blood against the walls of vessels is commonly referred to as blood pressure. Blood pressure involves arterial pressure, pressure in capillaries, and pressure in veins. In arteries blood pressure consists of two components, systolic pressure and diastolic pressure. Systolic pressure is the greater and is measured at the time that the ventricles of the heart contract. Diastolic pressure is related to relaxation of the ventricles. A typical measure such as 130/90 is interpreted to mean that the systolic pressure is 130 millimeters of mercury, the diastolic 90 millimeters of mercury.

Blood pressure increases when a person is emotionally aroused. The lie detector records blood pressure as one indicator that a subject may be under stress because of a certain question.
—Joel F. Lubar, *University of Tennessee*
See also Lie Detector.

BODY LANGUAGE. Psychoanalysts and other therapists believe that unconscious conflicts may be expressed by symptoms involving parts of the body. For example, asthmatic breathing may be said to show that the patient "can't get the load off his chest," and vomiting shows the need to get rid of something that is emotionally indigestible.

Both literature and everyday life are full of examples of what appears to be communication of conscious and unconscious feelings through postures and gestures, as when a father greets his son "with open arms" but shows an enemy his clenched fist. Books have been written assigning meanings to a wide range of positioning of the limbs and rest of the body.
See also Emotion.
Consult (8) Callum, 1971; Dittman, 1972. (13) Rosen and Gregory, 1965.

BODY TYPE. *See* Constitutional Types.

BORDERLINE MENTALLY RETARDED. *See* Mental Retardation.

BORING, EDWIN GARRIGUES (1886–1968), American psychologist. Born in Philadelphia, he studied for his Ph.D. under E. B. Titchener at Cornell University (1914). He was professor of psychology and director of Harvard Psychological Laboratory.

Described by himself as a "psychologist-at-large," Boring was active as an experimental psychologist, a teacher and administrator, a historian of psychology, and an editor. Boring's early experimental work centered on learning in schizophrenics, return of nerve function, and intelligence testing with R. M. Yerkes. Later work included the moon illusion, a study on the status of American women in psychology, and extensive work on sensation and perception.

At Harvard, Boring was instrumental in having the Psychology Department established independently of the Philosophy Department. But perhaps Boring had his greatest influence as an editor and writer. From 1925 until 1964, he was a member of the Board of Editors of *American Journal of Psychology*. Subsequently he was editor of *Contemporary Psychology* (1956–1962). His most important writings include *A History of Experimental Psychology*, 2d ed. (1957); *Sensation and Perception in the History of Experimental Psychology* (1942); *The Physical Dimensions of Consciousness* (1933); *Psychologist at Large: An Autobiography and Selected Essays* (1961).

BRAIN, the organ of the central nervous system responsible for the processing and coding of sensory and motor information, for the control of regulatory processes in the body, and for the mediation of complex processes, such as motivation, emotion, learning, and memory.

Structures. For anatomical convenience, the brain may be subdivided into three major divisions: the forebrain, midbrain, and hindbrain. The forebrain consists of the telencephalon, which is further subdivided into the neocortex, the basal ganglia, and the limbic system. The forebrain also contains the diencephalon, which is further subdivided into the thalamus and hypothalamus. The midbrain stands as a separate portion of the brain responsible for the integration of eye movements and vestibular functions. The hindbrain contains the cerebellum, the pons, and the medulla oblongata.

Various hindbrain structures are quite similar in all vertebrates. Considerable changes occur in the relative size and development of forebrain structures as one ascends the phylogenetic scale. In higher animals, such as carnivores and primates, there is tremendous development of the neocortex relative to other brain systems.

One of the most important aspects of brain development is that as one ascends the phylogenetic scale one finds that less of the cortex, the outermost covering of the telencephalon, is concerned with purely sensory and motor functions and more is concerned with complex integrative functions that seem to be the basis for complex learning. In the rat most of the cortex is relegated to sensory and motor aspects of behavior, whereas in the human most of the cortex is relegated to associative and integrative functions, with only a small percentage involved directly in sensory and motor processes.

Research Techniques. The brain is studied primarily through three basic methods: ablation, stimulation, and recording. All three methods are used in conjunction with one another by brain researchers in order to obtain a picture of how various systems in the brain function dynamically in the mediation of specific behaviors.

Ablation, an experimental technique for animals, involves selectively removing portions of the brain and trying to determine what the sum total of remaining parts can or cannot do. In this way it is possible, for example, to map out regions of the cortex responsible for auditory or visual functions or to determine which portions of the thalamus are involved in sensory or motor functions. Ablation has the advantage that it is sometimes possible to assign specific functions to specific regions but the disadvantage that it produces an abnormal organism. Thus, compensation for losses can and often does take place as a result of the interaction of the remaining structures.

The *stimulation* technique essentially involves placing small electrodes in specific portions of the brain and electrically activating them to observe the effect on some behavior or performed task. An alternative method of stimulation is through the implantation of cannulae, small tubes that can carry chemicals to specific regions of the brain. Stimulation in certain portions of the hypothalamus with cholinergic drugs will elicit drinking, whereas

stimulation of the identical regions with an adrenergic substance (norepinephrine) will elicit eating. As in the case in ablation, stimulation also produces an alteration in the normal functioning of the brain.

A third method, *recording,* is passive and produces the least change in ongoing cerebral activity. Recording involves placing recording electrodes in specific brain structures and observing the electrical activity of these regions as a function of different activities. It has been found, for example, that the electrical activity of the brain is markedly different during the various stages of sleep and certain aspects of learning and that it is related to attentional state.

The Hypothalamus. A large body of brain research has dealt specifically with hypothalamic functions. The hypothalamus acts as a funnel or channel that carries information from the cortex and the thalamus to the spinal cord and, ultimately, to the motor nerves or to the autonomic nervous system, where it is transmitted to specific target organs. These target organs can release into the bloodstream specific hormones that alter bodily functions. The autonomic nervous system also acts on smooth muscles to produce changes in blood flow or pressure.

Research has indicated that the hypothalamus is divided into many dual centers, which act oppositely with respect to a given behavior. For example, in the lateral hypothalamus stimulation elicits eating if food is available. In contrast, stimulation of the medial portion of the hypothalamus will cause the cessation of ongoing eating, and the animal will actually spit out food. Often stimulation and ablation of a structure produce opposite results. For example, destruction of the medial hypothalamic region will lead to *hyperphagia,* extreme overeating, whereas ablation of the lateral hypothalamic "feeding center" will lead to *aphagia,* starvation. Dual centers have been found for the initiation and stopping of movement, for hunger, for thirst, and for aggressive behavior.

Self-Stimulation. One particularly interesting aspect of recent research is work on electrical self-stimulation of the brain. It has been found that animals will seek stimulation of certain portions of their own brains. Most of these areas lie in a system known as the *limbic system,* a series of structures that surround the central core of the brain and are believed to be primarily responsible for control of motivational and emotional states. If an animal is given the opportunity to press a lever in order to deliver an electrical stimulus to portions of its own limbic system, it will acquire this response readily. In rats response rates as high as 6,000 per hour have been recorded. The function of these "pleasure centers" in the

BRAIN

The relations of the brain to the rest of the central nervous system and to the peripheral system are discussed and illustrated in the article NERVOUS SYSTEM. Parts of the brain are described in such entries as CEREBRAL CORTEX, CEREBELLUM, HYPOTHALAMUS, THALAMUS, LIMBIC REGION, SEPTAL REGION, and TEMPORAL LOBES.

Studies of brain activity are reported in CHEMICAL STIMULATION OF THE BRAIN, ELECTRICAL STIMULATION OF THE BRAIN, and BRAIN WAVES. Further investigations of the electrical activity of the brain are discussed in SLEEP AND DREAMS. For theories of how the brain functions in memory, see BRAIN STORAGE.

A variety of problems can afflict a person whose brain is damaged by head injuries, clots, tumors, poisons, infections, or other causes. See BRAIN DISORDERS and MENTAL RETARDATION.

Operations on the brain as a treatment for mental illness are discussed in PSYCHOSURGERY.

Brain

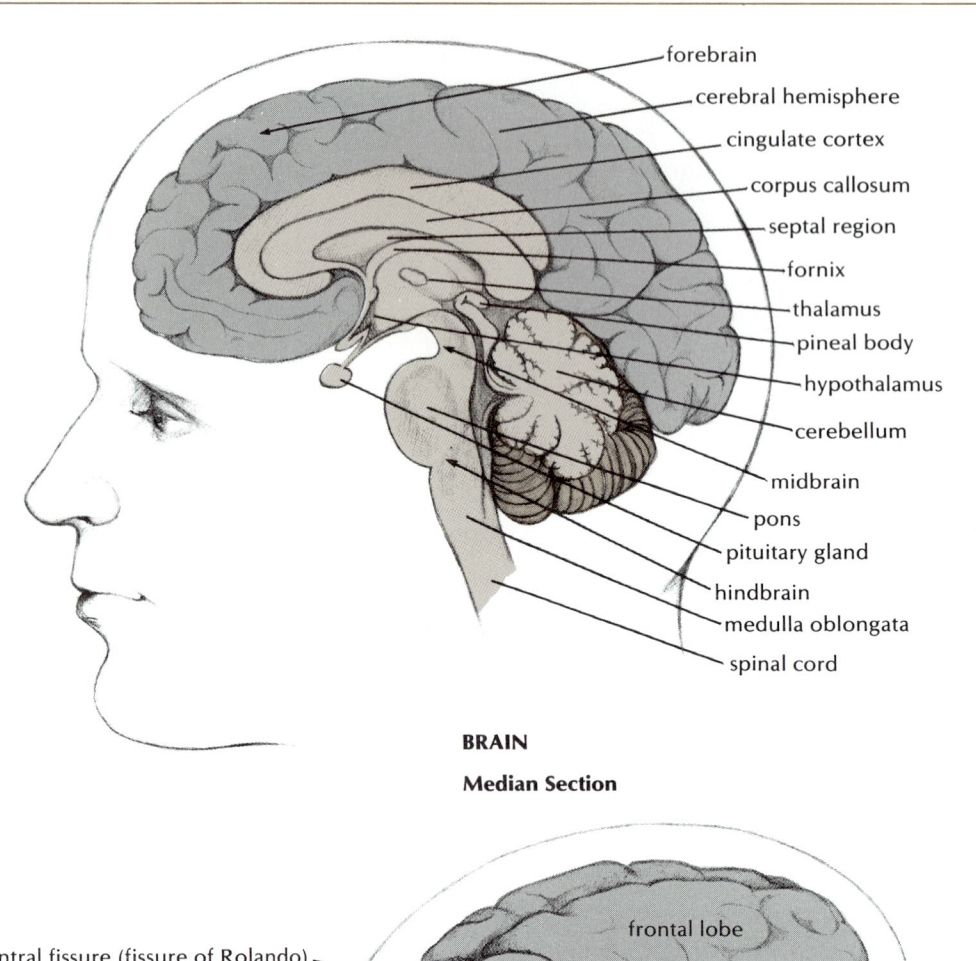

BRAIN

Median Section

forebrain
cerebral hemisphere
cingulate cortex
corpus callosum
septal region
fornix
thalamus
pineal body
hypothalamus
cerebellum
midbrain
pons
pituitary gland
hindbrain
medulla oblongata
spinal cord

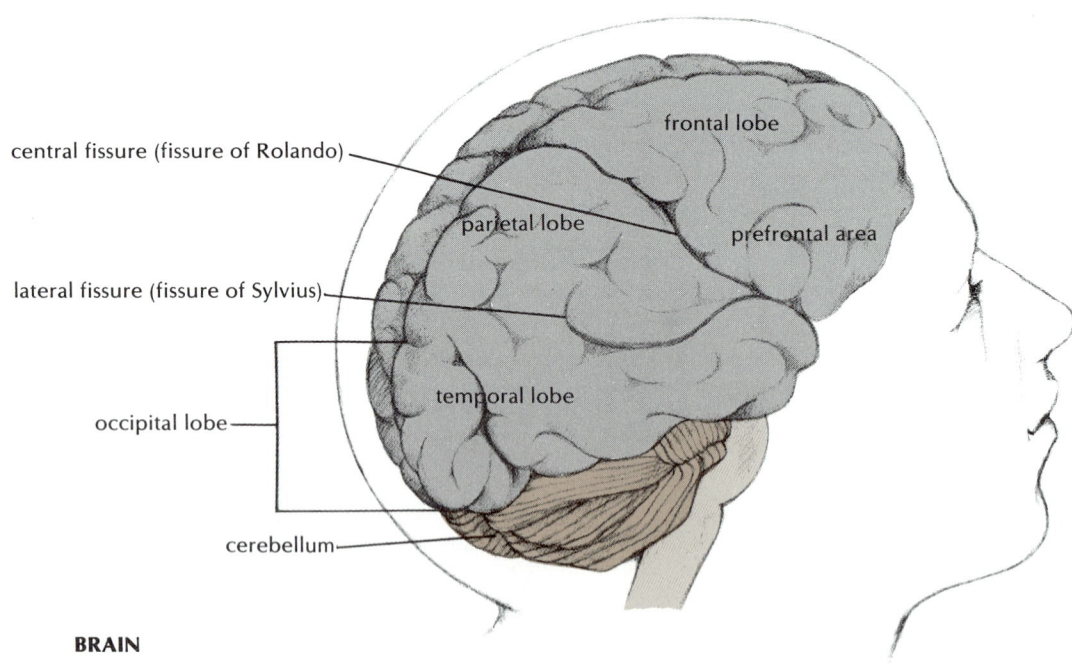

central fissure (fissure of Rolando)

lateral fissure (fissure of Sylvius)

occipital lobe

cerebellum

frontal lobe
parietal lobe
prefrontal area
temporal lobe

BRAIN

Surface of the Cerebrum

brain, as they are commonly called, is not well understood. Stimulation in certain portions of the human brain during neurosurgical procedures often produces pleasurable reactions over large portions of the body. This feeling is frequently one of euphoria or complete elation; at other times it is similar to sexual excitement.

—Joel F. Lubar, *University of Tennessee*
See also Brain Storage; Chemical Stimulation of the Brain; Electrical Stimulation of the Brain; Nervous System; *articles on individual regions of the brain.*
Consult (3) Gardner, 1968; Isaacson, *et al.,* 1971; Teitelbaum, 1967; Wooldridge, 1963.

BRAIN DISORDERS. The scope of mechanisms and manifestations of brain disorders is almost cosmic in extent. Depending on what part of the brain is affected, more or less characteristic signs are expressed. Thus the trained neurologist can identify the nature and locus of the lesion. Examples of neurological manifestations include convulsions, blindness, paralysis, and numbness.

Two basic questions are posed when the neurologist confronts a patient with a brain disorder: Where is the lesion? What is the lesion?

Localization

Determination of the site of the disease requires intimate knowledge of the inimitable function of each segment of the brain. For example, if the right arm is paralyzed, the lesion is in the lower part of the cortex, just in front of the *Rolandic fissure.* The latter, one of the many recognized landmarks on the surface of the brain, is about midway between the front and back and runs laterally from the top of the brain to near the bottom. It is one of the many clefts within and around which brain cells aggregate. All of these subserve specific functions.

Behind the Rolandic fissure is the sensory area of the brain. Damage to it causes loss of perception of sensation in the opposite part of the body. Damage to the most posterior tip of the brain causes impairment of vision.

In the most frontal part of the brain the higher processes—for example, thinking, reasoning, self-control—are localized. Prefrontal lobotomy causes alteration in these higher mental and ethical functions.

Deep within the substance of the brain compact collections of nerve cells serve to integrate thought, motivation, feeling, and movement. The last is profoundly affected in Parkinsonism or any disease that destroys the cells in the basal ganglia, the integrative center for organization of smooth, controlled dextrous movements. When these structures are damaged or diseased, the patient develops tremor, rigidity, involuntary movements, and other patterns, often bizarre, of movement disorder.

Causes

Eight categories encompass almost every possible neurological disease process. **Congenital,** for example, mongolism, cerebral palsy, malformation of cerebral blood vessels. **Traumatic,** for example, laceration of the brain, or *contusion.* The latter is bruising of the brain, whereas *concussion* is shaking up of the brain. *Subdural hematoma,* which may be caused by injury, is a progressively enlarging blood clot that slowly presses down on the surface of the brain. It is usually fatal if not removed. Treated promptly however, the patient usually survives without further complications.

Neoplastic, that is, traumatic growths. Subsumed under this category are *metastatic tumors,* that is, those originating in remote organs (for example, cancer of the lung) and carried by the bloodstream to the brain, where the cancerous cells embed and proliferate; and *primary tumors,* that is, those originating from cells indigenous to the brain itself. These abnormal cells undergo malignant change and rapidly multiply. Either type causes damage by destruction of the local area where the tumor is embedded and by causing pressure within the unyielding bony skull.

Vascular, that is, *thrombosis,* closure of a cerebral vessel because of clotting within the vessel. Less common are *embolism,* that is, breaking off of a fragment of tissue or blood clot, which is carried to the brain, where it becomes lodged, closing off the blood vessel and depriving the local area of nutrition; and *hemorrhage,* that is, destruction of brain tissue due to rupturing of a blood vessel, causing vigorous outpouring of blood into the surrounding tissue, which destroys contiguous areas.

Toxic, that is, poisons, including lead. This may occur in children who eat paint or dirt. Convulsions, blindness, coma, and death may result because of damage to brain cells. Alcohol is probably the most common brain poison, and it too can cause convulsions as well as staggering, blindness, paralysis, and intellectual deterioration. Solvents such as carbon tetrachloride are highly toxic to the nervous system, as are such insecticides as DDT and chlordane. Drugs are a common cause of brain disorder, for example, LSD and Benzedrine. Carbon monoxide is another dangerous poison for the brain.

Metabolic Disorders. Some of these are congenital. PKU (phenylketonuria), for example, is an inborn error, often heritable, that blocks the normal utilization of glucose of the brain cells. Since the brain can burn only glucose, any obstruction to the pathways that bring that substance to the brain cells or any interruption in the cycle that converts it to energy will damage, destroy, or alter the function of the brain cells. Hypoglycemia, that is, low level of blood sugar, can also disrupt normal brain cell metabolism and function, resulting in coma, convulsions, or death. Malnutrition associated with inadequate vitamin intake is another possible cause of metabolic brain disorder.

Infections of the Brain. When *acute,* for example, meningitis due to meningococcus or pneumococcus, these may cause inflammation and accumulation of pus over the surface of the brain, resulting in severe headache, convulsions, focal paralysis, and so on. Examination of the spinal fluid will show a large number of white blood cells, high protein content, and low sugar values; the last results from bacteria that consume the sugar in the spinal fluid. *Chronic infections* include tuberculosis of the brain and syphilis. The latter causes scarring over the surface of the brain, inflammation of the inside of the small arteries of the brain. Furthermore, live spirochetes attack individual cells, causing paralysis, blindness, convulsions, and dementia. If diagnosed in time, both of these chronic diseases can be completely cured, TB by streptomycin and syphilis by penicillin.

Degenerative. This final category includes a large number of diseases, many of them quite mysterious. For example, multiple sclerosis implicates both gray matter (cells) and white matter (nerve fibers that transmit the impulse from the cells). The spinal cord as well as the brain is attacked in an intermittent but usually relentless destruction of nerve tissue. Uncoordination, blindness, paralysis, and loss of bladder control may develop. Huntington's chorea is a hereditable degenerative disease eventuating in bizarre and often violent flinging and writhing movements, associated with progressive dementia.

These etiological groupings are not exhaustive but include almost all causes or mechanisms of brain disorder.

Diagnosis

In addition to the neurological examination, specific tests are often helpful. These include the *EEG* or *brain wave test.* The brain is composed of about 14 billion cells, each a small battery discharging electricity in a complex and constant electrical display that can be picked up and magnified. When wires are pasted on to the scalp of the patient and the electrical pulse is translated into a written graph, the neurologist is provided with a meaningful indication of where and what the lesion is.

Brain scan, another informative test, utilizes a radioactive substance that is injected into the patient. Preferentially, it concentrates in abnormal areas. An instrument moving back and forth over the patient's head scans the brain and automatically records the spot where the radioactive emanations are strongest.

Other tests are *arteriograms,* in which an x-ray film is taken after a radio-opaque substance has been injected into the carotid arteries, and the *pneumoencephalogram.* In the latter procedure, air is injected into the spine and bubbles up into the head, outlining the contours of the brain; x-ray examination can then disclose any abnormal mass or alteration of brain structure.

Recent research has brought many new successful therapies to cure or mitigate the neurological disease, particularly Parkinsonism and epilepsy. Both these common disorders are responsive to drugs.

—Harold Stevens, M.D.

See also Aphasia; Brain.

Consult (13) Karczmer and Eccles, 1972; Lennox, 1941.

BRAIN STEM. *See* Brain.

BRAIN STIMULATION. *See* Chemical Stimulation of the Brain; Electrical Stimulation of the Brain.

BRAIN STORAGE. Modern research dealing with memory function is now asking: What is memory? Where is it stored in the brain? How does it work? There is considerable evidence that memory is a cellular or organic process and that it is chemical in nature.

A number of important substances may be involved in the memory process. These include the amino acids, proteins, RNA (ribonucleic acid), and DNA (deoxyribonucleic acid). DNA is a genetic material that is responsible for passing physical characteristics from one generation to another; it is also important in forming specific kinds of RNA. RNA, in turn, directs the formation of proteins, which consist of organized sequences or linkages of amino acids. Amino acids are involved in the metabolism and formation of neurotransmitters.

Modern theories of memory storage are based on the premise that information is stored in the neuron in the form of specific proteins or RNA sequences, which are laid down as a result of stimulation. These RNAs or proteins are important for coding the release of neurotransmitters, which determine which pathways in the brain are activated.

Experimentally it has been shown that when an animal learns a specific task, such as walking a tightrope inclined from the floor to a food dish, specific RNA changes take place in those portions of the brain that are most involved in mastering the task. In this example the vestibular nuclei of the brainstem were found to be particularly active. Furthermore, chemicals that interfere with RNA and protein synthesis (such as puromycin) will block learning following their administration.

Recent work has led to the hypothesis

that memory is a two-stage process involving *short-term memory,* which is weak and easily disrupted, and a more stable *long-term memory.* Experimental brain damage, certain drugs, or electronconvulsive shock can interfere with short-term-memory functions but leave long-term-memory storage intact.

—Joel F. Lubar, *University of Tennessee*
See also Memory.

BRAIN WAVES, electrical responses that can be recorded directly from any portion of the brain or from the scalp with special electrodes. It is believed that these responses represent total activity from dendrites—specifically, the summed excitatory and inhibitory postsynaptic potentials.

For convenience, the brain wave of the waking adult human is divided into several frequency bands: the *delta* rhythm, less than 4 hertz; *theta* rhythm, 4 to 8 hertz; *alpha* rhythm, 8 to 14 hertz; and *beta* rhythm, 14 hertz and above. The most prominent of these rhythms is the alpha rhythm, which is best recorded from the occipital portion of the skull with the eyes closed. However, it does occur in some individuals from widespread regions with eyes open or closed.

Brain waves are useful for monitoring different stages of sleep and for the clinical detection and localization of certain epilepsies, brain tumors, or other abnormal conditions. During activation or arousal the electroencephalogram (or EEG, the record of electrical activity) from widespread portions of the brain shows a shift from high-voltage slow activity to low-voltage fast activity. During relaxed, quiescent, or sleepy states the EEG contains a larger proportion of lower frequencies.

Recent research has shown that it is possible for an individual to control the amount of alpha or theta rhythm present in his EEG. The subject is given feedback in the form of lights or tones when the desired rhythm is present. Through mental effort he can learn to increase or decrease the amount of alpha or theta rhythm. Increased alpha rhythm appears to be associated with mental relaxation.

—Joel F. Lubar, *University of Tennessee*
See also Brain; Sleep and Dreams.
Consult (3) Teitelbaum, 1967.

BRAINWASHING, also referred to as thought control, became a matter of widespread concern during and after the Korean War, when a number of U.S. soldiers in prisoner of war camps confessed to waging "germ warfare" and refused to be repatriated following the cease-fire. Subsequent studies of soldiers who did return and of people discharged from Chinese prisons revealed certain common practices in brainwashing that psychologists could relate to existing knowledge of how attitudes are formed and changed under normal circumstances. People normally develop and maintain those attitudes and beliefs that are functional, or useful, for them in their social environment. Attitudes are functional in that they help us get along with people (be liked and accepted) or avoid those we would dislike, sometimes help us deal with inner psychological problems or needs, and give us a sense of who we are and what we value—essential aspects of what is called our *identity.*

The major element in brainwashing is a deliberately calculated attempt to render the victim's existing attitudes and beliefs nonfunctional or useless, and to then replace them with attitudes, presented by his captors, which will be adopted because they are functionally useful in the new social environment created by the brainwasher. The captive is brought to a state of "debility, dependency, and dread" by being starved, physically abused, cut off from social contacts, and threatened with death, injury, or permanent imprisonment. These procedures are planned to bring about a childlike state of dependency in which only the captors can satisfy the victim's basic psychological needs. The victim is asked to "confess" and, after his resistance is worn down, he may try to find a way out of his dilemma by admitting trivial or absurd things. However, his captors are never satisfied and continue to abuse and threaten him. Often, fellow prisoners who have already been brainwashed will be used to belittle or condemn the victim and urge him to make a full confession. This increases the probability that the victim will come to feel "guilty" and therefore deserving of punishment. If he then confesses and, at the urging of his captors, even implicates others falsely, self-recrimination will increase his feelings of guilt and loss of identity.

Once the victim begins to adopt the attitudes and beliefs suggested by his captors, they reward him with better food, more comfort, and friendship. Threats of death or punishment stop and the captors work to provide the victim with a new identity, based upon the new attitudes and values that are now functionally useful to him. The victim may then be released from captivity and allowed to return home.

While there is evidence that many individuals have been successfully brainwashed by such procedures, there is still some doubt as to how effective the procedures really are or can be. The process typically involves several years of intense effort and complete control over the victim, both of which may be difficult to fully maintain. In the case of American POWs during the Korean War, the Chinese and North Koreans were largely inefficient in their attempts at indoctrination. Many people resisted being changed much, if at all; others emerged

BRAIN WAVES

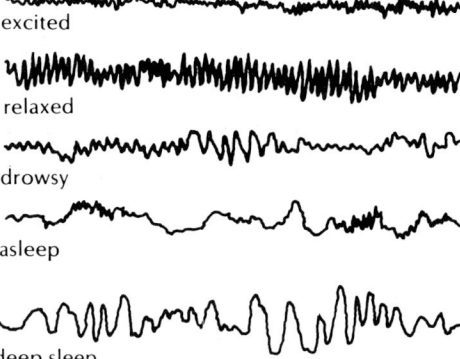

excited

relaxed

drowsy

asleep

deep sleep

|— 1 second

Normal electroencephalograph records typical of various sleep-wakefulness stages.

Jerome Bruner's experiments and theories on factors influencing cognitive growth have had worldwide impact on experimental and educational psychologists.

Viennese physiologist Joseph Breuer's observations on cathartic treatment of hysterics, reported to Freud, laid the groundwork for psychoanalytic theory.

confused, disorganized, and unsure of their real identity; relatively few became apparent converts. Resistance to change was more likely when the prisoner was part of a group who remained cohesive and provided each other with social support for resistance. Moreover, some attitudes seemed less dependent than others on current functionality and persisted despite extreme physical and mental stress.

Most social psychologists doubt that it is realistically possible to apply brainwashing techniques to large populations, even when the mass media are totally controlled. However, it is more likely that the education of the young could be structured in such a way as to develop those attitudes and beliefs that would be functionally useful and rewarded in a given social environment.

—Bruce Muller, *Southern Connecticut State College*
See also Attitudes and Attitude Change.
Consult (10) Farber, *et al.,* 1957.

BREATH HOLDING, an immature bit of behavior that may appear in the first two years of life as an expression of anger. It declines as the child becomes older. Breath holding occurs as a response to frustrating situations, as when the child's demands are not fulfilled. It may also be motivated by an unconscious desire to attract attention. Studies suggest that this behavior pattern is related to disturbances in parent-child relations.

BREUER, JOSEPH (1842–1925), Austrian physician and physiologist, born in Vienna. He practiced in Vienna and was elected to the Vienna Academy of Science in 1894.

Breuer's work has been viewed by many, including Freud himself, as laying the foundation for the development of psychoanalytic theory. It was Breuer who first reported the successful treatment of a hysterical patient by means of the cathartic method. While treating a young women for hysterical symptoms, including a "nervous cough" and the inability to drink water, Breuer discovered that many of the symptoms disappeared when the patient, under hypnosis, called forth the circumstances of their original occurrence. He theorized that neurotic symptoms derived from unconscious processes and lifted when the processes became conscious and the patient's feelings about them were discussed. Excited by his discoveries, he reported his findings to Freud, who pursued the technique with his own patients.

Breuer himself did not continue with this work, but he did collaborate and consult with Freud, leading ultimately to the publication in 1895 of *Studies on Hysteria,* a seminal work in the psychoanalytic movement. Breuer's association with Freud, in large part,

marked the first step in the change from a strictly neurophysiological to a psychodynamic approach to the understanding of neurotic symptoms.

—Michael Rothenberg, *The City College of The City University of New York*

BRUNER, JEROME S. (1915–   ), American cognitive and child psychologist. Born in New York City, he earned his Ph.D. at Harvard and was later director of Harvard's Center for Cognitive Studies. In 1972 Bruner joined the faculty at Oxford University in England.

An innovative experimenter and theorist, Bruner developed ideas on child development and thinking that have influenced educational as well as experimental psychologists the world over. In contrast to Jean Piaget's description of the maturational stages in cognitive development, Bruner has emphasized discovering the environmental and experiential factors that facilitate or deter effective reasoning and thinking. In one influential theoretical paper, Bruner distinguished between three *modes* of representations or "symbolizing" in human thought. [*Consult* (6) Bruner, 1964.]

1. *Enactive—amplifiers of human motor capacities, such as using tools.*   2. *Iconic—amplifiers of sensory capacities, such as smoke signals or radar.*   3. *Symbolic—amplifiers of reasoning capacities, such as language.*

Some of the experimental work done by Bruner and his associates at Harvard is summarized in *Studies in Cognitive Growth* (1966). His work has tended to complement rather than contradict Piaget's contributions to cognitive devleopment. Taken together, the work of Piaget's Geneva school and Bruner's Harvard group have enormous implications for education.

Bruner's publications (as author or coauthor) include *A Study of Thinking* (1956), *On Knowing* (1964), and *Toward a Theory of Instruction* (1966).

—Roland Siiter, *Montclair State College*
See also Cognitive Development; Concept Learning; Piaget.

BUILT-IN BEHAVIOR. *See* Instinct.

BURT, SIR CYRIL LUDOVIC (1883–   ), British psychologist and researcher, born at Stratford on Avon. He studied psychology at Oxford under William MacDougall and taught at University College, 1924–1950.

Burt's signal contribution to psychology was his pioneering work in the development of *factor analysis,* a method of analyzing data by reorganizing a number of interrelated performance scores into larger groups called factors. This approach was a major step in the history of the construction of standardized psychological tests. To all of his research he brought an originality of approach that was reflected in the creation of many invaluable statistical methods of data analysis.

Burt was not content to limit himself to laboratory research, however. He persistently devoted himself to the application of psychological principles to practical social problems. Most particularly, he conducted extensive investigations into the problem of juvenile deliquency in England. His major publications include *Mental and Scholastic Tests* (1921), *The Young Delinquent,* (1925), and *Factors of the Mind* (1940).

—Michael Rothenberg, *The City College of The City University of New York*

BYSTANDER APATHY. Diffusion of responsibility and perceived loss of control are both significant factors in the failure of bystanders to become involved, which is really a special case of apathy-indifference. But bystanders are often afraid as well as apathetic in help-requiring situations. Witnesses to crimes often fear reprisals if they volunteer information to police, and they are afraid of personal injury if they interfere in a physical disturbance.

The results of J. Darley and B. Latané's research has indicated that under many conditions bystanders are often very reluctant to offer help to others in need, or even to report fires. However, other research has shown that individuals who observe a real accident will stop to offer help if the situation seems real and if they perceive the situation as unthreatening and really requiring help.

The degree of bystander intervention apparently depends on a variety of factors. People perceived as sick, well-dressed, and female are more successful in eliciting help from bystanders than individuals perceived to be drunk, "hippies," or male. Another major factor involves location: people in small towns are approximately three times more responsive to a request to use the telephone than are city dwellers; girls are almost twice as successful as boys in being granted entrance in both locations.

—Brenda B. Bankart and C. Peter Bankart, *Wabash College*
See also Apathy-Indifference.
Consult (10) Altman, *et al.,* 1970; Darley and Latané, 1968; Latané and Darley, 1970.

CANNON, WALTER BRADFORD (1871–1945), American physiologist. Born in Prairie du Chien, Wis., he received an M.D. at Harvard in 1900 and was professor of physiology there from 1906 to 1942.

Cannon was prominent in the development of physiology in the United States. He introduced the term *homeostasis,* referring to the regulation of the internal environment. His

numerous studies made it possible to describe some of the physiological mechanisms involved in the regulation of the internal environment of animals. In particular, Cannon studied the mechanisms involved in hunger and thirst regulation and the role the brain and the rest of the body play in emotional states such as fear and rage. In the case of thirst and hunger, Cannon identified bodily states, such as dryness of the mouth and throat or contractions of the stomach, that might be responsible for initiating these primary drive states.

Cannon's most important research, however, was concerned with the development of his thalamic theory of emotion. This theory maintains that sensory impulses as they pass through the thalamus enroute to the cortex receive emotional coloring and that the role of the cortex is to modulate a continuously active thalamus. His other contribution to understanding emotion was the development of an emergency theory of emotion. This theory proposed that through the activation of the sympathetic nervous system, the organism mobilizes its resources to act in emergency situations.

Major Works. Cannon's publications include *Bodily Changes in Pain, Hunger, Fear, and Rage,* 2d ed., 1929, *The Wisdom of the Body,* 1932, and *The Way of an Investigator,* 1945.

—A. Ronald Seifert, *University of Tennessee*
See also Emotion.

CASTRATION ANXIETY, or castration complex. According to psychoanalytic theory, children develop a fear that they will lose—or have already lost—the male sex organs. For example, when a boy first observes that a girl does not have a penis, he may conclude that she originally had one and that it was taken away as a punishment. When a boy feels sexual attraction to his mother, he may fear that his father will castrate him as punishment. This fear of punishment may spread to sex activities such as masturbation. Freud believed that girls might interpret the lack of a penis as a result of punishment and develop "penis envy."

Some theorists argue that the castration fear in males is a factor in homosexuality and in problems such as exhibitionism and sadism. For example, a man who fears he lacks potency may turn to sadistic behavior to make an impression on a sex object.

See also Oedipus Complex.
Consult (13) Coleman, 1964.

CATALEPSY, a state in which a patient maintains one physical position for considerable periods of time. The general condition is stuporous or trancelike, and the muscles are semi-rigid. Catalepsy may be induced by drugs or by

Bystander apathy. A mason observing two drunk males fighting in a metropolitan area (above) continues to work (below), apparently unconcerned.

Study of the body's mechanisms for controlling internal environment led physiologist Walter Cannon to theories on the development of emotional states.

As researcher, teacher, journalist, James Cattell was a major trend-setter for American psychology in his emphasis on testing and practical application.

Raymond B. Cattell, notable for his work in personality.

hypnosis, may occur in hysteria, but is most often seen in cases of schizophrenia. The condition is sometimes called waxy flexibility.

See also Schizophrenia.

CATATONIC SCHIZOPHRENIA. *See* Schizophrenia.

CATHARSIS, in psychotherapy, the release of emotional stresses that are causing problems. The release of anxiety or tension may be achieved by "talking out" a problem the patient is conscious of. If traumatic material is deeply buried, however, hypnosis or drugs may be used to help the patient get at the problem. Abreaction—reliving an emotionally charged experience—may be used to achieve catharsis.

See also Abreaction.

CATHEXIS, a psychoanalytic concept first developed by Freud: the attachment of psychic energy to an external object or person, or to some aspect of the self. According to Freud, one of the earliest cathected objects for an infant is the mother's breast. At the same time, he cathects his own mouth and the very process of sucking. Any object or person that provides for the gratification of instincts becomes cathected. Freud contended that all infants are born with a supply of psychic energy housed in the id and stemming from a combination of sexual and aggressive needs. This energy is at first objectless, but as the infant develops, it is bound into a variety of cathexes.

There are times when a highly cathected object can become a source of conflict for the child. For example, a five-year-old boy who experiences sexual desires for his mother will be vulnerable to extreme anxiety. In such cases, *anticathexes* are formed: these transpose all thoughts about the forbidden cathected object to the unconscious level. Thus, cathexes serve to motivate the individual in specific ways, while anticathexes tend to reduce anxiety.

—Michael Rothenberg, *The City College of The City University of New York*

CATTELL, JAMES McKEEN (1860–1944), American psychologist, one of the pioneers in the area of intelligence testing. Born in Easton, Pennsylvania, he did graduate work under the European psychologist Wilhelm Wundt at Göttingen and Leipzig and taught psychology at Columbia for almost thirty years.

Cattell was very much influenced by Darwin's evolutionary theory and the trend in America at that time toward dealing with practical issues. His work focused on the study of the relative capacities of human beings to function effectively in various situations. In pursuit of this aim, he directed his efforts toward the development of objective methods of measuring abilities, both physical and mental. He conducted extensive research in such areas as association, attention span, reaction time, and psychophysical measurement. At the request of E. L. Thorndike at Teachers College, he also pioneered in the development of mental tests for children. These were the precursors of contemporary intelligence tests.

Even more important than his own research was the influence Cattell wielded on the direction of American psychology. He served as the first president of the American Psychological Association in 1895. At various times in his career, he edited six major scientific journals. In 1924 he founded the Psychological Corporation, a major force in the construction of applied psychological tests. The list of students who studied with and were influenced by him included Thorndike, R. S. Woodworth, and E. K. Strong. Many of his students went on to make major contributions in the area of tests and measurements and to make the application of psychology to practical problems one of the main thrusts of twentieth-century American psychology.

—Michael Rothenberg, *The City College of the City University of New York*

CATTELL, RAYMOND BERNARD (1905–), English psychologist. Born in West Bromwich, he received a Ph.D. (1929) and D.Sc. (1939) at the University of London. He has been research professor at the University of Illinois since 1945.

Cattell is best known for his personality trait theory and the resulting personality tests—the Sixteen Personality Factor Questionnaire, the IPAT Anxiety Scale, the Contact Personality Factor Test, and the IPAT Neurotic Personality Factor Test. Cattell formulated a list of 171 traits—the personality sphere—and then grouped together those traits that were highly correlated in an individual; the result was thirty-five groups called surface traits. After groups of subjects were rated on these traits and the results subjected to factor analysis, Cattell had twelve basic factors—the source traits. These traits could then be used to predict the thirty-five surface traits in a person.

Using these groupings, Cattell devised a series of tests to describe a specific personality. The personality ratings obtained from these trait analysis tests, however, cannot be generalized from one person to another, nor can they give a complete picture of personality.

Other areas of Cattell's work include evaluating genetic and cultural influences on personalities and discovery of the evidence for the fluid ability concept. Among his publications are *Description and Measurement of Personality*, 1946; *Personality*, 1950; *The Scientific Analysis of Personality*, 1965; and *Objective Personality and Motivation Tests*, 1967.

CAUTIOUS SHIFT. *See* Risky Shift.

CENTRAL NERVOUS SYSTEM. *See* Brain; Nervous System.

CEREA FLEXIBILITAS, waxy flexibility, a condition observed in patients with catatonic schizophrenia. *See* Schizophrenia.

CEREBELLUM, a major division of the brain, located above the lower portion of the brainstem. The cerebellum is connected to the brain by large fiber bundles known as cerebellar peduncles. Its main inputs are from the spinal cord, vestibular system, and cerebral cortex. It projects to these same structures. The cerebellum plays an important role in coordinating eye movements with input from the vestibular system and, therefore, is involved in sensorimotor coordination. Most importantly, it also coordinates the movements of the eyes with body movements and thus helps to program motor movements so that there is a good linkage between the eye movements and the operation of striated muscles.
—Joel F. Lubar, *University of Tennessee*
See also Brain.
Consult (3) Isaacson, *et al.,* 1971.

CEREBRAL CORTEX, a recently evolved portion of the brain, prominent in mammals. The neocortex of mammals contains six relatively well-defined layers. The cortex can be divided into specific regions: sensory, motor, and associative. One portion receives input from the somesthetic system and processes information regarding touch, thermal sensation, pressure, and pain. There is a representation of the entire body surface point-by-point on the somatosensory cortex, which is located posterior to the Rolandic fissure in the human brain. Lying in the temporal lobe region is the auditory cortex, which processes information important for the perception of speech, sound, and complex auditory discrimination. The occipital lobe contains the visual cortex, which is important for visual processing.

The sensory cortex can be divided into a primary area, which receives direct projections from the thalamus, and a secondary area, which receives many of its projections from the primary sensory cortex. The secondary area can also receive inputs from more than one sensory region.

The main motor cortex is located in the human brain anterior to the fissure of Rolando. It contains an orderly point-by-point projection of the body surface, with the feet toward the mid-line and the head lying on the lateral surface. Stimulation of the motor cortex produces discrete movement of specific muscle groups.

Association areas make up a vast portion of the remaining cerebral cortex of the human brain and are important in the integration of sensory and motor processes. The most complex association area in primates and man is the prefrontal association cortex. This region is neither sensory nor motor, yet damage produces profound deficits in the ability to perform complex abstract tasks. The prefrontal association cortex also plays an important role in emotional behavior.
—Joel F. Lubar, *University of Tennessee*
See also Brain.
Consult (3) Isaacson, *et al.,* 1971; Teitelbaum, 1967.

CEREBRAL HEMISPHERES. *See* Brain.

CHAINING, a process that involves linking together responses in a learning task. Each response gives rise to a new stimulus, which is associated with the next response in the series. In mastering a maze a rat must learn to associate its response at the preceding choice point. Hence, turning left at one choice point will give rise to internal stimuli that will help the animal at the next choice point. Chaining, or simple association between adjacent responses, is a factor in serial learning.
—Joel F. Lubar, *University of Tennessee*
See also Operant Conditioning.

CHARACTER, a term that has several meanings in psychology and in general usage. Character often means the sum total of an individual's traits, whether rated productive or destructive, normal or neurotic. In this sense, character is equivalent to the inclusive term *personality*. In this encyclopedia, theories of personality traits and development are treated under the heading of personality (except that entries on psychoanalytic theories use the Freudian term "character"). What are sometimes called character disorders are grouped as personality disorders.

Character can also be defined in a more selective sense as the relatively enduring traits of personality that are of ethical and social significance. This topic is discussed in articles on moral development and conscience. The psychoanalytic theory of development—the progression through stages from oral to genital—is covered under the heading of character development.
See also Character Development; Conscience; Moral Development; Personality.

CHARACTER DEVELOPMENT. Character may be defined as relatively enduring traits of personality that are of ethical and social significance. In psychoanalytic theory, character develops out of the gradual socialization and eventual genital focusing of sexual impulses. Originally autoerotic and polymorphously per-

CEREBELLUM

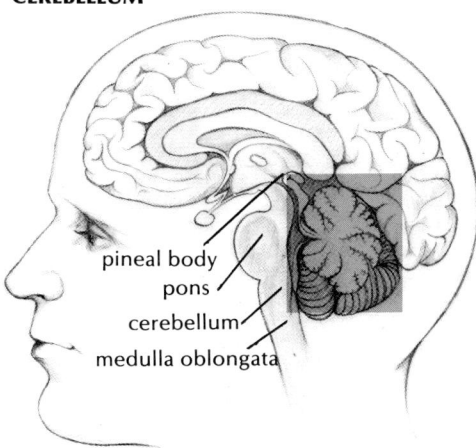

pineal body
pons
cerebellum
medulla oblongata

CEREBRAL CORTEX

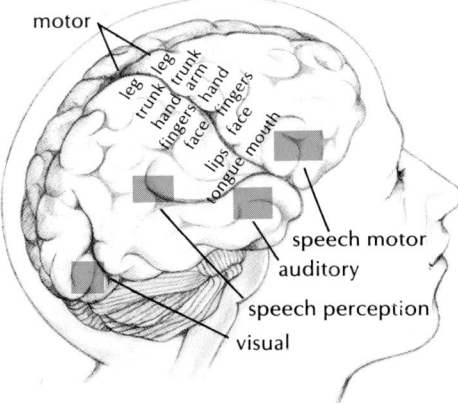

motor
leg leg
trunk trunk
hand arm
fingers hand
face fingers
lips face
tongue mouth
speech motor
auditory
speech perception
visual

verse, the individual, under the influence of social and biological forces, emerges from the oral, anal, phallic, and latent stages eventually into genital maturity. To the extent that he is over- or under-indulged in any of these erotogenic stages, he will exhibit physical and psychological characteristics typical of that stage, defining his character type. These traits are neither "good" nor "bad" in themselves; their value is defined by social goals and degree of presence. Everyone carries remnants of each of these stages in his character. Their expression may be direct—as in sexual foreplay—sublimated, or disguised by the expression of the opposite tendency.

The oral period, one of passivity, dependence, trust, and failure to distinguish oneself from others, focuses on mouth activities. As teeth grow, sadistic orientation develops as the individual takes pleasure in biting. Oral fixation in the adult is characterized by passive dependence, trust (perhaps gullibility) and pleasure, perhaps in eating, drinking, kissing, smoking, and talking. Sarcasm (biting remarks), satire, gossip, and gum chewing reflect oral sadistic influences, according to Freudian theory.

The anal character reflects problems of self-gratification vs. submission to authority, focused in the anal area with the help of toilet training and spanking. Orderliness, parsimoniousness, and obstinacy are characteristic. Or their opposites—sloppiness, spendthriftiness, indecision—may develop through reaction formation.

The resolution of the Oedipal conflict in the phallic stage and the finalization of this resolution in adolescence produce the final development of character. Failure to achieve this final resolution results in character disorder.

Other theories of personality deemphasize sexuality, accentuating learning, internal growth forces, and continuing character development throughout life.

—M. G. Affinito, *Southern Connecticut State College*

See also Anal Character; Genital Character; Oedipus Complex; Oral Character; Personality; Phallic Character; Psychoanalysis.

CHARACTER DISORDERS. *See* Personality Disorders.

CHARCOT, JEAN-MARTIN (1825–1893), French physician. Born in Paris, he received his M.D. from the University of Paris (1853) and was subsequently professor of pathological anatomy at the University of Paris and director of Salpêtrière Hospital.

Charcot's work centered on relating the clinical symptoms of patients to the normal and diseased anatomy of the nervous system, and he is often regarded as the father of neurology. He also is famous for his studies of hypnosis and hysteria and as a teacher of Sigmund Freud and Pierre Janet. Charcot began his investigations of hypnosis in 1875 with the belief that hypnosis was a symptom of hysteria, thus founding the so-called Salpêtrière school of hypnosis. (The Nancy school, represented by A. Liebeault and H. Bernheim, more correctly believed that hypnosis resulted from sleep suggestion and that the symptoms exhibited under hypnosis were the result of hypnotic suggestion.) By identifying and describing the stages of hypnosis—lethargy, catalepsy, and somnambulism—on a neurological basis, Charcot refuted the questionable animal magnetism basis of hypnotism as practiced by Mesmer and put it on a respectable basis for study and treatment.

Although hysteria was regarded as a female disease at the time, Charcot did discover some male patients with the disease and he did hint at the idea that sexual problems were an important factor in producing psychological problems—a suggestion that his pupil Freud developed more fully in his own work. In addition to his work on hypnotism and hysteria, Charcot did significant work on multiple sclerosis, spinal cord injury, paralysis, and identifying the causes of cerebral hemorrhage and the functions of the cerebrum.

See also Freud; Hypnotism.

CHEMICAL STIMULATION OF THE BRAIN. Because the brain operates on the basis of both electrical and chemical coding, neuroscientists are able to trace pathways by means of chemical stimulation. To transmit electrical impulses from one neuron to another a chemical substance is often released at the junction between two neurons, the synapse. This chemical acts as a stimulator to produce electrical excitation in other cells in neural circuits. One way to mimic the effect of such transmitters is to implant a cannula, a small hollow tube through which chemicals can be introduced directly into the brain.

By injecting chemicals into different brain regions, various behavioral changes can be elicited. For example, Neal Miller, at Rockefeller University, has reported that injection of testosterone, a male hormone, directly into the hypothalamus of female rats can lead to the exhibition of male behaviors in the rats. Similarly, chemical stimulation of other portions of the hypothalamus will elicit either drinking or eating, depending on whether the chemical used is related to acetylcholine, one type of naturally occurring chemical transmitter, or norepinephrine, another neurotransmitter.

—Joel F. Lubar, *University of Tennessee*

See also Electrical Stimulation of the Brain.

CHEMOTHERAPY, the use of drugs such as

Often termed "father of neurology," French physician Jean-Martin Charcot made important studies of hypnosis and hysteria.

tranquilizers and antidepressants to treat mental disorders. *See* Drugs and Behavior; Manic-Depressive Psychosis; Schizophrenia.

CHILD DEVELOPMENT. This area of study gathers knowledge about social, emotional, and intellectual change to help ensure a full, healthy, and satisfying life for all children. The basic premise of the developmental psychologist studying children is that qualitatively different processes and principles govern behavior as the child grows. The identification of these processes and the rules for change from one to another are his main work.

History. The scientific study of children, like psychology itself, is of relatively recent origin. As late as the eighteenth century children were accorded no special place in the arts or philosophy but were seen as "little people," indistinguishable from adults except by size. The first attention to the period of childhood arose from medical concern over high infant-mortality rates coupled with a religious concern for saving young souls and preparing children better to withstand adult temptations. Later, philosophers such as John Locke and Jean-Jacques Rousseau granted childhood a unique place in society and considered its philosophical nature and importance.

Child development as a science began when Charles Darwin proposed, as a corollary to his theory of evolution, that the origins of the human species might be found in its children. Thus, the initial interest of child psychology was an attempt to find parallels between animal, primitive, and modern man. By 1900 the so-called *child-study movement* was in full swing, led in the United States by G. Stanley Hall, who is often called the "father of child psychology in America."

Before many years had passed, it became clear that the analogy between individual development and species development was not very precise and that there was no way to test it directly. Child psychologists began to turn their attention to the problems that confront children as they grow toward maturity, not so much as a way of understanding the origins of the race as for the intrinsic benefit of the children themselves. This second phase has been called the *child welfare movement,* and it was the main focus of child psychology until mid-century.

Probably more than any other single figure, Sigmund Freud influenced this shift in emphasis in child psychology from academic to applied concerns. In Europe Freud had for some years been examining and describing the damaging influences that childhood traumas had on mature adults. This view was brought to the attention of the American academic and lay communities by the same man who was the most powerful spokesman for the Darwinian approach to childhood, G. Stanley Hall. Hall

invited Freud to speak at Clark University in 1909, and that date marked the shift in emphasis in child psychology from child study to child welfare.

The other major influence on child psychology early in the century came from France, in the form of the Binet intelligence scales (later to become the Stanford-Binet test), which made the measurement of intellectual standing a more objective matter than it had previously been. It became possible to determine with reasonable accuracy the progress that children were making intellectually in comparison with their peers. It was during this period that the term "retardation" took on its current meaning, as did "gifted" (which is actually a misnomer, since the scales measured precocity rather than great intelligence itself). Many child psychologists devoted their careers to improving the life situation of retarded and disturbed individuals as well as to providing greater intellectual challenge to precociously bright children. Child welfare research stations were established at several academic institutions, including Iowa, Minnesota, Yale, Clark, and Washington.

A more recent shift in emphasis in child psychology occurred soon after the end of World War II and may be conveniently dated by the publication of the first edition of Benjamin Spock's enormously popular child-care manual in 1945. Prior to the war American *behaviorists,* led by J. B. Watson, had advanced a reconceptualization of child development intended to be more scientific in approach than the Freudian psychoanalytic view. In his 1928 book *Psychological Care of Infant and Child,* Watson argued that by careful attention to sequences of reward and punishment, parents could guide the development of their children and produce any planned outcome. He urged parents to keep their children on strict schedules for feeding, weaning, toilet training, rest, and play and to avoid easy-going discipline and indulgent affection, which he felt resulted only in dependence and insecurity.

Spock presented an alternative to these behaviorist rules and declared that, within reasonable limits, mothers and fathers should feel comfortable with whatever child-rearing decisions they made. The main thing was for parents to want, care for, and love their children. Many have called this change in philosophy of child rearing a move toward "permissiveness," but this misrepresents Spock's message. Recognizing the importance of rules and consistent behavior on the part of the parents, Spock did not recommend permissiveness: he argued that parents should decide on a reasonable child-rearing philosophy and then have the courage of their convictions even if this or that "expert" recommended otherwise. Spock's message, above all else, was

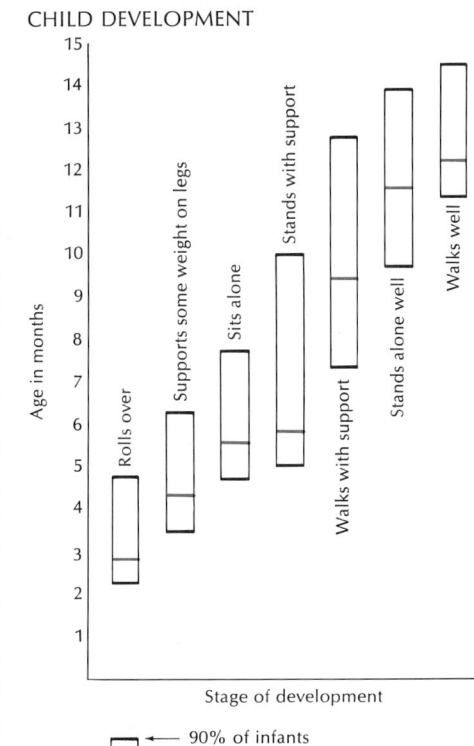

CHILD DEVELOPMENT

The dividing mark on each bar shows the age by which half the number of children attain the indicated stage of development.

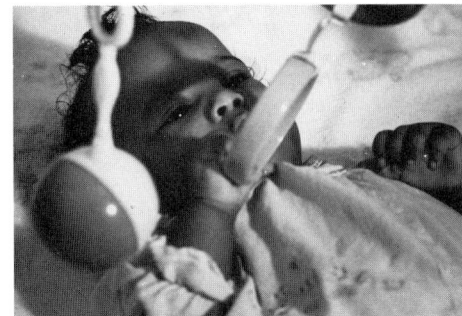

The infant, from birth, seems to be trying to understand his world, using senses that are functional much earlier than had been thought.

In the first year the child becomes able to move about to inspect the world. He may walk alone by his first birthday.

The sociable toddler may enjoy the company of another child but will rarely work cooperatively with him in any joint undertaking.

The preschooler, now a master of highly complex coordinations, has also learned to solve problems by using ideas rather than acts.

one of moderation. Trusting the child's natural regulation mechanisms and responding to the physical and emotional needs of both parents and child in a consistent, comfortable manner, he said, was more important than specific decisions about breast or bottle feeding, time of weaning and toilet training, or specific schedules for eating, sleeping, and play.

More than any other single figure, Benjamin Spock helped relieve parents of anxiety over the real and imagined effects that early traumatic experiences might have on their children. He directed attention to positive goals that could be defined and aspired to for all children. Spock introduced a new era in child psychology, from concern with preventing trauma and treating exceptionalities to concern with the determinants of normal healthy change in children. The fact that the field has now taken on the name *child development* signals this change. "Development" means benign intervention by adults into the world of children to ensure a full and healthy adulthood, and it is to knowledge of the basic principles of healthy development that most child psychologists have turned since 1945.

Recent Approaches. Along with the increased interest in normal development came more sophisticated methods of measuring and analyzing child behavior. Much earlier work, most notably that of G. Stanley Hall and his influential student Arnold Gesell, had attempted to trace first the evolution of the species and later the maturational development of children through extensive, detailed observation and cataloging of normative data. Child psychologists now began to examine and identify processes other than maturation that might cause behavior to develop.

The publication of Erik Erikson's book *Childhood and Society* in 1950, for example, extended Freud's concern with erotic preoccupations to include the importance of the culture and the establishment of positive social relations. Thus, in addition to their concern with oral, anal, and phallic behavior, psychologists began to study more intensely the resolution of psychosocial conflicts centered on trust, autonomy, initiative, identity, and integrity in the course of human development.

While Erikson and the other ego psychologists concentrated on healthy social and emotional development, American psychology also discovered the ingenious work of the Swiss psychologist Jean Piaget, the most penetrating observer of normal intellectual development. Piaget has searched for those universal aspects of intellectual development that all children may attain. His equilibration model provides a mechanism for intellectual growth resulting from the child's maturation *and* active interaction with his environment. Play and imitation for Piaget are not simply physical or mental exercise but two methods of coming to

know the world through action—a concept central to early cognitive development and crucial to later intellectual growth.

Although these two approaches emphasize other processes, they retain maturation as an important aspect of development; other influential views have placed much less emphasis on its role. Social learning theory, for example, grew out of John Dollard and Neal Miller's integration of learning theory principles (as espoused by J. B. Watson and later B. F. Skinner) with the problems presented by a Freudian approach. The aim was to uncover principles of behavior change operating uniformly from birth to death that will account for learning and social behavior. Though not strictly a developmental approach, social learning theory, because of its emphasis on precise measurement and control, has proved to be especially useful in prescribing behavioral therapy treatments for a variety of childhood disturbances, such as autism and some types of childhood psychoses.

The era of increased sophistication in measurement and analysis of child behavior also produced far-reaching advances in the study of infant development. Through the use of operant conditioning and ingenious application of technology, researchers have begun to unlock the secrets of the infant mind, and it is already clear that the child's first behavior is organized and structured, not random, as many had previously assumed. The infant seems to be trying to understand his world from birth. His senses are functional earlier than had been thought, and his ability to test guesses about what the world is like is remarkable. From these beginnings other investigators have continued the painstaking collection and analysis of data that lead to new knowledge of the process of normal development.

Current Research. A particularly difficult issue that remains to be satisfactorily resolved, even after fifty years of controversy, is the question of the relative contribution of heredity and environment—of genetics and learning—to the course of normal development. Though no contemporary researcher advocates either extreme position, views on the relative contributions of each of these factors vary considerably with the particular research question. While certain physical and motor changes, neurological and perceptual developments, and (to a certain extent) language skills are thought to have large genetic components within existing environmental conditions, severe sensory deprivation or physical trauma may alter the course of natural growth. Other differences in emotional and intellectual development have been related to less severe environmental influences, such as maternal deprivation or overprotection, father absence, or birth order and family size, but genetic predispositions are probably involved here as well. Some sex-related differences can be traced to cultural factors, some seem more closely related to biological factors, and still others are believed to result from the complex interaction of biology and culture, which operates as early as the first few days after birth. The so-called nature-nurture controversy may never be resolved in its original uncompromising form. Instead, child psychologists and geneticists are examining extremely subtle and complex interactions and asking how heredity and environment combine to produce a given effect rather than how much each contributes.

Partly as a logical outgrowth of the renewed interest in normal development and partly in response to the political demands of recent decades, child psychologists have focused attention most recently on poor and minority children as well as on the right of *all* children to adequate nutrition, health care, and education. The most notable result of the increasing concern for the welfare of children was the formation in 1970 of the Office of Child Development in the Department of Health, Education and Welfare of the United States government. For the first time the activities of the government on behalf of children, including day care as well as Head Start and other intervention programs, were brought together into a single agency under the leadership of Edward Zigler of Yale University, a prominent child psychologist.

The field of child psychology thus has passed through periods marked by different emphases, from the academic comparison of children with animal and primitive groups to a concern with exceptional children; from a focus on normal development to a commitment to provide the knowledge and skill necessary for the full development of all children and the enjoyment of childhood as an intrinsically valuable time of life.

—David H. Feldman and Samuel S. Snyder, *Yale University*

See also Cognitive Development; Heredity and Environment; Intrauterine Environment; *other articles listed under* Developmental Psychology *in the Item Guide. The state of development after childhood is discussed in* Adolescence.

Consult (11) Bronfenbrenner, 1970; Erikson, 1963; Freud, 1920; Ginsburg and Opper, 1969; Kessen, 1965; Spock, 1968; Stone and Church, 1968; Watson, 1928; Weiner and Elkind, 1972.

CHILD PSYCHIATRY. The majority of child psychiatrists in the United States are in private practice, with a small minority in community facilities and in academic work. Traditionally, play therapy with the child has been their main technique. In recent years, however, there has been an upsurge in other modalities: behavior modification (with and without parents as therapists), drug treatment, group treatment, family therapy, and educational therapy.

At least part of the reason for the emergence of these new modalities has been the lack of demonstrated effectiveness of more traditional approaches. Follow-up studies of psychiatrically disturbed children indicate that those with conduct disorders and psychoses do rather poorly with or without treatment, while those with neurotic disorders do comparatively well without treatment. Follow-up studies of psychiatrically disturbed adolescents indicate that the concept of "adolescent turmoil" is unfounded. The minority of adolescents who develop psychiatric disorders are just as ill as adults who do so, and intensive treatment is indicated.

Making psychiatric services for children accessible to more people is the major service need, and systematic evaluation of what therapies are effective for which children is the major research need of the future.

—Dennis P. Cantwell, M.D., *University of California, Los Angeles*

Consult (13) Barker, 1971; Chess, 1969; Howells, 1965; Howells, 1969; Kanner, 1972; Miller, 1966; Quay and Werry, 1972; Shaw, 1971. Also journals such as the *Journal of Child Psychology and Psychiatry,* the *American Journal of Orthopsychiatry,* and *Child Development.*

CHILD PSYCHOLOGY. Theories about emotional, intellectual, and social growth are covered under the heading of Child Development. Clinical psychologists working with children share the interests of child psychiatrists. *See* Child Development; Child Psychiatry; Developmental Psychology.

CHILDREN'S THINKING. *See* Cognitive Development Theory.

CHLORPROMAZINE, an antipsychotic agent, one of the phenothiazines, used to treat mental disorders. *See* Drugs and Behavior; Schizophrenia.

CHOICE SHIFT. *See* Risky Shift.

CHOMSKY, (AVRAM) NOAM (1928–), American linguist, born in Philadelphia. He received his Ph.D. from the University of Pennsylvania and has been at M.I.T. since 1955.

Chomsky's book *Syntactic Structures* (1957) revolutionized modern linguistic theory and, along with other writings, had great impact on psychologists. Though his work is highly technical and of primary interest only to specialists in linguistics, several of his general ideas remain popular in psychology.

Chomsky distinguishes between language *competence* (ideal knowledge of a language as rules and structure) and *performance*

The child in early school years is progressively more able to think in abstract terms. His memories are no longer isolated episodes and he is increasingly able to think ahead.

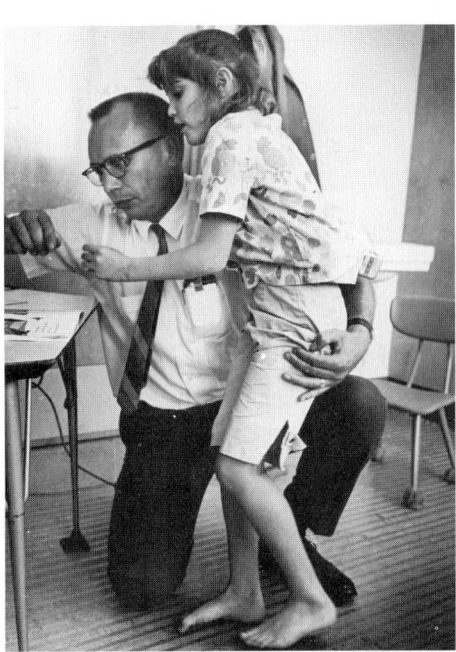

The noted child psychiatrist O. I. Lovaas working with an autistic child.

The revolutionary linguistic theories of Noam Chomsky have caused many learning and developmental psychologists to reexamine their methods and assumptions.

CHROMOSOME

Chromosomes of a normal human male, showing the 23 pairs, including the XY pair of sex chromosomes.

(how a speaker-listener uses language in practice). Linguists study competence, while psycholinguists study performance. The distinction can be debated, but it is useful in clarifying the division of labor between linguistics and psycholinguistics.

Furthermore, Chomsky and others have strongly criticized the ability of traditional learning theories to account for how children acquire language so rapidly (most of the basic rules and words by age four), much faster than their learning of other intellectual abilities. To explain this, Chomsky and his followers have stressed the possibility that humans are born with a large built-in capacity for acquiring language. Though some evidence supports this contention, it is an extremely difficult notion to test. Nevertheless, criticisms from linguists have caused learning and developmental psychologists to reexamine many of their methods and assumptions.

The cognitive psychology movement has also received a boost from the importance that Chomsky and his followers have attached to *rules* in acquiring language. Chomsky's "generative" approach to language indicates that rules generate the almost infinite variety of orders and sentences the child has never heard before. This "creative" aspect of using language presents difficulties to traditional learning principles, which are hard-pressed to account for the novelty of language by means of conditioning, reinforcement, and feedback from the environment.

Chomsky's major publications include *Current Issues in Linguistic Theory* (1964), *Topics in the Theory of Generative Grammar* (1966), and *Language and Mind* (1968).

—Roland Siiter, *Montclair State College*
See also Cognitive Psychology; Language.

CHROMOSOME, a threadlike body in the nucleus of the cell that carries the genes, the basic heredity factors. Thousands of genes may be arranged linearly along the human chromosome. Chromosomes are less than 1/1000 of an inch long and are formed of deoxyribonucleic acid (DNA) and structural proteins. During cell division, the chromosomes replicate themselves, resulting in a duplicate set of chromosomes that is distributed to the two daughter cells.

Each species has a characteristic number of chromosomes; man has forty-six, arranged in pairs. Recent experiments show that abnormalities in number or shape of the chromosomes in man can be correlated with behavioral and physiological disorders.

—Nina Adams, *Yale University*
See also DNA; Heredity and Environment.

CHRONIC BRAIN DISORDERS, conditions re-

sulting from relatively permanent impairment of the function of brain tissues. *Chronic* disorders are distinguished from *acute* in that the acute cases typically do not cause irreversible damage. The Standard Nomenclature of the American Psychiatric Association lists a number of conditions that may produce chronic brain disorders: congenital problems such as prenatal infectious disease or birth injury causing mental deficiency; syphilis that affects the central nervous system, as in general paresis; intoxication by such agents as lead, arsenic, mercury, carbon monoxide, and alcohol; permanent damage from a head injury; cerebral arteriosclerosis; other circulatory disorders, for example, due to a cerebral hemorrhage; epilepsy; senile brain disease; disturbances of metabolism, growth, or nutrition—for example, pellagra, or complications of diabetes or adrenal disorders; brain tumors; diseases of unknown cause, such as multiple sclerosis.

See also Acute Brain Disorders; Brain Disorders.

Consult (13) American Psychiatric Association, 1952; Coleman, 1964.

CHUNKING. *See* Memory.

CINGULATE GYRUS, a portion of the brain cortex lying between the two hemispheres. It is located directly above the corpus callosum, a large band of fibers separating the two hemispheres of the brain. Removal of the cingulate gyrus may lead to profound changes in emotionality and in some cases to disturbance of some motor and autonomic factors.

See also Brain.

CIVILIAN CATASTROPHE REACTION. Earthquakes, fires, floods, and crashes of trains, planes, or cars may produce the same symptoms in civilians that combat sometimes does in soldiers. The American Psychiatric Association lists civilian catastrophe reactions and combat reactions as two forms of gross stress reactions. These stress reactions come under the more inclusive heading of transient situational personality disorders. These disorders develop when a personality is temporarily overwhelmed by the stress of a disaster. The disorder is likely to be most serious in people who have tendencies to be immature or unstable, or who have previously gone through extreme stress.

The survivor of a disaster may go into a stage of shock. After a plane crash people wander off, unable to help themselves or to try to rescue others. They may temporarily forget who they are and where they are. Later they may go into a stage of dependence, wanting help and taking orders from others. Sometimes the symptoms of shock do not develop for days after the disaster. One survivor of the Coconut Grove fire in Boston, which killed more than

400 in 1943, was treated in a hospital and released but later showed guilt feelings over the death of his wife in the fire and committed suicide.

Fires such as this are likely to cause panic. Facing a sudden danger, for which they were not at all prepared, causes many individuals to lose control. There is less chance of panic reactions in disasters such as hurricanes, where people have warning of the danger that they must face.

Treatment for a disaster syndrome typically consists of rest, sedation, and talk sessions with a psychotherapist. The procedure may be much the same as with cases of combat reactions in servicemen.

See also Combat Neurosis.
Consult (13) Coleman, 1964.

CIVIL RIGHTS. For discussion of discrimination and racism, *see* Prejudice.

CLAIRVOYANCE (one form of extrasensory perception, or ESP), a direct response to an object or event not explainable by perception, memory, or inference. Anecdotes often report clairvoyance, as when Swedenborg "saw" the location of a document hidden by someone who died unexpectedly, or when a dowser locates underground water or minerals. However, any one report may be coincidence (or misstatement). The occurrence of clairvoyance can be established only by careful experiments, where, for example, a computer is programmed or a machine built to select random targets and the subjects who try to guess those targets are able to succeed at levels significantly higher than chance.

—Gertrude R. Schmeidler, *The City College of The City University of New York*
See also Extrasensory Perception; Parapsychology.
Consult (14) Schmidt, 1969.

CLASSICAL CONDITIONING. *See* Pavlovian Conditioning.

CLAUSTROPHOBIA, a morbid fear of being in an enclosed space. *See* Phobia.

CLIENT-CENTERED THERAPY, the nondirective approach to psychotherapy advocated by Carl Rogers. In this method, much of the responsibility for the course and outcome of the treatment of a mental disorder is placed on the patient. The therapist guides and encourages, taking a less authoritative role than he would in the directive form of therapy.

Rogers outlined five steps in treatment. In the first, the client or patient goes to a therapist for help. This step is very important because it shows that the client wants to improve his mental health. Second, the patient expresses his feelings—becomes able to vent hostile emotions—helped by the accepting attitude of the therapist. Third, the patient slowly comes to understand his problem, to gain insight into his life situation. Fourth, he begins to take steps that will make a positive improvement in his way of life. Finally, the client takes full responsibility for his life and ends the sessions with the therapist. This contrasts with classic psychoanalytic procedures.

See also Rogers.
Consult (13) Coleman, 1964; Rogers, 1942; Rogers, 1951.

CLINICAL PSYCHOLOGY. More than one-third of psychologists in the United States are involved with the study and treatment of problems of mental health, and Division 12 of the American Psychological Association (Division of Clinical Psychology) has a large membership. Clinical psychologists work in mental hospitals, outpatient clinics, community mental health centers, and child guidance clinics. They may also serve on the staffs of schools and colleges, welfare agencies, juvenile courts, or prisons. A considerable number are in private practice as counselors or psychotherapists. There is growing insistence that anyone practicing psychotherapy be licensed, and licensing may require a Ph.D. degree in psychology plus years of clinical experience.

As part of their diagnostic work, clinical psychologists often administer tests of intelligence and personality.

Clinical psychologists may share the duties of psychiatrists. However, psychiatrists are medical specialists with M.D. degrees and can carry out measures such as psychotherapy that are beyond the scope allowed to psychologists. It is difficult to separate clinical work from the broad field of abnormal psychology. Hence, in this encyclopedia one Subject Map covers the abnormal and clinical areas. *See* Abnormal Psychology and the accompanying Subject Map.

See also Counseling Psychology.

CLONE, a group of cells or organisms derived from a common ancestor by asexual cell division (for example, bacteria or amoeba). In asexual reproduction one cell, with its chromosomes, divides to produce two cells of the same genotype. Because there is no recombination of chromosomes and genes, as occurs in sexual reproduction, asexual reproduction provides no basis for variability.

CLOSED-MINDEDNESS. *See* Prejudice.

CLUSTERING. *See* Free-Recall Learning; Memory.

COCAINE, a stimulant drug found in the leaves of the coca tree. It does not produce the degree

CINGULATE GYRUS

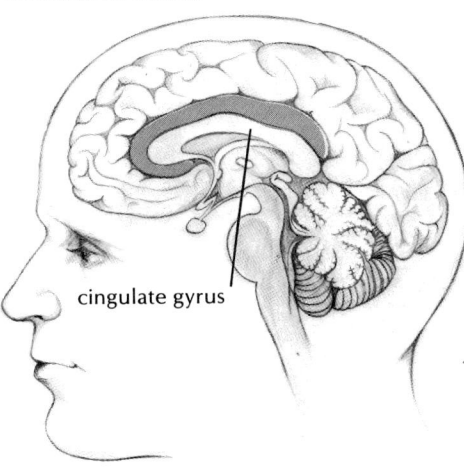

cingulate gyrus

In a clairvoyance test of ESP, the girl guesses that the card held by the experimenter is a star.

of physiological addiction caused by narcotics such as heroin, but it may cause habitual dependence. Prolonged use may lead to psychotic symptoms.

The coca tree is found in South America and some peoples of that region frequently chewed the leaves to relieve fatigue and hunger. The drug became widely used as a local anesthetic, but has largely been replaced by a synthetic, Novocaine.

See also Drugs and Behavior.

CODABILITY, a psycholinguistic concept referring to how few words of a language are needed to name or "code" a quality or category. Concepts requiring the fewest number of words to name are "highly codable."

This idea grew out of a study showing that college students recognized colors named by a single word (like "red") faster than colors named by several words (like "dark red-or-ange"). Further comparisons with other languages have shown that people have no difficulty remembering and recognizing colors that are highly codable in their own language but more trouble doing the same for colors poorly coded in their own language (but highly codable in some other language).

Since languages differ greatly in their codability for specific qualities like color, codability is one way in which a language may affect remembering and even thinking. However, the coding of qualities in a particular language is probably in turn determined by the cumulative experiences of its native speakers. For example, Australian Aborigines have many words for "kangaroo" because discriminating between kangaroo species and types is important in their culture and even to their survival.

—Roland Siiter, *Montclair State College*
See also Language.

COGNITION, the aspect of mental activity involving perceiving, thinking, and knowing. *See* Cognitive Psychology.

COGNITIVE DEVELOPMENT THEORY. Progressive changes can be observed in intellectual growth from infancy through childhood and into adolescence and adulthood. Many views of cognitive development exist, but two theories, those of Piaget and Bruner, warrant detailed attention.

Piaget's Theory

Jean Piaget describes cognitive development in terms of a series of successive, overlapping stages that summarize major changes that take place in the thinking of normal children. Four concepts are basic to his description. In *assimilation,* information is absorbed ("assimilated") by the brain; thus, thinking is the function of not only incoming stimulation but also what is already happening in the brain. In *accommodation,* mediating (thinking) pro-

cesses are themselves changed by incoming stimuli as experiences are accumulated; thus, the brain is "accommodating" environmental experiences. The *schema* (pl. "schemata") is a structural unit of cognitive activity; it makes up the existing framework onto which sensory data are fit but that changes as assimilation and accommodation take place. *Equilibration* is the process by which schemata (cognitive structures) change from one state to another. Using these general concepts, Piaget summarizes the changes in cognitive development that take place in terms of four identifiable stages. His theory emphasizes the importance of biological maturation of cognitive structures and internal processes in development and assumes that the order of the stages is invariant.

Sensorimotor Period (birth to about two years). Perceptions become organized, but thoughts are externalized—tied to objects. The child develops an understanding of objects and actions or "sensorimotor schemata": he can manipulate objects, move around, and initiate events. Gradually he learns that objects have *permanence,* even when they are taken out of his immediate vicinity. The infant learns about relationships between time, space, and shapes, but he lacks internal and symbolic representations of these things. The child's thinking also tends to be "animistic," that is, to ascribe life to inanimate objects that move (for example, seeing clouds as self-propelled). This period ends when internal imagery and language begin.

Preoperational Thought (two to seven years). Once language and internal representations of the world begin to develop, mental as well as physical objects acquire permanence. But thinking still has little flexibility and usually proceeds step by step in only one direction. Thinking is "irreversible" in that the child can follow a sequence of operations but cannot trace the sequence back to the original starting point. At this stage categorization is very simple, usually related to the child's own experiences rather than adult concepts. In other words, thinking is *egocentric*: the child cannot assimilate another person's point of view.

Concrete Operations (seven to eleven years). The child begins to apply logic to concrete ideas and to master the *conservation* abilities: when water is poured from a tall, narrow glass to a short, wide one, he knows that the amount of water stays the same (whereas at age four or five the same child would have said the tall glass held more water). Mastery of the concepts of conservation of length, mass, and finally volume occur in the same order in all children and usually are stable by age eleven or twelve. Thinking is reversible and less egocentric, and the child can make simple generalizations and abstractions that are still rooted to events and objects that are concrete.

Until about age seven children have difficulty in applying logic to concrete ideas. This child witnessed the pouring of equal amounts of liquid into two vessels but insisted that the narrower vessel contained more. When one of two equal-sized balls of clay was rolled out to an elongated shape, the child asserted that the new shape contained more clay.

Formal Operations (eleven years and after). Fully adult powers of reasoning, abstraction, and symbolization emerge, and gradually the capacities for using logical laws of argument, drawing implications, and reasoning hypothetically ("what if. . .") appear. The concepts of morality, social justice, and proper modes of social conduct become clarified to the individual.

Bruner's Theory

Jerome S. Bruner's work at Harvard in the 1960s yielded a picture of children's thinking as more flexible and adaptable than Piaget's theory would have it. He stresses environmental factors and does not believe the stages are invariant in order. One statement from an influential paper, "The Process of Education" (1960), has become famous: "any subject can be taught effectively in some intellectually honest form to any child at any stage of development." Emphasizing the origins of cognitive abilities as having arisen from man's tool-using capacities, Bruner also has advocated investigating cultural factors and anthropological data relevant to cognition.

More recently, Bruner and his colleagues at Harvard have been studying cognitive processes in very young, even newborn infants. Evidence is accumulating that neonates are not as passive and merely receptive to stimulation as once was thought: they can make discriminations, learn simple responses, and actively control stimuli presented to them—provided that conditions are arranged to take advantage of an infant's limited response repertoire. For example, very young infants can learn to control visual stimuli with their own sucking responses. Under these conditions, the sucking infant will suck faster or slower to view more novel or less novel stimuli—whichever it prefers.

From a broader perspective, both Piaget's theory and Bruner's work form the basis of many of the fundamental theoretical notions in developmental psychology today.

Another trend that is helping make the study of cognitive development one of the most active research areas in psychology is the impact of psycholinguistics and new theories of language acquisition on psychology. These developments are discussed in the article on Language.

—Roland Siiter, *Montclair State College*
See also Bruner; Cognitive Development; Language; Piaget.
Consult (7) Bruner, 1960; Phillips, 1969; Piaget, 1962. (11) Dinkmeyer, 1965; Watson, 1965.

COGNITIVE DISSONANCE.

COGNITIVE DISSONANCE. The theory of cognitive dissonance was developed by Leon Festinger. He postulated that an individual strives for internal harmony and consistency within himself, so that his attitudes, values, beliefs, and opinions are consonant with each other and with his behavior. If a person, for instance, believes that college education is necessary, he will try to provide it for his children. It was also noted in the theory that, although there is a consistency, or consonance, between cognitive elements, in some instances, inconsistency, or dissonance, occurs. An example would be continuing smoking although being aware of its negative effects on health.

According to the theory, the existence of nonfitting relations or dissonance among cognitions produces psychological discomfort, which will motivate the individual to reduce it in different ways. He might change his behavior (stop smoking), change an aspect of the environment (change to a filter-tip cigarette), or add a new cognitive element (gather new information in an attempt to negate the notion that smoking is dangerous to his health).

—Ragaa Mazen, *Southern Connecticut State College*
See also Attitude and Attitude Change.
Consult (9) Festinger, 1957.

COGNITIVE PSYCHOLOGY.

COGNITIVE PSYCHOLOGY. A traditional classification in philosophy and psychology divides mental activity into three aspects: *cognitive,* involving perceiving, thinking, and knowing; *affective,* involving feelings and emotions; and *conative,* involving acting, doing, and striving. Cognition is a general term designating all the various modes and aspects of knowing, including perceiving, recognizing, remembering, imagining, conceptualizing, judging, and reasoning. Thus it potentially includes all the inner mediating systems whereby an organism processes stimulus information and construes, represents, organizes, interprets, and responds to ongoing events. At the human level, this includes thought processes involving imagery, language, and symbols.

Range of Investigations. The field of cognitive psychology investigates on many levels how individuals structure and organize their environments, and the basic processes involved. The range of investigations is very broad, including such topics as: information processing in visual and auditory perception; memory or information storage and retrieval; language acquisition and psycholinguistics; imagery, fantasy, and stimulus-independent thought; altered states of consciousness; individual differences in styles of perceiving and thinking; and the dynamics of cognitive restructuring when conflicting or dissonant information is provided. This is only a small sample of the kind of topics investigated.

Theories. With so many aspects, it is evident that a unified general theory of cognition will be difficult to achieve. At present there are many outstanding cognitively oriented psychologists investigating problems and developing theories, but there is no single dominant

COGNITIVE PSYCHOLOGY

As the article COGNITIVE PSYCHOLOGY explains, this is not a simply defined field of study. Cognitive psychology might be described as a point of view about learning and thinking—how a person perceives stimuli and then organizes, selects, processes, stores, and uses information.

Examples of the viewpoint of cognitive psychology can be found in the following articles: LEARNING THEORY (contrasts connectionistic and cognitive theories of learning); COGNITIVE DEVELOPMENT THEORY (describes Piaget's ideas about how the child perceives and interprets his surroundings); CONCEPT LEARNING; PROBLEM SOLVING; LANGUAGE; COMPUTER SIMULATION; ATTITUDES AND ATTITUDE CHANGE and COGNITIVE DISSONANCE (showing the influence of cognitive theory in social psychology); and GESTALT PSYCHOLOGY (the organizing role of the perceiver in seeing or otherwise sensing his environment).

cognitive theory. However there are some widely shared views. Most would hold that whatever an organism "knows" about its environment has been mediated or transformed, not only by the sense organs but by complex systems that interpret and reinterpret sensory input. Cognition thus concerns the means whereby information is transformed, reduced, elaborated, stored, recovered, and used.

In the view of cognitive psychologists, the individual organism is not simply a passive and automatic recipient of stimuli presented from without. Rather it is an active participant in constructing the meaningful stimuli that it selectively organizes and to which it selectively responds. The ways in which stimulus information is processed—or, in other words, cognitive activities—play an extremely important role in determining behavior. The nature of cognitive processing and organization is therefore basic for understanding the ways in which man actively encounters his complex physical and social environment. It is the view of cognitive psychologists that these basic mental operations are organized and have general characteristics that can be discovered through systematic theory and research.

Origins. The study of cognition is a very old concern of psychology with an impressive background of theory and research. Yet for a considerable period it was relatively neglected and unfashionable, and only in recent years has it again become a central focus of psychological investigation. The origins of cognitive psychology can be traced far back into the history of philosophy. A major traditional field is *epistemology,* or inquiry into the origins, nature, methods, and limits of human knowledge. In the late nineteenth century, when psychology first developed as a distinct field emphasizing research and experimentation, it was generally defined as "the science of mental life." In that period psychologists were not loath to investigate and speculate about inner "mental" events. However, the techniques and findings of the early structuralist school—with its painstaking introspective analysis of the elements of consciousness—proved sterile. This period was followed by the ascendance of behaviorism after World War I. Psychology was redefined as "the science of behavior" and many experimental psychologists rejected speculation about inner processes and subjective experience as too "mentalistic," unobservable, and incapable of scientific verification.

Yet a number of important exceptions to the dominant behavioristic trend maintained and furthered the development of cognitive psychology. The early work of Otto Külpe and the Würzburg School demonstrated the significance of mental sets or determining tendencies in influencing reactions. The school of Gestalt psychology investigated the active selective and organizing forces in perception. The re-

lated field theory of Kurt Lewin and his students was concerned with the structuring and restructuring of the "psychological life space" of the individual. The organismic or holistic school of Kurt Goldstein studied the manner in which thinking was impaired by organic brain damage and psychopathology. In developmental psychology the extended investigations of Jean Piaget and Heinz Werner into the cognitive and intellectual development of the child were of enormous significance. In social psychology the concept of "attitude" was central, and the large body of research regarding the characteristics, formation, and modification of attitudes was basically cognitive in its concern with the way individuals interpret and respond to objects in their social worlds. And even in behavioristic learning theories there was a gradual shift toward the acceptance of hypothetical intervening events between stimulus and response, reflecting mediating processes within the organism. Internal processes are represented by Edward C. Tolman's "sign learning" and "cognitive maps" and Donald O. Hebb's "cell assemblies" involved in perceptual learning.

Recent Contributions. Since the early 1950s, cognitive approaches have again become central in psychological research and theorizing. A few of the outstanding contributions should be noted as representative of recent work: Jerome Bruner on the nature of perceptual coding, categorizing, and concept development; D. E. Berlyne on curiosity and information seeking as a motive; Leon Festinger on the motivating effects of cognitive dissonance; George Kelly's theory of personal constructs; Stanley Schachter on the role of cognition in appraising and labeling emotional states; and the research of Herman Witkin, Riley Gardner, and George Klein on individual differences in perceptual and cognitive styles and their theoretical relation to psychoanalytic ego psychology.

Central in many recent advances are the information-processing models and computer simulation of cognitive processes that have come through the development of the modern electronic computer and cybernetics. Among the significant contributions are Newell, Shaw and Simon's information-processing theory of thinking and problem solving; D. E. Broadbent's information theory of attention, learning, and memory; and Miller, Galanter, and Pribram's analysis of planning and problem solving.

Cognitive psychology is presently in an exciting period when many of its traditional problems are being reformulated in novel and promising ways, and many new avenues of investigation are being explored.

—Alden E. Wessman, *The City College of The City University of New York*
See also Cognitive Development The-

ory; Cognitive Dissonance; Computer Simulation; Concept Learning; Imagery; Language; Learning Theory; Problem Solving.

Consult (7) Harper, et al., 1964; Mancuso, 1970; Neisser, 1967; Warr, 1970.

COGNITIVE THEORIES OF LEARNING. See Cognitive Development Theory; Learning Theory.

COLITIS. Both ulcerative colitis and mucous colitis may be gastrointestinal reactions to psychological stress. See Psychosomatic Disorders.

COLLECTIVE UNCONSCIOUS. See Unconscious, Collective.

COLOR BLINDNESS, the partial to total inability to distinguish colors. Some individuals have a defect called color weakness; they have normal perception of bright primary colors but cannot distinguish pale colors such as pink and tan. From 4 to 8 percent of males have red-green color blindness and see all colors as yellow or blue. This is the most commonly observed form of the defect. A few individuals have blue-yellow blindness and see all colors as red or green. There are still fewer cases of total color insensitivity (monochromatism), in which everything looks gray.

See also Color Vision.

COLOR VISION. Physicists often depict light in terms of waves, somewhat like idealized waves on an ocean. Such lightwaves can be said to vary along any of several dimensions, but for color perception only one of these dimensions, wavelength, is crucial. This measurement is taken from the peak of one wave to the trough of the next and can be used to describe all of the energy known as visible light. The wavelengths involved are so short, however, that they must be measured in nanometers (nm.), a nanometer equaling one ten-millionth of a centimeter. Visible light varies, approximately, from 350 nm. to 750 nm., although the practical limits are more like 400 nm. to 700 nm. [Consult (4) Held and Richards, 1972.]

Color Perception. Human vision and the visual processes of some other animals (including some insects) are capable of distinguishing among different wavelengths of light. Although the wavelength is not the sole determinant of color perception, people consistently describe different wavelengths in characteristic ways; a light at 700 nm. is called "red" by most people, while one at 500 nm. is usually labeled "green." Even so, the naming of colors is regarded as a complex and frequently imprecise business. Sometimes we call an object by a given color name simply because we have always called it by that name. For example, we might describe a brick as "red" even though it is more accurately a reddish orange.

Color Qualities. The problem of describing the experience of color is amplified when one considers that "color" describes more than a single dimension. Most classificatory systems describe color in terms of three dimensions: hue, brightness, and saturation. Hue refers to the common notion of color, such qualities as green, blue, or purple. Sometimes "hue" refers to the so-called spectral colors (red, orange, yellow, green, blue, indigo, and violet), although there is no uniform agreement on the matter. In addition, a color may vary along the range running from white through gray to black, the brightness dimension. Finally, the amount of hue present in a given color sample describes its saturation; for example, both lemon juice and lemon peel are yellow (both have the same hue), but the peel is more highly saturated than the juice, and may be a bit brighter as well. F. A. Geldard claims that when colors are analyzed along these three dimensions, human beings are capable of discriminating approximately 7,500,000 different colors. [Consult (4) Geldard, 1972.]

The Anatomical Process. The mechanism by which the nervous system analyzes color information is far from completely understood, but even the small amount that is presently comprehended suggests a complex process. Only the essential features of color reception can be presented here.

Color reception is limited entirely to cone cells concentrated in the central areas of the retinas. Unlike the rod cells, which are more numerous in the periphery, cones operate during periods of high relative illumination. There are probably three types of cone cells, each sensitive to a particular portion of the visible spectrum. In fact, recent evidence suggests that one type absorbs principally red light, a second green light, and a third blue light. [Consult (4) Rushton, 1962.]

But if there are only three receptors, how is it that we can perceive so many colors? The answer may be related to a phenomenon called additive color mixture, which was known as early as the nineteenth century. Unlike the relatively unfamiliar subtractive color mixture (an example would be mixing blue paint and yellow paint to obtain green), additive mixtures are seen mostly by mixing lights. In this way it can be shown that any three lights, in various concentrations, are capable of producing all of the hues, provided that the lights are distributed along the spectrum. Perhaps the outputs of visual receptors combine to produce the perception of certain colors in an analogous way. The remainder of the visual system may utilize the retinal information in more complex ways, though this subject has yet to be fully understood.

Research. The psychologist studies color vision for a variety of reasons, but one impor-

COLOR VISION

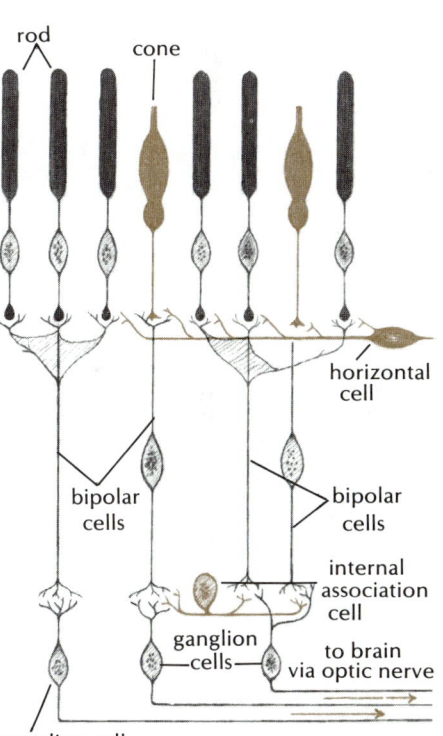

Color vision. Color reception is a function of the cone cells, which operate during periods of relatively high illumination. The cones of the fovea, the area of greatest visual sensitivity, have their own direct paths through bipolar cells with single endings. Outside the fovea larger bipolar cells with multiple endings collect signals from a number of sensors. Note how the rods, cones, and bipolar cells of the retina are also interconnected by internal association cells and horizontal cells.

tant one is that wavelength is not the sole determinant of color perception. Sometimes factors such as the colors of objects surrounding an object to be judged will influence perception of the object and must be considered from a point of view slightly different from the physicist's or physiologist's.

—Mark B. Fineman, *Southern Connecticut State College*
Consult (4) Geldard, 1972.

COMBAT FATIGUE. *See* Combat Neurosis.

COMBAT NEUROSIS. Personality disturbances related to the catastrophes of war have been given various diagnostic labels (shell shock, operational fatigue, combat exhaustion, war neurosis), but it is now generally accepted that these personality disturbances did not present significantly new symptoms. There is no specific neurosis or psychosis created exclusively by war experiences. Reactions to combat stress include psychosomatic disorders, neurotic breakdowns, depressions, and schizophrenic symptoms. The conditions under which these breakdowns occur are relatively transparent and develop rapidly. It has been estimated that 10 percent of men in combat during World War II developed combat neurosis.

A British medical officer, Frederick Mott, who introduced the term "shell shock" during World War I, believed that the symptoms resulted from minute hemorrhages of the brain from concussion from nearby shell blasts. Before the close of the war, however, it was recognized that this diagnosis was not appropriate for the majority of psychiatric casualties, many of whom had never been in the vicinity of exploding shells. Following World War II, the term "gross stress reaction" became the official American Psychiatric Association nomenclature for transient personality disturbances from combat and from civilian catastrophes as well.

Stress. Prior to the immediate onset of the symptoms, there is usually a history of conflict and anxiety. The general stress of adjustment to the war is undoubtedly a factor. The soldier develops fear concerning his nation, his local community, and his family and close friends. There are economic changes for himself and his family, the threat of separation from the family, the fear of food shortages, and the decline of the usual luxuries. There is also the stress caused by a change of occupational roles and identification and the adjustment to military discipline, routine, and group living. When the soldier reaches a combat area, other sources of stress and anxiety occur: prolonged and violent sensory and emotional experiences, excessive fatigue without opportunity for relaxation, and a sense of personal inability to control what he is being subjected to while under the ever-present fear for his own life.

Some writers describe the essential conflict as one between a sense of duty and a fear of death. In addition, there is grief over the loss of buddies and officers on whom the soldier had become emotionally dependent.

Symptoms. The first symptoms of combat neurosis are usually increased irritability and fitful sleep or inability to sleep. Soon hypersensitivity, a jumpy overreaction to unexpected noises or movement, develops. Battle dreams may occur. The individual becomes increasingly apprehensive, may develop tremors, and begins to feel that he cannot cope with his situation. Some become confused, others mute and stuporous. Most are dejected and have feelings of guilt and extreme anxiety about their own adequacy. (Soldiers with severe wounds seldom show symptoms of combat neurosis.)

Treatment. Treatment experience during the Spanish Civil War, World War II, the Korean conflict, and Vietnam found that the symptoms subsided most rapidly if the soldier was treated as close to his combat assignment as possible. Drug-induced sleep, the use of sodium pentothal to induce the acting out of combat fears and guilts (narcoanalysis), strong reassurance, and suggestion were typical treatments employed in forward zones. Group psychotherapy became a popular addition to treatment employed in military and veterans hospitals away from combat zones.

—Austin E. Grigg, *University of Richmond*
Consult (13) Bartemeir, *et al.,* 1946; Coleman, 1956; Grinker and Spiegel, 1945; Kardiner, 1941; Miller, 1943.

COMMUNICATIONS THEORY. *See* Information Theory; Language.

COMMUNITY MENTAL HEALTH CENTERS. The federal Mental Health Study Act of 1955 authorized the surgeon general to conduct a comprehensive study of the nation's mental health programs and resources. The group appointed to carry out the study, the Joint Commission on Mental Illness and Health, issued its final report, *Action for Mental Health,* in 1961. The recommendations of this commission served as the basis for congressional passage of the Community Mental Health Centers Act in 1963. The act authorized a system of matching grants with local communities for the construction and staffing of the centers. Federal funding has been approved until June 1973.

Within the Department of Health, Education and Welfare, the National Institute of Mental Health (NIMH) was responsible for implementing the Community Mental Health Centers Act. NIMH required that each center had to service an area with a population of between 75,000 and 2,000,000. Each center had to provide inpatient and outpatient services,

The personal conflict of adjusting to war and the anxiety and stress of being in a combat area may cause the personality disturbance labeled combat neurosis.

partial hospitalization, twenty-four-hour emergency services, and education and consultation facilities. The guidelines implied that each center had to demonstrate its accessibility to a nearby general or mental hospital, a requirement that further indicated that the medical model was the treatment approach for dealing with mental illness.

Within this framework, each center was free to determine the kinds of services it wished to offer. However, it had to provide "a reasonable volume" of services to the indigent. A critical evaluation of the centers appeared in the 1971 report sponsored by Ralph Nader.

—Daniel Kirk, *Marist College*

See also Community Psychology; Mental Health.

Consult (13) Joint Commission on Mental Illness and Health, 1961; Chu and Trotter, 1972.

COMMUNITY PSYCHIATRY, a special field of psychiatry that works to mobilize all the resources of a community to treat mental illness and promote mental health. Specially trained psychiatrists, with clinical psychologists and psychiatric social workers, try to involve all parts of a town in the program—not just mental hospitals and clinics but also general hospitals, schools and colleges, courts, welfare agencies, churches, labor organizations, and all interested citizens. One aim is to study patterns of mental disorders in the community with a view to planning prevention. Another is to treat as many cases as possible in the community rather than in institutions, using clinics and home care, for example.

See also Community Mental Health Centers; Community Psychology; Mental Health.

Consult (13) Hume, 1966.

COMMUNITY PSYCHOLOGY. The specialized area of community psychology began formally in 1965 with the Boston Conference on the training of psychologists in community mental health and was formally established as an interest area of the American Psychological Association with the founding of Division 27 (the Division of Community Psychology) in 1966. The area arose out of the work of clinical psychologists in the community mental health movement, which grew up between 1963 and 1965, and the experience of a variety of psychologists in President Lyndon B. Johnson's war on poverty program.

There are two frames of reference in community psychology: individual behavioral adaptation in community settings and the need for change of functioning of components of the community (or the society). This latter aspect has tended to be organized into two camps: community mental health vs. community action and community development.

As a specialized area, community psychology resembles industrial psychology in its interest in organizations and structures, but it is more identified with the consumers than with management. Its theory is generally based on an ecological view of man in his natural settings. There is also some emphasis on social-systems theory as separate from ecology. In more basic terms, the theory is global, transactional, and derived from relativity theory.

Training, in its early stages, has been discussed in most detail by a conference on training held in Austin, Texas, in 1967. One of the most theoretically based training programs is that in Transactional-Ecological Psychology at George Peabody College for Teachers (Nashville, Tennessee), where the theory is a combination of ecology and transactionism and construes the development of community psychology as part of a new field of psychology. Other approaches include community psychology as an applied social-psychology program (Boston College) or part of the clinical-psychology training programs.

—J. R. Newbrough, *George Peabody College for Teachers*

See also Community Mental Health Centers; Mental Health.

Consult (13) Adelson and Kalis, 1970; American Psychological Association, 1971; Bennett, *et al.,* 1966; Cook, 1970; Golann and Eisdorfer, 1973; Iscoe and Spielberger, 1970; Newbrough, 1972.

COMPARATIVE PSYCHOLOGY, the study of similarities and differences in the behavior of different animal species. Historically, two major divisions are recognized. In Europe, especially Germany, ethology, as practiced by Konrad Lorenz and others, has been concerned with the more instinctual, or genetic, aspects of animal behavior as it occurs in the natural environment: highly stereotyped behaviors controlled by specific stimuli. In the United States *animal psychology* has concentrated on the more experiential, or environmental, aspects of behavior as shown in a controlled laboratory setting: flexible behaviors controlled by arbitrary stimuli. Thinking in both camps recognizes that all behavior, no matter how simple or complex, is affected by both genetics and the environment. Thus, neither should be disregarded by a student of comparative psychology.

One goal of comparative psychology is to determine the genetic relations among all species in the animal kingdom, based on behavioral similarities and differences. Such an approach does not oppose the traditional classifications based on physical characteristics but attempts to correct, confirm, and complete what has been learned from biology. Other goals are to facilitate understanding of human behavior by studying animals when the neces-

Comparative psychology seeks to understand human behavior by studying animals. Preening and grooming are important in the courtship behavior of many animals. Even an attack can be changed into friendly grooming—in the case of these Laysan albatrosses by presenting the head and preening.

sary data would be difficult to obtain from human subjects, to test the generality or limitations of psychological theories across species, to enrich our appreciation and understanding of our animal kin, and to facilitate the conservation of our natural environment.

Methodologically, comparative psychology is closely related to developmental and cross-cultural research. In designing experiments for all three, the variable of primary interest (species, age, or culture, respectively) is an unalterable characteristic of the subjects rather than the experimental conditions to which they are randomly assigned. Developmental psychology is also aligned with comparative psychology because a complete understanding of the behavior of any species requires that it be described not just for mature members of the species but for all age levels.

—Earl Rodney Rees, *Western Washington State College*

See also Ethology; Experimental Animals; Heredity and Environment; Imprinting; Instinct.

Consult (3) Hess, 1959; Warren, 1965.

COMPENSATION, a psychological defense mechanism by which an individual attempts to defend himself against feelings of inferiority and to achieve a sense of security and self-esteem. When used by a relatively healthy individual, compensation may develop as intense striving and effort to achieve success in some aspect of life. For example, a person who feels physically inadequate or unattractive attempts to compensate for these feelings by achieving success in his profession. Many athletes developed their skills as compensation for physical shortcoming or disabilities that handicapped them early in their development.

Other individuals, functioning at a less effective level, respond to the same feelings of inadequacy by attempting to compensate through fantasies, wishful thinking, and, in extreme cases, even delusions. Such a person might exhibit antisocial behavior, such as derogation of others or increased aggressiveness, in order to enhance his own self-esteem.

—Michael Rothenberg, *The City College of The City University of New York*

See also Defense Mechanism.

COMPETITION, a drive that early in this century was labeled an instinct. Assault upon this labeling by psychologists, sociologists, and cultural anthropologists has shown not only that the competitive drive is learned, rather than instinctual, but also that its expression is dependent on a large number of factors. These include early upbringing, social pressures, cultural values, and reinforcements and rewards. In one culture competition can be dominant, while in another it is practically nonexistent.

See also Instinct.

COMPLEX, in psychiatry and psychoanalysis, a group of ideas or memories, with strong feelings attached, that have been repressed. *See* Castration Anxiety (or Complex); Inferiority Complex; Oedipus Complex.

COMPULSION. *See* Compulsive Personality; Obsessive-Compulsive Reaction.

COMPULSIVE PERSONALITY, a disturbed personality characterized by the extreme recurrence of particular thoughts and actions. A compulsive individual feels moved to repeat certain behaviors or words to a degree that is often irrational and unexplainable by standards of normal behavior.

A common compulsion centers around cleanliness. In the case of one thirteen-year-old boy, this began with frequent hand washing. Subsequently, he began to bathe several times each day and then to rub iodine on his face and hands to "avoid infection." In its extreme form, his compulsion was expressed in the conviction that his skin was of a special sort that retained germs and needed to be constantly scrubbed.

Such compulsions usually cannot be resolved simply by attempting to cajole, persuade, or order the person to renounce them. Psychotherapy is required to unearth the repressed underlying conflict from which the compulsive behavior derives. For example, the hand-washing boy was discovered to be suffering from guilt feelings over his participation in sexual activities with some of his friends at an earlier age. Once these feelings were explored and resolved, the compulsive behavior diminished rapidly.

—Michael Rothenberg, *The City College of The City University of New York*

See also Personality Disorders.

COMPUTER SIMULATION, the designing of computer programs to imitate or replicate such human psychological processes as verbal and concept learning, problem solving, and game playing.

Note that the simulation is performed by the program, not by the computer itself, which merely runs the program through its steps. Simulation also differs from computer *algorithms,* which are programs designed to solve some problem in an efficient way—not necessarily in the same way a person would solve it.

Simulation work has the expressed purpose of copying human psychological processes. If the programs are well devised, they may qualify as theories or models of how humans think. Thus, it is one outgrowth of the application of computer technology to the principles of cognitive psychology. Programs have already been devised to solve logic problems, to learn concepts, to "read" and "comprehend" English text, and to play games like chess—all in ways that parallel human thinking.

As theoretical models, computer simulations have met with criticism and are not without their difficulties. It is actually hard to tell when a simulation represents an adequate theory. One proposed test of simulation models is as follows: if an observer cannot tell the difference between computer simulation responses and a human subject's responses to a problem, the program can be considered a minimally "good" theory. Furthermore, the "thinking" displayed by most of the simulation programs that have been developed is much more rigid and inflexible than human more rigid and inflexible than human thought.

Though future research will have to determine to what degree computer simulations can help explain human thinking and learning, simulations do have the advantage of being able to incorporate the enormous complexity of human cognitive processes. Most other theories are very limited in their scope. This ability of computer simulation programs to do justice to the complexity of human thinking has encouraged other theorists to be more careful in specifying and describing the precise nature of their own theoretical descriptions.

—Roland Siiter, *Montclair State College*
See also Cognitive Psychology; Concept Learning; Problem Solving.
Consult (7) Hovland and Hunt, 1960; Newell and Simon, 1958.

CONATION. Philosophers and psychologists used to describe behavior as having three aspects: *affective,* referring to feelings or emotions; *cognitive,* referring to perceiving, knowing, and thinking; and *conative,* involving acting, doing, willing, striving. Conation is no longer regarded as a separate aspect of behavior, because drives and activity are involved in everything an organism does.

CONCEPT LEARNING, the acquisition of the capacity to identify and use the attributes that objects or situations have in common. Though the word "concept" refers to almost any definable (concrete, abstract, imaginary) regularity whatsoever, psychologists have devoted most of their attention to class concepts.

Terminology. The term *class concept* refers to any attribute that partitions objects or situations into distinct groupings. When only two groupings are possible (for example, members vs. nonmembers, living vs. dead), the two are commonly referred to as positive and negative *instances* of the concept. When one dimension (such as color) specifies many possible groupings (red, yellow, blue, green, and so on), the specific groups are designated as *values* of that dimension. More complex concepts can be defined by combining dimensions into *conjunctive* concepts (for example, red triangularity, blue circularity) or *disjunctive* concepts (redness and/or triangularity, blueness and/or circularity). Finally, when an object is presented to a subject, the dimensions (values, concepts) that are to be learned are deemed *relevant,* while other possible attributes of the stimuli are deemed *irrelevant.*

Learning Procedures. The ability to distinguish between relevant and irrelevant dimensions even before they can be identified as such is basic to the process of learning concepts. In a *discrimination-learning* situation the learner is presented with pairs (or more) of stimuli, one of which he must choose. Because he is rewarded each time he selects the stimulus designated as correct by the experimenter, the subject gradually learns to choose only that stimulus. If, for example, the learner correctly chooses a triangle every time one appears, he is said to have "acquired the concept" of triangle.

In humans this process of learning concepts through discrimination is usually bound up with language acquisition, since useful concepts are almost always indicated by a word. When the individual can consistently apply linguistic labels correctly to objects and qualities, then he has learned the concepts underlying those words. However, our normal discriminative capacities usually exceed the range and number of labels we use, since labels are applied only to the degree that they are useful. Thus, for example, we can discriminate between hundreds of thousands of different colors, but we use less than a hundred color names at most.

In another procedure, a learner is presented with one stimulus at a time and is told to respond to each with one or two (or more) arbitrary labels, such as X and Y. Beginning with guesses, he is expected to discover the rule that will consistently identify each stimulus as an X or Y. Thus, when the learner can consistently label each stimulus correctly, he has learned the two (or more) concepts.

In a third procedure (called *self-selection*), many or all of the stimuli are presented to the learner, who must choose any one and be told whether or not it is an example of the concept. Again, he selects repeatedly until he can consistently choose only instances of the concept without error. The advantage of this procedure is that the experimenter can observe not only when the subject is right and wrong but which choices he makes in the sequences of trials leading to discovery of the concept.

Theories. Before the 1950s theories of how concepts are identified and learned tended to view the process as primarily associative and rather passive: after familiarization and discrimination, a subject would come to associate the correct label with the relevant

CONCEPT LEARNING

One task in concept learning is to distinguish relevant dimensions. A rat, a chimp, and a child, taught to recognize the triangle above, all recognize the triangle below. The rat cannot view the rotated figure as a triangle; only the child can abstract the triangular form from the bottom figure.

1

2

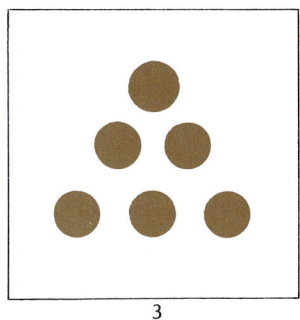

3

The cat acquires the concept of "triangle" by being rewarded with food each time it selects the correct stimulus.

CONCEPT LEARNING

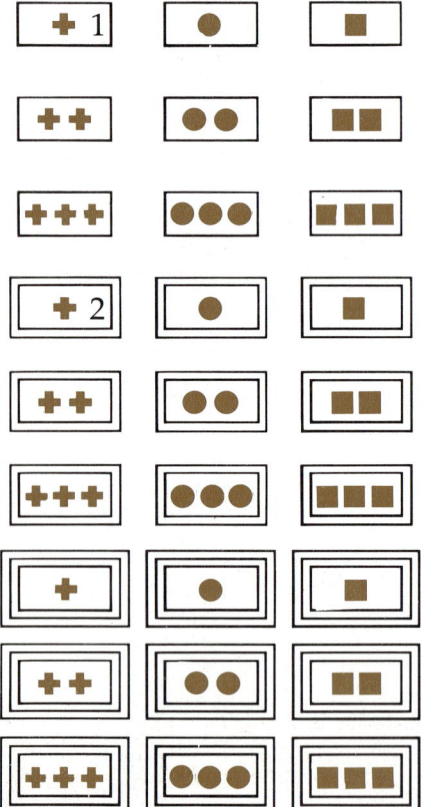

Cards used by Bruner and his colleagues in their studies of concept learning. The array of cards shown, which differ in included shapes, number of shapes, and number of border lines, was used in three different colors.

attribute involved. In 1956 Bruner, Goodnow, and Austin of Harvard University published *A Study of Thinking,* which revolutionized theoretical views of concept learning and inspired a large number of subsequent studies by many researchers.

Using the method of self-selection, Bruner *et al.* observed that different subjects used very different approaches or strategies to discover and learn concepts. Some learners, for example, developed approaches that were eminently logical but placed too large a burden on memory. Some of these subjects adjusted to this limitation by concentrating on one stimulus attribute at a time, hence reducing memory load. For example, if stimuli varied in shape, size, and color, a subject might attend only to the shape of stimuli until he decided that that dimension was or was not relevant to the concept. With conjunctive concepts, the learner continued to examine one attribute at a time until he reduced the possibilities to the correct combination of stimulus attributes. This strategy was termed *focusing* on one attribute at a time.

Other subjects adopted a riskier approach, changing two attributes (such as size and shape) on each trial. When the dual choice was correct, the subject gained more information than if he changed only one attribute. But if the choice was incorrect, he gained almost nothing because he did not know which of the attributes he had chosen might be correct. Another trial was needed to determine this. Such *focus gambling* was more commonly used by subjects who were forced to work under time pressure.

Thus, Bruner and his colleagues emphasized the role of thinking and planning in concept identification and learning. They viewed it as an active process in which the learner tests out "educated guesses" about what dimension might be relevant in a concept learning task. *A Study of Thinking* introduced the notion of learning *strategies,* organized sequences of responding designed by the subject to discover the relevant attributes in a conceptual task. Concept learning is apparently often deliberate (not passive), conscious, highly structured, and difficult to analyze in associative terms. In other words, discovering and using concepts involves complex thinking much like that involved in solving other kinds of intellectual problems. Conditioning and associative theories, while not necessarily incorrect, often seem too limited to account for certain behaviors.

—Roland Siiter, *Montclair State College*

See also Associationism; Codability; Cognitive Psychology; Language; Problem Solving.

Consult (7) Bourne, *et al.,* 1971; Bruner, *et al.,* 1956; Deese and Hulse, 1967; Smith and Rohrman, 1970.

CONCRETENESS, as a factor in memorization. *See* Memory Improvement.

CONDITIONED RESPONSE. *See* Pavlovian Conditioning.

CONDITIONED STIMULUS. *See* Pavlovian Conditioning.

CONDITIONING, a term applied to two forms of learning. One, first investigated by a Russian, Ivan P. Pavlov, is called Pavlovian or classical conditioning. The other, often associated with the experiments of two Americans—E. L. Thorndike and B. F. Skinner—is called instrumental or operant conditioning.

While there are similarities in the two kinds of learning, there are also important differences. In a typical classical conditioning experiment, two stimuli (such as meat and the sound of a bell) are presented almost simultaneously. The subject responds with an "automatic" response (such as salivating). After a number of pairings of the meat and the tone, the tone alone results in salivating. The subject has little or no control over the situation. In a case of operant conditioning, the experimenter might wait for a certain action (such as escaping from a puzzle box) and then reward this behavior with food. Thus the subject's actions are instrumental in gaining a reward. He can control the step that leads to the reward; the consequences determine his behavior.

See also Behavior Therapy; Biofeedback; Pavlovian Conditioning; Programmed Learning; Operant Conditioning; Reinforcement.

CONFLICT (within the person). Stresses in an individual caused by opposing wishes, needs, drives, or outside pressures are a principle cause of anxiety. In psychoanalytic theory, conflicts are at the root of neuroses. *See* Anxiety; Defense Mechanisms; Psychoanalysis; Psychoneurotic Disorders; Psychosomatic Disorders.

CONFLICT, SOCIAL. The study of social conflict is an interdisciplinary enterprise, involving sociologists, political scientists, and game theorists as well as psychologists. Psychologists have looked at conflict in a number of ways. Some view it as a manifestation of individual aggression, which is usually attributed to frustrations experienced by the individual.

Others see it as arising from images that individuals or groups have of one another—for example, the mutual perception of threat. Considerable interest has also been taken in methods of conflict resolution such as bargaining.

Three *image theories* have made particularly significant contributions to the understanding of conflict between groups. Ralph White attributes conflict to diabolical images of the enemy, virile and moral images of the self, selective inattention, and the absence of empathy. He points out that each group's perceptions of itself and its adversary tend to be "mirror images" of the other group's perceptions.

According to M. Sherif and C. W. Sherif, group competition fosters ingroup solidarity, pride in the accomplishments of one's own group, and unfavorable attitudes and images of the other group. These developments typically produce conflict, which is most effectively resolved when circumstances force the groups to collaborate on "superordinate goals. . .that cannot be achieved by a single group through its own efforts and resources." Charles Osgood sees conflict developing in "spirals" as untrustworthy behavior by one party engenders tensions in the other party who responds with untrustworthy behavior, to which the first must react with further untrustworthy behavior. Such spirals can be reversed if one party initiates a dramatic series of tension-reducing moves, a strategy Osgood terms "Graduated Reciprocation in Tension-reduction" (GRIT). After tension has been reduced in this fashion, it is possible to resolve the details of the conflict by means of negotiation.

Psychological research on conflict has mostly employed experimental gaming techniques.

—Dean G. Pruitt, *State University of New York at Buffalo*

See also Aggression; Bargaining; Power.
Consult (10) Berkowitz, 1962; Osgood, 1962; Pruitt, 1965; Raven and Kruglanski, 1970; Sherif and Sherif, 1969; Swingler, 1970; White, 1970.

CONFORMITY. When an individual's behavior is governed by a social norm, adherence to that norm is called conformity. Most human social behavior is influenced by cultural norms, although in most instances the norms are so well established that people do not recognize their conformity. The fact that most people sleep between six and eight hours every twenty-four hours is not conformity, but the fact that most people tend to get their sleep in one long night-time session is regulated by social norms and is therefore conformity.

In studying conformity in the laboratory, psychologists usually investigate the impact of various social factors on enforcing or instituting a norm. It has been found, for example, that conformity to an artificial group norm will occur only under conditions of uncertainty with ambiguous stimuli. If an individual can make an absolute judgment about a stimulus or situation, he will be much less prone to influence by group norms.

One of the principal functions of groups is to assure some degree of behavioral conformity among their members. Studies of group processes show, for example, that a group will devote more attention to a nonconforming new group member than to a conforming new group member. If the deviating individual does not eventually conform, however, the group will tend to exclude him actively in the future.

Conformity has been demonstrated to present a special problem in psychological experimentation. The norm of pleasing the "higher status" professor by behaving as the subject thinks he should can have very strong effects on the outcome of research.

—Brenda B. Bankart and C. Peter Bankart, *Wabash College*

See also Attitudes and Attitude Change.
Consult (10) Asch, 1955; Asch, 1956; Sherif and Hovland, 1961.

CONNECTIONISTIC THEORIES OF LEARNING. *See* Learning Theory.

CONSCIENCE. Self-regulation of behavior—in particular, resistance to temptation—is determined in large measure by the development of conscience. Representing the internalization of the rules of society, conscience is experienced by feelings of anxiety and guilt that accompany anticipated or actual transgression. Two major theories of its origins have been developed.

The *psychoanalytic view* of conscience is found in Freud's writings on the superego, which is one of the three main personality components, along with the id and the ego. The *superego* is said to be the internalized representation of the values and ideals of the society. It demands goodness over pleasure and tends to be reflected in an individual's view of his ideal self.

The *behavioristic view* of conscience is suggested in a number of experiments relating resistance to temptation and self-punishment to classically conditioned fear of transgression. In this view, conscience is seen as stemming in part from conditioned anxiety and fear of punishment and in part from experiences where self-punishment and guilt were effective in avoiding or lessening external punishment from parents, teachers, and others in authority.

A third view of conscience stresses developmental aspects of moral behavior.

—Brenda B. Bankart and C. Peter Bankart, *Wabash College*

See also Moral Development; Pavlovian Conditioning; Superego.
Consult (9) Aronfreed, 1968; Bandura and Walters, 1963.

CONSCIOUSNESS, the state of being aware, of experiencing what is going on. A person can be conscious at a range of levels, from coma up to the highest pitch of arousal. A person asleep is not unconscious because he can experience and recall dreams. A person under the influ-

A pigeon in a Skinner box used in experiments in operant conditioning.

Pavlov and his staff demonstrating their conditioning experiments.

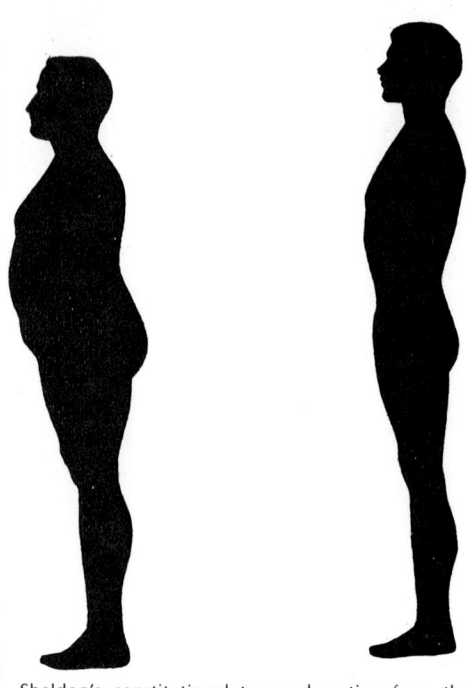

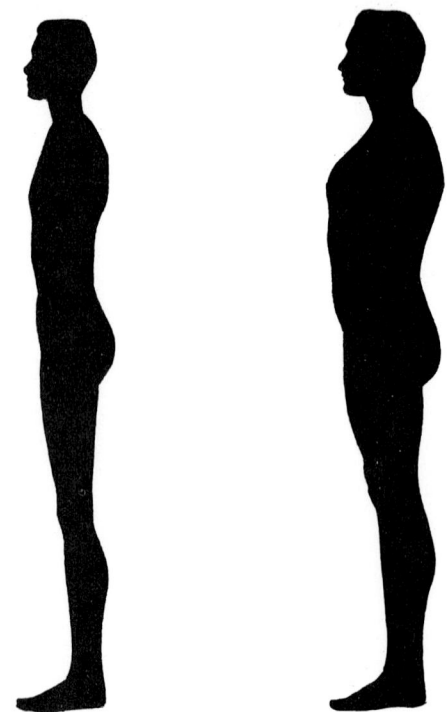

Sheldon's constitutional types, departing from the idealized (top right), are the endomorph (top left), ectomorph (bottom left), and mesomorph (bottom right).

ence of drugs may still be conscious—in fact, psychedelics such as LSD are described as "consciousness-expanding."

"Consciousness" has been used in various senses in philosophy and psychology. Some have spoken of consciousness or mind as if it were a thing in itself rather than a name for what is going on in an organism. The concept of consciousness has been at the center of controversies. For example, some psychologists held that they could study conscious processes by introspection. Behaviorists countered by arguing that the only proper subjects for study are overt, quantifiable bits of behavior.

Sigmund Freud distinguished levels of awareness—the conscious, of which the individual is fully aware, and the unconscious, in which are found feelings or thoughts that have been pushed out of awareness. These repressed memories or desires still have powerful effects even if unrecognized.

Psychologists are interested in studying altered states of consciousness, such as those produced by drugs or through the practices of Yoga and Zen Buddhism.

See also Drugs and Behavior; Hypnosis; Mind; Philosophical Psychology; Sleep and Dreams; Unconscious; Yoga; Zen.

CONSTANCY, PERCEPTUAL. *See* Perception.

CONSTANCY OF THE IQ. A much-debated question is the constancy, or stability, of intelligence as measured by tests. Do scores remain stable as people get older? Can they be changed by giving special training or otherwise modifying the environment?

As to changes with age, test scores show some decline after adolescence, but these results probably do not reflect any real decline in ability through the middle years. As to efforts to raise the IQ, studies have shown that school-age children who score high at one testing tend to score in the high range on retests, while those at the lower end of the scale tend to remain low. (Differences in administration and errors in scoring may produce a range of five points or so in test-to-retest scores.) Yet it does not follow that any individual's score cannot be changed. When dramatic improvements are made in a child's physical or mental health, or when he is given special motivation and training, IQ scores may go up by 20 points or more.

See also Child Development; Intelligence and Intelligence Testing; Middle Years.

CONSTITUTIONAL TYPES, classifications based on the notion that there is a relationship between physical structure and personality characteristics. This idea has intrigued scientists for thousands of years and was first elaborated by Hippocrates.

Early in the twentieth century, Ernst Kretschmer, a German psychiatrist, conducted a systematic investigation of the connection between body type and psychopathology among his patients. He first identified four such body types:

Asthenic—frail, angular physique

Athletic—muscular and well-developed physique

Pyknik—squat, plump, flabby physique

Dysplastic—those individuals who have strikingly deviant physical characteristics.

Kretschmer discovered that those patients with pyknik physiques tended to be manic depressives, while those with asthenic, athletic, and dysplastic physiques tended to be schizophrenic. [*Consult* (9) Kretschmer, 1925.]

While these findings are suspect because of the informality of Kretschmer's research, his efforts toward a systematic framework for classifying physical structure provided the foundation for the work of William H. Sheldon, the foremost constitutional psychologist.

After studying thousands of photographs of male college students in an attempt to identify the major components of physique, Sheldon finally arrived at three:

Endomorphy—The person high on this component and low on the others tends to be soft, round, and flabby in appearance (much like Kretschmer's pyknik category).

Mesomorphy—A person high on this component tends to be hard, muscular, and built for physical stress (like Kretschmer's athletic type).

Ectomorphy—A person high on this component is thin, frail, and angular (like Kretschmer's asthenic type).

Unlike Kretschmer, Sheldon did not see these as mutually exclusive categories but as dimensions along which all human beings could be measured. He developed a comprehensive methodology for measuring these characteristics.

Sheldon claimed that his research suggested a relationship between these physical components and various personality types. Thus, endomorphs tend to be warm, affectionate, and gluttonous for food; mesomorphs to be aggressive, adventurous, and courageous; and ectomorphs to be restrained, inhibited, and self-conscious. Although these alleged relationships have never been fully accepted, Sheldon's careful and systematic classification system has left its mark on psychology and has proved to be a useful measurement technique in a variety of studies in such areas as self-concept and body image.

—Michael Rothenberg, *The City College of The City University of New York*
Consult (9) Sheldon, *et al.*, 1954.

CONSULTING PSYCHOLOGY. A consulting psychologist is a specialist who provides professional advice about problems in industry and business, education, government work, or other fields. Often the consultant works as an individual on a fee basis, but he may also be a member of a consulting firm.

Division 13 of the American Psychological Association is the Division of Consulting Psychology, and the APA publishes the *Journal of Consulting Psychology.*

See also Consumer Psychology; Industrial Psychology.

CONSUMER PSYCHOLOGY, a branch of applied psychology concerned with questions about the optimal means for making goods and services available, providing information about them, developing and testing methods for promoting interest in their acquisition, and investigating how they might be consumed with maximum satisfaction and benefit to the customer.

Focus. From the broadest point of view, consumer psychology is concerned with the individual's behavioral expressions of value—that is, the ways in which he spends his time and money. These range from candy and toothpaste to savings for college education, from spending a few hours viewing television or reading the newspaper to the philatelist's seemingly endless absorption with old or rare stamps. Therefore, whatever the individual consumes—however he uses his time or spends his money—is fair game for study by the consumer psychologist.

The consumer psychologist is concerned with the psychological determinants of the individual's behavior as a consumer. In this context, the term *consumption* includes the individual's actions such as purchaser of goods and services, his reactions to efforts to influence his purchasing behavior, his perceptions of the shape of packages and the messages on their labels, and his preferences for or reactions to the news and entertainment comprised by the nonadvertising content of the mass media.

Beyond *marketing research,* consumer psychologists have been called upon to study the consumer's attitudes toward and the means for influencing his acceptance of devices or behaviors that are generally considered to be in his best interest, particularly in the fields of health and safety. Among the many illustrations of this relatively new area of study are the individual's responses to seat belts and shoulder harnesses in automobiles as well as his attitudes concerning air pollution, smoking, and other health hazards. The consumer psychologist may also be consulted for studies aimed at understanding how attitudes may be changed.

Applications. Since the techniques and procedures for conducting consumer research are very similar to those used in opinion research or public opinion polling, psychologists engaged in consumer research are often engaged in public opinion studies as well. Opinion research is supported by foundations, government agencies, universities, the mass media, political organizations, and individuals and organizations hoping to shed light on social problems, propaganda, and group behavior.

Rarely does the consumer psychologist operate alone. Because consumer behavior is interdisciplinary, it is common to find him working in the same office with advertising copywriters or account executives, public relations experts, statisticians specializing in sampling and survey research, experts in marketing research, economists, and sociologists.

Since the government's solicitude for the consumer's welfare has grown exponentially in the last decade, the psychologist now not only conducts some of the more traditional survey research studies for departments such as Agriculture but participates in many newer endeavors, a number of which are concentrated in the Department of Health, Education and Welfare. There is concern for providing clear information to the consumer regarding products and services vitally affecting his health, safety, and general well-being. Other agencies concerned with facets of consumer behavior are the Federal Communications Commission, among whose interests is the effect of violence in television programs upon the behavior of children and adults; the Federal Trade Commission, which is mounting a massive campaign to examine and reduce what it considers to be deceptive advertising; and the Food and Drug Administration, whose interest in determining the relationships between consumer perceptions and expectations from foods and drugs should be a challenge. Other branches of the government are also involved in consumer acceptance studies of foods, clothing, and equipment, like those conducted by the U.S. Army Research Institute of Environmental Medicine.

Expectedly, the heaviest use of consumer psychology occurs in business and industry, principally by advertising agencies, the mass media, private consumer marketing and public opinion research firms, and manufacturers themselves. Among the multitude of highly specific problems to which the consumer psychologist addresses his attention for such organizations are the testing of advertising copy, the assessment of likes and dislikes for television programs, and the determination of the likelihood of the public's acceptance of new brand names, a new product, or a new package style.

On a more macroscopic level, the consumer psychologist may be invited to assay what has come to be known as the "image" that one public group or another may have of a business firm, an agency of the government, or even of an educational institution. Perhaps a nationally known manufacturer of appliances is interested in determining the effect a large strike had upon its "image." The Peace Corps might wish to determine how it is viewed by college seniors, or the president of a state university, concerned with his institution's budget, might wish to ascertain what the members of the state legislature think of higher education, professors, and students.

Outlook. Consumer psychology is attracting students and developing its own literature. Consumer activities are becoming integrated into all phases of government. Manufacturers, advertising media, educational institutions, hospitals, and communities are all thinking in terms of their "public images," seeking to improve the way they are being looked at. It is now possible to secure research support and grants for investigations and fellowships in the area of consumer psychology. All of these indicators support a distinct feeling that consumer psychology's time has come, and that consumer psychologists can now spend more of their time in *doing* consumer psychology than in *selling* the proposition that it is worth doing.

—Robert Perloff, *Graduate School of Business, University of Pittsburgh*
See also Engineering Psychology.
Consult (14) Britt, 1966; Kassarjian and Robertson, 1968; Engel, Kollat, and Blackwell, 1968; McNeal, 1969.

CONTIGUITY, LAW OF, the principle that if two or more events occur close enough together they may become associated. According to many theories, contiguity is the basis on which learning takes place. For example, a hungry cat will soon learn which response is most effective for opening a trap door to a source of food. Those responses associated with food getting will be reinforced. As a basic principle of learning, the law of contiguity assumes that stimuli associated with specific responses become linked together in terms of their neural representation in the brain.

—Joel F. Lubar, *University of Tennessee*
See also Learning Theory.

CONTRAST EFFECT

CONTRAST EFFECT, the enhancement of one stimulus by another. For example, although the gray center in the figure is the same, its brightness seems to vary according to the surround.

Understanding contrast effects has practical value. Because yellow and black have the least contrast effect, they are the clearest color combination for road signs. For rich, deeply saturated colors, often used in school pennants, complementary contrasts (red/green, blue/yellow) are best.

—Nina Adams, *Yale University*

CONTROL GROUP. *See* Experimental Design.

CONVERSION REACTION (HYSTERIA), a psychoneurotic disorder marked by symptoms for which no physiological cause can be found. For example, patients say they are blind, and act blind in some or all circumstances, but examination of the eyes does not reveal any defect.

Conversion reactions may take many forms. Blindness and deafness are common *sensory* problems. It has been noted that the impaired vision, though real to the patient, may not be total. A pilot may be unable to see in a plane at night but have normal vision by day. Less common sensory symptoms are anesthesias of parts of the body. In glove anesthesia, the patient reports that he has no feeling beyond the wrist (and may not feel pain when tested); the nerves conducting sensations from the hand do not have any terminal at the wrist.

Paralysis of an arm or leg is one of the more common *motor* symptoms. Also observed are tremors, difficulties in walking, and impairment of speech such as aphonia, the inability to talk above a whisper.

Visceral symptoms have been known to include pain in the abdomen and other signs of acute appendicitis. In fact, many needless operations have been done on patients whose trouble was neurotic.

Such patients are not malingering or deliberately deceiving their doctors. They are not aware of the psychological origin of their symptoms.

The causes of conversion reactions—as with other psychoneurotic disorders—are believed to lie in the anxiety caused by severe conflicts. For example, a soldier caught between his sense of obligation to his country or his unit and his fear of combat might develop a paralysis of one leg. This will give him a way out of his stressful situation and also may get him some welcome rest and attention.

It may be difficult to distinguish cases of conversion reaction from psychosomatic disorders. Anorexia nervosa (inability to eat that may lead to starvation) is classed as a psychosomatic problem in this encyclopedia, though some authorities call it hysterical. However, distinctions can be made on several bases. Psychosomatic problems frequently involve organs that are linked to the autonomic nervous system, while hysterical symptoms often involve other parts of the body such as the skeletal muscles. In psychosomatic illness there is likely to be observable physiological damage. For example, a man with a neurotically caused ulcer has an actual lesion in his stomach, while a man with a conversion reaction may be reporting an abdominal pain though no organ damage can be found.

The study of hysteria has a long history. Ancient Egyptians and Greeks believed that some emotional disorders in women were caused by a displaced uterus. The Greek physician Hippocrates held this view, and the English term "hysteria" comes from the Greek work for uterus (*hysteron*). Centuries later Sigmund Freud and Joseph Breuer developed the theory that hysteria is produced by repressed emotional problems, and Freud adopted the term "conversion hysteria" (the conflict is converted to a new outlet).

Treatment for conversion reactions follows the pattern of therapy for other neurotic problems.

See also Combat Neurosis; Psychoneurotic Disorders; Psychosomatic Disorders.

Consult (13) Alexander and Selesnick, 1966; Breuer and Freud, 1957; Coleman, 1964.

CORRELATION, a concept used in discussing relationships between variables. Two sets of measurements on the same individuals or events or on matched pairs of individuals are compared, and a *correlation coefficient,* a measure of the extent to which the two variables are related, is calculated. The value of the correlation coefficient varies between +1.00 and −1.00; both of these represent perfect relationships between the variables, while 0.00 represents the perfect absence of a relationship. A high positive correlation indicates that the two variables vary together, while a high negative correlation indicates that the two variables vary oppositely.

CORTEX. *See* Cerebral Cortex.

COUNSELING PSYCHOLOGY. Counseling psychologists provide information and guidance with problems of educational planning, choosing and getting jobs, and adjusting to personal and marital requirements. They are often employed by school and college guidance offices, vocational guidance agencies, and marital counseling organizations. They may give tests such as vocational aptitude measures in addition to providing information and discussing plans and problems.

The work of counseling psychologists may overlap that of school psychologists, though school counselors usually work with younger children. When counseling psychologists deal with problems of individual or marital adjustment, they approach the area of clinical psychology. The usual distinction is that counselors work with normal individuals whereas clinicians help those who are suffering from a behavioral or mental disorder.

Division 17 of the American Psychological Association is the Division of Counseling Psychology, and the APA publishes the *Journal of Counseling Psychology.*

See also Marriage Counseling.

CREATIVE THINKING. *See* Creativity.

CREATIVITY, the ability to discover or produce new solutions to problems, new inventions, or new works of art. While directed thinking (problem solving) has finding the "correct" solution or answer as its goal, creative thinking is open-ended in that solutions are not predefined in their scope or appropriateness.

Older approaches to creativity described and analyzed the stages involved in the thinking of famous scientists and other gifted individuals. Graham Wallas presented one notable summary of these stages.

1. *Preparation*—studying previous work, defining the problem, finding leads

2. *Incubation*—mulling the problem over, periodically leaving it to encourage subconscious ideas to rise to the surface

3. *Illumination*—sudden insight or discovery of a possible solution

4. *Verification*—testing the idea out, comparing it with other possibilities, evaluating its worth and appropriateness.

More recent investigations have tended to show the difficulty of any simple definition of creativity and have shown that, above minimum levels of intelligence, it is not related to intelligence as measured by IQ tests. Researchers have commonly stressed either the abilities involved in creative thought or the personalities of creative people.

One concentrated research attack on creative abilities has been carried out by J. P. Guilford and his associates at the University of California, who developed many new tests and administered them to students and other individuals. Guilford identifies creativity as "divergent thinking abilities" and has used factor analysis to break these three abilities into three basic elements: fluency, flexibility, and originality. *Fluency* involves producing many solutions of a given type in a short amount of time, as in naming words starting with a given letter. *Flexibility* involves considering many alternatives, such as finding geometric figures embedded in a complex pattern. *Originality* refers simply to the uncommonness or remoteness of responses, as in the first word that occurs to a subject in response to a stimulus word.

In terms of personality, creativity has been related to the greater independence, nonconformity, receptivity to new ideas, and lesser anxiety shown by such individuals as prominent architects or composers. There is little evidence to support the traditional idea that creative people are somewhat mentally disturbed.

The chief unresolved difficulty in studying creativity is that no systematic, valid, or commonly agreed-upon way of measuring creativity has yet been devised. It is probable that creativity is not one-dimensional ability but is composed of a number of ability and personality factors.

—Roland Siiter, *Montclair State College Consult* (7) Guilford, 1967; Wallas, 1926.

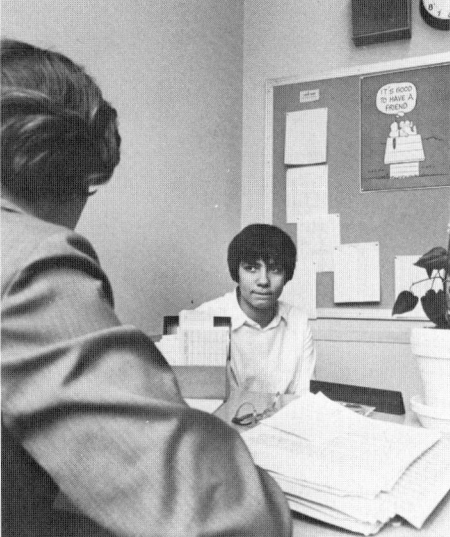

College guidance offices often employ a counseling psychologist, who may provide students with information, discuss plans and problems, and administer tests.

CRETINISM, retardation of mental and physical development caused by a deficiency of thyroid production during the fetal period or infancy. The use of iodized salt has reduced the incidence of cretinism. Children who have this condition can show marked improvement if treated in the first six months of life.

CRISIS INTERVENTION CENTER, a service designed to give immediate help to people with drastic emotional problems. Examples are the suicide prevention services established in many parts of the country. Staff members are available twenty-four hours a day to aid anyone who feels in danger of taking his own life. *See* Suicide.

CRITICAL PERIOD. An animal may be more susceptible to certain kinds of experiences at one stage in its life history than another, and these effects are relatively long lasting. For example, a white-crowned sparrow will not, as an adult, know how to sing its species-characteristic song unless it has heard that song before it was two to four months old. When all factors are excluded except chronological age and normal developmental processes, then a critical period for that behavior exists. Some scientists prefer to call this the "optimal" or "sensitive period," but the thrust behind all these terms is similar.

Although many species and behaviors show critical periods, many have not been throughly studied, and alternative interpretations exist. Learning the characteristics of "mother" through imprinting may take place in a few hours, but learning the cues that will later cause the organism to seek out a mate may take several months. Puppies will never become good pets—that is, socialized to humans—unless they have had contact with people by four months of age. It is currently thought by some psychologists that language, certain motor skills, and mother-infant attachments are optimally acquired at certain ages, measured in months or years.

Exact definition of the concept of critical period is hampered by the great diversity among species, behaviors, and time intervals. Inferences joining these three aspects cannot be made safely. For example, in contrast to the white-crowned sparrow, song sparrows reared by canaries in the absence of all song sparrows still produced songs indistinguishable from wild birds.

—Gordon M. Burghardt, *University of Tennessee*
See also Imprinting.
Consult (3) Bowlby, 1969; Hinde, 1970; Scott, 1962.

CROSS-SECTIONAL STUDY. One way to study people or behavior is to focus on the whole group of variable factors as they are at one time. A cross-section method in child development might involve studying the characteristics of a large number of children at each of several age levels. Psychological testing often requires that norms be established for age groups or grade levels in school. In contrast, the *longitudinal* method consists of following one subject over a period of growth and development.

CULTURE-FAIR TEST. Intelligence tests have been criticized for being unfair to members of minority groups. Obviously, a child who has difficulty with English will be at a disadvantage when taking a test that requires hearing or reading instructions in English and using the idioms of this language. Moreover, some items used in tests are more intelligible and relevant to middle-class children than to slum children. In response to such observations, measurement experts have tried to prepare tests that will avoid cultural bias. They have, for example, constructed tests that use pictures or symbols instead of words. They have tried to avoid items that are outside the normal interests of minority group members. They have worked on special tests for special groups, rather than assuming that one test can be standard for all children.

See also Intelligence and Intelligence Testing.
Consult (12) Cronbach, 1970; Hilgard, *et al.,* 1971.

CURIOSITY DRIVE. Curiosity refers to a motive or need for stimulation. Research has indicated that monkeys will actually acquire a learned response, such as lever pressing, in order to observe other monkeys engaged in various behaviors. Both animals and humans spend a great deal of time manipulating objects and examining them, and it is believed that the level of curiosity increases as one ascends the phylogenetic scale. In humans curiosity is associated with such attributes as intelligence and creativity. Curiosity is readily observed in the infant as he rapidly scans the visual field or fixates on moving objects.

—Joel F. Lubar, *University of Tennessee*

CUTANEOUS SENSES. *See* Skin Senses.

CYBERNETICS, a multidisciplinary research approach to the structure and functions of data- or information-processing systems. These systems aid the understanding of man's ability to record, process, and transmit information. The term "cybernetics" was brought into prominence by the mathematician Norbert Wiener (1894–1964). The field of cybernetics is divided into three fundamental subdisciplines—control theory, information theory, and algorithm and automata theory—each of which has, in turn, led to specific developments in such areas as learning systems, semantic information theory, formal language theory, and artificial intelligence.

Using the means and methods of *control theory* analysis, highly practiced and learning-dependent sensorimotor coordination processes can be modeled and machines built to duplicate normal functions. These man-machine systems may then be applied to specific problems in the training or relearning of specific sensorimotor processes.

The problems of language generation and linguistic communication in psychology are better understood with more precise *information theory*. This can be specifically applied to signal-recognition processes, choice-reaction experiments, or complex pattern recognition.

Algorithm and automata theory is used to build computer simulation models (robots) to simulate perception, thought, and problem-solving processes. Psychologists hope that such models provide a better understanding of man.
—A. Ronald Seifert, *University of Tennessee*
See also Computer Simulation; Information Theory.
Consult (7) Wiener, 1948; Wiener and Schade, 1963; Wiener and Schade, 1965.

CYCLOTHYMIC PERSONALITY, a tendency toward alternating moods of cheerfulness and exhilaration, on the one hand, and mild depression, on the other. These variations in mood tend to be cyclical and regular rather than related to specific events in the life of the individual. For each person the frequency and duration of the "up" and "down" phases of the cycle are different. What is common to all cases is the oscillating pattern of mood states.

The cyclothymic personality is very much like that of the manic-depressive psychotic individual except that the range of his mood swings does not reach such pathological extremes. However, some "cyclothymes" are predisposed to develop manic-depressive reactions and will do so under conditions of severe stress. In general, the cyclothymic person can function within the normal range without hospitalization. Individuals who are commonly called "moody" may well have cyclothymic tendencies.
—Michael Rothenberg, *The City College of The City University of New York*
See also Manic-Depressive Psychosis; Personality Disorders.

DARK ADAPTATION, the gradual improvement in perception after one has moved from a brightly lit area to a dark one. This process is due partly to enlargement of the pupil but primarily to chemical changes in the retina.

In the bright light most of the retina's visual pigments are chemically bleached. In the dark, as the pigments are resynthesized, visual sensitivity increases in two stages: visual pigments of the cone within five minutes; visual pigments of the rod in twenty to thirty minutes. Since the rods are more sensitive, maximum visual ability in the dark requires at least twenty minutes.
—Nina Adams, *Yale University*

DARWIN, CHARLES ROBERT (1809–1882), British scientist and naturalist. Born in Shrewsburg, he studied at Cambridge under John Stevens Henslow, who later recruited him as naturalist on the H.M.S. *Beagle* for a scientific expedition around the world. His major work was *The Origin of the Species* (1859).

Darwin's evolutionary theories changed the course of thinking in almost every scientific discipline. Perhaps most significant for psychology was Darwin's principle of natural selection: those organisms survive that are best suited to their environment and its requirements for living. His emphasis on the capacity of an organism to function effectively in order to survive influenced the thinking of men like John Dewey and James Angell in America, and together with several others, they founded the functionalist movement at the University of Chicago. Extending Darwin's thinking, they rejected the abstract orientation of Wilhelm Wundt and Edward Titchener and contended that psychology must concern itself with the mind and how it serves to help the organism adapt to its environment. This led, in turn, to the question of individual differences in capacities, the touchstone of mental testing.

Darwin also contended that there was continuity of mind and body between humans and all other species. This idea opened the way for the development of animal psychology as a viable means of studying factors affecting human functioning. Darwin himself published a treatise on the subject, *Expression of the Emotions in Man and Animals* (1872), in which he demonstrated from observational data that emotional behavior in man was dependent upon the inheritance of responses that had proved useful at earlier stages in the development of the human species. Much of this behavior, he claimed, was no longer functional in man. For example, the human habit of curling the lips in a sneer was related to the tendency of the carnivorous animal to bare his teeth in rage before attacking. The field of comparative psychology has its roots in this work.
—Michael Rothenberg, *The City College of The City University of New York*

DAYDREAMING, the process by which a person attempts to remove himself from an un-

DARK ADAPTATION

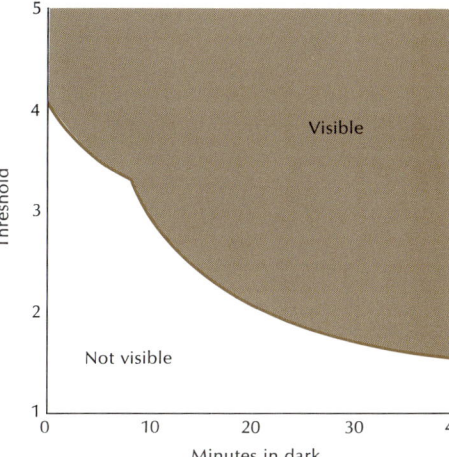

The graph shows the intensity of light required to be barely seen by a subject who has adapted to bright light and then been placed in total darkness. The threshold of intensity falls in two stages.

Among Charles Darwin's evolutionary theories, the principle of natural selection had the greatest impact on psychology and was the core of Functionalist thinking.

pleasant or potentially threatening situation by diverting his conscious attention from whatever he is experiencing into a variety of fantasies. These usually take the form of imagining himself in a time and place quite different from the one where he actually is. Often he will imagine himself doing things that reality and his own limitations prevent him from achieving in life.

Children who find school threatening or in some way unpleasant often lapse into periods of daydreaming. The adult most likely to engage in excessive daydreaming is a person who is unhappy and unsuccessful at work and in his social relationships and finds gratification in imagining himself performing heroic or distinguished feats. James Thurber's *Walter Mitty* has become a classic example in literature of the use of this form of defense mechanism.

—Michael Rothenberg, *The City College of The City University of New York*
See also Defense Mechanism.

DAY HOSPITAL, a mental hospital in which patients receive treatment in the institution during the day but return to their homes for the night. This program has several advantages as compared with full-time hospitalization. It reduces costs. It gets the family into closer contact with the hospital staff and in general brings hospital and community closer together. Since the patient is not cut off from his life outside the hospital, he does not face a major problem of readjusting after treatment ends. Also, he is less likely to develop dependence on the institution as a refuge.

D-DEPRIVATION (Dream Deprivation). *See* Sleep and Dreams.

DEAFNESS. There are many variables in the extent of the psychological problems that may evolve in children and adults whose hearing is impaired.

Teaching Children. For the child born with a congenital hearing defect, the most serious probelm is that of the acquisition of speech and language. Experts disagree on the methodologies for teaching such children. The basic question in this debate is whether the child should receive stimulation through an oral approach or by means of total communication, which combines oralism with some type of manual communication system. Successes and failures have been reported for both methodologies, and there is no scientific basis at this time for determining which will be most successful for a particular child.

Among the factors that influence learning ability are the severity of hearing loss, its duration before habilitation is implemented, the age at which it occurred, and the benefit

The most serious problem for the child born with a hearing defect is in the acquisition of speech and language skills.

provided by hearing aids. Although the situation involves some conflict, the child should receive a medical evaluation, an audiological evaluation, and a hearing-aid evaluation. In some cases, the professional team may describe the various methodologies to the parents and allow them to choose which procedure should be used. It is not uncommon for other professionals in psychology, psychiatry, and social work to be involved in the habilitation process. The ultimate goal is to make the child a productive member of society as he goes through the various phases of growth and development.

Treating Adults. Most acquired hearing losses are gradual and are most commonly caused by the aging process. The adult should be viewed in terms of numerous social roles—as a parent, spouse, worker, or participant in other activities—in order to determine the extent of the communication breakdown in any of these areas. All hearing-impaired adults do not experience the same kinds of problems.

The adult with hearing impairment should avail himself of a number of services, beginning with an examination of the ear by an otologist in order to determine whether or not there can be any medical or surgical treatment. (Sensory-neural [nerve] hearing losses are not reversible.) Such an evaluation will indicate the extent of the hearing loss and determine whether or not a hearing aid should be recommended. Rehabilitation services such as speechreading (lipreading), auditory training, and counseling should also be considered; all of these are provided by audiologists certified by the American Speech and Hearing Association. Associated vocational and psychological problems may result in the need for referral to a vocational rehabilitation counselor, a psychologist, a psychiatrist, or a social worker. The goal of such treatment is total rehabilitation for the hearing-impaired adult.

—Jerome G. Alpiner, *University of Denver*
See also Hearing.
Consult (4) Alpiner, 1963; Alpiner, 1969; Alpiner, 1970; Alpiner, 1971; Graunke, 1970; Morkovin, 1960; Rainer, *et al.,* 1963; Vernon, 1968; Vernon, 1969.

DEATH INSTINCT. Sigmund Freud introduced his theory of the dual life and death instincts in *Beyond the Pleasure Principle* (1920), a major reformulation of the psychoanalytic theory of motivation. Respectively, they were considered to represent the forces underlying sexual and aggressive behavior.

The life instinct, or *eros,* referred to the biological urge to unite—the parts binding together to form greater unities, as in sexual reproduction—and was seen as analogous to anabolism or biological buildup. The death instinct, or *thanatos,* was defined as the tendency of organisms and their cells to return to an inanimate state, analogous to catabolism, or biological breakdown. Inasmuch as the destiny of all biological matter is to return to an inanimate state, Freud regarded the death instinct as the dominant force.

Although Freud conceded that the death instinct was hypothetical and not directly verifiable, he held the concept was substantiated by certain phenomena, particularly human destructiveness and aggression and the peculiar fusions of destructiveness and sexuality in sadism and masochism. He also pointed to the tendency of neurotic individuals to repeat past behavior even if maladaptive, which he termed *repetition compulsion.* This he saw as an innate conservative and regressive reinstatement of earlier conditions.

The death instinct is a controversial aspect of Freud's theories. While regarded as a profound insight by some psychoanalysts, it has not been generally accepted.

—Alden E. Wessman, *The City College of The City University of New York*
See also Life Instinct.
Consult (13) Freud, 1933; Freud, 1950.

DECAY THEORY. *See* Memory.

DEFENSE MECHANISM, an unconscious attempt by an individual to protect himself from extreme states of anxiety caused by unacceptable wishes, impulses, or desires. Because the conscious awareness of these desires would be very disruptive to his functioning, the individual uses various defense mechanisms to prevent himself from experiencing them. It is important to note that whenever a defense mechanism is used, there is some degree of distortion of reality.

Defense mechanisms were first identified by Freud in 1894. He defined them as a function of the ego, which mediates between the primitive impulses of the id and the moral demands of the superego. When these two forces come in conflict, there is a sudden increase in tension. The ego will use a variety of techniques to reduce the tension—and it was these Freud called defense mechanisms.

Originally viewed by psychoanalysts as characteristic of neurotic functioning, defense mechanisms have more recently come to be regarded as part of adaptive functioning as well. Everyone uses defense mechanisms every day, without being aware he is doing so. It is the extent to which they are used and the degree to which reality is distorted that determine the level at which a person is functioning. Well-integrated individuals have more defenses available and use them more effectively, with less distortion of reality, than less well-adjusted persons, who respond in a more rigid,

stereotyped way, using only a few of the most primitive defense mechanisms.

Specific mechanisms are described in separate articles.

—Michael Rothenberg, *The City College of The City University of New York*
See also Compensation; Daydreaming; Denial; Displacement; Dissociation; Identification; Intellectualization; Projection; Rationalization; Reaction Formation; Regression; Repression; Sublimation; Withdrawal.
Consult (13) Coleman, 1964.

DEINDIVIDUATION. *See* Anonymity.

DELAYED REACTION (delayed response), an experimental situation in which the subject is presented both correct and incorrect stimuli and is then required to wait for an interval to pass before he is allowed to make a response. This task has been used to measure learning ability. It is also valuable in assessing the effects of brain damage, particularly in the prefrontal lobes, and has been used with hyperkinetic children. It is one of the most widely used methods of ascertaining certain types of brain damage in both man and other animals.

—Joel F. Lubar, *University of Tennessee*

DELGADO, JOSE MANUEL RODRIGUEZ (1915–), American neurophysiologist. Born in Ronda, Spain, he received an M.D. (1940) and D.Sc. (1942) at Madrid. He later became professor of physiology at Yale Medical School.

Delgado has developed electrodes for permanent implantation in the brain and methods for radio stimulation of the brain. He has studied autonomic and somatic functions, individual and social behavior, and emotional behavior evoked or modified by electrical stimulation of specific brain structures. He is widely known for a dramatic demonstration of the effectiveness of brain stimulation: he stepped into a bull ring in Spain and stopped the offensive charge of the bull with radio stimulation of the brain via previously implanted electrodes.

He is the author of *Physical Control of the Mind: Toward a Psychocivilized Society,* 1969, and editor of *International Review of Neurobiology.*

—Nina Adams, *Yale University*

DELIRIUM, a state marked by restlessness, excitement, confusion, and fear. There are likely to be frightening dreams, disorders of perception, and hallucinations. Periods of delirium are likely to alternate with times of sleepiness or coma.

Delirium is often caused by infectious diseases such as typhoid fever. The degree of disturbance depends to a great extent upon the seriousness of the toxic condition in the body.

Spanish-born neurophysiologist José Delgado developed techniques for control of emotional behavior by electrical stimulation of the brain.

However, an individual with a weak personality adjustment may be more likely to become delirious than a better integrated personality.

Delirium can also be caused by after-effects of operations, by exhaustion, by alcohol and other drugs, and by poisons such as lead and carbon monoxide.

See also Delirium Tremens.
Consult (13) Coleman, 1964.

DELIRIUM TREMENS, a psychotic reaction that occurs in chronic alcoholics, usually in people who are over thirty and have been drinking excessively for a number of years. The following symptoms may be observed: the patient does not know where he is or what time it is and cannot recognize people. He has hallucinations, "seeing pink snakes" or rats and roaches, and feeling great fear of these creatures. He readily believes that he sees strange animals if it is suggested to him that he does. He shows tremor (*tremens*) of the hands and mouth, sweats, and is feverish.

The symptoms last for three to six days, after which the patient goes into a deep sleep. There is danger of death from heart failure or pneumonia.

Consult (13) Coleman, 1964.

DELTA WAVES. *See* Brain Waves.

DELUSION, a false belief that persists in the face of evidence that it is irrational. Such beliefs are often symptoms of mental illness. A paranoid patient, for example, may have delusions of grandeur, being convinced that he is the Messiah or the secret power in the government. Also found in paranoid psychosis are delusions of persecution, such as an elaborately detailed belief that hidden enemies have been plotting against the patient for years. Delusions of extreme worthlessness, sin, and guilt are found in depressed patients. Many delusions center around sexual problems.

Delusions may be greatly detailed and may persist for years, as in the case of paranoia. On the other hand, delusions may be temporary, as in states of delirium.

It is necessary to distinguish a delusion from a hallucination, which is a reported sensory impression when no external stimulus exists to justify the sensation. Patients with alcoholic psychosis have been known to suffer from delusions (that the walls are covered with dangerous roaches). Both delusions and hallucinations are different from illusions, which are mistaken perceptions of actual stimuli and occur often in normal life.

See also Paranoia; Psychotic Disorders.
Consult (13) Coleman, 1964.

DEMENT, WILLIAM (1928–), American psychiatrist and educator. Born in Wenatchee, Washington, he received an M.D. (1955) and a

Ph.D. (1957) from the University of Chicago. He was founder (1969) and editor of the Sleep Reviews Project of the Brain Information Services and the cofounder of the Association for the Psychophysiological Study of Sleep. Later he became professor of psychiatry at the Stanford School of Medicine.

Dement is best known for his investigations of sleep, particularly the studies of dreaming and rapid eye movement (REM) sleep. By waking subjects when their electroencephalograph shows fast activity but muscle tone is low and eyes show rapid eye movement and asking whether they are dreaming, Dement (like Eugene Aserinsky and Nathaniel Kleitman) has shown a correspondence of REM and dream imagery. A classical example is a sequence of twenty-six regular eye movements shown by a subject who reported dreaming of a Ping-Pong game. Dement has also shown a correspondence between dream deprivation and increased dreaming on subsequent nights.

—Nina Adams, *Yale University*

DEMENTIA, severe deterioration of mental abilities as a result of damage to the brain by injury, disease, or atrophy. *Senile dementia,* or *senile psychosis,* comes on gradually in old age if brain tissues deteriorate. *Dementia paralytica* (general paresis) is the result of syphilitic infection of the central nervous system.

Dementia should be distinguished from *amentia,* or failure to develop normal mental ability. The noun "dementia" and the adjective "demented" were formerly used for all varieties of mental illness. For example, dementia praecox is an old name for schizophrenia.

See also Brain Disorders; for amentia, *see* Mental Retardation.

DEMENTIA PRAECOX, a term formerly applied to the group of psychotic disorders now described as forms of schizophrenia. *See* Schizophrenia.

DENDRITE. *See* Neuron.

DENIAL, a defensive reaction usually invoked in response to some immediate fear-producing stimulus (person, object, or thought). It involves behaving as though whatever is causing the fear either does not exist or is not true.

Denial is quite common in children, for whom it is one of the more primitive defenses, but it is more pathological when it occurs frequently in adults. Such individuals must continually deny the existence of important aspects of their experience or environment. Parents who have an emotionally disturbed child, for example, will often deny their own roles in the child's development, attributing his problems entirely to other factors.

In more extreme cases, denial can be more harmful than adaptive. If thoughts of real and imminent danger are denied, the danger still remains, and the possibility of more functional behavior is precluded.

—Michael Rothenberg, *The City College of The City University of New York*
See also Defense Mechanism.

DEPENDENCE AND INDEPENDENCE. These concepts are derived from the mathematical notion that two sets of events are related to one another in a specific way. If changes in one set of events determine what a second set of events will be, then the first set of events is labeled independent and the second set of events dependent. A specific example is that the early experiences of children, which are independent events, determine their behaviors and performance capabilities as adults. In the realm of motivation, it has been established that the magnitude of such incentives as the amount and type of food, which are independent variables (events), determine the strength of a response such as running toward a goal.

An important problem concerning independence and dependence is that they are not a perfect dichotomy. Many dependent events are not determined by a single independent event but by many. Furthermore, only a few of these independent events can be identified in many cases.

—Thom Herrmann, *University of Tennessee*

DEPENDENCY NEEDS, needs for gratification that an individual actually cannot, or feels he cannot, satisfy by himself. Observation of infants reveals that their activity level increases at those times when bodily discomfort (hunger, thirst, and so on) is greatest. Those persons who respond to the needs of the infant, most frequently the parents, become figures of central importance in his life. Initially he is almost totally dependent on them for gratification of his needs.

As he grows older, a child becomes capable of satisfying some of his own needs by himself. Different children develop these capacities at different rates—and to different degrees. However, no individual ever reaches the point at which he is completely free from dependence on others for the gratification of emotional needs. To the extent that he remains tied to persons who once were sources of love and protection, he is motivated by dependency needs. To the extent that he demonstrates an ability to function autonomously and to form new peer relationships, he is behaving independently. Thus, dependence and independence are opposite ends of the same continuum; the same individual may exhibit either type of behavior in different situations and with different persons.

—Michael Rothenberg, *The City College of The City University of New York*

DEPRESSANTS, drugs that decrease the activity of the central nervous system. Included are a variety of sedative-hypnotics—alcohol, gaseous anesthetics, barbiturates, and tranquilizers. *See* Drugs and Behavior.

DEPRESSION, a state that can range in seriousness from dejection in a normal person to a pattern found in severe mental illness. Sometimes a distinction is made between *melancholy,* a sad mood that most people experience, and *melancholia,* which is an exaggerated and pathological state of depression. *See* Asthenic Reaction; Cyclothymic Personality; Depressive Reaction; Manic-Depressive Psychosis.

DEPRESSIVE REACTION, a term that applies to psychoneurotic (neurotic) and psychotic disorders marked by severe depression.

A *depressive reaction* (also called *neurotic depressive reaction* or *reactive depression*) is a psychoneurotic disorder that occurs as a reaction to a distressing circumstance such as loss of a job, loss of a great deal of money, divorce, or death of a loved person. Symptoms typically include feelings of apprehension, gloom, helplessness, worthlessness, and inability to enjoy life or even to cope with routine duties. The sufferer is likely to lack appetite, to be listless, and to complain of bodily ailments (hypochondria). The depressed person may threaten suicide. All this may be seen as responding to anxiety by "copping out" rather than by increased activity or outwardly violent manifestations of stress.

Neurotic reactive depressions can usually be treated successfully by such means as antidepressant drugs, supportive counsel, and psychotherapy. However, it is possible for the psychoneurotic problem to become more serious and develop into a psychotic reaction.

A *psychotic depressive reaction* is more severe and more persistent than a neurotic reaction. The patient often loses contact with reality, suffering delusions of sinfulness and guilt and various hallucinations. Threats of suicide and attempts at suicide are often made. Behavior resembles that in the depressive phase of a manic-depressive psychosis. However, the depressive psychotic does not show cycles of elation (manic stages) alternating with depressed states. Moreover, the depressive reaction typically occurs as a response to some painful or guilt-producing experience. These two diagnostic clues differentiate the depressive state from manic-depressive psychosis. Treatment may include electroshock followed by psychotherapy.

See also Hypochondria; Manic-Depressive Psychosis.

DEPRIVATION, MATERNAL. *See* Maternal Deprivation.

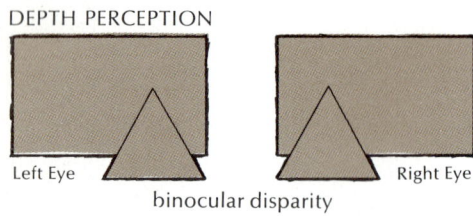

DEPTH PERCEPTION

Left Eye   Right Eye

binocular disparity

Figure 1
The slightly different retinal image in the two eyes provides a visual cue to depth.

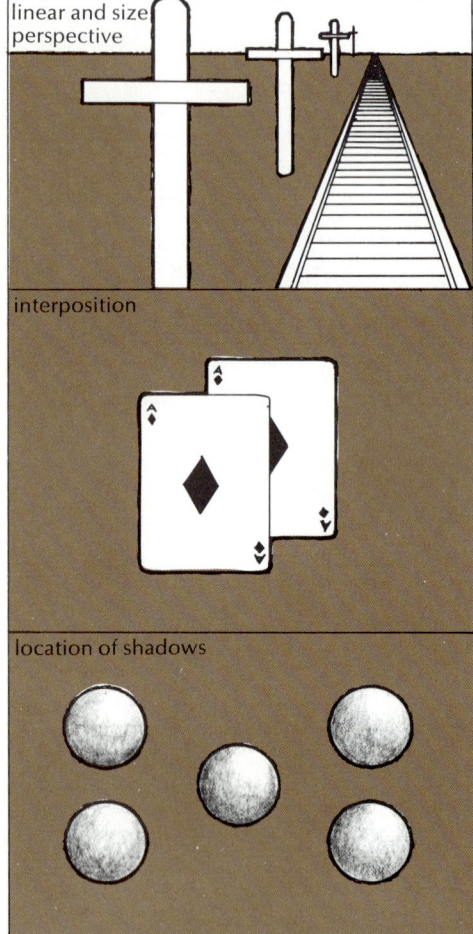

linear and size perspective

interposition

location of shadows

Figure 2
An adult viewer can perceive depth in a scene from pictorial cues such as linear and size perspective, interposition, and shading.

DEPRIVATION, RELATIVE. See Relative Deprivation.

DEPRIVATION, SENSORY. See Sensory Deprivation.

DEPRIVATION OF SLEEP OR DREAMS. See Sleep and Dreams.

DEPTH PERCEPTION, the experience of the third dimension of visual space. Experts in the field of perception sometimes use the term to refer only to the impression of the *relative* distances of things from the observer—for example, that the book is farther away than the pencil. The term *distance perception* is then reserved for the *absolute* distance of a single object from the observer.

Various determinants (or *cues,* as they have been called) of the perception of depth and distance have been isolated. Historically, *accommodation* (the lens of the eye automatically adjusts for the distance of the object viewed in order to yield a sharp image) and *convergence* (the angle at which the two eyes focus necessarily varies as a function of the distance of the object) were the first to be discussed. Later, *binocular disparity* (or *stereopsis*), the fact that the retinal images in the two eyes will differ slightly for an array of objects in depth, was discovered. Recently much attention has been paid to the change in the retinal image that occurs as a result of movement of the observer, referred to as *motion parallax* or *motion perspective.*

While all these cues have been shown to contribute to the perception of the third dimension, none is necessary, at least in adult humans. When a scene is viewed through a pinhole with head stationary, all of these factors are eliminated or minimized, but the scene is still perceived as three-dimensional. Therefore, it is now believed that the so-called pictorial cues first described by Leonardo da Vinci as rules for artists are also quite important in the perception of depth. Among these are *linear* and *size perspective, interposition* (or overlapping), and *the location of shadows.*

Recent evidence, chiefly from research using the so-called *visual cliff* has settled an age-old controversy about whether or not depth perception is innately determined or must be learned. Virtually every species of animal tested perceives distance at or shortly after birth.

—Irvin Rock, *Rutgers University*
See also Ames Room; Visual Cliff.
Consult (4) Gibson, 1960; Woodworth and Schlosberg, 1954.

DEPTH PSYCHOLOGY, the orientation of psychologists and psychotherapists who believe that it is not the surface appearance but what lies "within" or "beneath" the surface that denotes the true personality. In general, the analyst tries to guide the patient to uncover what is buried beneath defense mechanisms in order to discover his real personality and the causes for his conflicts.

Depth psychology is practiced by Freudian psychoanalysts as well as by those in the schools of Alfred Adler, Carl Jung, Karen Horney, and Harry Stack Sullivan.
—Thom Herrmann, *University of Tennessee*

DESCARTES, RENE (1596–1650), French philosopher and mathematician, born at La Haye, near Poitiers. Descartes' development of a mechanistic explanation for the human body stimulated a scientific approach to man, and his work was a major stimulus to the growth of modern psychology. Descartes is also regarded as the father of physiological psychology and of the study of reflexes.

Descartes saw the human mind and body as being separate and different but also as interacting with each other. The mind, or soul, said Descartes, contained innate ideas, such as God, and could perceive and will, while the body was mechanical in nature—an automation. The mind affected the body, and the body affected the mind; the site of interaction between mind and body was identified by Descartes as the pineal gland in the brain. (Descartes believed the soul to be unitary, so it could not affect the body at the two separate points that the right and left sections of the brain would represent.)

Descartes explained the emotions—the passions of the soul—in the mechanical terms of brain, blood, and organs of the body. He described nerves as tubes that carried "animal spirits" to and from the muscles and sensory organs, thus foreseeing the concept of the reflex arc. He also demonstrated that the crystalline body of the eye is responsible for forming the light image on the retina.
Consult (1) Boring, 1950; Murphy, 1949.

DETECTION THEORY. See Signal-Detection Theory.

DETERMINISM, the doctrine that every event has a cause or causes and that these antecedents completely explain the event. In philosophy, this brings up the question of free will: does man have any control over his destiny, or is it shaped by circumstances outside him?

Without necessarily answering this question, scientific psychology assumes a degree of determinism in behavior. Three categories of determinants are studied, usually as they interact to influence behavior. Biological factors include heredity, bodily constitution, and physiological health and disease. Psychological determinants include emotions, drives, attitudes, conscious and unconscious conflicts and traumas, and learning experiences. Social and cultural factors include economic status, social status, customs and mores, and social conflicts.

The interaction of causes is discussed in articles such as the one on Heredity and Environment.

See also Heredity and Environment; Philosophical Psychology.

DEVELOPMENT. *See* Developmental Psychology.

DEVELOPMENTAL PSYCHOLOGY, the study of the growth and changes in behavior of organisms from conception to death. Originally this field concentrated on child development, but the scope has been extended to the whole life span. The findings and theories of developmental psychology are described in articles that begin with the intrauterine environment and proceed through childhood, adolescence, the middle years, and aging.

Principles of Development. Development, sometimes conceptualized as "the forward thrust of life," is an extremely complex process that begins at conception and proceeds through maturity or adulthood. It results from the interaction of genetic or biological traits, predispositions and potentialities, on the one hand, and environmental factors, both physical and social, on the other. Within each species the sequence, timing, and direction of development proceed in a lawful predictable manner that, especially at the human level, takes into account individual variations, both normal and deviant.

Development involves the interplay of several complementary processes, most notably growth, maturation, and learning. *Growth* refers to normal, quantitative changes that occur in the physical and physiological aspects of a healthy child with the passage of time (for example, increase in height or weight). *Maturation* involves anatomical, neurophysiological, and chemical changes of the body that occur with time and over which we have only slight control. As these innate potentials unfold, certain body parts, functions, and behavior forms "ripen" or "reach fruition." Thus, maturation triggers changes in the capacity to function, rather than mere changes in quantity (for example, the capacity of the sexual organs to reproduce after puberty). *Learning* refers to relatively permanent modifications of behavior (change in performance) that result from experience, special training, observation, or exercise (for example, speaking a foreign language).

In the developing organism, these three factors are interdependent. For example, motor behaviors, such as sitting, require both maturation of back muscles and environmental opportunities; psychosocial tasks, such as toilet training, depend on neuromuscular maturation and social demands; cognitive skills rely on both earlier muscular activity and objects to manipulate.

The Critical Periods. This approach to development attempts to delineate the nature and timing of the *interaction* between external, environmental forces and the internal "unfolding" processes. It hypothesizes, essentially, that normal development proceeds through a series of phases or stages, each of which is marked by an increased receptivity toward certain environmental conditions (or "readiness" for certain experiences). What happens during each phase can have profound and far-reaching effects on the course of later development and learning potential. Critical periods occur not only in motor, sensory-perceptual, and physical development (such as cell differentiation) but also in the development of behavioral systems and processes (such as socialization and sex-role typing).

The *critical period* for any body part or behavioral system usually corresponds closely to its time span of most rapid development. Vulnerability to environmental influences (both positive and negative) increases precisely because the system is being organized or formed. For example, the drug thalidomide alters or stops the development of limb "buds." Thus, if it is in the mother-embryo's blood system during the time of limb formation (sixth to eighth week of prenatal development), limbs cannot form properly. Prior to or following this "critical period" the drug would have no effect.

The critical-periods principle may be used, with caution, to account for certain individual variations in forms of behavior, personality characteristics, skills, and even learning potential. However, it should be remembered that the detrimental effects of environmental variables on behavior are not likely to be irreversible or inalterable, though they can be very severe.

Some psychologists prefer the term maturational "readiness" to critical period. This concept indicates the "time" or stage when the individual is most prepared to benefit from certain learning experiences.

Patterns of Development. Although development is continuous and proceeds in an orderly, predictable, sequential pattern similar for all human beings, its rate varies both within a given body structure and between body systems. The latter is referred to as asynchronous growth and may contribute to phases of behavioral disequilibrium. Within a normal range, growth rates tend to vary from one individual to another as well.

Sensory and motor development proceeds according to three clearly definable trends: *cephalocaudal* from the head region downward through the body; *proximo-distal*

In the early 17th century, French philosopher René Descartes presented a scientific approach to the study of man and the interaction between mind and body that spurred the growth of modern psychology.

DEVELOPMENTAL PSYCHOLOGY

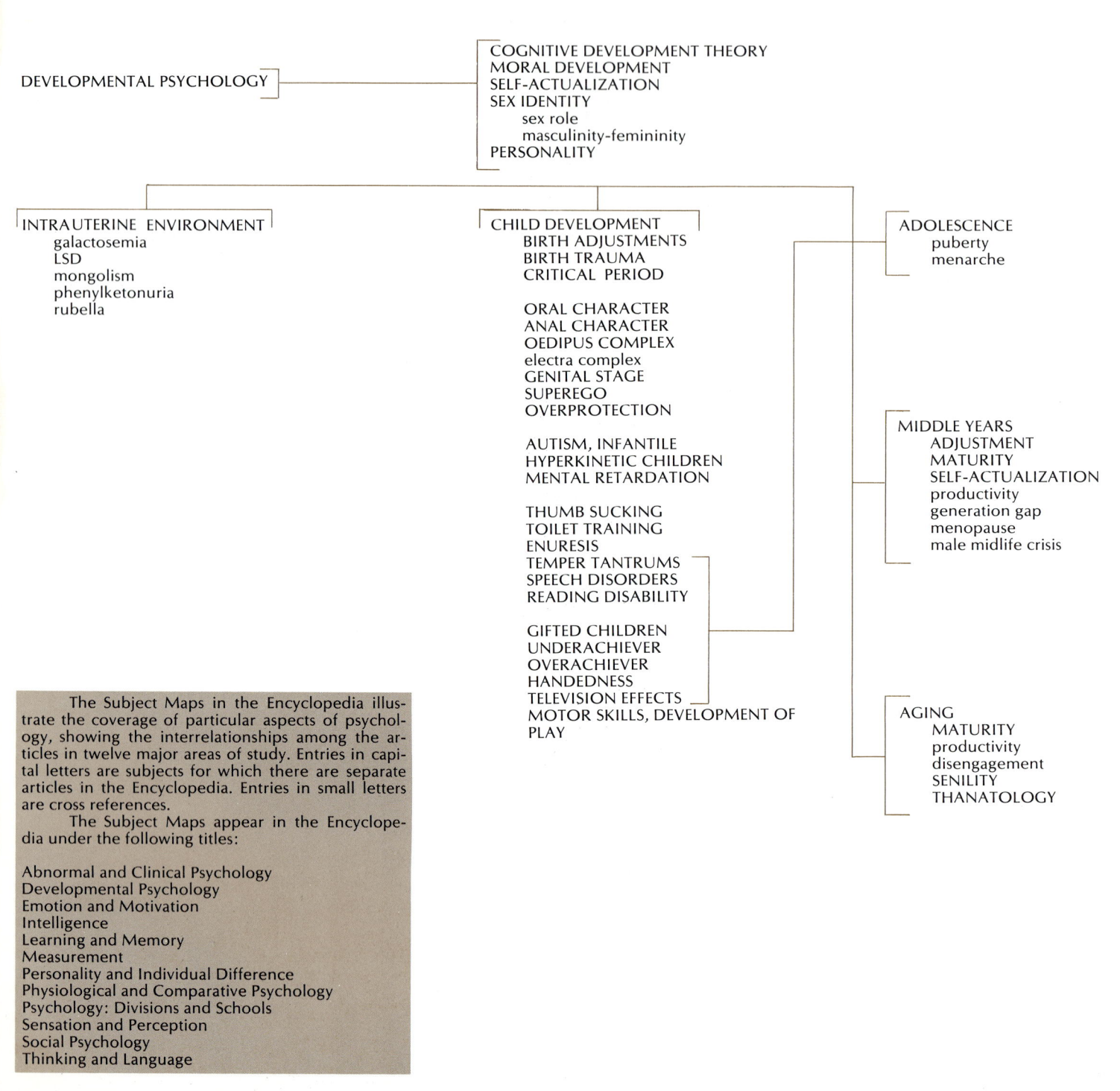

DEVELOPMENTAL PSYCHOLOGY

COGNITIVE DEVELOPMENT THEORY
MORAL DEVELOPMENT
SELF-ACTUALIZATION
SEX IDENTITY
    sex role
    masculinity-femininity
PERSONALITY

INTRAUTERINE ENVIRONMENT
    galactosemia
    LSD
    mongolism
    phenylketonuria
    rubella

CHILD DEVELOPMENT
    BIRTH ADJUSTMENTS
    BIRTH TRAUMA
    CRITICAL PERIOD

    ORAL CHARACTER
    ANAL CHARACTER
    OEDIPUS COMPLEX
    electra complex
    GENITAL STAGE
    SUPEREGO
    OVERPROTECTION

    AUTISM, INFANTILE
    HYPERKINETIC CHILDREN
    MENTAL RETARDATION

    THUMB SUCKING
    TOILET TRAINING
    ENURESIS
    TEMPER TANTRUMS
    SPEECH DISORDERS
    READING DISABILITY

    GIFTED CHILDREN
    UNDERACHIEVER
    OVERACHIEVER
    HANDEDNESS
    TELEVISION EFFECTS
MOTOR SKILLS, DEVELOPMENT OF
PLAY

ADOLESCENCE
    puberty
    menarche

MIDDLE YEARS
    ADJUSTMENT
    MATURITY
    SELF-ACTUALIZATION
    productivity
    generation gap
    menopause
    male midlife crisis

AGING
    MATURITY
    productivity
    disengagement
    SENILITY
    THANATOLOGY

The Subject Maps in the Encyclopedia illustrate the coverage of particular aspects of psychology, showing the interrelationships among the articles in twelve major areas of study. Entries in capital letters are subjects for which there are separate articles in the Encyclopedia. Entries in small letters are cross references.

The Subject Maps appear in the Encyclopedia under the following titles:

Abnormal and Clinical Psychology
Developmental Psychology
Emotion and Motivation
Intelligence
Learning and Memory
Measurement
Personality and Individual Difference
Physiological and Comparative Psychology
Psychology: Divisions and Schools
Sensation and Perception
Social Psychology
Thinking and Language

outward from the central axis toward the extremities), and *mass specific* (from gross movement to fine muscle coordination, from undifferentiated to differentiated).

—Cynthia MacRitchie, *Southern Connecticut State College*

See also articles listed in the Subject Map.

Consult (11) Olson, 1959.

DEVIATION, SEXUAL. *See* Sexual Deviations.

DEVIATION, STANDARD. *See* Standard Deviation.

DEWEY, JOHN (1859-1952), American philosopher and educator, born near Burlington, Vermont. He was at the University of Chicago (1894-1904) and Columbia (1904-1930). Dewey was president of the American Psychological Association (1899-1900) and was first president of the American Association of University Professors (1915).

Dewey is generally regarded as the individual most responsible for establishing functionalism as a movement in American psychology. Originally trained in philosophy, he became increasingly convinced, under the influence of men like James and Darwin, that philosophy must concern itself with man as he struggles for survival in the environment. His article on the reflex arc, published in 1896, attacked the molecularism and reductionism of Wundt and Titchener. He claimed that human experience cannot be understood by attempting to reduce it to ever simpler and more basic units. In the article, Dewey maintained that the behavior involved in a reflex response cannot be meaningfully reduced to stimulus and response elements. He viewed the reflex as an indivisibly integrated unit, neither part of which had any function without the other. He went on to state that the reflex, like all other forms of behavior and experience, should be interpreted in terms of its significance for human adaptation. In establishing these principles, Dewey set forth the first statement of the functionalist doctrine.

Dewey was also in the vanguard of those who pressed for a science of education. His presidential address to the American Psychological Association convention in 1900 mapped out the framework for the first program in educational psychology. His philosophical commitment to practicality in the study of human functioning led to the development of his theory of "instrumentalism" in education, popularly known as learning by doing. Much of the current enthusiasm for individualized instruction and experiential learning can be traced directly to Dewey's theories.

Dewey changed the direction of American psychology from the academic and the abstract to the practical and the functional. As founder of the functionalist school, he started a movement that extended the range of psychology from the laboratory into the public school classroom and the psychiatric clinic. It literally established applied psychology. His importance to the field cannot be overestimated. His numerous books include *The School and Society* (1899), *How We Think* (1910), *Democracy and Education* (1916), *Experience and Nature* (1925), and *Experience and Education* (1938).

—Michael Rothenberg, *The City College of The City University of New York*

Consult (1) Brickman and Lehrer, 1965.

DIENCEPHALON, part of the forebrain, which includes the thalamus and the hypothalamus. *See* Brain; Hypothalamus; Thalamus.

DIFFERENTIAL PSYCHOLOGY, the study of the psychological differences between individuals and between groups. Psychologists in many fields are interested in individual and group differences, hence this is a focus of study rather than a distinct specialty. Psychologists, for example, have long been interested in individual differences in intelligence—degrees of difference, their causes, and their importance. This kind of study has been extended to groups, using developing techniques of statistical analysis. Differences attributed to sex, race, ethnic background, training, and social and economic status have all been studied.

Although the causes of variations in abilities, traits, and performance may be disputed, the recognition of individual and group differences is essential in education, measurement, personality study, and other fields.

See also Constitutional Types; Intelligence and Intelligence Testing; Temperament.

DIRECTIVE PSYCHOTHERAPY, a form of treatment in which the therapist takes the role of a teacher, guiding, probing, and interpreting as work with the patient proceeds. This technique is contrasted with the nondirective or client-centered approach.

See also Client-Centered Therapy.

DISADVANTAGED. *See* Culture-Fair Test; Intelligence and Intelligence Testing.

DISASTER SYNDROME. *See* Civilian Catastrophe Reaction.

DISCRIMINATION. *See* Prejudice.

DISCRIMINATION LEARNING. *See* Concept Learning; Operant Conditioning.

DISENGAGEMENT THEORY. *See* Aging.

John Dewey, American philosopher and educator, was chief founder of Functionalism and thus applied psychology. His learn-by-doing theory profoundly affected doctrine and practice in U.S. education.

A century ago, American humanitarian Dorothea Dix strove successfully for reforms in the handling of insane persons, formerly imprisoned and mistreated.

DNA
NUCLEIC ACIDS

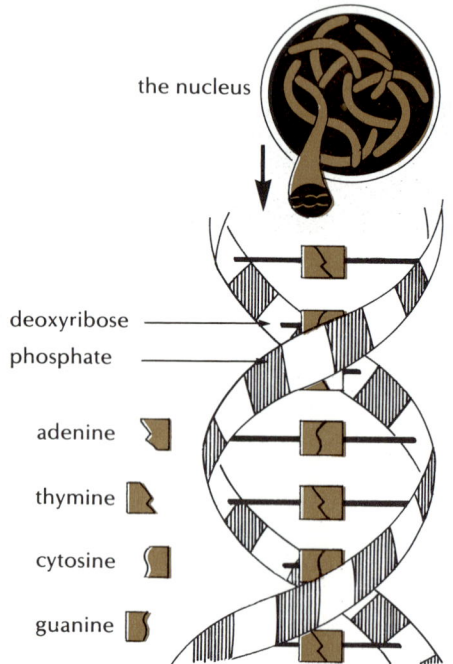

the nucleus

deoxyribose

phosphate

adenine

thymine

cytosine

guanine

The DNA molecule consists of long coiled chains of deoxyribose and phosphate linked by bridges of purines (adenine and guanine) and pyrimidines (thymine and cytosine). The sequence of the purines and pyrimidines, or bases, constitutes a genetic code.

DISPLACEMENT, the process by which an emotion originally attached to a particular person, object, or situation is transferred to something else. The unacceptable feelings are usually transferred from an object that is of central importance in the individual's life to an external object that is relatively harmless. A boy who is angry at his parents may kick a dog, or clout a baseball, instead of striking his mother or father. He remains unaware of where his anger was originally focused.

Displacement is the defense mechanism often found at the root of phobias. For example, a person with a morbid fear of dogs or horses may originally have been defending himself against anxiety created by hostile impulses toward his father. The displacement of these feelings onto animals enabled him to live comfortably with his father and remains unchanged even after he leaves home and is living independently.

—Michael Rothenberg, *The City College
of The City University of New York*
See also Defense Mechanism; Phobia.

DISSOCIATION, the process of separating a portion of the personality that is causing undue emotional stress from the rest of the normally functioning personality. The troublesome portion is not completely repressed, however, and periodically may break into consciousness. Thus, a person may demonstrate characteristics and behavior completely out of keeping with his typical functioning. He will do so without remembering anything once the episode is over and the conflicting impulses have been successfully overcome. In such circumstances a quiet or shy person may become angry and aggressive. The defense mechanism of dissociation is responsible for such conditions as sleepwalking, temporary amnesia, and multiple personalities.

—Michael Rothenberg, *The City College
of The City University of New York*
See also Defense Mechanism; Multiple Personality.

DISSOCIATIVE REACTION, a psychoneurotic condition in which one part of a person's psychic activity is blocked off from the rest. This term is sometimes treated as a synonym for dissociation. The dissociative reaction can take the form of amnesia, fugue, multiple personality, or somnambulism (sleepwalking). *See* Amnesia; Dissociation; Fugue; Multiple Personality; Sleepwalking.

DISSONANCE THEORY. *See* Cognitive Dissonance.

DISTRIBUTION, in statistics. *See* Frequency Distribution.

DISUSE OR DECAY THEORY. *See* Memory.

DIX, DOROTHEA LYNDE (1802–1887), American humanitarian. Born at Hampden, Maine, she founded Dix Mansion, school for girls (1817–1835), and was superintendent of women nurses under the U.S. surgeon general (1861–1865).

Ranked with Philippe Pinel in her work to alleviate the plight of the mentally ill, Dorothea Dix devoted over half her life to the reform of mental institutions in the United States and in Europe. In 1841, while teaching a Sunday school class at the East Cambridge, Massachusetts, House of Correction, Dix observed that the insane were imprisoned with criminals and treated as subhuman creatures. She immediately began a two-year investigation of jails and almshouses in Massachusetts. By exposing the inhumane treatment and conditions in these institutions and forcing them upon the public attention, she succeeded in having legislation passed to reform the treatment of mental patients in Massachusetts and then in other states. The result was the founding of state asylums for the treatment of mental diseases, rather than the previous practice of imprisoning mental patients. Her work helped dispel some of the fears and lack of information about the mentally ill, thus making possible more effective treatment of their conditions.

Dix visited Europe from 1854 to 1857 and the results of her work there included an investigation of treatment of the mentally ill in Scotland and the establishment of mental hospitals in Rome and on the island of Jersey. *See also* Mental Hospitals.

DNA (DEOXYRIBONUCLEIC ACID) has been called the building block of life. An extremely complex molecule with a high molecular weight, it is chemically classified as a polynucleotide. Each such nucleotide is composed of a phosphate group, a base, and a sugar. The sugar is deoxyribose, and the bases are adenine, guanine, cytosine, and thymine. The backbone of DNA consists of phosphate and sugar linked together and attached to these bases. The appearance of the DNA molecule is that of a double-stranded helix.

Functionally, DNA forms the basis for genetic organization in both the plant and the animal kingdoms. It specifies the sequence of nucleotides in a related molecule RNA (ribonucleic acid), which is responsible for determining the sequence of amino acids that form proteins. Proteins are the building blocks for many biological structures, including the nervous system. The complex structure of DNA had been studied for many years and was sufficiently resolved by James Watson and Francis Crick in 1953. As a result of their establishment of the double helix, they were awarded the Nobel Prize.

DNA has a number of interesting properties. For example, if a single strand is placed in an environment containing nucleotides, this strand of DNA can build itself a new companion strand. This process, known as *replication*, forms the basis on which genetic information is passed from one generation to another. If any error occurs in the sequence of the nucleotides formed during the process of replication, it might constitute the structural basis for another process, *mutation*, which is responsible for minute progressive changes in the genetic composition of organisms.

    —Joel F. Lubar, *University of Tennessee*
See also Brain Storage.

DOMINANCE RELATIONSHIPS, a system of status within a social organization in which individuals occupy different ranks in respect to one another. Such systems, found in both human and animal societies, are sometimes called "pecking orders." The relationships may be based only on physical characteristics, such as strength or cunning, as in the case of most animal social organizations, but in the more complex human societies they usually depend on the acquisition of prestige symbols, such as titles or material possessions.

    Dominance relationships are usually hierarchial in nature and are subject to change through competitiveness by the members of the society. Psychologists and sociologists believe such an organization of relationships allows the group to remain intact and assures its survival against outside pressures.

    —Thom Herrmann, *University of Tennessee*

DOUBLE BIND. *See* Psychotic Disorders.

D-PERIOD OR D-STATE. *See* Sleep and Dreams.

D-PRESSURE. *See* Sleep and Dreams.

DREAM DEPRIVATION. *See* Sleep and Dreams.

DREAM INTERPRETATION. *See* Sleep and Dreams.

DREAM NEED. *See* Sleep and Dreams.

DRIVE, a need or urge that motivates behavior. The term has been defined in several ways. Some drives can be explained as responses to basic bodily needs—hunger, thirst, elimination. Others involve social pressures and complex forms of learning—aspiration, competition, conformity. For discussion, *see* the articles on Motivation and Emotion. For information on specific drives, see the individual articles listed below.

    Achievement Drive
    Activity Drive
    Affectional Drive
    Affiliative Drive
    Aggression
    Anger
    Aspiration, Level of
    Competition
    Conformity
    Curiosity Drive
    Dependence-Independence
    Dominance Relationship
    Drive-Reduction Theory
    Elimination Drive
    Exploration Drive
    Gradient
    Homeostasis
    Hunger Drive
    Instinct
    Maternal Drive
    Operant Conditioning
    Pain Drive
    Pleasure Principle
    Sex Drive
    Sleep Drive
    Specific Hunger
    Thirst Drive
    Valance

The dominance of the breeding male lion works for the survival of the group.

DRIVE-REDUCTION THEORY. Clark Hull first proposed the principle that learning takes place only when a fundamental drive or need is reduced. For example, when an animal learns to avoid shock, its performance of the avoidance response reduces the fear of being shocked. This fear reduction strengthens the avoidance response. Drive-reduction theory has been proposed generally to account for learning that occurs when punishment is employed.

    See also Operant Conditioning.

DRUG ADDICTION. *See* Drugs and Behavior.

DRUG DEPENDENCY. *See* Drugs and Behavior.

DRUGS AND BEHAVIOR. In this post-LSD era, it seems superfluous to state that drugs are capable of altering behavior. In fact, the term *psychopharmacology* has been introduced to describe that branch of science that studies the effects of drugs on sensation, mood, consciousness, or other psychological or behavioral functions.

    Yet, even though the behavioral effects of drugs can be described, difficulties arise when one attempts to demonstrate the biochemical or physiological basis of the drug action. We possess only minimal understanding of the essential nature of psychological and behavioral functions and their relationships to underlying physiological processes. The effects of drugs on behavior are secondary to their action on neuronal mechanisms in the brain. Similarly, these actions on biochemical or physiological processes provide some understanding of the problems that result from the

Drive reduction. The grid in the Skinner box can be electrified for experiments in shock avoidance.

DRUGS AND BEHAVIOR

The comprehensive article DRUGS AND BEHAVIOR surveys the kinds of psychopharmacologic agents, their effects, their uses in therapy, and their possible abuses leading to dependence or addiction. Other articles fill in details on aspects of this major topic.

For example, the action of stimulants such as the amphetamines involves the normally present neurotransmitter norepinephrine. See AUTONOMIC NERVOUS SYSTEM.

The very ancient and widely enjoyed and abused drug alcohol is discussed in ALCOHOLISM, with additional notes in ALCOHOLICS ANONYMOUS and ANTABUSE THERAPY.

The importance of chemotherapy—using drugs to treat mental disorders—is pointed out in the treatment sections of PSYCHOTIC DISORDERS, SCHIZOPHRENIA, PARANOIA, MANIC-DEPRESSIVE PSYCHOSIS, and PSYCHONEUROTIC DISORDERS.

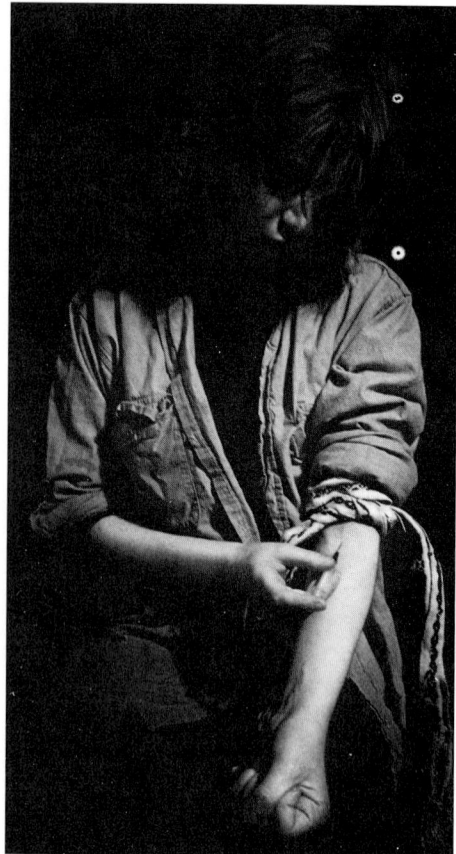

Although the effects of behavior-altering drugs can be described, the biochemical or physiological basis of their action is poorly understood. Above, a model simulating drug injection.

social misuse of psychopharmacological agents.

Sedative-Hypnotics. These drugs produce a state of behavioral depression that correlates with drug-induced depression of chemical transmission (synaptic transmission) between nerve cells in the brain, especially in that part of the brainstem that mediates wakefulness (the reticular formation). At low doses, all sedative-hypnotic drugs produce a state of drowsiness, with some behavioral excitation and loss of inhibition. This progresses as the dosage is increased to behavioral sedation, hypnosis (sleep), anesthesia, coma, and eventual death from depression of respiratory control centers in the brainstem.

Therapeutically, the sedative-hypnotic compounds are used for induction and/or maintenance of general anesthesia (barbiturates and volatile or gaseous anesthetics), induction of sleep (barbiturates and nonbarbiturate hypnotics), relief from anxiety (antianxiety agents), prevention of epileptic seizures (barbiturates), and recreationally to induce a state of disinhibition (alcohol). It is important to note that sedative-hypnotic compounds do not alleviate pain and, in fact, may lead to delirium by dulling consciousness without specifically blocking the transmission of pain. Sedatives, however, may relieve anxiety and alleviate muscle spasms, thus potentiating the effect of other analgesic drugs.

With all of these sedative-hypnotic compounds, *tolerance* (a condition in which the response to a certain dose of a drug decreases with repeated use), *physical dependence* (characterized by withdrawal symptoms when administration of the drug is stopped), and *psychological dependence* (a compulsion to use the drug for a pleasurable or otherwise enjoyable effect) occur. Tolerance of and dependence on these compounds are in some respects similar to opiate narcotic dependence, although barbiturate (and alcohol) withdrawal symptoms are frequently more severe and (unlike the opiates) may result in convulsions and death. Since all sedative-hypnotic compounds are similar in their effects on brain function and behavior, the effects of any two compounds are additive with each other, and a remarkable degree of *cross-tolerance* (a condition where tolerance developed to one drug results in a lessened response to another drug) and *cross-dependence* (a condition in which one drug can prevent the withdrawal symptoms associated with physical dependence on a different drug) are exhibited. Thus, any drug in this class can substitute for any other compound in it.

All compounds classified as sedative-hypnotics are highly liable to compulsive abuse. Indeed, they combine to form the most widely used psychoactive drugs in our society and are the causes of tens of thousands of

accidental or intentional deaths annually in the United States. For example, 400 tons of barbiturates are produced annually in the United States, and approximately 3,000 deaths occur because of overdosage. Damage by alcohol to the brain, liver, and other tissues is the cause of death in 12,000 Americans yearly, 50 percent of our highway deaths involve alcohol, and alcohol intoxication is a factor in 70 percent of homicides. There are an estimated 70 million users of alcohol in the United States, 7 to 10 million of whom are classified as chronic alcoholics. Similarly, over $750 million is spent annually merely on the promotion of antianxiety agents to the 180,000 physicians in the United States. The extent of misuse of these agents has not been calculated but is presumed to be high.

Stimulants. The amphetamines and cocaine are generally classified as *CNS* (central nervous system), *psychic, psychomotor,* or *behavioral stimulants.* These compounds elevate mood, induce euphoria, increase alertness, reduce fatigue, and, in high doses, produce irritability, anxiety, and a pattern of psychotic behavior.

At low doses, *amphetamines* evoke an alerting, arousal, or activating response not unlike one's normal reaction to emergency or stress. This latter response is not surprising, since amphetamines closely resemble in structure one of the brain's normal neurotransmitter substances, *norepinephrine (NE)*. Indeed, the behavioral actions of amphetamine and cocaine result from the ability of both compounds to mimic or potentiate the action of NE in the brain.

The *clinical antidepressants,* although structurally unlike amphetamine or NE, have a similar ability to elevate mood (only in depressed patients, not in normal patients or animals). This is apparently secondary to augmentation of the effect of NE at the synapse.

Because the common denominator of these stimulant agents is an action on NE nerve cells, resulting in potentiation of the synaptic effect of NE, a specific role of NE with regard to emotional behavior has been proposed. The *NE theory of affective disorders* states that, in general, behavioral depression may be related to a deficiency of NE, while mania results from excessive NE. In other words, NE is identified as the chemical mediator responsible for maintaining one on a continuum with mania and depression at the extremes and "normalcy" in the middle:

Behavioral State
Depression — Normal — Stimulation — Mania

NE Levels
Deficient — Normal — Slight Excess — Great Excess

Thus, agents that potentiate, augment, or otherwise increase NE activity (amphetamine, cocaine, clinical antidepressants) result in varying degrees of behavioral stimulation, depending on the concentration of NE at the synapse. Conversely, agents that deplete NE (reserpine) induce a serious depressed state and even suicide attempts in man. More recently, the effectiveness of lithium in the treatment of the manic phase of manic-depressive psychosis has been proposed to result from removal of NE from its site of action, as would be predicted according to this NE hypothesis.

Therapeutically, amphetamines are useful in the treatment of narcolepsy (a disorder characterized by sudden attacks of weakness and sleep) and of hyperkinetic children. This latter use has been subjected to increasing controversy: many experts feel that amphetamines and methylphenidate (Ritalin) are being used indiscriminately and argue that this misuse serves to introduce youngsters into the drug culture at an early age. As a diet aid, amphetamines are largely ineffective; their appetite-suppressing action usually disappears within about two weeks unless the dose is continuously increased. Amphetamines are widely used and misused to achieve a heightened degree of mental alertness. But such increases are usually accompanied by agitation and anxiety, loss of sleep, and depression upon withdrawal. Because of this agitation, the amphetamines are of little use in the treatment of severe depression. The clinical antidepressants, however, have limited use in the treatment of emotional depression, although electroconvulsive therapy appears to be more effective in cases of severe depression.

It appears that little if any physical dependence on either amphetamine or cocaine develops although fatigue, profound sleep, brain-wave (EEG) changes, lethargy, and emotional depression may be observed upon withdrawal. Tolerance of cocaine does not occur, but the tolerance of amphetamines that develops becomes marked, often reaching daily doses of thousands of milligrams intravenously. The potential for psychological dependence on both compounds is quite high. Tolerance and dependence do not appear to be problematic with the clinical antidepressants.

The other stimulants (caffeine, nicotine, and the convulsants) do not appear to exert a primary action on the NE system, and the behavioral effects of these agents are not thought to involve the continuum from depression through mania. These latter compounds are less selective in their action: their general stimulation of cerebral cortex, brainstem, and/or spinal cord results in increases in behavioral excitation.

Opiate Narcotics. Medically defined, the term "narcotic" refers only to drugs having both a sedative and an *analgesic* (pain-reliev-ing) *action* and is essentially restricted to the opiates and opiatelike drugs. The opiates are primarily used for the relief of pain, the treatment of diarrhea (due to a constricting action on the intestine), and the relief of a cough. Many opiatelike agents have been synthesized in attempts to duplicate the therapeutic usefulness of morphine and codeine and avoid the dependence liabilities associated with the opiates. In general, these attempts have proved unsuccessful.

The psychological effects of the opiates include euphoria or dysphoria (a sense of ill-being), nausea, drowsiness, dizziness, inability to concentrate, apathy, and lethargy. Higher doses produce a turning inward and sleep. Often a pleasant dreamlike state occurs. The analgesic effect does not result from a decreased input of painful impulses to the brain but from altered psychological reactions to the impulse: pain is still felt but it is not appreciated as being a negative or painful input. In addition to relieving the anxiety of pain (and therefore the motivation to avoid it), the opiate narcotics tend to decrease other primary motivations associated with sex, food, and aggression.

In chronic use of the opiates, considerable tolerance of the sedative, analgesic, euphoric, and respiratory-depressant (potentially lethal) effects develops, but there is less tolerance of the constipating and pupil-constricting effects. Cross-tolerance exists among all the opiates. Occasional use of opiates produces little or no tolerance.

The extent of physical dependence induced by these agents is closely related to the extent of tolerance developed. An individual who has developed little or no tolerance of the opiates (infrequent use) will exhibit little dependence, and withdrawal symptoms may be absent or resemble those symptoms of a mild flu. Withdrawal of the opiates after chronic high dosages, however, is followed by a severe and painful (although not life-threatening) pattern of responses ("cold turkey"), which persists for about one week. Psychological dependence on the opiates is great and appears to be more difficult to treat than either tolerance or physical dependence. Before a user may be permanently withdrawn from the opiates, his underlying motivations for seeking the drug's positive reinforcing or reward potential must be satisfied through other nonpharmacological means.

Thus, the opiates are not attractive or euphoric in themselves. The danger of physical and/or psychological dependence resides in the person, not in the drug. Hence, the treatment of the opiate user should not focus solely on efforts to withdraw the user from the drug but also attempt to remove the positive reinforcements associated with opiate use (euphoria and use of the needle). Methadone (an

---

Classification of Psychopharmacologic Agents

1. **SEDATIVE-HYPNOTICS**

   Barbiturates
       Phenobarbital
       Pentobarbital (*Nembutal)
       Secobarbital (*Seconal)
       Thiopental (*Pentothal)
   Nonbarbiturate Hypnotics
       Glutethimide (*Doriden)
   Antianxiety Agents
       Meprobamate (*Miltown, *Equanil)
       Chlordiazepoxide (*Librium)
       Diazepam (*Valium)
   Others
       Ethyl alcohol, bromides, paraldehyde, chloral hydrate, volatile and gaseous anesthetics (ether, halothane, methoxyflurane)

2. **STIMULANTS**

   Amphetamines (*Benzedrine, *Dexedrine, *Methedrine)
   Clinical Antidepressants
       Monoamine oxidase (MAO) inhibitors, (*Parnate, *Nardil)
       Trycyclic Antidepressants (*Tofranil, *Elavil)
   Cocaine
   Convulsanta (strychnine, *Metrazol, picrotoxin)
   Caffeine
   Nicotine

3. **OPIATE NARCOTICS (OPIATE ANALGESICS)**

   Opium, heroin, morphine, codeine, synthetic opiate derivatives, i.e. *Demerol, methadone

4. **ANTIPSYCHOTIC AGENTS**

   Phenothiazines (chlorpromazine)
   Reserpine (*Serpasil)
   Butyrophenones (haloperidol)
   Lithium

5. **PSYCHEDELICS & HALLUCINOGENS**

   LSD (lysergic acid diethylamide)
   Mescaline
   Psilocybin
   Substituted amphetamines (DMT, DET, DOM, STP, MDA, MMDA)
   Phencyclidine (*Sernyl)
   Cannabis (marijuana, hashish, and tetrahydrocannabinol)

* Trade Name

Mixed reactions greet a campaign to legalize the possession and use of marijuana.

U.S. CIVILIAN NARCOTICS ADDICTS*

1970	
Total	68,864
Age: average 30.6	
Under 21	5,714
21-30	35,542
31-40	19,311
41 and over	8,297
Race:	
White	35,275
Black	33,348
Other	241
Sex:	
Male	58,445
Female	10,419
Drug used:	
Heroin	66,040
Morphine	697
Other	2,127

*Compiled from reports voluntarily reported to Bureau of Narcotics and Dangerous Drugs by police or hospital authorities. Does not include estimated 60,000 addicts in armed forces.

opiate narcotic that is administered orally and produces little or no euphoria) combined with extensive psychological counseling may prove to be an effective method of treatment. Hopefully, once positive reinforcements are found outside the use of opiates, the methadone can be withdrawn.

Antipsychotic Agents. The treatment of psychiatric disorders entered a new era in the mid-1950s with the introduction of the phenothiazines (chlorpromazine) and reserpine into medicine. Chlorpromazine, which originated in France, improves mood and behavior in psychotic patients by inducing an indifference to external stimuli and a reduction of initiative and anxiety without requiring excessive sedation and without causing dependence or tolerance. In addition to its antipsychotic action, chlorpromazine is a potent antiemetic used in the treatment of nausea and vomiting; it also possesses antihistamic properties and is useful in the treatment of severe itching. In the laboratory, chlorpromazine decreases hostility and impairs conditioned response behavior—actions that correlate with the drug's antipsychotic action in humans.

In agreement with the NE theory of affective disorders, chlorpromazine is thought to block access of NE to its receptors in the brain. In general, the phenothiazines are remarkedly safe agents, with incidents of side effects placed as low as 3 percent. Potentially serious side effects include blood dyscrasias (1 in 10,000 patients), liver jaundice, and allergic skin rashes. To repeat, tolerance and dependency do not appear to be therapeutic problems.

Reserpine (Serpasil) was introduced into medicine concurrently with chlorpromazine. This agent induces an antipsychotic effect that correlates with a drug-induced depletion of NE in the central nervous system, as would be predicted by the NE hypothesis. Therapeutically, reserpine induces a number of troublesome side effects (including mental depression), hence it is currently established only as a substitute for chlorpromazine in those few patients who cannot tolerate the phenothiazines.

In 1967, haloperidol (a butyrophenone) was introduced into the United States as the prototype of a new class of antipsychotic agents. Its behavioral action is similar to that of chlorpromazine. The biochemical basis of the antipsychotic action of haloperidol has not been determined.

More recently, lithium has been introduced into the treatment of mania. As mentioned earlier, this agent appears to remove NE from its site of action in the brain. However, since no available animal model of behavior correlates with the human manic-depressive state, the action responsible for lithium's therapeutic usefulness is unclear.

Despite their behavioral effects, the antipsychotic drugs are rarely used nonmedically. They have served as powerful tools, contributing to our knowledge of the physiological and biochemical basis of psychology.

Psychedelics and Hallucinogens. Psychoactive agents have been used by man for centuries. Mescaline (from the peyote cactus), psilocybin (from Mexican mushrooms), morning glory seeds, marijuana (from *Cannabis sativa*), DMT and DET (dimethyl- and diethyltryptamine) all were included in various sacramental rites and in some instances were even considered divine. More recently, such synthetic compounds as LSD and phencyclidine and the synthetic amphetamine derivatives have been introduced. Only since 1960 have these agents received general public attention.

To date, although behavioral and psychological responses to these agents have been described in both animals and man, little is known of the underlying physiological basis of their action. Currently it is the thought that the hallucinogenic effect of LSD is secondary to an action on brain serotonin (a neurotransmitter localized in the raphe nuclei and apparently involved in emotional activity, including sensory perception). Aside from its well-known psychological effects, however, the physiological effects of LSD are few (widened pupils, hyperreflexia, muscular incoordination, increased heart rate and blood pressure) and seldom serious. The possibility that deformities may occur in the offspring of pregnant women taking high doses of LSD has not been eliminated.

Tolerance to LSD develops on repeated use, but physical dependence does not develop. Psychological dependence may occur in individuals who become preoccupied with the drug. Because use of the drug is usually intermittent, however, psychological dependence is not considered a serious problem. There is currently no authorized medical use of LSD, although many efforts have been made to establish its role as an adjunct to psychotherapy. Carefully controlled studies have not substantiated the early claims of merit.

Mescaline, peyote, and the other naturally occurring psychedelic agents (morning glory seeds, nutmeg) and synthetic psychedelics (substituted amphetamines) produce syndromes similar to LSD but considerably less severe.

Marijuana is the least potent of the psychedelic agents. At low to moderate doses it is a mild sedative-hypnotic that resembles alcohol and the antianxiety agents in its physiological and psychological effects. Unlike the sedatives, however, high doses of marijuana may produce effects similar to a mild LSD experience. Also unlike the sedatives, high doses of marijuana are not lethal. Since no cross-tolerance occurs between LSD and marijuana, the two compounds are necessarily different in their mechanism of action.

Recent reports indicate that a mild tolerance can develop to marijuana, but physical dependence has not been demonstrated. Some degree of psychological dependence may develop, but it is not considered serious. It has now been amply demonstrated that marijuana does not itself lead to the use of more powerful drugs, does not increase hostility or aggression or increase crime, and does not cause mental or physical deterioration, although loss of motivation and impairment of driving skills may be observed. Medically, marijuana has been claimed to possess antianxiety, antidepressant, antiepileptic, analgesic, and appetite-stimulating effects. To date, however, these claims remain largely unsubstantiated.

In this brief discussion no mention has been made of the effect of drugs on learning and memory. The topic is extensive and complicated, and introductions to it can be found in the Bibliography (see *Consult* list below).

Furthermore, no mention has been made of the anticholinesterase or anticholinergic agents (atropine, scopolamine, and DFP). Acetylcholine is a neurotransmitter that appears to be involved in the inhibition of behavior. Impairment of this system leads to nightmares, confusion, amnesia, hallucinations, and slowing of intellectual and motor processes.

Many other examples of drug effects on behavior could be given. However, this review has introduced the concept that a great variety of pharmacologically active agents may alter behavioral performance both in animals and in man. These alterations occur subsequent to changes in physiological and biochemical equilibria in the brain.

—Robert M. Julien, *California College of Medicine, University of California, Irvine*

Consult (13) Cooper, *et al.*, 1970; Goth, 1972; Interim Report of the Commission of Inquiry into the Non-medical Uses of Drugs, 1970; Lennard, *et al.*, 1971; Rech and Moore, 1971.

DRUGS IN THERAPY (chemotherapy). *See* Drugs and Behavior; Manic-Depressive Psychosis; Schizophrenia.

DUAL PERSONALITY. *See* Multiple Personality.

DYNAMIC PSYCHOLOGY, the orientation of those psychologists who have not been content to study consciousness alone and who are interested in what is sometimes called human nature. They do not form a school and have no leader or founder. Rather, they are a loose band of experts who regard motivation as the most important aspect of man.

Included in this broad grouping are psychoanalysts who, following Freud, provided its basis. Also included are psychologists such as McDougall, Tolman, Lewin, and Woodworth.

—Thom Herrmann, *University of Tennessee*

DYNAMISM, a mode of behavior also called a defense mechanism, adjustment device, ego defense reaction, or coping mechanism. *See* Defense Mechanism.

DYSGRAPHIA. *See* Aphasia.

DYSLEXIA. *See* Reading Disability.

DYSPHASIA. *See* Aphasia.

DYSSOCIAL REACTION, a form of sociopathic behavior. *See* Personality Disorders.

EARLY EXPERIENCE. *See* Child Development; Cognitive Development Theory; Developmental Psychology.

EBBINGHAUS, HERMANN (1850–1909), German experimental psychologist. Born in Germany, he took his Ph.D. in 1873 at the University of Bonn, in philosophy.

The scientific study of verbal learning and memory begins with Ebbinghaus, whose methods and principles are still used today. The major portions of his contribution are contained in a single short volume, *On Memory* (1885), a work that is probably the single most-often-cited sourcebook in the history of psychology.

Impressed with Gustav Fechner's use of psychophysical methods to study perception and sensation, Ebbinghaus embarked on a long series of systematic studies of memory, using himself as the sole subject and experimenter. He invented nonsense syllables, such as "myk," "fim," and "zap," which minimized the effects of previously formed associations attached to ordinary words and made the task of memorizing practically the same for all subjects. Over a period of years Ebbinghaus memorized countless nonsense syllables and then tested himself for recall at various lengths of time following original learning.

During his research Ebbinghaus obtained many important findings, often for the first time in psychology. He plotted some of the earliest *learning and forgetting curves,* which show that the greatest memory loss occurs immediately after initial learning. He made early measurements of *memory span* or *immediate memory,* showing that a subject could typically recall about six to eight items after one look. He demonstrated that meaningful materials (words and sentences) could be learned much faster and retained much longer than nonsense materials. He showed that, ev-

An educational psychologist, attempting to develop a new instructional strategy, works with a child with a learning disability.

erything else being equal, spaced practice tended to produce faster learning and better recall than massed practice. But his greatest contributions were the methods he used, both for learning and for measuring recall.

Appreciated in his own time, Ebbinghaus also helped found the first German psychology journal (1890), devised one of the earliest sentence-completion tests, and wrote a highly successful textbook, *Foundations of Psychology* (1902).

—Roland Siiter, *Montclair State College*
See also Associationism; Forgetting; Language; Meaningfulness; Memory; Paired-Associate Learning; Serial Learning.

ECOLOGICAL NICHE. *See* Behavioral Ecology.

ECOLOGY, HUMAN. *See* Behavioral Ecology.

ECTOMORPH. *See* Constitutional Types.

EDUCABLE MENTALLY RETARDED. *See* Mental Retardation.

EDUCATIONAL PSYCHOLOGY, the discipline concerned with the study of the learner, the learning process, and instructional strategies as interactive aspects of education. It involves the systematic analysis of the dynamics of pupil behavior, characteristics of effective teaching, and the psychological atmosphere of the classroom. Some specific objectives of educational psychology include application of principles of psychology to the educational process; improvement of the teaching-learning processes by initiating research and experimentation designed to contribute to the body of knowledge of these processes as well as to provide new methods and techniques with which to implement them; development of new theories and models that integrate pupil behavior and instructional strategies into potential exemplary programs and innovative curriculum developments.

Educational psychologists typically serve as members of instructional and research staffs at teacher training institutions, in psychology departments, or in educational research bureaus. Primary professional concerns and areas of research interests include teacher training, learning theory, innovations in instructional strategies, and the development of learning aids.

Specific subject matter areas traditionally taught in educational psychology courses include *the child and his development* (for example, growth processes and patterns, cognitive development, socialization processes), *the learning process* (for example, forms or types of learning, hierarchies of learning activities, learning and motivation, effective instructional procedures), *evaluating pupil growth* (for example, the measurement-evaluation process, techniques of assessing pupil learning and achievement and behavioral outcomes, diagnosis and recognition of individual differences, identification and remediation of learning problems), and *mental health in the classroom* (for example, personality integration, dealing with adjustment problems of the learner, teacher-pupil relations). In studying these areas, the prospective teacher is assumed to acquire information and skills he will need to deal with various classroom situations and to cope with trait differences among children.

During recent years there has been a trend toward more "humanistic" approaches to educational psychology. These focus on the "total child" and tend to place greater emphasis on increasing the teacher trainee's awareness of and sensitivity to the learner's affective or emotional needs while providing knowledge related to cognitive processes.

Major textbooks in the field are listed in the Bibliography. Professional journals include *Journal of Educational Psychology, Educational Psychologist, Educational Researcher, Review of Educational Research,* and *American Educational Research Journal.* Division 15 of the American Psychological Association is the Division of Educational Psychology.

—Frank T. Vitro, *University of Maine*
See also Child Development; Cognitive Development Theory; Gifted Children; Intelligence and Intelligence Testing; Measurement; Programmed Learning; Reading Disability; School Psychology; Slow Learner.
Consult (14) Cronbach, 1954; De Cecco, 1968; Klausmier and Ripple, 1971; McDonald, 1965.

EEG WAVES, electrical activity of the brain as measured by the electroencephalogram. *See* Brain Waves.

EFFECTORS, the output organs that the nervous system supplies. These may be subdivided into two main classes, somatic and autonomic. *Somatic* effectors supply the striated musculature of the body, which is responsible for powerful motor movements. The muscles of the arm and back, for example, are striated muscles. The *autonomic* effectors consist of the smooth muscles, such as the iris of the eye or the muscles that lie within the walls of blood vessels and glands.

The origin of the somatic effector system is the *ventral horn cell,* a large neuron located in the ventral portion of the gray matter of the spinal cord. Axons of ventral horn cells exit through the ventral roots of spinal nerves and are distributed to all portions of the body musculature.

The autonomic effector system originates in the lateral portion of the gray matter of the spinal cord. These fibers also exit via the ventral root but pass through a ganglion located outside of the spinal cord. After synapsing in this ganglion, these fibers are distributed to glands and smooth muscles.

The smooth muscles play an important role in such functions as maintaining the vasomotor tone of blood vessel walls. Changes in the diameter of blood vessels play a role in blood pressure regulation. Secretory functions controlled by autonomic effectors include the secretion of sweat from sweat glands and the control of many internal secretions, such as the release of epinephrine from the adrenal medulla.

—Joel F. Lubar, *University of Tennessee*
See also Autonomic Nervous System.
Consult (3) Isaacson, *et al.,* 1971; Jacob and Francone, 1970.

EGO. The term *ego* is used with differing meanings by various theorists. Derived from the Latin word for "I," the word generally designates the individual person as the center of all his psychological activities and characteristics. Many writers distinguish between ego as the executive functions and organizational processes of personality, while "self" designates the individual's conception of his personal identity and characteristics. The most detailed theory of ego characteristics and development comes from psychoanalysis. Freud's early ideas are suggested by his concepts of ego-defensive resistance and repression (1895) and of the reality principle (1911). Not until 1923, however, in *The Ego and the Id,* did he explicitly formulate the concept. Freud held that the id, the hypothetical source of biological drives and impulses, operated according to the pleasure principle seeking immediate gratification. Inevitable frustrations of the id, together with what the child learns from his encounters with external reality, generate the ego, which operates according to the reality principle to minimize frustration of biological drives in the long run.

According to Freud, ego processes have both conscious and unconscious aspects, and they include sensory perception, thinking, memory, and voluntary motor controls. The ego's function is to find ways to satisfy biological id drives in the real world within limitations imposed by the superego, or conscience, so as to relieve tensions without incurring guilt. Generally discharge of an impulse is simply postponed to a suitable situation; but when impulses cannot be discharged directly the ego utilizes various unconscious defense mechanisms to avoid anxiety and protect itself from conflict.

Freud held that the ego had no energy of its own, its dynamics originating in the id. But later psychoanalysts of the *ego-psychology*

school (for example, Anna Freud, Heinz Hartmann, David Rapaport, Erik Erikson) have argued for *autonomous ego functions* as adaptive capacities present from birth and not necessarily developed solely to avoid psychic conflict.

Representing the set of active organizational processes concerned with realistic perception, effective functioning, and personal integration, the concept of ego is central in most dynamic formulations of personality.

—Alden E. Wessman, *The City College of The City University of New York*
See also Id; Psychoanalysis; Superego.
Consult (13) Freud, Anna, 1937; Freud, Sigmund, 1933; Munroe, 1955; Symonds, 1951.

EIDETIC IMAGERY, the technical term for what is commonly called "photographic memory." Such thinking occurs in a small percentage of the population and is almost entirely limited to children. The capacity is usually lost with the onset of puberty. The individual with eidetic imagery can totally recall a visual field. For example, if a complex picture containing people, trees, buildings, and many different colors is presented to an eidetic child for several minutes, he will be able to recall any part of the scene with perfect clarity and accuracy. If questioned, he may describe the exact relationship between people and buildings. Another simple test for eidetic imagery is to write a long word on the blackboard, then erase the word, and ask people to quickly spell the word backward. The eidetic subject does this perfectly, while the individual who does not possess this ability haltingly tries to reconstruct the sequence again and again. If questioned, the eidetic reports that he sees the word projected in front of him and is simply reading it off backward.

Eidetic imagery is highly selective but is not due to persistent visual afterimages. If it were, eidetics would be plagued by visual fields filled with overlapping projections of literally thousands of images.

—Joel F. Lubar, *University of Tennessee*
See also Memory.

ELECTRA COMPLEX, in psychoanalytic theory, the unconscious incestuous desire of the daughter for her father, accompanied by animosity toward the mother. The name is taken from a figure in Greek legend and literature. Electra was strongly attached to her father, Agamemnon, and plotted to avenge his death at the hands of her mother, Clytemnestra. The Electra complex is analogous to the Oedipus complex in males, and the problem is usually discussed under that title. *See* Oedipus Complex.

ELECTRICAL STIMULATION OF THE BRAIN. In

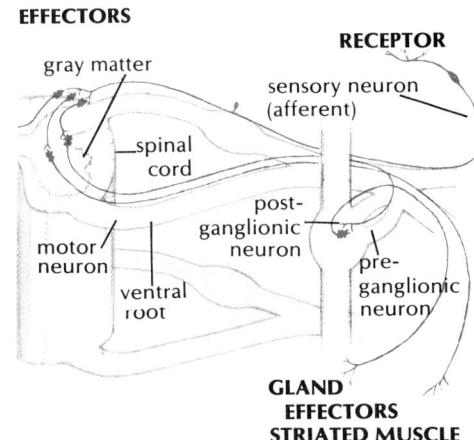

EFFECTORS

RECEPTOR

gray matter

sensory neuron (afferent)

spinal cord

post-ganglionic neuron

motor neuron

pre-ganglionic neuron

ventral root

GLAND EFFECTORS STRIATED MUSCLE

this procedure very tiny wires (electrodes) are implanted in different brain regions, and weak currents, which mimic impulses flowing through neural pathways, are introduced through them.

Electrical stimulation has been carried out in humans during brain surgery. Although the patients remain awake and alert, they are prevented discomfort by means of local anesthetics.

Electrical stimulation of the human visual cortex leads to visual sensations, such as flashes of light and colors. Stimulation of the auditory cortex will yield sound sensations; and stimulation of the motor cortex can elicit arm, leg, or other body movements.

Occasionally, stimulation of regions designated as "association areas" will yield complex perceptions, such as the recall of memory sequences or vivid scenes that the subject has once experienced. It appears that the association areas act to integrate material from the many sensory and motor regions and to aid in the interpretation of stimuli.

In animals, electrical stimulation of the brain has been used to map connections from one brain region to another. Stimulation of motor regions will elicit movements; stimulation in the hypothalamus might lead to attack, defensive acts, or other emotional responses. Stimulation of other regions, such as the reticular formation in the brainstem, can put the subject to sleep.

One of the most interesting findings about electrical stimulation of the brain is that stimulation applied to certain cerebral areas is rewarding for the subject. As a result of work by Olds and Milner at McGill University, this interesting fact was put to use in their studies of electrical self-stimulation. Rats were allowed to stimulate their own brains by pressing a lever that was connected to a switch that activated a stimulator circuit. If the area of the brain being stimulated resulted in a sensation that was rewarding to the animal, it continued to stimulate. Rats have been known to stimulate their own brains as much as 8,000 times in one hour. If, on the other hand, the stimulation led to unpleasant effects, the rat immediately stopped pressing; it might even attempt to turn off a stimulator that had been turned on by the experimenter.

—Joel F. Lubar, *University of Tennessee*
See also Chemical Stimulation of the Brain.

Consult (3) Olds, 1958; Olds and Milner, 1954; Teitelbaum, 1967.

ELECTROENCEPHALOGRAM (EEG), the record of electrical activity in the brain. Electrodes are attached to the scalp or to the brain if part of it is exposed. Changes in electric potential are amplified so that they produce wavelike trac-

Electroconvulsive therapy being administered to a patient.

ings. Also called electroencephalograph. *See* Brain Waves; Sleep and Dreams.

ELECTRO-OCULOGRAM (EOG), a graphic record of eye movements, used in studying stages of sleep and dreaming. *See* Sleep and Dreams.

ELECTROCONVULSIVE THERAPY. ECT (also called electroshock therapy) has been a major procedure in the treatment of specially selected mental patients since its introduction in 1933. The treatment consists of applying a rectified current of 110 volts but 20–30 milliamps to the temperofrontal region of the brain until there is evidence of a grand mal seizure. The first stage of the seizure is a *tonic contraction* of the body, most often evidenced by curling of the toes. The second, or *clonic phase,* follows. As soon as it ends, resuscitation is facilitated by administration of oxygen. As respiration is restored, consciousness returns.

Patients are usually drowsy after treatment and sleep for a short while. After awakening, there is a period of temporary confusion. Most memory is gradually recovered during the ensuing twenty-four hours.

With progressive treatment, the period of confusion between treatments increases. Some feel that cure is related to the development of "organicity." Most memory deficit returns within several months after termination of therapy, but some gaps may remain for an indefinite period.

While many methods have been devised for applying the current to the brain, the most successful appears to be bilateral use of electrodes on the temperofrontal region. The intensity of muscular reaction is controlled by intravenous application of a muscle relaxant immediately prior to treatment. Because of the marked anxiety caused as throat muscles contract and respiration ceases (the result of a curarelike effect), an ultra short-acting barbiturate is simultaneously administered. Current is applied as soon as the patient falls asleep.

Applications. ECT is the treatment of choice for severely depressed patients where there is a marked suicidal risk, since it rapidly produces amelioration of symptoms in more than 80 percent of cases. When depression is not as severe, other treatment modalities, such as antidepressant drugs, may first be given a trial. Shock treatment is also used as a life-saving measure when there is exhaustion secondary to markedly overactive behavior, either with an elevated mood (mania) or with bizarre motor patterns (catatonia). It is also useful in the treatment of acute delusional psychoses, since it may break the pattern of thinking before the delusions become firmly fixed. It has a limited use in the treatment of neurotic patients.

There are few contraindications to ECT.

In the physically healthy person there is a low mortality rate and, since the introduction of muscle relaxants, minimal likelihood of fracture. At times it is necessary to treat patients who have had myocardial infarction or congestive heart failure. These, too, are usually successfully treated.

Treatments are usually given several times a week but may take place several times a day if necessary to control a hyperactive patient. While the number of treatments in a series depends to a large extent upon the patient's responsiveness, it is possible that marked improvement may follow the first or second session. Quite often six to eight treatments are necessary to prevent an early relapse. In schizophrenia the series is usually longer, extending to fifteen or twenty treatments. Some patients also require supportive treatments in order to prevent the return of more serious pathology.

—Edwin Robbins. M.D., *New York University Medical Center*
Consult (13) Kalinowsky, 1967; Kalinowsky and Hippius, 1969; Sargent and Slater, 1963; Stern and Robbins, 1973.

ELECTROSHOCK THERAPY. *See* Electroconvulsive Therapy.

ELIMINATION DRIVES. Although the removal of bodily waste through urination and defecation is clearly defined biologically, these simple and basic processes have unfortunately generated myriad complex and vague theories concerning their psychic import. Some theorists, especially those of the psychoanalytic school, consider infantile experience with these drives a hallmark for psychological development. While evidence indicates that elimination is intimately associated with emotional expression during periods of stress or intense emotionality, it is perhaps best studied in terms of the taboos that the society has imposed on it rather than of the drives themselves.

—Thom Herrmann, *University of Tennessee*
See also Anal Character; Toilet Training.

ELLIS, (HENRY) HAVELOCK (1859–1939), British man of letters. Ellis' most influential writings are the seven volumes of his *Studies in the Psychology of Sex*, published from 1897 to 1928. These books, written from both the biological and the anthropological point of view, did much to promote the scientific study of sex.

He also studied dreams and concluded that the images in dreams might derive from the deeper levels of the mind not apparent when a person is awake; but he also believed that dreams were aroused by sensations from the stomach. A pioneer in studying states of consciousness, Ellis was one of the first researchers to experiment with mescaline, shortly after its isolation in 1888. Ellis is also well known as the editor of the Mermaid Series of Old Dramatists and the Contemporary Science Series.

EMOTION. There is today no satisfactorily precise definition of "emotion," although the term has been widely employed by psychologists since the late nineteenth century. The concept was not a technical label invented by psychologists but has been employed since ancient times. The Latin *emovere* means to stir up, to excite, to agitate. At least for as long as recorded history, man has recognized in himself and in others such reactions as depression, fear, anger, delight, love, and jealousy, and there has been agreement that these reactions are examples of emotion. There has also been agreement that emotions involve a subjective awareness of feelings, a high probability of changes in overt behavior, and physiological changes.

The belief has persisted that some generalized process called emotion underlies fear, rage, joy, and other reactions. This notion of a single underlying process called emotion fitted easily into the style of thinking of the founders of modern experimental psychology during the nineteenth and early twentieth centuries, when phenomena were categorized into such concepts as cognition, perception, and memory. The difficulties in formulating a precise definition of emotion, however, have caused some psychologists to wonder if it will be fruitful to continue to seek a single unifying process. Nevertheless, investigations in the area are increasing, but the emphasis now is on studying reactions influenced by rather specific states, such as anxiety or rage, or on examining the effects of altering specific sites of the brain and nervous system, such as the reticular formation or the limbic system.

Bodily Changes. The physiological reactions associated with certain emotions are evident in everyday experience. Under certain emotion-provoking stimuli persons may report palpitations of the heart, sensations from the stomach, changes in rate of breathing, sweating, trembling, perhaps even a feeling of being chilled, dryness of the mouth and throat, a marked shift in modulation of the voice, and general muscle tension. There is a positive correlation between the intensity of the emotional experience and the magnitude of the physiological changes.

Emotion appears to be a reaction of the whole organism. In anger, for example, nervous impulses are activated in both the autonomic nervous system and in higher brain centers. The medulla of the adrenal gland, near each kidney, is activated and secretes an in-

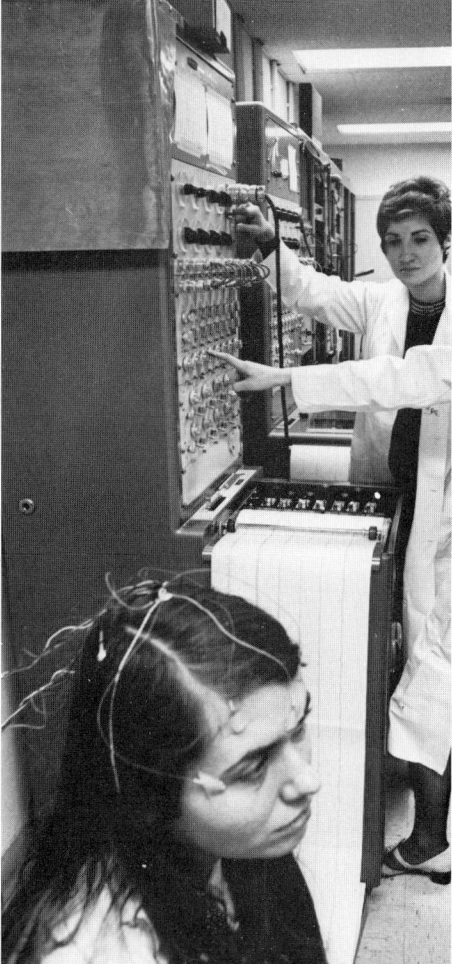

Electroencephalograph electrodes being placed at various sites on the outside of a subject's skull. She is to be placed in an isolation chamber for study of her brain functions during sleep.

EMOTION AND MOTIVATION

Bodily Processes in Emotion

EMOTION
AUTONOMIC NERVOUS SYSTEM
ADRENAL GLANDS
BRAIN
LIMBIC REGION
ELECTRICAL STIMULATION OF THE BRAIN
DRUGS AND BEHAVIOR
LIE DETECTOR

Theories of Emotion

EMOTION
JAMES-LANGE THEORY
    Cannon-Bard Theory
    Neural Activation Hypothesis

Emotional States

EMOTION
ANGER
ANXIETY
FEAR
STRESS
APATHY-INDIFFERENCE
DEPRESSION
TEMPERAMENT
HUMOR
BODY LANGUAGE

Emotional Factors in Functioning and Health

Emotions can serve as useful, adaptive drives—"energies of man." Intense emotional states can also be factors in behavior disorders ranging from depressed moods to the manic-depressive condition that is sometimes called an "affective psychosis." *Affect* is a term for feeling.

EMOTION
PREJUDICE
PSYCHONEUROTIC DISORDERS
ANGER
FEAR
ANXIETY
STRESS
GENERAL ADAPTATION SYNDROME
COMBAT NEUROSIS
REPRESSION
PHOBIA
PSYCHOSOMATIC DISORDERS
HYPERTENSION
EMOTIONALLY UNSTABLE PERSONALITY
SENSITIVITY TRAINING
MANIC-DEPRESSIVE PSYCHOSIS
SCHIZOPHRENIA

Motivating Behavior

DRIVE
    ACHIEVEMENT DRIVE
    ACTIVITY DRIVE
    AFFECTIONAL DRIVE
    AFFILIATIVE DRIVE
    CURIOSITY DRIVE
    ELIMINATION DRIVE
    EXPLORATION DRIVE
    HUNGER DRIVE
    MATERNAL DRIVE
    PAIN DRIVE
    SEX DRIVE
    SLEEP DRIVE
    THIRST DRIVE

Motivation Concepts

AGGRESSION
ANGER
ASPIRATION, LEVEL OF
COMPETITION
CONFORMITY
DEPENDENCE-INDEPENDENCE
DOMINANCE RELATIONSHIP
DRIVE-REDUCTION THEORY
GRADIENT
HOMEOSTASIS
INSTINCT
OPERANT CONDITIONING
PLEASURE PRINCIPLE
SPECIFIC HUNGER
VALENCE

The Subject Maps in the Encyclopedia illustrate the coverage of particular aspects of psychology, showing the interrelationships among the articles in twelve major areas of study. Entries in capital letters are subjects for which there are separate articles in the Encyclopedia. Entries in small letters are cross references.

The Subject Maps appear in the Encyclopedia under the following titles:

Abnormal and Clinical Psychology
Developmental Psychology
Emotion and Motivation
Intelligence
Learning and Memory
Measurement
Personality and Individual Difference
Physiological and Comparative Psychology
Psychology: Divisions and Schools
Sensation and Perception
Social Psychology
Thinking and Language

crease of adrenalin into the bloodstream. When the adrenalized blood reaches the liver, there is a rapid discharge of sugar into the bloodstream, which assists the body in withstanding fatigue and in energy output. Other changes enable the blood to clot more readily and the lungs to increase their capacity for intake of air, and there is an increase in pulse rate and in blood pressure.

A practical application of the use of bodily changes under conditions of stress is demonstrated by the lie detector, which is essentially a polygraph for recording physiological changes under emotion-provoking questioning. The polygraph measures changes in the electrical potential of the skin (GSR), rate of breathing, and pulse rate. A fourth scale indicates time intervals. The subject is asked questions, and the recordings of the effects of the questions on his heart rate, rate of breathing, and GSR are observed. A base line of reactivity is established by asking the subject neutral questions, such as his name, age, address, and educational history. Then questions that are specifically related to some critical incident or crime are asked. The assumption is that a person involved in a crime or critical incident will have a more emotional reaction when questioned about the event than will someone who was not present at it. The test, in actuality, does not measure lying but detects emotional reactions to questions that are related to some critical event under investigation.

The Nervous System. Both the central and the autonomic nervous systems are involved with emotion. Investigators of physiological correlates of emotion have tended to stress the role of the autonomic nervous system in precipitating the involuntary shifts in the rate of functioning of various body organs. More recent interest has focused on determining the role of specific neural structures in emotional reaction. There has been considerable interest in the hypothalamus, thalamus, reticular formation, and limbic system.

Research indicates that there is a reticular activating system that plays an important role in arousal or excitement that occurs under emotion-provoking conditions. The reticular formation, which runs through the center of the brainstem, is interconnected with the thalamus, hypothalamus, and other areas of the brainstem. Data from experimental stimulation and ablation (or removal) suggest that discharges from the reticular formation are projected rather diffusely into the cerebral cortex and maintain wakefulness and alertness.

Intense interest has been focused on the limbic system since a 1954 report that, when electrodes were implanted in the central area of the limbic system of rats, the animals would work to stimulate themselves by pressing a bar

to activate the area. [*Consult* (8) Olds and Milner, 1954; Olds, 1958.] Based on this and other results, this portion of the limbic system became known as the "pleasure center" of the brain. Electrical stimulation of human subjects undergoing brain surgery has yielded reports of highly pleasurable sensations from the central region of the limbic area.

Another researcher, J. I. Lacey, has pointed out that psychologists and physiologists overstress the role of the autonomic nervous system in sending messages to the organs of the body and tend to neglect its role in conveying messages back to the brain and central nervous system. He argues that the effects on brain functioning of these inputs to the brain from the thoracic and abdominal cavities must be considered before there can be an understanding of physiological changes during emotion. Lacey is especially intrigued with the manner in which the heart communicates to the brain. He believes that cardiovascular responses should not be regarded always as signs of arousal or emotion, but may be signals of a physiological attempt to restrain excitatory processes, to limit or to bring an end to what he calls "the turmoil produced inside the body." [*Consult* (8) Lacey, 1967; Lacey and Lacey, 1970.]

Electroencephalographic (EEG) studies of brain-wave patterns have found that under conditions of strong emotional excitement (rage, fear, or intense anxiety), the brain-wave pattern tends to be desynchronized, with low to moderate amplitude and fast, mixed frequencies.

Facial Expressions. Certain patterns of facial expression, such as crying, laughing, and frowning, appear to be unlearned. Those who have been deaf and blind since birth display such basic facial expressions. The startle pattern also has been found to be universal, the most persistent reaction being a closing of the eyes and a widening of the mouth, as in a grin. There are also social-cultural factors: the Chinese register surprise by sticking out their tongues, whereas most Americans raise their eyebrows and widely open their eyes. Judges can reliably categorize photographs of facial emotional expressions as reflecting pleasantness-unpleasantness, acceptance-rejection, and certainty-uncertainty. [*Consult* (8) Schlosberg, 1952; Frijda, 1969.]

Research Methods. The search for the mechanisms that underlie emotion has attracted investigators from a wide variety of fields. Physiological psychologists may implant electrodes into various brain structures of animals and study the effect of intracranial stimulation on behavior, employ ablation and destroy certain neural sites, or inject certain chemical substances into the bloodstream and observe whether emotional response occurs, is

Emotion. Certain patterns of facial expression, such as on the faces of these angry men, appear to be unlearned.

intensified, or is diminished. Other psychologists study human subjects in the laboratory under carefully controlled stimulations to ascertain the effects on their EEG, PGR, respiration, blood pressure, heart rate, and ability to perform a mental task; they may also ask the subjects to report subjective feelings during the experiment.

Theories. There has been controversy about an acceptable theory of emotion. The James-Lange theory, formulated independently by William James (1884) and the Danish physiologist C. G. Lange (1885), proposed that the perception of an emotional stimulus leads reflexedly to visceral reactions and muscular responses and that the feedback of these bodily responses to the brain is the experience of emotion. In other words, the emotional experience is a consequence, not the antecedent, of the visceral and muscular reactions. In a literal sense, we are frightened because we run; one first has the bodily changes and emotion is the feeling of these changes as they occur. [*Consult* (8) James, 1884.]

W. B. Cannon claimed that his work showed that visceral reactions are too diffuse to provide for the various distinctive emotions, and in 1927 he formulated his theory that emotional experience depended upon release of impulses from the thalamus into the cerebral cortex as well as to body organs and muscles. [*Consult* (8) Cannon, 1927; Cannon, 1931.] Bard in 1934 elaborated on this theory. Decortication studies have since refuted the Cannon-Bard theory, because complete removal of the thalamus has no effect upon rage patterns of animals. [*Consult* (8) Bard, 1934.]

A more recent researcher, Donald Lindsley, introduced a neural activation theory of emotion, which holds that the mechanisms of arousal of the reticule-thalamo-cortical systems underlie emotions. Worry and anxiety reflect emotional arousal at the cortical level; weeping and sweating reflect cortical, diencephalic, and brainstem arousal; and facial expression and muscle tension reflect somatomotor arousal. Lindsley stresses that the reticular system must be activated. [*Consult* (8) Lindsley, 1951; Lindsley, 1970.]

A study reported in 1962 showed that the same physiological background produced by a drug (adrenalin), when combined with identical behavior toward those in the experiment by a stooge, resulted in quite different behavior in two groups who had been told to expect different things from the drug injections. The researchers concluded that when the person has no appropriate explanation for his physiological arousal, he will interpret the state in terms of the particular situation in which he finds himself, but when he understands the basis for his physiological arousal he shows no such dependence on the environment.

K. M. B. Bridges and others have concluded that the capacity to communicate emotions follows a developmental sequence. Beginning with generalized emotion in the newborn infant, the ability to communicate distress and delight appears within three months, followed several months later by fear, disgust, and anger and by the end of the first year by elation and affection. Although the capacity to communicate emotions appears to be maturational, the objects that elicit emotions are learned. Studies of children's fears and those of their parents indicate high correlations. [*Consult* (8) Bridges, 1930.]

Emotions are related to mental and physical health. Prolonged or intense emotionality has been found to precipitate a loss of coordination between the sympathetic and parasympathetic nervous systems. In laboratory animals, prolonged emotional stress produces enlargement of the adrenals, stomach ulcers, kidney and heart disorders, circulatory and digestive disturbances, and disruption of hormone balance. [*Consult* (8) Gellhorn, 1943.]

Under emotional stress, Hans Selye found that many organs show involutive or degenerative changes. He described a general adaptation syndrome following stress: an initial alarm reaction is followed by a resistance stage and finally by a stage of exhaustion. [*Consult* (8) Selye, 1953; Selye, 1956.] Others report that some individuals to avoid emotional stress withdraw into isolated passivity, a reaction called emotional insulation.

—Austin E. Grigg, *University of Richmond*

See also Aggression; Anger; Autonomic Nervous System; Fear; James-Lange Theory; Lie Detector; *other articles listed in the Item Guides under* Emotion; Drive; Motives.

Consult (8) Arnold, 1960; Mandler, 1962; Young, 1961.

EMOTIONALLY UNSTABLE PERSONALITY. This term may be applied to at least three different kinds of reaction. It may describe a person who *overreacts* to emotional stimuli. Having failed to develop good inner controls in the process of development, he seems emotionally at the mercy of his momentary environmental situation.

Or it may refer to a tendency to *break down under stress*. The controls that enable the individual to deal adequately with everyday life are apparently not sufficient in a crisis.

Finally, the term may describe the cyclothymic's unpredictable emotional responses, which seem unrelated to real environmental stimuli. Perhaps *overcontrolled*, he tends to be conscientious, outgoing, sociable, energetic, overly self-demanding, and self-critical. In periods of elation he is apparently trying to escape his difficulties in a whirl of activities.

Often life experiences have apparently reinforced a constitutional tendency toward exaggerated mood swings.

—M. G. Affinito, *Southern Connecticut State College*

See also Cyclothymic Personality; Personality Disorders.

EMPATHY, broadly defined, is the ability to appreciate how someone else feels by putting yourself into his position and experiencing his feelings. Empathy, then, is feeling the same way that another person is feeling because you have been in a similar situation previously, because you are very close to the other individual, or because you have developed some special interpersonal skills. Empathic feelings can take any form, but there must be close correspondence between an observer's feelings and those of someone else, and the observer's feelings must be attributable to a knowledge of or a sensitivity for the same stimuli that caused the other individual's feelings.

Sympathy differs from empathy in several important ways, the most specific of which is that in this case a knowledge of the stimuli affecting the other person's feelings is not necessary. Sympathetic responses are feelings caused by observing the emotion displayed by another. The sympathetic feeling need not be similar to the original feeling, merely caused by it.

In some forms of psychotherapy empathy between the patient and the therapist is considered essential to the establishment of a helping relationship; it is believed that if the therapist cannot empathize with the patient's feelings and needs, the success of the therapy will be limited.

One goal of sensitivity training is often to increase awareness of others' feelings through training in empathy. This can be accomplished in a variety of ways, most commonly by emphasizing feedback about feelings that occur in interpersonal interactions.

—Brenda B. Bankart and C. Peter Bankart, *Wabash College*
Consult (13) Rogers, 1961.

ENCEPHALITIS, inflammation of the brain tissues. *Epidemic encephalitis (*also called *encephalitis lethargica* and *sleeping sickness)* is an inflammation caused by a filterable virus. This disease can cause mental retardation in children and serious personality disorders in children and adults.

Symptoms of the disease are fever and prolonged sleepiness or stupor. Sometimes patients experience insomnia, agitation, and delirium. Postencephalitic problems in adults include twitchings of the arm, hand, and face muscles and spasms in which the eyes turn upward. These organic problems sometimes lead to states of depression or withdrawal. Intelligence is usually not impaired. Epidemic encephalitis can cause Parkinson's disease in adults.

In children under five, encephalitis can cause severe mental retardation. Other children become so delinquent, aggressive, and unmanageable that they have to be put in hospitals. These effects are attributed to brain damage caused by the infection.

There was an epidemic of the disease in Europe and America after World War I, but it is now relatively rare.

See also Parkinson's Disease.
Consult (13) Coleman, 1964.

ENCODING. *See* Memory.

ENCOUNTER GROUPS. Encounter sessions are similar to those in group psychotherapy in that individuals aim to change their personal lives through confronting others and talking about their own emotional conflicts, but differ in that leaders are rarely trained mental health professionals. Thus, participants receive no screening or follow-up, enjoy no legal protections, and receive no individualized planning, evaluation, or goal setting.

Many encounter groups occur at "growth centers," such as the Esalen Institute in California. They use a series of "games" to generate extremes of emotion through the simulation of such ordinary human experiences as aggression, affection, dependency, and trust. The encounters tend to avoid intellectuality, personal history, and external experiences not in the "here and now."

Such groups often become coercive and encourage promiscuity, conformity, and ritualized emotional expression. There is little evidence to support claims that the lives of vast numbers of people have been greatly improved by them. Indeed, many people have been emotionally and physically damaged in encounter sessions.

—Bruce L. Maliver, Author of *The Encounter Game*

See also Human Potential Movement; Sensitivity Training.
Consult (13) Maliver, 1972.

ENDOCRINE GLANDS, glands of internal secretion, which produce hormones, important regulators of body functions. *See* Adrenal Glands; Parathyroid Glands; Pituitary Gland.

ENDOMORPH. *See* Constitutional Types.

ENERGIZER, a stimulant drug used as an antidepressant. *See* Drugs and Behavior.

ENGINEERING PSYCHOLOGY, a branch of ap-

Encounter group, a form of group psychotherapy often conducted in the absence of trained leadership.

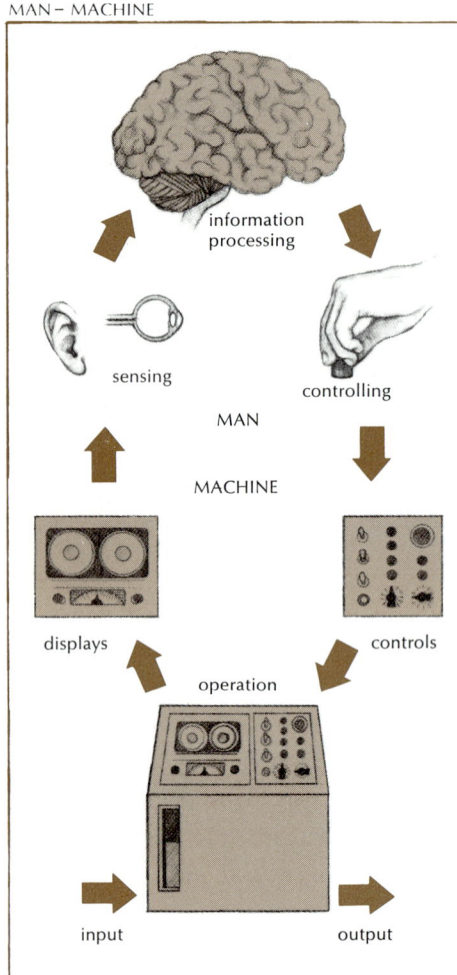

MAN – MACHINE

information processing

sensing

controlling

MAN

MACHINE

displays

controls

operation

input

output

The engineering psychologist examines man as an element in the man-machine system, treating him as a sensor, as a processor of information, and as a controller.

plied psychology concerned with the discovery and application of information about human behavior to the design of machines, tools, jobs, and environments so that they best match human abilities and limitations. The field has also been referred to, from time to time, as *psychotechnology* or *applied experimental psychology,* but these two names appear to be gradually dropping out of use.

Although engineering psychology may be properly thought of as a part of *industrial psychology,* it is more closely allied with *human-factors engineering.* This field is generally known as *human engineering* on the North American continent and is usually called *ergonomics* throughout the rest of the world. The broad area of human-factors engineering includes, in addition to engineering psychology, portions of such human sciences as anatomy, anthropometry, applied physiology, environmental medicine, and toxicology.

The distinctions between engineering psychology, industrial psychology, and human-factors engineering are more academic than real. In practice, the engineering psychologist needs to know enough about related disciplines to use them in arriving at sensible and informed design decisions. Rather than treating engineering psychology as a distinct entity, it would be more correct to say that this name is more a convenient focus around which training is offered in many universities.

Historical Development

Engineering psychology was born during World War II. New machines of war—such as radar, sonar, high-altitude and high-speed aircraft, naval combat information centers, and air traffic control centers—placed demands upon their human operators that were often beyond the capabilities of human senses, brains, and muscles. Research on ways of narrowing the gap between machine demands and human abilities was undertaken first in several British universities through the Medical Research Council and the British military services. Parallel efforts in the United States were made by the National Defense Research Committee, which, through the Office of Scientific Research and Development, set up similar research contracts in numerous universities and industries. At the same time, all three American military services incorporated psychologists into their research and development laboratories so that research findings could be put to immediate use.

Since World War II the growth of engineering psychology has been steady. The Society of Engineering Psychologists, Division 21 of the American Psychological Association, had nearly 400 members in 1972. Over 900 psychologists are members of the Human Factors Society; indeed, they make up over 60 percent of the membership of that organization. Psychologists also figure prominently in such for-

eign organizations as the Ergonomics Research Society (centered in Great Britain), the Société d'Ergonomie de Langue Française (centered in France), the Nederlandse Vereniging voor Ergonomie, and the Japanese Ergonomics Research Society. Engineering psychologists are employed in many universities, in every branch of the military service, in many independent research and consulting organizations, and in the aviation, automotive, electronics, communications, and home appliance industries.

In recent years, engineering psychologists have turned their attention to a variety of urban problems, such as street and highway design, rapid-transit facilities, hospital and urban health facilities, architecture and housing, pollution control, education, law enforcement agencies, postal systems, and airports. These developments are the result of a new awareness that, in the final analysis, all man-made systems are effective only insofar as they serve man safely, comfortably, and conveniently. This is consonant with the underlying philosophy of engineering psychology: technology must be designed for human use and against possible misuse.

The Man-Machine Model

In their work engineering psychologists regard man as an element in a man-machine system. This model is basically an elaboration and adaptation of the S–R (stimulus-response) paradigm found in many textbooks of elementary psychology. In effect, the engineering psychologist's model considers the human operator as an organic sensor, information processor, and controller located between the displays and controls of a machine.

Displays. The outputs of machine operations are signals that are made to appear on one or more displays. A machine display may be any of a thousand different things, such as the position of a pointer on a dial, the printout of a digital computer, a voice coming over a loudspeaker, a red light at a street intersection, or the resistance felt in a certain kind of control.

Information Processing. Having sensed a machine output on display, man has to interpret what the display means, understand it, perhaps do some mental computation, and reach a decision of some sort. These functions are ordinarily subsumed under the heading of *higher mental processes* in psychology textbooks. Engineering psychologists, who often use machine terminology instead of more customary psychological terms, refer to all these higher mental processes collectively as information processing.

Controlling. Having reached a decision, the human operator takes some action. The action is normally exercised on some sort of control, such as a push button, lever, crank, pedal, switch, or handle. The control actions, in turn, alter the behavior of the machine to produce an output and further changes in the displays, thus causing the whole cycle to be repeated.

Environmental Effects. A man-machine system does not operate in isolation but in an environment. Because the nature of this environment influences man's efficiency and performance, the engineering psychologist must be concerned with this area as well.

Example. A man driving an automobile is a good example of a man-machine system. The driver reacts to the displays on his dashboard as well as signals from the road and outside environment, noise from the engine and the vehicle, and feedback to his body from the controls and the vehicle. From these inputs he makes decisions about control actions, such as steering, braking, and shifting. These control actions affect the movements of the automobile, which, in turn, furnish new and different inputs to the driver.

Research Areas

The man-machine model provides a convenient framework for classifying some of the main content areas of engineering psychology.

Displays. Machine displays represent the starting point of the cycle. Perhaps for this reason, a considerable amount of work has been devoted to studies of displays and the ways in which they should be selected and designed. The research on visual displays has been concerned with such problems as the design of mechanical indicators; scales; cathode-ray tubes (such as TV monitors and radar scopes); charts, tables, and graphs; warning lights and symbols; abstract visual symbols for coding information; and general and specialized lighting systems. The research on auditory displays falls into two main classes: that dealing with tonal or noise signals, such as sirens, bells, horns, and buzzers, and that dealing with speech communication systems, such as the design of efficient languages for communication, the design of such components as microphones and amplifiers, and the design of speech communication systems.

Information Processing. As more systems become automatic, man's role in the system becomes that of a monitor and decision maker. He may be required to perceive complex displays, assimilate large masses of data, evaluate or assess complex situations, and make decisions in the face of uncertainty. Since our understanding of the mechanisms by which people do these things is still imperfect, this area of engineering psychology contains the fewest principles and concrete recommendations about ways in which man can be best integrated into man-machine systems.

Controlling. Research on the design of controls has yielded a substantial number of useful and practical principles. These are concerned with such matters as the factors involved in selecting the correct control for a job, control-display ratios, direction-of-movement relationships, control resistance, ways of preventing accidental activation, and control coding.

Environmental Problems. Although the study of environmental problems is primarily the province of applied physiology and related medical specialties, psychologists have also studied the effects of a wide range of environmental factors on behavior. This research has been concerned with the effects on performance of variations in illumination, noise, anoxia, noxious gases and contaminants, heat and cold, acceleration, vibration, and g-forces.

The Systems Approach

However important it may be to achieve a good match between a single operator and his machine, some of the most challenging and intricate problems of engineering psychology arise in the design of large man-machine systems and the integration of man into those systems. Examples are a nationwide telephone system, an automated post office, a computerized banking system, or a large hospital. In dealing with such large systems, the engineering psychologist finds himself most closely allied with the industrial psychologist. Indeed, the interactions of machine design and selection, training, and operating procedures are complex and reciprocal.

Personnel. A man-machine system is not complete unless there are suitably qualified people available to operate and maintain it. In the past, occupational psychology accepted the job as a given. The personnel psychologist merely had to find people who could perform the particular tasks it involved. In systems design, the job is considered a variable, to be changed and manipulated until a final design has been realized. If a job is designed in such a way that it is complex, the criteria used in selection must be high. By redesigning the job to make it simpler, selection standards may be relaxed.

Training. Personnel training cannot be separated from personnel selection and job design. In general, the more rigorous the criteria applied during selection, the less training operators will need to do a job. Conversely, when selection is less rigorous, more training will be required. Both selection and training, in turn, interact with the complexity of a system. The more complex the system, the more stringent selection and training requirements must be. When a system is redesigned to be simpler, selection and training requirements may be reduced. Complete systems design also includes the definition of training objectives, the development of training techniques, the preparation of an appropriate training program, and sometimes the design of training devices and aids to provide training for operators on the tasks they are to perform.

Operating Procedures. Instructions, op-

Apollo command module control panel is a product of cooperation between space scientists and engineering psychologists.

erating rules, and procedures set forth and explain the duties of each operator in a system. Once again, the interactions with other elements of system design are many and reciprocal. For a given level of selection and training, complex systems generally require complex rules and instructions. Simplifying system design often means that rules, procedures, and instructions can be reduced. Similarly, if system design is held constant, highly selected and trained operators generally need fewer instructions than do those who are less stringently selected and trained. Relaxing selection and training standards requires more explicit rules and instructions.

Areas of Application

Some of the most impressive and dramatic uses of engineering psychology have been in the design of military systems and of vehicles, suits, and tools for the exploration of space. Somewhat less complex systems to which engineering psychology has contributed are aircraft, automobiles, automated postal systems, and computerized medical systems both for medical diagnosis and patient monitoring. Engineering psychology has also been applied to the design of a variety of smaller items, such as highway signs, telephones, typewriters, computer consoles, and a number of consumer items, such as sewing machines and stoves. The current interest in consumer rights, by increasing the attention given to a great variety of products, appears to be imparting new vigor and direction to the field.

—Alphonse Chapanis, *The Johns Hopkins University*

See also Accident Proneness; Consumer Psychology; Safety Psychology; Space Psychology.

Consult (14) Chapanis, 1965; De Greene, 1970; Morgan, *et al.,* 1963.

ENURESIS, persistent bedwetting. This problem is more common in boys and occurs only at night or both at night and during the day. Less than 10 percent of all cases are organically based, and there is a tendency for these cases to wet both at night and during the day. In Western societies 20 percent of four- to five-year-old children are still wetting, while the proportion of fourteen-year-olds still wetting is only 2 to 3 percent.

Emotional disorders are commoner in bedwetters than in nonbedwetters, but most children who are enuretic are psychiatrically normal. The relationship between emotional disturbance and enuresis holds true at all ages and is stronger for girl enuretics and for children who wet both at night and during the day. The nature of the association is unknown: some children may develop a psychiatric disturbance because of enuresis, others may be enuretic as a manifestation of a psychiatric

Psychoanalyst Erik Erikson's studies have focused on the concept of personal identity.

disorder, and in others both the enuresis and the psychiatric disorder may be due to common factors. Conditioning methods have been the most effective treatment, but the psychiatrically disturbed enuretics do not respond as well as the psychiatrically normal.

—Dennis P. Cantwell, M.D., *University of California, Los Angeles*
See also Pavlovian Conditioning.
Consult (13) Kanner, 1957; Kolvin, 1972.

ENVIRONMENT, all the states, conditions, and stimuli that are outside and around an individual organism. Any or all of these factors can influence behavior, but their effects vary greatly from one individual to another.

One of the longstanding arguments in psychology (and in biology and public policy) concerns the relative roles of heredity and environment in development. *Eugenicists* contend that inheritance is the prime determinant of capacity and that humans can be improved by selective breeding of the best stock. *Euthenists* maintain that most or all individuals have the capacity for high development and that the basic need is to improve the quality of the environment they live in. Most authorities believe that heredity and environment interact to produce an individual's levels of performance and other ways of behaving. However, the "nature-nurture" controversy has been revived in debates about intellectual abilities and intelligence tests.

A recent focus in psychology is on the interaction of an organism with its total, ecological environment. This field borrows concepts from biology.

See also Behavioral Ecology; Eugenics; Euthenics; Heredity and Environment; Intelligence and Intelligence Testing.

ENVIRONMENTAL PSYCHOLOGY. *See* Behavioral Ecology.

EOG, electro-oculogram, a graphic record of eye movements, used in studies of stages of sleep and dreaming. *See* Sleep and Dreams.

EPILEPSY (convulsive disorder), a brain disorder marked by recurrent seizures with a variety of symptoms. Four main types have been named. Some persons have more than one type.

Grand mal (from the French, meaning "great illness"). The person experiencing a grand-mal attack (the most common form of epilepsy) loses consciousness; his teeth clamp together, his muscles become rigid, and he falls. He momentarily stops breathing but quickly resumes and enters a stage of muscle spasms. Working of his jaws causes bubbles to form ("foaming at the mouth"). During the attack, he is in danger of biting his tongue or injuring himself by falling. After the attack he may regain consciousness or fall into a deep sleep.

Petit mal (from the French, meaning "small illness"). The patient does not completely lose consciousness but shows a temporary "flickering" in his activities and awareness. His eyelids may twitch, and he may drop anything he is holding. He then resumes his activity not necessarily aware that he has had an attack.

Jacksonian. The patient experiences in one part of his body muscle spasms and sensations of tingling or burning, which then spread over the side of his body. He may lose consciousness and have general convulsive seizures.

Psychomotor. Although the patient appears conscious and continues his activities, he is unaware of his whereabouts and lacks conscious control of his actions. He may, for example, walk for blocks and then find he does not remember where he has been. He may experience delusions or hallucinations. In rare cases he may become violent and dangerous to himself and others.

Causes and Treatment. Electroencephalograph (EEG) records show distinctive brainwave patterns for each of the four types of seizures. All epileptic patients show abnormal patterns.

The causes of these disturbances in the brain are not fully understood. In some cases brain damage, as from a head injury or an infection, can be detected, but epilepsy can occur without such brain damage. Many students of epilepsy believe that hereditary factors predispose a person to seizures and that some factor in the environment precipitates the attack.

Drugs that control the activity of brain cells are effective in controlling seizures. A patient may take anticonvulsant drugs for years. Doctors advise the patient to maintain good general health and to avoid stressful situations. Psychotherapy may also be advised.

With treatment most epileptics can lead normal lives, though they cannot work in some hazardous occupations and in most U.S. states cannot be licensed to operate cars. They do not generally show any lowering of mental abilities, except in the rare cases of epileptic deterioration, which may lead to hospitalization. History shows that a number of outstanding figures have had seizures—Julius Caesar, Lord Byron, Guy de Maupassant, Paganini, and Vincent Van Gogh are examples.

Consult (13) Coleman, 1964; Wright, 1962.

EQUILIBRIUM SENSE (Static Sense), the sense of the position of the body in space. Since the body is constantly subjected to a gravitational

pull, the equilibrium functions must be reflexive and automatic. Thus, this sense is different from all the others, for most of its operations are not accompanied by awareness.

The receptors for the equilibrium sense lie in the vestibular apparatus within the inner ear. The *semicircular canals* (which lie in three different planes) are tubes filled with fluid. Head movements cause movement of the liquid, which stimulates receptors in the canals and signals the need for reflex adjustments of eyes and body. The *macula* is a static receptor contained within the utricle. When one is standing erect, the macula, pulled by gravity, is nearly horizontal. Any change in head position leads to movement of the otoliths (small stones) of the macula, which stimulate the receptors. Nerves from the vestibular apparatus enter the central nervous system and make connections with the systems that control the delicate tension and adjustment of postural and eye muscles.

Perception of the orientation of the body in space also depends upon information from the visual and kinesthetic (joints and tendons) systems. A deficit in any one sense may impair but not destroy the sense of equilibrium. The congenitally blind are not disoriented in space if their inner ear is functioning; destruction of the inner ear only impairs balance if vision is also destroyed.

—Nina Adams, *Yale University*
See also Sensation.
Consult (4) Geldard, 1971.

EQUIPMENT DESIGN. *See* Engineering Psychology.

ERIKSON, ERIK HOMBURGER (1902–), American psychoanalyst. Born in Frankfurt, Germany, he studied psychoanalysis with the Sigmund Freud group, Vienna. From 1960 he was professor of human development and lecturer on psychiatry at Harvard.

Erikson's studies have centered around the concept of personal identity, and he introduced the term "identity crisis." His theory of how personality develops is similar to Freud's theory of psychosexual development. According to Erikson, personality is not finally formed in childhood crises; the process continues throughout life. The individual must solve eight different stages of problems—such as trust versus mistrust, intimacy versus isolation, ego integrity versus despair. Social relationships are keys to this process. Among Erikson's publications are *Childhood and Society,* 1950; *Insight and Responsibility,* 1964; *Identity, Youth, and Crisis,* 1968; and *Gandhi's Truth,* 1969—a "psychohistorical biography" that won a Pulitzer Prize in 1970.

EROS, in Freudian theory. *See* Life Instinct.

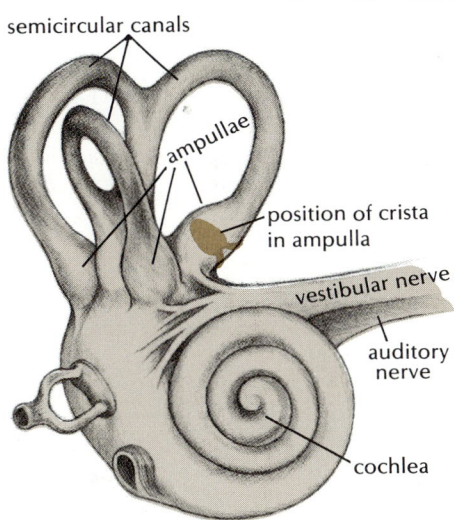

EQUILIBRIUM SENSE

position of vestibular apparatus in head

vestibular apparatus

semicircular canals

ampullae

position of crista in ampulla

vestibular nerve

auditory nerve

cochlea

The crista is located within the ampulla at the base of each semicircular canal. The fluid in the canal, when it is in motion, bends the gelatinous substance, which in turn bends the hair tufts and stimulates the hair cells to send nervous impulses to the brain.

crista

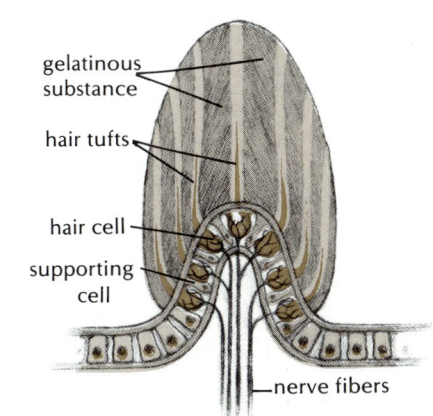

gelatinous substance

hair tufts

hair cell

supporting cell

nerve fibers

Jean Esquirol drafted the law (1838) that provided for humane treatment of mentally ill in France and authored a major treatise on clinical psychology.

EROTOMANIA. *See* Nymphomania; Satyriasis.

ESCAPE LEARNING, the acquired response of removing oneself from a noxious or unpleasant situation. A rat will readily learn to escape from a shock floor by running up a pole to a safe platform. The frightened child will readily run away from a yard where a vicious dog has tried to attack him.

See also Drive-Reduction Theory.

ESQUIROL, JEAN ETIENNE DOMINIQUE (1772–1840), French psychiatrist. He succeeded Philippe Pinel as director of Salpêtrière (1811) and became director, Royal Sanitarium, Charenton (1826).

Instrumental in the development of modern psychiatry, Esquirol made contributions on both the practical and the theoretical levels. With this draft of the law of 1838, humane treatment for mentally ill patients was legally established in France. At a time when doctors thought mental illness had an organic cause and the public believed it was caused by demonic possession, Esquirol proposed that emotional conditions were its source. He subjected his patients to statistical analysis in order to support this theory and then classified all psychoses into five main categories—mania, idiocy, dementia, lypemania, and monomania. He also introduced the term "hallucination."

In 1817, Esquirol established the first teaching clinic in psychiatry. *Les maladies mentales,* 1838, is considered the first modern treatise on clinical psychology.

ETHNOCENTRISM, rating one's own ethnic or racial group as superior to others. *See* Prejudice.

ETHOLOGY. Early in this century a few European zoologists started looking at and living with a wide variety of animals. They were fascinated by what animals normally do, including their patterns of courtship, maternal care, and fighting. These were not the first scientists to describe animal behavior, but they were the first who felt that such studies were of scientific importance. A dedicated group of workers with an integrated conceptual and methodological approach to behavior soon developed. The leaders of this new field, ethology, were Konrad Lorenz and Niko Tinbergen. After forty years, not only are these two men still active and contributing figures, but also the discipline they started, essentially from "bird watching," has become a conceptual and methodological movement affecting disciplines ranging from genetics and embryology to psychology, anthropology, and political science. This revolutionary approach to behavior is composed of three different interwoven concerns—attitude, method, and theory.

Approach. A characteristic attitude unites ethologists, although they may vehemently disagree on theory. They believe that animals must be studied on their own terms and not viewed as convenient substitutes for people, which is so characteristic of "rat psychology." Thus, they emphasize the normal behavioral repertoire or life style of the species and view the effects of the natural environment and ecology as intimately related to an understanding of behavior. The phylogenetic history of the species is also considered important; indeed, evolution is viewed as the integrating theory that is critical for understanding behavior. The ethological perspective, then, is a holistic biological approach focusing on behavior in the real world.

Method. The techniques of ethology cannot be easily summarized since diversity of methods is related to the diversity of species, behaviors, and questions asked. However, a typical procedure is followed in studying a particular animal. First the behavior patterns of the species are recorded and described objectively. How, when, where, and with whom or what does it hunt, eat, sleep, mate, build nests, fight, locomote, and so on? This descriptive record, the *ethogram,* is the basis for future study and experimentation.

Questions are then asked about each given behavior. What is the *adaptive function* of the behavior, both to the individual and to the species? What *causes* or *controls* this behavior, including such aspects as environmental stimuli, hormones, and the nervous system? What is the *ontogeny* of the behavior, that is, how does it develop? The answers cover such matters as imprinting, early experience, prenatal factors, and conditioning, as well as the interaction between genetic and experiential processes. A final question—How did the behavior evolve?—usually refers to the phylogenetic history of the species, but it is increasingly being broadened to include cultural evolution and tradition as ethology moves into human behavior.

To help answer these questions, ethologists may use ethograms gathered on related species in similar or different habitats as well as the published biological literature. In most cases, however, experiments are performed. But these differ radically from the experimentation of traditional animal psychology. Rather than forcing on the organism the problems and apparatus of the experimenter, ethologists take their cue from the animal itself and utilize natural units of behavior based on function or topography. Such experiments can be as simple as rearranging stones around a wasp's nest hole or as complicated as the analysis of ultrasonic communication in bats and moths. Most ethological experimentation involves modifying the natural environment, rearing and observing the animal away from the natural environment, or otherwise manipulating the organism to answer the four questions outlined above. The specific techniques vary, but all are focused on questions posed by the animal. Even when the studies occur in the laboratory, the natural situation is considered the touchstone for evaluating results.

Theory. Its generalized principles, particularly as applied to human behavior, are the most controversial aspect of ethology. Nevertheless, ethological theorizing, while incomplete and still evolving, has proved it can bring together observations and experimental evidence.

Ethology brought *instinct* back into psychology. The specific model of Lorenz and Tinbergen was based on an initial variable appetitive phase and the subsequently performed *fixed action patterns* (FAPs), highly stereotyped, unlearned behaviors released by rather specific cues from prey, mates, or shelter. Such cues are termed *signs* or *key stimuli*. Each FAP was motivated by its own motivating energy. The proper sign stimulus would release a given FAP via activation of an *innate releasing mechanism* (IRM). The sign stimuli involved in social behavior, termed *releasers,* were seen as particularly important. For instance, a submissive posture would terminate or inhibit aggression on the part of a dominant animal. If an animal was simultaneously aroused by two conflicting drives, then components of both behaviors might appear (ambivalence), an improper stimulus might be responded to, as in attack (redirection), or a third seemingly irrelevant behavior might occur (displacement).

Current Research. All these phenomena are still being studied today, but the implications behind the behaviors seen are not so readily ascribed to innate genetic processes. Nor are energy constructs as frequently employed. Indeed, even Lorenz and Tinbergen have modified their views. Nevertheless, work in behavior genetics is showing that even subtle differences in behaviors as between strains of mice can be under genetic control, and physiological studies are indicating that internal factors in the nervous system often can "drive" behavior without external influences. But the expression of any behavior is based on both evolutionary and environmental processes, and both need to be studied. The generalizability of mechanisms underlying behavior has become one of the major concerns of ethology, and the answers will have great ramifications for all of psychology.

—Gordon M. Burghardt, *University of Tennessee*

See also Critical Period; Imprinting; Instinct; Kinesis; Reflex; Taxes; Tropism.

Consult (3) Ardrey, 1970; Burton Jones, 1972; Eibl-Eibesfeldt, 1970; Hinde, 1970; Lorenz, 1965; Lorenz, 1952; Morris, 1967; Tinbergen, 1963.

ETIOLOGY, the study of causes. One of the main concerns of psychology and psychiatry is the study of the origins or causes of mental disorders. Articles on the major psychotic and psychoneurotic disorders include sections on the search for causes.

EUGENICS, a movement founded in the mid-nineteenth century as both a science and a proposal for the improvement of the physical, moral, and intellectual qualities of the human race through planned mating. Its ideas were an outgrowth of the concepts of "survival of the fittest" and the studies on genius by Francis Galton, the British scientist. Galton believed that the fact that many "geniuses" were closely related indicated that innate mental capacities were handed down within families, ignoring the advantageous effects of a stimulating environment. The eugenics movement advocated compulsory limits on the breeding of the feebleminded, criminals, paupers, and the insane and suggested incentives for the proliferation of "good stock." The movement gained influence in the United States and led to many state laws requiring sterilization of the feebleminded.

The basic weakness of eugenics as science was its ignorance of what traits are genetically controlled. During the Great Depression, dramatic differences among individuals were equalized by the economic situation, and scientists began to view the environment as the prime source of human variation. The movement also lost respectability as the laws were used and misused by the courts to include sterilization and castration of epileptics, drunkards, and drug addicts. The final horror was the Nazis' use of eugenics to "purify the Aryan race."

—Nina Adams, *Yale University*
See also Heredity and Environment.

EUTHENICS, the branch of science that attempts to improve man by maintaining or improving his environment. This approach is contrasted with eugenics, the view that selective breeding is the way to improvement. *See* Eugenics; Heredity and Environment.

EVALUATION. *See* Measurement.

EXCEPTIONAL CHILD, any child who is well above or below average in physical constitution, intelligence, emotional development, or other factors. Although the term logically applies to geniuses as much as to retarded children, it is most often used to mean handicapped. *See* Child Development; Mental Retardation.

EXCHANGE THEORY, a theoretical tradition based on the assumption that interpersonal behavior is a response to the rewards and costs

Konrad Lorenz, fascinated by what animals normally do, became a founder of ethology. He is shown accompanied by some of his famous subjects.

EXPERIMENTAL ANIMALS

Rat

Mice

Hamster

available to oneself and others. Fundamental concepts about the nature of reward and a useful notational system have been developed by J. W. Thibaut and H. H. Kelley.

A major assumption of this tradition is that each party's willingness to provide rewards to the other is contingent upon the other's willingness to provide rewards to the first. The exchange rate in such a contingency may be determined by a norm of reciprocity, by bargaining, or by a comparison of the inputs (credits) each party brings to the relationship. The reward provided by another party can be increased by means of ingratiation, a phenomenon that has been extensively studied by E. E. Jones.

Experimental gaming techniques are often used in research on exchange. P. F. Secord and C. W. Backman have attempted to reinterpret most social psychological phenomena in the terms of exchange theory.

—Dean G. Pruitt, *State University of New York at Buffalo*

See also Bargaining; Experimental Gaming.

Consult (10) Adams, 1965; Gouldner, 1960; Jones, 1964; Secord and Backman, 1964; Thibaut and Kelley, 1959.

EXHIBITIONISM, deliberate display of the genitalia by the male to the female under inappropriate circumstances. The exhibitionist characteristically displays his erect penis to a strange female, often an adolescent or young adult, in a public place, such as a street or in a car. Most exhibitionists expose themselves infrequently, usually at times of emotional stress. A few, however, exhibit with a high frequency, sometimes as much as several times a day. About 25 percent of exhibitionists are impotent, and most appear to have inadequate heterosexual adjustments. The apprehended exhibitionist is seldom able to offer an explanation for his behavior. Not infrequently he denies any sexual motivation.

—Eugene E. Levitt, *Indiana University School of Medicine*

Consult (13) Gebhard, *et al.,* 1965; Mohr, *et al.,* 1964.

EXISTENTIALISM, a school of thought that maintains that all human beings are at all times faced with the dilemma of making a choice of what actions to pursue when all of the information relevant to a decision is not available. In other words, at any point in time many alternatives are possible and can determine a rational decision. The existentialists believe that each individual manifests his or her own identity by choosing one specific course of action rather than others.

In this sense, existentialism deals with a study of the present and focuses on behavior occurring at any given instant in time. For example, at a specific moment one may decide to read a newspaper, to write a letter to a friend, or to work in a garden, choices made from any number of possible activities. In fact, the same individual might at that moment decide to engage in much more striking behavior: destroying all the furniture in the house, charging an expensive airline ticket to fly overseas, committing murder, or jumping off a bridge. The fact that each individual has an incredible amount of freedom and self-determination can lead to anxiety, defined as an inability to cope with so many possible alternatives at any one time.

The existentialist also recognizes that the individual's aims are never completely fulfilled. No action leads to complete self-satisfaction. Inner peace is therefore an ideal that is sought but never obtained, because as one redefines oneself constantly, all of one's goals keep changing. Each moment brings new challenges and more decisions.

Existential psychologists try to help people cope with the complex number of alternatives that always exist and to map out courses of action for dealing with an ever-changing environment.

—Joel F. Lubar, *University of Tennessee*

EXPERIMENTAL ANIMALS. Many factors make it impossible or unethical for psychologists to use human subjects in some experiments. For example, because of the possible physical and psychological dangers to humans in experiments that use drugs, prolonged early sensory deprivation, social deprivation, or surgery, it is necessary to use animals. The use of animals also allows for more precise control of extraneous variables, such as age, rearing practices, hereditary and environmental factors, food intake, and past learnings, than might be possible with human subjects. In addition, an animal is less complex than man, which makes it easier to simplify experimental procedures.

Any type of animal is a potential subject for a psychological experiment. The specific animal used in an experiment depends upon such factors as the time it takes the animal to reproduce (in order to study the effects of hereditary and environmental factors over several generations) and its physiological similarity to man. Its availability is related not only to the costs of acquiring and maintaining it but also to the particular hypothesis under consideration. For example, if the experiment is concerned with the effects of some glandular disturbance upon learning, the animal must have that particular gland.

Learning Research. Animals are used primarily in the area of learning, where research has been most productive in establishing data. Many experimenters believe that the same laws of learning apply to all organisms and that the discovery of basic principles of learning can be found through animal experimentation. From these basic and simpler principles more complex ones, which apply to learning in man, can be derived.

The most complex principles of learning explain human behavior. Some experimenters believe that, although there will be differences in learning between man and animals, the same laws apply to both organisms. Animals may modify principles of learning because of differences in structure and physiology, but the laws of learning will remain the same.

The most frequently used animal in learning experiments is the white rat. Other animals used include the rhesus monkey, chicken, pig, dog, pigeon, cat, goldfish, and chimpanzee.

Other Areas. Animals are also used in experiments on perception, abnormal and social behavior, as well as most other areas within the field of psychology.

One of the problems involved in using animals in experiments is that of how much generalization can be made from the behavior of animals to the behavior of man. There is no simple answer to this controversial problem in psychology. A generalization from an experiment means that data found and applied in one situation can also be reproduced and applied in another situation. The more similar the two situations, the more valid the generalization that can be made from one situation to another.

—Louis Snellgrove, *Lambuth College*
See also Experimental Design.
Consult (2) Underwood, 1966.

EXPERIMENTAL DESIGN, a set of precisely planned procedures for determining the relationships between variables, which allows for the prediction of the behavior of organisms. After establishing a *hypothesis*—a tentative belief or explanation of phenomena—the experimenter sets up procedures for testing it. This involves collecting and treating data after preliminary planning, so that the ultimate results can be adequately interpreted and given practical applications.

Hypotheses. One of the oldest but still used methods of stating a hypothesis is the "If. . .then" formulation. For example, an experimenter who was interested in determining whether there is any relationship between vitamins and a significant increase in intellectual ability might use the hypothesis "*If* vitamins are administered to individuals, *then* their intellectual ability will significantly increase."

A hypothesis can be stated in general or in very precise terms. For example, the vitamin hypothesis might be restated more precisely as "If vitamins are administered for a three-month period, there will be an increase of 15 points on the Wechsler Adult Intelligence Scale." The more precisely a hypothesis is

stated, the more exact the procedures that will be required in the experimental design.

Procedures. All experiments involve an *independent variable,* which sometimes is considered as the stimulus, and a *dependent variable,* the behavioral response that, according to the hypothesis, will change as a result of the independent variable. For example, the administering of the vitamins (independent variable) is supposed to increase the intellectual ability (dependent variable) significantly.

In order to know whether the independent variable is causing the dependent variable to change in some way, it is necessary to control other variables that might cause the dependent to change. To accomplish this, the experimenter establishes a control and an experimental group. The *experimental group* is the one on which the independent variable operates.

Ideally, the experimental and control groups should be matched as closely as possible on aspects that might influence the relationship between the independent and dependent variables. One way to achieve this is to use the same group of organisms in both categories. The control group is pretested to establish a quantitative measure of the dependent variable. Then the independent variable is introduced to the group, and a measure of the dependent variable is again taken to determine to what extent, if any, it has been changed by the independent variable.

Another method of design uses two groups that are equated in terms of possible factors that might influence the relationship between the independent and dependent variables (such as age, intellectual ability, sex, and interests). The data obtained from the experimental group are then compared with those obtained from the control group.

In more complex designs a number of independent variables are manipulated by the experimenter in order to determine if functional relationships exist between the independent variables and the dependent variables. All of the independent variable values may be applied to the same subjects in the experiment, or different values of the independent variables may be applied to different groups of subjects. Experiments in the *factorial design* are those in which two or more independent variables are manipulated in two or more ways.

Results. The ultimate goal of any experiment is to permit the prediction of events—specifically, in psychology, behavioral responses. If through experimentation, for example, it was known that certain environmental factors were primary in causing individuals to become criminals, then the alleviation of such environments would reduce crimes; conversely, if certain environments were related to law-abiding behavior, then the construction of these environments would also reduce crime.

Rabbit

Rhesus monkey

Pigeons

Computers are useful in evaluating the results of many kinds of experimental procedures.

EXPERIMENTAL PSYCHOLOGY

As the article EXPERIMENTAL PSYCHOLOGY notes, this term can mean laboratory research or, more broadly, experimental procedures in any area of psychological investigation.

Some of the greatest men in the history of psychology developed methods for the objective study of behavior. See, for example, the following biographies: WUNDT, WILHELM; WEBER, ERNST; FECHNER, GUSTAV; THORNDIKE, EDWARD L.; and PAVLOV, IVAN P. (also PAVLOVIAN CONDITIONING).

Experimental aims and methods are described in SCIENTIFIC METHOD and EXPERIMENTAL DESIGN, with further details in EXPERIMENTAL ANIMALS. The danger of the self-fulfilling prophecy in research is noted in EXPERIMENTER BIAS. Experimental studies in the natural environment, as opposed to the structured conditions of the laboratory, are discussed in ETHOLOGY.

Many articles describe laboratory apparatus and experimental techniques. For work on learning, see for example MEMORY DRUM, TACHISTOSCOPE, PUZZLE BOX, SKINNER BOX, and LEARNING CURVE. For some of the many studies of sensation and perception, see AMES ROOM, VISUAL CLIFF, and REACTION TIME. Recent work by physiological psychologists is noted in such articles as ELECTRICAL STIMULATION OF THE BRAIN and SLEEP AND DREAMS.

Data from experiments are presented in the form of a report and are based on statistical techniques, which may be either descriptive or inferential. Reports usually follow a formal structure, such as (in order) title, abstract summary of the experiment, state of the problem, history of the problem, experimental procedures, results, discussion of results, and a critical evaluation of experimental procedures.

Many experimenters use the *null hypothesis* to interpret the data from experiments. This hypothesis states that any differences found between the control and experimental groups occur only by chance or that there will be no differences between the two groups on the dependent variable. The use of statistical techniques, such as the *T*-test, analysis of variance, and chi-square, allows the experimenter to reject the null hypothesis at an appropriate statistical level.

Errors in data obtained from experimental designs can result from using inappropriate or inadequate apparatus, an insufficient or biased sampling of subjects, or an incorrect statistical technique for interpreting the data, as well as from the lack of a control group.

—Louis Snellgrove, *Lambuth College*
See also Experimenter Bias; Sampling; Scientific Method.
Consult (2) Candland, 1968; Postman and Egan, 1949; Snellgrove, 1967; Underwood, 1966; Woodworth and Schlosberg, 1954.

EXPERIMENTAL NEUROSIS, a mental disorder produced in laboratory animals by subjecting them to the stress of making difficult choices. This work began in the course of Ivan P. Pavlov's conditioning experiments. A dog had been conditioned to discriminate between a circle and an ellipse. Then the experimenter altered the shape of the ellipse, making it closer and closer to a circle. When the dog could no longer distinguish one from the other, it became agitated and disorganized, showing what Pavlov considered neurotic behavior. This study (1914) helped establish the view that mental disorders are of psychic origin.

More recent experimenters have succeeded in causing "nervous breakdowns" in animals that last for years after laboratory sessions were ended. Monkeys have developed ulcers and even died when kept in "executive" decision-making situations. Cats and monkeys have shown extreme anxiety reactions after being forced to choose between fear and hunger.

Consult (13) Brady, 1958; Liddell, 1960; Masserman, 1961.

EXPERIMENTAL PSYCHOLOGY, the use of experimental methods in psychological research. Originally the term had a more restricted meaning, being an equivalent to laboratory

psychology. In the nineteenth century scholars such as Wilhelm Wundt began using laboratory techniques to study topics such as reaction time, sensation, and the simpler forms of learning. Controlled laboratory studies have contributed enormously to knowledge of behavior, and today some psychologists still define the experimental field as a distinct specialty, closely associated with physiological and comparative psychology.

However, experimental methods can be used in almost any field where psychological research is going on, including clinical diagnosis, child development, and social problems. Therefore, it no longer seems appropriate to limit the experimental designation to study in the laboratory. The method of work rather than its location is distinctive.

Division 3 of the American Psychological Association is the Division of Experimental Psychology, and the APA publishes the *Journal of Experimental Psychology*.

See also Experimental Design *and other articles listed in the Item Guide.*
Consult (2) Boring, 1950; Brown and Ghiselli, 1965; Candland, 1968; Woodworth and Schlosberg, 1954.

EXPERIMENTER BIAS, the intentional or unintentional influences that the experimenter has on procedures used in an experiment, the collection of data, or its interpretation.

Objectivity is one of the cornerstones of research, and anyone who intentionally influences the results of an experiment so that results will agree with his hypothesis could not be called a scientist or psychologist. However, all scientists and psychologists are human, and sometimes their attitudes, behavior, or personal interests lead them, intentionally or unintentionally, to bias procedures to obtain the desired results. The problem is sometimes called *self-fulfilling prophecy.*

Causes. There are many ways in which an experimenter can unintentionally bias results from an experiment. For example, he may use a different tone of voice in reading directions to two different groups of subjects, read instruments incorrectly, allow too much or too little time for the control or experimental group, or use incorrect or inappropriate methods to test and interpret the hypothesis.

The experimenter can also give subtle clues to subjects so that they will know what is desired of them. For example, in one experiment graduate students were given two groups of animals. One group of students were told that their animals were "bright" and the other that theirs were "dull." The "bright" group of animals was found to learn faster, although originally there were no significant differences between the learning abilities of the two groups of animals. The "bright" group had been handled better by the students, and this treatment influenced the experimental results. Similar results have been obtained in teaching situations, where one teacher was given "bright" students and another teacher a group of "dull" students, although there were no significant differences in intellectual ability between the two groups.

Cures. Biases can be reduced or eliminated if the experimenter is made aware of the possibility of bias, can recognize it when it occurs, and actively resists any temptation to influence procedures or data intentionally.

—Louis Snellgrove, *Lambuth College*
See also Experimental Design; Scientific Method.
Consult (2) Rosenthal, 1966.

EXPLORATORY DRIVE, a drive related to curiosity. One authority classes exploratory behavior under three headings: The *orienting response,* or "what-is-it? response," occurs when an organism focuses attention on a new situation or object or person. New toys or strange pictures arouse attention and curiosity. *Locomotor exploration* can be exemplified by a cat or a child investigating a new house or a person manipulating a new object. Such exploring behavior has been observed in laboratory rats. The *investigatory response* refers to the specific actions involved in exploring and manipulating. It has been found that experimental subjects will manipulate and investigate for no reward other than what they get from this activity.

See also Curiosity Drive.
Consult (8) Derlyne, 1960.

EXTINCTION. If a stimulus that has been conditioned is now presented repetitively without reinforcement, a response that had been developed as a result of the previous pairing of that stimulus with a reinforcer will diminish in strength. Ultimately the response will disappear, and the extinction process is then complete.

Extinction operates in cases where both positive reinforcement or punishment have been used. For example, a cat trained to approach a visual stimulus, such as a triangle, for food reinforcement will eventually stop doing so if the food is no longer presented. Similarly, an animal that has been given avoidance conditioning using a buzzer followed by shock will no longer respond to the buzzer if it is presented enough times without the subsequent shock.

Extinction is not simply a weakening of a response because of disuse. Rather, it is believed to be an active process.

—Joel F. Lubar, *University of Tennessee*
See also Pavlovian Conditioning.

EXTRASENSORY PERCEPTION (ESP or psi), a direct response to something in the external world not due to sensory information or inference. It includes telepathy, clairvoyance, and precognition (and perhaps retrocognition) and is the area of parapsychology that has been most thoroughly investigated.

Evidence. For many years there was controversy about whether ESP occurred, but the evidence in support of it now seems conclusive. The sources of error in early research were corrected, and current investigations exemplify rigorous experimental controls. In a typical experiment, for example, subjects try to "call targets" (guess at stimuli). The targets might be five symbols (the "ESP cards": circle, plus, square, star, and wavy lines) arranged according to a random number table that was entered at random. A permanent record of the targets is made by someone ignorant of the subject's calls. The targets are concealed (in precognition experiments they are selected only after the subject has called them) both from the subject and from anyone in contact with him, including the experimenter. A permanent record of the subject's calls is made either by him or by someone ignorant of the targets. Standard statistics evaluate the data.

Using either unselected subjects or pretested "good" subjects, dozens of experimenters in many different laboratories have reported extrachance scores, with odds against chance astronomically high. Usually any individual's scores deviate little from chance expectation; only the accumulation of many scores makes the results meaningful. For example, with five ESP cards, the chance of being right is 1/5. In the typical ESP "run" with 25 calls, mean chance expectation is therefore 5. Typical scores average only about 5.2 (though exceptional subjects have been known to average 6 or 7 and in one case 18).

Recent Research. Instead of asking whether ESP occurs, current investigators tend to be concerned with the conditions that produce success or failure. Personality tests indicate that cooperative, interested subjects with an open, receptive attitude (that is, not overly tense or ego involved) tend to have scores that are both high and variable, while negativistic, withdrawn, or suspicious subjects tend to score lower than mean chance expectation (termed *psi-missing*). Scores significantly less than chance are informative too: subjects could not systematically avoid the targets unless at some unconscious level they had information about them. [*Consult* (14) Palmer, 1971.]

An interesting example of psi-missing is the "differential effect." Subjects required to use two ESP procedures tend to score higher with the one they prefer and often show psi-missing with the less preferred. Subtleties of mood or attitude apparently influence ESP scores.[*Consult* (14) Rao, 1962; Schmeidler, 1971.]

Tending a pigeon that will be used in an experiment.

EXTINCTION

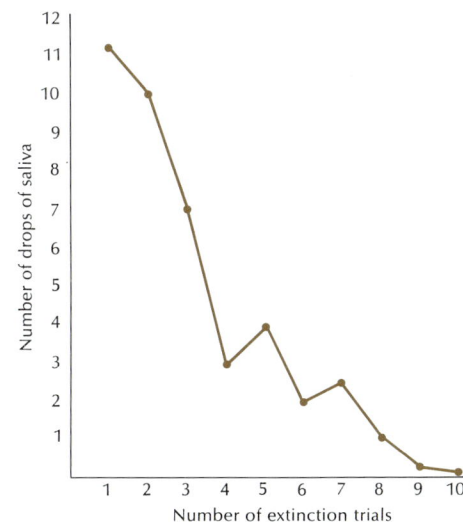

Pavlov found that when food reinforcement was no longer paired with the conditioned stimulus, the conditioned response gradually disappeared.

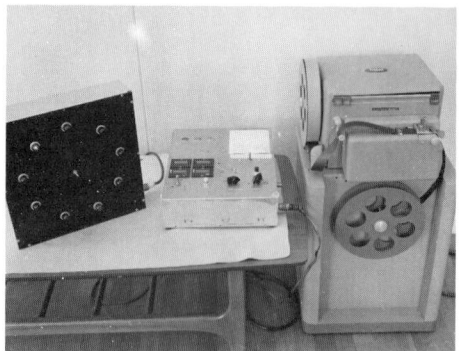

Electronic test machine for psychokinesis (PK). The subject tries to make the lamps light in one direction—clockwise or counterclockwise. They normally operate by chance.

No effect on ESP scores seems caused by changes in physical conditions, such as the distance or size of targets. Depressant drugs, fatigue, and oxygen deprivation produce chance scores or psi-missing, but neither stimulants nor hallucinogens seem to produce high scores. There is some evidence that ESP scores are higher when the EEG shows more alpha, after meditation, or (with a trained hypnotist) in hypnosis. This is consistent with the findings from personality studies: a relaxed but well-motivated mood seems most conducive to ESP success. [*Consult* (14) Honorton *et al.,* 1971.]

—Gertrude R. Schmeidler, *The City College of The City University of New York*

See also Clairvoyance; Parapsychology; Precognition; Telepathy.

Consult (14) Rhine and Pratt, 1957; Schmeidler, 1969.

EXTRAVERSION. *See* Introversion-Extraversion.

EYE MOVEMENTS, in studies of stages of sleep. *See* Sleep and Dreams.

EYSENCK, HANS JURGEN (1916–   ), English psychologist, born in Berlin, Germany. He received a Ph.D. from the University of London (1940) and became professor at the Institute of Psychiatry, University of London, in 1955.

Eysenck has concentrated on personality and learning theory and is known for his Eysenck Personality Inventory, which uses the factor theory of personality—the basic components of personality are isolated through statistical analysis of test results. The dimensions of personality that Eysenck uses are neuroticism, introversion-extraversion, and psychotism. Eysenck uses these dimensions as a basis of human typology (basic personality types) to provide an objective method of describing people.

Eysenck is also known for his application of learning techniques to behavior therapy. His publications include: *Dimensions of Personality* (1947), *Uses and Abuses of Psychology* (1953), *Dynamics of Anxiety and Hysteria* (1957), and the *Biological Basis of Personality* (1967).

FACTOR ANALYSIS, a statistical method that has been used in the study of intelligence and of personality. *See* Intelligence and Intelligence Testing; Personality.

FACULTY PSYCHOLOGY, the concept that a person has a mind composed of such distinguishable powers or faculties as intellect, will, memory, and feeling. This concept was developed when psychology was a province of philosophy. Thomas Reid, an eighteenth-century Scottish philosopher, held that the proper-

Hans J. Eysenck developed a personality inventory that isolates the components of personality through statistical analysis.

ties of mind could be analyzed into such powers as self-preservation, self-esteem, imagination, duty, judgment, and moral taste. Out of this view of mind grew such concepts as phrenology, which holds that traits of personality are directly associated with areas in the head.

The study of factors in intelligence and traits of personality continues in twentieth-century psychology, but the concept of mental faculties has been discarded.

See also Formal Discipline.

FAMILY CARE (Foster Care). *See* Foster Family.

FAMILY SIZE. In general, studies in this area differentiate between the characteristics of small families and large families and their impact on children. The differences have significant psychological effects on the interrelationships among family members. The nature of these relationships and the general climate of the home are affected by several factors, including sex, age, spacing of children, and the specific role each member plays.

In a small family a child is usually under pressure to measure up to family expectations. Considerable emphasis is placed on his development and achievement, and parents invest time and attention in his educational and recreational activities. This interest is facilitated by the fact that the economic status of a small family tends to be superior to that of a large family. Because there are few in the family, the parents are directly responsible for disciplining the children. Planning, democratic participation, and individualized attention are all characteristics of small families.

In large families emphasis is placed on the group rather than the individual, with discipline often administered by siblings. Children strive for recognition by adopting specific roles in the family, since there is less contact between the parent and any one child. Overindulgence and overprotection seldom occur. Children have the opportunity to cooperate with one another and develop responsibility. A greater degree of organization, authority, and administration seems to be inevitable in large families.

—Ragaa Mazen, *Southern Connecticut State College*

FAMILY THERAPY, a specialized form of group therapy that, as its name implies, deals with a person in his family setting, recognizing that his problems may have been caused by interactions with those closest to him. According to Dr. Nathan N. Ackerman, who originated the concept, family therapy is "not for one individual alone, but for the whole family. Usually this means father, mother, and children, but it can include other persons who participate within the home in the day-to-day life of the family group. It may, therefore, involve a grandparent, an aunt, or even a maid or a housekeeper."

The family therapist's goals are (1) to bring into the open the existence and probable causes of intrafamily conflicts; (2) to identify disturbed individuals in the family group and to clarify the nature and extent of their problems to the other members; (3) to mobilize and direct the resources of the family toward solving the problems of adjustment within the family and toward society in general; and (4) to direct the family's values in a constructive, healthy direction. To achieve these goals, the therapist invites the whole family to come and "talk it over," that is, participate in a group interview. Thereafter, he applies the general methods and techniques of group therapy, again utilizing individual therapy as well as pharmacotherapy whenever it is indicated.

—Emanuel Messinger, M.D., *U.S. Veterans Hospital, Northport, N.Y.*
See also Group Therapy.

FANTASY, imagination, often of pleasant states as in happy daydreaming. Fanciful reveries that give people a temporary escape from boring or unpleasant conditions are common defense mechanisms. Some degree of autistic thinking is found in normal people, but if fantasy reaches the stage of delusions or hallucinations, it is a symptom of mental disorder.

See also Autistic Thinking; Daydreaming; Delusions; Hallucinations.

FEAR, an intense emotional state aroused by anticipation of experiencing something menacing, such as pain or injury. A strong drive both in daily life and in laboratory experiments, fear is associated with many bodily symptoms, such as increased heart rate, rapid breathing, tenseness or trembling in the muscles, nervous sweating, and dryness of the mouth. In fact, William James concluded that what we call fear is an awareness of (or feedback from) these bodily changes. Although the James-Lange theory of emotions has been challenged, there is no doubt that extensive visceral changes accompany fear and other excited states.

Studies of children show that fears first appear around seven months of age, can be learned by imitating adults as well as through conditioning, and can be diminished through associations.

Some degree of fear is rational—even essential for survival. On the other hand, fears can reach the neurotic level of phobias. Fear and associated stress contribute to disorders such as combat reactions, civilian catastrophe reactions, and psychosomatic problems such as ulcers. Fear is related to states of anxiety.

See also Anger; Anxiety; Civilian Catastrophe Reaction; Combat Neurosis; Emotion; James-Lange Theory; Phobia.

FECHNER, GUSTAV THEODORE (1801–1887), German psychologist and physician. Born at Gross Sarchen, he received an M.D. in 1822 and was appointed professor of physics in 1834.

Fechner is often identified as the founder of experimental psychology because of his work in psychophysics. This represented only a portion of his research, which covered the range of the physical and biological sciences and extended to philosophy and aesthetics. However, the study of the relationship of "bodily energy" and "mental intensity" (psychophysics) was his abiding interest.

Fechner believed that there was a fundamental identity between mind and body and that it could be expressed mathematically. His studies resulted in the formulation of what has come to be known as Fechner's law, which states in essence that the relationship between the strength of a physical stimulus and the intensity of the sensation in the perceiver is a constant.

Among Fechner's other contributions was the development of an array of laboratory techniques involving the measurement of stimulus intensity and difference thresholds as ways of indirectly but objectively measuring sensation. His careful laboratory methodology became a model for psychologists. He was one of the first to provide support for the notion that human experience could be studied objectively, thus paving the way for the acceptance of psychology as a science.

—Michael Rothenberg, *The City College of The City University of New York*
Consult (1) Boring, 1950.

FEEBLEMINDEDNESS. See Mental Retardation.

FEEDBACK, a term used in cybernetics to mean automatic reporting to a control mechanism of the degree to which some function is being carried out. A standard example is a thermostat controlling a heating plant. If the temperature falls below a set point, this fact registers in the thermostat and the controlling mechanism turns on the heat.

The label "feedback" is now applied to well-known phenomena in psychology. Moving the body, walking erect, and keeping balance require feedback from receptors in the ear and in the muscles.

See also Equilibrium Sense; Kinesthetic Sense.

FEEDING BEHAVIOR. An infant's eating is regarded as the most important activity in the first year of life. It is associated with relief of hunger, reduction of tension, and other nonnutritive pleasures, such as being held, cuddled, and cared for. Studies in this area investigate differences between breast feeding and bottle feeding, fixed-schedule versus self-demand feeding, and early versus late weaning.

Gustav Fechner, 19th-century German physicist and experimental psychologist, stressed a laboratory approach to the scientific study of human experience.

Social psychologist and educator Leon Festinger is known chiefly for studies of cognitive dissonance.

No observable differences have been found between bottle-fed and breast-fed babies in respect to personality characteristics. There is no conclusive evidence as to the effects of fixed-schedule versus self-demand feeding, though it has been observed that a baby who is fed whenever he desires will eventually reduce the number of feedings and spontaneously adopt a somewhat regular schedule. Since sucking has been reinforced and established in an early stage of development, weaning a baby involves teaching him a new behavior and eliminating an old habitual pattern. According to psychoanalytic theory, early weaning may produce hostile reactions, anxiety, sleep disturbance, and thumbsucking, because the baby may not be ready at that particular time to give up this type of oral gratification.

While no research findings establish the type of relationship between feeding behavior and personality variables, we should not overlook the significance of parental attitude toward feeding and the general climate of the feeding situation on the child-parent relationship.

—Ragaa Mazen, *Southern Connecticut State College*

FEELING, in the sense of affect, is covered in articles on emotion. The term is also used for sense impressions. *See* Affect; Emotion; Sensation.

FEMININITY. *See* Sex Identity.

FERAL CHILD. *See* Wild Children.

FERENCZI, SANDOR (1873–1933), Hungarian psychoanalyst. An associate of Freud, Ferenczi introduced two new methods of psychoanalysis—active therapy and permissive therapy. Ferenczi's active therapy, an extension of Freud's privation theories, was to be used when the patient under analysis resisted free association. Ferenczi believed that abstinence from biologically pleasurable acts (such as eating, defecation, and sex) would increase the energy of the libido, providing more energy for therapy. Such privation would also make the patient's pathological defenses clearer to him. But such therapy was harsh and led to hostility in many patients.

By 1927 Ferenczi had decided that this treatment did not help his patients and turned to permissive therapy. He believed that a loving environment would encourage the neurotic patient to release his emotions. The lack of love and attention that the patient had suffered in his childhood would be counterbalanced by the permissiveness of the therapy. Among Ferenczi's publications are *Thalasso: A Theory of Genitality*, 1924; and *The Development of Psychoanalysis*, 1924.

FESTINGER, LEON (1919–), American educator and psychologist. Born in New York City, he taught at Stanford (1955–1968) and later was Else and Hans Staudinger Professor of Psychology at the New School for Social Research.

Festinger is well known for his studies on expectation, aspiration and decision making. He described the phenomenon of bringing belief and action into harmony in terms of reduction in dissonance and has done considerable research on the theory of cognitive dissonance. He has also devised laboratory techniques for studies of prejudice, rumor, and social influence. His major works include *Deterrents and Reinforcement: The Psychology of Insufficient Rewards* (with others), 1962; *Conflict, Decision and Dissonance*, 1964; *A Theory of Cognitive Dissonance*, 1957; and "When Prophecy Fails" (an article, with others), 1956.

—Nina Adams, *Yale University*

FETISHISM, an unusual form of sexual behavior in which gratification is obtained through the medium of an inanimate object. Common fetish objects are women's lingerie and footwear and garments made entirely of rubber, leather, or fur. The object may be employed alone or in connection with another individual. A man may masturbate by rubbing female undergarments against his penis, or he may become sexually excited only by a woman who wears certain specific garments.

The term is sometimes extended to include any unusual circumstance of sexual arousal, such as becoming sexually excited by watching a woman smoke or observing a woman's feet or being sexually attracted to statues.

—Eugene E. Levitt, *Indiana University School of Medicine*
Consult (13) Allen, 1962; Gebhard, 1969.

FIELD THEORY. One version of this broad orientation concentrates on the dichotomy between the idea that stimulus representations in the mind are connected by wires, circuits, tubes, and so forth, and the view that psychological and physiological processes are a patterning of many inputs into meaningful events. The *connectivist view* that it is a giant switchboard containing fiber tracts and individual neurons was clearly previewed in Descartes' early conception of a network of tubes carrying humors through different channels. This view has been stated more recently by D. O. Hebb, who sees the system as organized into discrete assemblies of cells. The field point of view, as typified by Wolfgang Köhler's Gestalt theory, considers the nervous system as a gigantic volume conductor that is permeated by fields of electrical energy and explains many perceptual phenomena more adequately.

Another version is typified by Kurt Lewin's field theory of motivation, proposed in

1935, which represents approach or avoidance forces as positive or negative vectors in the physical sense. *Positive vectors* are stimuli to which individuals are attracted; *negative vectors* are avoidances of threatening stimuli. Lewin believed that this mode of analysis motivation could be useful in visualizing sources of frustration in the environment. A specific example that lends itself to Lewin's vector analysis is the approach-avoidance conflict exhibited by an animal facing a source of food through which electric shock is delivered.

—Joel F. Lubar, *University of Tennessee*
Consult (8) Lewin, 1951.

FIGURE DRAWING TEST. Although it was originally developed as a parameter of intellectual functioning, this instrument is used essentially as a projective measure in personality assessment. Its administration is basically simple and straightforward, but many variations and elaborations have been introduced.

In all techniques the subject is asked to "draw a person" and then a person of the opposite sex. Careful observation is made of the mode of approach, spontaneous comments, and the time required for the task. Many examiners then request the subject to make up a story about the first figure drawn. Karen Machover, a sophisticated exponent of projective utilization of figure drawings, recommends a series of "fairly routine questions designed to elicit the subject's attitude toward himself and toward others" as a part of the story-telling process.

Careful analysis of the drawn figures, behavioral observations, and story associations (if included) enables the examiner to formulate hypotheses concerning major personality dimensions: self-concept, cognitive style, psychosexual identity, impulse control, and others. All data elicited during testing are relevant for interpretation. However, as S. Levy stresses, diagnostic formulations and definite conclusions concerning personality make-up should not be derived solely on the basis of the Figure Drawing Test.

—Randolph S. Kraft, *Federation of the Handicapped, N.Y.*
Consult (12) Goodenough, 1926; Levy, 1959; Machover, 1949.

FIGURE-GROUND PERCEPTION. A pattern, even when it does not portray an identifiable object, is usually perceived as a figure against a background.

The figure has contours, whereas the ground is formless and seems to extend continuously behind the figure. The figure is seen as a thing, the ground as a material.

Figure-ground relations are perceived in line drawings (Figure 1), geometric grays and whites (Figure 2), and abstract black-whites (Figure 3). The relations tend to be ambiguous

and reversible, though one element usually is dominant and may interfere with perception of the second: Figure 1 is either a Maltese cross or a pinwheel; Figure 4 is either a beautiful woman or an old hag.

The experience of figure-ground is also present in other senses. Everyone has heard the song of a bird against a background of noise or distinguished the melody of a violin against a full orchestra.

The ability to distinguish figure from ground seems basic and is probably innate. When congenital cataracts were removed from adults, enabling them to see for the first time, they could not describe or identify familiar objects or simple visual forms, but they could perceive a difference in the forms of two objects. An innate ability to see objects as unified and distinct from background is a basic concept of the Gestalt school of psychology, which theorizes that perception of the environment is based on perception of form.

—Nina Adams, *Yale University*
See also Gestalt Psychology, Illusion.
Consult (4) Bartley, 1969.

FIXATION, a term that implies arrest in development. According to psychoanalytic theory, a child passes through successive stages during which the major focus of psychological energy is related to a specific part of the body. The most important stages in personality or character development are the oral, anal, and phallic. In the oral stage, the mouth is the major source of pleasure; therefore, a great deal of psychic energy is related to this zone. As the child progresses through the stages, the focus of energy shifts to a different part of the body—for example, the anus during the anal stage and the genitals in the phallic stage.

Insufficient gratification or overindulgence at any one stage may lead to fixation at that level. For instance, a child who overindulged in sucking or who was weaned early may become fixated at the oral level. Therefore, fixation would hinder his normal psychological development.

—Ragaa Mazen, *Southern Connecticut State College*
See also Anal Character; Character Development; Oral Character; Phallic Character.

FORENSIC PSYCHOLOGY AND PSYCHIATRY. "Forensic" means having to do with courts of law. A major concern of forensic psychology is to determine whether legal evidence is reliable. This process involves such factors as perception and memory. Another concern involves decisions, sometimes called the domain of forensic psychiatry—for example, is a person to be judged sane and capable to stand trial? Is a person to be committed to an institution as mentally disturbed? See Psychology and the Law.

FIGURE-GROUND PERCEPTION

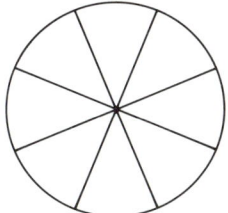

Figure 1.

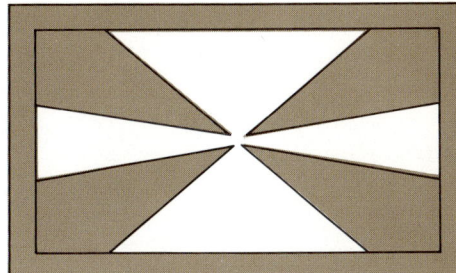

Figure 2.

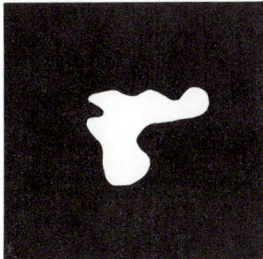

Figure 3.

Figure 4.

FORGETTING. The loss of ability to retrieve something that has been learned is a problem in the study of all learning and memory. There are also neurotic and pathological factors in the inability to recall past events or states, as in repression and amnesia. *See* Amnesia; Memory; Repression.

FORMAL DISCIPLINE, a theory of learning popular in the late nineteenth century, which regarded a subject as valuable if it helped a person learn other subjects. It was argued, for example, that what was learned by studying Latin would transfer to studying English. The argument was extended to claims that learning activities such as memorizing terms or studying math would strengthen a general power of learning, just as exercise strengthens the muscles. These arguments depend on the outmoded concept that there are separate mental faculties.

Psychologists have dropped the idea that memorizing, for example, strengthens a general memory faculty (or that such a faculty exists). But they have observed that practice in memorizing might show a student techniques and attitudes helpful for later learning tasks. Studies of school work have shown that there is little general transfer from one subject to others but that related elements and principles can be carried over.

See also Faculty Psychology; Transfer of Training.

FOSTER FAMILY, a temporary substitute family to a child whose parents cannot provide him with an adequate home situation because of such factors as economic hardship, death of a parent, illness, family breakdown, or psychological problems. The child's expenses are usually paid by a private or a public agency that has legal custody of the child.

Careful selection and preparation of a foster family are necessary to ensure the suitability and adequacy of the new home. While foster parents are expected to deal with their foster children with the care and affection they bring to their own offspring, they must also be prepared to face a situation where a child may be moved to another home because of circumstantial changes, incompatability, or other reasons.

More psychopathological symptoms have been observed in foster children than in children who were reared by their own families. This problem may result from negative experiences before placement, repeated moves to different foster homes, which may lead to feelings of being rejected or abandoned, or other causes. Studies in general, however, suggest that foster children are more responsive and adjusted than institutionalized children.

—Ragaa Mazen, *Southern Connecticut State College*

FREE ASSOCIATION, a therapeutic technique developed by Sigmund Freud. The patient is encouraged to say everything that enters his mind, without censoring it or attempting to make it seem socially appropriate, logical, consistent, or relevant. This technique is based on the theory that instinctual drives and repressed memories are dammed up and in search of a route for discharge. When external pressures become too great, the energy associated with those drives and memories is channeled into various defense mechanisms and release must be found. The psychoanalyst, by minimizing the requirement of conversation and interaction in therapy, attempts to encourage the patient to lower his defenses and to confront his repressed memories.

—Thom Herrmann, *University of Tennessee*

See also Associationism; Psychoanalysis.

FREE-FLOATING ANXIETY. *See* Anxiety.

FREE-RECALL LEARNING, a procedure used to study verbal learning and memory. The subject is presented with a list of items (words, nonsense syllables) to memorize, typically in a different (random) order in each study session. Then he is tested for recall by being asked to write down all the items he can remember in any order he wishes. Free-recall learning resembles serial learning, except the subject is not required to recall items in any particular order.

As a method for studying verbal learning and memory, free recall has often been used to determine how subjects organize or categorize items they wish to remember. When an experimenter deliberately provides them with potential categories, their use of these categories in recall is known as category clustering. For example, if the experimenter presents a jumbled list of animals, flowers, presidents, and countries, subjects tend to recall the items in groupings from one category, then another.

Later studies showed that, even when such category information is deliberately avoided by the experimenter, subjects will nevertheless attempt to organize the list of items, using their own systems or categories. For example, a subject might group items into sets of three. This phenomenon is called *subjective organization* rather than clustering. Subjective organization can occur in the manner of chunking. [*Consult* (6) Bousfield, 1953; Tulving, 1962.]

Clustering, subjective organization, and chunking in recall imply that a great deal of thinking goes on in the learning of simple lists of items. In other words, verbal learning and memory are not simply a matter of attaching verbal responses to specific stimuli: the subject applies and uses whatever organization and thinking that he can to his learning task. Describing the strategies, systems, and plans that subjects apply to learning and thinking tasks is one of the goals of modern cognitive psychology.

—Roland Siiter, *Montclair State College*
See also Chunking; Cognitive Psychology; Concept Learning; Memory; Serial Learning; Verbal Learning.
Consult (6) Deese and Hulse, 1967; Smith and Rohrman, 1970.

FRENKEL-BRUNSWIK, ELSE, sometimes listed as Brunswik-Frenkel (1908–1958), born in Lemberg, Austria-Hungary. She received her Ph.D. at the University of Vienna and was lecturer and research associate there from 1931 to 1938. After Hitler's invasion of Austria, she emigrated to the United States and was for twenty years professor of psychology at the University of California, Berkeley.

Frenkel-Brunswik, along with others, investigated prejudice and, in the process, developed new methods of assessing personality. The semistructured interview, the *E scale* (a test of ethnocentrism), and a test of authoritarian orientation known as the *F scale* (for fascist attitudes) were outgrowths of this work. The authoritarian personality, described as resistant to change and unable to tolerate anything new or different, was contrasted with the democratic personality, which was found to be more tolerant, flexible, and ready to take independent action. This research, with its new methods, new tests, and hypotheses concerning prejudice, formed the basis for *The Authoritarian Personality,* coauthored with T. W. Adorno (1950), her best-known contribution to the field.

FREQUENCY DISTRIBUTION, a statistical method for organizing and presenting data. The initial procedure consists simply of counting the number of times each item under study occurs. In psychological and educational measurement, a standard step is to tabulate the number of individuals receiving each possible score from low to high. (If large numbers of people have been tested, it is more practical to count the number of scores falling in groupings, such as ten-point intervals.)

Observing the distribution of scores is a step in analyzing test results. For example, when scores on an achievement test given to all students in a school system cluster toward the lower end of the range, many different factors might be accountable: errors in designing, administering, or scoring the test; distractions such as noise or heat; students' lack of motivation; teaching not as effective as it might have been.

Distributions are often presented graphically by plotting frequencies on a graph and drawing a line through the plotted points to form a frequency polygon. Scores can also be plotted to form a histogram (column diagram or bar graph).

The *normal frequency distribution* is an ideal situation in which half the scores fall above the midpoint and half below. When this distribution occurs, the mean (arithmetic average), the median (midpoint of scores), and the mode (most frequently occurring score) are all the same. The scores have a low standard deviation; that is, they cluster around the center rather than varying toward either extreme. When graphed, this distribution produces a symmetrical, bell-shaped curve.

Chance (probability) factors produce a normal distribution. The results of thousands of throws of dice yield a bell-shaped curve. Measures of the height of large numbers of people approach a normal distribution. (There are very few dwarfs and very few giants, with most people ranking nearer the center of the range.) Scores on intelligence and achievement tests for large numbers of subjects (a big school system, for example) also tend to follow the normal frequency pattern, though various factors may skew the curves.

See also Percentile; Standard Deviation.
Consult (12) Blommers and Lindquist, 1960; Hays, 1965.

FREUD, ANNA (1895–   ), British psychoanalyst. Born in Vienna, she emigrated to England in 1938 with her father, Sigmund Freud, and later became director of the Hampstead Child-Therapy Clinic in London.

Anna Freud has contributed to psychoanalytic theory and practice and to studies of child development. Her studies of the ego and defense mechanisms were important in the ego psychology movement in psychoanalysis. In working with children, she was an early user of play therapy. Her books have contributed to understanding the dynamics of childhood and adolescence and to improving techniques of therapy for members of those age groups. Her major works include *The Ego and the Mechanisms of Defense,* 1936; *Psycho-Analytic Treatment of Children,* 1946; and *Normality and Pathology in Childhood,* 1965.

FREUD, SIGMUND (1856–1939). Sigmund Freud, the founder of psychoanalysis, was born in Moravia, May 6, 1856, and died in London, September 23, 1939. For nearly eighty years, however, he resided in Vienna, which he left in 1938 when Nazi Germany invaded Austria. As a Jew, Freud's life was in grave peril from the Nazis.

Freud's personal life was uneventful. He married at the age of thirty, fathered six children (one of whom, Anna, became a psychoanalyst), and lived quietly in a modest apartment in the center of Vienna where he also saw his patients. His only personal tragedy was the appearance of cancer of the mouth when he

DISTRIBUTION OF IQ SCORES

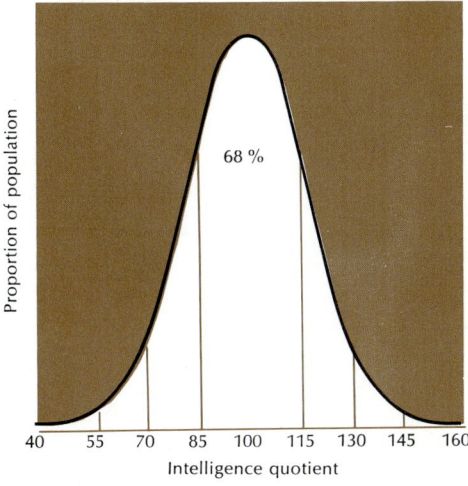

A normal distribution curve, with half the scores on each side of the midpoint.

Anna Freud, the youngest of Sigmund Freud's six offspring, became a specialist in the psychoanalysis of children.

The works and theories of Sigmund Freud, father of psychoanalysis, attracted a larger following—and more controversy—than any other psychologist's.

Erich Fromm developed the concept that many neuroses result from the increased freedom of choice in modern society.

was sixty-seven years old. This painful condition was never cured, despite numerous operations.

Work. After graduating from medical school in 1881, where he received basic training in science and research methods, Freud specialized in the treatment of mental patients. Dissatisfied with the techniques of treatment then being used, he developed, in collaboration with Josef Breuer, new methods, primarily those of free association and dream interpretation. These methods were used to disclose repressed wishes and conflicts that Freud regarded as the sources of neurotic and psychotic behavior. Freud became the first scientific investigator of the irrational forces in the unconscious mind.

In 1900 Freud's *Interpretation of Dreams* was published. This book, which is considered to be one of the most influential works of the modern era, described a method (free association) for exploring the unconscious through the analysis of dreams, provided a theory of dreams (they are wish fulfillments and guardians of sleep), and laid the foundation for a comprehensive theory of mental functioning. This volume was shortly followed by other books and articles, which soon attracted a small group of disciples. Among them were Carl Jung and Alfred Adler, who later defected and started their own movements.

Gradually, Freud's ideas became widely disseminated. In 1909, Freud received his first academic recognition, when he was invited to give a series of lectures at Clark University in Massachusetts. The International Psychoanalytic Association was founded in 1910.

Significance. The impact of Freud's writings on modern thought would be difficult to exaggerate. Not only did his ideas permeate medicine, psychiatry, psychotherapy, and psychology, but they also profoundly affected the social sciences, education, religion, and advertising and provided themes for literature, drama, motion pictures, and the plastic arts. Freud himself applied psychoanalytic findings to a wide variety of cultural phenomena: to society in *Civilization and Its Discontents* (1930), to religion in *The Future of an Illusion* (1927), to literature in *Delusions and Dreams and Other Essays* (1907), to art in *Leonardo Da Vinci* (1910), to anthropology in *Totem and Taboo* (1913), to social groups and institutions in *Group Psychology and the Analysis of the Ego* (1920), and to humor in *Jokes and Their Relation to the Unconscious* (1905).

Freud's ideas have always been controversial, and no scientist since Darwin has been treated with so much scorn and antipathy by his contemporaries. Freud was criticized for emphasizing sex as a motive force in human behavior and for his ideas on childhood sexuality. Despite the antipathy and criticism,

however, Freud is now generally considered to be the greatest psychologist of all times.
—Calvin S. Hall, author of *A Primer of Freudian Psychology*
See also Psychoanalysis.
Consult (13) Freud, 1953–1964; Hall, 1954; Jones, 1953–1957.

FRIGIDITY, in general, inability of the female to obtain gratification from sexual behavior. The term is often used loosely to cover individuals whose sexual reactions vary considerably. In its most severe form, frigidity is the condition of a woman who has never had an orgasm by any means and is repelled by any kind of sexual contact. In its mildest form, the term might be applied to a woman who is sexually normal in every way except that she usually fails to attain orgasm in coitus.

The term has been abandoned by Masters and Johnson, who prefer to speak of *orgasmic dysfunction*. Reasonably, the term should be reserved for those women who are unable to be sexually aroused by any partner. Frigidity may be temporary and not infrequently has a physical basis, such as pelvic pain associated with penetration of the vagina.
—Eugene E. Levitt, *Indiana University School of Medicine*
Consult (13) Masters and Johnson, 1970; Schaefer, 1969.

FROMM, ERICH (1900–), psychoanalyst and writer on social problems. Born in Frankfurt, Germany, he received a Ph.D. from Heidelberg University and studied later at Munich and at the Berlin Psychoanalytic Institute. Fromm moved to the United States in 1933 and was a professor at several United States schools as well as at the National University of Mexico.

Fromm's psychology combines psychoanalysis, culture theory, and historical materialism to describe how man can find the meaning of life not by sacrifice to machine and superstate but by personal relationships with people. Fromm stresses the role of social factors in development: social factors mold human character and, in turn, people mold the social processes. Drawing on Marx as well as on Freud and later psychoanalysts, Fromm places particular emphasis on how economic factors affect people's lives, in the sense that each person's work forces him to adapt to specific social conditions.

The "escape from freedom" is an important theme in Fromm's psychology. When an infant grows up and frees himself from his parents, his freedom gives him a feeling of isolation. The person then tries to escape from this freedom by particular orientations to the world—assimilation (relating to things) and socialization (relating to people). These orientations determine a person's character. Fromm regards the marketing orientation (a facet of assimilation) as particularly important because it leads to superficial, impersonal relationships and feelings of isolation. The impersonal nature of modern society makes man feel like a commodity or a small cog in a machine. To counter these feelings, he must become productive and capable of loving. Fromm's major works include *Escape from Freedom,* 1941; *Man for Himself,* 1947; *The Sane Society,* 1955; *The Art of Loving,* 1956; *The Heart of Man,* 1964; and *The Revolution of Hope,* 1968.

FRONTAL LOBE. *See* Cerebral Cortex; Psychosurgery.

FRUSTRATION-AGGRESSION HYPOTHESIS. *See* Aggression.

FUGUE, a dissociative state in which an individual reacts to a conflict by leaving the scene and apparently forgetting who he is. For example, a man who is facing a severe threat or stress in his home and job may disappear suddenly and wander about or even start a new life in some other town. Days, weeks, or maybe many months later he "wakes up," remembers his original identity, and returns to his family. He can then recall details of his life before the fugue but may be (or claim to be) amnesic for what went on during the dissociation reaction. Under hypnosis, however, he may recall details from the fugue period.
   See also Amnesia.

FUNCTIONAL DISORDER, a behavior disorder presumed to be psychogenic because no organic or structural cause can be found. All psychoneuroses, psychosomatic disorders, and gross stress reactions are classified as functional, primarily caused by emotional reactions. Some psychotic disorders, however, can be classed as *organic* rather than functional, because damage to brain tissue can be detected. Psychotic behavior problems following head injuries, infections, tumors, or poisoning are examples. On the other hand, schizophrenia, paranoia, and manic depressive psychosis are classed as *functional psychoses.*

   It must be emphasized that these classifications reflect the current state of knowledge and that disorders will be reclassified if new findings change the diagnostic picture. Some investigators believe that there are biochemical causes for schizophrenia, for example. If such factors are positively identified, schizophrenia may be shifted to the organic list.

   Thus, a classification of a disorder is not the same as a full explanation of causes. Some neuroses are called functional because of the absence of known organic problems, rather than because psychological causes have been demonstrated conclusively. In many cases a patient's history supports the belief in emotional origins. Sometimes it can be shown that no organic defect accounts for the reported symptoms—in hysterical anesthesia, for example, when nothing is wrong with the nerves where the patient reports loss of feeling.

   Many disorders show both organic and functional components. Psychotic states following brain damage may be more severe in persons with a history of emotional instability. Here, as elsewhere, behavior reflects the whole constitutional and personality structure of the individual. The fact that psychologists and psychiatrists classify disorders for convenience in planning books and holding discussions does not mean that they are proposing to separate "mind" problems from "body" problems.
   See also Psychosomatic Disorders.
   Consult (1) English and English, 1958.

FUNCTIONAL FIXEDNESS, the inability to solve an insight problem because the solver cannot perceive an unusual function for an object. For example, a subject might be given the task of completing an electrical circuit but not supplied with enough wire to make all the connections. Thus, the solution requires him to use some metal (wrench, pliers, or screwdriver) instead of a missing wire connection. Functional fixedness is said to occur when the subject fails to think of the novel property of the object relevant to problem solution (its conductivity in this example) because he is "fixated" on the common function of the object (its function as wrench, pliers, or screwdriver). This explanation of how functional fixedness inhibits problem solving was first presented in a classic monograph by the Gestalt psychologist Karl Duncker.

   More recently, however, psychologists at Princeton have conducted experiments to clarify more precisely the circumstances in which functional fixedness may be relevant or irrelevant. Their studies have shown that, although actual functional fixedness can occur in some situations, such analysis often does not apply. Other processes, such as whether or not the subject notices the presence of the relevant object at all, may inhibit solution.
   —Roland Siiter, *Montclair State College*
   See also Problem Solving.
   Consult (7) Duncker, 1945; Glucksberg and Weisberg, 1966.

FUNCTIONAL PSYCHOLOGY. A movement originated primarily by John Dewey around the turn of the century. In opposition to structuralism, this approach emphasized action and utility in man's adaptation to his environment. It stressed objective testing of theories as opposed to subjective introspection.

   Dewey believed that one "learns by

Because the problem solver cannot assign an unusual function to an object, he fails to see that the pliers can be used to complete the electric circuit.

Versatile Briton Francis Galton contributed to many sciences; toward eugenic goals he developed tests, methods, and apparatus for the measurement and statistical correlation of individual differences.

The one-armed bandit derives much of its income from those who subscribe to the "gambler's fallacy"— the notion that a win is due after a succession of losses.

doing" and regarded mental phenomena as activities or processes rather than experiences. Thus the causes of such activities as perceiving, feeling, and judging were objectively sought in the conditions from which they arose and the consequences they produced.

This point of view had great influence on the development of scientific psychology, although functionalism as a well-defined school of psychology no longer exists.

—A. Ronald Seifert, *University of Tennessee*

FUNCTIONALISM. *See* Functional Psychology.

GALACTOSEMIA. *See* Mental Retardation.

GALTON, FRANCIS (1822–1911), English scientist. Born in Birmingham, he received his medical training at Birmingham General Hospital and at Trinity College, Cambridge. He was knighted in 1909.

A versatile scientist who is credited with significant contributions to mechanics, meteorology, anthropology, statistics, exploring, genetics, and eugenics, Galton is also regarded as the pioneer in the study of individual differences. One of Galton's first major projects in individual psychology was detailed in *Hereditary Genius* (1869). Here he compared the backgrounds of both prominent and average citizens to show statistically that eminent men tend to have eminent offspring; he regarded heredity, however, as the main method of transference and did not take into account the effects of environment. Later, he did make the first psychologically based study of twins to show the influences of heredity and environment.

Galton originated mental tests for measuring individual differences and worked out the method of statistical correlation, thus making it possible for researchers to state their results in quantitative terms. The aim of these tests was to locate superior human characteristics. Galton believed that the species could be improved through eugenics—selective breeding of persons with desirable traits. In order to assess the resources of Great Britain, he opened a laboratory in 1882 where people could take a series of tests measuring their physical characteristics, reaction time, and senses, making this the first mental-testing center. In *Inquiries into Human Faculty and Development* (1883), Galton discussed many of his psychological ideas. He studied differences in mental imagery through the use of questionnaires. His experiments on association showed that childhood experiences had an important effect on adult thinking and that many associative processes occurred on the subconscious level. He developed several pieces of apparatus, including the Galton whistle to test for the highest audible pitch and the Galton bar for

testing estimates of visual extension. He was an originator of the concept of ideational types and discovered the phenomenon of synesthesia (a subjective sensation of a sense other than the one being stimulated, as in color hearing).

GALVANIC SKIN RESPONSE (GSR), also called *electrodermal response,* changes in the conductivity or electrical activity of the skin. These changes, which can be detected by a galvanometer, are indicators of emotional arousal. *See* Emotion; Lie Detector.

GAMBLING. Gambling may be defined as the risking of something of value with a hope of gain. Very little research has been done on gambling. Most of the findings are indirect, coming either from experimental psychologists who study risk taking and decision making among college students using small amounts of money or from psychiatrists who are treating severely disturbed gamblers. Only a handful of studies have dealt with individuals who gamble regularly but not excessively. These studies of social gamblers have shown that gamblers are responsible parentally, socially, and politically and are as well as if not better adjusted than nongamblers. [*Consult* (10) McGlothlin, 1954; Tec, 1964.]

Psychological Factors. Although the findings of the experimental psychologists are not necessarily applicable to real-life gambling, they are instructive in that they have revealed risk-taking behavior to be extremely complex. It has determinants in the cognitive, emotional, situational, and personality spheres. [*Consult* (10) Kogan and Wallach, 1967.]

Studies investigating *personality factors* in relation to risk taking suggest the existence of a general tendency or motive to either approach or avoid risk-taking situations. This motive is apparently independent of the kinds or styles of behaviors an individual may exhibit once he finds himself in such a situation. [*Consult* (10) Knowles, *et al.,* 1972.]

The general tendency to approach risk-taking situations is similar to the *utility of risk* notion, which claims that risk taking is a rewarding activity in itself. Empirical support for a utility of risk comes from studies where people show a greater preference for risk than for gain. It has been postulated that this preference for risk reflects a need to reach an optimum level of physiological arousal. *Emotional arousal* as measured by heart rate has in fact been found to increase with the size of the wager, and greater risk taking has been observed under low than under medium arousal conditions. [*Consult* (10) Berlyne, 1960; Cohen, 1972; Goodnow, 1955; Rule, *et al.,* 1971; Rule and Fischer, 1970; Von Neumann and Morgenstern, 1947.]

The operation of an approach-avoidance motive for risk taking helps to explain the lack of consistency in risk-taking behaviors found across different situations by some researchers. That is, the failure of individuals in a consistently risky or cautious manner is due to the operation of different risk-taking *styles*. These are differentially elicited by variations in the situations themselves and, at the same time, are moderated by cognitive and personality factors within the individual. [*Consult* (10) Weinstein, 1969.]

Greater consistency in risk taking is seen when risk approachers or avoiders are examined separately and when cognitive or personality factors are allowed to act as moderators. For example, individuals with a high need for achievement prefer moderately risky bets, while those with low need prefer either very risky or very safe bets. Also, subjects low in anxiety and in the need for social approval will adapt their risk-taking strategies, sometimes taking strong chances and other times betting conservatively, so as to maximize their gain. On the other hand, highly anxious subjects with a high need for social approval will stubbornly pursue a losing strategy without a desire to change. [*Consult* (10) Atkinson, 1957; Kogan and Wallach, 1964.]

Several *cognitive factors* have been found to moderate risk-taking behaviors. These include the perceived amount of chance or skill involved in the task; the belief in luck; the perceived certainty, subjective probability, or confidence of winning; and the belief in the *gambler's fallacy*—that is, the notion that a win is due after a succession of losses. [*Consult* (10) Cohen, 1972; Edwards, 1954; Knox and Inkster, 1972; Liverant and Scodel, 1960; Rotter, 1966.]

Situational influences on risk taking are numerous: the amount of money previously won or lost, the mathematical probability of winning, the amount that may be won or lost, the size of the bankroll, whether one is gambling alone or in a group, and whether one is gambling with one's own money or with someone else's. [*Consult* (10) Lupfer, 1970; Munson, 1962; Siegel and Goldstein, 1959.]

Pathological Gambling. Although the distinction is not clear, gambling may be considered pathological rather than social once it begins to disrupt an individual's normal personal, social, familiar, economic, or legal status. The incidence of pathological gambling in the general population is estimated at less than 1 percent. But as many as five varieties of pathological gambling have been identified: psychopathic, neurotic, impulsive, symptomatic, and subcultural. [*Consult* (10) Kusyszyn, 1972; Moran, 1972.]

The *psychopathic* variety seems the most common. Here gambling forms one part of the general syndrome of the psychopathic or antisocial personality. The *neurotic* form is the next most prevalent; this form of gambling usually results from a stressful situation, such

as loss of a job, or from an emotional problem, such as marital separation. These two varieties encompass over 60 percent of all gamblers seeking treatment. [*Consult* (10) Boyd and Bolen, 1972; Moran, 1972; Roston, 1965.]

Symptomatic gambling is just one indicator of a general mental illness, such as schizophrenia. *Subcultural* gambling is engaged in as a result of the individual's social background. In *impulsive* gambling, the individual becomes ambivalent toward his gambling and continues to gamble until he runs out of money.

The popular "compulsive" gambler is a clinical nonentity when one considers compulsive behavior in the usual sense, as part of an obsessional illness. [*Consult* (10) Lewis, 1936.]

Many treatment methods have been used with pathological gamblers, including psychoanalysis, group and individual psychotherapy, aversive conditioning, boredom or stimulus satiation, paradoxical intention, and drug therapy. The success of the various treatment methods has been fair to moderate. [*Consult* (10) Bergler, 1970; Moran, 1970; Peck and Ashcroft, 1970; Seager, 1972; Victor and Krug, 1967.]

—Igor Kusyszyn, *York University*
Consult (10) Kusyszyn, 1972.

GAME THEORY, the orientation that holds that behavior is based on decision making and that views its results in terms of specific "decision units": the situation and the individual, or groups and societies, involved in it. Game theory deals with both the rules used per se and with the rules for playing the game intelligently. It suggests that life is essentially a game of strategy, in which the outcomes depend largely on the individual decision process of the players.

A game occurs if the decision (or the results of a decision) of at least two participants results in a consequence for each. These consequences may be independent of the behavior or objectives of any one of the players; it is a result of the success or failure of the strategy used by both of them. Such consequences are termed "payoffs." An increased payoff for one participant is linked to a decreased payoff for an opponent.

Game theory is mathematical in form, relying heavily on the use of matrices. Some theorists believe that all social behaviors in humans are games and can be explained as such. This idea has met with mixed success, but the approach is relatively recent and may be a beneficial tool in the future.

—Thom Herrmann, *University of Tennessee*
See also Experimental Gaming.

GAMES, CHILDREN'S. *See* Play.

Gambling is defined as pathological, rather than as social, when it begins to disrupt the individual's normal status. The incidence of pathological gambling in the United States is quite low, perhaps less than 1 percent.

The "utility-of-risk" concept—that risk taking is a rewarding activity in itself—is supported by studies in which people show a greater preference for risk than for gain.

GANGLION. *See* Nervous System.

GASTRITIS. *See* Psychosomatic Disorders.

GENE. *See* Chromosome; DNA; Genetics; Genotype; Heredity and Environment.

GENERAL ADAPTATION SYNDROME (GAS), a response to great stress involving the mobilization of all an organism's biological and psychological resources. In the first stage of psychological adaptation a person responds to a stress alarm by efforts at self-control but also by agitation, fearfulness, anger, tension, and the use of ego defense mechanisms. If these measures do not cope with the stress, a second stage follows in which defense mechanisms may deviate into neurotic and even psychotic forms. If stress continues into a third stage, the person breaks down into exhaustion, stupor, or continuing violence.
See also Stress.
Consult (13) Coleman, 1964.

GENERAL PARESIS, or paresis, an organic psychosis caused when syphilitic infection damages brain tissue. The psychotic symptoms appear from five to thirty years after the person first contracts syphilis. The disorder comes on slowly, with the afflicted person showing such signs as headaches, irritability, confusion, impairment of work, memory, and judgment, and flattening of emotional responses. As the disease progresses, physical condition, abilities, and personality all deteriorate in varying degrees. The end is a vegetative state and death, if treatment is not successful. Penicillin produces improvement in many cases.

GENERAL SEMANTICS. *See* Language; Meaning; Semantic Differential.

GENERALIZATION, or stimulus generalization, a measure of the extent to which an organism has discriminated a learned response. It is essentially an indication of how intensely an organism will respond to stimuli other than the one involving the original conditioning. For example, if an animal has learned that a 100-hertz tone indicates food is available, a generalization study will determine the strength of the subject's food-getting responses when tones of other pitches, both above and below 100 hertz, are presented.

GENERATION GAP. *See* Middle Years.

GENETIC PSYCHOLOGY, a field dealing with the role of genetic and hereditary influences on behavior. Genetic psychology is also concerned with the questions of whether innate behaviors exist and how they can be identified and studied. It has been particularly interested in the development of intelligence and the relative contribution of hereditary and environmental factors for this mental faculty.
See also Genetics; Heredity and Environment; Intelligence and Intelligence Testing.

GENETICS, the study of the transfer of inherited characteristics from one generation to another. This discipline accounts for the differences and similarities that occur among related organisms. Geneticists study the chemical and physical nature of the transmitted genetic material, the processes by which it is transmitted, and the sites where it acts.

Two new fields investigate more specific questions. *Behavior genetics* attempts to correlate different behaviors with heredity. *Population genetics* examines the distribution of genes throughout a mating population and studies the basic characteristics of that population as determined by those genes.
—Nina Adams, *Yale University*
See also Heredity and Environment.

GENITAL STAGE, or genital level, in psychoanalytic theory, the culminating stage of psychosexual development. Following the oral, anal, and phallic stages, the genital stage begins at puberty and is distinguished by the ability to form a truly affectionate relationship with a sex partner. This stage is not the beginning of strong interest in the sex organs, already strong in the phallic stages. Some individuals do not achieve full genital sexuality—if, for example, their development is fixated at the oral or anal stage.

The concept of genital stage is sometimes combined with *genital primacy,* which means that the predominant sexual interest is in coitus rather than in such activities as masturbation or sadism.
See also Character Development.
Consult (1) English and English, 1958.

GENIUS. The term "genius" has two broad connotations. It is used loosely to identify individuals of exceptionally superior intellectual capacities (with extremely high IQ). It also applies to individuals who possess outstandingly creative productivity, usually demonstrated by recognized achievement in a particular field of endeavor.

The origin of the term has been traced to the word "genio," used during the early sixteenth century to denote a great artist, thus reflecting such an individual's exceptional abilities in a specific area. The first systematic attempt to study the phenomenon was presented in a publication entitled *Hereditary Genius,* by Francis Galton in 1869. Galton concluded that his data supported the thesis that there is a direct hereditary connection between eminence and genius, but his findings have remained inconclusive, largely because he ignored the influences of differential environmental factors in the development of genius.

The IQ definitions of genius are usually couched in terms of the highest points on the intelligence continuum, implying that few people could ever approach these limits. Typical IQ levels used to identify genius range from 140 to 180 and above. In one sense, it is unfortunate that the concept of genius has been equated with such extreme levels of intellect, because the connotation of superior intelligence has led to the concomitant notion that such individuals are frequently neurotic, psychotic, or otherwise maladjusted.

Perhaps the most appropriate use of the term "genius" would be to denote those gifted individuals who are preeminently creative, original, and productive in a given area. Reflecting this notion, Anne Anastasi defines genius as "a superlative degree of those abilities which have high social significance within a particular culture." Thus, in our culture, those individuals recognized for outstanding accomplishments in areas such as science, literature, music, and art are sometimes referred to as "men of genius."

—Frank T. Vitro, *University of Maine*
See also Gifted Children.
Consult (9) Anastasi, 1965.

GENOTYPE, the genetic structure that an individual has inherited from his parents and will transmit to his decendants, whether or not he actually manifests the associated traits. The manifestation of a trait (the phenotype) is due to the interaction of the genes with the environment (for example, suntanning of the skin is a change in phenotype but not in genotype). Changes in genotype occur through the recombination of genes that takes place during sexual reproduction or through mutation of the gene during cell division.

—Nina Adams, *Yale University*
See also Genetics; Heredity and Environment.

GERIATRIC PSYCHOLOGY AND PSYCHIATRY, the study of the psychological characteristics of older persons and treatment of disorders that develop in old age. See Aging.

GERONTOLOGY, the study of old persons and their way of life. This specialty draws on geriatric medicine, psychology and psychiatry, anthropology, sociology, and social work. For psychological aspects, see Aging.

GESELL, ARNOLD LUCIUS (1880–1961), American child psychologist. Born in Alma, Wis., he received a Ph.D. from Clark University (1906) and an M.D. from Yale (1915). He was director of the Yale Clinic of Child Development (1911 to 1948) and was later consultant with the Gesell Institute of Child Development.

Gessell was for many years *the* authority on child development in America. His career encompassed a prolific number of writings, the development of several psychological tests, the education of many child psychologists and pediatricians, and influential laboratory experimentation. Gesell stressed the importance of internal rather than environmental forces in child development. Though his theoretical work has largely been superseded by the ideas of theorists such as Jean Piaget and Jerome Bruner, he was an important pioneer in child psychology. He successfully bridged the gap between theoretical studies and practical applications.

His books, some of which sold widely, include *Infant and Child in the Culture of Today* (with Frances L. Ilg), 1943; *The Child from Five to Ten* (with Frances L. Ilg), 1946; and *Youth: The Years from Ten to Sixteen* (with Ilg and L. B. Ames), 1956.

GESTALT PSYCHOLOGY, a theory, school, or systematic point of view in general psychology. "Gestalt," the German word for "form" or "figure," is best rendered in English as "configuration." Gestalt psychology emphasizes totalities and dynamic organization in experience. When first formulated, it came into conflict with the older schools of structural and functional psychology—and, indeed, with its contemporary, behaviorism.

The genealogy of Gestalt psychology can be traced back at least to von Ehrenfels and the *Gestaltqualität* ("form-quality") movement of the late nineteenth century. Supporters of this viewpoint contended not only that experience was analyzable into local sensations (colors, tones, odors), a view they shared with W. M. Wundt and the structuralists, but also that experience contained within it certain additional elements or supralocal qualities, such as roundness, angularity, and turbidity in vision, melodic continuity in audition, and roughness in touch. The conventional analysis had considered these to be compounds (not elements) built up through association and dependent on past experience.

Theory. The emphasis by Gestalt psychologists on *wholes* and *organization* has led some to the belief that they oppose all psychological analysis, but it is only to "atomistic" approaches that they object. All sciences must use analysis to isolate their basic elements. Gestalt psychologists find what they consider the *real* units of experience, the true elements of their science, in subwholes or organized parts whose properties depend on the total configuration to which they belong. A first step into "real" analysis was taken by the Danish phenomenologist Edgar Rubin, who orginally stressed, in visual and auditory perception, the importance of the *figure-ground* distinction. Any visual field will spontaneously break down

GESTALT PSYCHOLOGY

If part of a contour is omitted, we tend to fill the gaps and organize the figure into a dog in a perceptual process known as closure.

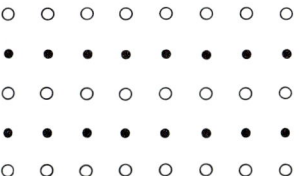

Spacing determines whether we see rows or columns (principle of proximity). When all dots are equally spaced we group similar items together—rows of circles and rows of dots (principle of similarity).

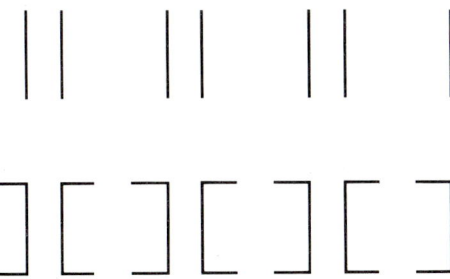

The principle of proximity causes us to group the lines into three pairs with an extra line to the right. The same lines, with extensions, pair oppositely under the principle of closure.

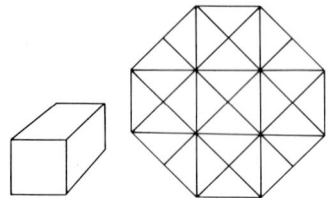

The larger figure is so dominant that it is difficult to see that it contains the smaller figure.

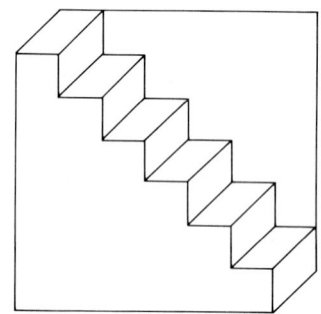

If you focus on the middle step, the figure of the staircase alternates with the ground.

into these two components; in reversible configurations the two portions will alternate with each other in predominating as figure.

Just as Gestalt psychology differs from the older introspectionism and behaviorism in its modes of description and analysis, it also departs widely from them on the explanatory side. Because it appeals to natural forces within the organism as originators of behavior, it has been thought to be more nearly aligned with *nativism* than *empiricism,* but Gestalt psychology rejects both extreme positions. Taking its leads from the physics of equilibrium states—whether found in hydraulics, thermal interchanges, or electrical phenomena—it tends to substitute dynamics for statics, free interplay of forces within the nervous system for order produced by artificial constraints and "machine" principles. Seen from this perspective, the central nervous system is less like a telephone switchboard than a set of electrical fields in a volume conductor.

Research. Prominently associated with Gestalt psychology are the names of Max Wertheimer, usually regarded as the originator of the approach through his revolutionary paper of 1912 on perception of visual movement; Wolfgang Köhler, its best systematizer and international advocate; Kurt Koffka, widely known for his perceptual researches; and Kurt Lewin, who extended Gestalt principles into the areas of personality study and developmental-social psychology.

Although visual perception was the field in which the basic ideas of Gestalt psychology were first developed and elaborated, its principles are by no means confined to this area. Indeed, other sensory and perceptual problems are readily attacked by them, and Gestalt theory is equally applicable to questions of the retention and reproduction of experience. Thus, the areas of memory and learning, thinking and concept formation, behavioral organization, and personality have all benefited by having their problems restated in this framework.

—Frank A. Geldard, *Princeton University*

See also Concept Learning; Figure-Ground Perception; Illusion.

Consult (1) Heidbreder, 1933; Koffka, 1935; Köhler, 1929; Köhler, 1969; Lewin, 1936.

GIFTED CHILDREN, a generic term usually used to refer to the 1 percent of children with intelligence quotients (IQs), as measured by tests, above 135 (100 is considered the average IQ).

The most extensive data available on gifted individuals were provided by a longitudinal study conducted by Lewis Terman and his associates, who attempted to resolve issues related to background variables and later development of gifted children. The investiga-tion, which began in 1921, involved the selection of over 1,000 California school children with IQs, as measured by the Stanford-Binet test, of 140 and above. The development of these subjects was appraised at intervals as they matured, the last assessment being at age forty-five.

The major conclusion was that the youngsters in this "genius" group achieved significantly more than children in the population at large. They were above average in physical development and health, leadership traits, and participation in extracurricular activities, and over 85 percent were accelerated in their school work beyond the level of their age mates. They eventually attended college with greater frequency than the general population, and an extraordinarily high proportion of them went on to graduate or professional study. As adults they tended to earn higher salaries and distinguished themselves through their writings and other achievements.

There are some who feel that IQ alone is not a sufficient basis for identification, since so many individuals with IQs below 130 tend to be "gifted" by virtue of various combinations of drive, self-direction, innovativeness, and curiosity. Thus, recent developments in the assessment of intelligence and in the definition of giftedness have expanded the concept to encompass multiple abilities rather than the single, generalized skill represented by an IQ score. While IQ is the predominate vehicle for specifying giftedness, educators have begun to assign more importance to various other abilities that the child may possess. For example, since 1960 research related to the gifted has shifted in focus from intellectual functioning to the creative process.

—Frank T. Vitro, *University of Maine*

See also Intelligence and Intelligence Testing.

Consult (5) Terman, *et al.,* 1925; Terman and Oden, 1947; Terman and Oden, 1959.

GLANDS. Although these organs may have more than one function, they can be classed as glands of external secretion (for example, the kidneys and sweat glands), which excrete through ducts to the outside of the body, and glands of internal secretion, which produce substances used in the body. The endocrine glands (ductless glands) produce hormones, which are discharged into the blood and act as regulators of many body processes. *See* Adrenal Glands; Gonads; Parathyroid Glands; Pineal Gland; Pituitary Gland; Thyroid Gland.

Glands and the nervous system are discussed in Autonomic Nervous System. Effects of glands on behavior are noted in the article on Emotion.

GLOSSOLALIA, "speaking in tongues," a phenomenon of religious ecstatic states in which a person discourses in language unintelligible to most others. In Christian tradition, the gift of tongues was conferred on Christ's disciples by the Holy Spirit on the day of Pentecost. Members of some Pentecostal churches still speak in tongues, and individuals in other denominations have shown interest in this form of religious experience.

The term "glossolalia" is also applied to fabricated language observed in cases of mental illness.

GOAL. *See* Drive; Motivation.

GODDARD, HENRY HERBERT (1866–1957), American psychologist, noted for his studies of mental deficiency. Born in Vassalboro, Me., he received his Ph.D. from Clark University (1899). He was founder and director of Vineland Training School for Feebleminded Children, Vineland, N.J., the first institution in the United States for training retarded children (1906–1918) and professor of psychology at Ohio State (1922–1938).

Goddard adapted the Binet intelligence test for use in the United States and worked on the classification of levels of retardation. He was the first to use the term "moron." One of his major contributions was showing that many defectives could be trained to hold productive jobs.

Goddard's studies led him to conclude that heredity was the prime cause of retardation. He reached this conclusion after tracing the ancestry of a New Jersey family (given the case-name "Kallikak") and finding one strain marked by retardation and other abnormalities. This finding did not prove that heredity was the cause of the retardation. However, Goddard almost entirely neglected the influence of environment on intellectual development. A later genetic study was marred by an incorrect view of how mental defects can be transmitted. Goddard assumed that a single gene was responsible, whereas, in fact, many genes interact to produce this result.

Goddard's major works include *The Kallikak Family,* 1912; *Feeblemindedness, Its Cause and Consequences,* 1914; *School Training of Defective Children,* 1915; *Human Efficiency and Levels of Intelligence,* 1920; and *The School Training of Gifted Children,* 1928.

See also Kallikak Family.

GONADS, the male and female sexual glands. In the female the ovaries, located in the abdominal region, produce two hormones, estrogen and progesterone, which are important for female sexual development, regulation of the menstrual cycle, and the production of the egg, or ovum. The male testes, small glands located in the scrotum in the adult, are important for the production of spermatozoa and testosterone, a hormone responsible for male sexual development and secondary sexual characteristics.

GOOFBALL, a slang term for a pill containing a barbiturate or a tranquilizer. *See* Drugs and Behavior.

GRADIENT, the changing strength of a drive to approach or avoid a goal. The gradual changes indicate the relative strength and direction (approach or avoidance) of the drive in terms of the relationship between the individual and the goal. The strength of the gradient is dependent on the individual's proximity to the goal.

GRAMMAR. *See* Language.

GRAPHOLOGY, handwriting analysis. Psychologists are interested in this subject because of the hypothesis that handwriting is a projection of personality. (Forensic graphology, the study of handwriting to determine who wrote what, is another specialty.)

The centuries-old attempt to read personality from handwriting has ranged from party game through pseudoscience to controlled investigation. Amateurs and self-styled experts have claimed they could study a sample of handwriting and describe the traits of the writer. Some have used long lists of specific signs, such as the weight and slant of letters and the length of bars on *t*s, relating each to a trait. Others have argued that it is necessary to integrate signs into patterns as a basis for diagnosis.

Psychologists have tested the claims of graphologists. A study by the French psychologist Alfred Binet led to a report that the graphologists were able to reach correct conclusions about personality. On the other hand, several investigations in the United States have tended to disprove these claims. Many psychologists in this country agree that although handwriting, like other behavior, reflects personality differences, much more investigation is needed before any pattern of relationships can be accepted.

Consult (9) Guilford, 1959; Allport and Vernon, 1933; Holt, 1966.

GREGARIOUSNESS. *See* Affiliative Drive.

GROSS STRESS REACTION, a personality disorder caused by the stress of combat in war or disaster in civilian life. *See* Civilian Catastrophe Reaction; Combat Neurosis.

GROUP BEHAVIOR. *See* Attitude Change; Bargaining; Choice Shift; Competition; Conflict; Conformity; Exchange Theory; Experimental Gaming; Field Theory; Power; Prejudice.

GROUP PSYCHOTHERAPY, often called group therapy, any form of psychological treatment

Henry Goddard studied the genetic transfer of mental deficiency and worked on the training of both defective and gifted children.

in which the therapist is involved in treating more than one patient at a time. Its goals and techniques have been employed for thousands of years, particularly by religious leaders, but it was not until the twentieth century that formalized systems of group psychotherapy were formed for the treatment of large numbers of people suffering from emotional and mental disorders. Psychodrama, originated by psychiatrist Jacob L. Moreno in Vienna shortly after World War I, was probably the earliest formalized system of group therapy. Psychodrama represented a protest against the impracticality of reaching large numbers of people with the individual psychotherapeutic methods of the Freudian school. Further, it affirmed the importance of social factors in the genesis and treatment of mental disorders.

Although the initial impetus for group therapy came from the unsatisfied needs of thousands of people for whom no real psychological therapy was available, experience with these methods soon revealed that the group structure itself offered some real advantages. In the United States, leaders in the development of group therapy methods were such teachers as S. R. Slavson, Paul Schilder, and Louis Wender.

Procedures. Current methods of group therapy involve either small groups (limited to between six and twelve patients) or larger (limited only by the capacity of the auditorium). In small groups, the setting is informal and intimate, and free interaction is promoted. The members meet (usually three to five times a week) in sessions lasting one to two hours under the unobtrusive guidance of a leader, who should be either a psychiatrist, clinical psychologist, psychiatric social worker, psychiatric nurse, or other psychiatrically trained professional. The leader tries to draw out shy, withdrawn members and restrain verbose, overexuberant ones. By listening to and responding to each other, the members learn to express their thoughts, feelings, fears, inhibitions, anxieties, and worries. They aim to develop understanding attitudes toward each other and to give each other support and encouragement. By recognizing others' thoughts, aberrations, and emotional difficulties, members may come to appreciate similar tendencies in themselves—to see themselves as others see them.

In large groups the leader needs to assume a directive or didactic role, though audience reaction and participation are strongly encouraged. Many clinics have both large and small group set-ups: a large or "general" group meeting once a week, divided into several small groups the other days of the week. In any well-run clinic, facilities would also be available for individual therapy sessions with experienced clinicians, to handle "crisis" situations and to provide more intensive therapy for those who need it.

—Emanuel Messinger, M.D., *U.S. Veterans Hospital, Northport, N.Y.*

See also Family Therapy; Psychodrama. Consult (13) Coleman, 1964; Slavson, 1946; Slavson, 1950.

GROUP THERAPY. *See* Group Psychotherapy; Encounter Group.

GSR RESPONSE. *See* Galvanic Skin Response.

GUIDANCE. *See* Counseling Psychology.

GUILFORD, JOY PAUL (1897–   ), American psychologist. Born in Marquette, Neb., he received a Ph.D. from Cornell (1927) and was professor of psychology at Southern California, and director (after 1949) of the Aptitudes Research Project. Guilford was president of the American Psychological Association (1949-1950).

Guilford's research has been in the area of psychological measurement of personality and intelligence. He has derived, through factor analysis, a model of the "structure of intellect," enumerating 120 specific intellectual factors. His books include *Psychometric Methods*, 1954; *Personality*, 1959; and *Fields of Psychology* (editor), 1966. He is coauthor of the *Guilford-Zimmerman Aptitude Survey, Guilford-Zimmerman Interest Inventory*, and *Guilford-Zimmerman Temperament Survey*.

—Nina Adams, *Yale University*

GUILT FEELINGS. Feelings of unworthiness and self-reproach may be factors in psychoneurosis. For example, if parents set high moral standards for a child and he fails to meet expectations, he may blame himself and develop anxiety. Conflicts between sexual drives and moralistic warnings have caused many emotional conflicts.

In Freudian theory the impulses of the id often clash with the standards of the superego. Guilt feelings develop when the ego, stirred by the id, violates an ideal of the superego.

Guilt can be a normal reaction to an actual fault. Failure to have guilt feelings is a mark of the antisocial person who has a weak conscience and who lives at odds with the customs and laws of society.

See also Oedipus Complex; Sociopathic Personality Disturbance; Superego. Consult (13) Lewis, 1971.

GUSTATION, the sense of taste. *See* Taste.

HABIT, any instrumentally learned response that occurs with regularity and in response to specific environmental cues. In some cases the habit is tied to a number of stimuli, while other habits may be tied to stimuli that occur relatively infrequently.

History. The concept of habit has a long history in experimental psychology. In the learning theories of Clark Hull and Kenneth Spence, for example, it played a central role as an established response tendency. Interacting with drive to produce behavior, habit was the know-how and drive the motivation. Learning was viewed as the accumulation and organization of response habits.

This concept of habit has received less attention in recent years because it has been recognized that habits can better be understood by means of a more operational analysis. This emphasizes their acquisition, modification, and generalization.

Although habit became less and less central to theories of human and animal learning as an intervening variable, it has remained an important aspect of all behavior theory. The questions that researchers pose about habit have changed, with modern interest focused on the factors that influence habit, especially the role of environmental cues in the establishment of habit.

One by-product of this change in emphasis has been a growing understanding of habitual behaviors. An important aspect of this change in focus is a growing concern about how behavior patterns became habits and how habits can be eliminated or modified.

Habit Acquisition. Building good habits is an essential part of the socialization process. Parents, teachers, and others have as one of their goals the teaching of good work habits, study habits, manners (which are social habits), and a variety of other habits that are valued by the culture. This can be expressed in slightly more technical terms by saying that parents and teachers are concerned with establishing a set of relatively permanent work behaviors, study behaviors, and social behaviors. Typical study-habit behaviors would include concentration, memorization, efficiency, neatness, and verbal skills. The goal is to establish these behaviors as virtually automatic responses to a set of stimuli associated with studying.

Acquiring these behaviors is essentially a two-part process. First the behavior in question must be learned. The individual must learn to concentrate, memorize, and attend to his work. These responses must become so well established, in fact, that they require little or no effort. In terms of operant conditioning, the establishment of a habit is entirely dependent upon the reinforcement of appropriate behaviors and the extinguishing or punishment of inappropriate behaviors. But this acquisitory stage may not be as obvious as it first appears.

The second aspect of habit acquisition is the pairing of the appropriate response with specific environmental cues. All of us have thousands of well-learned responses that cannot be considered habits because they are not tied to any specific external cues. To be considered a habit, such a response must occur when and only when a particular stimulus or set of stimuli are present. In this stage of habit building, the previously learned response is said to be brought under *discriminative control* of environmental cues; the habit becomes tied to events in the environment that determine when the response will occur. In building the study habit, for example, the responses of concentration, memorization, and so on become conditioned to a set of discriminative stimuli, such as a study hall, library, desk, open notebook, and so on.

The most common problem in establishing a habit is that the environmental cues often are not strong enough or salient enough to elicit the habit behaviors. Thus, school counselors often suggest that a student should have a room or small area that serves as a cue exclusively for studying. If the environment becomes a cue for only one habit, the probability that the desired behavior will occur is increased.

An even greater problem in the establishment of a habit may arise when the behaviors to be cued by the environmental stimuli are not sufficiently strong to be consistently emitted. The response may be so weak, in fact, that the environmental cues elicit an entirely different or even incompatible habit. Many otherwise good programs to build useful habits have failed because an inadequate amount of attention was given to strengthening the desired behaviors before getting them under strict control.

Habit Elimination. The elimination of habits can be more of a problem than their acquisition. Old habits, such as smoking, overeating, and unsafe work practices, are difficult to eliminate, but they can be extinguished by applying the same principles used to build habits.

First, the responses that the habit comprises may be weakened through punishment or extinction. In the case of overeating, the individual may deprive himself of some reward when he overeats, or he may join a weight-control group to provide external punishment.

Important environmental cues must also be eliminated, so that the habit will no longer be elicited by external factors. Smoking or eating cues, for example, can be catalogued by an individual and then systematically eliminated. Usually the weakest cues are eliminated first, followed by the more difficult. In one experimental program individuals learned to refrain from smoking in a variety of situations; the final step in the program was attendance at several no-smoking cocktail parties. Since

Elimination of undesirable habits requires the elimination of important environmental cues. If we substitute fruit juice for the coffee, the desire to smoke is reduced.

Credited with many firsts or near-firsts in American psychology, educator G. Stanley Hall also taught many who became distinguished in the field.

HEARING

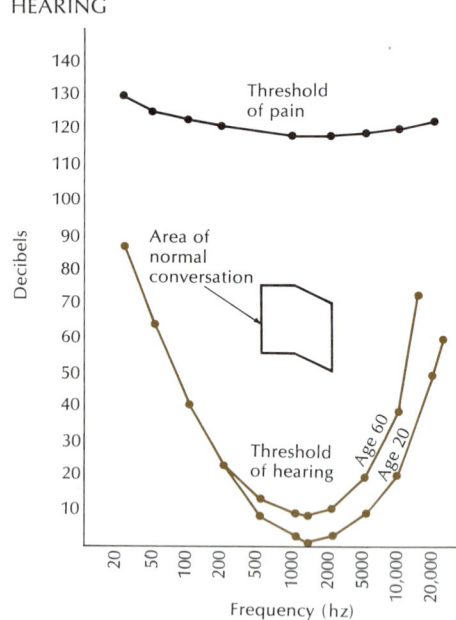

The human ear is able to sense frequencies in the range of 20 to 20,000 cycles per second. Note, however, how the volume must be increased to be audible to the older ear. Zero decibels represents a barely audible sound. Sounds above 100 decibels can be deafening.

cocktail parties serve as very strong smoking elicitors, this cue was an important one to eliminate. Such programs must be individually tailored to fit individual environmental hierarchies.

As with the building of habits, both the behavior and the environmental cues controlling the behavior must be effectively dealt with. Successful habit elimination ideally should also provide an alternative response for the old cues. The foreman concerned with unsafe work practices, for example, will be more successful if he trains the correct response at the same time that he tries to eliminate an inappropriate old habit.

—Brenda B. Bankart and C. Peter Bankart, *Wabash College*
See also Behavior Therapy; Operant Conditioning.
Consult (6) Kimble and Garmezy, 1968.

HALFWAY HOUSE, a facility for aftercare of patients released from mental hospitals. The house provides a place to live and helps people adjust to working and living in a community. Some houses provide continuing treatment for those who need it.

HALL, GRANVILLE STANLEY (1846–1924), American psychologist and educator. Born in Ashfield, Mass., he received his Ph.D. under William James and H. P. Bowditch of Harvard (1878) and studied under Wilhelm Wundt in Germany (1878–1880). He was professor of psychology and founder of the Psychology Laboratory (1884) at Johns Hopkins and was the first president of Clark University (1889–1920).

Hall's pioneering achievements in psychology include receiving one of the first American Ph.D.s in psychology; founding one of the first psychology laboratories in America; publishing innovative studies of childhood, adolescence, and human genetics; and founding the first American psychology journal—the *American Journal of Psychology* (1887)—the *Journal of Applied Psychology* (1915), and the American Psychological Association (1892). Hall was one of the first Americans to become interested in psychoanalysis, and in 1909 he brought Freud and Jung to Clark University. His students included John Dewey, James McK. Cattell, William Burnham, and Edmund C. Sanford.

Hall's own research efforts covered a broad area. Perhaps his most significant work studied children's minds through the use of questionnaires. Although his conclusions were drawn from samples of an ill-defined population, they represented the founding of the child-study movement. Hall was also particularly interested in applying the theory of evolution to psychology and concentrated on animal and human development and adaptation.

Hall's most important work is the two-volume *Adolescence: Its Psychology and Its Relations to Physiology, Anthropology, Sociology, Sex, Crime, Religion, and Education* (1904). Others include "Contents of Children's Minds," *Princeton Review*, 1883; *Founders of Modern Psychology*, 1912; and *Jesus the Christ in the Light of Psychology*, two vols., 1917.

HALLUCINATION, a sensory impression reported when no external stimulus exists to justify the report. Hallucinations are a symptom of mental illness; psychotic patients sometimes believe that they hear accusing voices when there is no sound, or see swarms of bugs on a bare floor or wall. Psychoactive drugs, such as LSD, can produce bizarre hallucinations.

A hallucination should be distinguished from an illusion, which is a mistaken perception of an existing stimulus, and a delusion, which is a persisting irrational belief.

See also Delusion; Illusion; Psychotic Disorders.

HALLUCINOGEN, a psychoactive drug such as LSD. *See* Drugs and Behavior.

HALO EFFECT, a tendency on the part of an experimenter to be unduly influenced by salient traits or characteristics (positive or negative) of a subject. Thus, in evaluating or rating the subject, the examiner's judgment of other aspects of his functioning or personality is (subconsciously) made to coincide with the most prominent impression.

HANDEDNESS, the preference for using one hand rather than the other to perform such fine motor skills as eating, writing, cutting with scissors, and swinging a baseball bat. Although approximately 95 percent of the world population is right-handed (very few persons are truly ambidextrous), there is no theoretically proven explanation for this tendency.

Cohen (1966) has indicated that infants who are above average in mental and motor development show a greater degree of hand preference by eight months of age than do babies who are less well advanced. This preference favors the right hand. But, despite this tendency, a definite hand preference is not usually established in infancy. Several studies have indicated that children display much bilaterality until the age of three and a half. They shift easily from use of one to the other hand, depending primarily upon the position of the person or the object they wish to grasp. A unilateral preference becomes predominate between the fourth and sixth years of life. [*See* H. Ames, 1964; Belmont, 1963; Brown, 1962; Palmer, 1964.]

—Cynthia MacRitchie, *Southern Connecticut State College*

HANDICAPPED. *See* Mental Retardation.

HANDWRITING ANALYSIS. *See* Graphology.

HARLOW, HARRY F. (1905–   ), American psychologist, born in Fairfield, Iowa. He is professor of psychology at the University of Wisconsin, where he is director of the Primate Lab and director of the Regional Primate Center.

Harlow's research with rhesus monkeys has concerned the areas of learning and motivation. His rhesus monkeys, in learning hundreds of different problems with different stimuli, exhibit continual improvement, which he has termed "learning to learn." He has also shown that rhesus monkeys are motivated to manipulate even with no food reward and has been critical of the "deprivation theory of drive."

Harlow's well-known films and papers on "surrogate mothers" show that young monkeys, when frightened, show preference for a cuddly surrogate rather than a wire-frame surrogate that delivers food. He also showed that unless monkeys have a peer group during their first six months, they exhibit bizarre or inappropriate adult behavior.

—Nina Adams, *Yale University*

HEAD INJURY. *See* Brain Disorders.

HEADACHE. Migraine headache is a psychosomatic disorder of the cardiovascular type. *See* Psychosomatic Disorders.

HEARING. The three major components of the hearing mechanism are the outer, middle, and inner ear.

Physical Structure of the Ear. The visible portion of the ear, the pinna, and the external auditory canal make up the outer ear. The canal, approximately 1¼ inches in length with a diameter of ¼ inch, transmits airborne sounds to the middle ear, in addition to protecting the eardrum or tympanic membrane. It serves as a resonator for sounds in the frequency range from approximately 200 to 5,500 hertz' (cycles per second).

In the tympanic membrane, which separates the middle ear from the outer ear, there are three layers of tissue: the outer cutaneous layer; the tendonous layer, which provides added strength to the membrane; and the mucous membrane, which is the innermost layer.

The middle ear is lined with a mucous membrane and is only one to two cubic centimeters in size. It is joined to the nasopharynx by means of the Eustachian tube. In other words, there is a direct connection from the nasal passage to the middle ear.

The three smallest bones in the human body are located in the middle ear: the malleus, which is connected to the tympanic membrane; the incus; and the stapes, which is fastened to the oval window. When airborne sounds reach the tympanic membrane, they cause this membrane to vibrate. This, in turn, causes mechanical vibration of the malleus, incus, and stapes bones.

The inner ear, or cochlea, is located in the temporal lobe and is referred to as a labyrinth because of its series of channels and chambers, both bony and membranous. The membranous labyrinth is located inside the bony labyrinth. Fluid called perilymph fills the bony labyrinth, and another fluid called endolymph fills the membranous labyrinth. The organ of Corti, the sensory mechanism for audition, lies inside and along the entire length of the membranous labyrinth.

The Hearing Process. When the vibration of the stapes causes the oval window, to which it is attached, to move, both fluids in the cochlea are affected. Activity in the organ of Corti is created by movement of pressure waves and affects a series of hair cells and other structures. There is a direct connection between the hair cells and the hearing or auditory nerve. Thus impulses are sent along the nerve, via the brainstem, to the brain, where speech is interpreted.

In summary, airborne sounds are conducted through the outer ear, are converted into mechanical vibrations in the middle ear, and are eventually changed into impulses in the inner ear. The impulses are conveyed for interpretation to the brain by way of the hearing nerve. The young healthy ear is able to perceive frequencies from 20 to 20,000 hertz although most speech in English is found within the frequency range from 500 to 2,000 hertz, which is often referred to as the speech frequency range.

—Jerome G. Alpiner, *University of Denver*

See also Deafness.

Consult (4) Davis and Silverman, 1970; Fletcher, 1953; Hirsh, 1952; Rose, 1971. (2) Stevens, 1951.

HEBB, DONALD OLDING (1904–   ), Canadian psychologist. Born in Chester, Nova Scotia, he began his career as a novelist then studied psychology at McGill, Chicago, and Harvard.

Hebb's predominant concern has been the relationship of the brain to intelligence. His *Organization of Behavior* (1949) was his major attempt to establish, at a physiologically molar level, integration of the brain and intelligence. He proposed that there are "cell assemblies," a brain process corresponding to particular sensory events. Activity in these assemblies can "reverberate"—continuing after the sensory event that started ceases—hence laying the basis for perception.

HEARING

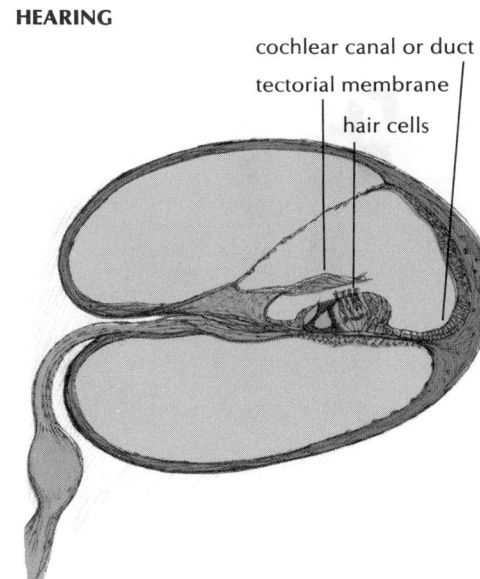

Cross-section of outer, middle, and inner ear with a detail drawing of the cross-section of the cochlea, showing the hair cells of the organ of Corti.

cochlear canal or duct
tectorial membrane
hair cells

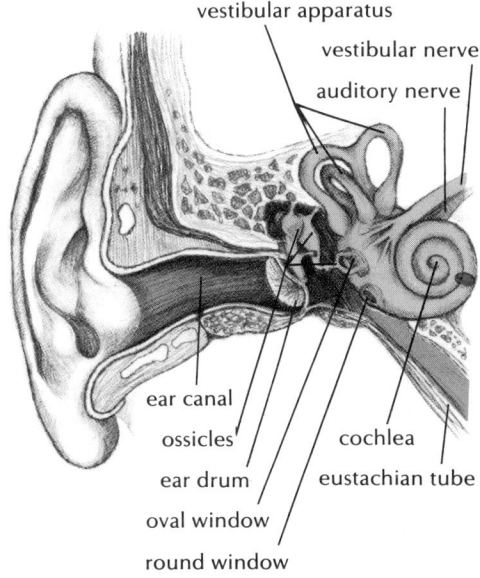

vestibular apparatus
vestibular nerve
auditory nerve
ear canal
ossicles
ear drum
oval window
round window
cochlea
eustachian tube

Herman Helmholtz, German physicist and physiologist, studied sensation, perception, and the development and structure of consciousness.

HEREDITY AND ENVIRONMENT

The mechanisms of inheritance, as they interact with environmental influences, are discussed in the general article HEREDITY AND ENVIRONMENT. Supporting details are provided in GENETICS, CHROMOSOME, DNA, RNA, GENOTYPE, and PHENOTYPE.

The general article also mentions one of the long-standing controversies in the history of psychology, the "nature-nurture" argument. In the 19th and early 20th centuries, some experts argued that heredity is the prime determiner of ability—see EUGENICS, JUKES FAMILY, and KALLIKAK FAMILY. There has been a recent revival of the controversy over inheritance versus environmental influences in discussions of mental abilities and aggression.

The great majority of students of this area believe that this is no simple either-or problem; the task is to trace the interactions of heredity and environment, what is innate and what is learned, as factors in behavior. See HEREDITY AND ENVIRONMENT, CHILD DEVELOPMENT, INTELLIGENCE AND INTELLIGENCE TESTING, AGGRESSION, ETHOLOGY (note the viewpoint of behavior genetics), and INSTINCT.

A recent concern of psychology is the study of the interaction of the individual with his surroundings, using methods from biology. This field is called BEHAVIORAL ECOLOGY, environmental psychology, or human ecology. Studies extend to such topics as the effect of building design on people, as noted in MENTAL HOSPITAL.

Hebb was the only Canadian to be president of the American Psychological Association.

—Thom Herrmann, *University of Tennessee*

HELMHOLTZ, HERMAN LUDWIG FERDINAND VON (1821–1894), German physiologist, physicist, and mathematician. Born in Potsdam, he received his M.D. in 1842, studying under Johannes Müller. He taught at Heidelberg and the University of Berlin and was first president of the Imperial Physico-Technical Institute at Charlo Henburg.

Helmholtz made fundamental contributions to the experimental psychology of sensation. However, he cannot be considered one of the founders of experimental psychology, for he viewed such research as an extension of physiology. His theories of vision and hearing derived from the concept of the specific energies of nerves, which states, in effect, that all sensations have different qualities and that different qualities can be localized in specific areas of the nervous system.

Helmholtz was in sympathy with the empiricists' contention that human conscious experience was the result of each person's interaction with his environment and not of some innate mechanism. He developed the concept of unconscious inference to describe the way in which past experience affects perceptions. Most of his research represented an attempt to study the development and structure of consciousness systematically. Among his technical contributions was the invention of the opthalmoscope, an instrument for the examination of the eyes. His major publications include *Psychological Optics* (3 vols, 1856–1866), and *On the Sensation of Tone,* 1862.

—Michael Rothenberg, *The City College of The City University of New York*

HEMATOPHOBIA, morbid fear of blood. *See* Phobia.

HEREDITY AND ENVIRONMENT. Heredity is the innate capacity of an individual to develop characteristics possessed by its ancestors. The laws of heredity were first described by Gregor Mendel in 1866. On the basis of his observations of pea plants bred in the garden of his monastery, Mendel stated that an offspring is not the result of the blending, like liquids, of parental characteristics. Instead, he showed that hereditary traits are independent of one another and are transmitted, by the laws of chance, as separate units from parent to offspring. Offspring may carry a given trait as a "recessive" unit of a pair and not show the characteristic, but it might emerge in later generations.

Basic Principles of Heredity. Genes are the basic material of heredity. They are combinations of organic molecules composed primarily of deoxyribonucleic acid (DNA). The genes lie along the threadlike chromosomes contained in the nucleus of the cell. Each cell in the human body contains forty-six chromosomes, with the exception of the *gametes* (sex cells), which contain half that number, twenty-three chromosomes. The gametes are formed by a process of cell division and reduction called *meiosis.* The fertilized cell from which an individual develops results from the joining of two gametes, one from the mother and one from the father. It then contains forty-six chromosomes, but in a combination different from either parent. Meiosis thus keeps the number of chromosomes constant. If it did not occur, each new generation of gametes would contain twice the number of chromosomes present in the preceding generation.

The genes control the development of enzymes, which are the basis of all chemical processes of the body. All the genes of an individual organism (the genotype) determine the range of physiological processes available to it under various environmental conditions. Most characteristics (the phenotype) depend on the combined action of many genes interacting with the environment. Only a few characteristics (such as eye color) are dependent upon the action of a single pair of genes.

Changes in the environment require accommodation by a given genotype or the emergence of a new genotype. New genotypes can result from the random alteration of a gene (*mutation*). Most mutants are not advantageous, and they die out. Darwin, in 1859, showed that those mutations that are more suitable to the environment will survive through natural selection. The Mendelian laws of the independence of hereditary units and the Darwinian laws of survival of the fittest and natural selection are the basis of modern understanding of inheritance and evolution.

Interaction of Heredity and Environment. A question of interest for both scientists and philosophers has been the comparative importance of hereditary and environmental factors in determining the characteristics of an individual. This question, sometimes known as the *nature-nurture controversy* is often filled with rhetoric and misinterpretation. The "nature" or "nativistic" argument states that man is fundamentally good or evil and that the environment is simply the background on which inborn instincts are acted out. Expressions like "it's in his blood" or "bad seed" reflect this approach. The "nurture" or "empirical" argument states that behavior is a consequence of experience and, in the extreme, that man is simply a mirror of environmental influences. The controversy usually swings from one extreme to the other.

Although many famous studies have

been done in this area, their conclusions often reflect the initial bias of the experimenters. Two projects in the early twentieth century traced intellectual and character defects in families. The Jukes family of feebleminded individuals, many of whom were unable to care for themselves, were traced for over 130 years by R. L. Dugdale and A. H. Estabrook, who concluded that an unwholesome environment plus heredity could account for the history of degeneracy. Henry H. Goddard's analyses of the Kallikaks, in which Martin Kallikak fathered two families, one with a normal woman and one with a feebleminded woman, led him to conclude that the involvement of the feebleminded genes was a sufficient explanation for the degeneracy found in that branch as compared with the normal branch. Most scientists agree that both studies show that it is impossible to separate the role of the inadequate environment from the role of the harmful genes in the families.

Other studies have shown that schizophrenia occurs more often in blood relatives of schizophrenics than in the general population. In addition, the closer the proximity of the relative, the higher the probability of occurrence. Identical twins have an extremely high incidence. It has often been argued that the closer the blood relation (genetic makeup), the more similar the environment will probably be. However, approximately the same proportions of incidence seem to occur even when identical twins are reared apart. Although the predisposition to schizophrenia seems to depend on some specific genetic factors, learned habits of interacting with conflict situations may elicit this predisposition.

Is intelligence inherited? Are there differences in intelligence among races? These two questions have been part of the political, psychological, and sociological literature for more than a century. In 1969 the controversy again emerged with an article by Arthur Jensen, "How Much Can We Boost IQ and Scholastic Achievement?" This showed a difference of about ten to fifteen IQ points between white and black students, even when differences in parental education and socioeconomic status are "balanced," and concluded not only that intelligence is an inherited quality but that black students have less of it. Serious questions and criticisms arose in reaction. Most psychologists do not equate IQ test scores and intelligence, particularly since IQ tests are never completely "culture fair." Some investigations have shown that scores on IQ tests vary with the amount of money spent per child in the school. (The money itself may not be the decisive factor, but spending is an index of interest in the support of schools.) Other studies revealed that both black and white students in the North score higher than many whites in the South.

Behavior genetics also show that genes do not transmit complex traits like intelligence. Complex traits are a product of the constant interaction between genetic material and the environment.

—Nina Adams, *Yale University*
See also articles listed in the Item Guide.
Consult (3) Levine, 1962; Robinson, 1970; Thiessen, 1972.

HEROIN. *See* Drugs and Behavior.

HESS, WALTER RUDOLF (1881–), Swiss physiologist. Born in Frauenfeld, he received an M.D. from the University of Zurich (1906). He was professor of physiology and director of the Physiological Institute, University of Zurich, 1917–1951, and received many awards, including the Nobel Prize for medicine and physiology in 1949.

Hess was a pioneer in the study of electrical stimulation of the brain and behavior. His systematic explorations of the thalamus and hypothalamus of the cat (1929) showed that varying the rate of stimulation of the hypothalamus produced behavior ranging from alertness to sleep. Some stimulation led to an integrated, directed attack, which he called "affective defense reaction." His early writings were published only in German. Later works include *Diencephalon*, 1954; *The Functional Organization of the Diencephalon, Hypothalamus and Thalamus*, 1956; *The Biology of the Mind*, 1964.

—Nina Adams, *Yale University*

HETEROSEXUALITY. *See* Character Development; Genital State; Sex Identity.

HIGHER-ORDER CONDITIONING. *See* Pavlovian Conditioning.

HILGARD, ERNEST ROPIEQUET (1904–), American psychologist. Born in Belleville, Ill., he received his Ph.D. at Yale, 1930. He was professor of psychology (now emeritus) at Stanford University and president of the American Psychological Association 1948–1949.

Hilgard's research has included studies of animal and human conditioned responses. His latest work concerns human motivation and unconscious processes, partly through experimental studies of the parameters of susceptibility to hypnosis. Hilgard is best known to thousands of college students studying psychology for his textbooks, particularly *Introduction to Psychology*, 1953, now in its fifth edition, and *Theories of Learning* (with Donald G. Marquis), 1948, rev. ed., 1966.

Hilgard's most recent books are *Hypnotic Susceptibility*, 1965, *The Experience of Hypnosis*, 1968.

—Nina Adams, *Yale University*

HEREDITY

Father's gamete (sperm) contains a single gene for each trait

Mother's gamete (egg) contains a single gene for each trait

Brown-eye gene

Blue-eye gene

Every cell of the offspring acquires a pair of genes for each trait

Heterozygous condition— one of each kind of gene

Brown-eye gene is dominant blue-eye gene is recessive therefore, this child is brown-eyed

If both parents are blue-eyed, all of their gametes will contain blue-eye genes

Homozygous condition— both genes of the same kind

All of the offspring are blue-eyed

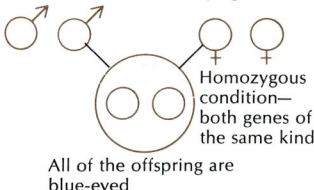

If both parents are heterozygous for brown eyes, each can produce both kinds of gametes

There are four possible gene pairs

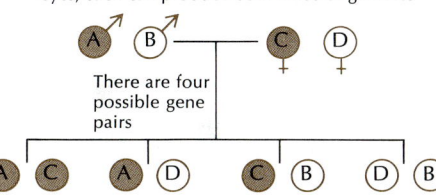

Since the brown-eye gene is dominant, three of every four births will be brown

HOLTZMAN INKBLOT TECHNIQUE

The Holtzman Technique employs forty-five blots similar to this.

Psychoanalyst Karen Horney, who deemed classical Freudian theory inflexible, stressed environmental causes and the context of neurotic behavior.

HOLISM, term applied to the basic assumption that a whole is more than the sum of its parts. In psychology, this implies that the experience of a whole, both in one's consciousness and in reality, has properties that are not simply the result of combining its parts. The early Greeks were the first to recognize the importance of "wholeness" as a concept necessary for understanding behavior. In more recent times holism has been a major orientation of both John Dewey and the Gestalt psychologists.

HOLTZMAN INKBLOT TECHNIQUE, a projective test used in personality study and diagnosis of mental disorders. Like the Rorschach Technique, the Holtzman uses inkblots to elicit responses from subjects. However, the Holtzman test uses ninety blots instead of the ten Rorschach blots and provides a more objective method of scoring responses. A subject gives one response to each blot. Analysis of responses has produced a scoring guide with norms for normal people and mentally disturbed people.

See also Rorschach Technique.

HOMEOSTASIS, the process of maintaining the constancy of the internal environment. The term was introduced by the American physiologist Walter B. Cannon to refer to any process that alters a given condition and thereby initiates other reactions that tend to reestablish the initial condition. A thermostat is an example of a simple mechanical homeostat.

Biological homeostasis is maintained by a number of complex physiological and biochemical mechanisms. Homeostats in the nervous system regulate such factors as body temperature, blood pressure, heart rate, and water balance.

Maintaining equilibrium in the body also requires regulatory behavior. If the body becomes dry, a homeostat in the hypothalamus starts a process that conserves water. However, the organism also needs to seek more fluids to maintain water balance. Similarly, homeostats step up metabolism if the body is cold, but overt behavior is also needed: animals seek shelter and humans go indoors. Homeostatic mechanisms and regulatory behavior are coordinated by the nervous system.

—A. Ronald Seifert, University of Tennessee

See also Hypothalamus; Thirst Drive.
Consult (3) Cannon, 1932; Richter, 1942–1943.

HOMESICKNESS, a form of regression frequently experienced by children, adolescents, and young adults, arises out of the emotional dependence of an individual on his family. While away from home for any extended period, he experiences loneliness, depression, and some anxiety. In young children, this often takes the form of a fear that they will be deserted or abandoned or that some disaster will befall their parents.

Homesickness often produces physical symptoms such as indigestion, loss of appetite, or headaches. These may sometimes be so severe that they make it necessary for the child to return home. Every individual experiences some degree of homesickness at various points in his life, but it is more debilitating in overly dependent people.

—Michael Rothenberg, The City College of The City University of New York

HOMOSEXUALITY, sexual interest in, or sexual contact with, a person of the same sex. It occurs among infrahuman mammals and in most preliterate societies. It is fairly common in the United States, especially among preadults.

Because homosexual behavior is harshly condemned, it is not easy to obtain an accurate estimate of its prevalence. The Kinsey surveys suggested that between 35 and 40 percent of American males and between 10 and 15 percent of females have experienced an orgasm as a consequence of homosexual contact at one time in their lives. [Consult (13) Kinsey, et al., 1948; Kinsey, et al., 1953.]

Homosexual activity is much more common among unmarried people of both sexes. A large majority of individuals who report homosexual contacts also have heterosexual experiences.

In the eyes of society, an individual is stamped as a homosexual even if his or her homosexual exploits are infrequent. Behavioral scientists restrict the terms "homosexual" and "lesbian" (female homosexual) to those individuals whose sexual contacts are exclusively or primarily with persons of the same sex and whose heterosexual life is very occasional or nil. It is estimated that between 2 and 4 percent of the adult male population and 0.5 to 1 percent of the female population have had only homosexual experiences.

Most homosexuals "pass" as heterosexuals for reasons of expediency. Less than 15 percent of homosexual males are identifiably effeminate; the "swish" is usually a man whose occupation does not discriminate against homosexuals. Only a small proportion of lesbians are identifiably masculine. The "butch" or "bull dyke" must also be in a position where identification as a homosexual will not lead to discrimination.

The promiscuous homosexual male who "cruises" in public toilets looking for partners plays the stereotyped feminine sexual role. Among homosexual partners of both sexes, however, there is seldom a permanent assignment of sex roles. Active-passive and dominant-submissive tendencies reflect themselves in the daily lives of a homosexual couple, but not necessarily in their sexual activity. The bull dyke especially will often assume a protective, masculine posture toward her "fem" partners, but she is not always more aggressive in the sexual sphere.

The earliest attempts at homosexual behavior in adolescence are usually no more than kissing among females and mutual handling of the genitalia among males. Among adult male homosexuals, kissing, caressing, and fellatio are the common forms of sexual behavior. Anal coitus is practiced only by about 20 percent of male homosexuals. Many lesbian relationships never go beyond kissing and fondling. Genital activities are cunnilingus and "bull dyking," an imitation of heterosexual ventral-ventral intercourse, in which the pubic areas are rubbed against each other.

Most states have laws declaring homosexuality a criminal act. Individuals incarcerated for homosexual acts with an adult make up about 15 percent of institutionalized sex criminals. All are males, and many were apprehended by police entrapment, a procedure in which a plain-clothes officer attempts to entice a cruising homosexual to solicit him. Entrapment of lesbians is unknown, probably because homosexual females rarely "cruise" public places, and because law enforcement agencies do not regard them as a threat to the community. A few states, notably Connecticut, are following the lead of Illinois in enacting statutes under which homosexual acts between consenting adults are no longer illegal.

—Eugene E. Levitt, *Indiana University School of Medicine*

Consult (13) Gagnon and Simon, 1967; Hooker, 1968; Marmor, 1965; West, 1967.

HORMONES, endocrine gland secretions that regulate body processes. *See* Adrenal Glands; Gonads; Parathyroid Glands; Pineal Gland; Pituitary Gland; Thyroid Gland.

HORNEY, KAREN (1885–1952), American psychoanalyst, born in Hamburg, Germany. She studied in Berlin under Karl Abraham, a friend and follower of Freud, and emigrated to the United States in 1932. She helped form the American Institute for Psychoanalysis in 1942.

Horney often spoke out against what she considered to be the excessively rigid constraints of classical Freudian theory. Her own modifications of that theory centered on the question of the development and expression of neurotic symptoms. She pictured the child's relationship to his mother as more varied than did Freud; that is, he was not bound inevitably to a single course ending in the Oedipal conflict. She also contended that early childhood experiences were not the sole factors involved in the determination of neurotic conflicts, but such problems as current fears and impulses are equally important. In addition, she stressed the importance of con-

sidering the environmental contexts in which neurotic behavior is expressed: what may be maladaptive in one cultural context might be perfectly appropriate in another.

Horney's views on personality allowed much more scope for development and rational coping than did Freud's determinism. She questioned the limitation of Freud's theory of instincts as motivating forces of behavior. Her flexibility and awareness of environmental factors made her a mainstay of the neo-Freudians. Horney tried to put her ideas in terms that the layman could understand. She is one of the most widely read of all the analytic writers. Her major works include *The Neurotic Personality of Our Times,* 1936; *Our Human Conflicts,* 1945; and *Human Growth,* 1950.

—Michael Rothenberg, *The City College of The City University of New York*

HOSTILITY. *See* Aggression; Anger.

HOUSE-TREE-PERSON (H-T-P) TECHNIQUE, a projective personality test developed by J. N. Buck. The subject is asked to draw a picture of a house, a tree, and a person. The examiner carefully observes the subject's behavior and verbalizations as well as sequence and size of the parts drawn. Time is also noted. Usually the drawing task is followed by a series of standard questions.

Interpretations are based upon analysis of pictorial material, relevant observations, and responses to the postdrawing inquiry. Theoretically, it is assumed that the house drawing reflects the subject's attitudes and feelings toward familial relationships and the home environment in general. The drawing of the tree appears to reflect the subject's relatively deeper and more unconscious feelings about himself and his interaction with the everyday world around him. Projection of an ego ideal is assumed to be reflected in the person drawing. Careful comparisons of the three drawings generate a more integrated conception of personality functioning.

—Randolph S. Kraft, *Federation of the Handicapped, N.Y.*

Consult (12) Buck and Jolles, 1956; Hammer, 1960.

HOVLAND, CARL IVOR (1912–1961), American psychologist. Born in Chicago, he received a Ph.D. from Yale and was affiliated with Yale throughout his career. He was appointed Sterling Professor of Psychology in 1947.

Hovland's early research concerned the parameters of presentation, cue differentiation, and generalization in memory, learning, and relearning. His later work dealt with attitude and communication. He was coauthor of *Experiments on Mass Communication,* 1949; *Communication and Persuasion,* 1954; *Order of Presentation in Persuasion,* 1957; *Personality*

HOUSE-TREE-PERSON TECHNIQUE

In the house-tree-person technique the subject is asked to draw three pictures and answer a series of standard questions.

and Persuadibility; and *Attitude Organization and Change,* 1960.

HULL, CLARK LEONARD (1884–1952), American experimental psychologist, born in Akron, N.Y. He taught for twenty-three years at the Yale Institute of Human Relations and was president of the American Psychological Association, 1935–1936.

Hull devoted his life to the study of motivation and learning. He developed a learning theory based on extensive observations of phenomena, from which he derived a number of primary principles. At the core of his theory was the concept of *intervening variables,* unobservable factors that the psychologist uses to explain observable behavior. He inserted the letter *O* in the learning paradigm to represent such intervening variables. Thus in *S–O–R, O* is related both to the antecedent stimulus conditions and to the subsequent observable responses.

The central principle of Hull's theory was that learning occurs only when reinforcement causes modification of an internal state (need or drive). Hull called this process *drive reduction* and constructed a system of seventeen postulates by which he hoped to quantify the learning process.

Although Hull's work was based primarily on simple conditioning, he believed his theory could ultimately be applied to more complex learning, for example, problem solving and concept formation. While many of the details of his arguments have been questioned, his systematic and comprehensive effort to quantify and explain learning continues to influence contemporary learning theorists. Hull's major works include *Principles of Behavior,* 1943, and *A Behavior System,* 1952.

—Michael Rothenberg, *The City College of the City University of New York*

HUMAN ECOLOGY. *See* Behavioral Ecology.

HUMAN ENGINEERING. *See* Engineering Psychology.

HUMAN-FACTORS RESEARCH. *See* Engineering Psychology.

HUMAN POTENTIAL MOVEMENT, the general designation for a wide variety of encounter, sensitivity training, and "human development laboratory" groups. All of these are intended to help people increase their capacity to cope with their own emotional problems and interact with others. An outgrowth of sensitivity training, this heterodox movement encourages experiences with Zen Buddhism, radical psychotherapies, astrology, mysticism, body manipulation and sensory experiences, art, dance, and theater games. In the United States over 170 "growth centers," such as the Esalen Institute, offer a range of such activities, but the encounter group experiences are at the heart of the movement. Basic groups, usually involving eight to fifteen participants and one leader, may assemble regularly for periods ranging from a few hours a week to a weekend (marathon) of full-time interaction or to several weeks of daily group interaction.

Although the human potential movement is intentionally eclectic, a common set of values and themes emerges. It emphasizes candor and interpersonal communication in the "here and now" and offers practice in human interaction and exposure to self-help psychic healing. It has been criticized for its stereotyped approach to human growth, in which ritualized steps toward individual change unwittingly repeat the very ills it sets out to destroy. Its commercialism, promiscuous sexuality, and circuslike atmosphere have also been attacked. The promise of "magical" personality changes may lure vulnerable people into emotional and financial exploitation.

On the other hand, the movement has also been praised as the vanguard of a new humanist revolution, and its advocates have brought group techniques into schools, government agencies, and industry. Positive results have been observed in individuals who have been able to use encounter experiences as a stimulant to personal growth, which they have often followed up with traditional psychotherapy. Negative results are seen in the significant number of people (estimated at 10 percent of participants) who have come away emotionally or physically damaged.

While many qualified mental health practitioners have long used or recently adopted some of the encounter techniques, serious problems have resulted from the widespread use of groups led by untrained persons. Some individuals evidently have found that the business of running such groups and promulgating the attendant "encounter culture" is both financially and personally rewarding.

—Bruce L. Maliver, author of *The Encounter Game*

See also Encounter Groups; Sensitivity Training.

Consult (13) Maliver, 1972.

HUMOR. Man is a zealous pursuer of laughter and humor. Yet, strangely, he does not know, nor does he really care to know, why humor gives him so much pleasure. As W. C. Fields put it, "The funniest thing about comedy is that you never know why people laugh. I know *what* makes them laugh, but trying to get your hands on the *why* of it is like trying to pick an eel out of a tub of water." It is a paradoxical fact that a small child has no difficulty in recognizing and responding to humor with laughter, while through the ages, sages, philosophers, writers of literature, and now behavioral scientists have tried in vain to understand it.

Psychological Research. Despite its importance in human affairs, humor has only recently become an area of research interest to behavioral scientists. One reason for this neglect is that such activities as humor, play, sports, curiosity, and the creative arts in general do not fit easily into most motivational theories, which emphasize behavior stemming from the deprivation of organic needs. Thus, they do not readily lend themselves to experimental research where the subjects respond because they are aroused by hunger, sex, anger, or anxiety. Humor, in contrast, relates to the environment in a pleasure-giving manner by reasserting man's cognitive and interpersonal competence.

Investigations have begun to show the importance of humor both in the development of the individual and as a social process. A number of studies have demonstrated that even the earliest smiles of the very young infant, out of which laughter and humor grow, reflect a basic process of communication as the expression of pleasure. Empirical data from different scientific areas provide meaningful support for the antithesis between humor as a gratifying sense of effectiveness and anxiety as a painful state of helplessness. Experimental studies of learned helplessness in animals and humans have demonstrated that when an individual's responses cannot control painful events or reinforcers, his behavior is characterized by depression, passivity, and an inability to use humor. Just as humor has often been viewed as a sign of faith in one's ability to master fate, so anxiety can be characterized as resignation to fate.

Conclusions. In short, research findings now support the view that humor is one of man's major modes of reasserting his mastery. A good example of this is seen in "gallows humor" in which man rises above his present state of pain. (For example, a man is about to be shot by a firing squad. When asked if he would like a last cigarette, refuses, saying, "No, thanks. I'm trying to give up smoking."). On this basis, individuals and groups stand apart from danger and make fun of their own foibles. This ability to laugh at oneself is the very essence of a healthy sense of humor, for it requires not only a strong ego to master fear in the face of threat but also an ability not to take oneself too seriously.

Similarly, the freedom to joke about them serves as an important outlet for forbidden feelings. Humor also serves to expose sham and pretense and can therefore be an important social force. Its ability to express basic truths and make them acceptable can

have both therapeutic and socially constructive effects.

—Jacob Levine, *Veterans Administration Hospital, West Haven, Connecticut*
Consult (9) Goldstein and McGhee, 1972; Levine, 1969; Mindess, 1971.

HUNGER DRIVE. The need for an organism to obtain food in order to survive is complexly determined. It depends upon such internal factors as the strength of stomach contractions, blood condition (including the level of glucose or blood sugar), and the state of the hypothalamus. There is evidence to suggest that the hypothalamus contains regions and receptors that detect blood sugar (glucoreceptors) and respond by initiating the search for food. Stimulation of these hypothalamic regions, particularly in the lateral hypothalamus, will impel an animal to seek food, whereas stimulation of the ventromedial hypothalamus will lead to the cessation of eating and the rejection of food.

—Joel F. Lubar, *University of Tennessee*
See also Specific Hunger.

HYPERKINETIC CHILDREN. The hyperkinetic child syndrome (hyperactive child syndrome, minimal brain dysfunction) is a relatively common disorder. It appears in early life (usually in infancy), is more common in boys, and is characterized by a symptom pattern of excessive motor behavior that is not goal-directed, by short attention span and easy distractability, and by impulsiveness. There are associated problems of impairment in perception and conceptualization and specific learning problems in the presence of normal intelligence.

Careful psychiatric, cognitive, motor, neurological, and academic evaluations of the hyperactive child frequently reveal that he is handicapped in a number of ways. These children come from parents with an increased incidence of psychiatric illness (alcoholism and sociopathy in fathers, and hysteria in mothers). The cause of the disorder is unknown, but recent studies suggest that in many cases a pathophysiological state of the central nervous system (for example, delayed maturation or low arousal level) may be a major underlying factor.

Stimulant drugs have been shown to produce a favorable response in 70 to 80 percent of patients, and tranquilizers are useful with others. Stimulant drugs improve attention, reduce inappropriate behavior, and increase positive teacher-pupil interaction in the classroom. They also improve cognition, as measured by psychological tests.

Contrary to what was formerly thought, hyperkinetic children do not outgrow the disorder in their early teens. If left untreated, it is a precursor to emotional and educational difficulties in adolescence and adult life, particularly to antisocial behavior and academic retardation. It less often leads to psychoses.

—James H. Satterfield, M.D., *Gateways Hospital, Los Angeles*

Consult (13) Bradley, 1957; Cantwell, 1972; Conners and Eisenberg, 1963; Laufer and Denhoff, 1957; Laufer, 1962; Laufer, *et al.*, 1957; Mendelson, *et al.*, 1971; Menkes, *et al.*, 1967; Millichap, 1968; Millichap and Fowler, 1967; Millichap, *et al.*, 1968; Minde, *et al.*, 1971; Morrison and Stewart, 1971; Satterfield, 1973; Satterfield and Dawson, 1971; Satterfield, *et al.*, 1972; Shetty, 1971; Stewart, 1970; Stewart, *et al.*, 1966; Weiss, *et al.*, 1971.

HYPERTENSION, a form of psychosomatic ailment involving a chronic state of high blood pressure that is not due to any identifiable organic causes. It results from an interaction of psychological and physical factors and can cause real damage.

Any strong emotional reaction has immediate and extensive impact on the circulatory system, usually in the form of increased heartbeat and heightened blood pressure. Studies have demonstrated, for example, that anxiety or anger will raise the blood pressure of any person. In the case of hypertension, the individual is chronically anxious and cannot reduce his tensions by the defense mechanisms that most people have available. Chronic high blood pressure, if left untreated, can lead to serious circulatory disorders or even heart attacks. Hypertension is usually treated with a combination of tranquilizers and psychotherapy.

—Michael Rothenberg, *The City College of The City University of New York*
See also Psychosomatic Disorders.

HYPERVENTILATION SYNDROME, a respiratory form of psychosomatic disorder. *See* Psychosomatic Disorder.

HYPNOSIS. At the present stage of knowledge, hypnosis (like electricity) can be defined only in phenomenological terms. It is a state of altered consciousness, induced in the subject (or patient) by the operator (or hypnotist) through verbal or (with deaf mutes and very young children) imitative means. The state is characterized by hypersuggestibility, amnesia, paralysis, positive and negative hallucinations, and various vasomotor phenomena. Any combination of these may be present and no single one is necessarily present. Negativism may, although rarely, replace hypersuggestibility.

Historical Background

Historically, most authorities compare hypnotic trance with religious ecstasy and equate it with white magic and the temple sleep of the Fertile Crescent in classical and preclassical times, and in the Middle Ages with black magic and demonism. With both, healing was believed to be caused by gods. Paralcelsus (1443–1541) and the alchemists displaced the cause to minerals (giving prescriptions for sulfur, lead, mercury, and iron) through a "universal spirit" that changed the chemistry of the body and (magnetically) polarized the patient. By the late eighteenth century magnets were in frequent medical use. F. A. Mesmer, who received his Ph.D. in (Jesuit) theology before studying medicine, was steeped in the current pre–Age of Enlightenment deistic philosophy of the healing goodness of God and the personal participation of the individual not only in religion but in the healing process. Without realizing it, Mesmer tapped psychological forces in the individual and made them accessible to study. Magnetism (later renamed mesmerism), under the social and economic pressures of the age helped bring to the fore the problem of what today we term psychological or emotional health.

By 1814 the Abbé Faria concluded that suggestion is the motive force behind magnetism. An interpersonal relationship therefore was postulated; this at first involved the all-powerful authoritarian Svengali and Rasputin type hypnotist; with Freud's studies of hypnosis it yielded to analytic psychology and transference-countertransference considerations.

But charlatans, pseudoscientists, and the lunatic fringe all exploited the subject—and at the same time made significant contributions to it. Mesmer felt that "grand crises" (the major convulsions he induced) resolved disease. In the 1820s the Marquis de Puyseguir discovered that sleep, not convulsions, could be induced by magnetic influence, named the phenomenon somnambulism, and "proved" that hypnotized somnambulists could be clairvoyant, foretell future events, and diagnose disease. Later hypnotists reportedly diagnosed and cured patients at a distance.

In 1826 a French Academy of Science committee (with Laennec, the inventor of the stethoscope, and Magendie, the pioneer neuroanatomist, among its members) characterized magnetism as "a therapeutic expedient" that as such had its place in medicine. This helped restore it to respectability. But by the 1840s, despite the giant contributions of James Braid of Manchester and John Elliotson in London, the never-ending stream of pseudoscientific faith healers and "inspired" self-styled psychologists had fused hypnosis with phrenology. Through carefully conducted "scientific" experiments with magnetic (that is, hypnotic) control the pseudoscientists believed they had demonstrated the existence of specific skull proturberances for such traits as combativeness, amativeness, and veneration. This work nevertheless helped revive

Anton Mesmer, in the process of trying to magnetize human beings, became the first to study hypnosis in the laboratory. His patients are shown seated around a drum filled with iron filings.

the intuitive insights of Paracelsus and Mesmer that mental disease is highly individualized and that the personality of the patient is a factor in its cause. This concept was underscored, although by implication, in the 1880s during the controversy between Jean Charcot, who equated hypnosis with hysteria, and A. A. Liébault, for whom it was suggestion. Sigmund Freud, who had already made significant contributions to both pharmacology and neurology, studied hypnosis under Bernheim, collaborated with Breuer in the hypnotic treatment of a patient, and used this as a steppingstone to the development of psychoanalysis. In the late 1950s and early 1960s, the British and the American Medical Associations and the American Psychiatric Association formulated statements of policy about hypnosis, characterizing it as a technique (not a method of therapy) with indications and contraindications for its use.

Current Status

Trance-Induction Techniques. These usually utilize progressive narrowing of the focus of conscious awareness, with a concomitant blocking of sensory input. With so-called classical techniques, subjects are repetitively and monotonously told to close their eyes (or that their eyes will grow heavy and close), to relax, and to go to sleep. If these suggestions are effective, the subject if challenged to open his eyes will develop eyelid catalepsy, moving the wrong muscles, and be unable to. With sensorimotor and other techniques, eyelid closure is not suggested even on the initial hypnosis. All techniques explicitly or implicitly set end-points as anatomically impossible as eyelid catalepsy.

The Hypnotic Trance State. Characteristics of trance induction and those of the trance state may differ. Some of the latter have been enumerated in the phenomenological definition in the initial paragraph of this article. Time manipulation (progression, regression, speeding up or slowing down of subjective time) is possible with hypnotized subjects, and so is intensification of emotion, posthypnotic suggestion, other abreactive techniques, visualization of plays or movies, and more than a score of other fantasy-evocation techniques.

Hypnosis is not sleep, hypersuggestibility, or role acting, although superficially with specific subjects it may seem so, and all three factors must be considered as definitions are formulated. Modern concepts are numerous and complicated. For these, reference should be made to the current literature.

Uses. Hypnosis is a potent tool in certain types of psychological research as well as in research on the nature of hypnosis itself. In the health sciences it can be utilized (1) as an anesthetic or analgesic agent in dentistry, surgery, and obstetrics; (2) as a tranquilizer to allay apprehension or anxiety, or to reduce tension; (3) for symptom suppression, to suggest away, for instance, the itch of a poison ivy or the agony of a severe burn; and (4) as an adjunctive technique in the treatment of patients with neurotic or psychotic disease or with character disturbances.

Abuses. Abuses and even malignant posthypnotic effects have been reported since 1920. There have been at least 205 cases during the past 20 years, of which three may be described.

In 1954 Camilio Weson Leyra was sentenced to death on the basis of an hypnosis-obtained confession to murder. The prisoner, after being incarcerated in Sing Sing on death row for five years, was released on habeas corpus by the U.S. Supreme Court. This case established the concept of a psychological third degree as contrasted with a physical third degree. The psychiatrist who did the hypnosis for the King's County, New York, district attorney was castigated by the court as being unaware of both due process of law and the democratic process.

A psychologist with pronounced sexual difficulties on a depressive basis requested hypnosis cure, but in view of his suicidal depression was instead referred for psychiatric treatment. He changed his mind, had another psychologist hypnotize him, and committed suicide.

In 1972, a luxury hotel and its insurance coverer together made an out-of-court $450,000 settlement in a law suit. A person with no history of prior emotional disease had developed a catatonic schizophrenic reaction necessitating psychiatric hospitalization after being hypnotized by a stage magician in the hotel's nightclub.

Medicolegal problems require further study. Research on hypnosis itself is badly needed. Every aspect of the subject is controversial and in a state of flux. And one authority even today seems to feel that hypnotic phenomena are artifacts of the investigative, research, or therapeutic process.

—Harold Rosen, M.D., *Johns Hopkins University*

See also Mesmer.

Consult (13) American Medical Association, 1958; American Medical Association, 1962; Barber, 1969; Hilgard, 1965; Rosen, 1953; Weitzenhoffer, 1953.

HYPNOTHERAPY. *See* Hypnosis.

HYPOCHONDRIA, a state of excessive concern with and complaints about one's physical state. The symptoms include a number of vague physical complaints, fear of impending serious illness, and a generally pessimistic attitude about one's well-being. While the hypochon-

The caption accompanying this photo from a French magazine reported that a self-styled "grand master of psychosomnia," who had hypnotized these people to believe that they were musicians, was bringing back old wizard's tricks calculated not to harm his subjects. The showman's claim to harmlessness is disputed by many psychologists.

driac seems to be suffering from a run-down physical condition, he is actually responding to persistent anxiety in the face of unresolved conflicts. This nagging anxiety can take its toll in such bodily reactions as indigestion, loss of appetite, minor aches and pains, and a feeling of fatigue. To date, no physical explanations have been found for the hypochondriacal reaction.

In one acute case, for example, a twenty-year-old college student with excellent grades developed a condition that increasingly made her feel that she would be unable to finish college. She experienced loss of appetite, insomnia, and extreme fatigue and melancholy. After physical examinations yielded no explanation, it was discovered that she was responding belatedly to the end of her first intense romantic experience. When this was brought to light, the symptoms began to diminish rapidly. In more chronic cases, hypochondria can be a part of the personality structure rather than a response to a particular conflict.

—Michael Rothenberg, *The City College of The City University of New York*
See also Psychosomatic Disorders.

HYPOGLYCEMIA, a low level of sugar in the blood. This disorder can be inherited and is a cause of mental retardation in children (idiopathic hypoglycemia). Hypoglycemic states can occur in persons who do not have the inherited problem. The chief cause is overproduction of insulin. See Brain Disorders.

HYPOMANIC PERSONALITY. In this character disorder a constant mild degree of mania is seen by others and the individual himself as an intrinsic part of his personality. Although this behavior differs from psychotic manic reactions in degree and suddenness of onset, it may be difficult to draw the diagnostic line. Excitement, energetic behavior, restlessness, and high productivity are characteristic. Denial of negativistic, destructive impulses and reaction formation against them are dynamically involved.

—M. G. Affinito, *Southern Connecticut State College*

HYPOTHALAMUS, a brain structure consisting of a very tightly packed group of nuclei and fiber tracts located in the diencephalon and lying just below the thalamus. It is believed that the hypothalamus has a regulatory function for both the sympathetic and the parasympathetic divisions of the nervous system. The various hypothalamic nuclei control many body processes, including water balance, sexual drive (to some extent), hunger, thirst, and even metabolic functions. The most complexly organized of the hypothalamic nuclei is the pituitary body, which consists of a glandular

portion and a neural portion. The pituitary acts as the master gland for the control of the entire endocrine system throughout the body.

—Joel F. Lubar, *University of Tennessee*
See also Brain.
Consult (3) Isaacson, *et al.,* 1971; Teitelbaum, 1967.

HYPOTHESIS TESTING. See Experimental Design.

HYSTERIA. See Amnesia; Conversion Reaction; Hysterical Personality.

HYSTERICAL PERSONALITY, a disorder of personality characterized by widespread repression of conflicts and feelings, which often find expression in various somatic complaints for which there is no apparent organic explanation. These are called *conversion symptoms,* and they usually take the form of sensory deficits (partial loss of vision or hearing), motor disabilities (partial paralysis), or such common ailments as headaches or sore throats. The hysteric demonstrates an apparent lack of disturbance in the face of these symptoms; instead, he adopts an attitude of cheerful resignation, which most persons suffering from genuine disabilities have great difficulty in achieving.

This suggests that, for the hysteric, conversion symptoms serve to ward off anxiety. A case in point is one in which a young man who had been studying singing for five years suddenly developed a chronic sore throat. Several specialists could find nothing physically wrong with him. But consultation with a psychiatrist uncovered strong feelings of ambivalence with respect to his chosen career. He had been unable to express these openly because he feared he would disappoint his family. Once the conflict was resolved, he was able to pursue his career with no further difficulty.

—Michael Rothenberg, *The City College of The City University of New York*
See also Personality Disorders; Psychosomatic Disorders.

IATROGENIC ILLNESS, a neurotic disorder caused by what a physician says to a patient or by his attitude toward the patient. A functional disorder (not to be confused with unwanted physiological side-effects of treatment, such as adverse reactions to antibiotics), an iatrogenic problem may develop in a patient when he is told about symptoms of heart disease. If he is prone to anxiety he may concentrate his fears on the condition of his heart and then experience the symptoms he has heard about. A neurotic patient under therapy may develop additional symptoms if the therapist's questions suggest additional problems.

ID. In Sigmund Freud's psychoanalytic theory

HYPOTHALAMUS

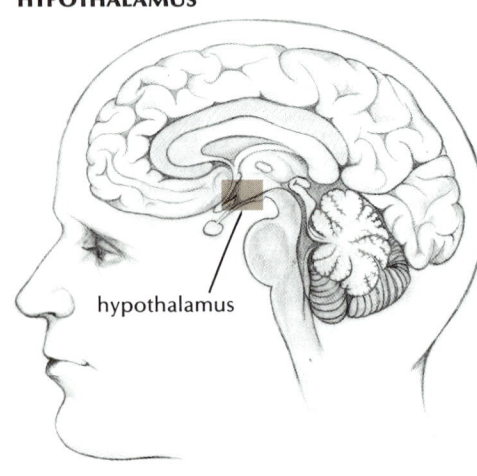

hypothalamus

of personality structure, the id is the original and most primitive basis of personality, from which the ego and superego become differentiated.

Derived from the Latin word for "it," the term *id* was used by Freud to designate the basic reservoir of psychic energy originating from biological impulses and bodily processes. These drives are not necessarily in harmony and seek gratification and release according to the pleasure principle of immediate tension reduction regardless of circumstances. Repeated frustration of these impulses gradually gives rise to the ego as a moderating and controlling agency of personality that functions in accordance with the reality principle.

According to Freud, the id is totally unconscious. It represents the inner subjective world of impulse and passion and has no knowledge of objective reality. It operates according to the "primary process" of hallucinatory wish fulfillment whereby vivid mental images substitute for actual desired objects—as in the dreams of normal individuals or hallucinations of psychotics. This process disregards logical connections, permits contradictions to coexist, knows no negatives, has no conception of time, and represents wishes as already fulfilled.

—Alden E. Wessman, *The City College of The City University of New York*
See also Ego; Superego; Psychoanalysis.
Consult (13) Freud, 1933.

IDEA, a term used in a variety of ways to refer to the content of thinking and to cognitive processes other than sensory processes. *See* Imagery; Thinking.

IDENTIFICATION, the unconscious act of attributing to oneself certain characteristics or traits that one perceives in someone else. This defense mechanism derives from the desire to be more like that other person.

Identification is often utilized by children, who characteristically identify with parents and other significant adults, such as teachers or older siblings, and can play an important role in their development. Persons who have ambitions in a particular area often identify with someone who has already achieved success in that area.

—Michael Rothenberg, *The City College of The City University of New York*
See also Defense Mechanism.

IDIOT, an old term for a person with the most serious degree of mental deficiency, having an IQ below 25 or 20. The preferred designation now is *profoundly mentally retarded. See* Mental Retardation.

ILLUSION, a false perception, one that does not correspond with the objective situation.

For example, in the well-known Müller-Lyer illusion the two horizontal lines are of equal length, but one appears to be appreciably longer than the other.

While perception is generally correct (or *veridical*) there are countless instances where it is illusory. For example, in moving pictures, no objective movement takes place. In induced movement a stationary object seems to move because the background is actually moving, as when the moon is in front of moving clouds. In successful camouflage, people see objects that are not present and fail to see those that are; in viewing photographs, drawings, and paintings, they perceive depth that is not there. It is now realized that the same principles of brain function that explain correct perception will also have to do justice to illusions. Thus, for example, because linear perspective is a cue to depth, an actual railroad track looks three-dimensional (veridical perception)—but so does a picture of one (illusion).

The better-known illusions are those involving geometrical patterns of various kinds, such as the Müller-Lyer illusion. A number of others have been extensively investigated. In the vertical-horizontal illusion the two lines are equal in length but the vertical line looks longer. In the Poggendorff illusion the oblique lines do not appear to be aligned, although they are, and in the Hering illusion the straight horizontal lines appear curved. In the Ponzo illusion the two equal horizontal lines appear of unequal length.

Research. While these illusions have been widely investigated and hypotheses abound, they remain unexplained for the most part. Certainly no one theory can explain all of them. One of the better-known explanations is the *eye-movement theory,* which asserts that impressions of length or curvature are based on either actual or intended scanning movements of the eyes and that such eye movements are often incorrect.

The *Gestalt theory* asserts that perception is the result of processes of organization in the brain in which the *relationship* among components of the stimulus are of central importance. Thus, for example, the relationship of a pattern to its context or frame of reference affects perception. In the last figure the inner shape in A looks like a diamond, but in B it looks like a square; yet the two are identical. This doctrine, while now widely accepted and relevant to the problem of illusions, is nevertheless too general to explain the specific effects obtained in most of the geometric illusions.

The *apparent-distance* or *perspective theory* asserts that perspective patterns or drawings give rise to an illusory impression of depth. As a result, the same mechanisms that ordinarily lead to constancy effects lead to false impressions of size. The lines perceived as

ILLUSION FIGURES

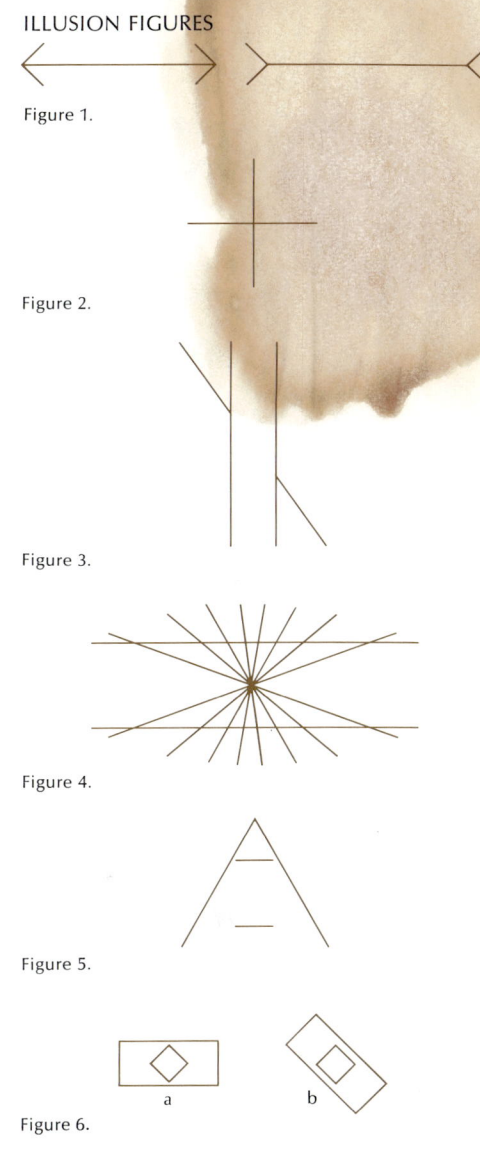

Figure 1.

Figure 2.

Figure 3.

Figure 4.

Figure 5.

Figure 6.

The Illusionator, a student demonstration device, includes a trapezoidal window frame, which when rotated creates the illusion of moving only 180 degrees.

farther away look larger than they otherwise would.

The *neural-displacement theory* asserts that a process in one place in the nervous system can block or inhibit a process in a neighboring place. As a result, contours may appear to be displaced from their actual locations. Thus, for example, if the sides of an acute angle were apparently displaced from one another, the angle would appear enlarged. This could explain illusions such as the Poggendorff and Hering illusions.

Various facts about illusions have been established. They occur in other senses, such as hearing and touch. Animals are subject to them, but people of different cultures seem to vary in their susceptibility to specific illusions. Children appear to experience even greater illusory effects than adults. Attitudes and instructions on how to view illusions have been found to have an effect, and illusions have been found to decrease with repeated exposure.

Illusions are not the same as delusions or hallucinations. An illusion is a mistaken response to a stimulus that actually exists. A hallucination occurs when, for example, a person sees "visitors" or hears "voices" that are not there. A delusion is a persisting belief that is not grounded in fact.

—Irvin Rock, *Rutgers University*
See also Ames Room; Apparent Movement; Depth Perception; Moon Illusion; Visual Cliff.

Consult (4) Gregory, 1968; Luckish, 1965; Segall, *et al.,* 1966; (1) Hilgard, *et al.,* 1971.

IMAGELESS THOUGHT, an idea introduced by Karl Buhler, a member of the Wurtzburg school, that initially shocked the pure experimentalists. Emphasizing the nonsensory character of many items in consciousness during cognitive tasks, Buhler argued that there were "thought elements" that did not belong to the same category as sensations or images. "Imageless thought" was the term assigned to these elements because, first, they could not be detected by introspection and, second, they did not depend on sensations or symbols.

IMAGERY, modes of thinking and remembering in which nonverbal (usually visual) representations are produced and used by an individual. During the era when behaviorism set the tone for American psychology early in this century, imagery became anathema to psychologists, who regarded such subjective experiences as unobservable and hence not accessible to scientific inquiry. With the recent rise of cognitive psychology, however, a substantial revival of interest in imagery blossomed forth in the 1960s. Current interest in the topic is diverse, with several notable research trends.

Allan Paivio and his associates at the University of Western Ontario in Canada have conducted many studies attempting to relate imagery to verbal and other processes in learning. They have shown, for example, that the imagery-evoking power (or concreteness) of words is an important variable in verbal learning—perhaps even more potent than meaningfulness. Thus, concrete words (for example, "tree," "rock," "door") are learned faster (as are associations between them) than abstract words (such as "truth," "justice," "freedom"). Paivio suggests that it is imagery that helps subjects learn such concrete words faster: concrete words evoke images that then function as mediation in memory and thinking.

Another trend has focused on the role of imagery in memory, especially as a mnemonic device.

Individual differences in imagery-evoking ability have interested many psychologists. When an individual has an exceptional ability to reproduce subjective images of his previous perceptions, such an ability is referred to as eidetic (or, sometimes, "photographic") memory. A detailed case study of one individual who possessed such an ability was described by the Russian psychologist A. R. Luria.

The role that imagery plays in ordinary thinking and problem solving is largely undetermined, but an increasing amount of attention is being devoted to the question.

—Roland Siiter, *Montclair State College*
See also Eidetic Imagery; Memory; Memory Improvement; Verbal Learning.

Consult (7) Luria, 1968; Paivio, 1971.

IMAGINARY COMPANIONS. The unseen friends "created" by many preschool children fulfill a variety of needs, ranging from companionship to scapegoating and self-aggrandizement. The imagined character, usually a person or an animal, has vivid, stable characteristics, often including a name. Such "companions" appear frequently among bright children and are more commonly observed among girls than among boys.

Consult (11) Jersild, 1968.

IMAGINATION. *See* Creativity; Imageless Thought; Thinking.

IMBECILE, an old term for a mentally deficient person with an IQ ranging from 25 to 50. The designation *trainable mentally retarded* is now preferred. *See* Mental Retardation.

IMITATION. In most discussions of learning, operant and classical conditioning are proposed as the two significant ways that an organism acquires new responses. It is now clear, however, that observational learning should be added to this list. This form of learning is often called *modeling* or *social learning*. Learning through observation and imitation can be considered a process quite distinct from both classical and operant conditioning. In observational learning neither conditioned reflexes nor conditioned stimuli play a major role in the acquisition of behavior, and learning can apparently occur even in the absence of reinforcement and practice.

Imitative learning seems to occur naturally in primates, but there is some controversy over whether nonprimate species can acquire new behavior patterns through observation. Although most experiments dealing with this question in terms of lower animals have been inconclusive, they strongly suggest that learning through observation requires a higher-level organization of the central nervous system than is found in most nonprimate species.

Effects. Imitation learning is generally considered to have three clearly different possible effects upon behavior. Each of these effects is determined by a separate set of variables. First, an individual observing a model may *acquire a new response.* This effect is demonstrated when an observer reproduces a novel, previously unexhibited behavior in a form essentially identical to the form of a model's behavior. Often a simple opportunity to observe the new response will cause the observer to acquire it though performance of the response may even be delayed for a time.

For example, when Albert Bandura and his colleagues exposed children to an aggressive model who was punished for his behavior, all of the subjects learned the novel aggressive response but did not display it until the experimenter told them that they would not be punished. Children exposed to an identical model who was not punished for his aggressive behavior displayed the novel behavior in the testing situation without prompting.

The second most common effect of imitation learning is the *inhibition and disinhibition of an already established response* through observation of a model. This depends on the outcome of the model's behavior. If he is rewarded for engaging in behavior that is normally inhibited, such as aggression, playing with a forbidden toy, or taking candy from a jar, then the behavior of the observer may be disinhibited, and the probability of his engaging in such behavior increases. If the observer sees that the model's behavior leads to a negative outcome, the opposite effect will take place; the observer's behavior is then said to be inhibited. The outcome to the model in either case is said to be a *discriminative cue* which determines the future occurrence of the observer's behavior.

The third major result of observational learning is the *facilitation* of previously learned responses, which differs from its other effects in two important ways. First, the behavior being exhibited is not normally inhibited, although it may be quite weak; and, second, the facilitation is caused by the observation of the behavior, and is not necessarily the outcome of the model's behavior. Highly positive outcomes may have an additional facilitative effect, but the main discriminative cue is the observation of the model's behavior. Response facilitation through modeling is demonstrated by the increase in altruism and help giving exhibited by children who are exposed to altruistic models.

Research. Albert Bandura and his associates have made the greatest contribution to the study of imitation and modeling. Their research has investigated how the characteristics of the model, characteristics of the observer, and the model's outcome work and interact to affect imitative behavior. Bandura has maintained that the acquisition of novel responses through modeling is largely a covert verbal process. He has found, for example, that while verbal coding of a model's behavior improves its later reproduction, engaging in an irrelevant verbal task (such as counting) interferes with later reproduction.

Human infants model their parents and others before they acquire verbal skills, however. This seems to suggest that imitation is not based solely on verbal coding. Future research in the area of imitative learning should yield much more precise information about the nature of the imitative learning process.

—Brenda B. Bankart and C. Peter Bankart, *Wabash College*

See also Aggression; Conscience; Learning.

Consult (9) Aronfreed, 1968; Bandura and Walters, 1963; (10) Bandura, 1965; Miller and Dollard, 1941.

IMPOTENCE, inability of the male to attain an erection in order to have sexual intercourse. The term refers to the incapacity to obtain full erection or to sustain an erection long enough to carry out a coital act. So-called *ejaculatory impotence* is the inability to reach a climax even though a sex act occurs.

Many males have an occasional experience of impotence. Chronic impotence before senescence is uncommon. It is defined by Masters and Johnson as the inability to obtain an erection for purposes of coitus in at least one of every four attempts. In *primary impotence,* the male has never been able to obtain an erection for coital purposes; this is a rare condition.

—Eugene E. Levitt, *Indiana University School of Medicine*

Consult (13) Masters and Johnson, 1970.

IMPRINTING. If goose eggs are hatched in an incubator and the young goslings are exposed to a human as their first moving object, they will follow the person and treat him as their "mother," to the complete exclusion of their

Learning by imitation and observation is one of the major ways humans acquire ideas, language, social habits, and skills.

natural mother. Such "learning" occurs rapidly (in a few hours), involves recognizing the characteristics of a species rather than an individual, is relatively permanent, and affects not only filial responses but also later sex partner choice.

Although such phenomena were noted earlier, Konrad Lorenz first clearly formulated the general characteristics of imprinting and noted its widespread occurrence in birds. Not until the 1950s, however, was extensive laboratory experimental work undertaken. We now know that imprintinglike behavior can involve many phenomena, such as song learning in birds, social attachments, food preferences, and nest site and habitat selection. It generally revolves around the relative efficacy of early over later equivalent experiences. Animals cannot be imprinted to just anything: unlearned or innate preferences play a role.

The research on imprinting is often confusing and contradictory, and there is controversy even among specialists. Although some experts use the term to refer to a broad class of phenomena, as outlined here, others use it to refer to an experimental operation regardless of outcome. Furthermore, widely different experimental procedures have been employed, making comparisons difficult.

Imprinting can also be viewed as a global process or theoretical construct, without reference to the species, behaviors, or specific mechanisms involved. This is particularly dangerous when attempts are made to extend research findings across widely different groups of animals, such as ducks and monkeys. As a matter of fact, different species of ducks can vary greatly in their imprintability, both filial and sexual.

Finally, imprinting phenomena have not been carefully studied in nature. This lack is beginning to be rectified, but more needs to be done.

—Gordon M. Burghardt, *University of Tennessee*

Consult (3) Burghardt and Hess, 1966; Hasler, 1966; Hess, 1972; Lorenz, 1935; Marler and Hamilton, 1966; Sluckin, 1965.

Imprinting. The noted ethologist Konrad Lorenz imprinted himself on young geese. They treat him as their mother, to the complete exclusion of their natural mother.

INADEQUATE PERSONALITY, a personality type for which there are no dramatic symptoms or disabilities. Rather, there is a general psychological malfunctioning of the individual. Inadequate personalities may score in the average range on any standard intelligence test and may be provided with average educational and social opportunities. Nevertheless, they seem to fail in all areas of adjustment—emotional, social, professional, and economic.

Such individuals are often congenial and unassuming but inevitably turn out to be ineffective in their daily lives and not strongly concerned with their pervasive failure. They demonstrate a singular lack of judgment, have no ambition or initiative, and spend much time in daydreaming or sleeping. Often when they begin something with a clear goal in sight, they lack the perseverance to see it through. Like children, they will neither work for nor tolerate any delay in the gratification of a need. They seem to want what they want immediately and without effort. Such individuals are extremely difficult to work with in psychotherapy.

—Michael Rothenberg, *The City College of The City University of New York*
See also Personality Disorders.

INCENTIVES. *See* Drive; Motivation.

INCEST, in general, sexual contact with a blood relative. In practice, the term is usually not applied unless the relationship between the sexual partners is at least that of first cousins. The most common form is father-daughter.

The incest offender against children is apt to be an ineffective, unaggressive male who is preoccupied with sexual matters. Incest offenders against adolescents and adults tend to be generally disinterested in sex. As is often the case in sex crimes, many instances of incest occur while the offender is under the influence of alcohol. Every state in the Union has laws prohibiting incest, and about 10 percent of institutionalized sex criminals are males convicted of this crime.

—Eugene E. Levitt, *Indiana University School of Medicine*
Consult (13) Gebhard, *et al.,* 1965; Weinberg, 1955.

INCIDENTAL LEARNING. Individuals tend to note and to remember items in the environment without special attention to them and with no specific intent to learn them. This phenomenon is termed incidental because it takes place without awareness or obvious reinforcement and is sometimes also known as *latent learning* because the information acquired remains hidden until an occasion for its use arises.

INCORPORATION. *See* Oral Character.

INDIFFERENCE. *See* Apathy-Indifference.

INDIVIDUAL DIFFERENCES. *See* Differential Psychology.

INDIVIDUAL PSYCHOLOGY, a school of thought founded by Alfred Adler upon his resignation from the "Vienna circle" in 1910. According to Adler, important conflicts often occur between the individual and his environment rather than within the individual, as Freud had held. Analysis of the mechanisms of the individual's adjustment were thus seen as a proper task of psychoanalysis, in both theory and practice.

See also Adler.

INDUSTRIAL PSYCHOLOGY, the application of psychological principles and findings to the world of work. Business, as well as industry, is covered by this field of specialization. Topics of study include job analysis, personnel selection and training, morale, management-employee relations, working conditions and efficiency, design of machines and work spaces (man-machine systems), consumer needs and preferences, and effects of advertising. Engineering psychology (human-factors research) and consumer psychology may be considered branches of the industrial field.

Earlier in this century *applied* psychology meant what is now called industrial psychology.

Division 14 of the American Psychological Association is the Division of Industrial Psychology.

See also Applied Psychology; Consumer Psychology; Engineering Psychology; Space Psychology; Work.

INFANTILE AUTISM. *See* Autism, Infantile.

INFERIORITY COMPLEX, a term first used by Alfred Adler to describe an individual's sense that he is not equal in competence to other people and is inadequate to meet the demands of the environment.

Adler felt that the motivating force of all life is the drive to assert oneself and master the environment and contended that the actual weaknesses and limitations of childhood produce some inferiority feelings in all of us. However, because of such factors as physical defects (real or imaginary) or overprotective parents, a child may come to regard himself as basically inferior.

The inferiority complex is often partially or totally unconscious and is manifested by efforts at compensation, which Adler saw as an extension of the tendency of weak body organs to compensate by excessive activity. Psychologically, an individual might attempt to compensate for feelings of inferiority by concealing them through feats of courage and achievement. Thus, a person who feels socially inadequate might strive to become a successful businessman. In extreme forms, efforts at compensation may result in aggressive or antisocial behavior.

—Michael Rothenberg, *The City College
of The City University of New York*
See also Compensation.

INFORMATION THEORY (IT), the mathematical and statistical study of communication and how messages are understood and controlled.

This designation is somewhat misleading: the "information" that is analyzed is purely a quantitative measure of the amount of uncertainty that is reduced by a message, and the set of methods and principles for analyzing quantifiable aspects of communicated messages of any kind do not constitute a true theory. The study grew out of ideas originally presented by C. E. Shannon and summarized by Shannon and W. Weaver. The initial work was done with telephone and other electronic communications systems, but IT analysis is equally applicable to human speech and language, writing, gestures, and codes.

The unit of analysis in IT is the *bit* (from *bi*nary dig*it*), defined as the amount of information that reduces uncertainty by exactly one-half. For example, if thirty-two different playing cards are placed face down, side by side, and the task is to find one card, say a heart ace, by asking the fewest possible yes-no questions, the most efficient question to begin with is whether the card is to the right (or left) of center. The answer to this question provides one bit of information because it cuts uncertainty in half, reducing the possibilities to sixteen cards. Repeatedly asking the same question for the remaining cards would reduce the possibilities to eight, then four, then two, then the answer. Thus, using this method, five bits of information are necessary to eliminate uncertainty entirely. In this example, the number of bits was easy to calculate because all alternatives were equally probable. When alternatives have different probabilities, the mathematics of IT become quite complex.

IT has been applied to problems in several areas of psychology, especially perception, speech, and language. For instance, when passages of ordinary English prose are quantified in terms of average uncertainty of forthcoming words, prose is about 75 percent "redundant"; that is, a great deal of information is repeated in terms of each word's capacity to reduce uncertainty about the next word to come. Thus, when a reader sees the word "the," he knows that the next word is more likely to be a noun than a verb, reducing the number of alternatives he might read. Longer passages may be necessary, but redundancy enhances communication considerably by ensuring that the reader or listener will understand the message even if he misses details here and there. Messages with no redundancy (as in computers) can afford no mistakes, since one error is enough to destroy communication. In language, redundancy is provided both by sounds (each language uses only a few of all possible sounds) and by grammar (rules make words interdependent).

—Roland Siiter, *Montclair State College*
See also Language; Speech.
Consult (7) Shannon, 1945.

The monkey solved the problem of reaching a piece of fruit not by trial and error, but in a flash of insight. He used the short stick to reach the longer one, and that stick to reach the fruit.

INHIBITION, restraint of an impulse, desire, drive, or activity. People are taught to inhibit the full expression of many drives and consciously or unconsciously apply checks. Aggression is restrained much of the time, although it may be reinforced during guerrilla warfare or international conflict. One of the anesthetic effects of alcohol is a lessening of inhibitions ("taking the brakes off behavior") and this may lead to acts that are not approved or allowed by society.

In psychoanalytic theory, inhibition means control by the superego of instinctual impulses from the id. This control is not the same as repression because restraint is applied before the impulse is expressed. If the superego prevents the sex drive from being expressed, this wards off a conflict that might arise between ego and the id over the guilt-producing effects of the impulse. If the impulse reaches the level of expression, then repression becomes necessary—the conflict must be pushed out of consciousness.

In learning theory, inhibition is used as an equivalent for interference: information stored earlier interferes with present learning (proactive interference or inhibition); newly stored information interferes with what was learned earlier (retroactive interference or inhibition).

See also Memory; Repression.

INNATE STRUCTURES. *See* Instinct.

INSANITY, a legal and social term for mental disorder that causes a person to be judged not capable of managing his own affairs and not responsible for his actions. In psychology, the term is no longer a correct synonym for psychotic disorder. In law, the term is important as a justification for putting people in institutions and as a defense against criminal charges. *See* Psychology and the Law.

INSIGHT, (1) in general, intuitive grasp of some subtle situation; (2) in psychotherapy, the achievement of understanding of one's own internal motives or unconscious sources of personal problems; (3) in problem solving, a sudden grasp of problem relationships leading to a solution, sometimes known as the "aha" experience.

In terms of problem solving, insight was first introduced into psychology by Wolfgang Köhler, whose reports on apes on the island of Tenerife during World War I are now classic. Köhler observed that chimpanzees would pile up boxes to reach a banana hanging from the ceiling or would put sticks together to pull in fruit lying outside their cage. He noticed that these solutions to their problems appeared to occur to the apes rather suddenly, with little apparent preparation, and dubbed this phenomenon "insight." Though it was noted that a chimp was more likely to solve its problem if it had previous experiences with the boxes or sticks, Köhler used the concept of insight to support the general contention of Gestalt psychology that the essence of problem solving is sudden reorganizations of the perceptual field rather than simple trial-and-error behavior, which E. L. Thorndike had implicated as fundamental to it.

Köhler's work inspired a brief, hotly contested debate in psychology as to whether learning or insight was more important for problem solving. This controversy is no longer active or relevant, since psychologists now recognize that any given problem may involve both trial-and-error and/or insight. The fact that insight does occur does not really explain what it is, or why it occurs, and the emphasis of modern studies of problem solving has shifted toward describing the processes underlying problem solving and thinking, rather than simply describing its occurrence. Gestalt psychology continues to be an influential force in theories of problem solving.

—Roland Siiter, *Montclair State College*

See also Gestalt psychology; Problem Solving; Trial-and-Error Learning.

Consult (7) Köhler, 1925; Thorndike, 1898.

INSTINCT. This term has been used and misused. Instinct has been both hailed as an explanation of behavior and condemned as a meaningless hangover from the scientific dark ages. Even today it is common to label as instinctive unconscious or habitual acts (as when someone says, "John instinctively avoided hitting the other car"). But since the time of Darwin, two other interpretations of instinct have predominated.

The first view emphasizes the urge, energy, drive, impetus, or motivation behind behavior. Thus, one reads about the "maternal instinct," "territorial instinct," or "sex instinct." Influential adherents of this view, such as Freud and McDougall, were impressed by the fact that while the behavior used to attain a goal or satisfaction could vary greatly, similar motivations and the discharge of some kind of internal tension or energy were involved.

The second interpretation restricts the term "instinct" to instinctive behavior. It emphasizes specific motor patterns, such as prey killing, courtship, and nest building, as well as the stimuli that trigger them. In many animals highly stereotyped behaviors common to all members of the species often appear in virtually complete form in the absence of any obvious opportunities to learn them: for example, ducklings reared apart from their parents walk, peck, swim, and recognize the maternal call. This more objective use of "instinct," unlike the first, could not deal adequately with the variability and modifiability of behavior seen in many mammals, including monkeys and humans.

Both of these approaches have come under heavy criticism—not only because they are contradictory but also because the idea of behavioral energy seems removed from scientific study. Furthermore, the view that complex behavior of animals could be based on innate-heredity processes was incompatable with the learning-environmental emphasis of behaviorism. Thus, when ethology first came to the attention of American psychologists, largely through Tinbergen's *The Study of Instinct*, scientists considered instinct a dead issue.

But ethologists forcefully presented evidence that many animals are able to perform complex natural behaviors—termed *fixed action patterns*—often in the absence of any opportunity for learning and that the evolutionary history of the species cannot be ignored. Moreover, they made a distinction between two phases of instinct: *appetitive behavior* is the highly variable and modifiable "search" for a specific stimulus situation, such as food or a mate; the *consummatory act* is the stereotyped specific movements involved in prey killing, copulating, or nest building. Although this distinction is far from absolute, it does help resolve the motivating and behavioral conceptions of instinct.

Today much evidence has accumulated that shows that "instinct" encompasses an enormous range of mechanisms underlying behavior and its development. Although all behavior is to some extent influenced and shaped by innate (genetic) and environmental factors, "instinct" is more and more used today to connote the natural behavior of animals (from sea slugs to humans) upon which natural selection must have acted. Popularizers of ethology have brought instinct back into the social sciences in general, often in a speculative manner. But the result has been the reconsideration of the evolutionary heritage behind the motivations and behavior of our species.

—Gordon M. Burghardt, *University of Tennessee*

See also Aggression; Ethology.

Consult (3) Bernard, 1924; Bowlby, 1969; Fletcher, 1957; Freud, 1915; Lorenz, 1970, 1971; Tinbergen, 1951.

INSTRUMENTAL LEARNING. *See* Operant Conditioning.

INTELLECTUALIZATION, an attempt to avoid confrontation with one's own real feelings and conflicts by developing superficial insight into one's problems. Not often found in children, this defense mechanism is most characteristic of adults with obsessive personalities.

The intellectualizing person can present a carefully detailed and well-reasoned analysis of himself and his motives. However, his report usually lacks insight into the unacceptable feelings and conflicts that are at the root of his problems. Intellectualization generally serves to isolate one from an awareness of his emotional experience: feelings are submerged, and rational thinking is offered in their place. Asked how he *feels* about something, the intellectualizer will tell you what he *thinks*. An example of this defense is found in the person who blames his inability to hold a job on the fact that he was deprived of love as a child.

See also Defense Mechanism.

INTELLIGENCE AND INTELLIGENCE TESTING. Few developments in applied psychology have had the sweeping impact of the so-called intelligence or mental ability test. This article will consider briefly the definition of intelligence, the devices used to measure it, and important issues in the interpretation of intelligence test performance.

The Nature of Intelligence

From early times to the present day, there is evidence that man has sought effective, meaningful ways of describing the behavior of his fellow man. Views about the nature of intelligence or what constitutes intelligent behavior were at first couched in the rather vague metaphysical terms of the philosopher. Plato, for example, defined intelligence as a spontaneous, immaterial power or Supreme God that ordered the process of nature. Aristotle, on the other hand, referred to "souls" or internal structures comprising matter that were the primary catalysts for various animal activities and processes. To cite still another early definition of intelligence, Saint Thomas Aquinas viewed it as "the ability to combine and separate."

The main difficulty with a construct as hypothetical as intelligence is that it cannot be observed directly. It can be verified only by specifying the operations that are to be used in measuring and by noting its manifestations in various situations devised to measure it. Thus, intelligence is said to be operationally defined by the measurement procedures used to assess it. [*Consult* Woodworth and Sheehan, 1948.]

Intelligence has gradually come to mean the higher-level abstract thought processes, as opposed to the simpler sensory or perceptual processes. H. B. English and A. C. English identify three abilities as the components most often suggested by the term "intelligence": the ability to deal effectively with abstract concepts, the ability to learn, and the ability to adapt and deal with new situations.

Measuring Intelligence

Early attempts at measuring intelligence were stimulated both by Darwinian biology,

Bird migration is instinctive behavior that is dependent on internal chemical (nutritional and hormonal) states and external releasing mechanisms (light and temperature).

INTELLIGENCE

The study of intelligence and intelligence testing is bound up with the study of thinking, learning, and measurement. For related articles, see the Subject Maps for THINKING AND LANGUAGE, LEARNING AND MEMORY, and MEASUREMENT.

INTELLIGENCE AND INTELLIGENCE TESTING
    intelligence quotient
    mental ability
    mental age
CONSTANCY OF THE IQ

MEASUREMENT
    standardized test
    testing

ACHIEVEMENT TESTS
SCHOLASTIC APTITUDE TEST
    aptitude tests
STANFORD-BINET SCALES
VOCATIONAL APTITUDE TEST
WECHSLER INTELLIGENCE SCALES

ABILITY

HEREDITY AND ENVIRONMENT
EUGENICS

CULTURE-FAIR TEST
EXPERIMENTER BIAS
    self-fulfilling prophecy
HALO EFFECT
SAMPLING
VALIDITY
NORM
PERCENTILE
STANDARD DEVIATION

CHILD DEVELOPMENT
COGNITIVE DEVELOPMENT

SKILLS, LEARNING OF
CREATIVITY
PROBLEM SOLVING

OVERACHIEVER
UNDERACHIEVER
SLOW LEARNER

EXCEPTIONAL CHILD
GIFTED CHILDREN
GENIUS
    prodigy

MENTAL RETARDATION
    feeblemindedness
    idiot
    imbecile
    mental deficiency
    mongolism
    moron

BRAIN DISORDERS
CRETINISM
MICROCEPHALY
PSEUDORETARDATION

The Subject Maps in the Encyclopedia illustrate the coverage of particular aspects of psychology, showing the interrelationships among the articles in twelve major areas of study. Entries in capital letters are subjects for which there are separate articles in the Encyclopedia. Entries in small letters are cross references.

The Subject Maps appear in the Encyclopedia under the following titles:

Abnormal and Clinical Psychology
Developmental Psychology
Emotion and Motivation
Intelligence
Learning and Memory
Measurement
Personality and Individual Difference
Physiological and Comparative Psychology
Psychology: Divisions and Schools
Sensation and Perception
Social Psychology
Thinking and Language

with its emphasis on individual differences, and by the establishment of psychology as a scientific discipline. Such early investigators as Galton, Cattell, and Jastrow all identified intelligence with the measurement of relatively simple sensory and perceptual phenomena. The results of their investigations were discouraging, since there was little relationship between performance on their tests and such external indices of intelligence as school success or teachers' ratings. It was only when Alfred Binet, a French physician, became interested in assessing more complex mental processes that intelligence and intelligence testing were launched on their present-day course.

Binet. Such complex functions as memory, imagination, and attention were first discussed in a paper by Binet and Henri published in 1895. This paper became the basis for the content of the *Binet-Simon Intelligence Scale* of 1905, which was developed to meet practical demands for a method of identifying mentally deficient Parisian school pupils. Binet's construction of a "metrical scale of intelligence" containing tasks graded in difficulty and (in the later 1908 and 1911 revisions) grouped by age levels greatly influenced all later developments in psychological measurement. The concept of mental age—that chronological age for which a given test score is the typical or average—was undoubtedly one of Binet's most significant contributions to the study of individual differences.

The Binet-Simon tests were introduced into America first by Henry Goddard and later by Kuhlmann and Lewis M. Terman. It was Terman's 1916 *Stanford-Binet Intelligence Scale* that proved most popular and initiated the intelligence quotient (IQ) as a method of expressing test performance. The 1916 Stanford-Binet and the subsequent revisions of 1937 and 1960 have formed the basis for evaluating the success of other group and individual tests designed to measure mental ability or intelligence. Binet emphasized the importance of attention, later defined as adaptation, in characterizing intelligent behavior; he also recognized that his scale did not measure "pure" intelligence but permitted only a sampling of the effects of many so-called intelligences. [*Consult* (12) Cronbach, 1970.]

Group Tests. Credit for developing paper-and-pencil group tests of intelligence goes to Arthur S. Otis, a graduate student of Terman's at Stanford University. Materials developed by Otis as part of his doctoral dissertation formed the basis for the *Army Alpha test,* which was used to screen and classify some 1,700,000 World War I Army recruits. This application of group testing techniques amply demonstrated their ability, and the 1920s saw the development of literally hundreds of group tests for use in American schools. Many of

these early tests contained serious weaknesses, frequently unrecognized by either their developers or their users. [*Consult* (12) Robertson, 1970.]

Paralleling the group test movement were developments in a branch of mathematical statistics known as *factor analysis.* Analysis of the relationships among various tests has resulted in several mathematically based models of intelligence. Charles Spearman, a British psychologist, postulated a general factor, termed *g,* and one or more specific factors in his two-factor theory; L. L. Thurstone, an American psychologist, postulated that eight or nine factors were necessary to account for intertest relationships; J. P. Guilford proposed 120 different cells, each representing a hypothesized factor, in his *structure-of-intellect model* of the late 1950s. The most reasonable formulation for the structure of human abilities seems to be that of Vernon and Burt, British psychologists who propose a hierarchical arrangement where broad factors on one level may be subdivided into narrower factors on a lower level. Factors emerging from factor-analytic investigations are hypothetical constructs imposed by the investigator to account for observed relationships among tests; they are not to be considered as discrete mental faculties. [*Consult* (12) Cronbach, 1970.]

The application of factor analysis to the development of ability tests for use in schools has been rather disappointing. Educators who administer such test batteries have often found a composite or total summary score most helpful in practical, day-to-day use of test results. At most, they can use certain verbal, quantitative, and reasoning subscores effectively.

Several varieties of group mental-ability tests are in use today. All of these measure broad, generalized reasoning abilities considered important for success in school; thus, they are often termed *scholastic-aptitude tests.* Some of these tests follow the Binet pattern and yield only a total or global score. Others subdivide their content and yield language and nonlanguage subscores in addition to a total score. Still others yield verbal and quantitative indices and, in some instances, a total composite. The fact that nearly all of these tests provide a total score supports the usefulness of *g,* the general ability factor emerging in most factor-analytic studies.

Present-day group tests almost without exception use the multiple-choice format first devised by Arthur S. Otis. Such an arrangement permits rapid, objective scoring by persons with little specialized training or by machines. A few typical examples of multiple-choice items used to measure broad verbal, quantitative, and figural reasoning abilities common to all group tests are illustrated on the following page.

Verbal Reasoning
Which word below does not belong with the others?
A-red   B-green   C-purple
D-color   E-orange   (Answer:D)

Quantitative Reasoning
Which number goes where there is a ? in the series?
1   3   ?   7   9   11
A-2   B-4   C-5   D-6   E-8
(Answer: C)

Figural Reasoning

△ is to ▲ as ☐ is to

A-▣ B-△ C-▣ D-☐ E-◇
(Answer: A)

Mention should be made of the distinction between so-called fluid and crystallized intelligence. *Fluid intelligence* refers to the ability to analyze and solve new, relatively novel problems, as opposed to *crystallized intelligence,* which refers to acquired knowledges and developed skills. It seems likely that both of these abilities are involved to varying degrees in most mental ability tests. [*Consult* (5) Eysenck, 1971.]

Using and Interpreting Test Scores

The score most associated with tests of mental ability is the intelligence quotient (IQ), first suggested by Stern, a German psychologist, and later introduced by Terman in the 1916 Stanford-Binet. More properly termed a *ratio IQ,* this index was obtained by dividing the subject's mental age, as obtained from a given test, by his chronological age. This quotient was then multiplied by 100 to eliminate the use of decimals. The resulting IQ, for which 100 was the average or norm (mental age equal to actual age), was viewed as a measure of rate of intellectual development, while mental age was viewed as a measure of level or power of intellect.

The deviation IQ, first introduced in conceptual form by Otis in his *Group Intelligence Scale,* has gradually replaced the ratio IQ. Difficulties in using the mental-age scale to calculate ratio IQs for adolescents and adults and other statistical difficulties argued for another method of expressing test performance. Wechsler first introduced the term "deviation IQ" in connection with his *Wechsler-Bellevue Intelligence Scale* designed to assess adult intelligence. [*Consult* (12) Wechsler, 1958.]

Otis was the first to suggest using individuals of a single specified age group as the reference frame for expressing an individual's brightness. To obtain a subject's IQ or "index of brightness," he simply added to 100 the algebraic difference between the subject's

score on the specified test (usually the number of questions answered correctly) and the average or typical score for subjects of the same chronological age. Deviation IQs on the Wechsler and Stanford-Binet individual tests and on the widely used group tests follow much the same procedure, with only slight modifications introduced to ensure comparability of the deviation IQs at successive age levels. The deviation IQ is best characterized as a standard score; percentile ranks are useful in its interpretation.

Areas of Controversy

The IQ aroused considerable controversy almost from its inception. Much of the difficulty has resulted from the fact that early psychologists wrongly considered the IQ an indicator of innate ability and viewed it as fixed and immutable. Unfortunately, these misconceptions are still with us and render the use and interpretation of IQs difficult at best.

The very nature of intelligence tests has encouraged not only the ranking of individuals and related comparisons but also comparison of the average performance of many diverse groups differentiated by socioeconomic level, race, geographic region, parental occupation, adult occupational status, educational attainment, type of instruction, and many other characteristics. Interpretation of these observed differences has been hindered by the erroneous belief that the differences that do occur are primarily the result of genetic or hereditary factors. Heated and bitter controversy has, understandably enough, frequently resulted from the implication that various racial, ethnic, or cultural groups are genetically inferior to others. Concern for the urban disadvantaged of recent years is a prime example of such controversy. Standardized tests, particularly those of intelligence, have often been viewed as a device used by white racists to impede the cultural advancement of nonwhite minorities.

Although space limitations prohibit full treatment of the various controversial issues here, the following points, at the very least, deserve mention:

Ability knows no racial, ethnic, or cultural boundaries; we find it wherever we find individuals. There is considerable overlap in the test performance of groups categorized in different ways, despite the fact that their average performance may differ considerably. Instances of gross misuse of mental-ability-test results are troublesome, but there is nevertheless persuasive evidence that such tests have called attention to many individuals whose outstanding intellectual qualities might otherwise have escaped notice by parents or educators.

Mental-ability tests by design measure a rather narrow spectrum of cognitive abilities—those important for succeeding in school.

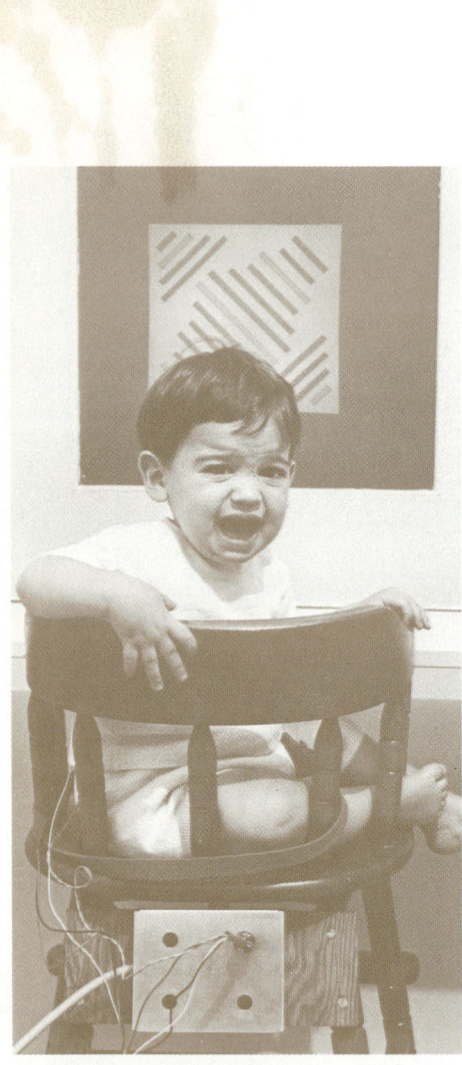

Despite innovative equipment and procedures, intelligence test ratings of very young children have low predictive value because of difficulties in sustaining their attention and cooperation.

Moreover, such abilities are in part learned and represent a complex blending of genetic and environmental determinants. Jensen and Eysenck have surveyed the body of research on this topic and both conclude that heredity is about four times as important as cultural environment in determining intelligence. But such quantitative statements seem premature, given our present methods for studying the problem. Far too little is now known of the etiology of brain functioning and of the role of biochemical processes as these relate to learning, thinking, and problem solving. [*Consult* (5) Jensen, *et al.,* 1969; Eysenck, 1971.]

There can be no denial that mental-ability tests have, for the most part, functioned as intended. Studies of high-level talent pools such as those identified by Terman and, more recently, by the National Merit Scholarship Corporation have demonstrated that persons scoring at high levels relative to their peers have performed at equally superior levels on a variety of other subsequently obtained criteria. Special studies have also been undertaken to determine the extent to which various measures of mental ability or school readiness are biased in favor of whites in their predictive efficiency. Results have generally shown considerable similarity of predictive effectiveness across various racial or ethnic groups. [*Consult* (12) Mitchell, 1967; Cleary, 1968; Stanley and Porter, 1967.]

In editing test items, test developers must be alert to any extraneous verbal or pictorial content that may mislead or confuse disadvantaged or minority-group testers. Furthermore, minority groups may quite rightly contend that they have been underrepresented in many test standardization programs. It has been only during the past ten years or so that scientific sample selection techniques have been applied to test norming studies in an attempt to obtain better representation of relevant population subgroups. Fortunately, this is no longer a major concern, since most of today's widely used standardized tests are based on well-defined, truly representative samples.

—Gary J. Robertson, *Test Department, Harcourt Brace Jovanovich, Inc.*

See also Genius; Gifted Children; Measurement; Mental Retardation; Stanford-Binet Intelligence Test; Wechsler Intelligence Scales.

Consult (1) Hilgard, *et al.,* 1971; (5) Eysenck, 1971; (12) Cronbach, 1970; Justman, 1967; Lennon, 1964.

INTELLIGENCE QUOTIENT (IQ), a unit showing the relative standing of an individual's abilities as measured by intelligence tests. The IQ is widely used for such purposes as evaluating students and classifying levels of ability from genius to retarded. *See* Gifted Children;

Intelligence and Intelligence Testing; Mental Retardation.

INTERDEPENDENCE. *See* Behavioral Ecology.

INTEREST INVENTORIES, tests that measure the preferences of an individual for some particular activity or group of related activities. Scores on such inventories are compared to a norm group to establish the relative strong and weak areas of interests.

Although interest inventories are sometimes related to other factors, they are primarily focused on vocational areas. They are widely used to help individuals plan their careers in education and the armed services and for job placement in industries and governmental agencies.

Unlike some other kinds of standardized tests, such as those measuring aptitude and achievement, the results of interest inventories can easily be biased by the average person. For example, if an individual wishes to show an interest in outdoor activities, he will choose any question or statement concerned with this area over other areas, or he can answer such items as "like." However, anyone who intentionally biases the results of an interest inventory is primarily hurting only himself.

Interest inventories are usually not administered until the senior high school level, because the interests of very young people are often unrealistic and unstable. Interests begin to stabilize in the late teens and are very stable by adulthood. As the individual becomes more mature, interests become more and more stable.

The results of interest inventories do not guarantee success or failure in a given occupation, although patterns of interests are related to specific occupations.

But, in addition to interest, some minimum amount of skill and knowledge is required to perform occupational tasks adequately. Although stronger interests and increased motivation to succeed may partially compensate for the lack of skill or knowledge, a certain aptitude for tasks used in the occupation would still be required.

Examples. One widely used interest inventory is the *Strong Vocational Interest Blank.* The items consist of statements that the subject answers by marking either "like," "indifferent," or "dislike." The responses can be scored for a large number of occupations for men and women. Norms were established for responses on this inventory for people who were successfully engaged in seventy-five different occupations. The more similar the interests of an individual to those who are successfully engaged in an occupation, the more likely he is to be successful in that occupation. Because an individual in a given occupation will be associating with others in the same occupation, who presumably share the same common interests, there is also more likelihood that the individual will be happier in that occupation.

Another widely used series of interest inventories are the *Kuder Preference Records,* which cover occupational, personal, and vocational areas. The occupation inventory provides scores for several specific groups, the personal measures five personal characteristics that are important for occupational choices, and the vocational covers general areas of interest.

—Louis Snellgrove, *Lambuth College*
See also Measurement.
Consult (12) Cronbach, 1970.

INTERFERENCE. Proactive and retroactive interference (or inhibition) are causes of forgetting. *See* Memory.

INTERNAL-EXTERNAL CONTROL (IE). Individuals vary consistently in how much they believe that their successes and failures (outcomes) are under their control. *Internal control* refers to the belief that outcomes are contingent upon one's behavior; in contrast, *external control* is the belief that outcomes are determined by luck, chance, fate or other powerful individuals. The IE concept is very similar to the sociological view of alienation as "powerlessness," which refers to an external orientation.

Relative to externally oriented individuals, those who assume a more internal locus of control are more likely to take calculated risks, to exert influence over others, and to resist others' influence attempts. They have fewer accidents, participate in social action campaigns, and seek instrumental information.

—R. Gary Bridge, *Columbia University*
See also Alienation.
Consult (10) Gurin *et al.,* 1969; Rotter, 1966; Seeman, 1959; Throop and MacDonald, 1971.

INTEROCEPTIVE SENSES, also known as organic senses or visceral senses, sensations arising within the body. These include hunger, thirst, visceral pain, nausea, and cramps. The interoceptive senses are poorly localized but serve a necessary function in arousing and sustaining behavior. For example, bowel and bladder pressure leads to emptying, stomach pressure initiates digestive reflexes, and dangerously hot or cold food in the esophagus is not swallowed.

The receptors for these senses are called *interoceptors* and respond to chemical, pressure, pain, and warm and cold stimulation. Interoceptors have been located in almost every organ of the body by recording impulses from the organ's sensory nerves, but the actual sensations have not all been described.

See also Sensation.

INTERPERSONAL ATTRACTION. Why do we like the people we like and dislike the people we dislike? Perceived similarity between ourselves and others seems to be a factor in our personal likes and dislikes. The commonsense aphorism that "birds of a feather flock together" has been supported by a wide range of research studies. Correlation evidence suggests that those who are mutually attracted to each other (for example, spouses, engaged couples, close friends) are very similar in their attitudes, values, personality traits, and social backgrounds. Experimental evidence also supports the conclusion that similarity fosters attraction. Indeed, one line of evidence suggests that attraction increases as a direct linear function of the proportion of similar attitudes that a person shares with another. [*Consult* (10) Bersheid, 1969; Byrne, 1969.]

The perceived similarity or dissimilarity of values and attitudes may also be a factor in prejudice. This finding has implications for the reduction of racism. If people reject members of other ethnic and racial groups chiefly because they believe that their beliefs are dissimilar, ethnicity may be less important in determining attractions and rejections than similarity of attitudes and values. [*Consult* (10) Rokeach, 1966; Triandis, 1961.]

The proposition that "opposites attract" has also been investigated but has generally not been supported. There are some obvious examples where dissimilarity does foster attraction; the sadist and the masochist cannot do without each other, for example, and most marriages are between people of the opposite sexes. [*Consult* (10) Winch, *et al.,* 1954.]

Specific Factors. Because proximity determines the *field of eligibles* with whom one can interact, one tends to come in contact with similar others more than with dissimilar others. Thus, largely extraneous factors, such as the architectural layout, can affect the pattern of interactions and subsequent attractions that develop within a building. The more people interact, the more similar they become because of shared information and common experiences.

Social-exchange theory suggests that individuals like those people who provide them with rewarding outcomes. And people who are similar provide the maximum outcomes, because it is easier (less costly and more rewarding) to interact with those who share goals and agree on how those goals should be achieved. [*Consult* (10) Levinger, 1972; Thibaut, 1959.]

Consensual validation is a third factor in interpersonal attraction. Finding that people agree with one or discovering that they hold similar views is rewarding because it signals that one's opinions, values, attitudes, and abilities are correct or adequate. Presumably people have a strong, learned drive to evaluate their abilities and opinions, emotions, and outcomes, but frequently their only source of comparison is with other people, not physical standards.

Both the consensual-validation model and the social-exchange theory assume that similarity maximizes outcomes, that we like those people who provide us with the most rewards and dislike those who mete out punishments. But recent research suggests that the *pattern* of outcomes is an important determinant of how much a reward or punishment facilitates attraction or rejection. Elliot Aronson's *gain-loss theory* predicts that an individual will prefer a person who is increasing his rewarding behavior to one who constantly provides high rewards and will dislike a person who is decreasing his rewards more than one who is providing a constantly low level of rewards. [*Consult* (10) Aronson, 1969.]

Finally, *balance* theory suggests that individuals desire relationships that are consistent. In this sense, people who hold similar likes and dislikes and possess similar characteristics provide the most balance. For example, an individual who strongly prefers GM cars will want his friend, whom he likes very much, to prefer GM cars too; this provides a balanced relationship. Perhaps similarity even of possessions as well as beliefs, values, and attitudes facilitates interpersonal attraction. [*Consult* (10) Heider, 1958.]

—R. Gary Bridge, *Columbia University*

INTERVIEW. Many research studies involve a conversation between two people. The interviewer asks the questions, and the interviewee answers them. The purpose of the interview is to obtain information pertinent to the topic under study. There are two types of interviews. In the structured interview every detail is planned in advance, and the sequence and the wording of the questions are fixed. The unstructured interview is more flexible: the interviewer is permitted more freedom in his choice of words, sequence of questions, and the use of alternate questions if necessary.

INTRAUTERINE ENVIRONMENT. Prenatal development is now a major area of study in biology, medicine, and psychology. What happens to the fetus can affect an animal not only in physiological constitution but also in behavior. Thus the study of the development of a child begins with the environment within the uterus.

Folklore. Among the oldest of human beliefs is the idea that an expectant mother can influence her unborn child through alterations in diet, mental impressions, shocks, fears, and ungratified desires experienced at any time during gestation. In the world of folktales, children demonstrating unusual musical or literary precocity are born of mothers preoccupied with Beethoven or Shakespeare while

pregnant, strawberry shaped birthmarks identify children whose mothers had yearned for strawberries in their fifth month of pregnancy, and clawlike deformities of an infant's hands or feet provide visible evidence of his mother's frightening encounter with live lobsters before giving birth. Written documentation of Western man's longstanding interest and belief in prenatal influences begins appropriately enough in the Bible. The Book of Genesis tells of Jacob culling Laban's flocks to his own advantage by carefully exposing the healthiest female cattle to the sight of spotted and striped rods at the time of conception. "And the flock conceived before the rods, and brought forth cattle ring-straked, speckled, and spotted." These, according to a previous contract with his "double father-in-law," Jacob kept as his own.

Belief in a Protective Environment. In the seventeenth century Sir Thomas Browne (in *Religio Medici*) recognized the vulnerability of the mammalian fetus in its uterine environment, where he considered it "subject to the actions of the elements and the malice of diseases." The bright light of Browne's inspired insight into prenatal development shone through the occult and mystical tales of midwives common during his lifetime. That light was to fade and disappear for several centuries. Except for old wives' tales, from Browne's time until the middle of the twentieth century, laymen and medical men alike pictured the fertilized mammalian ovum growing in a stable and protective environment. Whether one subscribed to the preformationist view, inherited from the Greeks, that a homunculus, or complete human embryo, was present at the time of conception, or the more contemporary and accurate view of a single cell advancing toward multicellularity according to a genetic blueprint, protection was considered a basic necessity for growth. Infant protection was seen as the primary function of the uterine environment. Together, amnion, chorion, placenta, and uterus were believed to filter out toxins, provide nutrients, remove wastes, absorb mechanical shock, and provide protection from light, cold, and tactile and auditory stimuli. Since it was only indirectly associated with its mother via the placenta, the human embryo-fetus was considered well protected against all but the most severe environmental disturbances—for example, radiation, or invasion by specific viruses such as rubella (measles). The need for protection was obvious especially during the embryonic (first eight weeks) stage of development, when most major organ systems are beginning differentiation.

Discovery of Environmental Effects. As early as 1832 biologists had found that eggs subjected to small changes in environmental temperature, oxygen, and salinity would produce bizarre deviations from normal develop-

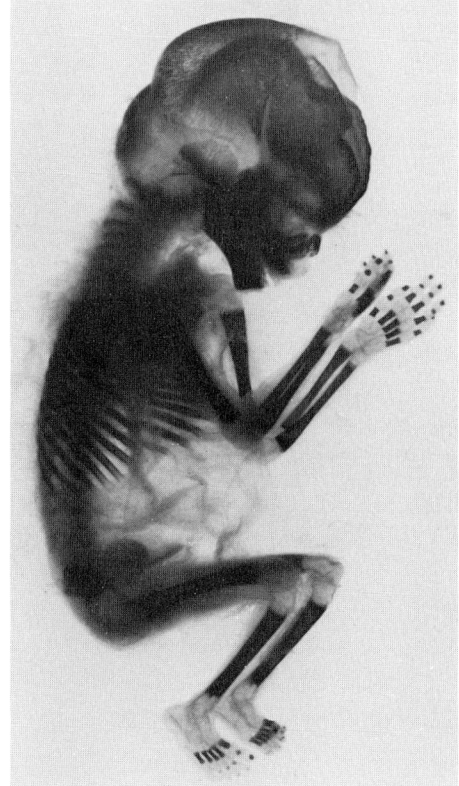

ment in oviparous animals (animals that reproduce by laying eggs). Two-headed fish and cyclopean (one-eyed) chickens could be produced on demand. By the 1950s viviparous animals (those giving birth to live young) including infrahuman mammals were found to be susceptible to embryological deformation (teratogenesis) induced through the treatment of pregnant females with chemicals that are normally used therapeutically in humans. Penicillin, streptomycin, actinomycin D, terramycin, sulphanilamide, sulphadiazine, meclizine (an antinausea compound previously freely used by pregnant women), and even Asian influenza virus were all found to cross the placental barrier and produce abortions or damage to eyes, brain, heart, and skeletal systems of fetal rodents. Interpretation and generalization of these results were tempered by the fact that they were produced in laboratory animals and were not obvious in humans. Species differences in genetic constitution were, in fact, known to play an important role in susceptibility to environmental agents. Many experts, including competent medical practitioners, felt that "if an unborn child were subjected to whims, outside influence, and ungratified desires of the mother, nearly every child would be born a monster." [*Consult* (11) de Lys, 1948.]

Viruses, Drugs, and Other Causes of Defects. It has required mass tragedy to emphasize that the human uterine shelter is *not inviolate*. Publicity given to the phoeomelic (producing seallike limbs) effects of thalidomide in 1961 brought to public attention the fact that in the United States alone more than 250,000 infants are born each year with defects so serious that they die in childhood or are handicapped for life. Suspected causes vary from fetal genotype, in the case of such disorders as phenylketonuria and mongolism, to commonly used tranquilizers such as chloropromazine, meprobamate, and reserpine, and other commonly used drugs such as folice acid, quinine, and aspirin taken by women during pregnancy. The relationship between cause and effect is not clear for most viruses and drugs, however, since the deformities they allegedly produce are indistinguishable from commonly observed malformations such as anencephaly (absence of brain), microcephaly (abnormally small head), and hydrocephaly (abnormally large head).

The effects of prescription drugs and other substances introduced into the bodies of pregnant women—for example, alcohol, tobacco, and marijuana—are currently undergoing extensive research. Since a great deal remains to be learned about the direct effects of those compounds on adult users themselves, prenatal effects upon the embryo are still unclear. Some evidence does show that chromosomal damage is higher among LSD users and their children than among nonusers, but no apparent congenital malformations were found among children studied. [*Consult* (11) Falkner and Reaser, 1970.]

Effects on Behavior. Possibly because of the high premium our culture places on "normal" physical appearance, more is known about prenatally induced morphological changes than behavioral changes. Until recently, the etiology of cleft palate was given greater emphasis than the depression of neonatal intelligence scores associated with dietary deficiencies suffered during pregnancy. [*Consult* (11) Harrell, *et al.*, 1955.]

Increasing scientific recognition is being given to the possibility that psychological variables such as stress experienced during pregnancy can affect the embryo-fetus and its later behavior. Maternal autonomic activity (considered to be an index of stress or emotionality) and fetal movement and cardiac activity patterns have been studied in detail. Mothers with high autonomic activity (as shown by the galvanic skin response, heart rate, respiration) are found to have more active fetuses. Experiments show a twofold increase in the activity of fetuses whose mothers are undergoing emotional stress. Infants whose mothers experience strong emotional distress or fatigue in late pregnancy are found to be more active, to cry more, to demand food more often, to spit up more, to have more frequent bowel movements, to weigh less, and to be more advanced in motor development than "average" infants during the first postnatal year. [*Consult* (11) Frank, 1966.]

These effects are attributed to steroidal hormones produced by the pregnant mother's endocrine system in response to stress. Hormones such as ACTH, corticosterone, testosterone, and epinephrine (adrenaline) are known to cross the placental barrier and alter postnatal emotional, aggressive, and sexual behavior. Much remains to be learned, however, about intrauterine effects upon postnatal behavior in humans. [*Consult* (11) Paschke, 1969.]

Overview and Summary. Approximately seven days after the union of sperm and egg in one of the Fallopian tubes the conceptus, now a hollow ball of cells (the blastocyst), begins to establish contact with its mother, finding its way into one of the folds of the uterus. The blastocyst, by virtue of the genetic contribution of the father, is histologically alien to the maternal uterine tissue and so must in some way conceal its immunological identity to avert abortion while inducing in the mother hormonal, metabolic, cardiovascular, and respiratory changes requisite to pregnancy. During its stay in the uterus the embryo-fetus develops the homeostatic mechanisms necessary to maintain its internal environment as a fetus and those additional mechanisms required for independent survival after birth. The fetus does not develop passively but rather actively, continuously demonstrating its autonomy in the face of a *relatively* stable and protective physiological environment modulated by variable material input.

The relative influences of the uterine environment and fetal genotype upon the neonate's behavioral development are presently an open area for research; we have many more questions than answers. It has been established that the experiences a mother has influence the behavior of animals as fetuses, as infants, and as adults prior to mating. [*Consult* (11) Denenberg and Rosenberg, 1967; Denenberg and Whimby, 1963; Joffe, 1965; Thompson, 1957.]

—Richard E. Paschke, *William James College*
See also Child Development; Heredity and Environment; Mental Retardation.
Consult (11) Joffe, 1969; Montague, 1962; Wolstenholme and O'Connor, 1969.

INTROSPECTION. A prevalent viewpoint during the early twentieth century characterized experimental psychologists who used introspective reports of the sensations produced by specific stimuli. In this view sensation is determined by consciousness and can only be understood through an individual's self-analysis of what a sensation means to him at a given time. Introspection is seldom used as a scientific approach in present-day psychology.

INTROVERSION-EXTRAVERSION. Carl Jung, psychoanalyst and founder of the school of "analytical psychology," first used these terms to express the basic dimension of personality types.

The *introvert* is motivated by and interested in only those things that relate to himself. Essentially self-centered, he sees both the physical and the social environment in terms of their effect upon him. He tends to be rigid in his thinking and behavior, and if he develops a neurosis, it is likely to be of the obsessive-compulsive type.

The *extravert* is oriented primarily toward the outside environment. He tends to be more adaptable and gregarious than the introvert and usually behaves in response to considerations of reality rather than personal or subjective concerns. If the extravert develops a neurotic reaction, it is likely to be hysterical in nature.

Following his consistent stress on the essential polarities in all personalities, Jung argued that the individual whose dominant personality characteristic is extraversion may be responding to a strong unconscious tendency toward introversion. It is important to

realize, however, that these two concepts are not present or absent in a person on an all-or-none basis. Jung saw them as endpoints of a continuum along which every human being could be placed. Although each individual may express one tendency more than the other, the normally functioning person will be able to permit both aspects of his personality to find expression. It is only in extreme cases that one becomes rigidly dominant and the other remains unavailable to the individual. In such instances one is likely to find neurotic functioning.

The introvert-extravert dimensions of personality have also been used by Hans J. Eysenck in his theory of neurotic behavior.

—Michael Rothenberg, *The City College of The City University of New York*
See also Psychoneurotic Disorders.

INVENTORY a device use to assess personality and interests. *See* Interests and Interest Inventories; Personality.

INVOLUTIONAL PSYCHOTIC REACTION, a psychotic disorder occurring in the middle years, marked by anxiety and depression and sometimes by paranoid delusions. The involutional period (from about forty to fifty-five in women and fifty to sixty-five in men) is a time of gradual decline in sexual and other bodily capacities. Men and women have to adjust to these changes and to social and personal facts, such as children growing up and leaving home and jobs turning out to lack an exciting future. A small number of people develop psychoses during the stresses of this time of life. Biological factors contribute to the disorder, but the chief cause is the way men and women react to their feelings and problems. Many patients who develop involutional psychoses have a history of being anxious, insecure, overconscientious, and rigid and narrow in their habits.

Many women go through periods of mild depression during the menopause. The involutional reaction in women and men is much more severe. Two forms have been described, the depressed and the paranoid. In the depressed type, feelings of worthlessness, sinfulness, and despair may become so great that there is a risk of suicide, even though patients may be well aware of their condition. This type of psychosis was formerly called involutional melancholia. Patients with the paranoid type are also depressed. In addition they have delusions, often of persecution.

Electroshock therapy and drugs have been used in treatment.
Consult (13) Coleman, 1964.

IQ, intelligence quotient. *See* Intelligence and Intelligence Testing; Intelligence Quotient (IQ); Mental Retardation.

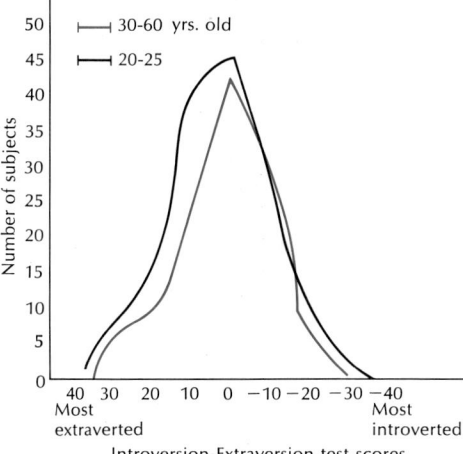

INTROVERSION-EXTRAVERSION

Two groups, the younger also with a higher educational level, show little difference in score distributions on an introversion-extraversion test. The curves approach normal distribution, with no concentrations at either extreme.

Philosopher William James, a pioneer in American psychology, rejected the Structuralist approach to the study of human consciousness and described it rather as individual, selective, and continuously evolving.

French physician Pierre Janet's efforts to unite clinical and academic psychology, and his theory of *idées fixes,* turned attention to the unconscious as a source of behavioral change as well as symptoms.

JAMES-LANGE THEORY. The first explicit psychological theory of emotions was published by William James in 1884 in the British journal *Mind.* A year later, Danish physiologist Carl Lange independently reported a similar theory. The theory became known as the James-Lange theory and was best described in James' *Principles of Psychology* (1890).

James argued that the perception of an emotional stimulus leads directly and reflexedly to visceral and muscular reactions and that the awareness of these bodily reactions is the emotion. He held that we feel sorry because we cry or are afraid because we tremble. In general terms, this theory states that emotional experience is a consequence, not an antecedent, of visceral and muscular reactions.

Walter Cannon, the most vigorous opponent of the theory, argued that different emotions seem to involve the same visceral changes, that experimentally induced visceral changes do not produce emotions, that separation of viscera from the central nervous system does not eliminate emotions, and that emotional reactions appear much more quickly than the visceral responses alleged to produce them.

—Austin E. Grigg, *University of Richmond*
See also Emotion.
Consult (8) Cannon, 1927; James, 1884; James, 1890.

JAMES, WILLIAM (1842–1910), American philosopher and pioneer psychologist. Born in New York City, he studied medicine and physiology at Harvard and abroad and taught psychology and philosophy at Harvard, 1872–1907.

James is regarded by many as the greatest of American psychologists. He was a precursor of the functionalist school. It was his conviction that, while the goal of psychology was the study of consciousness, this could not be accomplished by reducing the mind to elements. Rather, consciousness must be regarded as an ongoing process or stream. The mind, as expressed in habits, learning, and perception, is in continuous interaction with the environment; its primary purpose is to facilitate adjustment to the environment. James rejected the attempts of Titchener and the structuralists to subject human consciousness to scientific analysis.

James described human consciousness as having four characteristics. First, it is highly personal and unique with each individual. Second, it is forever changing. Because mind is a cumulative process, it is modified by each new sensory experience. Therefore, should the same sensory experience occur again, the mind that confronts it is not the same as it was previously. Third, it is continuous: changes in consciousness do not occur suddenly but evolve over time. Finally, James held that consciousness is selective, choosing from the environment on the basis of what is most "relevant" to the organism's adaptation.

James' practical or functional approach to the study of the mind derived from Darwin's theory of evolution. He believed that consciousness had developed like all other human functions, to aid the human species in its fight for survival. He said that consciousness "is to the highest degree improbable...that it should have no use."

Primarily through his writings, James influenced the development of major researchers such as John Dewey and William McDougall. His masterpiece, *Principles of Psychology* (1890), remains one of the greatest achievements in the history of psychology. Originally conceived as a manual for a laboratory course in psychology, it took ten years to complete and became a turning point in the development of American psychology. A sterile academic orientation was transformed into a vibrant practical force. Other works include *Talks to Teachers on Psychology,* 1899; *The Varieties of Religious Experience,* 1902; and *Pragmatism,* 1907.

—Michael Rothenberg, *The City College of The City University of New York*
Consult (1) Allen 1967.

JANET, PIERRE MARIE FELIX (1859–1947), French physician and psychologist. Born in Paris, he received an M.D. from the University of Paris and was director of the Psychological Clinic, Salpetriere (under Charcot).

In his work on hysteria, Janet attempted to unite clinical and academic psychology; he also came close to establishing a concept of the unconscious as a dynamic process. Janet recognized hysteria as a mental disease, and he used hypnosis to uncover the experiences responsible for the hysterical symptoms. He believed that mental conditions were caused by a decrease in a person's psychic energy due to physical stress. This decrease made a person unable to meet problems in his life, and neuroses would then result. A part of the personality would split off, and the person's field of consciousness would become smaller. The part of the personality that split off would remain active and could develop an autonomous system of dissociated ideas, or *idées fixes.* Janet considered the *idées fixes* responsible for the symptoms of the neuroses.

Although Janet spoke of *idées fixes* as "unconscious" and suggested that they could affect behavior, he cited physical weakness as the reason for their development. Thus, he did not really recognize a dynamic concept of the unconscious.

JEALOUSY, a feeling combining insecurity,

anxiety, and hostility. It can develop in small children in the form of sibling rivalry and is common in adolescence. Extreme jealousy shows up in paranoid delusions, such as a conviction that a husband or wife is continually being unfaithful.

See also Birth Order; Oedipus Complex.

JENSEN, ARTHUR ROBERT (1923-   ), American psychologist. Born in San Diego, Cal., he received a Ph.D. from Columbia University (1956) and was professor of educational psychology at the University of California, Berkeley, after 1958.

Jensen has studied individual differences in learning and the genetic factor in mental ability. His conclusion that inheritance is more crucial than training and surroundings involved him in a fresh outbreak of the nature-nurture controversy. His writings include *Environment, Heredity, and Intelligence* (with others) 1969.

See also Heredity and Environment; Intelligence and Intelligence Testing.

JOB ANALYSIS. *See* Vocational Aptitude Test; Vocational Counseling; Work.

JUKES FAMILY, the case name given to a New York State family with a notable record for retardation, delinquency, and crime. A study published by R. L. Dugdale and A. H. Estabrook in 1875 reported that more than 2,000 men and women "of Jukes blood" had been traced. Of these, 171 were classed as criminals, 458 were behind their age groups in school, and hundreds of others were labeled paupers, intemperates, and harlots.

Like the record of the Kallikak family, the story of the Jukes was taken as proof that heredity is a dominant factor in development. This conclusion has been challenged, however, on several grounds. The investigator based many of his classifications on opinion rather than objective evidence, and he did not allow for the influence of environment on the family members.

See also Heredity and Environment; Kallikak Family.

JUNG, CARL GUSTAF (1875–1961), Swiss psychotherapist. After receiving his M.D. from the University of Basel in 1900, Jung trained with Eugen Bleuler and Pierre Janet. Studies of schizophrenia and development of the *word-association test* to study unconscious emotional *complexes* soon established his reputation. Beginning in 1906, he worked closely with Sigmund Freud and from 1911 to 1914 was first president of the International Psychoanalytic Society.

Personal disagreements, particularly over his criticism of Freud's insistence upon the exclusively sexual nature of the libido or psychic energy, caused Jung to break with psychoanalysis. Thereafter he developed his own theory of depth psychology, called *analytic psychology* and for the next half-century investigated and wrote extensively on human personality, particularly its symbolic, mythological, and spiritual aspects. He died in Zurich.

Theories. Jung held that, in addition to the individual unconscious, there is a basic *collective unconscious,* consisting of the living symbols and images shared by all mankind that emerge in dreams, fantasies, delusions, and myths. These emotionally charged *archetypes,* or collective images, express fundamental aspects of human experience. Jung saw man as striving for *individuation* or self-realization, a psychic wholeness reconciling the tension of complementary opposites in personality. Among the opposed tendencies are the two attitudes of *introversion* versus *extraversion,* which respectively direct attention to inner and outer worlds, and the four functions of *sensing* versus *intuiting* as ways of knowing, and *feeling* versus *thinking* as ways of evaluating. Exaggeration of any of these *psychological types* or orientations in ego consciousness causes its opposite to become more powerful in the unconscious; and psychic wholeness requires their creative synthesis through personal transformation and self-discovery.

Status. Though he was often criticized for obscurity and mysticism, Jung's astounding breadth of scholarship and his remarkable revelations of the range of human experience and its symbolic expression assure his position as one of the most profound psychological theorists.

—Alden E. Wessman, *The City College of The City University of New York Consult* (13) Jung, 1933; 1958; 1964.

JUST-NOTICEABLE DIFFERENCE (JND), the minimum amount of difference between two stimuli necessary to tell them apart. One of the first principles of psychology was Weber's law, which states, "A stimulus must be increased by a constant *percentage* of its value to be just noticeably different."

KALLIKAK FAMILY, the case name of a family studied by the American psychologist Henry Goddard in his search for the causes of mental retardation. Impressed by Sir Francis Galton's theory that genius is hereditary, Goddard reasoned that the same might be true of deficiency. While he was director of the Vineland Training School for Feebleminded Children, he noticed that one of the inmates and various abnormal individuals in that part of New Jersey had the same name as a prominent and respected family. Goddard was able to trace the

Arthur R. Jensen has argued for the dominance of heredity over environment in determining individual differences and mental ability.

Breaking with Freud's psychoanalytic theory, Swiss Carl Jung developed his own philosophy of the nature and development of the human unconscious, stressing symbols and striving for spiritual goals.

Attitude measurement and industrial psychology are areas which Daniel Katz has given particular study.

Physiologist Nathaniel Kleitman conducted landmark research on sleep/wake patterns.

ancestry of both groups to a soldier in the Revolutionary War, whom he named Martin Kallikak (Kallikak is from Greek, meaning good-bad). Martin had an illegitimate son by a girl described as retarded. Of 480 descendants who could be traced, 143 were classed as defective and 46 as normal. The rest were not labeled, but illegitimacy, crime, alcoholism, and other mental disorders were reported to be common throughout the group. Martin later married and started a family tree in which only 3 of 496 traced descendants were classed as defective, while many were eminent.

In *The Kallikak Family* (1912) Goddard maintained that his study proved the primary role of heredity as a cause of mental deficiency. His findings, however, have been attacked on several grounds. The classification of individuals for more than a century back as "defective" could not be verified by objective tests. Moreover, Goddard almost entirely neglected to consider the role of environment in development. "Bad seed" children grew up in bad homes, or no homes, while children of the marriage grew up with the benefit of middle-class care, training, and example. Thus what Goddard thought was proof is not accepted, but his study is important as a pioneering effort to find the causes of mental retardation.

See also Heredity and Environment; Mental Retardation.

KATZ, DANIEL (1903–), American psychologist. Born in Trenton, N.J., he received his Ph.D. at the University of Syracuse (1928). He has been professor of psychology at Michigan since 1947.

Katz's research has been concerned with attitude measurement, industrial morale, and productivity. His works include: *Social Psychology* (with R. L. Schanck), 1938; *Political Parties in Norway* (with H. Valen), 1964; *The Social Psychology of Organizations* (with R. L. Kahn), 1968; he was an editor (with Festinger) of *Research Methods in the Behavioral Sciences*, 1953, and *Public Opinion and Propaganda*, 1954.

KINESIS, an undirected orientation that results in an animal's locating itself in one kind of environmental situation rather than another. In *orthokinesis*, for instance, the animal moves faster when in an unfavorable (negative) environment (for example, dry) and more slowly when in a favorable (positive) environment (moist). As conditions become more unfavorable, it locomotes faster and faster, thereby increasing its chances of coming upon favorable circumstances. In *klinokinesis* the same result is obtained. The animal turns more quickly in the favorable environment and less frequently in the unfavorable, all the while locomoting at a constant speed. The actual

evidence that animals utilize these mechanisms is sparse and is limited to invertebrates.
—Gordon M. Burghardt, *University of Tennessee*
See also Taxis.
Consult (3) Stasko and Sullivan, 1971.

KINESTHESIS, kinesthesia. *See* Kinesthetic Sense.

KINESTHETIC SENSE, the ability to appreciate the movements and steady positions of the joints in a remarkably accurate way. This sense is called kinesthesia, derived from the Greek word for movement, or alternately proprioception, muscle sense, or position sense.

The kinesthetic sense enables an organism to know whether its foot is pointed, its stomach distended, its fist clenched, or its neck tense. When humans use their hands to recognize objects with their eyes closed, this is a combination of touch and the kinesthetic input from the finger joints. The ability to make movements according to predetermined patterns (like the balancing movements of an acrobat or the hands of a watchmaker) is also aided by feedback from the kinesthetic sense. Kinesthetic control is trained in "mechanical" actions as braking a car or riding a bike. The blind, without visual input into their movements, compensate by relying more on their kinesthetic sensations.

The receptors for the kinesthetic sense are found in the joints and connective tissue around them. Recordings from the nerves of these receptors show three components of kinesthesia: some receptors discharge as a function of the rate of movement, others respond to the direction of movement, and still others to the position where movement stops. These recordings also show that most of these receptors are slow in adapting and continue to provide information over long periods of time.

At one time it was believed that receptors in the muscles gave information about the position and movement of the body. However, recent experiments show that muscle discharges are related to tension in musculature but do not supply kinesthetic information.
—Nina Adams, *Yale University*
See also Sensation.
Consult (4) Geldard, 1971.

KLEITMAN, NATHANIEL (1895–), American physiologist, born in Kishinev, Russia. He received a Ph.D. from the University of Chicago (1923) and was associated with the department of physiology at Chicago during his academic career.

Kleitman was a pioneer in research on the physiological aspects of sleep. He regarded the patterns of sleeping and waking as dependent upon the evolutionary development of the cerebral cortex. He distinguished between "wakefulness of necessity"—the arousal due to stimulation, either internal or external—and "wakefulness of choice"—the sleep/awake cycle of advanced organisms, due to the cortex.

Kleitman has published numerous articles. His book *Sleep and Wakefulness,* (1939, rev. ed., 1963), is one of the classic volumes in sleep research. *Sleep Characteristics* (1937) is an earlier work. Some of Kleitman's later research (in the 1950s) was done with William Dement.

—Nina Adams, *Yale University*

KLEPTOMANIA, compulsive stealing, usually without any economic motive. Kleptomaniacs, unlike ordinary thieves or shoplifters, do not steal because they intend to use or sell the stolen items. Nor do they plan their crimes carefully to avoid being caught—rather, they steal on impulse, and as a result they are easily and frequently caught. Some kleptomaniacs seem to gain erotic pleasure from the excitement and danger involved in stealing. Others appear to have a strong desire for punishment. Even if they are not caught, they punish themselves after stealing by feeling guilty, remorseful, and humiliated.

The great majority of kleptomaniacs are women. The articles they steal frequently have at least symbolic sexual significance—compacts and brassieres for example—and they tend to steal the same article repeatedly. Boys and men also steal fetishistic items such as women's underwear.

According to some theories, kleptomania is traceable to emotional deprivation in infancy. The act of stealing is an expression of revenge directed against symbols of the parent who withheld the breast or other pleasures from the infant. Again, the thief may be giving vent to hostility toward society or "the establishment."

KNOWLEDGE OF RESULTS. The practice of confirming the accuracy or inaccuracy of a response is important in psychotherapy and education, especially in programmed instruction. A subject who has immediate access to the results of a response is thought to be reinforced or corrected in a manner that produces a high probability that future responses will be correct, no matter what response was made under the earlier situation.

See also Reinforcement.

KOFFKA, KURT (1886-1941), American psychologist and researcher. Born in Berlin, Germany, he studied and taught at several European universities then emigrated to the United States. In 1927 he became professor of psychology at Smith College, where he taught until his death.

Koffka is known as one of the three founders of Gestalt psychology, along with Wolfgang Köhler and Max Wertheimer. His association with them began in Frankfurt in 1910 and continued throughout his life.

Most of Koffka's work was in the area of perception. In response primarily to the work of Edward Titchener, who spent years attempting to analyze perception into more basic units, Koffka argued that perception was a process that had to be studied in its complete configuration. He took the position that our perceptions are governed by laws that organize the environment around us. These are not learned but are innate in all human beings.

Koffka was the chief spokesman for the Gestalt school. He published the definitive statement of their position in a 1922 article for the *Psychological Bulletin*. He is also noted for his application of Gestalt theory to developmental child psychology. His major publications include *The Growth of the Mind* (1921) and *Principles of Gestalt Psychology* (1935).

—Michael Rothenberg, *The City College of The City University of New York*
See also Gestalt Psychology.

KOHLBERG, LAWRENCE (1927-   ), American psychologist. Born in Bronxville, N.Y., he received his Ph.D. from the University of Chicago (1958) and is now professor of education at Harvard.

Kohlberg is best known for his studies on the development of moral order and thought in the child. He has distinguished three different levels, each with two stages, of moral reasoning between the ages of seven and sixteen: preconventional or premoral; conventional or role conformity; and postconventional or self-accepted moral principles. He concludes that moral learning has maturational components, similar to Jean Piaget's stages in human development, and that each stage arises from an earlier one.

KOHLER, WOLFGANG (1887-1967), German psychologist and researcher, born in Revel, Estonia. In 1913 he was invited by the Prussian Academy of Science to direct the anthropoid station on Tenerife, one of the Canary Islands, where he remained for seven years. He went to the United States in the 1930s to escape Hitler.

Köhler, along with Kurt Koffka and Max Wertheimer, founded the Gestalt movement in Germany. Unlike his colleagues, however, he did much work in the area of animal perception and learning, particularly with apes and chimpanzees. Applying Gestalt principles, Köhler discovered that animals perceive and respond to relationships between stimuli rather than to their absolute size or other characteristics. This later was expressed as the Gestalt *law of transposition*. Köhler went on to

The best-known studies of Lawrence Kohlberg dealt with the maturational concept of moral learning.

German Emil Kraepelin classified psychiatric disorders by onset, symptoms, development, and outcome.

Best-known for descriptions of sexual pathologies, German psychiatrist Richard von Kraft-Ebing also deduced syphilitic infection as a cause of paresis.

describe what was called "insight" as the sudden perception of new relationships. In one of his most famous studies, he observed apes abruptly achieve new solutions to problems without any training. For example, an ape was shown a banana that was just out of reach and then given two poles, neither of which by itself was long enough to touch the banana. After a time, the animal had an "insight" that if they were put together, the elusive fruit could be reached. Köhler's work in this area formed the basis for further studies in concept formation. His publications include *The Mentality of Apes* (1925) and *Gestalt Psychology* (1929).

—Michael Rothenberg, *The City College of The City University of New York*
See also Gestalt Psychology.

KORSAKOFF'S SYNDROME, an organic psychosis involving amnesia, associated with chronic alcoholism but also caused by head injuries and other sources of brain damage. It is named for a Russian neurologist, Sergei Korsakoff.

See Amnesia.

KRAEPELIN, EMIL (1856–1926), German psychiatrist. Born in Neustrelitz, he studied medicine and then worked in Wilhelm Wundt's pioneering psychology laboratory in Leipzig. He was professor of psychiatry at Heidelberg, 1891–1903, and Munich, 1903–1926.

Adapting Wundt's laboratory methods, Kraepelin tested the effect of alcohol and other drugs on mental processes. He also studied the effects of fatigue and other factors on the efficiency of work, producing a work curve, a graph of variations in performance as work goes on.

Kraepelin's major effort, over a period of forty years, was devoted to classifying mental disorders. His premise that mental illnesses are analogous to physical ailments led him to a classification scheme based on onset, symptoms, development, and outcome. By studying thousands of case histories he isolated two basic complexes of symptoms: the disease with early onset that led progressively to dementia he termed dementia praecox (now called schizophrenia); the disease exhibiting extreme changes in mood from elation to depression he called manic-depressive psychosis.

Kraepelin believed that dementia praecox was caused by organic brain damage and was incurable. His generally organic approach to mental illness was soon challenged by psychodynamic theorists.

KRAFT-EBING, RICHARD VON (1840–1902), German psychiatrist, born in Mannheim. He was professor of psychiatry, at Strasbourg, Graz, and Vienna universities, and director, National Insane Asylum, Graz, 1873–1889.

Kraft-Ebing's most significant work was his *Psychopathia Sexualis* (1892), which contained clinical descriptions of sexual pathologies and did much to bring the subject of the sexual drive out into the open. This was a shocking and pioneering book in a period when even the medical profession did not publicly discuss human sexual behavior.

He also studied general paralysis, or general paresis. Although at first he attributed this condition to such causes as hereditary degeneracy, weak nerves, and menopause, he later concluded that general paresis indicated a previous infection with syphilis.

LAING, RONALD DAVID (1927–   ), Scottish psychiatrist. He has helped organize a group of therapeutic communities, called Archways, in Great Britain and has written a number of books describing his highly individual views of what mental illness is and how it should be treated. Laing objects to standard views of the mentally ill as necessarily abnormal. Instead, he maintains, a psychosis may be a reasonable protective reaction to the stresses of the world. He has been called the philosopher of madness.

His books include *The Divided Self: An Existential View of Sanity and Madness*, 1965; *The Politics of Experience*, 1967; *Self and Others*, 1969; *Sanity, Madness, and the Family*, 1970; and *Politics of the Family*, 1971.

LANGE, CARL G., Danish physiologist who in 1885 proposed a theory of emotions almost identical with one independently developed in the United States by William James. *See* James-Lange Theory.

LANGUAGE, means of communication involving vocalized sounds (speech) that embody units of meanings (words) arranged according to rules (grammar). Language itself and particular natural languages are studied by the science of linguistics. Language as an aspect of the behavior of individuals is studied by a branch of psychology called psycholinguistics. In this discussion three topics of primary interest in psycholinguistics will be emphasized.

Basic Language Properties. Though we often think of language in terms of writing or spelling, to linguists spoken language is primary, the written form secondary and derivative. Analysis of language is conducted at several levels: as sound, as meaning, or as structure.

At the level of sound, or *phonology,* any natural language employs a finite number of units of sound or *phonemes*. English has approximately forty-five distinct phonemes, roughly approximated by the variety of ways in which vowels and consonants are pronounced. Other languages use fewer or more phonemes, and different ones than in English. A native speaker's familiarity with the phonemes of his language is important in speech perception. Despite wide differences in phonemic pronunciation within a country (for example, North vs. South, urban vs. rural in the United States), native speakers easily decode dialect differences by using the overall, familiar verbal and situational cues provided by the context within which words occur.

Phonemes are the components of larger units—the root meanings or *morphemes* of a language. Morphemes include individual words (for example, "crab," "run," "word") and also the ways in which functions and relationships are indicated (for example, as a possessive morpheme, "-ness," a suffix morpheme in English). Word-morphemes that can stand alone are termed "free" morphemes, while prefixes, suffixes, and so on are "bound" and cannot stand alone. Sometimes one morpheme can use a variety of different sounds to convey the same meaning (the "-z" sound on the end of "buds," the "-ez" sound on the end of "bushes," the "-s" sound on the end of "mists"—all indicate plurality in English). In this case, each different sound is called an *allomorph* of the plurality morpheme. The entire network of relationships between sounds and meanings of a language is called its *morphology*. Psychologists have devoted much study to phonology, relatively less to morphology.

The structure or grammar of a language includes the morphological rules as well as *syntax,* the rules for putting the words of a sentence in order. Older approaches to grammar stressed only the syntactical rules derived from the obvious elements in a sentence, its *surface structure.* Since Noam Chomsky, modern linguistics has dwelled on the importance of less obvious elements, the *deep structures* that are thought to underlie the surface sentence. The concept of a deep structure can best be understood by considering an ambiguous sentence like "Flying planes can be dangerous." Which is dangerous, "flying" or "planes"? If the deep structure is conceived as something resembling the "real" meaning of the sentence, then there is no way to tell from the surface structure alone which meaning is indicated. Linguists attempt to solve this problem by developing grammars that specify the *transformational rules* (not just surface rules) by which deep structures (associated with meaning) can "generate" the surface sentence. This effort, begun by Chomsky, may have considerable consequences for psycholinguistics, though they are as yet largely undeveloped.

Language Acquisition. Language use in childhood evolves through a series of stages. Successive approximations to adult usage appear normally as follows:

4-8 weeks—vocalizations and cooing, with others and when alone.

6 months—longer vocalizations and repetitions or "babbling"; comprehension begins to emerge before production; understanding of "prosody" (intonations).

12-16 months—first words appear as imitations of adult speaking, usually nouns with emotional significance ("Mama," "Daddy").

18 months—vocabulary about fifty words; two-word phrases begin.

2 years—understanding is good; two- and three-word phrases are common.

3 years—two- to five-word sentences with child's own grammar; 1,000-word vocabulary; child is intelligible to strangers.

4-5 years—more adultlike grammar, with some complex constructions still missing; 5,000- to 7,000-word vocabulary.

6-12 years—grammar practically complete by age 12, the only changes throughout lifetime being vocabulary additions.

Three kinds of explanations have been cited to account for language acquisition: (1) Traditional learning theories use principles of reinforcement and conditioning. These principles probably account for the acquisition of individual words and their meanings but are hard pressed to explain grammar and the rules of language. (2) Cognitive psychology has emphasized the rule-learning or "hypothesis testing" approach, where infants supposedly try out different rules and grammars, gradually keeping those that work for the language they hear around them. This view has been supported by many linguists, including Chomsky. (3) Recently, some psychologists have also stressed the possibility that human infants may have a considerable built-in capacity at birth for language acquisition.

Language and Thinking. Though it might seem obvious that thinking depends on language, psychologists have found no simple way to summarize the general interaction of the two. Several views exist.

The early behaviorists suggested that thinking is merely internalized (subvocal) speech. However, a great deal of data, including studies of deaf people, have shown that language is not necessary for thinking, reasoning, or problem solving.

Benjamin Lee Whorf and others have advocated the "linguistic-relativity" or "Whorfian" hypothesis, which states that an individual's perceptions, thinking, and even his view of the world depend on the particular language he speaks. However, except for codability characteristics, there is little psychological evidence to support such a grandiose claim.

The Russian theorist L. S. Vygotsky and the Swiss Jean Piaget have suggested that language and thinking develop independently from different origins (language from communication with other people, thinking from interactions with objects in the environment) but become highly interdependent in adulthood,

LANGUAGE SUBJECT MAP
See the Subject Map for THINKING AND LANGUAGE.

where language functions largely "as the servant of" thought. This view is probably the most realistic description of a general relationship between language and thinking, though in particular circumstances either language or thinking *per se* may be most important for behavior.

—Roland Siiter, *Montclair State College*
See also Chomsky; Codability; Cognitive Psychology; Language Universal; Meaning; Piaget; Semantic Differential; Speech.

Consult (7) Chomsky, 1959; Langacker, 1967; Miller and McNeill, 1969; Slobin, 1971; Vygotsky, 1962.

LANGUAGE UNIVERSAL, a structural property common to all natural languages. Some examples:

"All languages have syntactical and morphological rules."

"Every language has some way of asking a question or indicating negation."

"Every language uses subjects and predicates."

The existence of language universals—some much more subtle than those listed—suggests that certain inborn cognitive or mental structures in humans may underlie the language universals and may help a human infant acquire the language he masters. In other words, at birth the human infant may already possess the most basic, general rules of any particular language he experiences in his environment, since these rules are universal to all languages he might hear.

—Roland Siiter, *Montclair State College*
See also Chomsky; Language.

LASHLEY, KARL SPENCER (1890-1958), American psychologist. Born in Davis, W. Va., he received his Ph.D. in genetics from Johns Hopkins (1914). He became involved in psychology and ended his academic career at Harvard as professor of neuropsychology. He was also director of the Yerkes Laboratories of Primate Biology (1942-1955).

Lashley is well known to psychology for a broad range of research. The Lashley jumping stand is a basic tool used in discrimination learning, which he studied extensively. (The stand is a platform facing several doors marked with different signs; a rat is trained to jump to the door that will swing open.) He also investigated the role of kinesthesis in learning and the functions of the cerebellum and motor areas in maze learning. He defined the law of mass action—that memory for a task is disrupted in rough proportion to the amount of brain destroyed—and other aspects of structure and function of the brain. Some of his pioneer work on the brain was done with S. I. Franz.

Lashley is also known for his work in comparative psychology, animal behavior and

instincts, and genetics. He wrote numerous monographs and *Brain Mechanisms in Intelligence,* 1927.

—Nina Adams, *Yale University*

LATENT LEARNING (or incidental learning), learning that appears to take place without reinforcement. For example, if a rat is allowed to wander aimlessly through a maze without reinforcement, it is found that when reinforcement is made available it learns the maze more rapidly than other rats who are not familiar with the maze. An explanation for latent learning is that even the unreinforced animal has formed a "cognitive map" of the maze, which helps it to learn the maze rapidly when reinforcement is presented for the correct response sequences.

—Joel F. Lubar *University of Tennessee*

LEAD POISONING, a cause of serious, often irreversible, brain damage. Children can get lead into their systems from lead-containing paint on walls, furniture, or toys. Adult painters and workers with metal have also been poisoned by lead. *See* Brain Disorders.

LEARNING. *See* Learning Theory *and articles listed in the accompanying Subject Map.*

LEARNING CURVE a graph of performance in some learning situation. On the vertical axis there is plotted some measure of proficiency—number of nonsense syllables recalled, number of trials required for a rat to run a maze, time for running a maze, words typed per minute by a typist, and so on. On the horizontal axis is plotted a measure of amount of practice—such as accumulating number of practice sessions in a maze or hours, days, or weeks of practice. From the shape of the curve it is possible to infer the rate of learning.

Many kinds of curves are obtained. A typical, or idealized, curve is S-shaped; it shows a slow rise in proficiency at first, then a rapid gain, followed by a leveling off as the learner approaches the limit of his capacity. Curves often show a *plateau,* a period of small gain or no gain followed by a resumption of progress. For example, in learning to type there may be good progress for two or three weeks. Then comes a period of several weeks in which there is no recorded gain in skill as measured by words typed per minute. Finally the student typist again shows increasing speed until he reaches an upper limit.

Graphs can also be drawn as indicators of forgetting. In his studies of memorization and retention of nonsense syllables, Ebbinghaus drew curves that showed rapid loss immediately after the learning session and a slow loss over the following days.

LEARNING THEORY, a systematic statement of

LEARNING CURVES

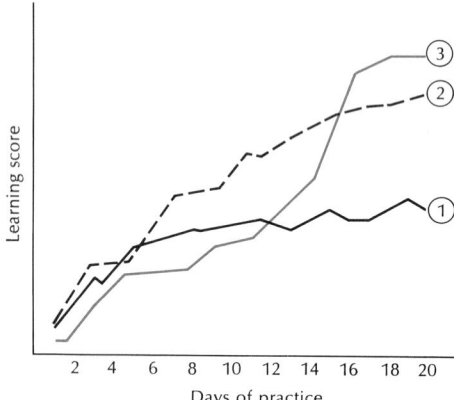

Maze learning in rats: Group 1 rats were permitted to roam the maze for a fixed period of time; no food was placed at the end of the maze. Group 2 rats always found food at the end of the maze. Group 3 rats received no reinforcement until the twelfth day.

LEARNING AND MEMORY

General Theories of Learning

LEARNING THEORY
  connectionistic theories
  cognitive theories
ASSOCIATIONISM
TRANSFER OF TRAINING
COGNITIVE PSYCHOLOGY
COGNITIVE DEVELOPMENT THEORY

Conditioning

PAVLOVIAN CONDITIONING
  classical conditioning
  conditioned stimulus
  unconditioned stimulus
  conditioned response
  higher order conditioning
  aversive conditioning
  REINFORCEMENT
  EXTINCTION

CONDITIONING

OPERANT CONDITIONING
  instrumental conditioning
  REINFORCEMENT
  shaping
  CHAINING
  EXTINCTION
  discrimination training
  TRIAL AND ERROR LEARNING
  PUZZLE BOX
  SKINNER BOX

Memory and Retention

VERBAL LEARNING
  PAIRED-ASSOCIATE LEARNING
  SERIAL LEARNING
  FREE-RECALL LEARNING
  TRANSFER OF TRAINING

MEMORY
  encoding
  chunking
  EIDETIC IMAGE
  clustering
  MEANINGFULNESS
  PRACTICE
  BRAIN STORAGE
  RNA
  short-term memory
  long-term memory
  forgetting
  interference
  REPRESSION
  SAVINGS OR RELEARNING
  MEMORY IMPROVEMENT

The study of learning and memory is bound up with the study of thinking, reasoning, problem solving, and language. For related articles, see the Subject Map for THINKING AND LANGUAGE.

Learning Concepts and Skills

CONCEPT LEARNING
  discrimination learning
  PROBLEM SOLVING

SKILLS, LEARNING OF
  LEARNING CURVE
  MEANINGFULNESS
  PRACTICE
  KNOWLEDGE OF RESULTS

Social Learning

IMITATION
  modeling

Applications of Learning Theory

BEHAVIOR THERAPY
  aversive counterconditioning
HABIT
  smoking
BIOFEEDBACK
  visceral learning
EDUCATIONAL PSYCHOLOGY
PROGRAMMED LEARNING
MEMORY IMPROVEMENT

The Subject Maps in the Encyclopedia illustrate the coverage of particular aspects of psychology, showing the interrelationships among the articles in twelve major areas of study. Entries in capital letters are subjects for which there are separate articles in the Encyclopedia. Entries in small letters are cross references.

The Subject Maps appear in the Encyclopedia under the following titles:

Abnormal and Clinical Psychology
Developmental Psychology
Emotion and Motivation
Intelligence
Learning and Memory
Measurement
Personality and Individual Difference
Physiological and Comparative Psychology
Psychology: Divisions and Schools
Sensation and Perception
Social Psychology
Thinking and Language

principles that explain learning, in general, as a relatively permanent behavior change, independent of maturation and such temporary "performance" factors as fatigue and sensory adaptation. Such interpretations of empirical laws of learning organize and integrate available knowledge and permit prediction of new relationships.

Although available theories differ in formality, comprehensiveness, the use of intervening variables, and the use of connectionistic vs. cognitivistic language, all of them tend toward abstraction in order to gain generality.

The following discussion will describe the major differences among the established theories in general terms and will note recent trends.

Single-Factor Theories. One issue raised by any large-scale attempt to explain all basic learning phenomena is whether there is more than one basic form or process of learning. Single-factor theories assert that one type of learning is predominant and that one basic process or principle (contiguity or reinforcement) underlies all forms of learning.

A theory based upon a *contiguity principle* argues that responding in the presence of a particular stimulus leads to learning. Thus if the stimulus is presented again, the response is likely to occur. The crucial principle, then, is that contiguity between stimulus and response leads to an association. Furthermore, this statement may be seen as an abstract and highly general representation of Pavlovian, or classical, conditioning. Such single-factor learning theories argue that contiguity is the principle underlying all basic learning phenomena, including operant learning.

But other single-factor theories (for example, those of Clark Hull and Neal Miller) focus upon a general *principle of reinforcement* represented in specific instances by the operant learning paradigm. In contrast to contiguity theories, reinforcement theories typically provide more detailed consideration of motivational factors in order to develop drive reduction (via the reinforcing stimulus) as the mechanism by which habits are formed. All reinforcement theories contend that drive reduction is central not only to operant learning but also to classical conditioning; thus the unconditioned stimulus in classical conditioning is interpreted in terms of a reinforcing function.

Two-Factor Theories. Several theorists (including E. L. Thorndike, B. F. Skinner, O. H. Mowrer, and K. W. Spence) were inclined not to focus upon only contiguity or reinforcement but, instead, to incorporate attributes of both factors, asserting that there were at least two major types of learning. In general, these theorists support the contiguity and reinforcement principles, with varying degrees of relative emphasis, and contend that at least both of

these constructs are necessary for analysis and prediction of behavior change.

Connectionism. Called connectionistic because the hypothetical unit that is learned is regarded as an association, habit, or stimulus-response "bond." The nature of the association, however, is regarded differently by the various theorists. For example, some argue that an association is acquired gradually; others contend that an association (or each subordinate "element" of an association) is either formed or not formed in a single trial, in stepwise, all-or-none fashion. Similarly, some theorists regard extinction as a weakening of association, but most would argue that any association, once formed, is permanent. The latter view extinction as an active process in which a newly acquired association leads to behavior that is antagonistic to that produced by the original association.

In strong contrast to these connectionistic approaches are the interpretations of learning presented by Gestalt psychology and E. C. Tolman. Rather than emphasizing the development of associations, the *cognitive* orientation focuses upon thoughts, ideas, and images as the basic units of learning. Instead of pointing to changes in strengths of habits or alterations of associative hierarchies, the theorist notes changes in cognitive structure (learning being viewed as a cognitive reorganization), such as understanding environmental features or expectation of environmental events.

Although pure connectionism and purely cognitive interpretation may be seen as extreme opposites, most theories lie between the extreme points on this continuum. Furthermore, many connectionistic constructs have their cognitive counterparts, the major difference being the type of language used in describing the construct. For example, "feedback" and "response-produced stimulation" ("cue") may be regarded as forms of mediation that are associationistic descriptions of symbolic operations. Similarly, the connectionistic construct of "fractional anticipatory goal response," a concept used to aid explanation of operant maze learning, is virtually tantamount to the cognitive term "expectancy."

Recent Developments. Other attempts to develop a comprehensive explanation of learning usually refine particular attributes of these major theories. Some eclectic admixtures have borrowed useful constructs from several available theories without incorporating the complete systems or their assumptions. Others resemble collections of functional relationships and specific learning principles with relatively little integration.

Currently, instead of a few comprehensive theories, there are several less ambitious treatments of limited aspects of learning. In most cases these have focused upon a particular learning paradigm or investigated a particular construct in depth. The results are smaller systems (models) that rely heavily upon empirical evidence, rather than speculation, for their premises.

For example, some theorists have attempted to determine why reinforcers "are reinforcing," and theories involving arousal, physiological mechanisms, and brain functions, plus certain extensions (in which responses are predicted to function as reinforcers), have emerged. A theory of frustrating nonreward (when an expected reward is omitted) has yielded a construct that may be seen as an energizer of behavior (facilitating understanding of partial reinforcement effects) as well as a source of mediators of extinction. Theories of specific paradigms, such as classical conditioning (using a construct of contingency) and discrimination learning (based upon the concept of attention) have also been developed.

Finally, there has been a recent trend away from connectionistic theories and inventories of functional laws of concept attainment, learning, forgetting, and transfer phenomena. Instead, models have been concerned with coding and retrieval, information-processing studies have used computer simulation, and cognitive analyses of learning strategies have regarded the learner as an active operator rather than as a storehouse of associations.

—Louis G. Lippman, *Western Washington State College*
See also Associationism; Cognitive Psychology; Memory; Operant Conditioning; Pavlovian Conditioning. *Other entries listed in the Item Guide under* Learning and Memory.
Consult (6) Hilgard, 1966; Hill, 1971; Marx, 1970.

LEARNING-TO-LEARN, the generalized improvement in the ability to solve a class of problems that results from working on some of the particular problems from the class—a form of nonspecific positive transfer. The learning-to-learn notion stems from work originally done by Harry Harlow and his associates at the University of Wisconsin.

They placed monkeys in a two-choice discrimination situation where, on any one trial, choosing one object yielded a food reward, while choosing the other object produced no reward.

The subject who has been given a series of such choices is said to have learned the task when he consistently chooses the one object that provides a reward. Once the subject has learned the task, the experimenter changes the problem so that some other object produces a reward when chosen. On early problems a subject may take many trials to begin to choose consistently the rewarded object, but on later problems consistency is achieved almost im-

mediately after the first trial (which is always a guess). Thus, over a series of different problems, learning-to-learn refers to the fact that the subject learns a rule for responding in the choice situation.

Harlow described this learning-to-learn process as the formation of a *learning set,* but this term is misleading because "set" is usually reserved for forms of specific rather than nonspecific transfer. Harlow argued that learning-to-learn cannot be explained with simple stimulus-response associations or generalization, and he contended that the store of rules gained in many situations forms the bases for thinking in humans.

More generally, it is now known that human beings can readily transfer rules and principles far beyond the specific task at hand. Rules apply to classes of problems or tasks regardless of the specific, concrete characteristics of the task. The data from learning-to-learn situations helped establish cognitive psychology, which emphasizes rules in learning and thinking, in contrast to traditional learning theories, which have difficulty explaining nonspecific transfer.

—Roland Siiter, *Montclair State College*
See also Cognitive Psychology; Concept Learning; Problem Solving; Transfer of Training.
Consult (6) Harlow, 1949.

LEFT-HANDEDNESS. *See* Handedness.

LEGAL PSYCHIATRY AND PSYCHOLOGY. *See* Psychology and the Law.

LESBIANISM. *See* Homosexuality.

LEVEL OF ASPIRATION. *See* Aspiration, Level of.

LEWIN, KURT (1890–1947), American psychologist, born in Mogilno, Germany. He received his Ph.D. from the University of Berlin, 1914, and emigrated to the United States in 1932. Lewin founded the Research Center for Group Dynamics at Massachusetts Institute of Technology.

Lewin is noted primarily for his extensive research in the area of human motivation and group dynamics. Using principles first expounded by the Gestalt psychologists, he developed a "topological" theory of human motivation. Central to this theory is the concept of "life space"— all the persons, events, ideas, needs, and so on that may be influencing an individual at a given point in time. Lewin believed that the greater knowledge one had of a person's life space, the more accurately one could explain and predict his behavior.

Lewin applied these ideas to an infinite variety of practical social problems: soldiers at war, marital conflicts, childhood emotional

Kurt Lewin studied human motivation extensively and applied his theories to practical social problems.

problems, and the like. In addition, he expanded his studies to include the behavior of groups. The sensitivity-training movement has its roots in his Research Center for Group Dynamics.

Lewin's influence and importance in the field of social psychology has continued to increase after his death. More than any of his colleagues, he put his ideas to work on practical social problems. He was also a voluminous writer. His major works include: *A Dynamic Theory of Personality*, 1935; *Principles of Topological Psychology*, 1936; and *Resolving Social Conflicts*, 1948.

—Michael Rothenberg, *The City College of The City University of New York*

LIBIDO, a term used in varying senses in psychoanalytic theory but generally meaning a psychic energy or instinctual force. This energy may have conscious or unconscious effects and may be helpful or hurtful to an individual. In Freud's earlier writings he used "libido" to mean sexual desires, but he changed his usage and the term came to relate to life force. In popular use the term means sexual, erotic impulse or pleasure.

See also Life Instinct.

LIBRIUM, the trade name for an antianxiety agent, chlordiazepoxide. *See* Drugs and Behavior.

LIE DETECTOR, often called the polygraph, a device designed for the measurement of many biological responses that are under autonomic control. These biological responses include the EEG (brain waves), heart rate, blood pressure, blood flow, respiration, and skin resistance (galvanic skin response).

The theory behind the device is that if one is anxious about the answer he might give to a probing question, significant deviations from normal values will occur in some or all of the measured biological indicators. Often this is the case, since one's emotional response to a question is determined largely through the functioning of the autonomic nervous system. Lie detectors are not foolproof. When individuals who are very apprehensive about being tested are asked "loaded" questions, they will often show a strong polygraphic response even if they are telling the truth. This is especially true if strong language is used in the wording of the question. Similarly, a pathological liar sometimes does not realize he is lying, does not care, or is not afraid of the consequences. Probing questions will elicit very little abnormal response in this type of individual.

Lie detectors are used by police departments to question suspects, and polygraph records have proved useful in persuading some individuals to confess. The courts generally have not allowed lie detector findings to be presented as evidence during a trial, and findings can never be used without the consent of the person tested. Lie detectors are also used by government security agencies and by private personnel departments for such purposes as screening job applicants and investigating leaks of information and thefts of money or goods.

—Joel F. Lubar, *University of Tennessee* Consult (10) Inbau and Reid, 1967.

LIFE INSTINCT. According to Sigmund Freud's final formulation of the psychoanalytic theory of motivation (c. 1920), the basic drives or instincts could be classified under two headings, the life instincts and the death instincts.

The *life instincts,* or "eros," serve the purpose of individual survival and species propagation; they include such drives as hunger, thirst, and sex. The form of energy for the manifestations of the life instincts is termed libido. Freud held that this postulated energy, which maintained all life processes, including those of organic function, self-preservation, self-love, and object-love, was basically homogeneous. He termed it eros, whether it was manifest as libido at the service of the sexual instincts or as ego-libido serving the functions of self-preservation.

The life instinct most emphasized by Freud was sexual. It was thought to encompass many separate needs located in different bodily regions (oral, anal, phallic, and genital). These were referred to collectively as the erogenous zones.

—Alden E. Wessman, *The City College of The City University of New York*
See also Death Instinct.
Consult (13) Freud, 1950.

LIFE SPACE, a concept of behavior developed by Kurt Lewin. *See* Lewin.

LIGHT ADAPTATION. When you walk from darkness into intense sunlight, the sight is dazzling. For a moment you cannot see well, and it almost hurts. Then your eyes adjust to the light. This process is the visual adjustment to the billionfold changes in illumination levels encountered daily.

Light adaptation is due partly to pupillary constriction but primarily to chemical changes in the retina. In response to bright light, the pupil constricts, reducing the light sixteenfold; the retina's visual pigments are chemically bleached, reducing visual sensitivity; and within three to five minutes the visual pigments are resynthesized. Thus vision returns to a steady level of sensitivity.

—Nina Adams, *Yale University*

LIMBIC REGION, a ring of interconnected structures in the brain located primarily around

LIMBIC SYSTEM

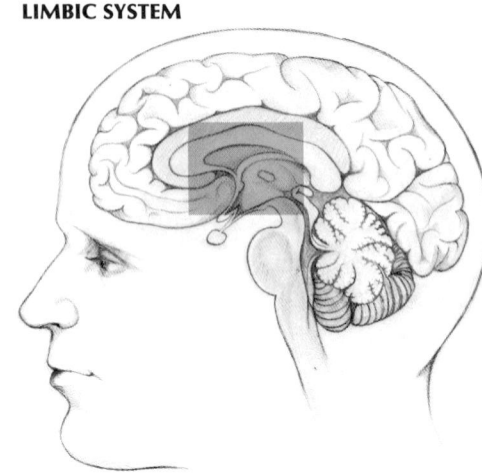

the central core of the thalamus. The limbic region is important for processing information regarding emotion and motivation. It consists of the *amygdala,* lying ventral and lateral; the *hippocampus,* lying ventral and posterior; the *septal region,* lying on the midline; and certain portions of the *hypothalamus.* There are also main fiber tracts, such as the *mammillothalamic tract* and the *fornix,* which carry information from one portion of the limbic system to others. Limbic stimulation and ablation (surgical removal) studies reveal that this region plays a primary role in the control of the hypothalamus, and limbic lesions lead to profound changes in emotional and motivational behavior.

—Joel F. Lubar, *University of Tennessee*
See also Brain, Emotion.
Consult (3) Isaacson, *et al.,* 1971.

LINGUISTICS. *See* Language.

LOBES OF THE BRAIN. *See* Cerebral Cortex; Psychosurgery.

LOBOTOMY. *See* Psychosurgery.

LOCALIZATION, the ability to discriminate where a stimulus comes from or the area of the body being stimulated. The ability to localize the direction and distance of a sound depends upon binaural (two-eared) hearing. Visual localization (acuity) is extremely sensitive in the center (fovea) of the eye and diminishes toward the periphery. The ability to localize stimulation of the skin varies: the face, tongue, and lips are so sensitive that two points separated by only a few millimeters can be distinguished; but two points separated by several inches on the trunk of the body cannot be. The visceral sensations are the most vague and difficult to localize.

—Nina Adams, *Yale University*

LOCKE, JOHN (1632–1704), British philosopher and one of the founders of associationism in psychology. His *Essay Concerning Human Understanding* (1690) is one of the classics in epistemology (the study of how we know) and contains his most important contributions to psychology.

Rejecting Descartes' doctrine of innate ideas, Locke adopted a thoroughgoing "empiricism" that traced all thinking and ideas to sensory experience. He argued that at birth the mind is merely a *tabula rasa* (blank tablet) on which experience writes itself; the contents of the mind or "ideas" all derive originally from sensory experience and are combined and made more complex by their associations with each other. Associationism subsequently became a whole school of thought carried on and elaborated by later British philosophers, such as Mill.

Locke also made an influential distinction between primary and secondary qualities of objects. *Primary qualities* are those perceived directly by the sense organs (shape, size) and are properties of the objects themselves. *Secondary qualities* do not exist in the objects themselves but come about as a result of the effect the object produces on the mind (color, tastes, sounds). Thus, secondary qualities are produced by the objects but are not in the objects. This distinction can be viewed as a precursor to the doctrine of the specific energies of nerves and to ideas in Gestalt psychology.

—Roland Siiter, *Montclair State College*
See also Associationism.

LONG-TERM MEMORY. *See* Memory.

LONGITUDINAL STUDY, a research method that involves following one subject over a period of time. For example, Lewis M. Terman used the longitudinal method in his study of the gifted, reporting on the ability and performance of the same individuals from childhood to adulthood. This procedure contrasts with the *cross-sectional* approach, which might involve studying the ability of all the sixth-grade children in a city.

LSD, lysergic acid. *See* Drugs and Behavior; Intrauterine Environment; Mental Retardation.

LURIA, ALEXANDER (1902–), Russian psychologist. Born in Kazan, he received an M.D. (1936) and D. Med. (1943) from Moscow University, where he is head of the department of neuropsychology.

A well-known neuropsychologist, Luria has studied and written about the analysis of brain injury and the particular role of languages and language disorders. In *The Nature of Human Conflicts* (1932) he described physiological correlates of lying by measuring finger movements, breathing rate, and pulse. Later major works include *Traumatic Aphasia,* 1947 (Engl. 1967); *Restoration of Functions After Brain Trauma,* 1948 (Engl. 1961); *The Role of Speech in Regulation of Normal and Abnormal Behavior,* 1961; *Higher Cortical Functions in Man,* 1962 (Engl. 1966); and *Human Brain and Psychological Processes,* 1963 (Engl. 1966).

—Nina Adams, *Yale University*

MACCOBY, ELEANOR EMMONS (1917–), American psychologist. Born in Tacoma, Wash., she received her Ph.D. from the University of Michigan (1950) and has been professor of psychology at Stanford since 1966.

Maccoby has been concerned with the growth and development of the child. She has measured the effects of love-oriented techniques (praise, withdrawal of love) and object-oriented techniques (rewards and physical

British philosopher John Locke viewed all thinking as derived from sensory experiences (empiricism) and their association with each other.

punishments) on behavior. She examined the development of "self-control" or "conscience."

Maccoby is the coauthor of *Patterns of Child Rearing* (with Sears and Levin), 1957; and *Experiments in Primary Education* (with Zellner), 1970; and is author of *Development of Sex Differences*, 1966.

MAIER, NORMAN RAYMOND (1900-), American psychologist. Born in Sebewaing, Mich., he took his Ph.D. at the University of Michigan (1928) and was professor of psychology there after 1945.

Maier's early research concerned a broad range of topics, including problem solving and reasoning in humans and rats, frustration, and stereotyped behavior. His later research deals primarily with executive and leadership development. His 1972 article "Innovation in Education" introduces methods for participation of students in large classroom situations.

Maier's works include *A Psychological Approach to Literary Criticism* (with Reninger), 1933; *Principles of Animal Psychology,* (with Schneirla), 1935; *Studies of Abnormal Behavior in the Rat,* 1939; *Frustration, A Study of Behavior without a Goal,* 1949; *Principles of Human Relations,* 1952; *Problem Solving Discussions and Conferences,* 1963; *Creative Management,* (with Hayes), 1962; *Psychology in Industry,* 1965.

Norman Maier's research and writings cover a broad spectrum, from frustration and problem-solving in rats to similar human behavior.

MAKE-A-PICTURE-STORY (MAPS) TEST, a projective story-telling technique developed by E. S. Shneidman. In a miniature theater in which various pictorial backgrounds and cardboard figures can be arranged, the examiner sets up the backgrounds one at a time, and the subject is allowed to select figures to be placed before them. He is then instructed to make up a story about the scene, including a description of the characters and events depicted, their thoughts and feelings, and the outcome of described events. Stories may be followed by a standardized inquiry.

Projective interpretation of the test results varies widely. Shneidman's formal scoring system, dealing essentially with interpersonal relationships, is sometimes utilized. Other examiners concentrate on the needs and attitudes of story heroes as a direct manifestation of the subject's true feelings and personality make-up. All interpretive approaches derive hypotheses concerning the subject's psychosocial development and significant intrapsychic dynamics.

—Randolph S. Kraft, *Federation of the Handicapped, N.Y.*

Consult (12) Fine, 1955; Shneidman, 1949.

MALE MIDLIFE CRISIS. *See* Middle Years.

MANIA. This term and its relatives "manic" and "maniac" are used in three ways. In general speech and writing, mania suggests abnormal behavior that is out of control and probably dangerous; but to call someone "a raving maniac" is a personal judgment rather than a professional diagnosis. *Manic* is used diagnostically in such terms as manic-depressive psychosis, referring to the excited phase of this disorder. *Mania* is also used technically to mean an uncontrolled urge, as to steal (kleptomania) or set fires (pyromania). *See* Manic-Depressive Psychosis; Kleptomania; Nymphomania; Pyromania.

MANIC-DEPRESSIVE PSYCHOSIS, the second most common form of functional mental disorders. It is surpassed only by the schizophrenias in frequency and importance. From 5 to 15 percent of total first admissions to U.S. mental hospitals still comprise cases that are at least initially categorized as manic-depressive psychosis. This term was originally proposed by Emil Kraepelin in 1896, to include cases of insanity characterized by periodicity—alternative disturbed emotional states showing either elation (the manic phase) or its opposite, depression.

Theories about Causes

Manic-depressive psychosis occurs twice as frequently in females as in males. First manic attacks usually occur between the ages of fifteen and twenty-five, while initial depressive attacks usually occur between the ages of twenty-five and thirty-five. The age of onset tends to be younger in women than in men. The aggressive woman with masculine strivings seems to be especially predisposed.

Undoubtedly, there is a strong hereditary factor in the occurrence of this disorder. The incidence of manic-depressive psychosis is twenty-five times as high among the siblings of manic-depressive patients as in the average population. According to one study, in nonidentical twins the expectancy of coexisting mental illness is 26 percent, while in identical twins the expectancy is approximately 100 percent. [*Consult* (13) Kallmann, 1952; Kallmann, 1958.]

Other researchers have found correlations of manic-depressive illness with body build or "constitution." Thus, Ernst Kretschmer in Germany, for example, found that about two-thirds of typical cases of manic-depressive psychosis fell into what he called the "pyknic" group, a body build characterized by roundness of contour, amplitude of body cavities, and a plentiful endowment of fat. [*Consult* (9) Kretschmer, 1925; Sheldon, *et al.,* 1954.]

An extraverted, cyclothymic personality is found in a large proportion of manic-depressive patients. Reports on their lives before they became patients show them as jovial, "hail-fellow-well-met" individuals, "big" and voluble talkers, jokers, pranksters, optimistic, excellent salesmen or promoters. Endowed with an exuberance of enthusiam and energy, they need little sleep. They tend to overindulge in eating, drinking, and sexual activity and are often socially popular. Along with these normal "high" states, they may also show "low" moods, which are not likely to be noticed as much by their friends since they will avoid social contacts at these times. Both the high and low emotional states are not attributable as a rule to any external situations or factors and are thus considered "endogenous."

The personality patterns just described are not in themselves proof of mental illness. As long as such individuals do not lose their ability to evaluate reality and do not form false judgments based on misevaluations, they cannot justifiably be considered mentally ill. If fact, many of them enjoy long, happy, and productive lives with no "breakdown." Many colorful, important, and highly successful "personalities" are cyclothymic individuals.

The Clinical Picture

When a person is diagnosed as mentally ill with a manic-depressive disorder, the clinical phases of the psychosis can best be understood as analogous to the opposite faces of a medal. The obverse or convex face corresponds to the manic phase, and the reverse or concave face corresponds to the depressive phase. The usual symptomatology is shown in the following table of opposites:

General Appearance and Behavior

Manic Phase, hyperactive, busy restless, impatient. Does everything in a hurry—walking, talking, eating, responding. Posture erect. Speech emphatic, accompanied with gestures. Quality of voice rich, variable, vibrant.

Dress: overdressed, flamboyant, decorative, but careless as to grooming; likely to be immodest.

Handwriting: large, wide, expansive, embellished.

Depressive Phase, underactive, sluggish, idle, and inert. Does everything at a markedly slowed pace—walking, talking, eating, responding. Posture stooped. Speech low in tone, often hardly more than a whisper.

Dress: dull, colorless, neglected.

Handwriting: small, cramped, crowded.

Stream of Mental Activity

Manic Phase, marked overproductivity, volubility, flight of ideas. However, wide-ranging thoughts remain connected to each other as distinguished from the dissociation of thought seen in schizophrenia. Speech tends to go on endlessly unless interrupted.

Depressive Phase, underproductive, paucity of thoughts and speech. Responses terse and abbreviated. Has to be "pumped" for information.

Emotional Reactions

Manic Phase, happy, elated, exalted, egotistical, boastful, overly optimistic, expansive, grandiose. Friendly and magnanimous if agreed with, but readily becoming irritable, hostile, impatient, and verbally abusive if frustrated or crossed.

Facial expressions: coincide with the mood of the moment.

Depressive Phase, obviously sad, depressed, readily crying. Hopeless, fearful, anxious, woebegone, overly pessimistic.

Facial expression: furrowed brow.

Mental Trend, Content of Thought

Manic Phase, grandiose and expansive ideas. Unrealistic feelings of strength, power, skill, work capacity, and efficiency. Readiness to assume excessively difficult tasks, burdens, responsibility. Overly sanguine of success. No feelings of self-blame; more likely to attribute misfortunes to external events or circumstances.

Depressive Phase, depressive, self deprecatory trends. Feelings of weakness, ill health, exhaustion. Work incapacity and inefficiency. Reluctance or refusal to assume simplest tasks, burdens, responsibilities. Overly fearful of failure. Marked feelings of guilt, self-blame, unworthiness, sinfulness, which frequently lead to suicidal thoughts and attempts.

In most cases of manic-depressive psychosis, auditory hallucinations are not prominent or persistent. Their content corresponds to the existing emotional state. When they are present, the patient is apt to recognize their abnormality and not insist on their reality, as the schizophrenic would do. Similarly, when persecutory delusions are expressed (usually only in disturbed phases), they are fleeting and are readily acknowledged as erroneous when improvement occurs.

From the clinical standpoint, several different varieties of "manic-depressive breakdowns" are seen. Probably, the most frequent pattern is that of an initial manic or depressive phase lasting several weeks to several months, followed by a more prolonged period of normality. Also, fairly common is the pattern of either an initial manic or depressive phase followed immediately by its opposite counterpart and then a period of normality. The frequency of attacks varies widely. Some patients have two a year, others one attack every few years, and some may only have one or two attacks in a lifetime. However, the pattern of the initial episode is likely to be repeated in subsequent attacks. In many instances a particularly stressful life situation seems to bring on an attack, but frequently this is not the case. Often, patients have gone through extreme stress periods without difficulty, and then have broken down after what should have been minor disappointments.

Milder episodes of the manic phase are called *hypomania*. Similarly, milder forms of the depressive phase may be called *hypomelancholia*. Such patients may not be noticeably slowed down, but they "don't fell well" and often have made the rounds of general practitioners and internists who can find no organic pathology for their vague hypochondriacal complaints. The "cyclic" history of these "sick" episodes is usually the clue that tells the psychiatrist that the patient is suffering from a mild form of manic-depressive psychosis, depressed phase.

Sleep disturbances, especially early interruptions, usually usher in and persist throughout an attack of manic-depressive illness. Normalization in sleep pattern is a good sign of improvement. Poor appetite is another characteristic sign of this illness, and dramatic weight losses are frequently seen as a consequence of the attack. Likewise, weight gain is a very reliable sign of improvement. Sometimes "depressed" patients sleep excessively, but they wake up feeling unrefreshed, worse than when they went to bed. Also, most patients find that they feel worse on awakening in the morning but tend to feel "not so bad" as the day comes to a close, and sometimes almost normal or good in the evening.

Treatment

The clinical features outlined here describe full-blown pictures of manic-depressive psychosis as it presented itself up to three decades ago. Prior to that time, there was no effective treatment available, and psychiatrists were forced to let each episode run its natural course. Since then the situation has markedly changed for the better. Since the early 1940s it has been found that most depressive attacks can be rapidly terminated (in two to four weeks) by courses of electroshock treatments. Since the middle of the 1950s it has been found that many (but not all) cases of depression can be also terminated by the use of newly discovered antidepressant drugs, specifically of the imipramine and the monoamineoxidase inhibitor groups. Since 1965, American psychiatrists have found that the judicious use of a simple chemical, lithium carbonate, would usually terminate a manic attack in a few days.

In addition to other forms of treatment, patients usually get emotional support and reassurance and counseling that will help them understand their problems.

—Emanuel Messinger, M.D., *U.S. Veterans Hospital, Northport, N.Y.*

See also Constitutional Types; Cyclothymic Personality; Drugs and Behavior; Electroconvulsive Therapy; Schizophrenia.

Consult (13) Arieti, 1966; Coleman, 1964.

MANIPULATIVE DRIVE. Psychologists have observed that experimental animals and children will handle, explore, and tinker with new objects for no reward other than whatever the activity does for them. *See* Curiosity Drive; Exploratory Drive.

MARIJUANA. *See* Drugs and Behavior.

MARRIAGE COUNSELING. As a specialized field, marriage counseling is relatively new. Among the first to define marriage counseling as a clinical specialty, the American Association of Marriage Counselors, founded in 1942, was at that time considered a radical group. The organization is now the American Association of Marriage and Family Counselors (AAMFC). Membership consists primarily of people in the disciplines of psychiatry, clinical and counseling psychology, social work, and religion or pastoral counseling. Marriage counseling may be thought of as a professional activity conducted by people representing various disciplines, although it is also practiced by those without specialized training.

The demand for marriage counseling has grown steadily and rapidly since the inception of AAMFC. Family and marriage counseling concern themselves with the larger context of the structure and function of the American family system. Recent changes, helping to legitimate marriage counseling as a distinctive profession, have been the licensing of marriage counselors in many states. In many other states marriage counseling can be practiced by anyone, whether professionally qualified or not, who wishes to set up a practice.

Underlying Theories

Just as there are many disciplines producing marriage counselors, there are many different theoretical viewpoints of what marriage counseling is and should be. In order to understand the nature of marriage counseling it is necessary to explore some of the assumptions that are basic to the various approaches.

Although marriage counseling has developed out of a social need and awareness of the conflict and stress within marriage, there is little agreement as to the factors necessary for a satisfying marriage. Marital problems are highly varied and diffuse. They encompass a range of areas that can be either intrinsic or extrinsic to the marriage, but generally marital problems involve both. Marital conflicts may be rooted in the purely psychological problem of one or both partners or may grow out of the nature of the marriage relationship itself.

The various approaches to marriage counseling and their underlying assumptions will be presented under three categories: psychodynamic, behavioral, and humanistic-experiential.

Psychodynamic Approach. The psychodynamic orientation rests on the assumption that the forces underlying marital dysfunction reside within the disturbed personalities of each of the marital partners. Each of the spouses is thought to bring unresolved neurotic and/or psychotic needs into the marriage, and these create stress.

Treatment based on this orientation is usually psychoanalytic and focuses on intrapsychic mechanisms. The goal of this form of treatment is the analysis of underlying motivation for the presently observed disturbances in functioning. Each person's personal history is extremely important and relevant to understanding the motivating forces at work in creating the marital disturbances.

A variant of the psychodynamic orientation assumes the position that dysfunction in marriage results from deficiencies in the ego strengths of one or both of the partners. Such deficiencies stem from defective socialization. Adult personal and interpersonal skills and coping mechanisms were not part of the socialization of one or both the spouses. Thus, current life experiences can lead to only limited gratification since it requires a sound and integrated ego structure to gain satisfaction from life experiences, including marriage.

Treatment aims at "building" the ego, that is, helping the individual face weaknesses, understand the causes (to gain insight), and finally adopt more appropriate ego mechanisms for coping with life.

Behavioral Orientation. The premise underlying the behavioral orientation is that marital problems consist of a set of dysfunctional behaviors. These behaviors are observable, measurable, and modifiable. It is assumed that what is needed in the marriage is, first, the identification of the undesirable behaviors and, second, their modification or extinction. The behaviors are learned and can therefore be unlearned. The dysfunctional behaviors in question may have been brought into the marriage by either or both of the partners. Marital unhappiness is also caused by interactions between spouses that can result in a distressing relationship. The specific behaviors of the couples' interaction can be modified to bring about a more satisfying relationship.

Treatment, using learning approaches, is varied but usually employs the systematic recording of behavior. Once the behaviors are explicated, a number of modifying procedures can be used. The counselor may employ external contingencies to reinforce functional behavior or extinguish harmful behavior. The counselor may ask the spouses to employ certain contingencies that will influence one another's behavior.

Humanistic-Experiential Orientation. Emanating from humanistic psychology and philosophy is the humanistic-experiential orientation, which regards shared human experience as being primary to sound marital relationships. Each human has needs, feelings, desires, and motives. If, in marriage, they are withheld from one another, the result is distrust, anger, and general marital unhappiness. The inability to share feelings openly and honestly and to fully experience one another is central to the description and definition of marital dysfunction. Essential to this orientation is an awareness of the constraints placed on the marital relationship by social norms, roles, and demands. Extrinsic social concerns keep the spouses from experiencing their basic humanness, hence causing marital stress.

Humanistic counseling procedures employ structured exercises and experiences and rely on feelings that are being experienced at the present time. The emphasis is generally on implementing communication skills. As two people become able to open and share these feelings with one another, they each experience the meaning of emotional honesty and openness.

Trends in Procedures

There are many variations in the structure of marriage counseling as well as the previously mentioned orientations. Some counselors prefer to see each spouse individually for one or more sessions and then see the couple together, while others prefer to see one spouse and have another counselor see the other spouse. Still others prefer to see one spouse as the primary client with the other spouse being seen only occasionally. Conjoint counseling, seeing the couple in joint interviews, is insisted upon by some marriage counselors. There is a growing trend toward pairs of counselors interviewing married couples, on the theory that the counselors' relationship will be a model for the couple. This has even extended to married cotherapists working with married couples. More recently, marriage counseling in groups has become a preferred mode of treatment. The assumption here is that couples can improve their relationships by sharing with and receiving help from other couples.

Certain types of research have led to new areas of counseling. Sex counseling has, until recent years, been part of more orthodox forms of marital counseling. The pioneering work of Alfred Kinsey in uncovering myths and facts about the sexual lives of married men and women produced attempts at direct intervention in sexual problems faced by many married couples. More recently, the work of Masters and Johnson has led to the emergent field of sex counseling. Sex counseling combines experiential, learning, and dynamic approaches. The couple, with the counselor's help, specifies the problems they are having. One or both partners are sexually behaving or not behaving in certain ways that affect the feelings of the other. The distress thus caused can frequently be helped by modifying sexual behavior and feelings about sex.

Newer notions of marriage counseling are leading theory builders and researchers, as

Early maternal deprivation has profound effects on the psychological well-being of children. Interesting experiments with surrogate mothers have been performed with Rhesus monkeys. The infant (above), though fed by the wire surrogate, preferred contact with the cloth-wrapped surrogate. Frightened by a mechanical toy (below), it flees to the softer form.

well as clinicians, to consider the process of counseling as one of growth rather than adjustment. Adjustment leads to the maintenance of the status quo, while growth implies that change may have to occur within and without the institution of marriage. Many of the problems brought to the counselor's office have their basis in the institutions on which marriage is built. Growth models lead counselors to help their clients to see the effects of these institutions on the marriage and to harness their energies to work to change them. Because of this approach, divorce is now being viewed by many as an alternative that is not necessarily destructive to either of the parties or the children. Research is currently under way on the long-term effects of divorce on the family members.

New forms of relationships are demanding new forms of counseling. Group marriage and communal living arrangements require approaches to interpersonal conflicts that differ from orthodox modes of marriage counseling. Colateral relationship arrangements require new ways of dealing with relationships that are outside of the social institution of formal marriage. Changing trends and emerging modes of marriage demand that counseling forms change to keep pace. Many counseling theorists and researchers firmly believe that it is their responsibility to lead the way in thinking of alternatives not only to counseling procedures but also to marriage itself.

—Constance R. Ahrons, *Mental Health Associates*, and Morton S. Perlmutter, *University of Wisconsin*

Consult (14) Carter and Glick, 1970; *Family Process* (periodical); Jackson and Lederer, 1968; *Journal of Marriage and the Family*; Rogers, 1972.

MASCULINITY-FEMININITY. *See* Sex Identity.

MASOCHISM, a desire to experience pain, either physical or psychological, as in humiliation, embarrassment, or degradation. The pain is usually associated with sexual activity, but this connection is not essential to the concept. In its mildest form, masochism is fairly common. About half of both the males and the females interviewed by Kinsey and his associates reported that being bitten during sexual arousal was pleasurable. The term should probably be reserved for the seeking of severe physical pain and inordinate defilement, including the infliction of burns and cuts, and severe body beatings. The ultimate extreme is the so-called ritual suicide in which the masochist strangles in a network of self-applied ropes or starves to death because he is unable to extricate himself.

Masochistic inclinations are often found to coexist with sadistic tendencies,

hence the common use of the combined term *sadomasochism*.

—Eugene E. Levitt, *Indiana University School of Medicine*

See also Sadism.

Consult (13) Gebhard, 1969; Kinsey, *et al.*, 1948; Kinsey *et al.*, 1953; Levitt, 1971.

MASTERS, WILLIAM HOWELL (1915–), American physician. Born in Cleveland, Ohio, he studied for his M.D. (1943) under Dr. George Washington Corner, University of Rochester School of Medicine and Dentistry. He was associate professor of obstetrics-gynecology, Washington University School of Medicine, St. Louis, after 1947 and director of the Reproduction Biology Research Foundation after 1964.

Although he did extensive research on hormone-replacement therapy for postmenopausal women, Masters is best known, along with his colleague Virginia Johnson, for his physiological studies of human sexual function and the application of these studies to provide therapy for sexually dysfunctional couples. This treatment has been described as behavioral psychotherapy using operant conditioning and desensitization. Masters and Johnson have written two books: *Human Sexual Response*, 1966; and *Human Sexual Inadequacy*, 1970.

MASTURBATION, self-stimulation of the penis in the male or the clitoris, labia, or vagina in the female, for purposes of sexual pleasure, usually leading to orgasm.

Masturbation is practiced at one time or another in their lives by 97 percent of males and 50 percent of females. It is a common sexual outlet in adolescence and occurs less and less frequently with age. It is much more prevalent among unmarried adults, but a substantial number of married persons of both sexes continue to masturbate occasionally.

There is no scientific evidence that masturbation is a cause of mental or emotional symptoms or illness. However, frequent masturbation as the sole sexual outlet may itself be a symptom of a more generalized psychological disorder.

—Eugene E. Levitt, *Indiana University School of Medicine*

See also Autoeroticism.

Consult (13) Dearborn, 1967; Katchadourian and Lunde, 1972.

MATERNAL DEPRIVATION, a term used to cover a wide variety of inadequacies in the mother-child relationship. These include extreme social isolation, cruelty, neglect, institutional upbringing (of varying quality), and separation. Though it is known that such early deprivation often has a profound effect upon the physical, emotional, social, and intellectual well-being of children, evidence regarding the permanence and reversibility of such damage is far less conclusive. [*Consult* (11) Clarke and Clarke, 1960.]

The argument that a warm, continuous, and intimate relationship between a child and his mother (or mother substitute) is essential for mental health must be reevaluated in light of recent studies that indicate that in some instances substantial recovery may occur. Among the complex factors that must be considered in assessing the modifiability of early deprivation are the intensity and duration of such experiences, the age of occurrence, the experiences both preceding and following deprivation, and the constitutional vulnerability/resilience of the child. [*Consult* (11) Bowlby, 1951.]

—Cynthia MacRitchie, *Southern Connecticut State College*

MATERNAL DRIVE. The drive to protect and care for offspring is dependent upon hormonal changes as well as external stimulation. There are variations across and within species, but for most animals four activities that can be observed are nest building, placement of affection, retrieving, and suckling. Animal behavior during these four activities has been shown to be dependent upon a number of specific hormonal and environmental changes, such as body temperature and presence of the young. But it is not enough to simply call maternal drive instinctual behavior.

Human maternal behavior is less dependent upon hormonal changes and consists mainly of providing the infant with nourishment, physical comfort, and security. How the human provides these is related to psychological and cultural attitudes as well as physiological conditions.

—A. Ronald Seifert, *University of Tennessee*

See also Instinct.

MATURATION, the process of growing, learning, developing. *See* Developmental Psychology.

MATURITY (mature personality). An ideal rather than an actuality, maturity is not an automatic accompaniment of age and physical development. Most psychologists would agree that the mature person realistically appraises the world and himself, finds them imperfect but open to change, and enjoys the "actual" as well as the "possible." A strong sense of identity with mankind enables him to experience joy and sorrow and to act spontaneously without fear of humiliation or losing control. Independent, nonconforming, creative, humorous, he perceives without distortion, enjoys

feelings of intimacy with a few people, and freely accepts alternative courses of action with flexibility.

—M. G. Affinito, *Southern Connecticut State College*

See also Middle Years; Self-Actualization.

MAY, MARK A. (1891–   ), American educational psychologist. Born in Jonesboro, Tenn., he received a Ph.D. in psychology from Columbia in 1917. He was professor of education psychology at Yale and became director of the Institute for Human Relations there.

May's early work was in learning theory, "the effect of set" on practice. Later he studied the nature of character traits and the effectiveness of motion pictures as teaching aids. His publications include *The Mechanism of Controlled Association* (1917); *Studies in the Nature of Deceit* (with others, 1928); *Human Reactions of Relief* (1936); *A Social Psychology of War and Peace* (1943); and *Learning From Films* (with A. A. Lumsdaine, 1958).

MAZE, apparatus used in studies of animal learning and performance. Simple single-choice devices, such as T-shaped and Y-shaped mazes, are the most widely used, with the animal (usually a rat) starting at the base of the T or Y and running either to the left or the right to goal boxes, which sometimes contain food. Multiple-choice mazes can be used in problems of learning serial habits.

McDOUGALL, WILLIAM (1871–1938), British psychologist. Born in Lancashire, England, and educated at Cambridge University, he was director, Psychology Lab, University College, London (1900–1906); reader, Oxford (1904–1920); and professor of psychology at Harvard University (1920–1927) and Duke University (1927).

McDougall made his most significant contributions to social psychology. In *Introduction to Social Psychology* (1908), he contended that human action and interaction come from instincts, which are inherited. Each of these instincts has a corresponding emotion and can be modified by experience. In his discussion of social life, McDougall also attributed different social responses, such as imitation, to instinct. This instinct theory became very popular, but it was in direct opposition to the behaviorist view.

McDougall's systematic ideas, as outlined in *Mind and Body* (1911), concentrated on purposive striving; the central fact of the mind was what one wanted to do, as shown by effort, will, and freedom. He believed in mind-body interactions and held that the mind could influence the body.

Many of the views that McDougall sup-

MAZE

Simple Y

Simple U

Simple T

Typical laboratory mazes used in studying animal learning and performance.

British social psychologist William McDougall attributed human action and interaction to instinct, in opposition to behaviorist theories.

Margaret Mead, noted authority on personality and culture.

ported were unpopular. He supported psychic research, including the ESP work of J. B. Rhine at Duke, and he conducted experiments with white rats in an attempt to prove Lamarckism (the inheritance of acquired characteristics).

McDougall was a prolific writer, producing 24 books and over 160 articles and notes. Among these are *Physiological Psychology* (1905), *Outline of Abnormal Psychology* (1926), and *Religion and Science of Life* (1924).

MEAD, MARGARET (1901–), American anthropologist. Born in Philadelphia, she received her Ph.D. from Columbia University (1929) and was chairman, Social Sciences Division, Fordham University from 1968 and adjunct professor of anthropology, Columbia University, from 1954.

Margaret Mead's work, as detailed in *Coming of Age in Samoa* (1928), *Male and Female* (1949), and *Childhood in Contemporary Societies* (1955), stresses the relationship between culture and psychology, particularly in adolescence. Mead contends that development is strongly affected by cultural factors and so it proceeds differently from culture to culture. Although biological and psychological factors affect the transition from childhood to adulthood, Mead puts a greater emphasis on cultural determinants. Thus, in more primitive societies, preparation for adulthood begins early in life and there is no stress during the adolescent period—development from childhood to adulthood is a continuous process. But in more advanced societies, as in the United States, the progression from childhood to adulthood is in stages, because the children do not assume their future roles early in life. As a result, the transition produces more stress and is generally more difficult than in primitive societies.

An autobiographical volume, *Blackberry Winter: My Early Years,* appeared in 1972.

MEAN, the sum of the scores in a set divided by the number of scores in the set. One of the most important properties of the mean is that it is the point in a distribution of scores about which the sum of the deviations (of scores from the mean) is equal to zero. The mean, therefore, is the point that balances all the scores on either side. It is similar to the median, but unlike the median is very sensitive to extreme scores. Thus the mean is a more sensitive measure of central tendency than the median and the mode.

See also Median; Mode.

MEANING, what symbols signify, especially the symbols that are language. Words can stand for objects ("bathtubs"), abstractions ("justice"), qualities ("red"), and functions ("toward," "from"). Commonly accepted, well-specified meanings of words are called *denotative* meanings. The analysis of denotative meanings (the problem of reference) has traditionally been relegated to philosophy and linguistics (i.e., semantics). Of greater interest to psychologists have been *connotative* meanings—the emotions, evaluations, and subtle implications suggested by words and their use in particular contexts by individual persons. One technique, for example, that has been used to measure connotative meanings and how they change under certain conditions is the semantic differential.

Presumably word meanings (denotative and connotative) are originally learned by means of the principles specified by learning theories, mainly instrumental learning and sometimes conditioning. However, meanings are also embodied in the grammatical structure of sentences, and there has been much recent speculation that part of language acquisition (acquiring grammar) may be dependent on some sort of inborn, "built-in" cognitive mechanisms in humans.

—Roland Siiter, *Montclair State College*
See also Chomsky; Language; Language Universal; Semantic Differential.

MEANINGFULNESS, the relative number of associations to which a word or concept immediately gives rise. Thus, a word that suggests many other words and meanings (such as "army") is more "meaningful" than a word suggesting only a few other words ("maelstrom"). Meaningfulness has often been used as a variable in studies of verbal learning, since it predicts rate of learning: the more meaningful the materials to be learned, the faster the learning.

A number of methods have been invented to measure meaningfulness. One of the most popular, first used by C. E. Noble, is to ask subjects to name as many associations as possible to a given word in a fixed amount of time—for example, one minute. When these data are pooled from a number of subjects, then the data become representative of the "average" amount of meaningfulness associated with the given word. In Noble's data, for example, the following relative meaningfulness values were obtained:

1.24	xylem
1.84	maelstrom
2.54	jetsam
3.91	ordeal
6.24	income
7.70	jelly
9.43	army

Similar procedures can be used with nonsense syllables. When this is done, it is found that even nonsense words vary in their meaningfulness values with "nev" being more meaningful than "yeq."

—Roland Siiter, *Montclair State College*
See also Nonsense syllables.

MEASUREMENT. Psychologists and educators use hundreds of tests, techniques, scales, and inventories to study ability, aptitude, achievement, interest, attitude, and other personality traits. Although "testing" is a term widely used to cover all these devices, many workers in the field prefer "measurement" or "evaluation" as a term for a great range of procedures. The word "test" tends to suggest a paper-and-pencil, question-and-answer instrument that yields a numerical score. While the field of measurement includes simple teacher-made tests, it also takes in personality inventories with 500 items. Many techniques do not yield a numerical score but require an interpretive report.

Even with tests that produce a numerical score, this result can seldom be used by itself as a criterion of ability or other characteristics of an individual. In studying college applicants, Scholastic Aptitide Test (SAT) scores are an important screening device, but admissions officers also consider school grades, extracurricular interests, and impressions formed in interviews with applicants. Intelligence-test scores are not to be taken as magic numbers that label a child dull, normal, or gifted. In clinical work, psychiatrists and psychologists measure intelligence and personality traits. But test results (which are often interpretations) are further interpreted along with a patient's physical health record, personal and family history, and judgments of his condition formed on the basis of talks with him.

Measurement has become a big business in the twentieth century. The first mass testing was the evaluation of intelligence tried by the U.S. Army during World War I. Since that time, large-scale testing has become a usual practice, particularly in schools. A major development is the use of *standardized* tests. These are administered to thousands of subjects. On the basis of the results, standard scores are computed so that the scores of one person, school, or region can be ranked against norms for an area or even for the country.

Measuring devices used in various fields of psychology are discussed in individual articles. *See the Subject Map on p. 158.*

Consult (12) Adams and Torgerson, 1964; Cronbach, 1970; Downie, 1967; Hilgard, *et al.*, 1970; Noll, 1965; Remmers, *et al.*, 1965; Thorndike and Hagen, 1961.

MECHANISM. *Adjustment* mechanisms are ways people act to adapt to the environment and achieve goals. *Defense* mechanisms are ways of dealing with doubts, frustrations, and conflicts—for instance, by denying a problem is important or blaming failure on someone else. *See* Adaptation; Adjustment; Defense Mechanism.

MECHANORECEPTION. *See* Touch.

MEDIAN, the score that divides a set of ranked scores into halves, so that half the scores fall below the median and half fall above it. The median, therefore, is the score at the fiftieth percentile. This figure is sometimes useful in describing central tendency in certain types of distributions where the mean cannot be used. One difficulty with the median is its insensitivity to extreme scores. For example, in the set of scores 2, 7, 8, 10, 48, the median is 8 despite the fact that the set contains the extreme score 48. *See also* Mean; Mode; Percentile.

MEDIATION, or "mediating response": hypothesized implicit associative responses that mediate between an overt stimulus situation and overt responses. For example, when asked to unscramble the letters IHCAR (an anagram stimulus) to form a word, the subject pauses and eventually utters "chair" aloud. Mediation refers to what supposedly went on during the pause between the stimulus and overt response.

Overt Stimulus—IHCAR

Mediating responses—CR. . . , CA. . . , RA. . . , HA. . . , CH

Overt response—"chair"

Mediation is one of the ways in which learning theorists have tried to analyze thinking, concept learning, and problem solving, as well as verbal learning. Thinking here is conceived of as a chain of internal responses that themselves generate further responses (overt or covert) by association. Theoretically, the length of such a chain of mediating responses has no upper limit.

The advantage of describing thinking in terms of mediation (that is, in terms of associationism) is that while retaining the main outlines of a theory to account for thinking, one can still discuss complex thinking processes that are not directly observable. Thus, according to associative (or stimulus-response, S–R) learning theorists, mediation plays the crucial role in describing how learned associations account for thinking, reasoning, and problem solving. More broadly, according to such theories, knowledge consists of association, and thinking is merely a rapid outpouring of implicit (unobservable) associative responses.

However, such an analysis of thinking is viewed by many psychologists as oversimplistic and inadequate. The major problem is the apparent structure of thinking: it is extremely difficult to describe some kinds of reasoning and the grammatical structure of language in purely associative terms. Many psychologists of the modern school of cognitive psychology have abandoned mediational explanations of thinking and prefer to use rules, strategies, plans, and related concepts instead. Much of the contemporary work on thinking, language, and problem solving has shown that, while mediating responses often occur, all of think-

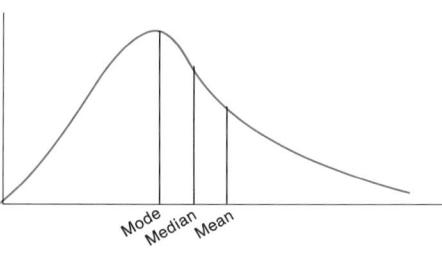

Positively skewed

A subjective test measuring a subject's ability to quickly evaluate various designs.

MEASUREMENT

MEASUREMENT
    testing
    standardized test

ACHIEVEMENT TESTS
BENDER-GESTALT TEST
SKILLS, LEARNING OF

CULTURE-FREE TEST
VALIDITY
EXPERIMENTER BIAS
    self-fulfilling prophecy
HALO EFFECT

ABILITY
READINESS TEST
PROBLEM SOLVING

INTELLIGENCE AND INTELLIGENCE TESTING
    mental age
    mental ability
    intelligence quotient
CONSTANCY OF THE IQ

SCHOLASTIC APTITUDE TEST
    aptitude test
    prognostic test
STANFORD-BINET SCALES
VOCATIONAL APTITUDE TEST
    aptitude test
    prognostic test
WECHSLER INTELLIGENCE SCALES

PERSONALITY
    PERSONALITY INVENTORY
    INTEREST INVENTORIES
    MINNESOTA MULTIPHASIC PERSONALITY
        INVENTORY
    RATING SCALES
    INTERVIEW
    SOCIOMETRY
    ATTITUDES
    ALLPORT-VERNON-LINDZEY
        STUDY OF VALUES

PROJECTIVE TECHNIQUES
    FIGURE-DRAWING TEST
    HOLTZMAN INKBLOT TECHNIQUE
    HOUSE-TREE-PERSON TECHNIQUE
    MAKE-A-PICTURE-STORY TEST
    RORSCHACH TECHNIQUE
    ROSENZWEIG PICTURE FRUSTRATION
        STUDY
    THEMATIC APPERCEPTION TEST
    TOMKINS-HORN PICTURE ARRANGEMENT
        TEST
    WORD-ASSOCIATION TEST

STATISTICS
    AVERAGE
    CORRELATION
    FACTOR ANALYSIS
    FREQUENCY DISTRIBUTION
    MEAN
    MEDIAN
    MODE
    NORM
    PERCENTILE
    SAMPLING
    STANDARD DEVIATION

The Subject Maps in the Encyclopedia illustrate the coverage of particular aspects of psychology, showing the interrelationships among the articles in twelve major areas of study. Entries in capital letters are subjects for which there are separate articles in the Encyclopedia. Entries in small letters are cross references.

The Subject Maps appear in the Encyclopedia under the following titles:

Abnormal and Clinical Psychology
Developmental Psychology
Emotion and Motivation
Intelligence
Learning and Memory
Measurement
Personality and Individual Difference
Physiological and Comparative Psychology
Psychology: Divisions and Schools
Sensation and Perception
Social Psychology
Thinking and Language

ing cannot be described in associative terms. Thinking reflects past learning, but subjects also think while they are learning; that is, neither process can be explained entirely in terms of the other.

—Roland Siiter *Montclair State College*
See also Associationism; Concept Learning; Language; Problem Solving; Verbal Learning.

Consult (7) Bourne, 1971.

MEDICAL PSYCHOLOGY. In many countries, particularly Great Britain, medical psychology may mean psychiatry, the branch of medicine concerned with psychic disorders. In the United States, however, the term means the application of psychology to all phases of medical research, treatment, and prevention. For example, psychologists serve as consultants to physicians and nurses treating chronic disorders and rehabilitating orthopedic cases. Psychologists work with medical men to study drug effects and drug use and addiction. They are members of teams investigating patterns of mental illness in communities. Psychologists teach courses in medical schools on such topics as doctor-patient relationships, problems of perception and meaning in diagnosis, personality, psychotherapy, and research methods. Insights from psychology have helped build the study of psychosomatic illness. Another field of study is psychological reactions to sickness, disability, or impending death.

Medical psychology thus has a wider scope than clinical psychology, which focuses on the study and treatment of mental disorders.

MEDIUMS. *See* Parapsychology.

MEDULLA OBLONGATA, a portion of the brainstem lying directly above the spinal cord and below the pons. It is the point of exit for four cranial nerves: the glossylophyrangeal, the vagus, the spinal accessory, and the hypoglassal. The medulla also contains many neurons that play a vital role in the control of respiration and blood pressure. Medullary damage as a result of trauma often leads to death because of respiratory failure.

MELANCHOLIA, a term used for depressed states in mental illness since the time of the Greek physician Hippocrates (about 460–377 B.C.). In current practice, terms such as "depression" are preferred. *See* Depression; Depressive Reaction; Involutional Psychotic Reaction.

MEMORY. An experimental demonstration of memory involves three stages: encoding, storage, and retrieval.

Encoding. The memory of everyday experience is for the most part effortless and involves little more than direct perception. Such direct encoding, however, is not usually sufficient for the retention of detailed verbal information, as is often required in memory experiments or in educational situations.

There are reputed to be a few individuals, rare among children and extremely rare among adults, who retain a complex visual display in a clear picturelike memory trace (called an *eidetic image*) for minutes or even days; but most persons lose such detailed visual information within seconds of the experience. In many situations, therefore, successful encoding requires that the perceived information be transformed into some more stable form. A skilled reader does not deal with a printed message on a strictly visual level; the visual pattern may be transformed into a pattern of sounds, into individual word meanings, and finally into highly structured thoughts.

Memory experiments have shown that subjects will use any or all of these levels of encoding, depending on the requirements of the task. The limits of memory are determined not by the amount of information presented, but by the number of familiar units, or *chunks,* into which it can be organized. Letters are remembered more easily than nonsense forms, words more easily than anagrams, and clichés more easily than unfamiliar sentences because letters, words, and clichés constitute chunks, while nonsense forms, anagrams, and unfamiliar sentences do not. One can remember about as many clichés after a single exposure as one can remember random letters—yet each cliché is "information-rich" in that it stands for several words, numerous letters, and an extremely complex pattern of line segments. Since *chunk formation* depends on the familiarity of the unit, it can be considered an example of the positive transfer of previous learning to a new situation.

Once verbal information has been given a semantic interpretation, it can be transformed into a visual scene in which objects, rather than printed letters, are represented. The concrete idea expressed in the sentence "The boy ate the bee" is remembered far better as a vividly imagined scene than as a sentence. The retention-enhancing power of encoding in *visual imagery* was known to the ancient Greeks but has only recently come under systematic experimental scrutiny.

Storage. This stage, which follows the encoding of a memory trace and precedes its retrieval, is particularly difficult to study because if adequate precautions are not taken, an experimental subject may rehearse. *Rehearsal* involves retrieval of the stored information and, possibly, further transformations of the form in which it is encoded. The effects of

MEMORY

Principles that apply to learning and memory are discussed in LEARNING THEORY. For ways of studying remembering and forgetting, see FREE-RECALL LEARNING, PAIRED-ASSOCIATE LEARNING, SERIAL LEARNING, LEARNING CURVE, and the biography of Hermann EBBINGHAUS.

Factors affecting retention are covered in CODABILITY, IMAGERY, EIDETIC IMAGE, MEANINGFULNESS, and PRACTICE.

Theories about how the brain stores information are noted in BRAIN STORAGE and RNA.

For techniques that help retain information (mnemonic strategies) see MEMORY IMPROVEMENT.

More can be involved in forgetting than losing material over a period of time. Ideas can be pushed out of consciousness, as explained in REPRESSION and AMNESIA.

MEDULLA OBLONGATA

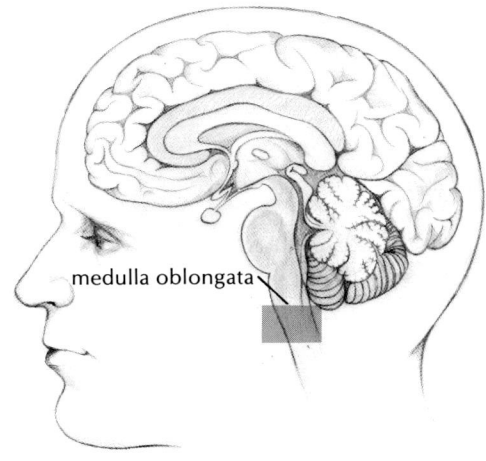

medulla oblongata

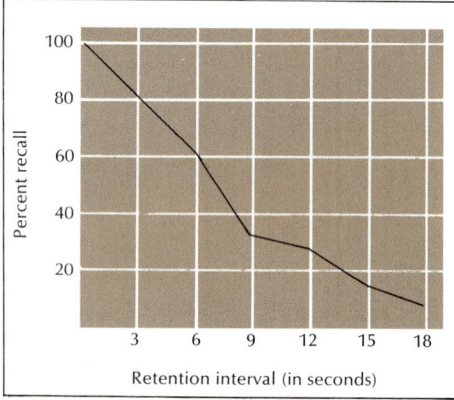

SHORT-TERM MEMORY
When a subject is prevented from rehearsing information, for example, by having him perform irrelevant tasks immediately after learning, his ability to recall falls off rapidly (above). The retention curve (below) for nonsense syllables learned with repeated practice is in striking contrast.

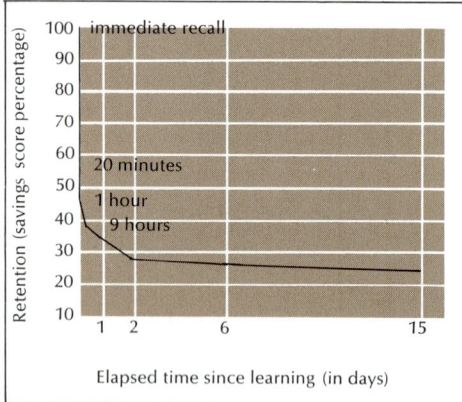

RETENTION

these operations are not easily separated from whatever passive changes in the memory trace might be characteristic of storage *per se.*

A question of current theoretical interest is whether there are two distinct processes involved in storage—*short-term* and *long-term memory*—or only one. Proponents of the two-process view cite experimental evidence for a number of differences between the two: they are said to differ in capacity, in rate of forgetting, in the cause of forgetting, in the form in which the information is encoded, and in the susceptibility of the trace to disruption by injections, electrical shock, and blows to the head. Evidence interpreted as supporting the two-process view has come from work with amnesic patients and with animals, as well as with normal human subjects.

Alternative interpretations of the various findings have been offered, however, and opponents of the two-process theory, encouraged by experiments seeming to support a one-process view, remain unconvinced. This controversy has been fueled in part by semantic confusion. Both terms "short-term" and "long-term" are often used to refer to experimental situations involving retention intervals as short as seconds and as long as minutes or even days. Two-process theorists point out that "short-term memory" experiments very probably tap both hypothetical memory processes and not just the short-term process, as some investigators have apparently assumed.

Retrieval. One influence of the analogy between human memory and that of an electronic computer has been an increasing emphasis on the retrieval stage as important for a complete understanding of memory. The fact that information that is in memory cannot always be retrieved is illustrated by the familiar *tip-of-the-tongue* phenomenon. The success of memory retrieval depends critically on the specificity of the cues that are available on the retention test.

Consider two common experimental situations, in both of which a list of words is first presented for memorization. In *recognition memory*, the subject is then presented with test words and asked to indicate which ones were in the list. In *free recall*, the subject is simply asked to remember as many words from the list as he can. Recognition performance is typically much better than free-recall performance, because the words themselves are available as retrieval cues. But free-recall subjects apparently construct their own retrieval cues, as is illustrated by the phenomenon called *clustering*. Semantically related words tend to be recalled together (in clusters), even when they were not presented together in the list.

Loss. A central problem in the study of memory is the analysis of the causes of forgetting. Early psychologists assumed that forgetting was due to time-dependent decay. Although some modern investigators attribute loss of short-term memory to decay—a matter of considerable debate—it is now generally accepted that the most important cause of forgetting in long-term memory is interference from other, similar material. The effects of information stored prior to the encoding of the to-be-remembered material is called *proactive interference;* those caused by information stored afterward are called *retroactive interference.* Experimental findings suggest that proactive interference takes place primarily at the retrieval stage and is partly due to confusion regarding which memory traces are more recent. Retroactive interference, by contrast, appears to involve both storage and retrieval. The effect on storage seems akin to partial destruction of the memory trace during the learning of the interfering material.

—Douglas L. Hintzman, *University of Oregon*

See also Ebbinghaus; Imagery; Learning Theory; Memory Improvement.

Consult (6) Adams, 1967; Cermak, 1972; Norman, 1969.

MEMORY DRUM, a device that presents items to be memorized, such as words or nonsense syllables; used especially in serial learning.

See also Serial Learning.

MEMORY IMPROVEMENT. The mnemonic devices that some professional "mentalists" use to amaze their audiences and those that are taught to aspiring businessmen in commercial memory-improvement courses are not much different from methods that were known to the ancient Greeks and Romans. Experimental psychologists have recently become interested in mnemonic strategies, not so much for their practical applications as for what their systematic investigation can reveal about the nature of memory.

Mnemonic devices do not strengthen one's memory in the way exercise strengthens a muscle. Rather, they are tools that are applied selectively to information that one especially wants to be able to recall. The various methods stress elaboration of the to-be-remembered information and transformations of the form in which it is encoded, with the goal of aiding later retrieval of the information from memory.

Techniques. Most mnemonic devices rely on one or more of the following: (1) relationships with previously learned material, (2) rhymes, and (3) visual imagery. One version of what is known as the *peg-word system,* used to remember an ordered list of objects, will serve to illustrate all three.

In this case, the *previously learned material* consists of the number system. The names of concrete objects are first associated with the numbers through the use of *rhymes*—

e.g., *one-gun, two-stew, three-tree,* and so on. Once memorized, these objects serve as permanent "pegs" to which any other ordered set of objects may be attached to through visual imagery. For example, Delaware, the first state admitted to the Union, is associated with the number *one* through an image of Della, waving a *gun* and shouting, "Beware!" After all the appropriate images have been formed in this way, the first thirteen states can be recalled in order by using the peg words to retrieve the images.

The great advantage of such a system— like that of the *method of loci,* in which objects are imagined in a well-learned series of geographical or architectural locations—is that it imposes a ready-made structure on retrieval. This aids recall of an unordered set of objects, such as a shopping list, as well as that of an ordered one. For by proceeding through the numbers (or locations) in order, one can be certain that none of the objects has been missed.

The use of *visual imagery* to facilitate the association of ideas is common to several mnemonic devices. Experiments have shown that pairs of concrete ideas (e.g., duck-sofa) are much easier to encode in this way than are pairs of abstract ideas (e.g., commerce-hatred). The lore of mnemonics holds that the most effective images are bizarre. Experiments suggest, however, that this quality is irrelevant; what is important is the interaction between the imagined objects. A duck dancing on a sofa (raising clouds of dust) is much better remembered than a duck sitting on a sofa, no matter how unusual the elements of this passive scene may be.

The businessman or politician seeking to improve his memory for people's names will be given varied advice. Fashion prominent facial characteristics into a link with the name. Develop a rhyming description of an imaginary scene in which the subject appears ("Mr. Morgan plays the organ with his toes"). Above all, attend to the name while being introduced, rehearse it, and strive to create a stable association with the face. This last recommendation reveals the main drawback of mnemonic devices; their use requires considerable effort.
—Douglas L. Hintzman, *University of Oregon*
See also Memory.
Consult (6) Bower, 1970; Normal, 1969; Nutt, 1941; Yates, 1966.

MENARCHE, the beginning of menstrual periods in girls. See Adolescence; Sex Identity.

MENINGITIS, infection of the membranes covering the brain and spinal cord. See Brain Disorders.

MENOPAUSE, "change of life," the period

when the menstrual cycle ceases for normal reasons. In some cases, psychological stresses develop. See Involutional Psychotic Reaction; Middle Years.

MENSTRUAL CYCLE. See Adolescence; Involutional Psychotic Reaction; Middle Years; Psychosomatic Disorders; Sex Identity.

MENTAL ABILITY. See Intelligence and Intelligence Testing.

MENTAL AGE (MA), level of ability as represented by a score on an intelligence test; used in computing the intelligence quotient (IQ). See Intelligence and Intelligence Tests.

MENTAL AND EMOTIONAL DISORDERS, a broad term covering brain disorders, psychoses, psychoneuroses, personality disorders, and other problems. See the classified list of articles in the Subject Map for Abnormal and Clinical Psychology. This map also lists articles dealing with causes and treatment. Note the major discussion in Mental Health.

MENTAL DEFICIENCY. See Mental Retardation.

MENTAL HEALTH. There is not much evidence that either the nature or the extent of mental disorders has altered significantly over time, but there have been striking changes in the way they are thought about and combated. The belief that the modern pace of life and social pressures have vastly increased mental disturbances is not statistically supported where consistent records are available. There has been no observable increase in patient rates from the mid-nineteenth to mid-twentieth century. Nevertheless, the mental health problem receives increasing attention. More vulnerable people are now kept alive, and mental disorders are considered more amenable to treatment. The present concern about mental health may not betoken an age of anxiety so much as an age of psychotherapy. [Consult (13) Goldhammer and Marshall, 1953.]

This way of thought is a rather recent development. What was until the late eighteenth century considered possession by the devil, witchcraft, divine vision, or simple moral degeneracy came to be regarded, under the impetus of Philippe Pinel, William Tuke, and Benjamin Rush, as a physical disease easily curable by humane "moral treatment." This rethinking, aided by the reform efforts of Horace Mann and Dorothea Dix, succeeded in removing mental patients from jails and workhouses into insane asylums—where they soon languished in often equally deplorable conditions—but it did not fully succeed in removing the moral element from the prevailing view of

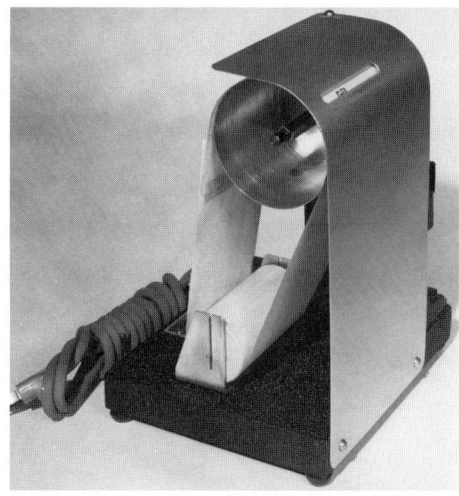

The memory drum is a device used in verbal learning experiments to present items to be memorized at a preset rate.

The enlightened French psychiatrist Philippe Pinel is shown removing chains from mental patients.

mental disorder. By the beginning of the twentieth century, a new reform movement, the National Committee for Mental Hygiene, founded by Clifford Beers, undertook to correct the abuses to which the earlier idealism had quickly deteriorated. The "disease" had not proved readily curable and, faced with disillusionment, narrow professionalism, social Darwinism, and unruly patients, treatment had given way to custodial care and mechanical restraints. [*Consult* (13) Caplan, 1969.]

Definition of Mental Illness. There are ways in which "mental illnesses" are not like physical illnesses at all, and some of the differences involve the impulse not to aid the afflicted so much as to remove them from view as frightening or threatening. Physical diseases generally have a known origin, standard symptoms, and an organic structure and follow a predictable course. Some of the more severe mental disorders also have regular symptoms and outcomes, but those showing organic lesions are no longer considered mental and are handled by specialists in neurology. Furthermore, there is far-ranging speculation about the causes of mental illness, which may include heredity, organic disease, physical or chemical agents, and psychosocial experiences either in one's past development or as present mental stress.

But it is the very inexplicability of mentally diseased behavior that is its hallmark. The mentally ill behave in ways that cannot rationally or emotionally be explained. As J. A. Clausen puts it, "It is the functions of the socialized person (rather than the organism)—thought processes, beliefs, motivations, feelings, interpersonal skills—that are disordered." When a person is malfunctioning socially so that he is ineffective or unhappy in ways unattributable to physical disease, he is said to have a mental illness. [*Consult* (13) Clausen, 1968.]

The further one gets from the most serious pathologies, particularly the psychotic states, the clearer it becomes that there remains a strong judgmental component to mental disease diagnoses. What is considered as unsatisfactory, bizarre, or irrational functioning depends to a great extent on the standards and expectations of culture and subculture or of the clinical observer. The strongest expression of this point of view contends that it is a form of psychiatric imperialism to label behavior a "disease" because we disapprove of it or cannot comprehend it. [*Consult* (13) Szasz, 1967.]

Logically, mental illnesses are not comparable to diseases of specific organ systems. However, there is another way of talking about disease—in its most general form, a dysfunctional way of being in the world—which can apply to physical disorders as well as the derangements without known organic manifestations. In common understanding, mental disorders are exemplified by the psychoses and neuroses. Jurisdictionally, mental disorders include all those usually diagnosed by psychiatrists and clinical psychologists. The *Diagnostic and Statistical Manual of Mental Disorders* (American Psychiatric Association, 1968) includes categories extending from mental retardation, organic brain syndromes, psychoses, neuroses, and personality disorders to psychophysiological disorders, "special symptoms," transient situational disturbances, childhood and adolescence behavior disorders, "conditions without manifest psychiatric disorder," and "nondiagnostic terms for administrative use." These categories lack system or consistency, but they do describe what clinicians observe in hospitals and have allowed the collection of national statistics with some internal comparability.

Treatments. In the United States, the National Institute of Mental Health's regular surveys of the mental patient population have recorded dramatic changes in treatment patterns. By the end of World War II, the public mental hospitals had become seriously crowded as the country's population increased and patients lived longer. The number of patients in state and county mental hospitals (then housing the overwhelming majority of psychiatric inpatients) grew about 2 percent a year in the decade from 1946 to 1955, despite rising release rates. [*Consult* (13) Kramer, 1969.]

The fact that increasing numbers of patients were released from "asylums" where commitment was traditionally a life sentence was one of the first marked results of the National Mental Health Act of 1946, which made federal funds available for outpatient clinics, psychiatric services in general hospitals and nursing homes, and other alternatives to the mental institutions. This program, combined with the introduction of widespread use of tranquilizing drugs in the early 1950s served to turn the tide. The peak public hospital census of residents, 559,000 in 1955, was reduced to 426,000 by 1967 and has continued to decline. There are now many more psychiatric admissions to general hospitals than to mental hospitals. New policies, such as open wards, closer liaison with community agencies, and easy discharge and readmission procedures, have also helped to reduce the average length of stay substantially. [*Consult* (13) Giesler, *et al.,* 1966.]

The most common diagnosis for admission to state and county mental hospitals is "organic brain syndromes," but almost one-half of the resident population is made up of schizophrenic patients, who enter at an earlier age and stay longer. In private mental and general hospitals, the leading cause for admission is depressive disorders, but there is a possibility that in doubtful cases, middle-class patients are more likely to receive that diagnosis than the more stigmatizing one of schizophrenia. [*Consult* (13) Kramer, 1969; Schwab, 1967.]

In 1966, 2,392,761 mental patients either were residents at the beginning of the year or were admitted during the year to any hospital or outpatient clinic, a rate of 1,235 cases for every 100,000 population. This is not dissimilar to the figures from the psychiatric register kept for residents of Monroe County, New York, which indicated that over a five-year period 4.9 percent of the population had psychiatric contact. [*Consult* (13) Gardner *et al.*, 1963.]

The lowest age-specific rate for the 1966 NIMH survey was in those under the age of fifteen, with only 609 per 100,000, and the highest rate, 2,098, was in the age group thirty-five to forty-four. Except for those twenty-five to thirty-four, the rate was higher for males than for females, but this may not represent a true difference: there is some evidence that key breadwinners in a family are more in need of treatment on arrival for care because their families have kept them at home longer. And there has been a consistent finding, noted for some time, that those who are married are admitted less often to mental hospitals and released more quickly than the unmarried or formerly married. [*Consult* (13) Hammer, 1961; Malzberg, 1940.]

Distribution. It is hazardous to draw conclusions from treatment rates about the quantity or distribution of mental illness in the general population. H. E. Lehmann has estimated that, in the case of depressive disorders, only one out of five cases comes to medical attention, and not necessarily the most severe ones. Treatment rates are strongly affected by the availability of treatment and by attitudes toward its use, which vary considerably among different subcultures. [*Consult* (13) Lehmann, 1970.]

The statistics on treated cases also fail to include those patients who are seen by private psychotherapists in their consulting rooms. The problems of this smaller but culturally significant middle-class clientele cannot easily be categorized in the terms of the official *Diagnostic and Statistical Manual* but tend, rather, to have an existential tone. People who seek private therapy complain of the meaninglessness and unfulfillment in their lives, of vague dissatisfaction and alienation. The goals of their treatment are different from the hospital therapist's objective of readjusting and returning his patients to society, since these private clients are often, it could be said, already too well adjusted. What they may be missing is the full actualization of themselves as individuals. [*Consult* (13) Smith, 1968; Wheelis, 1958.]

The human-potential movement,

guided by the theories of (among others) A. H. Maslow, Carl Rogers, and Rollo May, has been an attempt to contend with this psychological problem. Such an approach (and its spin-offs in sensitivity training and encounter groups) stresses the goals of heightened humanness, self-knowledge, and authenticity in interpersonal relations. Thus, it blurs the distinction between health and disease, rejects the medical model, and advocates the promotion of "positive mental health." The view of mental disorders as on a continuum with normality has probably helped promote more acceptance of the humanity of the afflicted, but specifying the positive side has been difficult and even more subjective than defining mental disease. [*Consult* (13) Jahoda, 1958; Menninger, 1958.]

The widely varying choice of cut-off points along the continuum, as well as the variety of methodologies, has produced varying estimates of psychopathology in the community. As the Dohrenwends note in a review of over forty-four epidemiological studies, these extend from 1 to 60 percent. The two most ambitious American studies were conducted on random samples of the adult populations in midtown Manhattan and in the pseudonymous Stirling County in Nova Scotia. The former found 23.4 percent of midtowners aged twenty to fifty-nine significantly "impaired" psychologically, and the latter judged that 57 percent of the Canadian sample qualified, according to the manual, as "psychiatric cases," though only 2.9 percent were at least "moderately impaired." In Sweden, a ten-year follow-up study done by a single psychiatrist found a mental disorder rate of 15.6 percent. One could not conclude, however, that Manhattanites were sicker than Nova Scotians or Swedes, because the investigators used different approaches and standards. [*Consult* (13) Dohrenwends and Dohrenwends, 1969; Hagnell, 1966; Leighton, *et al.*, 1963; Srole *et al.*, 1962.]

The primary value of such epidemiological research is not in its total disorder rates but in the comparative distributions, established in each study, of different disorders among different subpopulations. Such results provide clues about the etiology of these conditions. The Dohrenwends conclude that there is one strongly consistent demographic finding among all these investigations: the relationship between low socioeconomic status and high rates of schizophrenia and personality disorders. Otherwise, they note discrepant results for age, sex, race, rural-urban, and other geographical differences. There is, however, a tendency for the youngest age groups to have low pathology rates and for women to have higher rates of neurosis and men higher rates of personality disorder.

The mental disorder differential be-

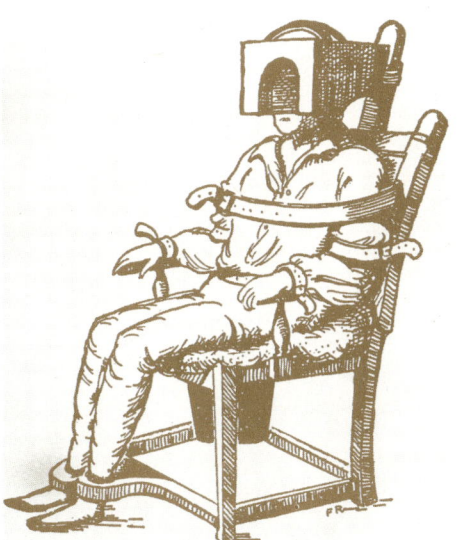

The "tranquilizing chair" was used in the 18th century by physician Benjamin Rush to restrain difficult patients.

tween the classes is susceptible to interpretations. A. B. Hollingshead and F. C. Redlich, who found the treated prevalence of schizophrenia in New Haven eleven times greater among the lowest social class than in the uppermost class, also found that members of the latter entered treatment earlier, were referred through medical rather than legal channels, were treated with psychotherapy rather than organically (with drugs or shock), and recovered earlier. The middle classes show a greater propensity to define their problems in psychological terms and are more able to afford the time and money for treatment; these factors may gain them the prompt and appropriate treatment to mitigate the more serious consequences of mental stress and disorder. [Consult (13) Gurin, et al., 1960.]

The economically underprivileged may also be least protected from the physical and social degradation of the environment, which is believed to affect mental functioning. Focusing strictly on the physical aspects, however, a recent review concluded, "Aside from the literature on lead (the ingestion of which produces mental disturbances), there is little that can be said with confidence on the effects of pollution and a deteriorated physical environment on mental health." There are some suggestive results implicating aircraft noise and substandard housing, but the pattern is not yet clearly convincing. When class and ethnicity are held constant, it is found—contrary to expectations from some animal studies—that overcrowding (in terms of people per acre) is not associated with mental hospital admissions. [Consult (13) Galle, et al., 1972; Williams, et al., 1972.]

It is clearly a difficult task, and possibly a misleading one, to attempt to isolate as psychologically pernicious a single aspect of the physical environment, separate from the others with which it is associated and from the sociocultural milieu in which it occurs. Even in the heredity studies, where there is some evidence for the genetic transmission of both schizophrenia and manic-depression, the results imply that the biological factor must occur in a stressful environment for the illness to develop. Many studies have related mental illness to aspects of the social environment. For example, when R. E. L. Faris and H. W. Dunham found that in Chicago mental hospital admission rates (particularly for schizophrenia) were highest in the central slum district, they attributed the increase to the "social disorganization" of this area—high crime, family instability, unemployment, single-room occupancy, residential mobility. The association of mental disorders with poverty and other indices of social pathology need not, however, be interpreted as the effect of the social environment on individual functioning. The relationship

may result, rather, from a tendency for those predisposed to mental pathology to "drift" into the more disorganized parts of a city because of their inability to maintain family relationships or gainful employment.

[Consult (13) Faris and Dunham, 1939.]

Community Approaches. Whatever the causal model, it has become clear that certain mental disorders are clustered with social ills among underprivileged segments of the population. The Mental Retardation and Community Mental Health Centers Construction Act of 1963 attempted to contend with this large-scale human ineffectiveness and deprivation. The consequent growth of community psychiatry and psychology reflects a situational or environmental mode of help where the mental health problem is not seen only as an individual or intrapsychic one. The role of professionals from the new community mental health centers in offering consultation to schools, welfare and housing boards, and other social agencies marks a reformist commitment to changing the environment in the service of mental health. It also reaffirms the notion of mental disorder as a transactional phenomenon between a person and his surroundings, a relationship rather than an entity. This movement responds to the inadequacy as a goal of merely returning the patient to the community, where he will again encounter the social forces that originally brought him to the hospital. Short of changing the community, some believe that an alternate living environment (whether it is a residential drug control center or a Skinnerian commune) providing social supports and free of the pathogenic pressure of the larger society is, at least temporarily, necessary for sound mental health. In some ways, this represents a full turn of the wheel from the antiasylum movement of the previous generation. [Consult (13) Levine and Levine, 1970; Newbrough, 1969.]

It is planned by 1980 to have a mental health center for every 100,000 population in the United States. The new approaches to treatment that were their mandate—confronting the manifold problems of living, allowing greater decision making by community members, providing on-the-spot care for the socioeconomically deprived—may take time to make themselves fully evident. Their founding principle is that an effective response to the mental health problem in the 1970s will require attention to the community context. Such a cross-disciplinary, culturally sophisticated approach may vastly expand the range and ambition of both remedial and preventive efforts, providing more acceptable, less disruptive services. It may also offer a systematic, inclusive foundation for testing more advanced etiological theories. It cannot, however, be expected to solve the problem of mental health. That, when ultimately encompassed, is perhaps nothing less than the problem of the human condition.

—Roger Christenfeld, *College of Physicians and Surgeons of Columbia University*

See also Adjustment; Behavioral Ecology; Community Mental Health Center; Community Psychology; Human Potential Movement; Mental Hospital; Psychiatry; Psychology and the Law; Psychoneurotic Disorders; Psychotherapy; Psychotic Disorders; Self-Actualization. *Other articles listed in the Item Guide under* Mental Health.

Consult (9) Coleman, 1966; McKinney, 1960; (13) Coleman, 1964; Encyclopedia of Mental Health, 1963; Joint Commission on Mental Illness and Health, 1961; Stern, 1968.

MENTAL HEALTH CLINICS AND CENTERS.

Clinics provide outpatient psychiatric care for persons who need treatment but are not judged to require hospitalization. United States clinics have been treating about a million patients each year. Mental health centers give outpatient treatment plus a wider range of services. They may admit patients for emergency treatment. They may treat patients on a day basis (letting them go home to spend nights) or on a night basis (letting them leave the center to work). They cooperate with hospitals, doctors, public health officers, and community leaders to prevent and treat emotional problems and to rehabilitate patients. The centers are also intended to carry on research.

See also Mental Health.

MENTAL HOSPITALS.

For many centuries society has had the problem of what to do with people who are classed as mentally disordered. Western society has often decided to put them in institutions, formerly called by such names as asylums or bedlams, but now mental hospitals.

History

The beginnings of mental institutions appeared in fifteenth-century Europe and spread from Spain to other countries and thence to the American continent. The early hospitals were similar to medieval dungeons with torture chambers and made abundant use of whips, shackles, and chains to control the incarcerated. The rationale for this approach was that physical force was necessary for both treatment and control, since patients were dangerous and of little value to society. This view was consistent with, and received support from, the major religions, governments, and medical experts of the period.

Shifts in political, philosophical, and legal climates during the nineteenth century saw humanitarian reforms emerge in the attitudes toward and treatment of mental disorders. Those who were formerly regarded by society as unmanageable beasts were now seen increasingly as human beings. The use of dungeons and many of the restraining devices declined. Good care reached a peak in some hospitals in the mid-1800s, when so-called moral treatment incorporated kindness and a wholesome physical environment within small institutions.

However, with an increasing population came overcrowding, which resulted in the construction of larger and larger hospitals. These institutions sought quick, expeditious means of improving behavior via medical intervention. The large patient populations could not in fact have close contact with and individual attention from small staffs. Hence oversized, overpopulated institutions emerged. Far removed from the extrahospital community, they provided little more than custodial care.

In the last two decades a reaction against that type of care and treatment set in. It was clearly recognized that "institutionalizing" a person for years created a greater disability than that for which the patient was originally admitted.

New Goals

Goals and plans have now changed. Hospitals are to be used as last resorts, with the burden of proof on the committing agents as to why other forms of treatment—mental health clinics, private practitioners, halfway houses, day care centers, and night care centers—were not used. And when hospitalization is indicated, the goal is to admit people, whenever possible, voluntarily, as is done in general hospitals, rather than through involuntary commitment.

The current ideal model involves a short stay in the more personal and pleasant surroundings of smaller hospitals designed to provide a total milieu that is more conducive to the individual's return to the community. Moreover, extensive psychotherapeutic, psychopharmacological, vocational, occupational, and physical programs are utilized. Finally, there has been an increasing awareness and protection of the civil rights of the patient and former patient.

If plans can be put into use, mental hospitals will no longer be the warehouses for society's unwanted and feared. On the contrary, they now have as a primary goal rehabilitation and return to the community of all patients.

Environmental Studies of Hospitals

The new approach to mental hospitals can be illustrated by studies of the physical environment of institutions. Men and women everywhere react to the environment, both psychologically and physiologically, and less than stressful stimuli can still elicit responsiveness. Psychologists for many years focused on the interpersonal environment. Discussion of

MENTALLY ILL PATIENTS BY TYPE OF FACILITY

Item and year	All facilities	Hospitals, inpatient services				Outpatient psychiatric services
		Mental		General	VA	
		State and county	Private			
Patients (1,000):						
1955	1,675	819	123	266	88	379
1965	2,637	805	125	519	116	1,071
1966	2,764	802	104	549	123	1,186
1967	3,140	801	124	579	128	1,507
1968	3,381	792	118	559	134	1,779
1969	3,650	767	124	535	187	2,037
Percent distribution:						
1955	100.0	48.9	7.3	15.9	5.3	22.6
1965	100.0	30.5	4.8	19.7	4.4	40.6
1966	100.0	29.0	3.8	19.9	4.4	42.9
1967	100.0	25.5	4.0	18.4	4.1	48.0
1968	100.0	23.4	3.5	16.5	3.9	52.7
1969	100.0	21.0	3.4	14.7	5.1	55.8
Rate per 100,000:						
1955	1,032	505	76	164	54	234
1965	1,374	420	65	271	60	558
1966	1,427	414	54	283	64	612
1967	1,604	410	64	296	66	771
1968	1,711	401	60	283	68	901
1969	1,828	384	62	268	94	1,020

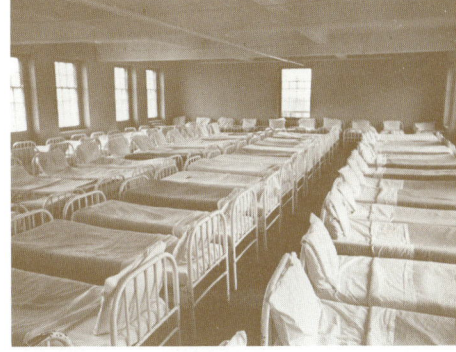

A typical dormitory of an overcrowded mental health hospital common during the early post World War II period.

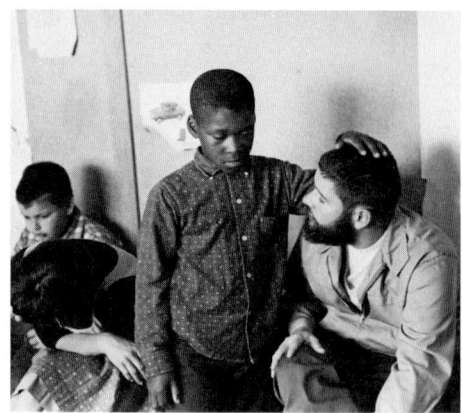

A therapist works closely with his patient at a center for emotionally disturbed children designed to provide a meaningful therapeutic environment.

A child engaged in solitary play in the boy's ward of a mental health hospital.

the physical environment largely took place among conservationists, architects, and urban planners. It is only in recent decades that psychologists, and more specifically mental health professionals, have addressed themselves to this topic. In New York State, which initiated an enormous construction program for state hospitals, rehabilitation centers, state schools for the retarded, and children's psychiatric hospitals, there has been a call for a wedding of architecture and psychology: designing for space must follow function. [*Consult* (13) Lee, 1966; Saper, 1968.]

Planners have realized that physical environments provide the tone and climate in which treatment takes place. Mental health settings in both the past and in recent years have been distinctly antitherapeutic.

If we accept the assumption that society often indicates its value of the individual by the setting and material it provides, it is easy to see how the self-regard of the patient, generally at a low level, is decreased substantially by prisonlike, custodial institutions. On the other hand, a facility drawn to human scale, with warm and not overpowering sensory stimuli, can facilitate a healthy return to the community. Semiprivate and private rooms can be helpful as appropriate stimuli for interpersonal contact. Often sex and age, in addition to emotional condition, relate to the room of choice for the individual. Lighting of a residential type is certainly preferable to institutional or factory fixtures, again taking into account the decrease in visual functions with age.

The tendency for hospitals to have long corridors, tunnels, or dayrooms has been found particularly troublesome. They militate against normal social interaction and communication. The typical dayroom has chairs arranged arm to arm around its periphery, which makes for easier cleaning, but certainly impels the residents to adapt to institutionalized living. It is not the model of the arrangement one expects to find in the community, since it affords no face-to-face contact between people. [*Consult* (13) Spivack, 1967.]

Offensive noises and odors, although adapted to readily, are unwholesome. Noise interferes with concentration, and even when adapted to produces an accrued negative effect. This is compounded by call and public address systems amid patients who may very well have been or are close to auditory hallucinations. Unpleasant smells make it quite difficult to recruit personnel in addition to discouraging visiting on wards with incontinent, aged, or disordered residents.

A variety of additional physical factors are important in setting the climate of a mental health facility. Although human beings have a remarkable capacity to adapt to the most pathogenic conditions, further psychological

research involving physical stimuli should be used to create situations that permit the emotionally disordered to return to the daily, extra-hospital community more effectively.

—Howard M. Cohen, *State University College, New Paltz, N.Y.*

See also Community Mental Health Centers; Community Psychology; Mental Health; Psychology and the Law.

Consult (13) Goffman, 1961; Levinson and Gallagher, 1964; Ullmann, 1967. (14) Proshansky, *et al.*, 1970.

MENTAL HYGIENE MOVEMENT. Mental hygiene can be defined as a program to improve the treatment of mental illness and to promote mental health. Some of the pioneers working in this direction were aroused by the shocking state of the asylums in which mental patients were locked up. For example, Dorothea Dix began in 1840 a long campaign in America and Europe for humane treatment. The mental hygiene movement in its modern form, however, can be dated from the efforts of another American, Clifford W. Beers. He experienced mental illness and unhelpful or harsh treatment in three institutions, finally recovering in a private home. To educate the public about the problems of mental illness and the need for enlightened treatment, he published his own story, *A Mind That Found Itself,* in 1908. In the same year he founded the Connecticut Society for Mental Hygiene, helped by the psychologist William James and the psychiatrist Adolf Meyer. Beers established the National Commission for Mental Hygiene in 1909 and thereafter worked to spread the movement.

From Beers' original emphasis on public understanding and humane treatment, the movement broadened into the current federally supported mental health programs.

See also Beers; Mental Health.

MENTAL ILLNESS. Articles on kinds, causes, and treatment are listed in the Subject Map for Abnormal and Clinical Psychology. Note the major discussion in Mental Health.

MENTAL RETARDATION. The retarded (or mentally deficient) are a major concern for psychologists, psychiatrists and other physicians, social workers, teachers, and parents. A variety of problems of maturation, learning, and social adjustment fits under the heading of retardation.

Definitions

Prior to 1960, none of the definitions of mental retardation was completely satisfactory to all of the many disciplines involved in the field. The American Association on Mental Deficiency published a manual on terminology (1961) that has been well received. The AAMD defines mental retardation as subaverage general intellectual functioning that originates during the developmental period (here meaning up to age sixteen) and is associated with impairment in adaptive behavior. "Subaverage" refers to performance that is more than one standard deviation below the mean of measures of general intellectual functioning. Five levels are specified: *borderline* (Binet IQ range 83–68); *mild* (67–52); *moderate* (51–36; *severe* (35–20); *profound* (below 20).

There is no reference in the definition to intellectual capacity (simply to test scores). Nor is there a judgment about constitutional origin or incurability of the condition.

The subaverage intellectual functioning must be reflected by impairment in one or more of the following aspects of adaptive behavior: maturation, learning, social adjustment. *Maturation* refers to the development of self-help skills such as walking, talking, and habit training. A delay in maturation is of prime importance as a criterion of mental retardation during the preschool years, while impaired *learning ability* is particularly important as a criterion during the school years. *Social adjustment* is of particular importance at the adult level, where it is assessed in terms of the degree to which the individual is able to maintain himself independently in the community.

Approximately 16 percent of the population will exhibit subaverage performance on measures of general intellectual functioning, but the majority will probably not show significant impairment in adaptive behavior, particularly in maturation and social adjustment. At present, the most commonly quoted estimate of mental retardation is 3 percent of the population.

As of 1969, 52 percent of the mentally retarded were receiving special educational services. For educational purposes, mental retardates are classified as educables or trainables. In a small number of cases (profoundly retarded) the severity of the defect precludes educational services within the public schools. The terms "moron" ("feeblemined" in England), "imbecile," and "idiot" were used to designate these groups at one time, but they have become so unacceptable to most professionals that they are seldom used today.

Educable mentally retarded children (IQ 50 to 75 or 80) are seldom diagnosed as retarded prior to entering school. They comprise about 83 percent of the retarded population. They generally show no significant physical stigma and most do not evidence demonstrable abnormalities of the brain. Educables are much like their nonretarded peers in physical characteristics and appearance. Their greatest problems usually arise during the school years. Their academic achievement is usually between a second- and fifth-grade ability level at

maturity. Special education programs for educables usually consist of full- or part-time placement in special classes in neighborhood schools with as much integration as possible.

The great majority make a satisfactory adjustment in the community at the adult level. No more than 1 percent of this group ever enters a residential institution for the retarded. Most educables are employed in unskilled and semiskilled job areas. Many marry, and their children are usually not retarded.

Trainable mentally retarded children (IQ 25 to 50) come from homes that resemble those of a cross-section of the general population. They are usually diagnosed during the preschool years. They comprise about 12 percent of retardates. About one-third are mongoloid and another third have known brain injury from varying causes. School programs for trainables are oriented toward the skills necessary for successful living in the home, school, and immediate neighborhood and eventually in a sheltered workshop.

At maturity they will generally not have learned to read or compute to any usable extent, beyond the recognition of certain signs (Men, Women, Danger) and very simple number concepts. Trainables will usually need some care, support, and supervision throughout life.

Profoundly retarded individuals (IQ below 20 or 25) usually do not learn to take care of their bodily needs. Many are bedridden or in wheel chairs. They are unable to guard themselves against ordinary physical danger. They require complete care and supervision throughout life. These cases make up about 5 percent of retardates.

Causes

In a majority of cases of mental retardation, the cause is unknown or in dispute, particularly as regards educable retardates.

Environmental Factors. The majority of educables do not evidence demonstrable abnormalities of the brain and they tend to come from homes of a low socioeconomic level, often being victims of poverty. These individuals are frequently referred to as *cultural-familial* retardates. The occupations of the parents are generally in unskilled and semiskilled areas, and their level of formal education is often rather low. Inadequate medical care, serious complications of pregnancy, and premature births are common to these families.

For many years, heredity was assumed to be the major cause of retardation in these cases. While the emphasis on heredity has tended to decrease, some writers contend that research will eventually uncover as yet unrecognized genetic or biochemical abnormalities within this group.

In recent years, attention has focused on environmental factors that may play a causal

MENTAL RETARDATION

The major article MENTAL RETARDATION describes classifications of mental deficiency and discusses causes of subaverage intellectual functioning. Supporting information on causes can be found in BRAIN DISORDERS and INTRAUTERINE ENVIRONMENT. Further discussion of the reasons for differences in mental ability will be found in INTELLIGENCE AND INTELLIGENCE TESTING, CHILD DEVELOPMENT, and HEREDITY AND ENVIRONMENT.

READING DISABILITY covers problems that in some cases involve retardation. Other pertinent articles are SLOW LEARNER and PSEUDORETARDATION.

role. Cultural-familial retardates usually reach school age with neither the experiences nor the language skills necessary for systematic school learning. Certain researchers feel that the language deficits occurring in the early preschool years constitute the greatest hazard to later school learning, and these deficits may be irreversible if not counteracted early. They believe it is necessary to reach the very young child through preschool programs during the crucial period of language development occurring between ages two and a half and four and a half. Increasing chronological age simply adds to the pervasiveness of the problem. It is hoped that an emphasis on language and sensory-perceptual training will combat the sociologically induced mental retardation of many children.

Genetic Problems. A variety of genetic factors are recognized as causes of retardation. Several of these are being controlled as a result of medical research.

Among the genetic syndromes, *phenylketonuria* (PKU) is probably the best known. There is a one in four chance a child will be affected when both parents are carriers of the recessive gene. One in fifty in the population is a carrier; PKU occurs once in every 10,000 births. The child is normal at birth but when he is placed on milk, he is unable to metabolize phenylalanine, an essential amino acid found in protein. By age three, most are severely retarded, if untreated. Reports on the effectiveness of a low phenylalanine diet appeared in the mid-1950s. A blood test that can detect PKU several days after birth provides a means of routinely screening infants. This is now legally required in hospitals in a majority of states. If the diet is started early in life and is well controlled, mental retardation can be prevented or greatly lessened.

Galactosemia, another inherited metabolic disorder, can be controlled through a diet free of milk sugar. Again, early detection through several available tests is vital, since after several months irreversible damage may have occurred.

Mongolism (Down's syndrome, trisomy 21) is the most common clinical condition associated with mental retardation. It occurs once in every 700 births. One-third of the children enrolled in classes for trainables are mongoloid. (Mongolism is more likely to occur with advancing maternal age. In mothers under thirty, the incidence of mongoloid births is one per thousand, while in mothers over forty-five, the incidence is one in every forty births.) Malformations of the heart and respiratory problems are common to the condition. The mental age range in adult mongoloids is approximately three to seven years.

Most mongoloids (more than 90 percent) have a chromosomal count of forty-seven instead of the normal forty-six, including three 21s. This results from the fertilization of an abnormal ovum. Trisomy 21 is the result of an error in cell division and not an inherited disorder.

There are two additional types of mongolism, both resulting from extra 21 chromosomal material.

Mosaicism (about 2 percent of mongoloids) results from an error in cell division after fertilization. Some cells contain an extra 21, while other cells are normal. Mosaic mongoloids can vary physically and mentally from obvious mongolism to near normalcy.

In *translocation mongolism* (4 percent of cases) the total chromosome count is forty-six. In addition to two separate, unattached 21s, there is an extra 21 attached (translocated) to another chromosome, usually a 15. Thus there is the equivalent of forty-seven. Translocation mongolism has aroused great interest since in many cases a parent, more often the mother, has an abnormal chromosomal pattern. In these instances the risk of having another mongoloid is increased tremendously, as high as one chance in three. In a succeeding pregnancy, the chromosomal pattern of the fetus can be determined by an examination of cells obtained from the amniotic fluid.

At present there is no effective medical treatment for mongolism.

Viruses and Other Causes. Certain viral agents can damage the unborn child. Rubella may cause a syndrome of cataracts, heart disease, mental retardation, and deafness in the developing child if the mother is infected during the first three months of pregnancy. The risk may be as high as 50 percent in the first month, 25 percent in the second month and 17 percent in the third month. Rubella vaccine should eventually eliminate this virus as a cause of defects.

Thousands of infants die or suffer defects each year as a result of an Rh factor blood incompatibility between the mother and the fetus. The defects include mental retardation, cerebral palsy, and deafness. The artificial introduction of antibodies to the Rh factor into the mother's bloodstream after the birth of her first child shows promise of eliminating this problem as a cause of defects within the next generation.

Prematurity (especially if the child weighs less than three and one-half pounds at birth) and serious complications of pregnancy are responsible for a variety of defects, including mental retardation. A greater availability of medical services and a utilization of these services by all pregnant women could prevent many of these defects.

Anything that reduces the supply of oxygen to the fetus (anoxia), such as premature separation of the placenta or pinching of the cord, may cause brain damage.

Retardation may result during childhood from a number of factors, including meningitis, encephalitis, and lead poisoning.

Increasing Awareness of the Problem. During the past twenty years several events have helped to increase interest in mental retardation. The National Association for Retarded Children, a parents' organization founded in 1950, pressed for the passage of mandatory special education legislation for retarded children through 700 local chapters across the country. This helped to increase awareness at the local level.

A number of stories on PKU children in national publications, emphasizing the value of a low phenylalanine diet, has helped to create a more positive public attitude toward retardation.

In 1961, President Kennedy appointed experts from a variety of disciplines to a Panel on Mental Retardation. Their charge was to explore all possibilities and pathways to prevent and cure retardation. Their recommendations have stimulated interest and research and have led to a greater involvement at the federal level.

Organizations concerned with problems of retardation include: American Association on Mental Deficiency (headquarters at George Peabody College, Nashville, Tenn., and chapters throughout the country); Council for Exceptional Children (Arlington, Va., with chapters throughout the country); National Association for Retarded Children (Arlington, Tex., and more than 700 chapters across the country). Another source of information is the supervisor of special education in the local school district. In 1972 the American Psychological Association formed a division for psychologists working in the field of retardation (Division 32).

—Walter Cheetham, *Southern Connecticut State College*

See also Brain Disorders; Intrauterine Environment.

Consult (13) Ellis, 1968; Farber, 1968; Haywood, 1970; Kolstoe, 1970; Robinson and Robinson, 1965; Rothstein, 1971; Stevens and Heber, 1964. Also periodicals such as *American Journal of Mental Deficiency, Education and Training of the Mentally Retarded,* and *Exceptional Children.*

MESCALINE, a psychedelic agent. *See* Drugs and Behavior.

MESMER, FRANZ (OR FRIEDRICH) ANTON (1733–1815), German physician. Born in Iznang on Lake Constance, Baden, he received a medical degree from the University of Vienna (1766) and practiced treatment by "animal magnetism" in Vienna and later in Paris.

What Mesmer called animal magnetism was later renamed mesmerism and is now called hypnosis. Mesmer believed that magnetic forces from the planets and stars could affect the human body. He developed his theory while he was studying medicine, influenced by the teachings of Paracelsus, a sixteenth-century doctor. In Vienna, Mesmer began treating patients for nervous disorder, at first using magnets to attract the rarefied fluids that he believed flowed from celestial bodies. Controversy developed, the Vienna Faculty of Medicine expelled him, and he moved to Paris in 1778.

In France, Mesmer built a famous practice. His patients sat in wooden tubs with iron rods projecting from the covers and magnetized water flowing around them. Mesmer touched each patient in turn with an iron rod. The patient would then twitch and convulse in a "grand crisis," which, according to Mesmer, produced a cure.

The French Academy of Sciences and Faculty of Medicine reviewed his work, concluding that "magnetism minus imagination is nothing." Later a royal commission, with Benjamin Franklin and Antoine Lavoisier as members, investigated Mesmer's work. They reported that he had apparently achieved cures, but they warned about dangerous effects from the grand crisis. Mesmer was virtually branded a quack and left France to live in obscurity.

Mesmer apparently believed sincerely in his theories of magnetic influences and did not realize the role of suggestion in his treatments. His work was important, however, because he had roused interest in new approaches to therapy. Later studies of the trancelike states he had produced contributed to the modern uses of hypnotism.

See also Hypnosis.

MESMERISM. *See* Hypnosis; Mesmer.

MESOMORPH. *See* Constitutional Types.

MESSAGE. This broad term refers simply to the type of information that is transmitted from one being to another in the process of communicating. Messages may be verbal or nonverbal. The complex dance of the bees contains an intricate message telling the members of the hive the exact distance and direction to a source of food. The emotional responses commonly labeled anger or annoyance quickly transmit a message from one individual to another. Physical gestures and postures convey a variety of messages or symbols, and this mode of communication has been commonly referred to as "body language." Smells and tastes also carry information: the smell of perfume carries one message, whereas the smell of sweat transmits a different type of information.

Friedrich Mesmer believed that one human could impose his will on another's unconscious through "animal magnetism."

All the sensory processes are capable of receiving and coding information from the environment. Each of these channels carries messages of different types.

—Joel F. Lubar, *University of Tennessee*
See also Body Language; Language; Sensation.

METAPSYCHOLOGY. As metaphysics goes beyond physics, metapsychology goes beyond empirical psychology to consider philosophical issues such as the nature of mind and will and the mind-body problem.

Freud used "metapsychology" in another sense, a combination of descriptive and explanatory terms to denote mental processes comprehensively. This approach attempts to incorporate explanations derived from all of the varied orientations (systematic, dynamic, economic, and structural) that can and have been used to interpret phenomena, especially dreams.

—Thom Herrmann, *University of Tennessee*

METHADONE, a synthetic opiate narcotic. It has been used to reduce the severity of withdrawal symptoms suffered when an addict is taken off heroin. It is also used in programs for all-around treatment of addiction. *See* Drugs and Behavior.

MEYER, ADOLF (1866–1950), American psychiatrist. Born in Niederweningen, Switzerland, he received his M.D. from the University of Zurich in 1892. He moved to the United States and served in several hospitals and universities and was professor of psychiatry and clinic director at Johns Hopkins, 1910–1941.

Meyer's influence became so great that he was called "dean of American psychiatry." One of his contributions was stressing the holistic approach to a patient, trying to view "the whole individual in action." He introduced the making of case histories covering facts about the patient's constitution, background, family life, work life, and so on. Meyer also encouraged visiting the patient's home to study the milieu from which he came and to which he would return if released from treatment. Meyer held that environmental factors might be a cause of ineffective functioning and that patients could be taught more efficient ways of behaving.

As another contribution, Meyer encouraged and worked with Clifford W. Beers in founding the mental hygiene movement.

His writings have been published as *Collected Works,* 1951.

See also Mental Hygiene Movement.

MICROCEPHALY, the condition of having an abnormally small head, usually associated with mental retardation. About 5 percent of cases of deficiency fall in this category. Microcephalics are usually classed as severely or profoundly retarded and are usually put in institutions. It is believed that the condition may be caused by a recessive gene or by environmental factors such as infectious disease in the mother during pregnancy or exposure to radiation during pregnancy. A number of microcephalic children were born to women who were in Hiroshima when the atomic bomb was exploded over the city.

MIDDLE YEARS. Most social, economic, educational, scientific, and political policy is set by men and women in their middle years. The majority of people receiving psychotherapy are probably in this age group. For such reasons, it might be expected that psychologists would give a great deal of attention to the middle-aged group. Yet the years from about thirty-five to sixty have had far less organized study by developmental psychologists than is true of childhood and old age. The middle years are strongly influenced by the experiences of childhood and adolescence that preceded them and by the expectations of old age and death that will follow. However, middle age can be a highly dynamic and productive period.

One reason for a concentration on the early years can be found in Sigmund Freud's emphasis on the importance of childhood experiences in personality development. Yet while Freud was focusing on early childhood, Carl Jung was stressing the middle years and anticipating many contemporary theories and observations about them. Seeing the individual as composed of many conflicting, inherent potentials striving for realization, Jung described the focus in the early years as on the practical requirements of acquiring skills, finding an occupation, and establishing a family. In the middle years, when these tasks have been largely accomplished, the person's other potentials strive for realization. Spiritual and social values become important, and the need for integration of all one's possibilities becomes paramount. Time perspective broadens to include not only time since birth but time to retirement and time until death. The middle years are best understood not as the static result of preceding developments but as a time of reorganization, reevaluation, and change.

The possibilities for such a healthy approach to middle age are limited, however, by the extent to which earlier choices and experiences have left the individual free to be flexible and realistic. For the poor, middle age may offer very few opportunities.

Trend of Abilities in the Middle Years. Intelligence test scores rise to the age of eighteen and then decline, but vocabulary tests hold up well with aging. According to reports, they continue to show gains until at least the

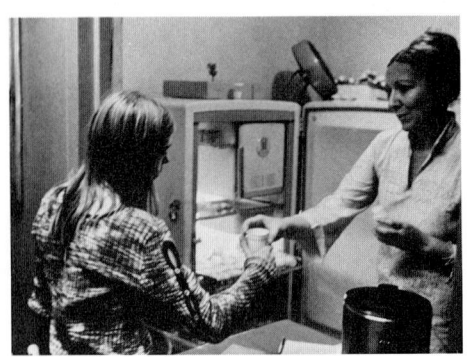
Methadone being dispensed at a clinic.

late thirties and perhaps as late as fifty. Performance IQ begins to decline for females, but not for males, in the late twenties. Declines during the fifties involve speed and perhaps immediate memory, exemplified by the deterioration with age of digit symbol tests that require the marking of symbols below paired numbers. This effect may, however, be due more to the older person's extracareful checking. Intelligence tests are designed primarily for children and are extended to adulthood largely by shortening time requirements. There is reason to believe that they fail to measure the synthesizing ability required especially for tasks of the middle years. This suggestion is further supported by the observation that the IQ predicts school grades well, but neither IQ nor school grades are very accurate predictors of adult achievement.

Rather than despairing that one loses some of the intellectual and cognitive abilities of earlier years, the person in the middle years might better recognize that the demands of this time of life require integrating rather than concrete kinds of abilities. It is those functions no longer required for his ongoing activities that seem to deteriorate.

Earlier reports have suggested that most of the best work in mathematics and physical sciences seems to be done by young people, with a greater capacity of novelists and playrights to continue their crafts into later years, perhaps related to the tendency for vocabulary tests to hold up with age. [Consult (11) Heim, 1970.]

Later reports, however, indicate that with the exception of the arts, the decade of the twenties is roughly the period of least productivity, with the forties being the decade of highest output for almost all areas of work. Productivity of scholars showed little decrement even after sixty, but that of scientists decreased and output of persons in art, music, and original literature dropped appreciably. [Consult (11) Dennis, 1968.]

Generation Gap. The "generation gap" may also be accounted for partially by the changing tasks of the middle years. Older people tend to be more susceptible to social influence and more likely to believe that certain behaviors are more appropriate for certain age groups. A certain rigidity may be seen here, or perhaps a greater awareness of the reality of life's situations and the close integration between oneself and the larger society. The task of young people to establish their "identity" as separate from others may be seen by the older person as "selfishness."

The generation gap may also represent the extent to which parents have focused on the parental role to the exclusion of their other potentials. For the parent who sees little in life beyond raising a family, the future may lie in the children and he or she may demand that they should meet his or her own unsatisfied expectations. To the extent that this cannot be, dissatisfaction and anger are experienced.

Midlife Crises, Toward the end of the middle years, the individual may become especially aware of crises of this period of life. For women there occur the obvious gradual changes of the climacteric, usually beginning in the forties, with menopause occurring at the average age of fifty. Hormonal changes lead to irregularity in occurrence and amount of menstrual flow and its eventual cessation. There may also be flashes of temperature change, some pain in intercourse, and loss of skin elasticity producing changes in appearance. Today estrogen-replacement therapy can relieve these secondary symptoms, and for most women the menopause causes no special psychological problems. [Consult (11) Neugarten, 1968.]

Yet for the woman who has seen herself narrowly as a sexually attractive potential bearer of children, these changes—along with her children's growing up and leaving home—may create a feeling that there is nothing left in life. With an average life expectancy of seventy-five, she sees twenty-five useless years ahead. The extreme feeling of dissatisfaction, bitterness, and depression characteristic of involutional melancholia is directly related to this narrowed view of oneself.

Similar feelings may be experienced by the male as he observes his own declining abilities and anticipates retirement. To the extent that his view of himself is limited, he too will experience depression, as will the exclusively "career" woman.

But for the person who has been able to develop many of his potentials and to incorporate aging and death into an overall philosophy of life, who has adjusted well to a wide range of family, community, and social demands, the midlife crisis will culminate in a reevaluation and integration of personality and a graceful and positive anticipation of age.

—M. G. Affinito, *Southern Connecticut State College*

See also Adolescence; Aging; Child Development; Developmental Psychology.

Consult (11) *Developmental Psychology Today,* 1971; Glass and Kase, 1970; Gray, 1967; Maddi, 1968; Neugarten, 1968.

MIGRAINE, a severe "sick headache," with pain usually occurring on one side of the head only. It is described as a cardiovascular form of psychosomatic disorder. *See* Psychosomatic Disorders.

MILD MENTAL RETARDATION. *See* Mental Retardation.

MILGRAM, STANLEY (1933–   ), American experimental social psychologist. Born in New

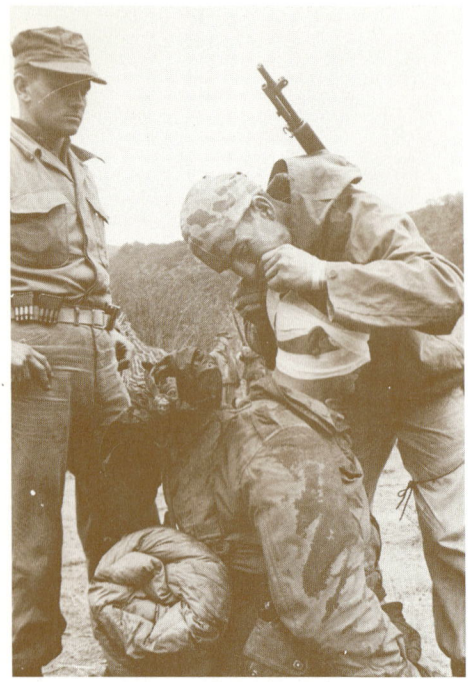

Military psychologists have been called on to develop elaborate training exercises to simulate war situations.

York, he studied for his Ph.D. at Harvard (1960). He is professor of psychology, City University, New York.

Milgram's studies of obedience, conformity, and crowd behavior have been cross-national. Especially well known is his series of controversial investigations of obedience to authority done at Yale in 1960–1963. The subjects, playing "teacher," administered punishment to other "subjects" learning lists of words. Though the actual punishment was false, the subjects heard pleading, cries, and screams. The experimenter's role was to urge the subjects to continue administering shocks. Milgram concluded that most people do what they are told to do so long as the command comes from legitimate authority. Controversy centered on the social implications and the ethics of conducting such a study. Publications of this study are "Behavior Study of Obedience," *Journal of Abnormal Psychology,* 1963; "Some Conditions of Obedience and Disobedience to Authority," *Human Relations,* 1965; "Issues in the Study of Authority; A Reply to Baumrind," *American Psychologist,* 1964.

—Nina Adams, *Yale University*

MILITARY PSYCHOLOGY, the application of psychology in the armed forces. Psychologists in this specialty are concerned, for example, with selecting personnel, using tests, studying training programs, evaluating morale, analyzing activity and performance in military jobs, exploring the social systems of men in organizations, and designing automated or man-machine systems. In some respects applications of engineering psychology are required.

Division 19 of the American Psychological Association is the Division of Military Psychology.

MILLER, GEORGE ARMITAGE (1920–   ), American experimental psychologist, an important contributor to theory and research in language and memory. Born in Charleston, W. Va., he studied for his Ph.D. at Harvard.

Miller's "Magic Number Seven" article (1956) introduced the concept of chunking and provided impetus to research on short-term memory. His book *Plans and the Structure of Behavior* (1960), with Eugene Galanter and Karl Pribram, is one of the cornerstones of modern cognitive psychology. In the 1960s Miller did much to convince psychologists of the importance of principles of linguistics for psychological theory. He served as president of the American Psychological Association in 1969–1970.

—Roland Siiter, *Montclair State College*
See also Cognitive Psychology; Language.

MILLER, NEAL ELGAR (1909–   ), American psychologist. Born in Milwaukee, he received a

George Miller's work in areas of language and memory has had major impact on cognitive psychology.

Ph.D. from Yale University (1935). He was professor of psychology at Yale, 1952–1966, and at Rockefeller University after 1966.

Miller has made a number of contributions by his studies of learning. With John Dollard, he has worked on a theory of social learning, or imitation. Miller has also done significant work on hunger motivation and learning. His more recent work on visceral responses has shown that the autonomic nervous system is subject to conditioning. Attempts have been made to apply visceral learning, or biofeedback, in medical practice by teaching patients to control their blood pressure.

Publications include *Social Learning and Imitation* (coauthor with Dollard) 1941; and *Personality and Psychotherapy: An Analysis in Terms of Learning, Thinking, and Culture* (with Dollard) 1950.

MIND, the term used in pretwentieth-century psychology and still common in popular culture to refer to the collective attributes and contents of "consciousness"—what one thinks, feels, desires, perceives, wills, remembers.

When behaviorism became prominent, the vague and general term "mind" was discarded and actually "forbidden" in academic and scientific psychology. However, it has persisted in the adjectival form "mental," as in "mental test." More recently, "mind" has occasionally been revived by cognitive psychologists in order to contrast their approach with traditional behavioristic and S–R viewpoints.

MINNESOTA MULTIPHASIC PERSONALITY INVENTORY (MMPI), a psychometric instrument designed to measure all the more important phases of personality. It consists of 550 statements covering a wide range of subject matter—from the physical condition to the morale and the social attitudes of the individual being tested. The subject must respond with "true," "false," or "cannot say" to each statement. Although the inventory can be individually administered, using a card-sorting technique, the group form is usually used, as it is less time-consuming and can be machine-scored. There is a great deal of information available on the test's validity, interpretive significance, and use. [*Consult* (12) Hathaway and McKinley, 1951.]

As the inventory was originally developed in a clinical setting, eight of the fourteen scales on which responses are keyed are based on diagnostic nomenclature: hypochondriasis (Hs), depression (D), hysteria (Hy), psychopathic deviate (Pd), paranoia (Pa), psychasthenia (Pt), schizophrenia (Sc), and hypomania (Ma). The ninth clinical scale, the interest or masculinity-femininity (M-F) scale, "measures the tendency toward masculinity or femininity of interest pattern." Other nonclinical scales that are used to develop a profile are the social introversion-extraversion scale (Si) and the four validity scales: the lie (L) score (response inconsistencies indicating subjects' attempts to "look good"), the question (?) scale ("cannot say" responses), the validity (F) score (a check on response validity), and the K score (a correction factor for the entire record).

—Randolph S. Kraft, *Federation of the Handicapped*, N.Y.

Consult (12) Dahlstrom and Welsh, 1960; Hathaway and Meehl, 1951.

MINORITIES, ATTITUDES TOWARD. *See* Prejudice.

MNEMONIC STRATEGIES. *See* Memory Improvement.

MODE, the most easily obtained measure of central tendency, simply the score that occurs most frequently in a set of scores. For example, in the set 2, 5, 5, 6, 7, 7, 7, 9, the mode is 7.

When all of the scores in a set occur with the same frequency, there is no mode. When two different adjacent scores both occur more frequently than any other scores, the mode is the average of the two adjacent scores. When there are two nonadjacent highest scores, there are two modes, and the group of scores is said to be *bimodal*.

See also Mean; Median.

MODELING, a form of learning also called *imitation* and *social learning. See* Imitation.

MODERATE MENTAL RETARDATION. *See* Mental Retardation.

MONGOLISM. *See* Intrauterine Environment; Mental Retardation.

MONOTONY. *See* Work, Studies of.

MOON ILLUSION. The moon appears to be much larger when it is near the horizon than when it is seen in elevation. Yet, as attested by photography, the image of the moon cast on the retina is always approximately the same size. Therefore, the great difference in perceived size of the moon as a function of its elevation in the sky is an illusion.

Men have known about and speculated about this illusion since antiquity, but these speculations can be reduced to either of two major explanations. According to the *eye-elevation hypothesis*—espoused and experimentally tested by E. G. Boring—raising the eyes to view a distant object makes it appear smaller. It is not clear, however, why such an effect of eye elevation on perceived size should be expected to occur. According to the *apparent-distance hypothesis*—first stated by the as-

tromoner Ptolemy—the illusion results from the fact that the moon at the horizon appears to be farther away because of depth cues provided by the terrain. Since it is now known that the perceptual system takes distance into account in assessing the size signified by the retinal image, the illusion would then be predictable in terms of contemporary knowledge about size perception. Recent experiments have been widely interpreted as supporting this theory and contradicting the eye-elevation hypothesis.

—Irvin Rock, *Rutgers University*

See also Depth Perception.

Consult (4) Boring, 1943; Kaufman and Rock, 1962.

MORAL DEVELOPMENT. The study of moral development has received increasing attention in recent years, but widespread agreement on how the problem should be researched has not yet been reached. In general, the study of moral development has concentrated on how individuals come to adopt the standards of right and wrong that are laid down by their cultures and how they resist the temptation to transgress the rules of acceptable conduct. Investigations have centered on how moral standards are developed in children, although it is generally assumed that the processes observed in children are paralleled in adults. These studies have taken two essential directions: developmental research, which focuses on stage theory, and conditioning research, which focuses on environmental and experiential factors.

The developmental view stems largely from the work of Jean Piaget, who has reasoned that moral development could also be conceptualized as occurring in stages, through which the individual progresses in a manner roughly paralleling cognitive development.

Kohlberg's Stages. Piaget's view was adopted by Lawrence Kohlberg, who distinguished six stages of moral development. These six stages have been classified as representing three primary levels of moral thinking, with two stages at each level.

At level I, stage 1 is characterized by an orientation to obey rules in order to avoid punishment. Stage 2 is characterized by hedonistic motives; the individual conforms to obtain rewards and have favors returned. Level I is classified as "premoral" because there is no concept of right or wrong and behavior is judged only in terms of the pleasurableness of personal outcomes.

At level II, stage 3 is characterized by the approval motive; the individual behaves morally to avoid disapproval and dislike by others. Stage 4 is characterized by adherence to authority and a fear of censure by legitimate authority. Guilt is first experienced at this stage when the individual comes to feel anticipatory

The moon illusion, in which the moon at the horizon is seen much larger than when it is higher in the sky, is a product of subjective compensation by the viewer.

Rumanian-born psychiatrist Jacob Moreno gave early impetus to group therapeutic methods, psychodrama.

MOTIVATION

Motives, incentives, needs, drives—these are important in all kinds of behavior. Emotions have been called "the energies of man," and the effects of strong feelings are well known—see for example, ANGER, FEAR, and AGGRESSION. Drives are used to motivate learning, as described in INSTRUMENTAL CONDITIONING, DRIVE-REDUCTION THEORY, REWARD AND PUNISHMENT, and BEHAVIOR THERAPY. People's interests motivate them in school and on the job—see INTEREST INVENTORIES.

Numerous drives have been named and classified. Some arise out of bodily needs, for example, ELIMINATION DRIVE, PAIN DRIVE, SLEEP DRIVE, HUNGER DRIVE, and THIRST DRIVE. Nervous-system controls for such drives as hunger and thirst are noted in BRAIN, HYPOTHALAMUS, and HOMEOSTASIS. Other drives are the ACTIVITY DRIVE, CURIOSITY DRIVE, and EXPLORATORY DRIVE. Many incentives involve social pressures—for example, ACHIEVEMENT DRIVE, AFFILIATIVE DRIVE, and CONFORMITY. See the list of articles under DRIVE.

Theories about the origins of motives are discussed in INSTINCT and ETHOLOGY. Freudian beliefs about drives are noted in LIFE INSTINCT and DEATH INSTINCT.

fear of punishment. Level II is considered to be "conventional" in orientation, since moral behavior demonstrated at this level is still almost completely dependent on external rules and standards.

Level III moral thinking is characterized at stage 5 by concern with individual rights and democratically accepted law. At stage 6 moral behavior is based entirely on individual principles of conscience, with self-condemnation as the principal enforcer of moral behavior. Level III represents the highest level of individual moral reasoning. Here moral thinking is based almost exclusively on personal moral standards and one's own beliefs.

Kohlberg's position is supported by a variety of evidence, including cross-cultural studies.

Learning. An alternative to the stage theory views moral development as the result of a number of learning experiences in which parents, teachers, and other significant members of the culture teach its rules and standards by rewarding moral behavior and punishing nonmoral behavior. Justin Aronfreed, a researcher in this area, has suggested, for example, that conscience develops as a way of avoiding punishment for transgression. This view emphasizes the role of models and observational learning as well as the importance of classical conditioning in the acquisition and development of morally based responses and feelings.

—Brenda B. Bankart and C. Peter Bankart, *Wabash College*

See also Conscience; Superego.

Consult (9) Aronfreed, 1968; Bandura and Walters, 1963; Kohlberg, 1963; Kohlberg, 1964.

MORALITY. See Conscience; Maturity; Moral Development.

MORENO, JACOB LEVY (1892-   ), psychiatrist, born in Bucharest, Rumania. He studied for his M.D. at the University of Vienna, 1917, and did postgraduate work in the Psychiatric Clinic in Vienna. He is the director of the Moreno Institute and Theater of Psychodrama, Beacon, N.Y.

Moreno is one of the founders and major proponents of group therapeutic experiences, particularly psychodrama. His extensive writings trace the encounter-group method back fifty years, to the institute, under Sigmund Freud, in Vienna. His works include *Who Shall Survive*, 1934 (rev. ed., 1953); *Psychodrama*, 1946 and 1956; *Group Psychotherapy*, 1947; *Sociometry, Experimental Method and Science*, 1951; *Sociometry and the Science of Man*, 1956; and *First Book on Group Psychotherapy*, 1957. He was editor of *International Handbook of Group Psychotherapy*, 1966, and *Psychodrama of Sigmund Freud*, 1967.

MORGAN, CONWAY LLOYD (1852-1936), English biologist and psychologist. Born in London, he received a doctor of science degree at Bristol University and was subsequently professor of psychology and ethics there.

A founder of comparative psychology, Morgan, influenced by the theory of evolution, worked to establish the study of animal behavior. In order for biology to advance, Morgan believed that a study of comparative animal behavior much like comparative anatomy must be established. In order that anthropomorphical interpretations of animal behavior would not cloud experimental and observational conclusions, Morgan formulated a guiding principle—Lloyd Morgan's canon—to guide researchers. As described in *Introduction to Comparative Psychology* (1895), it states: "In no case may we interpret an action as the outcome of the exercise of a higher psychical faculty, if it can be interpreted as the outcome of the exercise of one which stands lower in the psychological scale."

Much of Morgan's work was careful observation of animals with the environment slightly modified to create the necessary conditions. Perhaps one of his best-known studies was his description of a dog lifting a gate latch. Among his publications are *Animal Life and Intelligence*, 1890; *Habit and Instinct*, 1896; *Animal Behavior*, 1900; and *The Animal Mind*, 1930.

MORON, an old term for a mentally deficient person with an IQ in the range from 50 to 75 or 80. This is the least severe category of mental defect. The designation "educable mentally retarded" is now preferred. See Mental Retardation.

MORPHEME. See Language.

MORPHINE. See Drugs and Behavior.

MOTHERING. See Child Development; Maternal Deprivation; Maternal Drive; Overprotection.

MOTIVATION, a term used to cover explorations of the "why?" of behavior. Many psychologists have tried to list the drives or needs that explain the direction, vigor, and persistence of behavior.

One of the briefest lists was made by a social psychologist, William I. Thomas. He grouped motives under four heads: a wish for security, a wish for recognition, a wish for response from fellow beings, and a wish for new experience. A. H. Maslow used six categories: physiological needs (such as hunger and thirst); needs for safety; needs for love, belongingness, and acceptance; needs for esteem, achievement, and status; needs for self-actualization; and cognitive needs (such as curiosity). Henry A. Murray extended the list to forty motives—twelve that he called *viscerogenic* or physiological needs and twenty-eight *psychogenic* needs. The psychogenic forces (many labeled by newly created terms) include acquisition, achievement, recognition, avoidance of inferiority, dominance, deference, aggression, abasement, nurturance (helping others), play, and cognizance (satisfying curiosity). [*Consult* (10) Maslow, 1954; Murray, 1938; Thomas, 1923]

Ernest R. Hilgard grouped motives under three broad classes: *Survival* motives include the hunger drive, thirst drive, drive to avoid pain, and needs to breathe and to eliminate wastes. Also included in this category are drives with less obviously bodily origins, such as needs to be active and to explore. *Social* motives include the maternal drive, sex drive, needs for dependency and affiliation, needs for dominance and submission, and aggression. *Ego-integrative* motives center around goals, the need to achieve. [*Consult* (1) Hilgard, 1962.]

Many psychologists have pointed out that it is impossible to make neat and simple distinctions between motives. Hunger can involve more than a need to fill up on food. Physiologists have noted the phenomenon of *specific hunger*—that is, organisms will tend to select balanced diets if given a choice. On the other hand, humans sometimes overeat so much that they become obese and endanger their own health. Those with another kind of psychoneurotic problem may undereat to the verge of starving. People can learn to want substances that are dangerous, such as alcohol and other drugs. To further complicate the problem of sorting out motives, drives may express themselves indirectly. According to Freudian theory, the sex drive may be sublimated into artistic creativity, or a frustrated sex drive might explain overeating.

Many attempts have been made to explain motives. Some theorists have tried to find the why of behavior in reflexes and instincts. Others have stressed human will and creativity. Most now see motives as involving both physiological needs and varying amounts and layers of learning. A discussion of what may be called "inborn" vs. behavior that is learned can be found in the article on Aggression.

See also Aggression; Emotion; Instinct. *Specific drives listed in the Item Guide.*

Consult (1) Hilgard, 1962. (8) Maslow, 1954; Murray, 1938.

MOTOR SKILLS, LEARNING OF. *See* Skills, Learning of.

MÜLLER, JOHANNES (1801-1858), German physiologist and anatomist. *Born in Koblenz, he studied medicine in Bonn, where he became professor of anatomy and physiology.*

Müller is best known to psychologists for the "doctrine of specific energies." Since the Greeks, people had assumed that stimulation impresses itself directly on the brain. Müller noted that sensory quality depends on which nerve is stimulated and that each sensory nerve has a characteristic sensation no matter how it is stimulated (for example, pressure on the eyeball leads to sensation of light). His work laid the base for research in sensation and perception by experimental psychology.

Müller is also known as a founder of modern physiology and conducted research in voice, hearing, lymph and blood systems, cartilage, embryology, and many other areas of physiology and anatomy.

—Nina Adams, *Yale University*

MULTIPLE PERSONALITY, a pathological condition resulting from the splitting off of an unacceptable segment of the personality by means of dissociation. Thus, certain aspects and functions of the personality are removed from the conscious control of the individual and tend to act as a separate or secondary personality.

An individual who expresses this disorder can appear to others to have developed a second, totally different personality. The nature of the second personality can be diametrically opposed to that of the primary personality. This is not surprising, since it usually comprises thoughts and feelings that the primary personality has rejected as anxiety provoking.

In some reported cases, as many as two or three secondary personalities coexisted with the primary one. One twenty-eight-year-old woman admitted to a hospital after a suicide attempt became angry and abusive several days later and informed doctors that the depressed, suicidal patient was "Mary" while her name was "Cynthia." In such cases, the secondary personality often recognizes the existence of the primary personality, but the reverse is not true. A famous instance of multiple personalities is depicted in the book and movie *The Three Faces of Eve.*

Although much talked about, this disorder is very rare in psychiatric case records.

—Michael Rothenberg, *The City College of The City University of New York*

MULTIPLE SCLEROSIS, a disease that is among the degenerative class of causes of brain disorders. *See* Brain Disorders.

MUNSTERBERG, HUGO (1863-1916), German psychologist. Born in Danzig, he was a student of Wilhelm Wundt (1992-1885). He was a lecturer at Freiberg University (1887-1892) and director, Psychological Laboratory, Harvard (1892-1916).

Described as the founder of applied psychology, Munsterberg made an important

Manipulation seems to be a motive in its own right. The monkey takes the latches apart even though no reward is offered.

Johannes Müller's work on senses and sensation laid the groundwork for perception research.

German Hugo Munsterberg was among the first to apply psychology to education, law, and business.

contribution in applying psychology to education, business, and law. But he was also interested in philosophy, psychic research, and social psychology. Among his important achievements is the *action theory* which tried to establish the physiological correlates of mental acts. The conclusion that mental acts always consist of a complete circuit from sensory receptor to motor response stimulated psychological research in the area of physiological processes. Munsterberg also did pioneer studies of group behavior and promoted the mental testing movement. His publications include *Psychology and Life,* 1899; *Science and Idealism,* 1906; *Psychology and Industrial Efficiency,* 1913 and *Psychology and Social Sanity,* 1914.

MURRAY, HENRY ALEXANDER (1893–), American psychologist, born in New York City and educated at Harvard (A.B. 1915), Columbia (M.D. 1919), and Cambridge (Ph.D. 1927). He taught psychology at Harvard for nearly forty years.

Murray is primarily noted for his theory of personality, which he called "personology," and for having developed the Thematic Apperception Test (TAT). As a theorist he was eclectic, seeing personality as emerging from physiological, intrapsychic, and environmental influences. He conducted an elaborate two-and-a-half-year study of fifty individuals at the Harvard Psychological Clinic, one of the most systematic investigations of motivation and personality ever produced by psychology. One of the techniques used in this study was the TAT, which consists of a series of pictures for which the individual is required to make up stories. The themes that emerge from these stories reveal much about a person's own needs and desires. While Murray's theory of personality has not gained widespread acceptance, the TAT has become one of the classic projective techniques, ranking second in popularity only to the Rorschach.

Murray's major publications are *Explorations in Personality* (1938) and *Personality in Nature, Society, and Culture* (1953).

—Michael Rothenberg, *The City College of The City University of New York*
See also Personology; Thematic Apperception Test.

MUSCLES. *See* Effectors.

NAIL BITING, a common behavior among normal school children. It increases in adolescence, after which it declines considerably.

An outlet for aggression, fixation at the oral level, or an aid to tension reduction—these are some of the suggested explanations for nail biting. Whether or not one would consider it a neurotic symptom, depends on its severity, persistence, and the overall evaluation of the personality of the biter.

NARCISSISM, self-love in a degree beyond self-esteem. The condition is named for Narcissus, a youth in Greek legend who fell in love with his reflection in a pool and pined away to death while admiring himself.

In his psychoanalytic theory, Freud distinguished earlier and later stages of narcissism. He considered *primary narcissism* normal in infants, who focus on their own bodies and gratify their pleasure drives by such activities as sucking and eating. If character development proceeds normally, children turn their pleasure-seeking drives to other people. However, if love objects are lost, an immature or disturbed person may develop *secondary narcissism* and revert to absorption with self.

Schizophrenic patients may turn away from the rest of the world and live in fantasies of their own grand achievements.

NARCOTICS, drugs having sedative and pain-relieving effects, chiefly the opiates: codeine, opium, morphine, heroin, and synthetics such as Demerol. *See* Drugs and Behavior.

NATIONAL ASSOCIATION FOR MENTAL HEALTH, a voluntary organization "devoting itself exclusively to the total fight against mental illness and to the advancement of mental health." Activities include sponsoring research on prevention of mental disorders and care of patients, promoting training of experts to work in hospitals and clinics, and helping to establish clinics. Publications include *Mental Hygiene,* a quarterly.

The association was formed in 1950 by a merger of the National Committee for Mental Hygiene (founded in 1909 as a result of the efforts of Clifford Beers), the National Mental Health Foundation, and the Psychiatric Foundation.

NATIONAL INSTITUTE OF MENTAL HEALTH (NIMH), one of the major operating divisions of the Health Services and Mental Health Administration in the US Department of Health, Education, and Welfare. "The Institute provides national leadership for the improvement of mental health through the conduct and support of programs for the discovery and demonstration of new knowledge, the training and development of specialized manpower, and the inauguration, demonstration, and support of services to promote and sustain mental health, prevent mental illness, and treat and rehabilitate mentally ill persons." (*US Government Organization Manual*).

The institute has conducted or supported research on such problems as alcoholism, narcotics addiction, suicide, delinquency and crime, and problems of city living. The institute has also been involved in developing community mental health centers.

The institute began operations in 1949, under plans authorized by the National Mental Health Act of 1946.

See also Community Mental Health Centers; Mental Health.

NATURE-NURTURE CONTROVERSY, the debate over the roles of heredity and environment as determiners of abilities and behavior. The argument has been particularly hot where intelligence is the topic of study; but there has also been sharp discussion of the causes of aggressive behavior, some citing instinct and others learning. *See* Aggression; Child Development; Eugenics; Heredity and Environment; Intelligence and Intelligence Testing.

NECROPHILIA, sexual intercourse with a dead human body. This is undoubtedly the rarest sexual behavior. Understandably, the necrophiliac is likely to be psychotic and in most recorded instances has murdered a woman in order to satisfy his unusual desire.

—Eugene E. Levitt, *Indiana University*
School of Medicine
Consult (13) Allen, 1962.

NEED. *See* Drive.

NERVE. *See* Nervous System.

NERVOUS BREAKDOWN, a colloquial generic term used to refer to a wide variety of lapses of functioning. It has no precise or scientific connotations. Sometimes it refers to an acute organic illness, sometimes to a psychotic episode, sometimes to neurotic reactions such as acute anxiety or lethargy and depression. Generally it is used in cases that do not reach extremes of dysfunction. Family doctors, patients, and families of patients often use the term either for lack of a more precise diagnosis or to mask what they consider to be an embarrassing condition. Studies have suggested that there are no established criteria for determining nervous breakdowns and that two persons may have something quite different in mind when they use the term.

Nervous breakdowns are often ascribed to "overwork." However, in the majority of cases it is not overwork but persistent anxiety experienced in the fact of a stressful situation that leads to the lapse in effective functioning.

—Michael Rothenberg, *The City College*
of The City University of New York

NERVOUS SYSTEM, system responsible for the control and maintenance of all bodily (somatic) and mental functions. This system is divided into two main portions: the central

nervous system (CNS) and the peripheral nervous system. The central nervous system consists of the brain and the spinal cord; the peripheral nervous system is subdivided into a *somatic* portion, concerned with sensory and motor functions, and an *autonomic* portion. The latter is further subdivided into the parasympathetic and sympathetic divisions. The autonomic nervous system is primarily responsible for the regulation of visceral functions, smooth muscles, and glandular secretion.

The nervous system is composed of two primary types of tissue, gray and white. The gray tissue consists of neurons, the individual cells responsible for the transmission of electrical impulses that carry information to and from the body. The white matter consists of fibers and is further subdivided into the axons and dendrites, which are the input and output processes, respectively, of neurons.

In the peripheral nervous system bundles of axons that arise from neurons are called *nerves.* Clusters of cell bodies are grouped into *ganglia.* In the central nervous system bundles of axons are referred to as *tracts,* and collections of neurons are referred to as *nuclei.*

Peripheral nerves carry information to or from the body. A peripheral nerve may be a sensory, or *afferent,* nerve, which conducts impulses toward the central nervous system, or it may be a motor, or *efferent,* nerve, which conducts impulses toward the periphery. Some nerves are mixed, containing both afferent and efferent fibers. The terms "afferent" and "efferent" are also relative with respect to a particular part of the nervous system under consideration. For example, fibers that carry impulses into any region are said to be afferent to that region, and fibers carrying impulses from any region are said to be efferents of that region.

Major Divisions of the Nervous System
Peripheral Nervous System. The peripheral nervous system consists of two basic portions, the somatic and the autonomic. The somatic portion is made up of afferents that arise from specific receptors. These sensory receptors are subdivided into two main types, general sensory receptors and special sensory receptors.

The general sensory receptors are located over the entire body surface and are found in the skin, muscles, tendons, joints, and bone coverings. These are responsible for sensations of hot, cold, touch, pressure, pain, and movement sensation.

The special sensory receptors are located in specialized sensory organs and in higher animals are found in the head region. These more commonly are the classical sense organs for vision, audition, gustation, olfaction, and vestibular sensations.

The efferent portion of the somatic nervous system consists of fibers that arise in the brain

NERVOUS SYSTEM

For additional text and diagrams describing the central nervous system, see BRAIN and related entries such as CEREBRAL CORTEX and HYPOTHALAMUS. The Item Guide with BRAIN also lists articles on such topics as BRAIN WAVES and BRAIN DISORDERS. Many articles not only describe structures but also explain how the nervous system regulates behavior.

Further details on the peripheral nervous system are given in AUTONOMIC NERVOUS SYSTEM and RECEPTORS. See also articles on the senses, as listed under SENSATION.

The article EFFECTORS notes somatic and autonomic effectors. Details on components of the nervous system are given in NEURON, SYNAPSE, and ALL-OR-NONE LAW.

NERVOUS SYSTEM

Nerves of the peripheral nervous system. The cranial nerves, which mainly carry sensation and control the muscles of the head and neck, are unique in not passing through the spinal cord after leaving the brain.

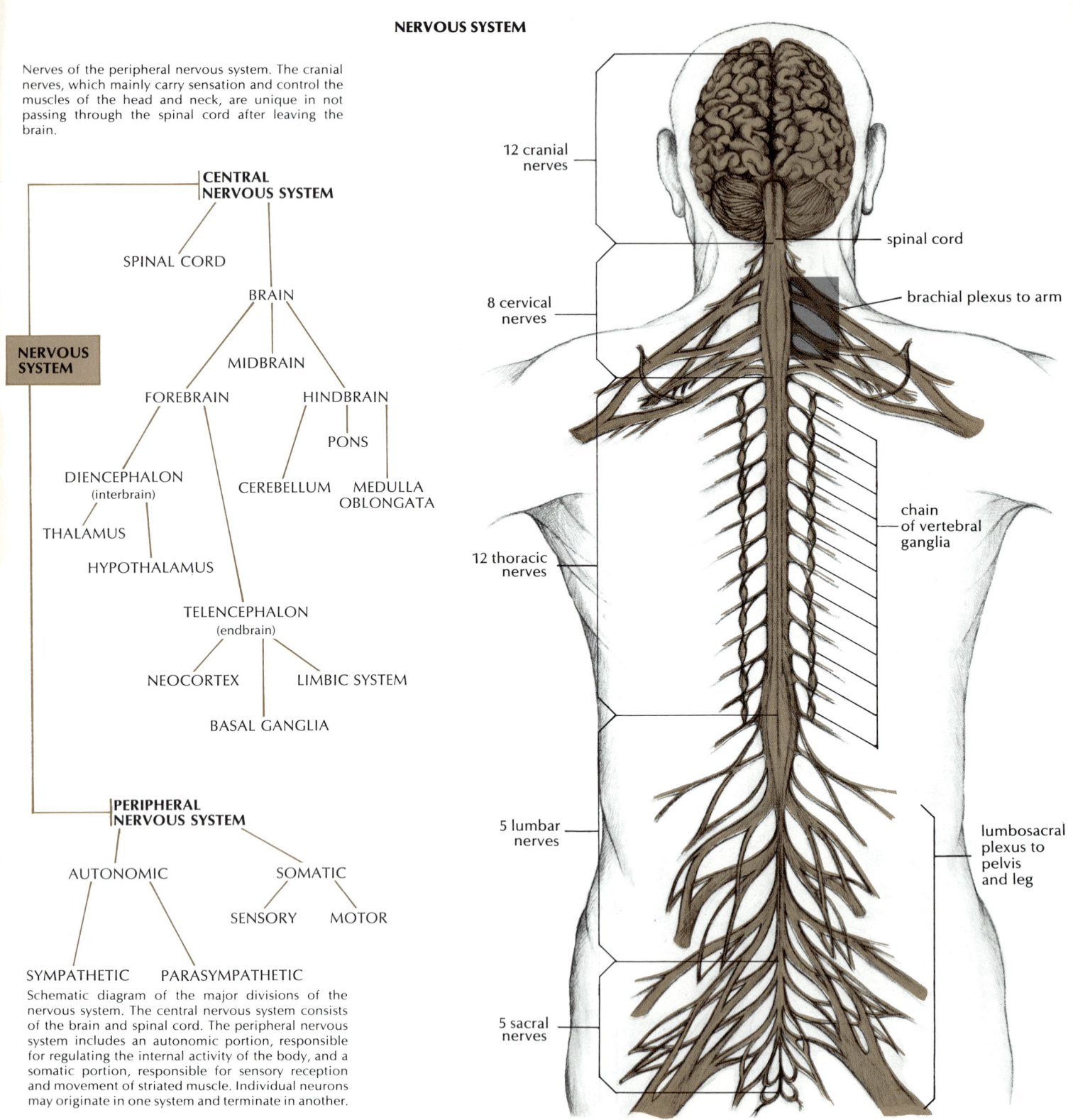

CENTRAL NERVOUS SYSTEM

SPINAL CORD

BRAIN

MIDBRAIN

FOREBRAIN   HINDBRAIN

PONS

DIENCEPHALON
(interbrain)   CEREBELLUM   MEDULLA
OBLONGATA

THALAMUS

HYPOTHALAMUS

TELENCEPHALON
(endbrain)

NEOCORTEX   LIMBIC SYSTEM

BASAL GANGLIA

NERVOUS SYSTEM

PERIPHERAL NERVOUS SYSTEM

AUTONOMIC   SOMATIC

SENSORY   MOTOR

SYMPATHETIC   PARASYMPATHETIC

Schematic diagram of the major divisions of the nervous system. The central nervous system consists of the brain and spinal cord. The peripheral nervous system includes an autonomic portion, responsible for regulating the internal activity of the body, and a somatic portion, responsible for sensory reception and movement of striated muscle. Individual neurons may originate in one system and terminate in another.

12 cranial nerves

spinal cord

8 cervical nerves

brachial plexus to arm

12 thoracic nerves

chain of vertebral ganglia

5 lumbar nerves

lumbosacral plexus to pelvis and leg

5 sacral nerves

and travel to the spinal cord. Motor nerves exit out of the spinal cord to terminate upon the motor end plates of striated muscles. These fiber tracts are responsible for direct movement of a muscle or the control of the strength, intensity, or duration of a motor response. **The autonomic nervous system** consists of the sympathetic and parasympathetic branches. Generally these two divisions work in opposition to one another. The sympathetic system is primarily responsible for emergency functions and the expenditure of large amounts of energy; the parasympathetic is important for regulatory functions, such as digestion and sleep.

Central Nervous System. This system consists of the brain and spinal cord. The brain may be subdivided into specific portions based on the embryological development of that structure.

The forebrain is the most anterior portion and consists of the telencephalon and diencephalon. These are recently evolved structures that are important in the processing of sensory and motor information.

The midbrain lies posterior to the diencephalon and consists of a series of tracts and nuclei primarily responsible for the control of eye movements and vestibular function.

The hindbrain contains the cerebellum, the pons, and the medulla oblongata, which are important for the control of visceral functions, such as blood pressure and respiration, for the control of coordination and movement, and for the maintenance of sleep and wakefulness.

The telencephalon is covered by the neocortex, the most recently evolved portion of the brain, in which much of the processing of specific sensory and motor information take place. It also contains the *basal ganglia,* a series of nuclear structures that are important in the finer control of motor functions, and the *limbic system,* a ring of structures that lie around the central core of the brain. The limbic system is believed to be largely responsible in motivational and emotional behavior.

The diencephalon contains the thalamus and hypothalamus. The thalamus is largely responsible for the processing of specific sensory information, and the hypothalamus for the regulation of the autonomic nervous system and visceral functions throughout the body.

The Spinal Cord. The other major part of the central nervous system mediates three basic functions: afferent somatic functions (sensory), efferent somatic functions (motor), and autonomic functions.

The input-output system of the spinal cord consists of thirty-one pairs of spinal nerves. Each pair is subdivided into a dorsal branch and a ventral branch. The *dorsal branch* (dorsal root and dorsal root ganglion) carries sensory or afferent information into the spinal cord, where it is relayed by the central nervous system to the thalamus and appropriate portions of the cortex. *The ventral root* carries motor information from large motor neurons located in the ventral horns of the spinal column. These motor neurons receive their input from the motor cortex. The ventral root transmits these motor impulses to specific striated muscles.

The autonomic portion of the cord consists of both sympathetic and parasympathetic divisions. *The sympathetic division* is located in the central portion of the spinal cord (the thoracic and lumbar regions), and *the parasympathetic division* is located in the lower portion of the cord (the sacral portion). Autonomic information leaves the spinal cord and enters a ganglionic chain. From there the information is relayed to the specific smooth muscles, viscera, and glands throughout the body.

—Joel F. Lubar, *University of Tennessee*
See also Autonomic Nervous System; Brain; Neurons; Synapse.

Consult (3) Gardner, 1968; Isaacson, *et al.,* 1971.

NEURASTHENIA. *See* Asthenic Reaction.

NEURON, the basic element responsible for the reception, transmission, and processing of sensory, motor, and other information of physiological and psychological importance to the individual. The adult human brain contains approximately 12 billion neurons. In the central nervous system neurons do not regenerate and hence are not replaced if they die.

A neuron typically consists of a cell body, or *soma,* and two process areas, *dendrite* and *axon.* The dendrite is the *afferent,* or input, process and may have anywhere from one to several thousand branches. The axon is the *efferent,* or output, branch and consists of one main trunk, which may have collateral branches and many terminations. The terminations of the axon consist of the end button, which is believed to contain the biochemical constituents for the synthesis of neurohumors. The neurohumors are stored in the synaptic vesicles that are released from the end button upon the arrival of an action potential. These neurohumors cause polarization (excitatory or inhibitory) of postsynaptic cells. Thus, the neurohumor acts as a transmitter of information from one neuron to another.

—Joel F. Lubar, *University of Tennessee*
See also Synapse.

NEUROSCIENCE. *See* Physiological Psychology.

NEUROSIS, or neurotic disorder. *See* Neurotic Personality; Psychoneurotic Disorders.

NEUROTIC DEPRESSIVE REACTION. *See* Depressive Reaction.

NEURON

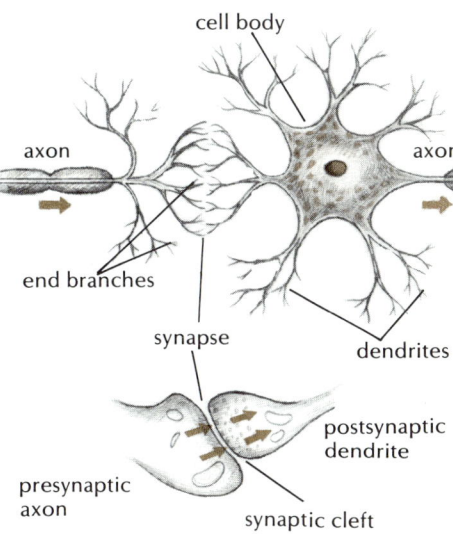

The upper drawing shows the cell body, axon, and dendrites of a typical neuron. Below it is shown the synapse, the junction between the axon of one neuron and the dendrite of another.

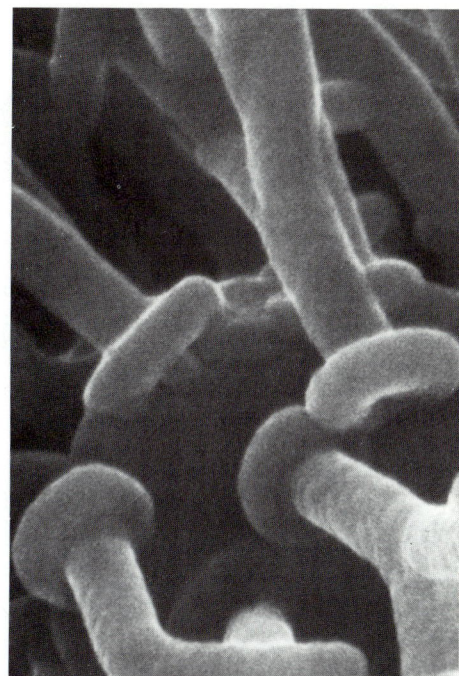

Photo made with the scanning electron microscope shows the ends of many axons, called synaptic knobs (a millionth of a millimeter in diameter), synapsing on a cell body.

Social psychologist Theodore Newcomb gave special study to impact of the group on individual attitudes.

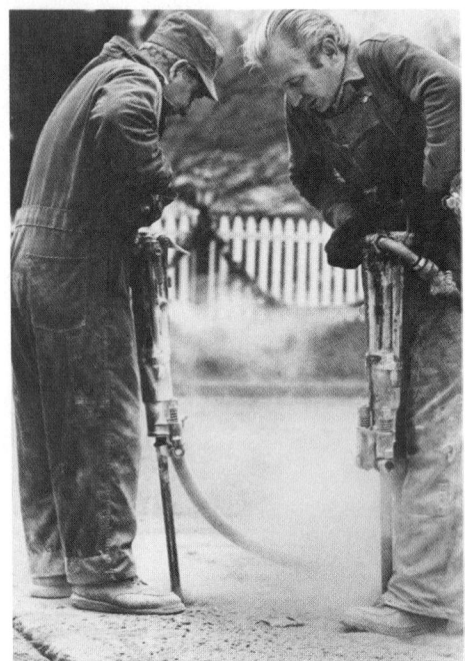

Workers with jackhammers probably suffer permanent hearing loss.

NEUROTIC PERSONALITY. The term "neurotic" (or "psychoneurotic") is a generic one and covers a wide variety of emotional disabilities. In all cases, some disruption of the effective functioning of the individual is accompanied by varying degrees of anxiety. The most comprehensive theory of the neurotic personality is provided by psychoanalysis, which states that neurosis is an expression of unresolved developmental conflicts in the form of tension and impaired functioning. This necessitates the repression of the unresolved conflict and the attendant loss of energy to deal with day-to-day needs.

Every individual, to some extent, is the victim of childhood conflicts and desires, but the neurotic differs from the normal person in several important respects. His conflicts are repressed, whereas the normal's are more conscious. His energy level is seriously depleted. He has far greater difficulty in dealing with the everyday frustrations of his life. He is troubled by chronic feelings of guilt; the normal is better able to accept himself
—Michael Rothenberg, *The City College of The City University of New York*
See also Personality Disorders; Psychoneurotic Disorders.

NEWCOMB, THEODORE, M. (1903–), American psychologist. Born in Rock Creek, Ohio, he took his Ph.D. at Columbia (1929) and was professor of sociology and psychology at the University of Michigan after 1946.

Newcomb's area of research has been personality, attitude change, and, in particular, the effect of the group on attitude. In 1952 (with Festinger and Pepitone) he introduced the term "deindividuation," the social process by which an individual gives up the usual standards of rational behavior within a group (as in lynch mobs or crowds).

Newcomb's books include *Experimental Social Psychology* (with Murphy and Murphy) 1937; *Personality and Social Change,* 1943; *Social Psychology,* 1950; *The Acquaintance Process,* 1961; *Persistence and Change,* 1967; *The Impact of College on Students,* 1969 (with Feldman).
—Nina Adams, *Yale University*

NIGHT HOSPITAL. In this program, patients who need psychiatric care go out to work during the day and then return to the hospital to get treatment and spend the night. This plan may be used with patients who are recovering after full-time hospitalization; they must get used to working and living out of the hospital but still need support. The night program is one of several alternatives to the traditional practice of shutting patients up in mental hospitals.
See also Day Hospital.

NIGHTMARE, a dream marked by feelings of terror so strong that the sleeper wakes up at the time of the dream. Nightmares are not typical dreams because they cause people to wake up spontaneously. People can sleep through longer sequences of less stressful dreams.

One theory explains nightmares as leftovers from emotion-arousing experiences, such as severe illnesses, car wrecks, or combat. Freud considered nightmares as the breaking out of repressed sexual or aggressive impulses.
Consult (3) Foulkes, 1966.

NOISE. When a sound is composed of different tones varying randomly in frequency, amplitude, and phase, it is distinguished from tones that have a clear pitch and is experienced as noise. A "pure" noise of totally random vibrations can be produced by amplifying the random emissions of electrons in a vacuum tube or by the hissing of a steam radiator.

Pure noise is also called *white noise* because like white light, it contains a whole range of frequencies. Most noise is not pure but has tonal components (for example, the tonal difference between the noise of hammering and the noise of dishwashing). White noise is often used in psychology experiments to mask the presence of random sounds that would distract the subject. Since background noise is always present, its effect upon intelligibility of speech depends upon the intensity of the noise compared with the intensity of the speech—the *speech/noise ratio.*

Continual noise, which can cause temporary and permanent shifts in the threshold of hearing, is considered a serious occupational health problem. If a noise is so high that conversation is impossible (in cabs of some trucks, on some assembly lines, in the area around pneumatic drills) the people who are subjected to it for eight hours a day, five days a week, will probably sustain a permanent, noise-induced hearing loss. The common myth that people learn to tolerate a noisy work atmosphere is probably a description of their increasing deafness. Continuous noise also can resonate the bones of the head and face, causing pain, swelling, and headaches. Low-frequency intense tones can affect circulation and breathing by resonating the heart and lungs. Noise also has significant effects on violence, patience, efficiency, and fatigue, though these are difficult to measure. Studies have shown that efficiency goes up and absenteeism goes down when noise is reduced in a workplace.
—Nina Adams, *Yale University*
Consult (4) Broadbent and Little, 1960; Jerison, 1959.

NONDIRECTIVE THERAPY. *See* Client-Centered Therapy.

NONSENSE FIGURE, a figure that does not closely resemble any familiar thing and has no conventional meaning. Nonsense figures are often used in experiments on learning, memory, and perception. In experiments, subjects make an effort to give meaning to nonsense figures, they note symmetry, repetitions, draw similarities to things, and then note differences (for example, the figure shown here is like a triangle with two chunks missing).

NONSENSE SYLLABLES, a letter combination (consonant-vowel-consonant, for example, *juk, nax, wib*) first used by Hermann Ebbinghaus in experiments on memorization and retention. These syllables are used because actual words have associations that could affect the rate of learning and forgetting.

See also Ebbinghaus, Hermann; Serial Learning.

NONVERBAL COMMUNICATION. *See* Body Language; Message.

NOREPINEPHRINE (NE), or noradrenalin, a substance that acts as a neurotransmitter. *See* Autonomic Nervous System; Drugs and Behavior.

NORM, in statistics, an indication of the common or average performance of a given group. In educational and psychological measurement, norms are used to interpret test results. For example, the achievement test scores of a large number of students might be compiled and from the central range of scores norms for age and grade groups could be established. Then any individual's score can be evaluated in terms of how far above or below the norm it falls.

See also Frequency Distribution; Normal.

NORM, SOCIAL. *See* Conformity.

NORMAL. Normality is a concept that is hard to define but has great influence in psychology, medicine, law, and other fields. Statistically, the normal can be defined as the average performance of a group. In measurement, the normal or norm is established by finding the central group of a large number of scores. On IQ tests, scores ranging around 100 are called normal, and scores well above or below this range can be considered abnormal. In this sense a genius with an IQ of 150 and a retarded child with an IQ of 50 are equally abnormal—away from the middle range.

The idea of a norm is also used in social psychology. Groups tend to put pressure on their members to conform to standards of behavior.

In terms of IQ or any other measure, there are no sharp cut-off points between normal and abnormal. These labels refer to ranges of scores or other ways of rating people. In custom and in law the line between normal (accepted or tolerated) and abnormal (penalized) may be particularly wavy—for example, in regard to sexual behavior.

Yet popularly and professionally something loosely called normal is set against a concept of the abnormal. Each term gets meaning by contrast with the other, and abnormal is most often used to label inferior ability or adjustment or some form of sickness or disorder. There are many practical reasons for having a field of abnormal psychology, concerned with mental deficiency, behavior problems, and mental illness. Clinical psychologists and psychiatrists have to give attention to those who are diagnosed as disturbed or ill, having left the normal range of behavior.

Currently, social scientists are trying to find more flexible and insightful criteria for normality and illness. At the same time, they are trying more than in the past to help all people live healthfully rather than waiting to give aid to the casualties. Behavioral ecologists and community psychologists are among those pushing in this direction.

See also Abnormal Psychology; Behavioral Ecology; Mental Health; Norm; Psychology and the Law.

NORMAL DISTRIBUTION. *See* Frequency Distribution.

NOSOLOGY, the classification of disorders; also the branch of medicine that deals with distinguishing and naming diseases.

In the nineteenth century, psychiatrists gave a great deal of attention to naming mental disorders and compiling what then seemed neat and definitive lists of symptoms. Emil Kraepelin was a leader in this effort. Current students of human problems realize that symptoms and causes can be so complex and varied that no system can pigeonhole all disorders, and diagnosticians are urged to look widely and deeply before they put a label on a syndrome. Nevertheless, classifications are needed as a guide to diagnosis, a means of reporting a patient's condition, and an aid in discussing cases and patterns of illness.

Examples of classification in this encyclopedia can be found in the lists of psychotic, psychoneurotic, and personality disorders, and brain disorders. *See* the Subject Map for Abnormal and Clinical Psychology.

Consult (13) American Psychiatric Association, 1968.

NULL HYPOTHESIS. *See* Experimental Design.

NYMPHOMANIA, an emotional disorder of

NONSENSE FIGURE

DECIBEL SCALE OF NOISES

Decibels		
150 120 110 100	Deafening	Jet engine at takeoff Rock music at discotheque Nearby riveter Loud power mower
90 80	Very loud	Police whistle Factory noise
70 60	Loud	Average radio Conversation
50 40	Moderate	Large office Classroom, church
30 20	Faint	Hospital, music room Recording studio
10 0	Very faint	Rustle of leaves Threshold of human hearing

women whose major symptom is an extremely high frequency of sexual acts, usually involving many partners, without regard for the desirability or other personal characteristics of the partners or for the dictates of reality.

True nymphomania seems to be characterized by an almost uncontrollable sex drive that is very easily and very frequently aroused and that must be fulfilled no matter what the circumstances or the consequences. The true nymphomaniac is always ready for further sexual exploits, regardless of the amount of sexual gratification that she has experienced immediately previously.

The term has been incorrectly applied to women who are simply gifted with lusty sexual appetites or active sexually for any reason, to prostitutes, and to those whose resistance to seduction is weak because of personality characteristics.

True nymphomania appears as a secondary symptom of psychosis and is rarely encountered outside of the mental hospital. Albert Ellis, for example, states that he had never had a true nymphomaniac as a patient in his many years of extensive treatment of sexual disorders.

Nymphomania has scant scientific value as a diagnostic label. Currently, the term is rarely used in psychiatry, psychology, medicine, or the behavioral sciences, though it is still popular in fiction and is used as an epithet.
—Eugene E. Levitt, *Indiana University School of Medicine*
Consult (13) Ellis and Sagarin, 1965; Levitt, 1973.

The obsessive-compulsive Captain Queeg, as portrayed by Humphrey Bogart in *The Caine Mutiny*, sought to control his stress by constantly rolling steel ball bearings in his hand.

OBESITY. Being seriously overweight can be a medical problem caused by a low level of metabolism. The majority of cases of obesity, however, fall in the province of psychology and psychiatry because they are psychophysiological or psychosomatic problems. The fat person may have a constitutional predisposition to put on weight. In addition, he overeats because he has learned to or because he wants a refuge from emotional problems.

A child can be taught to eat too much by a mother who feels that "food is love" and that refusing what she has cooked is rejecting her. A shy or awkward child may find that being fat is a defense against being expected to succeed in sports and social events. An insecure child or adult may feel safer inside a layer of fat. Obesity, however, is likely to lead to further social failure and to ridicule, and the fat person then responds to this anxiety by more compulsive eating. Treatment of obesity calls for psychotherapy directed at the whole personality pattern, in addition to diet control and exercise.

OBSESSION, an idea or preoccupation that is unwanted but hard to get rid of. Persistent

thoughts can bother a normal person, as when someone complains "I can't get that song out of my mind." In a time of stress, a person may be temporarily plagued by thoughts of accident, illness, or death.

Obsessive ideas and impulses can also reach an excessive degree, as in the morbid fears called phobias or in compulsive behavior. In such cases, the obsession is more irrational and more persistent and tends to take over an individual's behavior.
See also Obsessive-Compulsive Reaction; Phobia.

OBSESSIVE-COMPULSIVE REACTION, a neurotic disorder in which the anxiety stemming from unconscious conflicts is controlled by means of persistent thoughts and repetitive behavior. While these patterns seem irrational even to the person suffering from them, the obsessive-compulsive individual is apparently unable to control them. He is often beset by a persistent thought that causes him great anxiety. In many cases this takes the form of a fear of death, either for himself or for a member of his family. In other instances he is driven to perform some ritualistic act, such as repeated washing of the hands.

In some cases the obsessive thoughts and compulsive acts are related. The individual performs the act in order to alleviate the anxiety provoked by the thought. Thus someone obsessed by the fear of sickness or death through infection will compulsively wash and even sterilize every object with which he comes in contact.

The thoughts and behaviors that characterize an obsessive-compulsive reaction mask some other more basic conflict. If permitted to gain consciousness, this would cause intolerable stress to the individual.
—Michael Rothenberg, *The City College of The City University of New York*
See also Compulsive Personality.

OCCUPATIONAL THERAPY, treating patients with mental disorders by having them work at such activities as weaving, needlework, sketching, painting, modeling with clay, metalworking, or gardening. Sometimes patients practice a vocational skill, such as typing, printing, or operating a business machine.

If the occupation is to be treatment, not just a way to keep patients busy, a program should be planned to fit the needs of each individual. Some hospitals employ specialists who have taken a four-year college course in occupational therapy followed by nine months of clinical experience. A therapist who has completed this training can use the initials OTR after his or her name.

OEDIPUS COMPLEX. Following the oral and the anal, the third of the psychosexual stages in

Sigmund Freud's psychoanalytic theory of personality development is the phallic stage. In this period, roughly from three to six years of age, the child's erotic concerns focus on pleasurable genital sensations and masturbation, with active curiosity and fantasy regarding the origins and significance of sexual differences.

The critical development in this period is the Oedipus complex, which Freud considered one of his fundamental discoveries. It is named after the legendary king of Thebes who was fated unknowingly to kill his father and marry his mother. Based on his psychoanalytic findings, Freud held that the myth expressed a universal unconscious incestuous fantasy in which the son falls in love with and sexually desires his mother and wishes his father's death. Similarly, the daughter sexually desires her father and hates her mother. (The term "Electra complex" is sometimes used for incestuous feelings in girls.)

Freud held that the boy imagines his jealous father will remove his genitals, the source of his lustful feelings. This castration anxiety induces repression of these desires, bringing about an identification of the boy with his father, whereby he gains some vicarious satisfaction. This process is also critical in consolidating the superego as the internalized representative of the parents.

As for the girl, she blames her mother for her lack of a penis and transfers her love to the father, who has the valued organ she desires to possess. However, her love for her father and other males is mixed with penis envy.

Freud felt that unresolved Oedipal conflicts were critical in the psychodynamics of neurosis and that the Oedipus complex was basic to understanding male and female psychology. While most later writers credit Freud with monumental discoveries in revealing the dynamics of family life and showing its tremendous significance in personality development, many criticize various features of his formulation. It now seems established that gender identification begins at an earlier period. Also, many argue that Freud's views on the psychology of women were biased by the prevalent attitudes of his time regarding masculine superiority.

—Alden E. Wessman, *The City College of The City University of New York*
See also Sexuality.
Consult (13) de Beauvoir, 1957; Freud, 1920; Freud, 1935; Mullahy, 1948.

OLD AGE. *See* Aging.

OLDS, JAMES (1922–), American physiological psychologist, born in Chicago. He is professor of psychology at the University of Michigan.

In 1953, while doing brain-stimulation research, Olds discovered that stimulation of certain areas of the brain can reward or motivate animals in learning situations. This discovery led to an enormous research effort. Olds studied the anatomical loci of these reward areas and found some aversive spots as well. He studied the parameters of stimulation and showed that extremely intense stimulation can be aversive. He showed that rats will press a bar to turn on stimulation, sometimes for hours, and called this "self-stimulation." He compared the strength of this central stimulation with the food, water, and sexual drives and found that, depending upon placement, the central stimulation was sometimes more effective. He also found interactions between naturally elicited drives and central stimulation. His interests include a neural theory of learning.

—Nina Adams, *Yale University*

OLFACTION. *See* Smell.

OLIGOPHRENIA, "of feeble intellect." *See* Mental Retardation.

ONANISM, the practice of contraception by withdrawal of the penis from the vagina just prior to ejaculation. The term is sometimes confused with masturbation. Individual instances of onanism are technically known as *coitus interruptus*. It is performed occasionally by many couples but is seldom used as a regular contraceptive procedure. Its failure rate when used regularly has been estimated to range from l5 to 30 percent, much inferior to most mechanical or chemical methods of contraception. There is no evidence that the regular use of coitus interruptus is psychologically or physically harmful.

—Eugene E. Levitt, *Indiana University School of Medicine*
Consult (13) Neubardt, 1967.

ONLY CHILD. *See* Family Size.

OPERANT CONDITIONING, also called instrumental conditioning, a basic learning process in which a behavior that is followed by a positive consequence will increase in probability. For example, if a dog is rewarded with a piece of meat when it sits up and begs, it will be likely to exhibit that behavior more often. Similarly, if a behavior is followed by a negative consequence, its frequency or probability will decrease. If you receive a shock while trying to repair your own television set, you may prefer to call the repairman in the future. In operant conditioning the nature of behavior is determined by its consequences, whether positive or negative.

Behaviors can be acquired, maintained, or eliminated through such conditioning.

Behavior Acquisition. New behaviors can be learned through reinforcement, shaping, or chaining.

James Olds' discovery that stimulation of the brain can be rewarding, or aversive, depending on area and intensity, opened new doors in learning research.

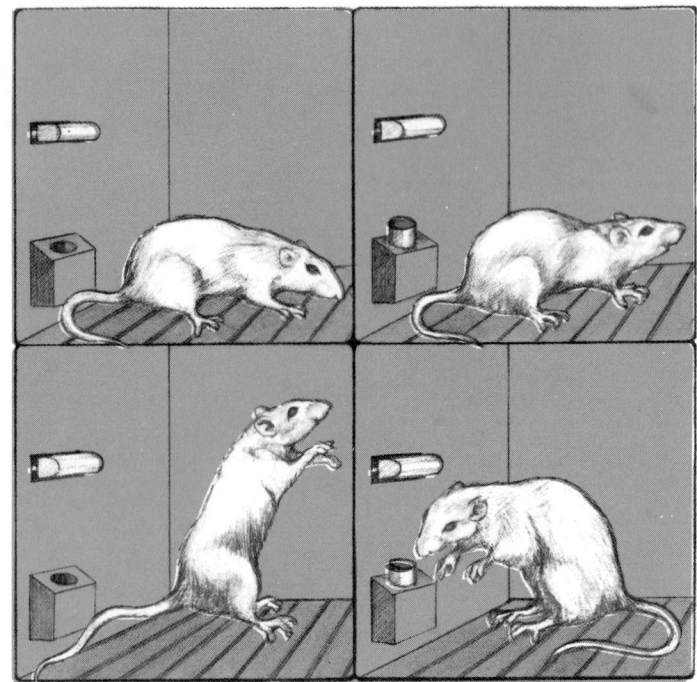

Because behavior that is reinforced tends to be repeated, the skillful trainer can modify an animal's behavior to his own ends. The goal here is to teach a rat to push a cart to the base of a tower, climb the tower, then ascend a ramp to receive its reward.

Reinforcement. The thirsty rat is taught to associate a loud click with the delivery of water from a dispenser. Eventually the click itself is sufficient to get the rat to approach the dispenser; it is a conditioned reinforcer.

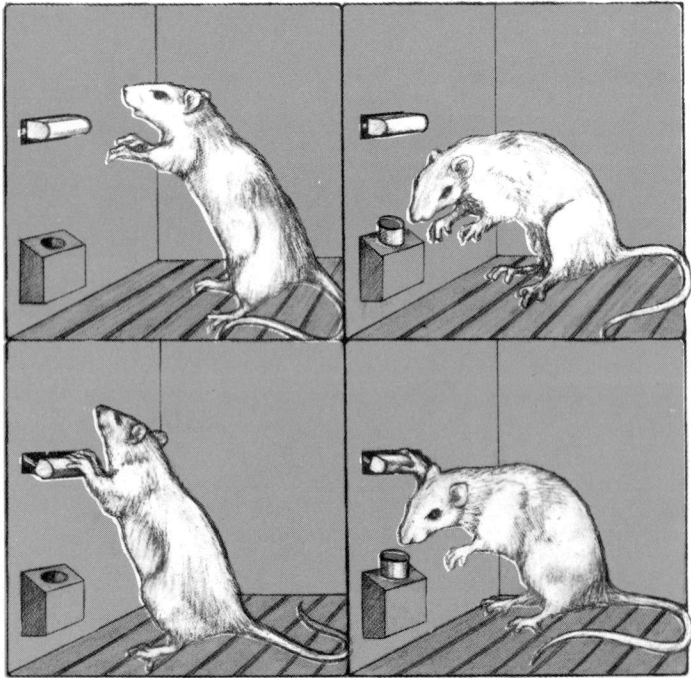

Shaping. Reinforcement is used to strengthen some of the animal's natural behaviors in order to teach him to press a bar. By selectively reinforcing closer and closer approximations to the desired activity—rising on its hind legs, bending forward, and so on—we can shape a bar press.

Chaining. After shaping each of the components of the routine, each component is linked with others in longer and longer sequences—the completion of each link in the chain serving as the cue for the next step.

Reinforcement is a consequence that increases the probability of the preceding response: either the presentation of something positive, such as food, money, or praise, or the removal of something negative, such as pain, ridicule, or being ignored. Reinforcing consequences, whether positive or negative, will increase the probability of new behavior. The attention and delight with which the parents respond to their baby's first few smiles increase the likelihood of future smiles. Picking up the baby when he stops crying and ignoring him while he cries will increase the likelihood of quiet behavior.

Once a new response has occurred, it is a fairly simple matter to reinforce it so it will be strengthened. In the case of many complex behaviors, however, the response rarely occurs so that it can be reinforced. In these cases either shaping or chaining can be used to bring about the desired response.

If you are teaching a small child to say "Daddy," you may start the *shaping* procedure by reinforcing any sound close to "da." You then shape the response by reinforcing closer and closer approximations to the final response such as "da da" and finally "Daddy." Each successive step involves utilizing operant conditioning principles.

Chaining is similar to shaping in that it involves reinforcing components of the final response. In this case, however, each component is a complete behavior, and the final response involves linking all of these separate behaviors together, as in learning to drive a car. You may know how to turn the ignition key, shift the gears, and steer, but these responses and many others must be performed in sequence before you can drive. By reinforcing longer and longer sequences, extremely complex behaviors can be acquired through operant conditioning.

Behavior Maintenance. Once new behavior has been learned, it can also be maintained through operant conditioning. During learning one typically reinforces the response every time it occurs. After the response has been learned, the reinforcement can be thinned out so that it occurs on a partial schedule. At first you can reinforce every second response, then every fifth, then every tenth response, and so on. Partial reinforcement is the kind typically encountered in everyday life, and it serves to produce stable responses.

Behavior can also be maintained by internalized reinforcement. In these cases, the individual rewards himself. For example, you may help someone in distress because it makes you feel good.

Through the process of socialization, certain behaviors are reinforced by parents and peers so that the individual gradually internalizes these reinforcers; that is, he learns that certain behaviors are desirable and receives internal satisfaction by engaging in these behaviors. Academic success often functions in this way. Frequently it is necessary to engage in long periods of class attendance, studying, and exam taking before one ever receives a tangible reward, such as a good grade or a diploma. For some individuals education is so valued that "knowledge is its own reward," and they maintain steady academic behavior because of strong personal internal rewards.

All behaviors are continually being maintained by subtle positive and negative controls. Skill in carpentry, for example, may be maintained because the tools do what the individual wants them to do (a case of positive control). Appropriate social behaviors are constantly being maintained on an irregular basis by peers, teachers, and parents. Negative control is frequent: you keep your room clean to avoid a disgruntled mother or roommate; you drive at the speed limit to avoid a traffic ticket; or you complete an assignment to avoid an angry teacher. Although we are not always aware of the controls that operate on operant conditioning principles, they occur continually and determine a great deal of our behavior.

Behavior Elimination. Operant conditioning also works to eliminate behaviors. If all reinforcement for a response is eliminated, that behavior will eventually disappear. This process is called *extinction*. If you studied hard for every exam and never passed, you would soon stop studying. If you called a girl several times for a date and she always refused, you would soon stop calling. All behavior requires at least some reinforcement, however minimal, to be maintained.

Extinction is frequently used to eliminate problem behaviors in home and institutional environments. Severe tantrum behaviors can be reduced by ignoring them, as can schizophrenic speech patterns and many other undesirable behaviors.

While extinction can be an effective tool for eliminating behavior, it is frequently a very slow process. In many cases a quicker remedy is needed. For example, some children engage in severe self-destructive behavior, such as head banging. In such cases, *punishment* can be used to eliminate the behavior. Electric shock applied to the back has been used with great success with children. A few, very brief intense shocks whenever the child bangs his head are sufficient to eliminate the behavior and, in many cases, save the child's life. Similar punishments have been used to treat homosexuality, alcoholism, and drug addiction.

Some behaviors are appropriate in certain situations but inappropriate in others. These inappropriate behaviors can be eliminated through *discrimination* training. Aggressive behavior is rewarded in many contact sports but punished at school or in the home;

both of these procedures make use of operant conditioning.

The term "conditioning" is also applied to another form of learning, *classical* or *Pavlovian* conditioning.

Glossary

Chaining— is the technique of reinforcing longer and more complex sequences of behavior to obtain a highly complex end behavior.

Discrimination—training in which a response is consistently rewarded in some situations and punished in others.

Extinction—the elimination of behavior through the removal of all reinforcement for that behavior.

Internalized reinforcement—reinforcement that comes from within the individual and not from an external source.

Partial reinforcement—reinforcement that occurs less than 100 percent of the time. It produces very resilient and stable behavior.

Punishment—any event that decreases the probability of a preceding event. It can consist of the presentation of an aversive event, such as shock, or the removal of a positive event, such as attention.

Reinforcement—any event that increases the probability of a preceding event. In the case of positive reinforcement a positive event such as food is presented, whereas in the case of negative reinforcement a negative event such as pain is removed.

Shaping—the technique of reinforcing successive approximations to a final behavior goal.

—Brenda B. Bankart and C. Peter Bankart, *Wabash College*

See also Behavior Therapy; Biofeedback; Conditioning; Learning Theory; Maze; Pavlovian Conditioning; Programmed Learning; Puzzle Box; Reinforcement; Skinner Box.

Consult (1) Hilgard, *et al.*, 1971; (6) Kimble, 1961.

OPERATIONAL ANALYSIS, a scientific approach that grew out of the viewpoint known as operationalism. This view maintains that the concepts of science become meaningful only in terms of the methods of investigation used to obtain those concepts and that it is therefore impossible to separate scientific definitions from the methods used to measure and obtain them.

The physicist largely responsible for the development of operationalism in the United States, P. W. Bridgeman, maintained that to ask, "What is gravity?" is a meaningless question. Gravity can only be defined by the operations used to measure it. Hence gravity is a process equal to a constant multiplied by the product of two interacting masses divided by the square of the distance separating them. In this view of science, one must not ask any question about the "real" nature of gravity, or why do two objects mutually attract one another, or where the gravitational force or field comes from. Operationalism has become a dominant method for defining concepts in many fields, including psychology. It leads to rigorous scientific analysis, but, because of its insistence that many questions cannot be asked, it also results in a certain narrowness of vision.

For psychologists, an operational analysis of emotionality would depend simply on measurements of the different responses that occur in the organism while specific stimuli are applied to it. These responses, to which such human labels as hate, fear, love, and anger are attached, would be described by the operationalist simply as approach, avoidance, attack, defensiveness, and similar terms. This approach makes no attempt to handle the subjective aspects of emotion, focusing only on its objective measurement.

Operationalism may be equally well applied in clinical psychology by defining such abnormal states as schizophrenia or manic-depressive psychosis solely in terms of specific tests that are used to measure them. The adage "intelligence is what intelligence tests measure" is the keystone of an operational approach to understanding the basis for intelligence. The limitations of such a definition are obvious.

—Joel F. Lubar, *University of Tennessee*

OPIATE NARCOTICS, codeine, opium, morphine, heroin, and synthetic drugs such as Demerol. *See* Drugs and Behavior.

OPINION. *See* Attitude and Attitude Change.

ORAL CHARACTER. Sigmund Freud's psychoanalytic theory of personality development postulates a series of psychosexual stages during childhood defined in terms of the dominance of certain erogenous zones of the body. In the first, or oral, stage, which persists into the second year of life, the mouth and eating are held to be the principal source and activity of pleasure or displeasure. The initial mode of pleasure is concretely expressed in sucking and swallowing and, more figuratively, in incorporating or *introjecting*—that is, symbolically making objects part of oneself. Displeasure or rejection is expressed by spitting out or, more figuratively, in *projecting*. Later, when the teeth erupt, the mouth is used for biting and chewing.

According to Freud and Karl Abraham, these two modes of oral activity, incorporation of food and biting, are basic to the psychodynamics of infancy and the prototypes from which many later character traits develop. Too much or too little gratification in this stage may produce an *oral character* that remains fixated in these activities and modes of relating to objects. For example, an infant overgratified in the incorporative stage may in later life be overly dependent and sanguinely optimistic that all his needs will be met. On the other hand, lack of early gratification may produce a pessimistic and distrustful individual. From frustration in the late oral, or biting, stage various ambivalent adult attitudes—for example, hostile-friendly or submissive-aggressive, are held to result.

Later psychoanalytic theorists, notably Erik Erikson, have expanded the psychodynamic formulation of the developments occurring in this period.

—Alden E. Wessman, *The City College of The City University of New York*
See also Anal Character; Oedipus Complex.

Consult (13) Erikson, 1959; Fenichel, 1945.

ORAL STAGE. *See* Oral Character.

ORGANIC BRAIN DISORDER. *See* Brain Disorders.

ORGANIC DISORDER, one that is attributed to observable damage to organs or tissues. For example, psychotic behavior related to head injury or to brain damage by poisoning or infection comes under the classification of *organic psychoses.* These are distinguished from *functional psychoses,* in which the cause is believed to be psychological. *See* Brain Disorders; Functional Disorders; Psychotic Disorders.

ORGANIC PSYCHOSIS. *See* Brain Disorders; Organic Disorder; Psychotic Disorders.

ORGANIC SENSES. *See* Interoceptive Senses.

ORGANISMIC THEORY. Rejecting the mind-body dualism often applied to man, this approach conceives of the human individual as a psychobiological entity endowed with certain capacities. Hence it holds that psychology should be a behavioristic or holistic study of man coming to terms with his environment.

Although the organism always acts as a whole, it cannot actualize all its potentials at the same time. The environment and the tendency for the organism to achieve optimal performance in that environment determine which potentials will be actualized. When a holistic method is adopted to analyze the relationships between man and environment, the organism may be examined only by proceeding from the whole to the parts, not from the parts to the whole. The organismic approach is thus placed in a dilemma: it insists that the organism must be perceived in its behavioral "wholeness," yet it must resort to isolated observations in order to secure more specific information.

—A. Ronald Seifert, *University of Tennessee*

ORIENTING RESPONSE, also called orienting reflex, orientation reflex, or orienting reaction. *See* Arousal; Attention.

ORTHOPSYCHIATRY, multidisciplinary approach to mental health, stressing prevention or early treatment of disorders. The American Orthopsychiatric Association includes psychiatrists, pediatricians, clinical psychologists, sociologists, social workers, nurses, and educators. The association publishes the *American Journal of Orthopsychiatry.*

OSGOOD, CHARLES (1916–   ), American psychologist. Born in Somerville, Mass., he received his Ph.D. from Yale (1945) and is currently professor of communications and psychology at the University of Illinois.

Osgood's best-known work is the use of the semantic-differential technique, developed in 1967. Using three basic dimensions—evaluation, potency, and activity—the connotative meaning of any work can be established, for English and other languages. The semantic differential can be used to distinguish different personality types clinically. Osgood's earlier work concerned "congruity theory"—the shifting of attitudes in order to resolve incongruity between action and idea. Osgood's major writings include *Method and Theory in Experimental Psychology,* 1953; *The Measurement of Meaning* (coauthor), 1957; *An Alternative to War or Surrender,* 1962; and *Semantic Differential Technique* (editor, with Snider), 1969.

—Nina Adams, *Yale University*
See also Semantic Differential.

OTIS, ARTHUR SINTON (1886–1963), American psychologist. Born in Denver, he received his Ph.D. at Stanford. He developed one of the first group intelligence tests and was editor of tests and mathematics for the World Book Company, Yonkers, N.Y., for twenty-five years.

When the United States entered World War I, five psychologists were selected to design a test that would sift out the mentally unfit from men called for military service and classify draftees by levels of ability. Lewis M. Terman was on the committee. Because administration of the Stanford-Binet tests to thousands of individuals was impractical, a group test was needed. Otis, one of Terman's graduate students, had developed a group IQ test as his doctoral dissertation and was therefore invited to join the committee. His group test served as a basis for the Army Alpha and

Charles Osgood's work in psychology and communications suggested that clinical distinction of personality types can be based on semantic indices.

Beta that were used to classify the almost 2 million drafted men.

Otis went on to develop the *Otis Self Administering Test of Mental Ability* and the *Otis Quick Scoring Mental Ability Test.* These tests have been widely used by the military and in American schools.

OUTGROUP. *See* Prejudice.

OVERACHIEVER, a categorical term that refers to the student whose scholastic achievement exceeds the expected level of performance for individuals having comparable intellectual abilities. Thus, his academic proficiency seemingly exceeds his measured intellectual abilities when compared to the achievement level of individuals with similar intelligence.

The term is considered by some to be a statistical "artifact," resulting primarily from the imperfections in our assessment techniques. Others suggest that its use is incongruous with the finite limits implied by the very concept of "abilities."

—Frank T. Vitro, *University of Maine*
See also Underachiever.

OVERCROWDING. High population density is one of the most devastating stressors known in lower animals and man. One of the principal outcomes of overcrowding is a very high incidence of physical aggression, which along with the possibilities for disease can completely destroy a community.

One researcher, J. B. Calhoun, has studied the effects of overcrowding on the behavior of albino rats. The rats lacked neither food nor water, but as the pressure of population increased, Calhoun observed increasingly bizarre behaviors, such as sexual abnormalities—hypersexuality, homosexuality, and bisexuality—cannibalism, extremes of aggressiveness and passivity, a breakdown in nest building, and failure of any of the offspring to survive to maturity. He termed this effect *behavioral sink* to convey the idea that as population pressure increased, the ability of the organisms to function normally increasingly broke down and ultimately reached the point of complete behavioral degradation. [*Consult* (10) Calhoun, 1962.]

Overcrowding is known to affect the physiological development of organisms. Its greatest effect is seen in the loss of function of the adrenal glands, which are responsible for producing hormones that enable the animal to cope with stress. In addition, overcrowding affects body size, resistance to infection, and the size and function of the reproductive organs.

—Brenda B. Bankart and C. Peter Bankart, *Wabash College*
See also Stress.
Consult (10) Beach, 1948.

OVERDEPENDENCE. *See* Overprotection.

OVEREATING. Destruction of a control center in the hypothalamus can produce *hyperphagia,* greatly increased appetite and extreme intake of food. Overeating can also be caused by a metabolic problem resulting from underactivity of the thyroid gland. The great majority of cases of obesity, however, are caused by psychological problems. *See* Brain; Obesity.

OVERPROTECTION. Overanxious and exaggerated care for a child can cause him to develop personality problems. Either parent or both can be overprotective, but the mother more usually takes the role and the problem is often called "momism."

Mothers can overprotect in many ways—for example, feeding, bathing, and dressing a child long after he can take care of these routines himself; escorting him to school and back; keeping him away from "rough" boys and "dangerous" games; fussing about his health and giving lavish care when he is ill; indulging him with food, presents, and privileges.

The overprotected child is emotionally handicapped because he has not been "psychologically weaned," has not learned to be independent. He is likely to be afraid of people outside his home. He may be so anxious about sickness that he develops hypochondria—at the same time, finding ill health a means of getting attention. Stories of overdependence can be found in many case histories of neurotic disorder. Some alcoholics, for example, have been so protected that they do not know how to function without props. Mother may have given them a sense of self-importance during childhood, but this breaks down if mom is not there to rebuild it.
Consult (13) Coleman, 1964.

PAIN, a very specific sensation that at low levels may be called stinging, burning, or tingling and at high levels is unpleasant and causes withdrawal.

Pain can be aroused by severe mechanical, thermal, chemical, or electrical stimulation. All of these probably cause release of some chemical, producing tissue damage. The sensation warns the organism that its body is being injured. The pain stimulus is received by naked nerve endings in the skin and transmitted by specific nerve pathways to the brain. In patients with severe pain, these pathways are sometimes cut to alleviate some of the pain.

Reactions to pain vary enormously among individuals, depending upon training, culture, attention, and mood.

—Nina Adams, *Yale University*
See also Pain Drive; Sensation.

PAIN DRIVE. Any stimulus that is aversive to an

Overcrowding is one of man's severest stresses.

animal can be employed to impel that animal to perform a given response. Psychologists have used pain, primarily inflicted as electric shock, for decades as a reinforcer in learning tasks. Acting as an unconditioned stimulus, shock produces the biologically adaptive unconditioned response of withdrawal or escape. It can be paired with a secondary reinforcer, such as a tone or a light, which will lead to the learning of an avoidance response. For example, a tone paired with a shock can be used to train a rat to learn to avoid a certain portion of a maze.

—Joel F. Lubar, *University of Tennessee*
See also Operant Conditioning.

PAIRED-ASSOCIATE LEARNING, procedure used to study verbal learning and memory. Items (words, nonsense syllables) are presented in pairs, and the subject must learn to give the second (response) item of each pair when the first (stimulus) item is presented. Two variations in this procedure are commonly employed.

In the *anticipation method* the subject tries to anticipate the correct response when the stimulus item is presented, one pair at a time. For example, the subject sees the stimulus item WOK and tries to think of its response, BIM. After a period of time (the anticipation or test interval), both items are presented together (WOK-BIM) for the subject to study.

In the *study-test* (or recall) *method,* the subject first sees all the pairs for a time, during which he studies the items. This is followed by a test in which each stimulus item is presented one at a time. This method differs from anticipation in that the subject receives no feedback about the correctness of his response until the next study session.

Paired associations have been used more often than any other technique to study verbal learning. Indeed, this procedure is often cited as the "model" for verbal-learning research, since the association of two items in memory can be considered a basic process of learning and thinking. According to a useful and influential theory, paired-associate learning involves two stages: a *response-learning* stage, where the subject learns what the responses are, and an *associative* stage, where the subject learns to associate the response item to the stimulus item. The advantage of this model is that different variables (such as study time, meaningfulness of items, interitem similarity) can be postulated to affect each stage in different ways; any one variable may facilitate one stage and possibly inhibit the other. Such a model is able to account for the complexities that occur in paired-associate learning data.

—Roland Siiter, *Montclair State College*
See also Memory; Serial Learning; Transfer of Training.
Consult (6) Deese and Hulse, 1967.

PANIC. *See* Civilian Catastrophe Reaction; Combat Neurosis.

PARAMNESIA, confusion of actuality and imagination in remembering something. For example, a person may hear so many stories about his early childhood that he comes to believe he himself can recall the events he has been told of.

One instance of paramnesia is the déjà vu experience ("already seen" in French). A person may have a sudden and mystifying feeling that he has walked down this street before or sat in this house before, even though he is sure he has never been near them until today. Déjà vu experiences have been called memories "of another incarnation," but logical explanations have been proposed. For example, a new street or house may hold cues (sights, sounds, smells) associated with similar experiences in another place. Thus the person has a hint of something familiar though he does not remember the earlier setting.

PARANOIA, a psychiatric term designating a characteristic combination of mental symptoms, often seen in many diverse types of mental and emotional disorders. There are two essential elements in reactions termed (1) unrealistic feelings of self-overevaluation, grandeur, or grandiosity; and (2) unrealistic and irrational beliefs of being persecuted. The word "paranoia" is derived from two Greek roots: *para,* which means "beside," in the sense of altered or changed, and *noia,* meaning "intellect" or "reason." The word thus implies a "mind beside itself."

Symptoms. Paranoid reactions develop under stress in people who are basically egocentric and conceited but, at the same time, possess innate feelings of inferiority that they are psychologically incapable of accepting realistically. Instead, they overcompensate for the inferior feelings by developing a sense of superiority in one sphere or another. When the external world does not agree with their overevaluation of themselves, they conclude that it is because of jealousy. When their plans and aspirations continue to be thwarted by a "jealous," unsympathetic world, they conclude that they are being persecuted, that malicious forces are working against them. In this frame of mind paranoiacs exaggerate, misinterpret, distort, and attach undue significance to everyday remarks and events, which they use as evidence to bolster their belief in the "machinations" against them.

Almost any type of serious mental dysfunction can manifest itself to some extent by paranoid reactions. Thus, they are frequent in the so-called functional psychoses, such as schizophrenia, manic-depression, and epileptic psychoses. Also, they often appear in the numerous different types of organic brain syn-

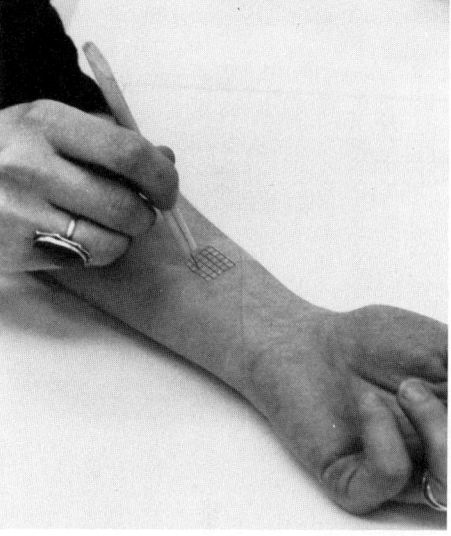

Mapping technique used to show spacing of pain receptors in the skin.

dromes. These arise from impaired cerebral circulation, senile changes, and endocrine, vitamin, or metabolic deficiencies, from delirious states due to infectious diseases, in drug or medicinal intoxications (where there has been excessively prolonged usage, overdosage, or where an individual has special susceptibility to certain drugs), and, especially during recent years, as a result of excessive use of stimulant, appetite-suppressing, and hallucinogenic substances (including alcohol). Toxic and "delirious" paranoid reactions *usually* subside when the causative agent is removed. However, in virtually all cases where chronic paranoid reactions result, one can find an underlying personality structure that psychiatrists feel predisposes them to develop.

The Paranoid Personality. Chronic paranoid reactions are invariably seen in individuals who have an exaggerated picture of their self-importance—of what they are, or at least of what they think they should be. These attitudes usually reflect the views and attitudes of at least one of their parents or parent surrogates. Surveys have shown that they come from distrust-provoking backgrounds, where the parents are cruel, unstable, and punitive or highly moralistic and demanding or indulging and pampering (convincing the child that he warrants special privileges).

Most paranoids have been raised in an atmosphere permeated by intolerance, bigotry, self-righteousness, and carping, critical attitudes. Their families remained aloof and disinterested in neighborly contacts and community affairs and explained their withdrawal by impugning the character, ethics, morals, and motives of people who are active in these spheres. Prone to condemn and decry in others faults they themselves possess, and of which they are completely unaware, such parents will set up excessively high achievement goals for the child and will tend to deprecate and minimize whatever he does accomplish. But they will not attribute the child's failures to lack of ability or application, or even poor fortune, but to "unfair" teachers and to "favoritism" for others who may have "important connections." (These same individuals will assiduously seek and utilize for themselves any "connections" that they believe might give their child an advantage over others.) Thus, the child will be taught to view the world as hostile, competitive, full of schemers, and beset with pitfalls for the naive and unwary.

Other prominent character traits seen in paranoid personalities and in their antecedents have been delineated by Sigmund Freud as the anal-erotic character triad. This consists of (1) orderliness, which is also expressed in preoccupations with physical cleanliness, meticulousness, and scrupulousness in little things; (2) economical, frugal, hoarding tendencies, which tend to become exaggerated into avari-

ciousness and miserliness; (3) obstinacy, which can progress to spitefulness, vindictiveness, and tendencies for violent and vengeful acts.

Coming from such a background, the future paranoid individual has generally displayed character traits that have made it difficult for him to get along with a group as a child. He is often a lonely, unhappy, brooding, insecure youngster, lacking the ability to make close friends or to participate in congenial play with others for any extended period. He is inclined to be suspicious, stubborn, secretive, obstinate, and resentful of discipline. When crossed he is likely to be sullen, morose, peevish, and irritable.

As he matures into adolescence and early adulthood, these personality characteristics become accentuated. The individual becomes increasingly sensitive about the attitude and behavior of others, "makes mountains out of molehills," and readily believes that others wish to do him injury. He lacks a sense of humor, becomes readily offended at well-meant jests, is egotistic, self-righteous, self-assertive, sarcastic, derogatory, querulous, embittered, and resentful. Characteristically, he has become argumentative, uncompromising, and aggressive.

As a result, the individual's relationships with other people readily become strained. He approaches them with a "chip on his shoulder." His achievement drive may be intense and impel him to seek goals that are well beyond his capacity. Intolerant of criticism and unable to accept suggestions, he readily criticizes and belittles others. Meticulous and precise, he is in some respects highly efficient, but, because of his jealousy and inflexibility, he is prone to difficulties in situations where he needs to work harmoniously with others. He is driven to demonstrate his superiority and, if placed in a position of authority, is very likely to become a petty tyrant.

Frequently one encounters persons handicapped by paranoid personality characteristics that have never developed beyond this level. In others these characteristics become gradually and insidiously intensified until the person is clearly psychotic. That is to say, the individual loses substantially, and for an extended period, the ability to counterbalance his misinterpretations of events and other people's motives with a realistic, objective evaluation of them.

Treatment. When paranoia is found in its pure form—that is, not as a manifestation of schizophrenia, manic-depressive psychosis, or secondary to some form of organic psychosis—it is extremely difficult to treat. The paranoid individual may tactfully be persuaded that other people interpret the world and his position in it differently than he does and that he should tolerate their point of view, just as the sympathetic psychiatrist is willing to listen to the patient's point of view. Although the patient's convictions about his false beliefs are not likely to be shaken by this reasoning process, his hypersensitivity and readiness to be affronted can be lessened to a considerable extent if he can be persuaded to accept tranquilizing medication, particularly of the phenothiazine type.

The treatment of paranoid schizophrenia and manic-depressive cases involving paranoid elements depends on the treatment of the more basic mental disease. Currently quite good results are obtainable in the majority of the schizophrenic cases by the use of phenothiazine tranquilizers, sometimes assisted by electroshock. In the manic-depressive cases with paranoid features, successful results can often be obtained by the use of antidepressant medication and electroshock therapy. Psychotherapy is considered helpful by most psychiatrists but is not in itself curative in these conditions.

—Emanuel Messinger, M.D., *U.S. Veterans Hospital, Northport, N.Y.*
See also Manic-Depressive Psychosis; Psychiatry; Psychotherapy; Schizophrenia.
Consult (13) Arieti, 1959; Coleman, 1964.

PARANOID PERSONALITY, a personality structure characterized by suspiciousness, aggression, and considerable insecurity and defensiveness. The paranoid individual, while not psychotic, exhibits to a less extreme degree many of the symptoms associated with paranoid schizophrenia. He is usually argumentative and tends to regard everyone as a potential enemy or competitor. He projects his own anger and hostility onto those around him, thus justifying his own aggressive behavior as necessary self-defense. Because he is so suspicious, his unpleasant manner tends to elicit hostile reactions and alienate those around him. But such responses serve only as evidence for his claims that everyone is "against" him.

While every individual exhibits some oversensitivity, irascibility, selfishness, and bickering, the paranoid personality displays these behaviors as consistent traits, and to an extreme degree. He alleviates his own anxiety and guilt by ascribing to others feelings he harbors himself, blaming them for his own failure and inadequacy. Although such individuals rarely require hospitalization, they have great difficulty in making a successful professional or social adjustment.

—Michael Rothenberg, *The City College of The City University of New York*
See also Paranoia; Personality Disorders.

PARAPRAXIS, a minor error such as making a slip in speaking or writing, forgetting something, losing an object, or having a small accident. In psychoanalytic theory, such a bit of behavior is thought to reveal unconscious motives or conflicts. "Freudian slips" in conversation are often noted, such as saying "orgasm" when "organism" is meant.

PARAPSYCHOLOGY, psychical research, the area of science that studies extrasensory perception, psychokinesis, and such related topics as survival after bodily death.

History. In 1882 the Society for Psychical Research (SPR) was founded in London. But the raw material of parapsychology studies had been reported from the earliest days. The witch of Endor saw the spirit of the dead Samuel. Croesus, King of Lydia, tested the Delphic sibyl by sending a messenger to ask what the King was doing on a certain day. Croesus tried to trick her by carrying out a bizarre, unkingly act—cooking a tortoise and lamb in a bronze caldron—but the sibyl described it. Socrates' "Daemon" told him one morning to avoid his usual route in Athens; and that day, when Socrates would otherwise have walked there, a dangerous herd of wild pigs ran through the city street. Saint John Bosco twice, as a schoolboy, dreamed the Latin assignment that would be dictated next day. Pope Pius V saw and described, in Rome, the Battle of Lepanto while it occurred. And lesser folk have reported similar extraordinary events as well as many others, such as hauntings, poltergeists, and levitations. Such wonders deserve scientific study—or if such reports are invalid, this too should be known. The SPR's purpose still seems worthy today: "to examine without prejudice or prepossession and in a scientific spirit those faculties of man, real or supposed, which appear to be inexplicable on any generally recognized hypothesis." It included, then or later, such dignitaries as Lord Balfour, Henry Sidgwick, Sir William Crookes, Charles Richet, Lord Rayleigh, and Hans Driesch. Related societies were soon founded, such as the American Society for Psychical Research (ASPR) with Simon Newcomb and William James.

Research Methods. The SPR used three major techniques of investigation: collecting and critically analyzing "spontaneous cases," studying intensively anyone who seemed especially gifted (psychics, sensitives, mediums), and experimentation. Spontaneous cases were examined as in a law court: independent evidence about what had occurred was sought, and both confirming and disconfirming statements were published. Many cases were well confirmed, with independent witnesses stating the experience was described before confirmation was known and with written evidence of the confirmation. Both the ASPR and SPR continue this work, and their stimulating collections are worth reading. Uncritical compilations, also interesting, have been published by L. E. Rhine. [*Consult* (14) Rhine, 1967.]

Studies of special sensitives yielded strong confirmation for at least some psychic claims. Face-to-face sittings are often suspect, because the sitter may inadvertently give cues; but some sessions produced accurate information not known to the sitter—for example, the size and location of someone else's book that contained a diagram of Indo-European languages. [*Consult* (14) Sidgwick, 1921.]

Modern research avoids cues by "double-blind" methods, in which a note taker holds "proxy sittings" for several individuals, all unknown to him. Copies of all transcripts (coded for anonymity) are sent to each "absent sitter," who marks each scorable statement true or false. Statistical analysis shows if more checks are given to the appropriate transcripts. [*Consult* (14) Pratt, 1969.]

Experimentation is now the major method of parapsychological research. Studies of telepathy, clairvoyance, and precognition use stringent controls and have amply confirmed that ESP occurs. Modern interest lies in finding the conditions that facilitate or hinder it.

Formal experimentation on psychokinesis (PK) was initiated by J. B. Rhine, who first studied whether a subject could, by "willing," control the fall of dice. Since no die is perfect, all faces of the die must be "willed" equal numbers of times for good research. Also, since muscular control is possible for the first two bounces, an apparatus must ensure that the die bounces many times. Even with these conditions, however, extrachance results appear, especially at the beginning of a series. The systematic decline of scores after the beginning of a series is one of the striking effects. Other procedures include "placement," where discs are released from a central mechanism and the subject hopes they will fall to the right or left, and tests of possible influence on the temperature of a distant thermometer or the decay curve of a magnetic field. PK effects in the laboratory are usually so slight that they demand sensitive equipment or thousands of trials; but the fact that they occur is of major theoretical importance. Some few well-controlled sittings with psychics and observations of poltergeists suggest that massive psychokinetic effects can also be produced. [*Consult* (14) Owen, 1964.]

Research in other areas of parapsychology is less clear. However, some good work on psychic healing has begun, as when Grad and his colleagues inflicted surgical wounds on mice and found faster recovery if a "healer" held their cages. Similarly, Watkins and Watkins found faster recovery from anesthesia for animals whom certain "talented" subjects tried to wake. This may be a special case of psychokinesis. [*Consult* (14) Grad, 1965; Watkins and Watkins, 1971.]

No good experimental design has yet been found to study survival after death. The basic difficulty is that if a message seems to come from a dead person, and if it is checked and shown to be accurate and also to have been known to no living person, it can still be explained away as successful ESP of the clairvoyant type. Evidence from spontaneous cases or psychics is interesting but inconclusive. [*Consult* (14) Hart, 1959.]

Significance. The present status of parapsychology is curious. There are few specialists in the area. The Parapsychological Association (which limits membership to serious workers) has only about 200 members, though it is affiliated with the prestigious American Association for the Advancement of Science. Most of the good research is published in the *Journal of the American Society for Psychical Research* or in the *Journal of Parapsychology*, but most psychologists never read those journals and therefore are uninformed. Only recently have psychology departments begun to introduce even a single parapsychology course. Popular writings are common, but spread misinformation as well as information. In short, parapsychology is well established scientifically but not yet accepted by the academic community as a whole.

—Gertrude R. Schmeidler, *The City College of The City University of New York*

See also Clairvoyance; Extrasensory Perception; Precognition; Psychokinesis; Telekinesis; Telepathy.

Consult (14) Murphy, 1961; Rao, 1966; Rhine and Pratt, 1957; Schmeidler, 1969; Thouless, 1971.

PARASYMPATHETIC NERVOUS SYSTEM. *See* Autonomic Nervous System.

PARATHYROID GLANDS, four small yellowish or brownish oval bodies located on the lobes of the thyroid gland. They are of primary importance for the regulation of calcium and phosphorous levels. Calcium is important for bone formation, blood coagulation, and electrical balance in nerves and muscles. Phosphorous is also important in bone formation.

PARESIS. *See* General Paresis.

PARKINSON'S DISEASE, a degenerative brain disorder that has also been called paralysis agitans or "shaking palsy." Symptoms include muscle tremors in one arm, spreading to one leg, then to the face and neck, and finally to the other arm and leg. The face appears masklike and speech becomes slurred. The patient tends to lean forward as he walks so that he appears to be starting to run, although he moves with mincing steps. Intellectual ability is usually not reduced, but the patient may develop problems such as apathy and withdrawal as a reac-

PARATHYROID GLANDS

thyroid gland

parathyroid glands

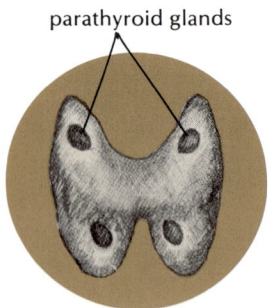

tion to his physical symptoms.

The disease is most common in persons between fifty and seventy. Drugs and psychosurgery have been used as treatment.

PARTIAL REINFORCEMENT. *See* Reinforcement.

PASSIVE-AGGRESSIVE PERSONALITY, a neurotic condition, generally related to immaturity of personality development, in which unacceptable aggressive impulses are expressed in one of several indirect ways.

A *passive-dependent* individual overtly expresses feelings of helplessness and inadequacy. He behaves irresponsibly and is constantly looking to others for support and direction. He is frequently very anxious and extremely demanding of these closest to him. Situations calling for aggressive or assertive behavior are avoided, and underlying hostility is masked by an outward appearance of timidity.

The *passive-aggressive* personality uses such passive maneuvers as stubbornness, procrastination, forgetfulness, and indecisiveness. When in psychotherapy, the individual will frequently arrive late or forget his appointment. He tends to be socially awkward. Again, these techniques serve to conceal more direct and intense feelings of hostility.

The *aggressive* form of this personality has low tolerance for frustration and is frequently engaged in arguments and complaints with those in authority. Verbal aggression substitutes for physical violence and is usually a reaction formation to serious dependency needs.

—Michael Rothenberg, *The City College of The City University of New York*

PASTORAL COUNSELING. For thousands of years religious leaders have offered advice and support to the sick and troubled. In the twentieth century, pastoral counseling has developed as a special field that combines insights and procedures from religion and from psychiatry and the social sciences. For example, major seminaries offer courses in principles of psychology and methods of counseling. Clergymen trained by such courses work with students, with patients in hospitals, with inmates of prisons, and with members of the armed forces. Some denominations have set up counseling centers to offer help with personal problems in the context of religion. Clergymen are also involved in community mental health programs and may be members of staffs of clinics and centers.

Consult (14) Bier, 1962; Cavanagh, 1962; Clinebell, 1968; National Association for Mental Health, *The Clergy and Mental Health;* Oates, 1959.

PAVLOV, IVAN PETROVICH (1849–1936), Russian neurophysiologist, born in Ryazan. He received a medical degree from the University of St. Petersburg (now Leningrad), 1883. He was professor at the Military Medical Academy and, after 1895, director of the Institute of Medicine, St. Petersburg.

Pavlov made notable contributions in the fields of medicine, physiology, and psychology. As director of the Institute of Medicine he devised operative procedures for studying the digestive system. He examined the operation of the salivary glands and became particularly interested in the salivary apparatus. His work was influenced in this area by an earlier physiologist, Sechenov, whose research had a profound effect on Pavlov's intellectual development.

In 1904 Pavlov was awarded the Nobel Prize for his combined research dealing with the nervous system and the digestive tract. His most important contribution to the study of the nervous system was the concept that during learning temporary connections might be formed in the cortex as a result of repetition of stimuli. Hence, stimuli and responses become linked together through channels or pathways.

The model Pavlov used to study temporary connection formation in the brain later became known as Pavlovian or classical conditioning. First a response was elicited by presenting an unconditioned stimulus, and then that response was conditioned by pairing the unconditioned stimulus with a neutral stimulus.

Pavlov was particularly interested in reflexes, and his work formed the basis for reflexive psychology, which is still a dominant theme in Soviet psychology today. He distinguished between natural unconditioned reflexes that are learned early in life and the artificially conditioned reflexes of the laboratory. The salivary response, he contended, is a response developed in infancy connected with the sight or smell of food. He showed that many naturally occurring internal reflexes could be conditioned.

Pavlov worked intensively with conditioned reflexes throughout the early decades of the twentieth century. Sir Charles Sherrington, another great figure in the history of neurophysiology, described Pavlov even at the age of sixty-five as "overflowing with energy although an elderly man. He was spare in figure and alert and humorous in manner."

Pavlov's early work in reflexology carried him into detailed studies of the function of the cortex and led him to postulate the concept of cortical inhibition, which he believed played an important role in initiating sleep. Pavlov was also responsible for the development of many of the electrophysiological tools used in this field.

Ivan Pavlov, Nobel-winning Russian neurophysiologist, studied digestive and nervous systems, made important discoveries about reflexes, conditioning.

Pavlov's major works (in English translation) are *Conditioned Reflexes,* 1927; *Lectures on Conditioned Reflexes,* 1928; and *Conditioned Reflexes and Psychiatry,* 1941.

—Joel F. Lubar, *University of Tennessee*
See also Pavlovian Conditioning.

PAVLOVIAN CONDITIONING. Also known as classical conditioning, this is essentially a two-step training process.

Procedures. In the first step an *unconditioned stimulus (UCS),* such as food, bright lights, loud sounds, pain, or tactile stimulation, is paired with a neutral *conditioned stimulus (CS)* that causes no direct effect, such as a click, a tone, or a dim light. In most cases the interval between the CS and the UCS is on the order of .5 second.

The response elicited by the UCS is called the *unconditioned response (UCR).* This response is an unlearned, biological reflex of the nervous system and usually takes the form of a glandular secretion or a smooth-muscle contraction. Knee flexion and eyeblinks are examples of smooth-muscle UCRs; salivation and skin-resistance changes are examples of glandular UCRs. The form and nature of the UCR is dependent upon the nature of the UCS and the organization of the nervous system of the individual being conditioned.

The combination of the neutral CS, the response-causing UCS, and the unlearned UCR is typically presented to a subject several times during conditioning. Eventually, the UCS is dropped from the sequence in the second step of the process, and the previously neutral CS comes to elicit the UCR. When conditioning is complete, presentation of the CS alone will successfully result in a *conditioned response (CR)* similar to but not always the same as the UCR. The only way an outside observer could tell if an observed response was a UCR or a CR would be to know whether the eliciting stimulus was a learned CS, in which case the response would be a CR, or an unlearned UCS, in which case the response would be considered a UCR.

In a later stage of conditioning the initial conditioned stimulus (CS^1) can now be closely associated with a second initially neutral stimulus (CS^2). Again, after several pairings of the two stimuli in close temporal contiguity, the new CS^2, when presented alone, will elicit a CR. This process, in which a previously conditioned CS serves as the UCS for the conditioning of a second CS, is known as *higher-order conditioning.* Researchers have worked up to CS^5, or fifth-order conditioning.

Research. The earliest and best-known experiments in classical conditioning were conducted by the Russian neurophysiologist Ivan Pavlov during the early years of this century. His experiments typically involved presenting a hungry dog with meat powder (UCS) paired with an auditory click (CS) to elicit salivation (UCR). After several pairings of the food powder with the click, the click alone elicited salivation (CR). Similar experiments using electric shock as the UCS and a muscle flexion as the UCR have also been used to explore the parameters of classical conditioning.

Applications. The classical conditioning paradigm has a variety of uses in training new responses and in psychotherapy. One of the most effective applications has been in the treatment of enuresis, chronic bedwetting. The patient sleeps on a moisture-sensitive electric pad; any moisture on the pad activates an alarm bell that wakens him. The bell serves as the UCS, the feelings associated with bladder tension as the CS, and the UCR is waking up. Therapy is terminated when the CS of bladder tension can elicit the CR of waking without the bell. Other therapeutic uses of classical conditioning include treatment of homosexuality, alcoholism, fetishism, and obesity.

The term "conditioning" is applied to another form of learning, operant or instrumental conditioning.

Glossary

Conditioned response—a reflexive response of the smooth muscles or glands that is elicited by the presentation of a conditioned stimulus; the conditioned response may or may not be identical in form to the unconditioned response.

Conditioned stimulus—an initially neutral (that is, nonresponse-eliciting) signal that comes to elicit a response through frequent pairing with an unconditioned stimulus.

Elicit—the term used to describe the relation between stimulus and response; for example, the salivation response elicited by the sound of the tone.

Higher-order conditioning—the process in which neutral stimuli become classically conditioned stimuli through pairing with other conditioned stimuli.

—Brenda B. Bankart and C. Peter Bankart, *Wabash College*

See also Behavior Therapy; Conditioning; Learning Theory; Operant Conditioning; Pavlov; Reinforcement.

Consult (1) Hilgard, *et al.,* 1971 (6) Kimble, 1961.

PECKING ORDER. *See* Dominance Relationship.

PEDOPHILIA, the use of a minor for sexual gratification by an adult. Sexual contact between adult females and nonadult males is known to occur, but persons convicted of the crime of pedophilia are, almost without exception, males. They constitute a third of all institutionalized sex criminals, one of the largest classifications.

Approximately two-thirds of the objects of pedophilic acts are prepubescent and adolescent girls, in about equal numbers. The act itself is seldom more than fondling. Sexual intercourse is rarely attempted, and actual penetration occurs only in about 2 percent of known cases. Genital acts such as anal coitus and fellatio occur more often when the pedophile's object is male. Pedophiles who have had contact with boys under twelve tend to have a basic heterosexual orientation, while those whose objects were pubescent boys are more likely to be true homosexuals.

Contrary to general belief, a large majority of pedophilic acts, especially involving females, are performed by relatives, neighbors, and acquaintances of the victim. The man who is sexually interested in young children is usually an unaggressive, inadequate individual. Those pedophiles who choose teenage girls as their objects, however, tend to be relatively stable, adequate persons.

—Eugene E. Levitt, *Indiana University School of Medicine*

Consult (13) Gebhard, *et al.,* 1965; Mohr, *et al.,* 1964.

PENFIELD, WILDER (1891–   ), American neurosurgeon. Born in Spokane, Wash., he received a D.Sci. degree at Oxford University (1935) and an M.D. at Johns Hopkins (1918). He was director of the Montreal Neurological Institute until 1960 and established the Laboratory of Neurocytology at Presbyterian Hospital, 1925.

Penfield specialized in neurosurgical alleviation of epileptic seizures. In the course of surgery, he examined, through stimulating electrodes, the differential responses of different areas of the cortex. He helped localize the motor and sensory areas of the cortex in man and demonstrated the different brain loci for speech arrest (a pure motor effect) and aphasic arrest (the forgetting of specific words). He is best known for the elicitation of memories through stimulation of certain areas of the temporal lobe, which led him to theorize about the neuronal basis of memory.

His major works include *Epilepsy and Cerebral Localization,* 1941; *Cerebral Cortex of man* (with T. Rasmussen), 1950; *Epileptic Seizure Patterns* (with K. Kristiansen), 1950; *Epilepsy and Functional Anatomy of the Human Brain,* 1954; and *Speech and Brain Mechanisms,* 1959.

—Nina Adams, *Yale University*

PENIS ENVY. According to psychoanalytic theory, girl children notice during the phallic stage of development that they lack the visible sex organs of the male. Girls blame the mother for this lack and feel envy of males. Boys at this stage develop castration anxiety. *See* Oedipus Complex; Sex Identity.

PEPTIC ULCER. a psychosomatic disorder, a gastrointestinal reaction to stress. *See* Psychosomatic Disorders.

PERCENTILE. In educational and psychological measurement, percentiles are used to compare test scores. Scores are first distributed on a 100-point scale, from highest to lowest. The scores can next be divided into 4 groups (*quartiles*), 10 groups (*deciles*), or 100 groups (centiles, but *percentile* has become the standard term). A score in the first quartile, first decile, or first percentile is toward the bottom of the range of scores.

Percentiles indicate the percentage of scores falling below a point on the scale. For example, if a student has a test score at the 99th percentile, his score is equal to or higher than the scores of 99 percent of cases. A score at the 20th percentile equals or exceeds the scores of only 20 percent of cases.

Consult (12) Blommers and Lindquist, 1960.

PERCEPTION, the experience of objects and events in the world based upon stimulation of the sense organs. In psychology, the field of perception is the study of the determinants of sensory impressions, such as those of size, shape, direction, orientation, distance, and movement.

In the past it was customary to distinguish sensation from perception (or interpretation). Sensation presumably referred to impressions directly caused by stimulation of the sense organs, whereas perception referred to the interpretations we learn to make of these sensations. Because of many newly discovered facts, this distinction is no longer considered valid. But in contemporary psychology, the field of sensory processes is still distinguished from perception. The former is concerned with the basis of sense impressions, such as those of color, brightness, taste, or olfaction, and emphasizes the physiological mechanisms in the sense organ or nerve fibers arising from it.

A central fact about the perception of objects in the world is that it remains more or less constant despite variation in the stimulus affecting the sense organ. Thus, for example, the size of the retinal image varies with the distance of the object from the observer, but the perceived size remains relatively constant; the shape of the retinal image varies with the vantage point of the observer, but the perceived shape remains constant. The finding that animals and infants also perceive in this way casts doubt on the classical theory that sensation is directly correlated with the sensory stimulus and that the mature adult learns to judge such properties as the constant size, shape, and color of objects. Rather, the prevailing view is that perception is a more complex process. It is now thought to be based on the

Wilder Penfield, a distinguished neurosurgeon noted for the elicitation of memories through electrical stimulation of the brain.

PERCEPTION SUBJECT MAP
See the Subject Map for SENSATION AND PERCEPTION.

combined utilization of various sources of sensory information, or on various relationships within the stimulus. Thus, for example, in the perception of size, the size of the retinal image of an object is detected *and* information about the distance of the object is taken into account.

The perception of object properties as constant is an achievement that is highly adaptive, since it means that perception is more often than not veridical. However, it is believed that the same perceptual mechanisms that generally lead to veridical perception also occasionally lead to illusions.

—Irvin Rock, *Rutgers University*
See also Depth Perception; Illusion; Sensation; Sensory Adaptation; Vision. *Other entries listed in the Item Guide under* Sensation and Perception.

Consult (4) Gibson, 1950; Gregory, 1966; Hochberg, 1964; Köhler, 1947.

PERCEPTUAL CONSTANCY. *See* Perception.

PERIPHERAL NERVOUS SYSTEM. *See* Autonomic Nervous System; Nervous System.

PERSONALITY. There have been almost as many attempts to define the concept of personality as there have been writers or theorists who have set out to do so. It is simultaneously one of the most fascinating and elusive of concepts confronting psychology. The history of philosophy is dotted with attempts to penetrate the mysteries of human nature and the human condition. The modern study of personality is but the most recent expression of this ageless concern. In its most general form, it is the application of the scientific method to the problem of human nature.

Theories

Theories of personality range broadly across the entire field of psychology. They represent differing traditions and belief systems. Debate among theorists often centers around what assumptions are useful or necessary for the development of an adequate theory. Despite the fact that these assumptions are usually based more upon belief than fact, they determine in large measure the form that the theory will take. Some of the most influential and divergent trends will be discussed here.

Type Theories. Early theories were often little more than crude attempts to formalize the various popular stereotypes about personality. Persons were categorized into broad *types,* generally with the implication that each type represented a different psychobiological constitution. Hippocrates (c. 400 B.C.) introduced a system of classification based upon temperament and physique. His four temperaments—melancholic, choleric, sanguine, and phlegmatic—resemble closely those suggested by modern theorists.

W. H. Sheldon utilized a threefold classification of physique and personality: the *morphological* (physical) characteristics—endomorph (fat), mesomorph (muscular), and ectomorph (thin)—correspond to the three *temperaments*—viscerotonic (easy-going), somatotonic (aggressive), and cerebrotonic (intellectual, artistic). This view has been subjected to considerable criticism, if not ridicule, from the mainstream of psychology. Sheldon's theory has been called simplistic and his methodology criticized for its lack of adequate control. For example, he used the same subjects to rate both morphological and temperamental characteristics and then made much of the high correlations between their judgments. Furthermore, he ascribed a causal significance to morphology, though alternative explanations of his data seem quite plausible. His judges might have relied upon common social stereotypes, such as "fat and jolly" or "frail and sensitive," in their personality ratings.

Typologies almost always involve discrete categories, and the individual belongs to either one or another. The problem for the typologist is to decide which of the pure (idealized) types is most appropriate for a particular individual, and this, of necessity, is almost always a forced fit. An obvious danger in this form of classification is its tendency to attribute *all* of the characteristics of the "type" to individuals displaying only *some* of those characteristics—not unlike the mechanism of stereotyping.

Trait Theories. This approach attempts to isolate certain *dimensions* of personality upon which individuals may vary with respect to the amount of a characteristic (trait) they might possess. It is rooted in the same tradition of measurement of individual differences (psychometrics) from which intelligence and aptitude testing developed. The trait psychologist is concerned with developing techniques for the identification and measurement of stable personality patterns.

Raymond B. Cattell has developed the most complete such theory to date. It relies upon the statistical procedures of *correlation* and *factor analysis* for the identification of traits. Characteristics that are highly intercorrelated (correlation clusters) are presumed to be controlled by the same underlying common factor. For example, a person's performance on a variety of verbal tests, such as vocabulary, reading comprehension or speed, and word naming, will tend to be relatively consistent; the surface connection among these various performances might be related to a single underlying factor, such as "verbal ability." Once these statistical procedures have established such underlying factors from a welter of correlational data, tests are devised for the measurement of the factors (which Cattell calls *source traits*), and personality is assessed ac-

PERSONALITY AND INDIVIDUAL DIFFERENCE

Theories of Personality

PERSONALITY
  Type Theory
  CONSTITUTIONAL TYPES
      body types
  TEMPERAMENT
  AUTHORITARIAN PERSONALITY

  Trait Theory
  FACTOR ANALYSIS

  Psychodynamic Theory
  PSYCHOANALYSIS
  ID
  EGO
  SUPEREGO
  CHARACTER DEVELOPMENT
  INTROVERSION-EXTROVERSION

  Behavior Theory
  BEHAVIORISM

  Pseudoscientific Theories
  PHRENOLOGY
  PHYSIOGNOMY

Personality Development
PERSONALITY
DEVELOPMENTAL PSYCHOLOGY
CHILD DEVELOPMENT
PSYCHOANALYSIS
CHARACTER DEVELOPMENT
SEX IDENTITY
    Masculinity-Femininity
ADJUSTMENT
SELF-ACTUALIZATION
SELF-CONCEPT
MATURITY
MORAL DEVELOPMENT

Assessment of Personality
PERSONALITY
PERSONALITY INVENTORY
MINNESOTA MULTIPHASIC PERSONALITY
    INVENTORY
INTERESTS AND INTEREST INVENTORIES
PROJECTIVE TECHNIQUES
    RORSCHACH TECHNIQUE
    THEMATIC APPERCEPTION TEST
RATING SCALES
INTERVIEW

Personality Disorders
PERSONALITY DISORDERS
    character disorders
    antisocial reaction
    dyssocial reaction
ALCOHOLISM
COMPULSIVE PERSONALITY
CYCLOTHYMIC PERSONALITY
DRUGS AND BEHAVIOR
    drug dependency or addiction
EMOTIONALLY UNSTABLE PERSONALITY
HYPOMANIC PERSONALITY
HYSTERICAL PERSONALITY
INADEQUATE PERSONALITY
NEUROTIC PERSONALITY
PARANOID PERSONALITY
PASSIVE-AGGRESSIVE PERSONALITY
PSYCHONEUROTIC DISORDERS
SCHIZOID PERSONALITY
SOCIOPATHIC PERSONALITY DISTURBANCE
SEXUAL DEVIATIONS

The Subject Maps in the Encyclopedia illustrate the coverage of particular aspects of psychology, showing the interrelationships among the articles in twelve major areas of study. Entries in capital letters are subjects for which there are separate articles in the Encyclopedia. Entries in small letters are cross references.

The Subject Maps appear in the Encyclopedia under the following titles:

Abnormal and Clinical Psychology
Developmental Psychology
Emotion and Motivation
Intelligence
Learning and Memory
Measurement
Personality and Individual Difference
Physiological and Comparative Psychology
Psychology: Divisions and Schools
Sensation and Perception
Social Psychology
Thinking and Language

cording to the relative amounts of the source traits found in a given individual.

Psychodynamic Theory. A major influence upon the development of modern personality theory derives from the clinical tradition in psychology. Clinicians have generally been less concerned with quantification than with the description of personality dynamics based upon their clinical impressions and case studies. The most influential of all such approaches was that developed by Sigmund Freud. From his extensive clinical observations of neurotic patients, as well as from his own lifelong self-analysis, Freud developed theories of personality structure and development and of neurosis, in addition to a method of psychotherapy.

Freud's neurological training inclined him to identify structure in terms of function. He isolated what he believed to be the three basic psychological structures—the id, ego, and superego—each responsible for its own set of personality functions.

The *id* was seen by Freud as the core of personality and the wellspring from which everything psychological emerges. It is the instinctive, primitive, animal basis for human behavior and the storehouse for all psychological energy (libido). The id seeks pleasure through the immediate gratification of instinctive impulses.

The *ego* restrains the id and aligns the individual's behavior with the demands of the real world (of which the id is blind). In order to accomplish this, Freud argued, the ego redirects impulses of the id, seeking and hopefully finding gratification in safe and socially acceptable behavior.

The *superego* corresponds roughly to what is usually termed "conscience." It represents the restrictions and ideals absorbed from the parents in childhood.

Since the functions of the three psychic structures relate to differing goals, the structures are usually in conflict. Thus, personality organization reduces to a dynamic interaction among the forces of the id, ego, and superego (psychodynamics). Freud believed that the basic patterns of personality dynamics are established very early in life with the child's early successes and failures in achieving gratification. He distinguished among six separate stages from birth through adolescence, each marked by its own form of impulse gratification.

Furthermore, Freud argued that the impulses could all be traced to one biologically determined source—the sexual instinct. Many of the post-Freudian psychoanalysts disagreed on this point, arguing instead for a more social and less instinctive base for human motivation. For example, Karen Horney suggested that neurotic conflict is frequently a consequence of the internalization of conflicting cultural tendencies. The current trend is to view the ego as prime mover, and a major concern is with the development of a theory of ego function consistent with this shift.

Behavior Theory. This approach to personality can be seen as an attempt to extend the insights, techniques, and methods of analysis developed in the learning laboratory to the study of personality. For the behaviorist, all behavior can be analyzed in terms of specific *inputs* or stimuli (Ss) affecting the organism and *outputs* or responses (Rs) made by the organism. When an S becomes capable of evoking a particular R, an S–R bond, or habit, is assumed to have been formed. Personality is seen as nothing more mysterious than a special patterning, albeit a complex one, of S–R bonds (habits).

For example, J. Dollard and N. E. Miller (1950) suggest that the Freudian concept of repression might be better understood as a *learned response* of "not thinking" in connection with anxiety-arousing stimuli. Behavior may be "modified" through the extinction of old habits or the addition of new habits. Thus, in a procedure labeled *reciprocal inhibition* by J. Wolpe and A. A. Lazarus, anxiety responses are replaced by stronger responses to relax following relaxation training and conditioning.

Phenomenology. This approach is more a method of study and a philosophical orientation than a specific theory about behavior. Phenomenologists reject the historical determinism found in psychoanalytic theory as well as the more mechanistic explanations of the behaviorists. The phenomenological method is subjective and introspective, relying upon the person's report of his experience (his inner world) as its primary source of data. Phenomenological theories are generally holistic rather than atomistic and emphasize the individuality and uniqueness of the person-in-particular rather than more general or universal tendencies. The basic causes of behavior are seen as directly knowable and can be discovered through the analysis of conscious experience. Existential psychology relies very heavily upon the phenomenological method.

Development

Personality theorists differ widely in the extent to which they focus upon developmental factors in the formation of personality. Freud saw personality development as nearly complete by the time the child reached the age of six. The behaviorists also stress the importance of early experience but view personality development as more continuous, emphasizing the total learning history of the organism. By contrast, phenomenologists tend to focus upon contemporary events (present experience) and are less inclined to search for explanations in terms of life history.

Two research strategies have been extensively used in the study of personality development. The *longitudinal* study plots the course of development for a given individual throughout his entire life cycle. Though this type of data is highly desirable, the method has so many obvious drawbacks—time, expense, and availability of subjects—that it is precluded. In practice, longitudinal studies generally focus upon a selected time span, such as infancy or adolescence, hoping to arrive at an overall picture through the piecemeal addition of information gathered in a large number of investigations.

In the *retrospective* (autobiographical) approach, the investigator depends upon subjects' recollections, associations, diary notes, and so on, to build a picture of personality development. Since personal accounts are likely to be biased and incomplete, the method is of questionable validity. Yet its ease and intrinsic appeal have contributed to its widespread use.

Assessment

Techniques of personality assessment often bear the earmarks of the theories from which they are derived. Projective tests, such as the Rorschach and TAT, are in the tradition of psychoanalysis and ego psychology, while personality inventories and scales derive from trait theory and the psychometric tradition. The *clinical interview* is the most informal of the procedures used. Its value lies chiefly in the skill and sensitivity of the interviewer as well as in the cooperativeness of the subject. *Projective tests* are based upon the assumption that when a person is confronted with an unstructured or ambiguous situation and asked to provide his own structure, he will do so in a way that is characteristic of himself, hence providing insights into his personality. Though the various assessment procedures all have their own special drawbacks, they are most useful when combined to form a test battery. When the results of several independently administered and scored tests concur, the personality assessment gains considerable credence.

—Gerald Tolchin, *Southern Connecticut State College*

See also Constitutional Types; Ego; Id; Interview; Introversion-Extraversion; Personality Disorders; Personality Inventory; Projective Techniques; Psychoanalysis; Superego. *Other articles listed under* Personality *in the Item Guide.*

Consult (9) Dollard and Miller, 1950; Sheldon, *et al.,* 1940; Wolpe and Lazarus, 1966.

PERSONALITY DEVELOPMENT. Psychoanalytic theories of development through stages are discussed in the article on Character Development. For a general discussion of theories, *see* Developmental Psychology; Personality.

PERSONALITY DISORDERS OR CHARACTER

DISORDERS are characterized by faulty traits that are regarded as an intrinsic part of the individual's personality. They do not represent a breakdown of behavior under stress. Because to the person with such a disorder his inadequate characteristics are part of his "normal" personality, he feels little or no anxiety about himself and is unlikely to seek psychotherapy. Thus "faulty" is largely socially defined in this context, and, because the traits exhibited have much in common with "normal" behavior at one extreme and "neurotic" or "psychotic" patterns at the other, it is often difficult to diagnose a character disorder.

General Personality Disorders. These are relatively mild and reflect a general failure to appraise oneself accurately, to interact realistically and adequately with others, and to deal efficiently and productively with one's environment.

The *paranoid personality* is characteristically suspicious, sensitive to the slightest hint of scorn, hostility, or accusation. The individual is unaware of how much he provokes others with his own aggressive and hostile reactions. The *schizoid personality* is a detached, solitary, secretive loner who avoids intimate contact, especially with the opposite sex. Unable to show hostility, he avoids competitive situations as much as he does intimacy. The *compulsive personality,* an inhibited, obstinate, inflexible conformist, is driven to crippling excesses of frugality, overwork, and cleanliness. The *cyclothymic (manic-depressive) personality* experiences mood swings or maintains a constant elated or depressed state without apparent cause.

While some constitutional factors may be involved in these disorders, individual developmental experiences within the family context are more important. Some experts feel that under sufficient stress they might develop into full-blown neuroses or psychoses. It is more likely, however, that the person will go on living his constricted or emotionally inadequate life without major change.

Sociopathic Disorders. These are characterized by an apparent lack of conscience and concern for other people.

The *antisocial (psychopathic) personality* is amoral, unreliable, irresponsible, deceitful, callous, impulsive, unconventional, thrill-seeking, often charming, and optimistic, with a good sense of humor. There is a wide gap between the individual's intelligence and his moral awareness. Able to impress and exploit others, he is contemptuous of those he exploits. Feeling no anxiety or guilt, he dissembles his way out of difficulties. The psychopath is sometimes highly successful, and frequently is a burden to friends, relatives, and spouse. He may have a record of difficulty with the law but is usually not a calculating criminal.

Usually the psychopathic personality

has suffered early sociocultural deprivation, a lack of warm interpersonal relationships within the family, even in apparently "good" homes. The parents failed to provide adequate ethical models.

The *dyssocial personality,* characterized by distorted ethical values, may be found in professional criminals. Capable of loyalty, courage, responsibility, the individual has good inner controls and a relatively strong conscience, which differs, however, from that of the larger society. This personality is probably the product of a lifelong environment that has fostered values that conflict with the larger society.

These descriptions of the antisocial and dyssocial personalities are extreme. Most sociopathic reactions fall somewhere in between.

The prognosis for the sociopath is usually unsatisfactory, though socializing influences over time and the realization of the self-defeating nature of his behavior may produce change with age.

Sexual Deviations. Seeking sexual gratification in ways considered undesirable by society—for example, *exhibitionism, voyeurism* (gratification through looking), *pedophila* (preference for a child object), *prostitution,* and *rape*—often brings the deviate into serious conflict with society. Recently questions have been raised concerning the extent to which homosexuality should be considered antisocial or a private affair.

The causes of these disorders vary widely. Typically, family and social experiences have interfered with mature sexual development and impulse control. The prognosis also varies, being fairly good for exhibitionists, for example, and poor for homosexuals.

Dependence on Alcohol and Drugs. These are marked by physiological (addiction) and/or psychological (habituation) need for an outside agent to provide release from inhibition and anxiety. Aspirations set unrealistically high, frustrating life conditions, and a family context leading to passivity and immaturity have left these personalities inadequate in dealing with frustration.

The prognosis is poor for morphine (and derivative) addicts, better for other drugs, and good for alcoholics who recognize their problem and want to change.

—M. G. Affinito, *Southern Connecticut State College*

See also Alcoholism; Compulsive Personality; Cyclothymic Personality; Drugs and Behavior; Emotionally Unstable Personality; Hypomanic Personality; Hysterical Personality; Inadequate Personality; Neurotic Personality; Paranoid Personality; Schizoid Personality; Sexual Deviations.

Consult (9) Coleman, 1960; (13) Coleman, 1964.

PERSONALITY INVENTORY, a device for assessing personality. An inventory may consist of a large number of questions such as "Do you blush easily?" or "Do you like to be with other people most of the time?" The subject responds to each by checking "Yes," "No," or "?". Other inventories require the subject to chose between pairs of statements.

Sometimes these measuring instruments are called "tests," but they have important differences from achievement or intelligence tests, on which answers can be scored right or wrong. There is no correct or incorrect answer to an inquiry about blushing. All the inventory can do is suggest what personality trait pattern an individual has.

See also Minnesota Multiphasic Personality Inventory; Personality.

Consult (1) Hilgard, *et al.,* 1970. (12) Cronbach, 1970.

PERSONNEL PSYCHOLOGY, a division of industrial psychology that specializes in selecting, evaluating, and training personnel and in morale and relations of management to employees. *See* Industrial Psychology; Vocational Aptitude Tests.

PERSONOLOGY, a theory developed by Henry A. Murray that views the personality as a continuously developing process spanning the entire lifetime of the individual. This process mediates between the person and his needs and the demands of the environment. Murray defined a variety of needs (derived from psychoanalytic conceptions of child development) that serve to motivate the individual and argued that, although everyone is motivated to some extent by the same needs, it is the particular combination of needs and the way in which they operate on the individual that define and determine each person's uniqueness. Thus, personology emphasizes both the continuity and generality of motivational variables as well as the distinctness of each human being.

—Michael Rothenberg, *The City College of The City University of New York*

PHALLIC STAGE. In psychoanalytic theory, the sexual dominance of the phallus (erect penis) emerges out of the pregenital stage at about age three or four. Such focusing of stimulation in one zone, overwhelming for the immature organism, may be experienced as anxiety. Instinctively and experientially the mother is seen as the wish-fulfilling object who can reduce this tension. Normally, however, she rejects her son's incestuous advances.

Recognizing that his mother is already possessed by his father, who is larger in body and genitals, the child perceives him as the powerful enemy who might punish, especially through castration. Frustrated and anxious, he resolves this Oedipal situation at about age six through sublimation and identification, which form the basis for intellectual and superego development. Character and civilization depend on the successful resolution of this stage.

The female experiences jealousy over the lost penis, blames her mother, turns to her father, and encounters a competitive situation somewhat analogous to the boy's.

—M. G. Affinito, *Southern Connecticut State College*

See also Character Development; Oedipus Complex.

PHARMACOLOGY. *See* Drugs and Behavior.

PHENOTYPE, the numerous features by which an individual is recognized. In addition to eye color, hair color, and body shape, phenotypic characteristics include the individual's biochemical processes, physiological qualities, and behavior. Phenotype must be distinguished from *genotype* or genetic makeup. *See* Genotype.

PHENYLKETONURIA (PKU). *See* Brain Disorders; Mental Retardation.

PHI PHENOMENON. *See* Apparent Movement.

PHILOSOPHICAL PSYCHOLOGY. Also known as philosophy of mind, this area of study is concerned with the conceptual and speculative problems involved in the science of psychology. It attempts to analyze and clarify fundamental concepts involved in the scientific explanation of mental events and process—namely, mind, consciousness, self, soul, memory, will, cognition, and perception.

Philosophical psychology attempts to answer certain broad questions. Is the mind a unique, irreducible substance or a state or process of the brain? How is the mind related to the body and to the soul? Are the customary distinctions between mind, brain, and soul illusory or valid? What is the nature of the self? What are the criteria for saying that a given self or person remains the same self or person? What is the will: is it determined or are beings with wills capable of free choice? What is an intentional state, and is there a difference between an intentional relation (that between an emotion and the object of an emotion) and a causal relation? Are emotions appraisals, and do they constitute types of cognition? Since these are primarily metaphysical and epistemological issues, the validity of answers to them rest heavily on the adequacy of the theories of meaning and knowledge presupposed by the philosophical psychologist, over which there is great controversy.

The American Psychological Association, the American Philosophical Association, and the Southern Society for Philosophy and Psychology all sponsor papers and symposia on problems in philosophical psychology at many of their annual meetings. Journals that frequently publish in the area include *Philosophy of Science, Mind, British Journal of Psychology,* and *The Philosophical Review.* The works of William James, Sigmund Freud, and B. F. Skinner contain uses and analyses of key mental concepts; Bertrand Russell's *Analysis of Mind* (1921), Gilbert Ryle's *The Concept of Mind* (1949), and Peter Strawson's *Individuals* (1959) are important landmarks in the field. A good selected bibliography can be found in Paul Edwards and Arthur Pap's *A Modern Introduction to Philosophy* (1965), pages 266–278.

—W. T. Blackstone, *University of Georgia*

PHOBIA, a persistent, intense fear of specific persons, objects, or situations accompanied by a wish to flee or avoid the fear-provoking stimulus. Defined in this way, "phobia" does not necessarily have pathological connotations. However, the term has generally come to suggest a fear that is irrational and unrealistic. Thus, not every fear is a phobia: to be afraid of a raging fire in one's home does not mean one is pyrophobic, for example. Fears that are realistic and based on sound judgment are not phobias.

At the root of all phobias is intense anxiety that stems not from an observable present danger but from one that is unconscious. The phobic person is continuously vulnerable to extreme states of anxiety. When the anxiety is associated with a particular person or situation, and when the recognition of that anxiety is totally unacceptable to the individual, it is displaced onto some other, less threatening person or situation. In Freud's report of the case of Little Hans, for example, a five-year-old child's morbid fear of his father was displaced onto horses; this allowed him to continue to live within his own family and express his anxiety in more acceptable ways.

In the case of a phobic reaction, the person usually is aware that his fear is irrational, but this in no way alleviates his anxiety. Instead, he attempts to rationalize it, to make it seem more like reasonable caution in the face of real dangers. However, even when the supposed dangers have been eliminated, the phobia persists. Thus, a claustrophobic person who is afraid of suffocating in a closed room will find little real comfort in the knowledge that the room is adequately ventilated.

Childhood phobias often resolve themselves with normal physical and sexual development. However, many phobias remain static or, in more pathological cases, become attached to a widening range of activities and objects as each of these comes to stimulate the underlying conflict. In the extreme, a person may not go outside of his own home.

One successful method for the treatment of phobic reactions is *desensitization*. With this technique, the patient is helped to gradually acclimate himself to stimuli associated with the phobic situation until he responds with less acute anxiety. Eventually he is able to tolerate the actual phobic situation. Training in relaxation is an integral part of desensitization. Unlike psychoanalytic therapy, no attempt is made to identify or resolve the conflict underlying the phobic reaction.

Glossary of Common Phobias

Acrophobia—excessive fear of heights.

Agoraphobia—excessive fear of open spaces.

Ailurophobia—excessive fear of cats.

Astraphobia—excessive fear of lightning or thunder.

Claustrophobia—excessive fear of enclosed spaces.

Hematophobia—excessive fear of blood.

Mysophobia—excessive fear of dirt or contamination.

Nyctophobia—excessive fear of the night.

Pyrophobia—excessive fear of fire.

Xenophobia—excessive fear of strange persons or places.

Zoophobia—excessive fear of animals.
—Michael Rothenberg, *The City College of The City University of New York*
See also Behavior Therapy.
Consult (13) Coleman, 1964.

PHONEME. *See* Language.

PHONETICS. *See* Speech.

PHRENOLOGY, a theory of personality and a method of studying personality traits that was very popular in the first half of the nineteenth century but is now considered pseudoscience. Phrenologists believed that personality could be divided into a number of specific traits and that each of these faculties was centered in a particular region of the brain. Maps of the head were drawn to show the location of faculties, and bumps on the skull were taken as evidence of strong development of the adjacent characteristic.

Although some of the concepts of phrenology are ancient, the field developed largely through the work of two Germans, Franz Josef Gall (1758–1828) and Johann Kaspar Spurzheim (1776–1832). Gall identified twenty-seven faculties, and Spurzheim refined the list to include thirty-five. Among these were "propensities," such as amativeness, philoprogenitiveness, and combativeness; "lower sentiments" (common to man and lower animals), such as self-esteem and cautiousness; "higher sentiments" (peculiar to man), such as benevolence and wit; "perceptive faculties," such as color, number,

A phrenologist's studio, circa 1830.

and language; and two "reflective faculties," comparisons and causality.

Spurzheim believed that he was developing a science of the mind (this is the meaning of his term "phrenology"). At the same time, many quacks entered the "head reading" business. After a surge of popularity, phrenology went out of fashion.

Twentieth-century studies of brain structure and function have shown no correspondence between phrenologists' maps and centers that regulate behavior. It is true that areas of the brain have been shown to relate to aggressive and other kinds of behaviors, but this is very different from supposing that there are distinct faculties called "combativeness" or "language" that are neatly governed by specific spots in the head and that these traits are inherited.

Although the specific beliefs of phrenology have been discarded, the school had an important influence on the development of modern psychology. Gall and Spurzheim stressed and advertised the concept that physiological factors can influence behavior. In psychiatry, this was a new and helpful approach at a time when mental illness was often attributed to possession by the devil. In psychology generally, the ideas of phrenologists stimulated the study of behavior by objective methods.

See also Brain.

PHYSIOGNOMY, the belief that personality traits can be judged from physical appearance, particularly the form and expression of the face. Literature and daily speech are full of examples of this belief. Shakespeare has Julius Caesar tell that he prefers "sleek-headed men" to Cassius, whose "lean and hungry look" suggests he is dangerous. It is common practice to stereotype people as "bull-headed," "weak-chinned," and "shifty-eyed," or as having a "generous mouth" or a "noble brow."

An Italian criminologist, Cesare Lombroso (1836–1909), claimed that he could identify "criminal types" by "degenerate" characteristics, such as low brows and eyes set closely together. His ideas had considerable popularity in the first part of the twentieth century, but they have since been rejected by scientists. Psychologists conducted experimental tests that found no validity in judgments of intelligence and other characteristics from facial expressions. Measurements of criminals have disproved Lombroso's theories. Physiognomy is now classed as pseudoscience.

See also Phrenology.

PHYSIOLOGICAL PSYCHOLOGY. This division of psychology is a hybrid field. A physiological psychologist must be well trained in the areas of psychology and physiology. Furthermore, he may need to be competent in other areas,

PHYSIOLOGICAL PSYCHOLOGY

NERVOUS SYSTEM

    central nervous system
    peripheral nervous system
    ganglion
    nerve
    spinal cord
    AUTONOMIC NERVOUS SYSTEM
    sympathetic nervous system
    parasympathetic nervous system

    NEURON
    SYNAPSE
    ALL-OR-NONE LAW

    RECEPTORS
    EFFECTORS
    REFLEX

GLANDS

    ADRENAL GLANDS
    GONADS
    PARATHYROID GLANDS
    THYROID GLAND

BRAIN

    CEREBELLUM
    CEREBRAL CORTEX
    CINGULATE GYRUS
    HYPOTHALAMUS
    LIMBIC REGION
    MEDULLA OBLONGATA
    PINEAL GLAND
    PITUITARY GLAND
    SEPTAL REGION
    TEMPORAL LOBES
    THALAMUS

    BRAIN WAVES
    BIOFEEDBACK
    BRAIN STORAGE
    CHEMICAL STIMULATION
        OF THE BRAIN
    ELECTRICAL STIMULATION
        OF THE BRAIN
    BRAIN DISORDERS
    PSYCHOSURGERY
    SLEEP AND DREAMS

SENSATION

    EQUILIBRIUM SENSE
    HEARING
    INTEROCEPTIVE SENSES
    KINESTHETIC SENSE
    PAIN
    SKIN SENSES
    SMELL
    TASTE
    TEMPERATURE SENSE
    TOUCH
    VISION

The Subject Maps in the Encyclopedia illustrate the coverage of particular aspects of psychology, showing the interrelationships among the articles in twelve major areas of study. Entries in capital letters are subjects for which there are separate articles in the Encyclopedia. Entries in small letters are cross references.

The Subject Maps appear in the Encyclopedia under the following titles:

Abnormal and Clinical Psychology
Developmental Psychology
Emotion and Motivation
Intelligence
Learning and Memory
Measurement
Personality and Individual Difference
Physiological and Comparative Psychology
Psychology: Divisions and Schools
Sensation and Perception
Social Psychology
Thinking and Language

Swiss psychologist Jean Piaget developed new techniques for child behavior study and new theories about the nature of their cognitive development.

including neuroanatomy, pharmacology, neurology, neurophysiology, and perhaps even biophysics. Physiological psychology is closely related to psychobiology, or biological psychology, which deals with the biological bases of behavior.

The physiological psychologist is interested in the physiological, biological, and anatomical mechanisms responsible for behavior. But his primary interest is in behavior, and his interest in physiology is secondary. Thus, he can be contrasted with the neurophysiologist, who, in studying phenomena such as the control of sleep, muscle, or glandular function, is primarily a physiologist employing behavior as a tool to gain an understanding of physiological mechanisms.

A new term, *neuroscientist,* has come into use, largely as a result of the formation of the Society for the Neuroscience. This organization of several thousand members has the goal of bringing together all sciences that deal with the study of the brain and the relationship between brain and behavior.

Currently physiological psychologists are asking such questions as what is the basis for memory function? How do drugs exert their effects on behavior? What are the brain structures responsible for mediating emotional and motivational states? What is the physiological basis for sleep and dreaming? Because many of their experiments are conducted with animals, their work is related to comparative psychology. Division 6 of the American Psychological Association is the Division of Physiological and Comparative Psychology.

—Joel F. Lubar, *University of Tennessee Consult* (3) Isaacson, *et al.,* 1971; Teitelbaum, 1967; Thompson, 1967.

PIAGET, JEAN (1896–), Swiss child psychologist. From 1929 he was director of studies at the Institut Jean-Jacques Rousseau of Geneva.

A prodigy, Piaget published scientific papers while in his early teens and developed wide-ranging interests in the physical sciences, philosophy, logic, and child development. Fascinated with the kinds of errors that young children make in solving problems, Piaget realized that children's thinking was qualitatively as well as quantitatively different from that of adults. Consequently, he developed an ambitious plan for investigating and describing the whole process of the development of thinking in childhood, from early infancy to maturity.

In a long series of studies, Piaget devised methods of study for observing children's behavior and developed concepts to describe the major processes and changes that take place in children's thinking. His general conclusion was that the thinking of children below the age of eleven years differs considerably from adult thinking and that normally children experience a series of crucial shifts or stages at predictable

ages. (These stages are summarized in the article on Cognitive Development.)

Although they were slow to gain influence in the United States, Piaget's ideas began to be taken seriously in the late 1950s, when many child psychologists were becoming increasingly dissatisfied with traditional explanations of thinking in childhood from the point of view of learning theories. Piaget's approach offered the advantage of respecting the child's subjective point of view on the world, but at the same time his theory accepts the complexity of thinking and its development. At present many of Piaget's assumptions and concepts are being challenged and put to the test in psychology. However, no one any longer questions the importance of Piaget's contribution, which is the most comprehensive and systematic treatment of cognitive development ever devised.

Major works by Piaget include *The Language and Thought of the Child* (1926), *The Origins of Intelligence in Children* (1952), and *Six Psychological Studies* (1968).

—Roland Siiter, *Montclair State College See also* Bruner; Cognitive Development.

PICA. A craving to eat such substances as clay, earth, starch, hair, plaster, and paint. Though the craving may sometimes be a response to a deficiency in the diet, most of the substances consumed are not foods at all. Children who eat paint chips from walls or chew painted toys are in danger of lead poisoning if lead-based paints have been used. Lead poisoning can cause brain damage and mental retardation.

PINEAL GLAND, or pineal body, a small structure located at the center of the brain, just above the thalamus. In the seventeenth century René Descartes suggested that the pineal gland controlled the flow of humors to all portions of the brain and body and hence acted as the seat of consciousness or "soul." Today we know it has the less grandiose function of controlling body biological rhythms (circadian rhythms) in most animals. In lizards and in some birds the pineal body is sensitive to light and controls the organism's responsiveness as a function of day-night cycles. In mammals, including man, the pineal gland releases hormones that may play an important role in maintaining body biological rhythms.

—Joel F. Lubar, *University of Tennessee See also* Brain.

PINEL, PHILIPPE (1745–1826), French physician. Born at Saint André, Tarn, France, he received his M.D. from the University of Toulouse (1773) and was director of Bicetre Hospital (1792) and of Salpétriere (1795).

While the French Revolution was sweeping away the monarchy, Pinel was creating his own revolution in psychiatry. Rather

PINEAL GLAND

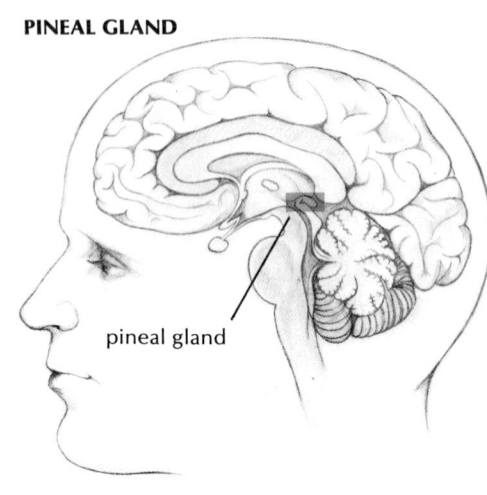

pineal gland

than keeping the mentally ill chained in hospital dungeons under conditions not fit for animals, Pinel released his patients from their chains and so laid the foundation for a method of effective and humane treatment. When Pinel asked permission of the president of the revolutionary Commune to free his patients from their chains at Bicetre, the president asked Pinel if "you are mad yourself that you want to unchain these animals." Pinel's historic answer was "it is my conviction that these mentally ill are intractable only because they are deprived of fresh air and their liberty."

Pinel believed that severe brain dysfunctions might be the cause of some psychological disorders; he also considered the effects of heredity and environment. Most importantly, Pinel believed each case should be treated separately. He wrote up case histories on each patient and he tried to build up a relationship between the physician and the patient by talking with each patient—the beginnings of psychotherapy. Violence, blood letting, purging, and the like were all discontinued as methods of treatment. Pinel described his method as the "moral treatment" and he described it fully in his *Traite Metaphilosophique sur la Manie* (1801). One of his most prominent students was Jean Esquirol.

PITUITARY GLAND, also known as the hypophysis, often described as the master control gland of the endocrine system. The pituitary is located at the base of the brain and has two divisions, a neurohypophysis and the adenohypophysis. The *neurohypophysis* controls the secretion of several important hormones. One is the antidiuretic hormone, which maintains water balance; the second, oxytocin, acts upon blood pressure and controls the ejection of milk from the mammillary glands. The *adenohypophysis* is entirely glandular and releases into the bloodstream many substances that act upon peripheral endocrine organs. An example is adrenocorticotropic hormone (ACTH), which controls the secretions of the adrenal gland.

—Joel F. Lubar, *University of Tennessee*

PLATEAU. *See* Learning Curve.

PLAY. The patterns of play in children closely parallel their cognitive, physical, sex-role, and social development. The "play" of infants is primarily of two types. *Solitary* activities consist of exploration and experimentation with simple household objects and toys. Adult-initiated "social" activities include "peek-a-boo" and "pat-a-cake."

Beginning in the second year, some children engage in *parallel play*. Thus when several toddlers are playing in proximity to one another (as in a sandbox), each engages in his own pursuits. Social interaction is usually limited to the demand for a desired toy being used by another child.

The play of three- to five-year-olds is characteristically active and vigorous, often making use of newly acquired skills. Early in this age range play is only vaguely planned and often lacks sustained purpose. Activities such as jumping, climbing, skipping, and even painting are enjoyed for the pure pleasure of the activity and the mastery of self and objects involved. Make-believe, or dramatic play, in which everyday family, school, and "marketing" activities are imaginatively reenacted is also highly characteristic of preschoolers.

As the youngster enters the middle childhood years, he begins to enjoy games with simple rules, competitive and, occasionally, cooperative activities. Children frequently adhere to the rules of games with such a ritualistic intensity that many games have been passed down from one generation to the next virtually unchanged since medieval times. Solitary as well as social play (which is now primarily restricted to children of the same sex) increasingly centers around constructing, manipulating, and creating objects that use real tools and materials.

—Cynthia MacRitchie, *Southern Connecticut State College*

PLEASURE PRINCIPLE. In 1911 Sigmund Freud postulated two basic principles of mental functioning that derived from the organism's need to maintain a constant state of equilibrium—the pleasure and the reality principles.

The *pleasure principle,* which Freud considered inborn, referred to the tendency of the organism to avoid pain and seek pleasure through immediate discharge of bodily tensions and drives. From psychoanalysis of free associations and dreams, Freud had observed that sexual instincts constantly strive for pleasure or avoidance of pain in a very primitive and demanding fashion. Even though the well-socialized adult ordinarily did not act out these wishes and might not be even aware of their existence, Freud held that such typically irrational, inexpedient, amoral, and childish urges were basic features of human motivation.

Opposing these impulses are the ego instincts, which operate according to the reality principle. It demands delay or postponement of immediate pleasure, with the aim of perhaps achieving greater pleasure in the long run.

—Alden E. Wessman, *The City College of The City University of New York*
See also Reality Principle.
Consult (13) Freud, 1925.

POSTHYPNOTIC SUGGESTION. A hypnotized subject can be instructed to carry out some act on a signal at a time after he is out of the hypnotic trance state. For example, the hypno-

Parallel play, in which the children stay near to one another but enjoy their own pursuits.

The child in early school years enjoys cooperative activities, usually with children of his own sex.

The active play of the five-year old makes use of newly acquired skills.

tist may suggest that the subject will resume his hypnotic condition when he hears a bell or when the hypnotist gives a signal. These suggestions are usually carried out. *See* Hypnosis.

POWER, the capacity of one party (the *source*) to influence the behavior of another party (the *target*) in a direction desired by the first. The parties referred to in this definition can be individuals, groups, or organizations.

A unitary concept of power does not seem useful for psychological analysis. Instead B. H. Raven and A. W. Kruglanski have distinguished six broad classes of power: (1) *legitimate power,* based on the target's belief that the source has the right to prescribe behavior for him in the matter at hand; (2) *informational power,* based on the source's possession of information that suggests ways in which the target can satisfy his needs and values; (3) *expert power,* based on the target's belief that the source is knowledgeable about the matter at hand; (4) *referent power,* based on the target's identification with the source, and hence the degree to which he respects the source and finds him attractive; (5) *reward power,* based on the source's capacity to satisfy the target's needs; and (6) *coercive power,* based on the source's capacity to punish the target. To this list can be added *cooriented power,* which is based on the target's belief that the source has values similar to his own, and *reciprocal power,* which is based on the source's provision of a prior benefit to the target.

In this classification scheme, power is not viewed as a property of the source but a feature of the relationship between source and target. Nor is this a one-way relationship with one party always the source and the other the target. Rather, each party in a relationship typically has some form of power over the other, and the parties alternate as source and target.

A combination of expert and cooriented power is often responsible for the target's willingness to accept suggestions from the source without fully understanding the rationale underlying them. This combination constitutes what is sometimes called *interpersonal trust.* Such trust is often the historical residue of the source's earlier displays of competence and his adherence to norms valued by the target. Political power is often based on such trust.

Empirical research has concentrated mainly on reward and coercive power. These types of power are ordinarily exercised in the form of promises and threats, which may be either explicit or implicit. Credibility is essential for the success of such moves. In other words, the target must believe that the source has the capacity and intention to follow through on his promises and threats. The source's capacity to maintain surveillance over the target's behavior is an element of credibility. The credibility of threats is also enhanced by the consistency of past enforcement and diminished to the extent that the source incurs costs by punishing the target. The use of coercive power tends to diminish other forms of influence, such as referent power.

—Dean G. Pruitt, *State University of New York at Buffalo*

Consult (10) Gamson, 1968; Hollander, 1971; Jones and Gerald, 1967; Mogy and Pruitt, 1973; Raven and Kruglanski, 1970; Tedeschi, 1970.

PRACTICE. Psychologists studying learning have investigated the efficiency of massed versus distributed practice. In *massed* practice, the learner sticks at his task for considerable periods of time; in *distributed* practice, he alternates rest periods with practice sessions or trials of a skill. In many cases, distributed practice has been found to give better results. Hermann Ebbinghaus, for example, reported this conclusion from his studies of memorization. There are exceptions, however; massed practice seems to be advantageous in dealing with some difficult learning materials.

See also Learning Curve.

Consult (1) Hilgard, *et al.,* 1972.

PRECOGNITION (one form of extrasensory perception, or ESP), a direct response to a future event that is not explainable by inference. Stories of prophecy are common in folklore, as are anecdotes of "dreaming true," as when Abraham Lincoln dreamed of his assassination. Such claims are inconclusive: perhaps they are normal inferences, fears, or hopes; they may be stated only after the event or may be coincidental. However, rigorous laboratory research has demonstrated precognition in experiments where subjects guess the order of "targets" that have been selected randomly (for example, by throwing dice to determine the point of entry, then following the order of a random number table).

—Gertrude R. Schmeidler, *The City College of The City University of New York*

See also Extrasensory Perception; Parapsychology.

Consult (14) Ebon, 1968.

PRECONSCIOUS. In Freud's earlier theories of psychoanalysis, he postulated three regions of the mind. In the *conscious* are thoughts of which we are fully aware. In the *preconscious* (or foreconscious) are thoughts that are not now in awareness but that can be recalled when wanted—memories of recent events, recollections of friends, and the like. Thoughts

Children doing a test of precognition. Before a story is told, they attempt to guess which one of the drawings is right for the story. "Chance" will determine the order of targets.

in the *unconscious* have been repressed and can be recovered only by hypnosis, free association, or other special techniques.

See also Unconscious.

PREDISPOSITION. Inherited factors may predispose an individual to develop in a certain way, but his environment influences his actual course of development. For example, one theory is that some people have a predisposition to develop psychosomatic illness. If they are put under sufficient stress, disorders appear. *See* Heredity and Environment; Psychosomatic Disorders.

PREGENITAL STAGE, in psychoanalytic theory, includes the oral (birth to about two years) and anal (about two to three or four years) stages. Sexual emphasis on oral incorporation and failure to differentiate self from other provide the prototype of identification. The anal stage contains conflicts typical of the active-passive dimension.

See also Anal Character; Oral Character.

PREJUDICE. To answer the question "What is prejudice?" it is necessary to distinguish two types of scientific definitions: A *conceptual* definition specifies what something is at an abstract level and is used in communication between scientists. An *operational* definition specifies a particular process by which a concept is measured. That is, it tells us what the concept means in terms of observable phenomena.

Conceptual Definition

Although conceptual definitions of prejudice differ in many ways, four factors occur in almost every one of them.

Prejudice Is a Negative Orientation. In everyday usage "prejudice" can mean a bias in favor of as well as against something. Social scientists, however, reserve the term for negative orientations.

Prejudice Is an Intergroup Phenomenon. Whereas in common usage we can speak of a prejudice against suburban houses or classical music, social scientists reserve the term for negative orientations toward groups of people and the members of these groups. That is, prejudice is basically directed at groups; individuals receive prejudicial treatment because they are perceived to be members of a particular group.

Throughout history the most common objects of prejudice have been minority groups. Originally, "minority" simply meant that the group was a numerical minority in a particular population—blacks are a minority group in the United States, comprising only about 12 percent of the total population. Over the years, however, the term has been broadened to mean any group that has an inferior political and economic (that is, power) position in a society. Blacks in the Republic of South Africa, for example, outnumber whites yet they are a minority group in that they occupy an inferior political and economic position in that society.

Prejudice is also commonly directed against racial groups. Although anthropologists define racial groups in terms of shared genetic features, prejudice is directed against socially defined racial groups. For example, many Indian or Pakistani visitors to the United States have received impolite and sometimes hostile treatment because their dark skin defined them as "Negroes"—even though anthropologists classify them as Caucasian in terms of their genetic makeup.

That prejudice is an intergroup phenomenon assumes that people think in terms of groups. Although each individual does respond to others as individuals, there is also a strong tendency to use categories in thinking about other people. Some of the most prominent categories are racial (for example, Negroes, whites, Orientals), ethnic (Catholics, Italians), and sexual (male, female). To some extent thinking in terms of categories of people is unavoidable. It is simply not possible for humans, even with their amazing intellectual capacity, to perceive all the uniqueness of every individual.

The categorization process involved in prejudice goes beyond that required for effective interpersonal functioning and in many cases interferes with such functioning. Categorization generally creates *stereotypes,* beliefs about the personality or behavior of people who are members of a particular group—for example, "Italians are emotional," "Turks are violent."

Prejudice Is Bad. All researchers concerned with prejudice and stereotypes see them as something to be reduced or eradicated. Some have argued that prejudice is bad because it is difficult to change and therefore is a somewhat irrational attitude (evidence that refutes stereotypes often does not yield reduced prejudice). Yet change is possible, and except for the most bigoted individuals prejudice is no more irrational than most other attitudes. This does not mean that prejudices are perfectly valid and logical attitudes. On the contrary, prejudice is bad for a number of reasons. First, the prejudiced individual ignores the range of variation in behavior and personality of the target group. Second, he thinks that his beliefs (stereotypes) about the group came first and that his negative attitude followed from and was based upon these beliefs. In fact, the reverse is generally true—children acquire negative attitudes toward outgroups and later learn the stereotypes appropriate to these prejudices. Finally, the preju-

Prejudice. Children generally acquire negative attitudes toward out-groups and later learn the stereotypes appropriate to these prejudices. Interaction among children of different ethnic groups often tends to reduce prejudice.

diced person assumes that people in the target group have certain jobs, behave in certain ways, and so on, *because of* their ethnic or racial background rather than because of cultural prescriptions or a history of discrimination.

Prejudice Is an Attitude. In psychology an *attitude* is an internal predisposition to respond favorably or unfavorably, positively or negatively, toward a particular class of objects. Prejudice is a specific type of attitude in which the object is a socially defined group.

It is important to note that attitudes—like feelings and other significant psychological variables—are internal and not directly observable.

By putting together these four factors, we arrive at the following definition of prejudice: "a negative attitude toward a socially defined group and toward any person perceived to be a member of that group." This attitude is invalid and undesirable. [*Consult* (10) Ashmore, 1970.]

Operational Definitions

Prejudice, like other attitudes, can only be seen indirectly in the way it shapes overt behavior. The psychologist must study overt behavior to infer whether the underlying attitude of prejudice exists. Five major types of prejudice measures have been used. [*Consult* (10) Cook and Selitz, 1964.]

Self-Reports. Prejudice is most often measured by asking people to answer questions or respond to statements. For example, a self-report measure of anti-Semitism might ask the respondent whether or not he agrees with such statements as "Jews are sneaky and conniving" and "It is simply not true that Jews are more clannish than other people." It is assumed that people who agree with the first statement and disagree with the second have more anti-Semitic feelings than those who show the opposite pattern.

Observation. Prejudice is also inferred from observations of how individuals behave toward a particular group or group member. For example, those who are more willing to help a Japanese or Chinese who needs directions in a strange city are assumed to be lower in anti-Oriental prejudice.

Performance on Objective Tasks. Many objective tasks such as memorizing words or judging how plausible a statement is can also serve to measure prejudice. For example, people high in antiblack prejudice are more likely to rate as implausible such statements as "Segregation leads to a waste of our human resources by decreasing the scientific and professional training given to capable Negroes."

Projective Techniques. Prejudice can also be assessed by asking people to describe or tell a story about unstructured, unclear stimuli. As with objective task measures, it is assumed that attitudes influence the descriptions given or stories told. A psychologist might measure antiwomen prejudice by asking people to describe what is happening in a series of pictures that show women in positions of responsibility and power (for example, a woman in a dark robe sitting in what appears to be a courtroom). Those high in antiwomen prejudice might deny that the woman really is a judge.

Physiological Measures. In recent years attempts have been made to use measures of bodily activity (such as heart rate and skin conductance) in the presence of the attitude object as indicators of prejudice. At present, however, physiological measures can indicate how much emotion a particular group arouses in a person, but they can not show whether the person is positively or negatively oriented toward the group.

Prejudice, Discrimination, Racism-Sexism

Obviously, other things besides attitudes help determine how an individual behaves toward a particular group and its members. Of these other factors, social pressures and legal restraints are probably the most important. That prejudice is just the determinant of hostile, harmful intergroup actions helps point up the difference between prejudice and the related terms "discrimination," "racism," and "sexism." While prejudice is an attitude, the latter three concepts all include at least some direct behavioral component.

Discrimination refers to behavior that keeps an individual from doing something (such as eating at a lunch counter) because of his membership in a particular group. *Racism* is "any attitude, action, or institutional structure that subordinates a person because of his or her color." *Sexism* can be defined as subordination of a woman on the basis of her sex. Thus, racism and sexism involve both negative attitudes and discriminatory behavior. And this discriminatory behavior may result from either prejudice or other factors such as social pressure (for example, a white store owner refusing to serve blacks for fear he will lose his white customers) or legal restraints (as one instance, prior to 1850 several Southern states had laws that prohibited teaching slaves how to read).

—Richard D. Ashmore, *Rutgers University*

See also Attitudes and Attitude Change.

Consult (10) Allport, 1954; Hecker, 1951; Harding, *et al.*, 1969; Jones, 1972.

PREMATURITY. See Intrauterine Environment; Mental Retardation.

PRENATAL DEVELOPMENT. See Intrauterine Development.

PRESCRIPTIVE LINGUISTICS, the traditional idea that some languages or dialects are "superior" to others in their clarity or possibilities for expression (for example, that languages of so-called primitive peoples are simpler than modern languages). Linguists completely reject such prescriptive value judgments, which are made largely on the basis of differences between cultures rather than between the languages themselves. In fact, as far as can be determined, any natural language or dialect has the same expressive potential as any other.

Some languages may require a few more words than others to say something, some a few less, depending on the cultural environment. But no one language is "better" than any other. Actually, many of the languages of so-called primitive peoples are much more complex in their rules and structure than the most familiar modern languages. Regardless of differences in rules and structural complexity, each language is equally capable of expressing the same meanings.

—Roland Siiter, *Montclair State College*
See also Codability; Language.

PROACTIVE INTERFERENCE. See Memory.

PROBABILITY SAMPLER. See Sampling.

PROBLEM SOLVING, (1) in general, behavior that is directed toward a goal whose attainment is not immediately available and involves some difficulty; (2) more commonly, human thinking directed toward finding the answer to a question, working puzzles, playing games, and the like. Concept learning and creativity are also frequently classified as problem solving but, because of their own unique properties, warrant separate classification. The following discussion, emphasizing the psychological study of human problem solving, will consider first problems that are often used and then turn to general theories of problem solving.

Problems and Tasks. Problems of every conceivable variety have been used to study thinking processes. The following have been particularly popular.

Word problems, especially anagrams—words whose letters have been scrambled; for example, IHCAR = "chair."

Numerical and arithmetic problems—for example, the famous water-jar problems used by A. S. Luchins.

Insight problems—those whose solutions usually occur quite suddenly after the solver sees some important relationship among problem elements. Two insight problems often used are the two-string problem and the candle problem.

The two-string problem requires the solver to find a way to tie together two widely separated strings hanging from the ceiling. The solution is to tie some object on the end of one string and swing it like a pendulum toward the other, enabling the solver to reach both strings and then tie them together. The candle prob-

lem is to attach candles to a screen in such a way that they stand upright. Insight comes when the solver realizes that among the objects provided for the experiment is a tack box that can be tacked to the screen to hold a candle.

Search tasks—which range from simple jigsaw puzzles to complex games like chess. The defining characteristic of these problems is that all possible alternatives are available to the solver; the problem is to choose or discover the "correct" or best alternative. With a jigsaw puzzle, for example, only one solution is correct for each piece. In chess, the "best" alternative cannot always be specified. Thus, the solver must depend on his past experiences and insights to give him rules of thumb, or *heuristics,* to help narrow down the possibilities.

Theories. Three different views of problem solving have been prominent in psychology, each stressing the importance of different kinds of processes. The differences between these approaches tend to determine not only which variables are examined, but also the problems and tasks that are used.

Learning theories have stressed the role of past experiences and previously formed associations in problem solving. In this view, the correct solution to a problem is considered to be a response low on the hierarchy of possible responses to the problem situation. In other words, problems take time to solve because the answer has low probability of occurrence and is likely to be aimed at only after those responses that are more immediately available to the solver have been attempted. "Thinking" is viewed as *mediation* leading to the desired response. In contrast to the cognitive approach, learning theories have tended to regard problem solving as a passive process in mediation, and associations are assumed to be primarily under the control of external stimuli and problem characteristics rather than internal thought processes.

The learning orientation basically classifies problem solving as a special instance of learning and memory and derives largely from traditional conceptions of *associationism.* Such analyses seem most appropriate for describing the solution of problems where the answer *necessarily* must come out of the subject's past memories, as in working out anagrams or other word problems. More complex problems, however, do not lend themselves well to analyses stressing memory and stimulus factors.

Gestalt psychology has stressed the role of perception and sudden reorganizations of the perceptual field, which are termed *insights,* in problem solving. In this view, past learning is less important than the solver's capacity to perceive the meaningful but often less obvious relationships involved in a problem, such as an

PROBLEM SOLVING

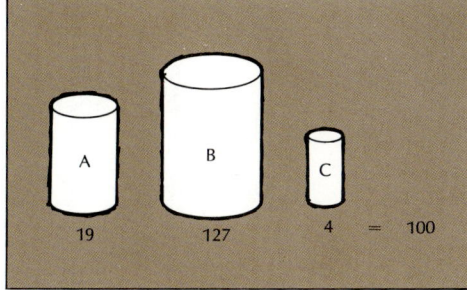

WATER-JAR PROBLEM
The water-jar problem is an arithmetic puzzle requiring the solver to obtain a specific amount of water using ungraduated measuring jars of known total capacity. For example, obtain 3 oz. of water, given A = 19 oz. capacity, B = 45 oz., C = 10 oz.

2 STRING PROBLEM
The two-string problem is an insight problem requiring the solver to tie two hanging strings together although he cannot reach one while holding the other. Insight comes when he realizes that he can attach an object to one string and swing it like a pendulum.

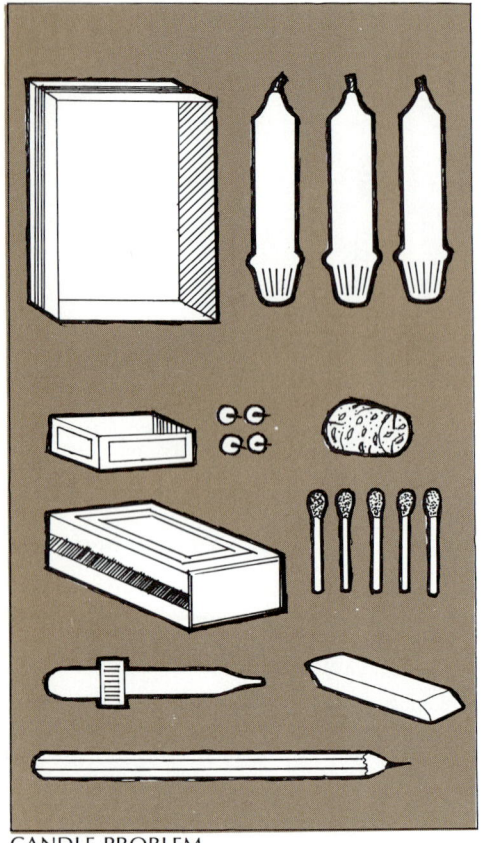

CANDLE PROBLEM

The candle problem, another insight problem, requires the solver to mount three candles vertically on a screen, using any of the items on the table. The solution requires that the boxes be tacked to the screen and the candle bases melted to them.

SQUARE PROBLEM

The solution to the square problem requires the solver to violate the organizing nature of perception. When asked to draw four straight lines that will pass through all the dots, without lifting his pencil from the paper, the solver unsuccessfully attempts to stay within the "confines" of the "square," although not instructed to do so.

unusual function for an ordinary tool (using pliers as a weight in the two-string problem) or a spatial relationship among problem elements (solving the "square" problem). Gestalt psychologists often refer to processes of insight and functional fixedness in problem solving.

Cognitive psychology, the most recent trend, regards problem solving as a series of stages or steps encompassing symbolic manipulations, operations, and feedback that are governed by strategies and heuristics. Not ignoring the role of past experience and learning, cognitive theories nevertheless attribute much more structure to thinking than associations and mediation. Also, unlike the learning version, the cognitive approach stresses problem solving as an *active* process, determined as much or more by internal rules and transformations of problem information as by external stimulus and situational factors. The attempt to construct models of the problem-solving process, as in computer simulation studies, typifies the differences of this approach from others.

—Roland Siiter, *Montclair State College*
See also Cognitive Psychology; Concept Learning; Functional Fixedness; Gestalt Psychology; Insight; Learning Theory; Learning-to-Learn; Transfer of Training.
Consult (7) Bourne, *et al.,* 1971; Duncker, 1945; Luchins, 1942; Maier, 1930.

PRODIGY. *See* Genius; Gifted Children.

PRODUCTIVITY, in work, arts, letters, and the like. *See* Aging; Middle Years.

PROFOUND MENTAL RETARDATION. *See* Mental Retardation.

PROGNOSTIC TEST, a measuring instrument that can be used to predict performance, as in college study or in a field of work. *See* Scholastic Aptitude Test; Vocational Aptitude Test.

PROGRAMMED LEARNING (also programmed instruction, autoinstruction, automated teaching), a self-instructional process accomplished by the use of textbook materials, mechanical apparatuses, or various forms of audiovisual monitoring devices (teaching machines). The object of the technique is to motivate the learner and facilitate the learning process by means of active involvement, individually paced progress, and immediate feedback and reinforcement. The programmed approach to instruction is largely the result of the theory and research of B. F. Skinner, who investigated operant (instrumental) conditioning, in which the control and direction of behavior are contingent upon reinforcement.

Most programmed instructional materials follow one of two major formats. In the *linear program,* each student, regardless of ability, proceeds through the program via a series of small controlled steps designed to eliminate almost any possibility of error. As he proceeds through the sequence of steps, the student constructs his own responses. The *branched program* varies the order of presentation of material, depending on the student's success or failure in responding. He is offered several answers to questions and must choose the one that he believes is correct. His selection will determine what material will be presented next. A correct response will direct him to the next step in the sequence of the program, whereas an incorrect response might lead to an explanation of his error, additional instructional review of related information, or even a retracing of previous steps. Such a program is designed to take the slower learner through the material by smaller steps than the more competent student.

Strong arguments exist both for and against programmed learning and instruction. Advantages over conventional programs that are frequently cited include: (1) its presentation of a logical, organized amount of material at a rate controlled by the learner; (2) its provision of continuous and immediate knowledge of results (feedback) and reinforcement; (3) its requirement of active participation in the learning process, which improves motivation and usually results in greater mastery and retention; and (4) its release of the teacher from responsibility for conveying so that he or she has more time for individualized instruction. One of the main disadvantages is that preparation of good programs is an arduous and often costly process (and autoinstruction is only as good as the program used). Furthermore, students have been known to tire of the technique, and their ability to think creatively is not directly stimulated. While programming relieves teachers of some of the repetitious tedium of teaching facts and information, it cannot replace the experiences and human interactions that can be provided by the teacher. To date, the research is, at best, equivocal and inconclusive regarding the overall inferiority or superiority of programmed instruction. It is probably best thought of as complementary to rather than a replacement for the classroom teacher.

—Frank T. Vitro, *University of Maine*
See also Operant Conditioning.
Consult (14) Lange, 1967.

PROJECTION, the process of turning outward one's own objectionable desires, attitudes, and motives and attributing them to others. The individual then sees these feelings as coming from sources outside of himself, even though they actually represent his own inner feelings.

Projected feelings can be interpreted as mirroring a person's own unconscious. For example, an individual who feels insecure, hostile, and uncomfortable with others may feel that nobody likes or will relate to him. Paranoid schizophrenics make excessive use of the defense mechanism of projection: they see an environment filled with hostile and suspicious individuals, though it is they themselves who harbor unconscious feelings of murderous rage.

—Michael Rothenberg, *The City College of The City University of New York*
See also Defense Mechanism.

PROJECTIVE TECHNIQUES, instruments for measuring personality designed on the theory that people will reveal their characteristics when they respond freely to stimuli that can be interpreted in many ways. For example, when taking the Rorschach technique, the subject is asked to tell what he sees in each of ten inkblots. The Thematic Apperception Test (TAT) consists of a series of pictures, and the subject is asked to make up a story about each scene. It is assumed that the person will project his own attitudes and feelings into the story that results from his interpretation of each picture. These and other techniques are described in separate articles.

Many of the projective instruments in use are called tests. Some authorities, however, prefer the label "technique" to differentiate these devices from school exams and others that have right and wrong answers. Projective techniques have to be interpreted rather than simply scored, and the interpretation may require extensive training.

A number of the projective methods are used in clinical work to provide clues for assessing personality problems and diagnosing mental disorders. They may also be used for such purposes as screening applicants for important positions.

See also Figure-Drawing Test; Holtzman Inkblot Technique; House-Tree-Person Technique; Make-A-Picture-Story Test (MAPS); Rorschach Technique; Rosenzweig Picture Frustration Study; Thematic Apperception Test (TAT); Tomkins-Horn Picture Arrangement Test; Word-Association Test.
Consult (12) Cronback, 1970.

PROPAGANDA. *See* Attitude and Attitude Change.

PROPRIOCEPTION. *See* Kinesthetic Sense.

PSEUDOCONDITIONING, or sensitization, the pattern that occurs when a stimulus not necessarily paired with a reinforcer leads to an increased probability of a response. For example, a loud noise might make a rat press a lever even if it is not paired with the food obtainable by pressing that lever. Pseudoconditioning is a particularly perplexing problem for psychologists who are trying to determine whether simple animals such as protozoa or flatworms are capable of true learning or are only sensitized by the presentation of conditioning stimuli.

—Joel F. Lubar, *University of Tennessee*
See also Backward Conditioning; Pavlovian Conditioning.
Consult (6) Kimble, 1961.

PSEUDOPSYCHOLOGY, subprofessional teaching and counsel, or outright quackery, in some field where psychology operates. Pseudoscientists are camp-followers of professional workers in most fields, but psychology has attracted a very large proportion of dubious practitioners. One reason, put bluntly, is that there is money in trouble and insecurity. Many people have serious fears and worries, and most people have times when they wish they could know more about themselves or lead more fulfilling lives. People will pay for what they think will help them. Thus there is a too-ready market for six steps to a perfect memory, ten ways to a charming personality, and courses of treatment guaranteed to win a partner or save a marriage. Activities in pseudopsychology range from traditional games such as palmreading, headreading, and dream books to elaborately fronted counseling by self-appointed experts on sex, marriage, and other complex personal problems.

To protect the public and the profession, the American Psychological Association has published standards for the practice of psychology. Most states now require by law that a person meet certification requirements before he can use the title "psychologist." [*Consult* (1) "Ethical Standards of Psychologists," 1968.]

Some caution should be used with labels such as "quack." Eminent men have been called charlatans in the period before their theories won respect—Freud is an example. Many fields have attracted both sincere students and quacks. For example, when Spurzheim was forming his theories of phrenology, he was sincere though (in the light of later findings about the brain) mistaken. One who now practices phrenology could be called a charlatan. Hypnosis is used by dangerous entertainers and ethical scientists. The qualifications and attitude of the person are what count.
See also Phrenology; Physiognomy.

PSEUDORETARDATION. Some children are mistakenly classed as mentally retarded. They may make low scores on intelligence tests and give other signs of deficiency, but retesting or observation later shows that they are of normal ability. The behavior that led to the first diagnosis may be due to lack of mothering, isolation and lack of stimulation, or emotional disturbance.

Note also the comment on cultural-

An effective teaching machine employing an ordinary typewriter with keys color-coded to pieces of colored tape on a child's fingers.

familial retardates in the article on Mental Retardation.

PSI-MISSING. *See* Extrasensory Perception.

PSYCHEDELIC DRUGS. *See* Drugs and Behavior.

PSYCHIATRIC SOCIAL WORKER, a professional who works with psychiatrists to help patients with mental disorders. These social workers are employed in hospitals, clinics, and community mental health centers. Typical duties include interviewing patients and members of their families (reports of the interviews are part of the background material used by psychiatrists in diagnosis and planning treatment); helping patients adjust to living in the hospital; counseling the patients' families; helping in rehabilitation programs.

Required training for a psychiatric social worker consists of four years of college (B.A. degree) plus two years in an accredited school of social work (M.A.) and a period of supervised experience.

PSYCHIATRIST. For training required and nature of careers, *see* Psychiatry.

PSYCHIATRY, the specialized branch of medical practice that deals with the diagnosis, treatment, and prevention of mental and emotional disorders. Consequently, a psychiatrist is a physician who has become especially qualified by training and clinical experience in the speciality of psychiatry.

Scope. In its scope, psychiatry embraces the following fields: mental deficiency, convulsive disorders, child psychiatry, problems of aging, legal responsibility and competency as regards financial matters, legal responsibility as to criminal activity, legal issues in commitments to mental hospitals, delinquency, family and marital maladjustment, military psychiatry, addictions (drug and alcohol), and all those social and environmental conditions that influence the development and course of psychiatric disorders.

The psychiatrist is primarily concerned with the treatment of psychotic and psychoneurotic disorders. In order to deal with them effectively—and more important, in order to avoid the possibility of making potentially lethal mistakes—it is essential that he possess a solid basic knowledge of general medicine. Not only do many physical disorders have symptoms that simulate psychiatric illness, but many physical illnesses have psychiatric components. The treatment plan must be designed to ameliorate both the physical and the mental (or emotional) components. No one suffering from a "nervous ailment" should commit himself to the care of a medically untrained individual such as a clinical psychologist or lay psychoanalyst unless he has been assured by a competent internist or psychiatrist that he does not have a physical illness that also needs attention. Since there is, and will be for the foreseeable future, a shortage of psychiatrists, then clinical psychologists, psychiatric social workers, psychiatric nurses, and counselors will have to be used extensively to manage the heavy psychiatric case load; but they should be used only when their activity is adequately supervised by a psychiatrist.

Requirements for Certification. The first prerequisite of a psychiatrist is that he possess the M.D. degree. This means that he has completed a "premedical course" of three to four years leading to at least a bachelor's degree, and then a four-year course in a grade A medical school. After graduating from medical school and thus getting his M.D. degree, he is required to pass either a state or national board examination in order to secure a license to practice medicine. Then, in order to meet the minimum requirements to become a "Diplomate of the American Board of Psychiatry and Neurology," he must spend at least five calendar years (comprising at least three years of training as a resident and two additional years of clinical experience) before he is eligible to apply for examination for certification as a psychiatrist. The examination consists of written and oral-practical parts, to be passed in that order. The examinations are exhaustive and difficult and constitute an almost insurmountable barrier for anyone who has had deficient training.

Thus, under the optimum conditions, and with maximum performance, the would-be psychiatrist will have spent at least thirteen years after his graduation from high school before achieving certification as a specialist. Assuming he has graduated from secondary school at the usual age of eighteen, he will be at least thirty-one before he has reached his goal. Nowadays, many psychiatrists take considerable more time than outlined above, since the intense competition to secure admission to the limited number of American or Canadian medical schools has impelled them to secure additional premedical qualifications by earning masters, or even Ph.D. degrees.

Needs and Opportunities. At present, there are about 10,000 board-certified psychiatrists "available" to serve the needs of a combined American and Canadian population of some 230,000,000. Even if we assume that there are three times as many physicians who are "noncertified"—that is, going through the training process—it is obvious that there must remain a tremendous unfilled need for psychiatrists. Staff positions are clamoring for applicants in private, federal, state, city, and county mental hospitals; mental hygiene clinics; community mental health centers; school, college, and university health services; the military services; large industrial corporations; and especially in recent years in drug addiction programs. Because of the demand, a qualified psychiatrist can readily secure a starting salary of $25,000 to $30,000 a year in an initial institutional appointment.

Many psychiatrists will work part-time (fifteen to twenty hours a week) in an institutional clinic or hospital for an assured income, and in addition maintain a private office where they can command fees for individual therapy ranging from $25 to $50 a session, (usually averaging forty minutes). If they choose to engage in "group" therapy, they can readily double or treble this rate of income.

Psychiatry, besides being a rapidly expanding field of medicine, is still one of the least developed, so great opportunities exist for research, experimentation, and new discoveries. Teaching ancillary workers in the mental health field is another area where psychiatrists are sorely needed. In this connection they are brought into a close pedagogical relationship with psychologists, social workers, nurses, aides, occupational therapists, vocational and rehabilitation specialists, recreational therapists, teachers, school and college counselors, probation officers, jurists, ministers, priests, and rabbis.

—Emanuel Messinger, M.D., *U.S. Veterans Hospital, Northport, N.Y.*

See also Child Psychiatry; Drugs and Behavior; Mental Health; Mental Hospitals; Psychoanalysis; Psychology and the Law; Psychoneurotic Disorders; Psychosomatic Disorders; Psychosurgery; Psychotherapy; Psychotic Disorders.

Consult (13) Arieti, 1966; Arieti, 1970; *Encyclopedia of Mental Health,* 1963; Freedman and Kaplan, 1967; Hinsie and Campbell, 1970; Noyes and Kolb, 1958.

PSYCHICAL RESEARCH. *See* Parapsychology.

PSYCHOANALYSIS is both a method of treating abnormal behavior and a theory for describing all behavior.

As a method of psychotherapy, psychoanalysis was originated by two Viennese physicians, Josef Breuer and Sigmund Freud, who described it in their *Studies on Hysteria,* published in 1893. It was not until 1896, however, that the word "psychoanalysis" was first used to designate the new methods of treating mental patients. By this time, Breuer had severed his connection with psychoanalysis, leaving its development and elaboration to Freud.

Freud's ideas met with considerable hostility from the medical profession, and he worked alone for a number of years. The publication of his *Interpretation of Dreams* (1900), *Psychopathology of Everyday Life* (1901), *A Case of Hysteria* (1905), and *Three Essays on Sexuality* (1905) attracted a small

group of disciples from various countries. This group, under the leadership of Freud, was responsible for initiating and guiding the psychoanalytic movement, which eventually spread throughout the world.

National associations of psychoanalysts were organized, and the International Psychoanalytic Association was formed in 1910. The objectives of these organizations include the dissemination of information about psychoanalysis and the sponsorship of institutes for the training of psychoanalysts. In the United States psychoanalytic institutes usually train only individuals who have a medical degree. Some of Freud's early disciples, notably Carl Jung and Alfred Adler, seceded from the movement and started their own schools of psychoanalysis, which developed in several directions.

Methods and Concepts. As originally conceived and practiced, psychoanalysis was a new method of psychotherapy. Among its techniques are free association, dream interpretation, overcoming the patient's resistances, and analyzing the transference relationship between patient and psychoanalyst. Orthodox psychoanalytic treatment requires seeing a patient daily for a period of several years.

Psychoanalysis also developed an explanation of neurosis. This theory holds that a neurosis has its inception in a traumatic experience during childhood. The memory of the experience is repressed and forgotten, but it still exists in the unconscious mind and produces neurotic symptoms later in life. Many of the traumatic experiences involve sexual conflicts. The aim of psychoanalytic therapy is to discover the childhood trauma and bring it back into consciousness, where it can be dealt with effectively and rationally.

Psychoanalysis does not restrict itself to the investigation and treatment of abnormal behavior. Freud intended that psychoanalysis should be a general psychology whose principles and theories would describe and explain the behavior of normal people. Psychoanalysis became a comprehensive system accounting for the organization, dynamics, and development of personality.

The personality organization consists of the id, ego, and superego. The *id* is unconscious and contains the instincts and repressed experiences. The *ego* is the executive of the personality; it tries to satisfy the instincts by appropriate interactions with the external world. The *superego* is a person's conscience, which develops as a result of social training by the parents. The personality organization is energized by the life and death instincts and their derivatives. A main source of energy is *libido* or sexual energy. The development of personality consists of a series of stages (oral, anal, and phallic) that the child passes through during the first five years of life. Other con-

Sigmund Freud, G. Stanley Hall, Carl Jung (front row), and A. A. Brill, Ernest Jones, Sandor Ferenczi (back row), at Clark University, Worcester, Mass., in 1909.

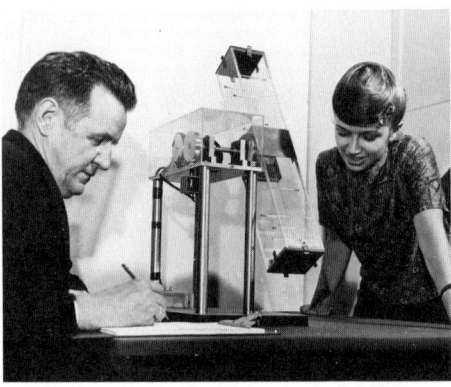

A test for psychokinesis using dice in a rotating cage. The girl is attempting to "will" the dice to fall with a designated face turned up.

Figure 1

JOURNALS SCANNED

The following list includes journals and reports which are scanned regularly and abstracted selectively.

Abstracts for Social Works
Academic Therapy
Academy of Management Journal
Accident Analysis & Prevention
ACT Research Report (American College Testing Program)
Acta Instituti Psychologici
Acta Medica Auxologica
Acta Neurobiologiae
Acta Neurobiologiae Experimentalis
Acta Neurologica
Acta Neurologica Belgica
Acta Neurologica Scandinavica
Acta Oto-Laryngologica
Acta Paedopsychiatrica
Acta Pharmacologica et Toxicologica
Acta Physiologica Polonica
Acta Psiquiátrica y Psicológica de América Latina
Acta Psychiatrica Belgica
Acta Psychiatrica Scandinavica
Acta Psychologica
Acta Psychologica Taiwanica
Acta Symbolica
Actas Luso-Españolas de Neurología y Psiquiatría
Activitas Nervosa Superior
Administrative Science Quarterly
Adolescence
Adult Development & Aging Abstracts
Adult Education
Aerospace Medicine
Afro-American Studies
Aging and Human Development
Agressologie
Alberta Journal of Educational Research
América Latina
American Annals of the Deaf
American Anthropologist
American Behavioral Scientist
American Educational Research Journal
American Foundation for the Blind, Research Bulletin
~an Foundation for the Blind, Research Series
~~·:~·tes of Research Report, Washingt~
→ Tʰ·

cepts that are employed in the psychoanalytic theory of personality are conflict, anxiety, rationalization, projection, repression, regression, identification, displacement, narcissism, masochism, sublimation, and the Oedipus and castration complexes.

The concepts and theories of psychoanalysis have been applied to a wide range of social and cultural phenomena.

Status. Since the death of Freud in 1939, psychoanalysis has changed in various ways. Greater emphasis is being placed on the autonomous integrative functions of the conscious ego and less emphasis on the instinctual impulses of the unconscious id. The concept of the death instinct has virtually been abandoned, although the analysis of the aggressive impulse has received increasing attention. Methods of treating patients in a shorter period of time have been devised. The psychoanalysis of children using play techniques has become more prevalent. Many new offshoots of psychoanalytic therapy, each with its own adherents and practitioners, have appeared.

Psychoanalysis, which was formerly shunned by medical schools and by academic psychology, has become more acceptable to them, although the training of psychoanalysts is still being done primarily by independent psychoanalytic institutes. The experimental investigation of psychoanalytic hypotheses by academic psychologists is a major trend, and an imposing body of research findings is rapidly accumulating.

The application of psychoanalytic theory in the social sciences and the arts continues unabated. Psychoanalytic ideas have penetrated all aspects of contemporary thought. Psychoanalysis has grown from a small and isolated group of disciples around Freud into a large and diversified movement of worldwide significance.

—Calvin S. Hall, Author of *A Primer of Freudian Psychology*

See also Adler; Ego; Freud; Id; Psychotherapy; Superego. *Other articles listed in the Item Guide under* Psychoanalysis.

Consult (13) Abraham, 1968; Brown, 1959; Freud, 1953–1964; Hall, 1954; Horney, 1939; Jones, 1953–1957.

PSYCHOBIOLOGY. There are a number of fields dealing with the relationship between the biological organism and behavior. The most broadly defined of these fields is psychobiology (sometimes also called *biopsychology*), which deals with the biological foundations of behavior. This vast and highly complex hybrid field analyzes behavior in terms of the biochemical and physiological factors that might play a role. It asks which anatomical structures and pathways might be involved in the mediation of specific behaviors.

Related but not exactly the same as

psychobiology is physiological psychology, dealing specifically with physiological mechanisms underlying behavior. Of a broader scope are the "neurosciences," dealing with all aspects of brain function—behavioral and medical, chemical and electrical.

—Joel F. Lubar, *University of Tennessee*
See also Physiological Psychology.

PSYCHODRAMA, a method of psychotherapy in which patients act out troublesome situations. The enactment may be done on an actual stage: the patient takes the leading role, trained assistants play other parts, and the therapist is the director. In another form of drama, a family group acts out problem situations. Taking roles in the drama helps people express emotions and gives insights into attitudes and motivations. The technique was developed by a psychiatrist, J. L. Moreno.

Consult (13) Moreno, 1947; Moreno, 1959.

PSYCHOGENIC, of psychic origin. Psychogenic disorders are contrasted with organic disorders, which can be explained by damage to an organ of the body. *See* Functional Disorder.

PSYCHOKINESIS (PK), a direct psychological effect upon a physical object that is not explainable by muscular or glandular response. Careful laboratory investigations show small but significant PK changes when subjects "will" a die face to turn up or a movement to change or a distant object to grow hotter or colder.

See also Parapsychology.

Consult (14) Pratt, 1960; Rhine, 1970; Schmeidler, 1972.

PSYCHOLINGUISTICS. *See* Language.

PSYCHOLOGICAL ABSTRACTS. One major tool in finding out more about psychology is *Psychological Abstracts,* a series published monthly by the American Psychological Association. *Psychological Abstracts* is a guide to the world's professional literature in psychology and related disciplines. It includes summaries of technical reports, journal articles, and books; in fact, it is very much like a mail-order catalog, with clear directions for finding whatever you may be looking for. The *Abstracts* are compiled into two volumes each year, with a cumulative index for each six-month volume. Each index starts with a list of all the national and international journals that are regularly searched for relevant material (Figure 1).

Using Psychological Abstracts. *Psychological Abstracts* provides summaries of journal articles and refers to books and specific chapters in books. In order to present this informa-

Figure 2

A Reader's Guide To Using Psychological Abstracts

Within the monthly issue, abstracts are arrange content headings as listed in the Table of Contents. month volume.

PA's author index is intended to be a name inde ly applied, consequently, "J. Smith" and "John Smi though they may in fact be the same person. By the J. Smith with two abstract numbers following it,

The subject index heading terms are reviewed ar the discipline shift and increase. For example, the terms when the increase of articles on the topic anc to the addition of this term these articles were place Therapy," and "Drug Addiction." Conversely, as a t delete a term or combine several terms into one ge

PA is computer-printed and because of necessar casion the abstracts representing articles from a si of PA, e.g., an issue of the Journal of Psychology may may appear in the May issue of PA, the other 3, in the

The following are examples of entries and expla- nations of their elements.

JOURNAL ARTICLE ENTRY

(1a) Brown, Mildred; (1b) Jones, John J., (1c) Wilson, J. T., & (1d) Carson, E. Norman. (2) (*Boston U.*) **(3) Single cell activity in the hypothalamus in intact and adrenalectomized rats. (4)** *Psychological Journal,* **(5a)** 1970(Jan), **(5b)** Vol. 13(6), **(5c)** 173–190.—**(6)** In this replication of a study by A. R. Arnold **(7)** (see **(7a)** PA, **(7b)** Vol. 42: **(7c)** 1791 and 45: **(7d)** Issue 1), 123 intact and adrenalectomized male Wistar rats were tested under urethane anesthesia. Adrenalectomy increased the mean spontaneous discharge and changed the pattern of firing of anterior hypothalamic neurons. The possible relation of these electrophysio- logical findings to the effects of adrenalectomy on the CNS is discussed. **(8)** (German & French summaries) **(9)** (97 ref.)—**(10)** *Journal abstract.*

1a-1d—Authors: Only four are listed; if there are more than four authors, the first author is listed followed by et al. Suc- cession marks are not given, e.g., Jr., II, III, etc.
2—Address: A mailable address is included for the first-named author **only.**
3—Title: Article title including subtitles. If the original article is in a foreign language, that title is given, followed by the English translation in brackets, e.g., [Parapsychology.].
4—Primary journal title in full.
5a—Year and month of the primary publication issue.
5b—Volume number followed by issue number in parentheses.
5c—Inclusive pagination of the article.
6—Text of the abstract.
7—Reference to a previous entry in **Psychological Abstracts.**
7a—**PA**=**Psychological Abstracts.**
7b—**PA** volume number.
7c—**PA** abstract number.
7d—**PA** issue number where abstract number is unavailable at time of publication. When only the issue number is given, one must consult the Author Index of the **PA** issue noted in order to determine the abstract number for the author and article cited.
8—Summaries included in the primary source are listed when in language(s) other than that of the article.
9—Number of references is included when 15 or more. May also appear as pages, e.g., (3 p. ref.).
10—Abstract source.

Figure 3

Subject Index

Ability (see also Childhood/Ability in)
ability attribution & impression formation in strategic game, primacy effect, 6676
ability estimates & risk, comparative & evaluative & task information, 10220
ability testing & complex skill acquisition, time & interpolated practice separating measurement from performance, flight students, 156
academic achievement & achievement related values & as- pirations, self-evaluated ability, high school seniors, 7741
academic achievement in chemistry, ability grouping vs. modified ability grouping, U.S. Military Academy students, 5793
acceptance of newcomers in success & failure work groups, race & high vs. low competence, 10770
adjustment & ability measurement as qualification criteria, Ss on alpine expeditions, (Germ) 9924
aptitude & draft vulnerability, Air Force enlistees, 7877
aptitude treatment interactions, remedial approach vs. in- ducement vs. preferential vs. compensatory models, 7839
attitudes & college orientations, Scholastic Aptitude Test scores & sex & socioeconomic status & environment, black students attending traditionally black vs. white institutions, 9611
attitudes toward school & class & work & peers & self, ability grouping in schools, superior vs. slow vs. heterogeneously grouped 10–12 yr. olds, 9859
attribution of greater riskiness to another, other's ability, college students, 8825
balance skill retention after 2 yr., a¹ ⁻ ' retesting of high school students ˙˙˙˙˙iuk's
˙˙ly, 6091

Figure 4

Brief Subject Index

Ability (see also Childhood/Ability in)
8140, 8231, 8681, 8825, 8916, 9602, 9611, 9758, 9788, 9799, 9828, 9834, 9844, 9859, 9883, 9888, 9899, 9903, 9924, 9938
Ability/Verbal (SEE Ability, Verbal Behavior)
Abnormal Behavior (SEE Behavior Disorder, Mental Disorder, Neurosis, Psychosis, spe- cific abnormalities)
Abnormal Psychology (SEE Clinical Psychol- ogy, Psychopathology)
Abortion
8743, 8744
Absolute Judgment (SEE Judgment/Percep- tual)
Abstraction (SEE Concept, Generalization, Thinking)
Academic Achievement (SEE Achievement/ Academic, Achievement/Academic– College, Achievement/Academic–Elemen- tary School)
Acceleration (SEE Movement)
Acceptance (see also Social Approval)
8837, 9193, 9245, 9320, 9413
Accident (SEE Driving, Safety˙
˙˙ ˙˙tion (SEE Adapta

Achievement (see also next headings)
8599, 8633, 8682, 8906, 8913, 94(
9513, 9899, 9906
Achievement Motivation (see also ment/Over & Under)
8123, 8673, 8683, 8698, 8702, 8˙
8878, 8893, 8906, 8912, 8922, 9
9638, 9799, 9817, 9852, 9861
Achievement Need (SEE Achievem vation, Aspiration & Aspiratic Need)
Achievement Test (SEE Test/Ac
Achievement/Academic (see also ment/Academic–College, Acl Academic–Elementary Schoo Learning, Sex Differences/ Achievement)
8675, 9326, 9367, 9447, 9608, ˙ 9664, 9711, 9793, 9797, 9798, ˙ 9804, 9805, 9807, 9813, 9815, ˙ 9850, 9861, 9889
Achievement/Academic–College Achievement/Prediction of Acac 9602, 9604, 9607, 9609, 9619, 9 9792, 9810, 9˙¹³ 9815 9816, 9 ˙˙˙¹ ˙˙˙

Figure 5

47: 9625–9634 *EDUCATIONAL PSYCHOLOGY*

9625. Temme, Lloyd V. & Cohen, Jere M. (Indiana U.) **Ethnic differences in high school friendship.** *Sociology of Education,* 1970(Fal), Vol. 43(4), 459–464.—Reexamines 1 of the hypotheses offered in *The ...lescent Society* through a reexamination of the data ...d in that study. Specifically, the suggestion ...ntation is greater in schools where valu... ...nic status (SES) is higher and other ... ...in a s... ...n area ...... *H. Mueller.*

9627. Vitro, Frank T. (U. Maine) **The relationship of classroom dishonesty to perceived parental discipline.** *Journal of College Student Personnel,* 1971(Nov), Vol. 12(6), 427–429.—Investigated the relationship between cheating and perceived parental discipline. Ss included 70 female college students who completed Epstein and Komorita's Parental Punitive Scale. 45.6

Also, a p... ...cating and low academic performance. *R. H. Mueller.*

9628. Walsh, Richard P. (Southern Illinois U., Edwardsville) **Comment on the Lin and McKeachie article.** *Psychological Reports,* 1971(Oct), Vol. 29(2), 601–602.—Considers Y. Lin and W. McKeachie's (see PA, Vol. 47:Issue 5) finding that there were no significant sex differences in test anxiety in their Ss.

Figure 6

RESEARCH

9627. Vitro, Frank T. (U. Maine) **The relationship of classroom dishonesty to perceived parental discipline.** *Journal of College Student Personnel,* 1971(Nov), Vol. 12(6), 427–429.—Investigated the relationship between cheating and perceived parental discipline. Ss included 70 female college students who completed Epstein and Komorita's Parental Punitive Scale. 45.6 of the Ss were identified as cheaters on the basis of grading their own exams and arriving at a grade discrepant from that determined earlier by the course instructors, without the Ss' knowledge. A chi-square analysis reveals no significant relationship between cheating and perceived maternal discipline; however, the relationship was significant between cheating and perceived paternal discipline. Thus, it appears that the "incorporation of values and standards of morality is most favorable when parental discipline does not involve extreme techniques." Also, a positive relationship was found between cheating and low academic performance.—*R. H. Mueller.*

REVIEW

6424. Smith, Richard A., Gelles, David B., & Vanderhaeghen, J. J. (U.S. Navy Medical Neuropsychiatric Research Unit, San Diego, Calif.) **Subcortical visual hallucinations.** *Cortex,* 1971(Jun), Vol. 7(2), 162–168.—Reviews clinical and experimental studies supporting the theory that visual hallucinations may result from subcortical lesions. A case report is presented which suggests that lesions at all levels of the neurovisual system may be associated with visual hallucinations. "Occurrence of the phenomenon of subcortical visual hallucinations is compatible with what is known about the complex integration of cortical and subcortical visual processes."—*Journal summary.*

THEORETICAL DISCUSSION

7451. Linehan, Marsha M. Toward a theory of sex differences in suicidal behavior. *Crisis Intervention,* 1971, Vol. 3(4), 93–101.—Proposes a theory of suicidal behavior which posits social acceptability and social expectations as the primary bases for explaining differences between males and females in the degree to which each sex attempts or commits suicide. It is concluded that research is needed to study relationships between cultural expectations and suicidal behavior.—*E. Pile.*

tion in abbreviated form, an easy-to-read code is used so that the reader can readily find the original source. This code is provided in detail on the opening page of each monthly issue (Figure 2).

Near the front of each monthly issue is a Table of Contents, which indicates the broad general areas under which each issue is ordered. If you are looking for a specific variable rather than a general area, however, it is more useful to use the Subject Index in the cumulative volume; this is usually bound at the end of most library copies. For the most recent unbound issues, the same information can be found in the Brief Subject Index at the end of each monthly issue (Figures 3 and 4).

Suppose, for example, that you have noted some relationship between attitudes that college students have toward their parents and toward cheating. When you look in the cumulative index for "cheating," you are referred to "deception," where you find an entry that appears to have the information you are after. The abstract number 9627 is given. Because this is the index for Volume 47, you look for the running head at the top corner of the page that includes the number 47:9267 (Figure 5).

Note, incidentally, that the illustrated entry is classified under the general heading Educational Psychology, which may provide further information for you in this or other volumes.

Any research article contains the following sections: introduction, method, results, and conclusion (the conclusion usually describes the inferences that the author feels he can legitimately make from his results). The *Abstracts* summary should include a statement representing each of these sections. Research articles are one of three general types of journal articles to be found in the summaries. In addition to *research* articles, there are also *reviews* of other investigations, and *theoretical discussions* meant to stimulate further research. These article types are often identified in the first sentence of the summaries (Figure 6).

Evaluating an Article From the Abstract. Like any other catalog, the *Abstracts* saves you time by giving you just enough information to decide whether or not to take the trouble to go to the original source. Although the article title may at first suggest that you have tracked down exactly what you were looking for, the summary might reveal that you were misled by the title. But if you have found the reference you want, the summary will rarely be adequate in itself—in most cases it will stimulate a number of questions (Figure 7) that will require careful reading of the original article.

Once you have found an article specific to your interests, the introduction will refer to related research that you may wish to follow

up, and the list of references at the end of each article should provide a number of excellent leads (Figure 8).

In addition, it is well to keep in mind that most researchers are specialists within a given area of interest. The chances are good that if you look in the Author Index of the *Abstracts* for the names of authors whose articles you have found useful, you will find references to further relevant research findings (Figure 9).

—Joseph Rubinstein, *Purdue University*

PSYCHOLOGICAL JOURNALS. Leading periodicals in branches of psychology at the ends of sections of the Bibliography. For a note on abstracts of the literature on psychology, *see* Psychological Abstracts.

PSYCHOLOGICAL TESTING. See Measurement.

PSYCHOLOGIST. For training required and nature of careers, *see* Psychology.

PSYCHOLOGY, the science of the behavior of organisms. As used in this definition, the term "organism" refers to any living animal, either human or subhuman. Basically, psychology is concerned with the behavior of human beings, but much about that subject can be learned from studying the behavior of other organisms, such as rats, monkeys, pigeons, chimpanzees, and even lower forms of life.

At one time psychology was defined as the study of the mind, but the word "mind" is difficult to define. Modern psychologists usually find it more profitable to talk about total behavior, including thinking, than to split behavior into mental and physical components.

Psychology and Philosophy. Like all sciences, psychology developed out of the study of philosophy, which through the centuries has tried to understand the ultimate nature of the world. As knowledge increased, persons who would formerly have been spoken of as philosophers came to be known as scientists. They have specialized in such areas of philosophy as physics, chemistry, biology, astronomy, and so on. Even today, with the termination of advanced study in any area, most scientists receive the Doctor of Philosophy (Ph.D.) degree, although in the science of psychology there have been some attempts to award a Doctor of Psychology (Psy.D.) degree. (Either of these degrees from the graduate school of a recognized university is not to be confused with high-sounding but meaningless and even dangerous "degrees" awarded by "schools" that are little more than diploma mills.)

Before the days of the scientific approach to psychology, the ancient philosophers were concerned with many of the same problems confronting psychologists today:

Figure 7

9627. **Vitro, Frank T.** (U. Maine) **The relationship of classroom dishonesty to perceived parental discipline.** *Journal of College Student Personnel*, 1971(Nov), Vol. 12(6), 427–429.—Investigated the relationship between cheating and perceived parental discipline. Ss included 70 female college students who completed Epstein and Komorita's Parental Punitive Scale. 45.6 of the Ss were identified as cheaters on the basis of grading their own exams and arriving at a grade discrepant from that determined earlier by the course instructors, without the Ss' knowledge. A chi-square analysis reveals no significant relationship between cheating and perceived maternal discipline; however, the relationship was significant between cheating and perceived paternal discipline. Thus, it appears that the "incorporation of values and standards of morality is most favorable when parental discipline does not involve extreme techniques." Also, a positive relationship was found between cheating and low academic performance.—*R. H. Mueller.*

1. What differences might there be between real and perceived parental discipline?

2. If there are differences between real and perceived parental discipline, what might account for these differences?

3. How typical are these subjects? Are we justified in generalizing from them?

4. What kind of items are on the *Parental Punitive Scale*?

5. What does "45.6 of the S's" mean? How do you get .6 of a subject? Could it mean percent?

6. How did noncheaters perceive parental discipline?

7. Cheating was not related to maternal discipline but was related to paternal discipline. These subjects were all female; how would it have been with male subjects?

8. From the abstract it would appear that "discipline" refers only to punishment. Is it appropriate for the author to refer to "extreme techniques?"

9. What relationships are there between perceived parental discipline and low academic performance?

Figure 8

REFERENCES

BARCLAY, D. Why children cheat in school. *New York Times Magazine*, January 19, 1958, 52.

BURTON, R. V., MACCOBY, E. E., & ALLINSMITH, W. Antecedents of resistance to temptation in four year old children. *Child Development*, 1961, *32*, 689–710.

CAMPBELL, W. G. Measurement in determining the personality and behavior of the college cribber. *Education*, 1933, *53*, 403–408.

EPSTEIN, R., & KOMORITA, S. The development of a scale of parental punitiveness toward aggression. *Child Development*, 1965, *36*, 129–142.

HARTSHORNE, H. (Ed.) *From school to college; A study of the transition experience.* New Haven: Yale University Press, 1939.

MACKINNON, D. W. Violation of prohibitions. In H. A. Murray (Ed.), *Explorations in personality.* New York: Oxford University Press, 1938. Pp. 491–501.

MUELLER, K. H. Can cheating be killed? *Personnel and Guidance Journal*, 1953, *31*, 465–468.

PECK, R. F. Family patterns correlated with adolescent personality structure. *Journal of Abnormal and Social Psychology*, 1958, *57*, 347–350.

SEARS, R. R., WHITING, J. M., NOWLIS, V., & SEARS, P. S. Some child rearing antecedents of aggression and dependency in young children. *Genetic Psychology Monographs*, 1953, *47*, 135–234.

TRABUE, A. Classroom cheating: An isolated phenomenon? *Educational Research*, 1962, *43*, 309–316.

VITRO, F. The effects of probability of test success, opportunity to cheat, and test importance on the incidence of cheating. *Dissertation Abstracts*, 1970, *30*(9), 3806-A.

Figure 9

Author Index

PSYCHOLOGY: DIVISIONS AND SCHOOLS

Divisions of Research and Application in Psychology

ABNORMAL PSYCHOLOGY
adolescent psychology. See
    ADOLESCENCE; DEVELOPMENTAL
    PSYCHOLOGY
APPLIED PSYCHOLOGY
BEHAVIORAL ECOLOGY
child psychology. See CHILD
    DEVELOPMENT; DEVELOPMENTAL
    PSYCHOLOGY
CLINICAL PSYCHOLOGY
COMMUNITY PSYCHOLOGY
COMPARATIVE PSYCHOLOGY
CONSULTING PSYCHOLOGY
CONSUMER PSYCHOLOGY
COUNSELING PSYCHOLOGY
DEVELOPMENTAL PSYCHOLOGY
        CHILD DEVELOPMENT
        ADOLESCENCE
        MIDDLE YEARS
        AGING
DIFFERENTIAL PSYCHOLOGY
EDUCATIONAL PSYCHOLOGY
ENGINEERING PSYCHOLOGY
environmental psychology. See
    BEHAVIORAL PSYCHOLOGY
ETHOLOGY
EXPERIMENTAL PSYCHOLOGY
geriatric psychology. See
    AGING
INDUSTRIAL PSYCHOLOGY
legal psychology. See PSYCHOLOGY
    AND THE LAW
MEASUREMENT
MEDICAL PSYCHOLOGY
MILITARY PSYCHOLOGY
PARAPSYCHOLOGY
PERSONNEL PSYCHOLOGY
PHILOSOPHICAL PSYCHOLOGY
PHYSIOLOGICAL PSYCHOLOGY
PSYCHOBIOLOGY
psychopharmacology. See DRUGS
    AND BEHAVIOR
PSYCHOPHYSICS
SCHOOL PSYCHOLOGY
SOCIAL PSYCHOLOGY
SOMATOPSYCHOLOGY

For another way of classifying the working areas of psychologists, see the list of professional divisions in the article on the AMERICAN PSYCHOLOGICAL ASSOCIATION. Careers in psychology are discussed under PSYCHOLOGY.

Influential Schools and Theories in the Development of Psychology

ACT PSYCHOLOGY
ANALYTIC PSYCHOLOGY
ASSOCIATIONISM
BEHAVIORISM
BIOFEEDBACK
COGNITIVE PSYCHOLOGY
CYBERNETICS
DEPTH PSYCHOLOGY
DETERMINISM
DYNAMIC PSYCHOLOGY
EXISTENTIALISM
FACULTY PSYCHOLOGY
FIELD THEORY
FUNCTIONAL PSYCHOLOGY
GENETIC PSYCHOLOGY
GESTALT PSYCHOLOGY
HOLISM
INDIVIDUAL PSYCHOLOGY
INTROSPECTION
METAPSYCHOLOGY
ORGANISMIC THEORY
PSYCHOANALYSIS
STIMULUS-RESPONSE PSYCHOLOGY
TOPOLOGICAL PSYCHOLOGY
WURZBURG SCHOOL
ZEN

Notable Figures in the History of Psychology

Alfred ADLER
Alfred BINET
Jerome BRUNER
Walter B. CANNON
James M. CATTELL
Noam CHOMSKY
Charles DARWIN
Rene DESCARTES
John DEWEY
Hermann EBBINGHAUS
Gustav T. FECHNER
Sigmund FREUD
Erich FROMM
Francis GALTON
Hermann von HELMHOLTZ
Karen HORNEY
William JAMES
Carl JUNG
Kurt KOFFKA
Wolfgang KOHLER
Kurt LEWIN
John LOCKE
Ivan P. PAVLOV
Jean PIAGET
B. F. SKINNER
Harry S. SULLIVAN
Edward L. THORNDIKE
John B. WATSON
Ernst H. WEBER
Max WERTHEIMER
Wilhelm WUNDT

The Subject Maps in the Encyclopedia illustrate the coverage of particular aspects of psychology, showing the interrelationships among the articles in twelve major areas of study. Entries in capital letters are subjects for which there are separate articles in the Encyclopedia. Entries in small letters are cross references.

The Subject Maps appear in the Encyclopedia under the following titles:

Abnormal and Clinical Psychology
Developmental Psychology
Emotion and Motivation
Intelligence
Learning and Memory
Measurement
Personality and Individual Difference
Physiological and Comparative Psychology
Psychology: Divisions and Schools
Sensation and Perception
Social Psychology
Thinking and Language

Socrates, for example, believed that the one true kind of knowledge was the knowledge of the self. Plato for the first time made a clear-cut distinction between mind and matter, but Aristotle found no sharp distinction between the two. Later, René Descartes (1596–1650) argued that there are two substances in the world and termed them "thinking substance" and "extended substance." He considered that these two interacted as mind and body. Thus, the problem of the relationship of mind and body runs far back in history and is not completely solved even today.

Schools of Psychology. In the early part of the twentieth century a number of systems of psychological thought developed.

Structuralism grew out of the work of a German psychologist, Wilhelm Wundt (1832–1920), who founded the first psychological laboratory. The structuralists tried to break complex behavior into basic elements, that is, into the specific experiences of the organism. This approach was scientific but proved to be too narrow in orientation.

Beginning about 1912, a system known as *Gestalt psychology* developed. The German word "Gestalt" is usually translated as "form," "pattern," or "configuration." The Gestaltists were concerned with the overall pattern of behavior and insisted that the whole of behavior was something more than the sum of its parts. They stressed the importance of insight in learning, as opposed to the trial-and-error approach, which was popular at that time.

Beginning about 1913, an American psychologist, John B. Watson (1878–1958), argued that psychologists should be concerned only with the objective study of overt behavior. The *behaviorists* stressed the relationship between stimulus and response and the importance of scientific methodology. They placed strong emphasis on animal experimentation. Their principles have greatly influenced modern experimental psychologists.

Although these various schools or systems of psychological thought, and others not mentioned, have had great influence on modern psychology, contemporary psychologists place little stress on such separate systems of thought. They are too narrow to include all that is now known about the science of behavior.

Psychology as a Science. At the higher levels of study, no sharp line can be drawn between the various sciences. For example, psychologists are concerned with the effects on behavior of the chemistry of the body and the effects of certain drugs on behavior. They also study the relationship between behavior and physiology, neurology, embryology, and genetics. Sometimes psychology is considered one of the biological sciences.

Also, psychology is often considered a social science, along with sociology and anthropology. Sociology is usually concerned with the development and behavior of groups, both formal and informal, in what is usually spoken of as literate societies. Anthropology deals with the origin and evolution of racial groups and the development of social institutions and behavior. Traditionally, anthropologists have been concerned primarily with nonliterate (primitive) societies, but this dividing line between sociology and anthropology is not as sharp as it once was.

Psychologists, especially social psychologists, are basically interested in research on the influence of the social group on the individual member of the group and the influence of the individual on the social group. Often psychologists prefer to work with smaller groups than those studied by sociologists and anthropologists, because in such settings more variables can be controlled than in large social groups. What is learned about behavior in small groups can often be seen operating in the behavior of large social organizations. Today, the three sciences of sociology, anthropology, and psychology are often grouped together as *behavioral science.*

Psychology and Psychiatry. The psychiatrist is trained in medicine and holds the Doctor of Medicine (M.D.) degree, with all its ethical and legal rights and responsibilities. He specializes in the diagnosis, treatment, and prevention of mental disorders, both mild and severe. If he sees fit, he can prescribe drugs or even perform surgery in his treatment of "mental" disorders. The psychologist is trained in methods of research and/or clinical practice but, with very rare exceptions, does not hold an M.D. degree as well as a Ph.D. degree. Without the medical degree he cannot prescribe medicine or perform surgery. Nevertheless, psychologists often work with psychiatrists in clinics where both strive, through individual and group therapy, to help individuals who are having difficulty in adjusting to the behavior of those in their immediate environment or to society as a whole.

Both psychology and psychiatry are sometimes confused with psychoanalysis, which actually developed out of medical practice. Sigmund Freud (1856–1939) is usually considered to be the founder of this system of thinking. His early writings had much to say about the mind, which he divided into three parts: conscious, foreconscious, unconscious. His later writings stressed the *id* (unconscious primitive urges, such as sex and aggression), the *ego* (the rational aspects of personality), and the *superego* (the ethical and moral aspects of personality, sometimes spoken of as conscience). Although Freud was not scientifically oriented, his teachings and those of his followers have had a marked influence on clinical psychology.

Training. Although psychology is usually thought of as a college-level subject, many high schools offer a course in the subject—mostly a one-semester course but taught for two semesters in about a third of the schools. As far back as the 1830s courses in mental philosophy were offered in secondary schools. Apparently these were the forerunners of modern psychology courses. High school textbooks with the word "psychology" in their titles first appeared in 1889.

Today the Educational Affairs Office of the American Psychological Association lists the names of some 10,000 teachers of psychology at the high school level. Not only are courses in psychology offered, but units or modules based on psychological material are often incorporated in various social studies courses. Some psychological material is even taught in lower grades, although not necessarily under the label "psychology." In fact, the American Psychological Association at its headquarters in Washington, D.C., has an office devoted to precollege psychology.

Careers. The kind of work a person is prepared to do after he has secured training as a psychologist depends in part on the specific graduate training he has received, and in part on his postdoctoral internship or other experience. Most states have laws governing the practice of psychology, and no one can practice in those states unless he has a license or certification.

The greatest number of psychologists in any single field practice *clinical psychology.* After receiving their doctoral degrees, they usually serve at least a year's internship in a mental hospital or other institution for individuals with severe psychological problems. This training prepares them to serve in such institutions as mental hospitals, prisons, mental health clinics for both children and adults, schools for the retarded or community schools with special programs for the retarded, and juvenile corrective programs. The clinical psychologist may establish an office and engage in private practice.

Closely related to clinical psychology is *counseling and guidance psychology.* Professionals in these fields usually work with individuals who have some problems of personal and/or social adjustment but who can, for the most part, be classified as normal. These psychologists are often consulted by individuals in need of educational or vocational guidance.

Educational psychologists are likely to do research on such problems as efficiency of learning, including motivation to learn. They usually work in university schools of education so that they can improve teacher training. *School psychologists* usually work directly with children, teachers, and school administrators. They often give intelligence and other psychological tests and interpret the scores with the objective of improving the learning efficiency of children. Also, they work with problems of undesirable child behavior. They often hold the Doctor of Education (Ed.D.) degree.

Experimental psychologists usually work in colleges or universities or in special laboratories where they carry on basic research concerned with behavior. Such work often involves the use of animals as subjects (*comparative psychology*) and very precise instruments and techniques of research.

Social psychologists, as the name implies, are concerned with problems of behavior in social settings. They may be especially concerned with the child's learning to live with other children and with adults and his general intellectual and physical growth (*developmental psychology*). One area of special interest is the measurement and evaluation of the characteristics that make up the unique individual (*personality psychology*). Sometimes social psychologists work in the fields of public opinion surveys and market research.

Today considerable attention is being given to what might be called *environmental psychology,* although it is closely related to social psychology. Workers in this field are concerned with man's use of space. How does environment influence choice of locality for a home? What is the effect on behavior of prolonged sensory deprivation as man explores outer space and ocean depths? These psychologists are much concerned with the general problem of ecology. Their field may be called *human ecology* or *behavioral ecology.*

Psychologists interested in the general area of business are often spoken of as *industrial psychologists.* They may work in personnel offices, where they strive to solve problems of employee disagreements among themselves or with administration. They strive to fit the right man to the right job. They may work closely with engineers in designing instruments that are easy to read and machines that can be operated with a minimum of employee error. Related specialties are called *consumer psychology* and *engineering psychology.*

Many psychologists devote much of their time to teaching psychology in colleges and universities, along with research, writing, or clinical work.

There are other areas and the young person considering psychology as a life work can be assured that he will find some niche. In many of these it is not necessary to hold a doctoral degree. There is an increasing recognition that some important psychological work can be done by individuals with a master's degree. They may work in schools as psychometrists or in various fields of special education for unusual children. They may administer and score psychological tests in schools and clinics, although responsibility for diagnosis and long-term planning is assigned to more fully trained individuals.

Individuals who have majored or even

minored in psychology may teach psychology, at least for a time until they secure a master's degree, in high schools and even elementary schools, provided that they otherwise meet teacher licensing requirements. Although not working directly in the field of psychology, such majors or minors may find vocational opportunities in business personnel administration or management training. They may find that even their limited training in psychology can be applied in such fields as sales and advertising.

There are even two-year college programs designed to train individuals for subprofessional work of a psychological nature in mental hospitals, homes for the aged, schools for the retarded, and child guidance clinics.

Professional Associations. Most of the qualified psychologists in the United States belong to the American Psychological Association (not to be confused with the American Psychiatric Association). The purpose of this organization is "to advance psychology as a science and as a means of promoting human welfare." It was founded in 1892 as a general organization of psychologists. Today members may belong to various divisions, depending on their specialized interests. The association encourages professional standards by awarding its diplomas to individuals who meet certain high standards of training and experience.

The American Psychological Association has three classes of membership, depending on the individual's training and experience: associates, members, and fellows. In addition, there are foreign affiliates and high-school-teacher affiliates. Also, undergraduate and graduate college students of psychology may attend the meetings of the association and subscribe to its journals at special rates, although they are not members. An *employment bulletin* informs them of job vacancies and permits them to place notices of their own availability.

In addition to the American Psychological Association, there are regional, state, and local associations. Other nations have their professional societies. The International Congress of Psychology holds meetings every four years, in various countries, and its *Proceedings* are published. Provisions are made for language differences at the meetings and in the publications.

Publications. All members of the American Psychological Association receive the journal *American Psychologist* and the newspaper *APA Monitor.* Much of the material in these publications can be read by students without undue difficulty. In addition, the association publishes a number of other professional periodicals such as *Journal of Applied Psychology, Journal of Educational Psychology, Journal of Experimental Psychology,* and *Journal of Abnormal Psychology;* the articles in these tend to

be rather technical. There are a number of professional psychological journals not published by the association; *Journal of School Psychology* and *Journal of Experimental Child Psychology.*

The American Psychological Association does not publish a nontechnical journal fitted to the reading interests and understanding of laymen. However, a magazine, *Psychology Today,* is directed to a popular audience, and some of the articles in it are written by leading psychologists in an easily understood style. The same publisher has a weekly newsletter, *Behavior Today.* A newsmagazine of the social sciences called *Human Behavior* is intended for both the professional reader and the educated layman. There is a magazine for teachers, *People Watching.*

—T. L. Engle, *Indiana University*
See also American Psychological Association (includes a list of the divisions of the association). *For an outline of the fields of psychology, with a list of articles in each field, see the Item Guide.*
Consult (I) Abrams and Stanley, 1967; American Psychological Association, *Directory*; American Psychological Association, 1970; Astin, 1972; Bardon and Bennett, 1967; Bardon and Walker, 1972; Bayton, Roberts, and Williams, 1970; Campbell and Soliman, 1968; Cates and Dawson, 1971; Engle, *Journal of School Psychology,* 1967; Engle, *American Psychologist,* 1967; Engle and Snellgrove, 1973; English and English, 1958; "Ethical Standards of Psychologists," 1968; Finger, 1969; Heidbredder, 1933; Hill, 1964; Howell and Murdock, 1972; Little, 1972; Long, 1970; Love, 1972; Lunneborg, 1968; McCollom, 1972; MacLeod, 1971; Manning and Cates, 1972; Meyer, 1972; Miller, 1969; Mosher and Sprinthall, 1970; Noland, 1967; Norton, 1972; Peck, 1967; Roen, 1967; Sargent and Stafford, 1965; Schein, 1971; Task Force on the Practice of Psychology in Industry, 1971; Thornton, 1967; Thornton and Colver, 1967; Trow, 1967; Traxler, 1967; Viteles, 1972; Woods, 1971.

PSYCHOLOGY AND THE LAW. Every person, in every society, is subject to some degree of regulation by others. Each society must strike a balance between the freedoms enjoyed by its members and the controls exerted over individuals by the government. Law consists of the formalization of social controls, which limit and regulate individual action and which, of equal importance, control the government in its exercise of power over the individual. Laws are justified by a variety of interlocking assumptions involving social, moral, and humanitarian issues. These assumptions are usually supported by existing social and political theories but are not necessarily supported by fact. [*Consult* (14) Tolchin, 1972.]

Both law and the social sciences are

continually evolving in response to immense pressures signifying changing conceptions of the human condition and changing ideas of social order and organization. The relationship between the scientific enterprise and law is complex and often only dimly understood. The complaint is sometimes heard that the law changes far too slowly in comparison with the rapidly made strides of science. Yet most, if not all, scientific theories eventually fall into disrepute and the law cannot be as fickle as the changing fads and fashions of science. It must nevertheless not be so rigid as to be unchangeable in the light of evidence.

There are numerous points of contact between psychology and the law. Some of the more important of these underscore the legal and social assumptions involved in the relationship between psychology and the law.

Responsibility

A fundamental assumption underlying the rule of law, in a free society, is that man is a responsible agent, that he can understand and follow rules and therefore be held accountable for his behavior. Questions of legal competency arise in connection with both civil and criminal law. In civil law the question is usually whether a person is competent to make legal decisions regarding his welfare, as in the making of contracts and wills and in guardianship. Though legal competency is decided by the court, judges rely heavily upon testimony presented by so-called expert witnesses, such as physicians, psychiatrists, and psychologists. Competency is generally evaluated in a specific situation or in relationship to a specific task. For example, at the moment when a person signs a contract, is he in sufficient contact with reality to understand the nature of the proceedings?

In principle, legal competency (as determined by the court) and the classification "mentally ill" (as determined by a psychiatrist) are separable, since they refer to different things. In practice, however, a diagnosis of mental illness generally leads to a judgment of "not competent" in civil proceedings. The question of who is qualified to judge competency often is reduced to the question of who can provide expert testimony as to the mental status of the individual in question. If we assume that mental illness is a disease and that diagnosis is a factual process, it is reasonable to ask a physician to provide expert testimony. Yet mental illness may have very little to do with "illness" in the physical sense except in those cases (a small percentage of actual cases) where a disease of the nervous system is known to exist. The situation is further complicated when we consider that a diagnosis is not a fact but an opinion and that the categories of "sane" and "insane," at best, describe the extremes of an ill-defined continuum rather than discrete categories. The concept of responsibility is so inextricably bound up with psychiatric, legal, and moral issues that it is too complex for any one individual to decide. [*Consult* (13) Szasz, 1961; (14) Goldstein, 1967.]

In criminal law the focus generally shifts from legal competency to legal responsibility. The question is whether a person should be held legally responsible for his actions rather than whether he is legally competent to conduct his affairs. Thus, if a person accused of having committed a criminal offense is judged "insane" or "not responsible," he is considered in the eyes of the law "not guilty" (by reason of insanity). The *insanity defense* has its origins in fourteenth-century Anglo-Saxon law: a person was considered not responsible when it was believed that he lacked sufficient reason (understanding) to know what he was doing. Legal tests of insanity concern the instructions trial judges give to juries in cases where the insanity defense is used and derive from case law precedents.

Based on an English case of 1843, the M'Naghten rule has been widely used. It states that "every man is to be presumed to be sane, and. . .that to establish a defense on the ground of insanity, it must be clearly proved that, at the time of the committing of the act, the party accused was laboring under such a defect of reason, *from disease of the mind,* as not to know the nature and quality of the act he was doing; or. . .that he did not know he was doing what was wrong." The rule has been criticized for being too restrictive and unwieldy to apply and for its excessive focus upon intellectual or cognitive disturbance to the exclusion of motivational and emotional factors. To deal with this latter issue, the *irresistible impulse rule—* which instructs jurors to acquit by reason of insanity those persons who have lost control over their behavior because of mental illness—has been added to the M'Naghten rule.

Recently, a newer and far more simple test known as the Durham rule has been gaining in popularity. It states that an accused is not criminally responsible if his unlawful act was the product of mental disease.

It is important to note that, when a person is acquitted by reason of insanity, he is not set free as in the case of persons simply judged "not guilty." He is committed (involuntarily) to a mental hospital for the treatment of his mental illness. The hospital incarceration is usually for an indeterminate length of time and often exceeds the maximum length of prison sentence for the particular crime for which the individual was originally accused. In most states, the question of sanity generally *precedes* the determination of guilt. Thus, if acquittal by reason of insanity occurs, there is actually no legal determination made as to the criminal accusations. In other words, a person may be declared "criminally insane" when in fact he was innocent of the crime of which he was accused. Further, since the current trend in prison reform is to offer extensive programs of rehabilitation (treatment) to convicted criminals, the advantages of mental hospital as opposed to prison incarceration appear questionable.

Commitment to Hospitals

The practice of involuntary hospitalization for mental illness entails so serious a deprivation of individual freedom and human rights that it deserves the most serious and soul-searching attention. In recent years the practices of involuntary civil commitment and involuntary treatment have come under increasing criticism. It is likely that some major changes will occur. [Consult, for example (14) Szasz, 1963.]

It is possible to identify a number of basic assumptions upon which the practice of civil commitment rests. Two important sets of assumptions involve (1) mental illness and (2) dangerousness to oneself and others.

Mental Illness. A glance at the American Psychiatric Association classification system is enough to indicate that an extremely wide range of behaviors are potentially classifiable under the rubric of mental illness. Mental illness does not refer to any single identifiable state of an organism but instead refers to a host of behaviors all of which differ to a greater or lesser extent from accepted cultural norms. In a case-finding study in midtown Manhattan, psychiatric criteria were applied diagnostically to a random sample of the population. Less than one in five persons were considered to be mentally healthy, with forty-five percent of the 1,660 persons sampled being judged moderately symptomatic to incapacitated.[Consult (13) Srole, et al., 1962.]

What does it mean to say that a person is behaving abnormally when the criteria for abnormality would apply to about half of the population? Either we have an epidemic of proportions equaled only by the Great Plague of the Middle Ages or our diagnostic criteria are so vague as to have become almost all-inclusive. Even if the epidemic theory were to be correct, the lesson medicine learned from infectious diseases is that by the time symptoms begin to appear in the population it is too late to prevent an epidemic. Control of a disease is achieved only after the conditions conducive to the flourishing of the disease are controlled. It can be argued that, by couching our social problems in terms of mental health and illness, we can avoid facing the possibility that our society is failing to meet some of the basic needs of its people. Also it can be said that the mental health movement has resulted in an enormous misallocation of resources and attention away from the substantive issues

producing unrest—social and economic inequities, racism, bigotry, bureaucratization, war, and other forms of institutionalized violence, to name but a few.

Perhaps even more fundamental is the question whether the concept of illness can be validly applied to persons who are psychologically or emotionally disturbed or whether it is being used merely as a convenient but misleading metaphor. Persons who are diagnosed as functionally mentally ill (about 70 percent of mental hospital admissions) have no known disease or organic pathology. "Since they do not suffer from disease, it is impossible to *treat* them for any sickness." Yet, hundreds of thousands of persons are involuntarily hospitalized for this purpose. [Consult (13) Szasz, 1968.]

There are really several intertwined issues at stake here: Are functional disturbances illnesses? If not, why do we use medical means to control such persons? Even if we grant that the illness model has some validity here—as with known organic disorders such as senility and brain traumas—we must still deal with the question of why hospitalization is involuntary. In the case of other illnesses such as heart disease or cancer or even highly communicable conditions such as venereal disease, it is accepted that the would-be patient has an undeniable right *not* to be treated or even examined. Such a *right to refuse treatment* does not as yet exist for the allegedly mentally ill individual. [Consult (14) Tolchin, et al., 1970.]

A related issue has to do with the legal principle of the *right to treatment,* first articulated by Morton Birnbaum (1960). It states that persons who are hospitalized involuntarily for mental illness have a constitutional (due process) right to receive treatment or at least adequate care. It follows that the denial of treatment or adequate care—as often occurs in custodial institutions—would be grounds for the dismissal of the involuntarily held patients. [Consult (14) Halpern, et al., 1972.]

The American Psychiatric Association has stated what it believes to be acceptable standards for care in terms of staff-to-patient ratios of 1 physician per 30 patients on intensive-care units and 1 to 150 on continued-care services. It is difficult to imagine how such case loads could lead to adequate treatment as specified in the right to treatment. Nevertheless, it is not uncommon to find case loads as high as 1 physician per 1,000 patients in public mental hospitals.

Danger. The concept of dangerousness is as fraught with ambiguity and emotionally explosive connotations as is the concept of mental illness. It is generally assumed that persons who are mentally ill pose such a significant threat to themselves or to others as to justify their control through incarceration in

PSYCHONEUROTIC DISORDERS

The comprehensive article PSYCHONEUROTIC DISORDERS describes the symptoms of neuroses and tells how these behavior problems differ from the psychoses. This article also discusses causes, treatment, and the expected outcome of treatment.

Further details on neurotic behavior can be found in ANXIETY, ASTHENIC REACTION (neurasthenia), DEFENSE MECHANISMS, DEPRESSION, DISSOCIATION, HYPOCHONDRIA, OBSESSIVE-COMPULSIVE REACTION, and PHOBIA. Other disorders such as AMNESIA, KLEPTOMANIA, and MULTIPLE PERSONALITY are often classed as neurotic. Freudian views of the conflicts that give rise to neuroses are described in such articles as PSYCHOANALYSIS, OEDIPUS COMPLEX, and REPRESSION.

Additional information on treatment is given in PSYCHOTHERAPY, PSYCHIATRY, PSYCHOANALYSIS, BEHAVIOR THERAPY, GROUP THERAPY, and HUMAN POTENTIALS MOVEMENT.

mental hospitals. The dangerousness hypothesis derives from a particular theory of mental illness that in the tradition of psychoanalysis, argues that mental illness is the consequence of a collapse of normal controls over primitive, animalistic drives. Such a view has been severely criticized for its neglect of man's positive adaptive nature. Very little data can be taken as support for the dangerousness hypothesis. A. Dershowitz was able to find no more than a dozen studies that followed up psychiatric predictions of antisocial behavior. In the studies cited, the evidence was clearly against the accuracy of psychiatric predictions, particularly when compared to other sources such as actuarial tables. An oft-cited study, which sorely requires replication, reports arrest data of former mental patients released from mental hospitals in New York State. The arrest rate for the former-patient group was less than one-twelfth that of the general population. [Consult (14) Dershowitz, 1969; Neier and Fabricant, 1969.]

One might argue, however, that to commit a dangerous act is, in and of itself, evidence of mental illness. Yet we do not usually incarcerate persons who are engaging in objectively dangerous behavior such as cigarette smoking or skydiving unless, in addition, their behavior clearly violates the law. Only in the case of persons alleged to be mentally ill (where the diagnosis of mental illness is taken as prima facie evidence of dangerousness) do we invoke the power of the state to incarcerate. Another assumption here is that psychiatrists and other mental health professionals can validly predict behavior, dangerous or otherwise. However, the lack of validity of clinical predictions based upon interview evaluation or psychological testing is well known. There is no reason to believe that psychiatrists are particularly accurate in predicting dangerousness and some reason to consider the contrary. There is great social pressure upon the psychiatrist to err in his predictions on the side of safety. Many would say it is prudent to observe a person more closely (in a hospital) if there is some doubt as to his potential harmfulness to himself or to others. [Consult (13) Meehl, 1954]

Law and Social Change

In the foregoing discussion emphasis has been placed upon the assumptions underlying law and public policy in the sphere of mental health. The purpose is to illustrate that many current practices in the mental health area appear to be based upon myth and theory rather than fact. Psychologists and other social scientists are called upon to participate in the legal process in a variety of ways—as expert witnesses to present testimony to the court or to evaluate a person in terms of competency or for civil commitment, or even to present a friend of the court (*amicus*) brief. They are also consulted for advice in the drafting of legisla-

tion or in the evaluation of current laws. It is tempting at such times to fall back upon familiar theories or explanations in order to conceal or deny ignorance. Yet, as has been argued, to confuse one's theories with facts is considered by many psychiatrists to be a fundamental symptom of mental illness. The social scientist has an ethical obligation to maintain his objectivity, particularly where his actions can affect the welfare of others. He also has an important opportunity to affect social change through the legal process by providing a sound base of evidence on which we can act.

—Gerald Tolchin, *Southern Connecticut State College*

Consult (13) American Psychiatric Association, 1968; Glidewell, 1971; Meehl, 1954; Srole, *et al.*, 1962; Szasz, 1961. (14) Birnbaum, 1960; Goldstein, 1967; Neier and Fabricant, 1969; Szasz, 1958; Szasz, 1963; Szasz, 1968; Tolchin, *et al.*, 1970; Tolchin, 1972.

PSYCHONEUROSIS. *See* Psychoneurotic Disorders.

PSYCHONEUROTIC DISORDERS, one of the most common forms of behavior pathology observed today. Present in all segments of the world's population, these disorders are considered functional in nature; that is, the neuroses are thought to be the result of psychological rather than physical causes. Anxiety is the dominant symptom in these disorders, and neurotic behavior is the result of attempts to cope with this subjective experience.

This class of psychopathology does not involve severe personality disorganization, and the condition often responds to treatment. As a result, neurotics are seen primarily on an outpatient basis rather than as institutionalized mental patients.

Symptoms. Although the various types of neurotic disorders display different symptoms, anxiety is common to them all. Although everyone experiences anxiety to some degree, it is felt that the neurotic possesses either a greater amount of anxiety or is less able to tolerate it. As a prime motivating force in psychoneurotic behavior, anxiety causes the individual to exaggerate basic defense mechanisms to avoid this discomfort. To a great extent the coping behavior employed distinguishes the major neurotic types.

In addition to anxiety, most neurotics relate to the world with inefficient behavior. This personality characteristic may take many forms, including extreme dependency, insecurity, and fearfulness. Because the neurotic evaluates most situations as threatening to his position in the world, he may experience strong feelings of inadequacy in the face of minor stress. These evaluations tend to add to his general level of anxiety.

Unsatisfactory interpersonal relation-

ships are part and parcel of neurotic adjustments. Since the neurotic is overly concerned with his inadequacies, he tends to think primarily of himself and his own needs (egocentricity). This life orientation leaves little time and energy to consider others and thus strains relationships badly.

Often in psychoneurotic disorders there are a number of vague *somatic complaints,* such as headaches, dizziness, or increased heartbeat (tachycardia). Common among these symptoms are fatigue, listlessness, and lack of excitement for living. (These complaints were formerly known as neurasthenia.) It is probable that somatic complaints afford the neurotic individual *secondary gains;* that is, examinations by physicians, the opportunity to complain, and an excuse from responsibility bring him attention from others.

Although the psychoneurotic individual may have vague feelings that something is wrong with his life, he usually demonstrates a *lack of insight* as to his own responsibility for this dissatisfaction. Thus, he tends to perpetuate his neurotic behavior in a rigid manner, often even following treatment.

Finally, the neurotic demonstrates *unrealistic perceptions of reality.* He may set goals for himself that are not consistent with his abilities, for example, or he may feel unworthy of love because of certain guilt feelings. It should be emphasized, however, that psychoneuroses do not involve a breakdown in the ability to distinguish the real from the not real. Rather, reality is misinterpreted or distorted by the neurotic process. This characteristic distinguishes the neuroses from more severe disorders.

Causes. It is generally agreed that neurotic disorders are caused primarily by psychological factors, both in early development and in later life situations. There are many theories as to the origin of neurotic behavior, but several views are dominant.

Until recently the *psychoanalytic* theory of Sigmund Freud was widely accepted. Basically, Freud felt that anxiety was the result of conflict between the desires of the individual and the social prohibition of expressing those desires. This conflict between two parts of the personality leads to anxiety. In order to reduce discomfort, *defense mechanisms* are employed. These attempt to satisfy both and thwart neither pole in the conflict.

Repression is the primary defense. The original conflict is forced to an *unconscious level* (out of awareness). Essentially, neurotic behavior occurs when repression is incomplete and the conflict threatens to gain awareness. At this point, neurotic symptoms are developed, in an effort to gain relief from anxiety.

Recently, alternate explanations of the origins of psychoneurotic behavior have come from advances in the area of learning and learning theory. These argue that neurotic behavior is learned through the principles of reinforcement, both positive and negative. An individual who has been confronted by a traumatic situation may respond with anxiety or fear that is appropriate to that situation; but when the behavior persists in the absence of the feared situation, his reaction becomes neurotic. For example, if a child is badly frightened by an angry dog, he will cry, scream, and either run or seek protection. If, in adulthood, and faced with friendly dogs, this behavior persists, he may be said to have developed a *phobic reaction* to dogs.

Hans Eysenck has developed this approach further. His research has indicated that personalities may be categorized as either *introvert* or *extravert* (using terms made famous by Carl Jung). The introvert, he has found, possesses a more reactive autonomic nervous system and therefore is susceptible to easily conditioned (learned) responses. Eysenck believes that this renders him prone to develop certain neurotic behavior patterns. [*Consult (13) Eysenck, 1963.*]

Other researchers have emphasized different factors in the cause of neurotic behavior. John Dollard and Neal Miller, for example, discuss the role of competing drives in the origin of neuroses. They have outlined certain conflict situations that may give rise to maladaptive responses. For example, an individual who has been offered a better job at a higher salary might fear that he will fail at the new responsibility. In this situation he may be unable to reach a decision, and this may possibly lead to neurotic behavior. [*Consult* (13) Dollard and Miller, 1950.]

All of these theories and research concerning etiological factors in the psychoneurotic disorders have both positive and negative aspects. No single position has been able to account for all the vagueness of neurotic symptomatology. It is likely that each position has its merits and validity and that a multitude of factors enter into the question.

Treatment and Outcome. Because neurotic disorders typically do not involve severe personality disorganization, most neurotics are treated on an outpatient basis through public or private agencies.

Chemotherapy (using tranquilizers and antidepressants) has become a major aid in the treatment of neuroses. These medications are effective in helping to alleviate various symptoms, such as depression, and have come to replace such techniques as electroshock therapy. However, tranquilizers and stimulants alone are ineffective in the complete rehabilitation of a neurotic personality. Chemotherapy may permit the individual to function more comfortably, but it can also lead to certain physical and psychological dependency, which only increases the problem.

It is generally agreed that medication in combination with some form of *psychotherapy* is the most effective treatment for the neurotic disorders. Psychotherapy was developed by Freud through his experience with neurotic (primarily hysterical) patients. Although there have been many modifications of Freud's technique (for example, by Carl Rogers), the basic principles remain the same. In psychotherapy the patient is encouraged to talk about his problems, feelings, and past experiences. It is believed that when they are expressed in a safe, neutral situation, the traumatic situations recalled will lose their emotional sting. In addition, interpretations by the therapist at the proper time will help the individual to gain insight into the nature of his difficulties. Once insight, or understanding, has been achieved, the patient can be encouraged to deal more effectively with life situations.

A major departure from classical psychotherapy has been the *behavior-modification* technique of Joseph Wolpe. This treatment procedure is based on the learning theory approach to neurotic behavior. Its basic principle is that if neurotic symptoms are learned, then they can be unlearned through the same principles. For example, one of Wolpe's treatment techniques for anxiety involves *systematic desensitization,* in which the patient is first taught to relax as completely as possible. Once this has been achieved, the therapist asks the patient to visualize certain anxiety-arousing scenes while remaining in the relaxed state. It is felt that this procedure aids the individual in overcoming his learned reaction to anxiety about threatening situations. In technical terms, the anxiety response to certain stimuli is *extinguished.* Behavior therapy has been reported to be less expensive, more efficient, and more effective than traditional treatment methods. [*Consult* (13) Wolpe, 1969.]

Still another treatment technique for psychoneurotic disorders involves the use of *group therapy.* This procedure brings groups of eight to ten persons together to discuss their difficulties under the direction of a professional leader. Each individual has the opportunity to relate to others, share experiences, and help his fellow group members through support and *feedback,* or evaluations of each person's behavior. The group setting also provides a relatively safe atmosphere in which to experiment with alternate forms of behavior that the neurotic may be reticent to attempt in other situations. It should be emphasized that there are many theories of group treatment. [*Consult* (13) Gazda, 1968.]

Among the most recent innovations in this technique are the *Gestalt therapy* of Frederick Perls and transactional analysis, developed by the late Eric Berne. [*Consult* (13) Perls, 1968; Berne, 1966.]

The prognosis, or outcome of treatment, in the neurotic disorders is generally more optimistic than in either personality disorders or psychotic reactions. This statement, however, must be qualified: without treatment a neurotic disorder can often worsen to psychotic proportions. Occasionally, this may be true even with treatment. Taking all things into consideration, however, neurotic disorders do respond well to treatment, and the individual can be restored to more positive personality functioning.

Glossary of Psychoneurotic Disorders

Anxiety neurosis—a type of neurosis in which anxiety is consciously felt in a variety of situations. Occasionally this anxiety is of sufficient strength to cause a panic reaction.

Depressive neurosis—extreme depression triggered by internal conflict or external loss of a cherished object or person.

Hypochondriacal neurosis—neurotic condition in which the individual focuses abnormal attention upon his body and body functions and fears that he has contracted various diseases. Examination reveals no such disease entities, but reassurance fails to assuage the individual.

Hysterical neurosis—neurotic disorder characterized by involuntary, and psychologically caused, loss of function. This loss may involve, for example, paralysis, blindness, or anesthesia of certain body parts.

Neurosis—a relatively common mental disorder in which anxiety is the chief complaint. Anxiety in this condition may be consciously experienced or translated into other symptoms by means of defensive operations. There is no gross misinterpretation of reality or personality disintegration.

Obsessive-compulsive neurosis—a condition of neurotic proportions in which persistent unwanted thoughts, urges, or actions intrude upon the individual. The thoughts (obsessions) and/or actions (compulsions) must be carried out to prevent severe anxiety.

Phobic neurosis—a neurotic reaction in which the individual demonstrates intense fear of an object or situation. It is usually recognized that this fear is irrational; however, it persists.

—Richard E. Dimond, *Sangamon State University*

See also Anxiety; Behavior Therapy; Defense Mechanisms; Personality Disorders; Phobia; Psychoanalysis; Psychosomatic Disorders; Psychotherapy.

Consult (13) Arieti, 1959; Beck, 1967; Dollard and Miller, 1950; Freud, 1933; Kisker, 1972; Masserman, 1967; Rogers, 1961; Thigpen and Cleckley, 1957; Wolpe, 1969.

PSYCHOPATHIC, a term sometimes applied to any form of mental disorder. The term "psychopathic personality" may be used for cases of antisocial behavior. *See* Personality Disorders; Sociopathic Personality Disturbance.

PSYCHOPHARMACOLOGY. *See* Drugs and Behavior.

PSYCHOPHYSICS, the field of study dealing with the measurement of sensation. Investigations of the sensory organs are compared with individual judgments to determine the magnitude of sensation.

Psychophysical methods developed early in the history of psychology. The German psychologist Ernst Weber (1795–1878), who contributed much to this field, was interested in determining how sensory organs function and, particularly, in finding ways to measure their sensitivity. He established that humans respond to relative differences in the weights of two objects rather than to the absolute magnitude of their difference. His further studies of weight discrimination showed that the relative difference that could be detected by the subjects was equal to a constant ratio between the two weights. For example, the difference between one weight and another might be just barely detectable when the second weight exceeds the first by a fixed relative amount. For weights Weber found this ratio to be 1 in 40, and he called this fraction a "just noticeable difference" (JND). The findings formulated by Weber dealing with the estimation of stimulus magnitude have been referred to as Weber's law.

During the nineteenth century Gustav Fechner further developed psychophysical measurements for many different sensations, including the visual and auditory. He formulated his measurements in terms of a law that stated that the intensity of a sensation is proportional to the logarithm of the intensity of the stimulus.

Since the time of Weber and Fechner many other equations have been proposed to explain the relationship between physical events and perceived stimuli. Psychophysics has shown that one cannot equate the physical stimulus to the perceived one. For example, the pitch of a sound is not identical to its frequency but is a function of frequency and loudness. Sound also has other qualities: its density, for example, is not a quality of its volume or its intensity but a subjective judgment of how much space is occupied by the sound and how "thickly" the sound is distributed within the space.

Among the numerous techniques determining the magnitude of sensations are the method of constant stimuli and the method of limits. These are now standard laboratory procedures in experimental psychology.

—Joel F. Lubar, *University of Tennessee*

PSYCHOPHYSIOLOGICAL DISORDER. *See* Psychosomatic Disorder.

PSYCHOSEXUAL DEVELOPMENT. For the psychoanalytic view of stages in development, *see* Character Development. For a broader view, *see* Sex Identity.

PSYCHOSIS. *See* Psychotic Disorders.

PSYCHOSOMATIC DISORDERS (or psychophysiological disorders) a variety of body (soma) reactions that are assumed to be very closely related to psychological phenomena. Stress, for example, is known to be accompanied by various bodily changes, such as rapid respiration, shortness of breath, upset stomach, and diarrhea. In extreme forms, particularly if one cannot express one's emotions more directly through anger or flight, these bodily reactions produce such problems as asthma and urticaria. Although the most common psychosomatic disorders effect the gastrointestinal and respiratory systems, any part of the body may be involved. Clearly these body reactions are as real and potentially as harmful as such physical injuries as fracture or infection.

Theories. The three most prevalent explanations of the development of psychosomatic disorders emphasize organ weakness or inferiority, psychosomatic specificity, and an interaction effect between various physical predispositions and psychological factors.

The *organ-weakness theory* suggests that emotional responses tend to injure an inadequate body part or that some parts of the body seem to be overused during times of emotional stress. Over a prolonged period of time, the weak organ continues to deteriorate, culminating in the specific psychosomatic disorder.

Psychosomatic specificity proposes that certain physiological or psychosomatic characteristics are unique or specific to certain physiological or psychosomatic reactions. Thus, asthma is thought to be related to the child's suppression of crying because of his fear of maternal rejection. The basic personality of the duodenal ulcer patient, for example, suggests that his wishes for love and dependence have been frustrated; he overcompensates by appearing excessively responsible, independent, and hard-working.

The *two-factor theory,* the most recent explanation, suggests that a certain somatic predisposition, probably of an inherited nature, interacts with psychological factors to produce any given psychosomatic disorder. This hypothesis proposes that in the absence of some undetermined amount of both somatic predisposition and psychological stress, no psychosomatic disorder will develop. These two sources of stress are related, however, in the sense that an increase in one source of stress reduces the amount of stress needed from the other source.

Treatment. The adequate treatment of the individual with a psychosomatic disorder is exceptionally difficult. First, the identification of the physiological condition is often particularly difficult with disorders whose symptoms may vary considerably over time (for example, neurodermatitis or asthma). In fact, there is often no unanimous agreement as to the criteria needed for the diagnosis. Once the proper diagnosis has been made, the possible approaches include symptomatic treatment alone, which at times may be of life-saving importance (as in severe attacks of asthma or perforated ulcers), symptomatic treatment in conjunction with psychotherapy, or primarily psychotherapy.

The most desirable treatment, combining medical and psychological efforts, requires collaboration among the professionals involved and the patient. Psychological treatment might be primarily symptomatic (for example, teaching an ulcer patient to relax and avoid becoming very anxious), or it might emphasize resolution of those early, often childhood, conflicts that are thought to underlie the specific psychosomatic disorder. Finally, treatment might focus on the patient's current relationships and defenses against anxiety and conflict with others.

Glossary of Psychosomatic Disorders
Gastrointestinal Reactions

Peptic ulcer—an open sore (ulcer) in the intestinal tract that develops because of excessive or prolonged gastric secretion. It is assumed that persistent emotional stress, through its influence on the vagus nerve, is responsible for the excessive gastric secretion.

Ulcerative colitis—the mucous membrane of the colon becomes very fragile, resulting in ulcers and bleeding. Emotional stress, by virtue of its effects upon both digestive and eliminative functions, aggravates this condition.

Mucous colitis—the main symptom is the elimination of stools containing mucus. Additional symptoms include indigestion, loss of appetite, and nausea.

Chronic gastritis—symptoms of indigestion, hyperacidity, belching, and nausea are most common. These symptoms are closely related to anger, anxiety, guilt, and other forms of psychological stress.

Anorexia nervosa—in its more extreme form, this condition is marked by progressive weight loss and lack of appetite in the absence of organic disease. In less severe forms, it is manifested by loss of appetite during periods of such psychological stress as conflict or guilt.

Respiratory Disorders

Hyperventilation syndrome—there is a marked increase in both depth and rate of breathing. Subjectively people feel they are about to faint, feel lightheaded, and often have visual disturbances. This syndrome is most often related to acute anxiety.

Bronchial asthma—breathing difficulties, wheezing, and a sense of constriction of the chest are the most common symptoms. While allergic factors are often of major importance, interpersonal conflicts and anxiety appear associated with both the development of bronchial asthma and the incidence of subsequent attacks.

Cardiovascular Disorders

Tachycardia—this condition is marked by both speeded-up activity of the heart and irregularity of the heart rhythm. Breathing difficulties and feeling weak and faint are also present at times. These episodes may appear at any time; sometimes the stress situation is apparent, but at other times there is no readily apparent source of stress and anxiety.

Hypertension—neither the exact cause nor the specific nature of the interaction between psychological and physiological factors in the development of the condition are known. There is considerable agreement, however, that emotional stress, particularly that due to the ineffective expression of anger and hostility, sharply increases blood pressure.

Migraine—type of headache accompanied by severe pain, nausea, vomiting, and various gastrointestinal and/or genitourinary symptoms. While there appears to be a genetic predisposition involved in migraine, such psychological factors as unhappiness, anxiety, and guilt aggravate the condition. The incidence of migraine is considerably greater among individuals with hypertension.

Genitourinary Disorders

Menstrual disturbances—the range of symptoms includes premenstrual tension, with increased restlessness, irritability, and emotional overreactions; dysmenorrhea, which is painful menstruation; and iamenorrhea, in which there is a decrease or complete cessation of menstruation without adequate physiological basis.

Sexual disturbances—perhaps the most common symptoms are impotence and frigidity. *Impotence,* or the inability to perform and enjoy sexual intercourse, may manifest itself through occasional inability to achieve an erection (which is not uncommon) to more severe cases in which there is no sexual arousal under any conditions. *Frigidity* is essentially the female equivalent of impotence. The major symptom is lack of sexual feeling or responsiveness. This may manifest itself in degrees, ranging from occasional lack of interest or desire for sexual intercourse to vaginal spasms that may make sexual intercourse impossible.

Skin Disorders

The skin appears to be one of the most sensitive parts of the body in reacting to psychological stress. Reactions such as neurodermatosis and eczema are common inflammations of the skin. While allergic factors are sometimes involved, most frequently these reactions seem to occur in individuals with various degrees of emotional instability.

—Michael Hirt, *Kent State University*

Consult (13) Arieti, 1959; Coleman, 1964.

PSYCHOSURGERY, operations on the brain as a form of treatment for mental illness. The most common form of surgery is the lobotomy, which involves cutting the nerves connecting the frontal lobes of the brain with the thalamus.

The rationale for psychosurgery was based upon research reports in 1935 that prefrontal lobotomies made monkeys placid in the face of frustration. The first operation on the human being was performed in Portugal shortly afterward. The possibilities of such surgery were further explored by W. Freeman and J. W. Watts, who firmly established it as a psychiatric modality in 1942.

Psychiatrists have been cautious about recommending this procedure because it permanently alters the structure of the brain by severing brain tissue. In spite of the alteration of cortical tracts, psychological testing does not verify extensive evidence of dysfunction. Those areas in which some deficit may be found include impaired ability in conceptualization and abstracting. Intelligence tests do not show a drop of total scores. Some subtest scores may actually improve, perhaps as a secondary effect of relief from anxiety.

Since the advent of tranquilizers, psychosurgery has become less popular, because fewer people require "heroic" treatment.

Prognosis. Patients selected for psychosurgery include chronic schizophrenics who have been refractory to any other treatment. Uncontrollable behavior, often aggressive or assaultive in nature, is a second indication. Psychosurgery has also provided relief for severe obsessive compulsive or hypochondriacal symptoms, particularly when there is high level of anxiety or tension. It has also been recommended for the treatment of depression.

As with many forms of psychiatric treatment, the procedure has proved most effective in patients who have warm, accepting families capable of providing a suitable environment in the convalescent period and afterward. Better results are obtained in patients who have had a good premorbid adjustment, including a stable work record, than are obtained in the underachieving population, who usually cannot compensate for the many lost years after recovery brought about by surgery.

Postoperative Complications. These can be serious and extensive. To some degree, they depend upon the method of surgery and upon the location and extent of the surgical lesions.

Neurological defects include seizures, particularly when there has been bilateral surgery. Preexisting brain damage, postoperative infection, and operative complications such as hemorrhage are associated with seizures in at least 15 percent of the cases. Usually this complication can be controlled with antiepileptic medication.

Adverse personality changes include a period of postoperative shock in which patients become apathetic. Some unfortunately do not recover but remain apathetic for the rest of their lives. In others there may be loss of appetite regulation, leading to marked obesity. At times incontinence is a postoperative sequel. One of the more common outcomes is a decrease in ability to judge social situations—which is a function of impaired ability to conceptualize and abstract. Tactless remarks, inconsiderateness for others, and inappropriateness of sexual behavior are some manifestations of this behavioral defect.

Surgical Approaches. These vary from transorbital procedures, which require no distinct opening of the vault of the brain and can be performed under light anesthesia, to techniques requiring major surgery, in which the brain is fully exposed. Instruments utilized range from an icepick in the blind, transorbital approach to scalpel, electrocoagulation, and sonic techniques performed under direct operative vision. The goal of all procedures is to produce the most favorable clinical result with the smallest possible lesion.

—Edwin Robbins, M.D., *New York University Medical Center*

Consult (13) Freeman and Watts, 1950; Greenblatt, 1967; Kalinowsky and Hock, 1952.

PSYCHOTHERAPY, a procedure for treating psychological problems through psychological methods—that is, by a trained therapist's talking with a patient. Psychotherapy is distinguished from the advice giving and support offered by friends in that the therapist guides his own behavior by a systematic understanding of what he should do and why. The interaction between the expert and the sufferer should not be termed psychotherapy unless the patient has sought help of his own free will; attempts to change a person's behavior because someone else is distressed about it do not fall into this category. [*Consult* (13) Szasz, 1965.]

Problems. Various difficulties in living can cause a person to seek psychotherapy. Often the individual experiences distressing feelings, such as anxiety, depression, or loneliness. Sometimes he knows that he is not getting along well with people who are important in his life. A mother may be concerned that she is not handling her children well; a husband may find his wife dissatisfied with their marriage. Sometimes the individual is dissatisfied with what he has been able to achieve in his work: a student cannot keep his mind on his studies; an artist cannot be as creative as he would like. Sometimes the individual has distressing inhibitions: a man cannot get sexually interested in his wife; a woman finds herself unable to achieve orgasm.

At times the individual is plagued by thoughts that he cannot rid himself of. He may have irrational fears—of riding in elevators, for example. Sometimes there are physical symptoms, such as headaches or a stomach ulcer, for which there is no sufficient physical explanation.

Methods. Advice giving and encouragement have been used for centuries to help people with their psychological difficulties. It is only in recent times, however, that a so-called *dynamic psychotherapy,* based on an understanding of unconscious conflicts and their expression through symptoms, has been developed. We owe this development to Sigmund Freud.

In trying to help neurotic patients by psychological methods, Freud first made use of *hypnosis.* Some psychotherapists still use this technique, either to remove symptoms directly or to overcome the inability of patients to remember thoughts and feelings that are connected with these symptoms, in order to understand the origin of the symptoms and thus alleviate them indirectly. Freud abandoned hypnosis, however, for four reasons. First, relatively few patients can be hypnotized deeply. Second, the ability to hypnotize fails just when the material being dealt with is most important. Third, the hypnotic method tends to conceal the underlying conflicts both from the patient and from the therapist. Finally, the results of hypnosis are usually short-lived. [*Consult* (13) Gill and Brenman, 1959; Jones, 1953.]

Freud then developed the *psychoanalytic method,* which aims at restoring to the patient's awareness the important thoughts and feelings that he had to put out of his conscious mind. When this has been achieved, the patient is in a position to adapt more effectively, to feel greater contentment, and to give up the symptoms through which he attempted to resolve his conflicts.

There are other ways of alleviating symptoms. If some of the unconscious wishes that affect the patient can be given satisfaction, he may no longer need the symptoms. For instance, the fellowship of Alcoholics Anonymous may meet his needs for a close, dependent relationship with other human beings, thereby relieving his need to drink. Although participation in Alcoholics Anonymous cannot be considered psychotherapy, the same principle can apply when a therapist allows his patient to become dependent on him. Relief of

guilt because the therapist takes a benign attitude toward his patient is also often helpful. At times symptoms can be alleviated by frightening a patient into conformity, as when an authoritarian therapist shows his disapproval of his patient's sexual or aggressive actions. If the patient's drives are not too strong, such disapproval may help him to resist temptations, thereby feeling less guilt and having less need of symptoms. [*Consult* (13) Dollard and Miller, 1950.]

Since about 1950 many psychologists in universities have attempted to apply the principles of the psychology of learning to the alleviation of symptoms and the teaching of more effective adaptation. Some researchers have relied almost completely on the principle that responses that are regularly followed by reward are more likely to occur again on the next occasion when the same situation is presented. Others have utilized more complex strategies involving attempts to deal with the patient's conflicts, to alleviate anxiety (which they believe to be a precondition for symptoms), or to provide a human model for the patient to copy, or to punish unwanted responses and thereby eliminate them. These attempts to apply learning principles to the alleviation of symptoms are known as *behavior therapy* and *behavior modification* (even though psychoanalytic therapy also is intended to change behavior). [*Consult* (13) Bandura, 1969; Kanfer and Phillips, 1970; Rachman and Teasdale, 1969; Wolpe and Lazarus, 1966.]

Results. Although thousands of therapists have practiced psychotherapy during the past eighty years, well-documented knowledge of the results of psychotherapy is scarcer than we would like. There have been hundreds of studies of the results of psychotherapy. [*Consult* (13) Meltzoff and Kornreich, 1970.]

All but a handful of the studies fail to meet the highest standards of research design and measurement methodology. This handful—which includes studies by Rogers and Dymond, by Koegler and Brill, by Strupp, Fox, and Lessler, and by Karon and VandenBos—supports several conclusions. The effectiveness of therapy varies from one therapist to another, but psychotherapy *is* helpful, on the average. Neurotic sufferers do *not* get better when they have no treatment at all. Tranquilizing drugs produce more alleviation of the symptoms of schizophrenic patients in the short run than psychotherapy by inexperienced therapists does, but psychotherapy produces greater long-run improvement in schizophrenics and, when the therapists are experienced, even produces more short-term improvements. As to behavior therapy, the great methodological skills of researchers have yet to be applied in a rigorous way to answer the question whether such procedures are generally effective in treating neurotic patients. [*Consult* (13) Karon and VandenBos, 1972; Koegler and Brill, 1967; Rogers and Dymond, 1954; Strupp, *et al.,* 1969.]

—Frank Auld, *University of Windsor*
See also Behavior Therapy; Electroconvulsive Therapy; Mental Health; Mental Hospital; Psychiatry; Psychoanalysis; Psychosurgery.

Consult (13) Coleman, 1964; Strupp, 1971.

PSYCHOTIC DEPRESSIVE REACTION. *See* Depressive Reaction.

PSYCHOTIC DISORDERS. These are generally considered the most severe of all mental disorders. While psychotic behavior may be the result of organic or physical factors, the major psychoses are functional in nature; that is, they have no known organic cause and appear to be purely psychological reactions to various forms of stress. The dominant characteristics of a psychosis are personality disorganization and an impaired ability to perceive reality. In combination, these factors result in the need for treatment in a hospital as opposed to an outpatient setting.

Symptoms. The psychotic individual demonstrates a severe *personality deterioration.* This is usually manifested by an inability to function according to a daily routine that for most individuals presents no difficulty. Interpersonal relationships are severely affected and may be fraught with conflict, suspicion, or cessation of all contact. Occasionally the psychotic individual becomes physically dangerous to society in general.

Loss of contact with reality is a major symptom that distinguishes psychotic disorders from other functional disorders. This impaired ability to distinguish the real from the not real may be evident in the form of *severe withdrawal,* which renders the individual uncommunicative and unresponsive to environmental stimuli.

Autistic thinking is also a common hallmark of a break with reality. Thus, the psychotic responds to the world on the basis of internal cues that render his reactions inappropriate to a given situation. While this type of thinking may appear illogical, Silvano Arieti has pointed out that it may constitute another type of logic, which he called *paleological.* [*Consult* (13) Arieti, 1948.]

Loss of reality contact may also be seen in the form of *disorientation.* The individual may not know who or where he is; in some instances, he may lose track of time so completely that he no longer knows what year it is.

Frequently, a psychotic disorder is accompanied by *hallucinations,* a state in which a person hears and/or sees things that do not exist in objective reality. Auditory or visual hallucinations may appear to be symbolic rep-

resentations of the internal conflict with which the person is struggling. Thus, a psychotic who is suffering extreme guilt may "hear" voices that accuse and downgrade him. Similarly *delusions*—beliefs that the psychotic holds and defends against onslaughts of logic or physical impossibility—often give clues to an internal conflict. Generally, delusional thoughts are classified according to content. Therefore, a person who feels that he is Napoleon or God is said to be suffering from *delusions of grandeur.* Similarly, one who holds *delusions of persecution* feels that people, even total strangers, intend to do him great physical harm. Both delusions and hallucinations may be viewed as exaggerations of basic *defense mechanisms,* which all persons possess to some degree. But while the "normal" often engages in pleasant fantasying, the psychotic loses his ability to distinguish between fantasy and reality, eventually believing to be real what was originally imaginary.

These symptoms may occur in different combinations in a given psychotic individual. To a great extent, symptom combinations represent the basis of *classification* of the various types of psychotic disorders.

Causes. A great deal of research has been devoted to the etiology of psychosis. However, to date there is no single, definite answer to what causes a psychotic process.

One possible explanation involves *hereditary factors* as important in the subsequent development of a psychosis. F. J. Kallmann has contributed many findings concerning this hypothesis. He has discovered that a psychotic condition known as schizophrenia is more likely to occur in individuals whose identical or fraternal twins are schizophrenic than among unrelated members of the general population. Similarly, he has reported a higher incidence of manic-depressive psychosis among families in which a member possesses this disorder than in samples not related by family ties. [*Consult* (13) Kallmann, 1953.]

A second approach to the etiology of psychotic disorders has been to analyze the various body functions (the *constitution*) of psychotics (mainly schizophrenics) and to compare these to nonpsychotic individuals. Unfortunately, although certain differences among the populations in regard to vitamin deficiency, kidney malfunction, hormonal and enzymatic processes, and many other areas have been found, these results have proven unreliable and open to methodological criticism. On the whole, they have led nowhere.

Investigations of *neurophysiological differences* between psychotics and nonpsychotics have led to equally equivocal findings. For example, Heath and his colleagues report changes in nonpsychotic individuals upon the administration of *taraxein,* a substance present

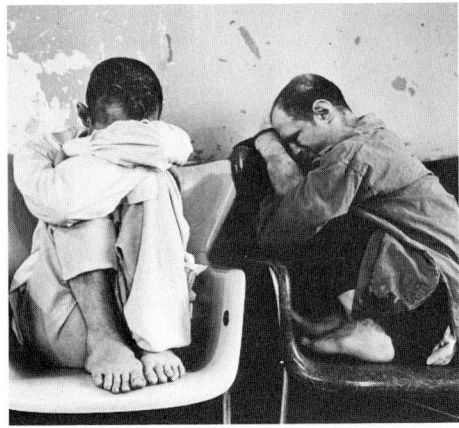

Severe withdrawal, in which the patient is uncommunicative and unresponsive, is symptomatic of psychotic disorders.

PSYCHOTIC DISORDERS

An overview of the psychoses—the symptoms and causes of the mental illnesses that most often are so severe as to require hospital treatment—is given in PSYCHOTIC DISORDERS. Supporting articles discuss what are called the FUNCTIONAL PSYCHOSES: SCHIZOPHRENIA (including simple, hebephrenic, paranoid, catatonic, and shizo-affective types), MANIC DEPRESSIVE PSYCHOSIS, and PARANOIA. Psychotic states can also be caused by damage to the brain. See BRAIN DISORDERS and articles such as GENERAL PARESIS and SENILITY, MENTAL DISORDERS OF.

Treatment of psychoses is discussed in the general article on psychotic disorders and in SCHIZOPHRENIA and other articles on the functional psychoses. Further details are given in PSYCHOTHERAPY, PSYCHIATRY, ELECTROCONVULSIVE THERAPY, and PSYCHOSURGERY. Chemotherapy is noted in DRUGS AND BEHAVIOR and in the main articles on the psychoses. The role of hospitalization is covered in MENTAL HOSPITAL. For an overview of the problem of treating and preventing mental illness, see MENTAL HEALTH.

in the blood of schizophrenics. These behavioral changes closely resemble those found in psychotic disorders. However, these findings have been difficult to replicate in other laboratories. Therefore, despite the fact that all three of these approaches have led to positive findings, it is difficult to make specific conclusions concerning their etiological significance.

A fourth body of research on causes of psychosis (again, dealing mainly with schizophrenia) is contributed by investigators such as Jay Haley, G. Bateson, and R. D. Laing. These scientists have approached the question through the study of *family relationships,* especially the verbal interactions among family members of psychotics. For example, Laing has found that there is a correspondence between the content of hallucinations and delusions and beliefs that family members have instilled in the psychotic individual. In interviews with numerous families he discovered such pathological interactions as the refusal of the parents to believe the child's statements, their fostering of dependency as opposed to personality integration and autonomy, and the establishment of secret systems of communication between two or more family members, which is then denied to exist if questioned.

Bateson's studies report communications based on the *double-bind.* In this situation the child is given messages that are incompatible, such as a warm friendly voice while being spanked or punished. In this way the child learns to react with behavior that appears bizarre or strange to other members of society. While research of this sort can be considered still in its infancy, it does seem to be yielding fascinating as well as fruitful results. [*Consult* (13) Bateson, 1960; Haley, 1959; Heath, *et al.,* 1957; Laing and Esterson, 1964.]

Treatment and Outcome. As mentioned earlier, psychotic disorders are of such severity that they warrant hospitalization. Treatment in this situation usually involves *chemotherapy,* which makes use of major tranquilizers, energizers, and other antipsychotic medications. Pharmacological agents in the phenothiazine group are most common.

Recently other forms of therapy have been added to the treatment of psychotic cases. A growing number of hospitals have begun to institute *token economies,* like those reported by J. M. Atthowe and L. Krasner. In this procedure the hospital ward is arranged so that all rewards, such as food, clothing, bedsheets, or privileges, must be purchased with tokens rather than being simply supplied. Tokens, in turn, are received for desirable ward behavior. In a sense, the psychotic is "paid" for "acting" (behaving) more sanely. Token economies appear quite effective and represent a major change from typical ward organizations, which are primarily custodial and may "foster"

psychotic behavior. [*Consult* (13) Atthowe and Krasner, 1965.]

Another innovative intervention is the *therapeutic community.* One such program is described by R. Almond. In this setting the ward is operated and managed by the patients themselves (not all of whom may be psychotic). They possess complete responsibility for all decisions and actions taken. By this procedure the psychotic is drawn from isolation and urged toward the acceptance of greater responsibility for his own behavior. [*Consult* (13) Almond, 1971.]

A more traditional, yet still important, treatment of psychosis is *psychotherapy,* both individual and in groups. Especially in conjunction with other programs, psychotherapy aims to aid the psychotic in reestablishing personality organization and more effective functioning.

While psychotic disorders have historically been considered to present a poor chance of recovery, such treatment methods seem to have improved this situation. It must be emphasized, however, that a favorable prognosis in these cases depends upon many factors, not the least of which is the availability of intensive-treatment programs.

Glossary of Psychotic Disorders

Affective psychoses—characterized by pronounced mood disorders, which are the chief factor in the person's loss of contact with his environment.

Catatonic schizophrenia—a severe form of schizophrenia, generally characterized by cessation of all behavior. During these stuporous states, the person may be unreachable by social contact and may demonstrate *waxy flexibility,* the tendency to remain for long periods of time in a physical position fixed by others.

Childhood schizophrenia—demonstrated by the onset of schizophrenic behavior prior to puberty.

Hebephrenic schizophrenia—dominated by shallow, inappropriate emotional responsivity, especially a frequent and unpredictable giggle that may occur at any time.

Manic-depressive psychosis—an effective disorder, usually of longstanding nature. It is displayed by severe mood swings from elation to severe depression over a period of time. In each case, the present mood is exaggerated to the point where it represents a break with reality.

Paranoia—an extremely rare paranoid state in which a complex delusional system is the only symptom. The individual may appear to possess no mental disorder other than this one, delusional thought process. Authorities are divided as to the actual existence of this type of psychosis.

Paranoid schizophrenia—characterized by the presence of delusions that consistently affect the person's behavior. Hallucinations may be present, but severe personality deterioration is rare.

Paranoid state—a condition of psychotic proportion in which delusional thinking plays a paramount role.

Psychosis—a severe mental disorder characterized by personality disintegration, distorted or inaccurate perceptions of reality, and marked difficulty in daily functioning. The major types of psychosis are schizophrenia, paranoid states, and affective illnesses.

Schizophrenia—the most common of all psychoses, characterized by disturbances in thinking, withdrawal from reality and social contact, and inappropriate emotional responsiveness. Delusions and hallucinations are frequently present.

Simple schizophrenia—a type of schizophrenic process in which the general behavior patterns are regressive in nature. Loss of social contacts and a low level of adjustment are the chief symptoms.

—Richard E. Dimond, *Sangamon State University*

See also Manic-Depressive Psychosis; Mental Health; Mental Hospital; Paranoia; Psychiatry; Psychotherapy; Schizophrenia.

Consult (13) Arieti, 1959; Coleman, 1964; Kesey, 1962; Kisker, 1964; Laing and Esterson, 1964; Rokeach, 1967.

PUBERTY. *See* Adolescence.

PUBLIC OPINION. *See* Attitude and Attitude Change.

PULSE RATE. As a result of the contraction and expansion of arterial walls, a pulse can be felt at certain points in the skin overlying an artery. The pulse wave is a direct result of the ejection of blood from the heart into the arterial system. Medically, pulse rate can be used to detect irregularity in heart function as well as to determine the strength of the heart beat. The pulse rate typically increases in time of stress.

PUNISHMENT, and learning. *See* Operant Conditioning; Reward and Punishment.

PUZZLE BOX, a box from which an animal can escape by correctly manipulating one or more latch devices. The classic example is the puzzle box used by E. L. Thorndike with cats.

See also Operant Conditioning; Problem Solving; Trial-and-Error Learning.

PYROMANIA, a compulsion to start fires. This disorder has been called an obsessive-compulsive reaction or a symptom of an antisocial personality. Whatever the cause, persons with this mania have been responsible for millions of dollars of fire damage and numerous deaths.

The unconscious motivation for pyromania may be defiance of a particular authority figure or of "the establishment," a more general expression of aggression, or sexual drives that do not find another outlet. Some compulsive arsonists watch the fires they start and become sexually aroused to the point of orgasm.

RACISM. *See* Prejudice.

RAPE, sexual intercourse, in the broadest sense of the term, accomplished by force or, occasionally, by fraud. The essential aspect, that the victim either did not consent or could not understand, is sometimes difficult to establish. So-called statutory rape is intercourse with a female who is not an adult and is therefore incapable of giving consent.

A large majority of those convicted of rape have no distinguishing characteristics except the attitude that it is legitimate to take by force whatever is desired. Only 10 to 15 percent of imprisoned rapists are seriously psychologically disturbed individuals. Men convicted of rape involving prepubescent females are intellectually dull, emotionally disturbed, and frequently alcoholic.

—Eugene E. Levitt, *Indiana University School of Medicine*

RAPID EYE MOVEMENTS. One stage of sleep is marked by rapid eye movements (REM sleep). *See* Sleep and Dreams.

RATING SCALE, a device used in evaluating personality. Rating simply means that an observer makes judgments about the person being assessed. The scale focuses the rater's attention on specified traits and provides a place to record judgments. A graphic rating scale lists ranges of descriptions of personality traits from one extreme to another. For example, a subject's manner could be rated along a line from "avoided by others" to "sought out by others." The rater checks the point on the line that corresponds to his opinion of the subject.

Various errors can enter into rating, particularly the "halo effect." If a subject ranks high (or low) on a few traits, there is a tendency to give him high (or low) ratings on other traits.

RATIONALIZATION, the process by which behavior or attitudes prompted by unrecognized motives are explained away by excuses or reasons that place the person in a more favorable light. In using this mechanism, an individual defends himself against truths that are uncomfortable or painful. For example, a student who should be studying for an important examination but wants to go to the movies will rationalize by saying that he needs the relax-

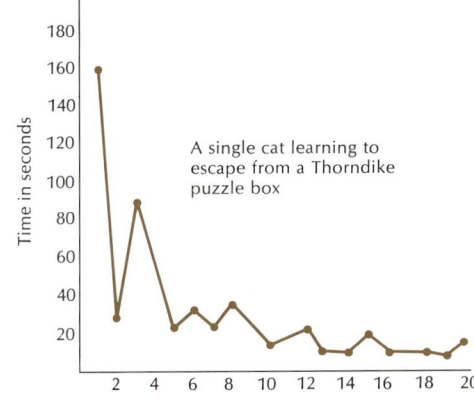

A single cat learning to escape from a Thorndike puzzle box

The graph shows that with successive trials the cat requires less and less time to escape from the puzzle box.

ation. Thus, he can attend the movie without guilt.

Rationalization is quite commonly used by everyone in situations that are difficult or embarrassing. However, when carried to an extreme, it may become detrimental to effective functioning. If questionable motives are continually rationalized, the likelihood of personal growth and change of behavior is minimal.

—Michael Rothenberg, *The City College of The City University of New York*
See also Defense Mechanism.

REACTION FORMATION, a process in which an unconscious painful or undesirable character trait or attitude is masked by an excessive and inflexible demonstration of an opposite trait or attitude. For example, a person who persistently presents himself as pleasant and anxious to please, even in the face of conditions that would justify anger, may be attempting to cover up or defend against the anxiety caused by his unexpressed rage and resentment. A mother who unconsciously feels hostility toward her child may cope with these feelings by relating to the child in an overly solicitous and overprotective manner.

Reaction formation can usually be identified by a single-mindedness of purpose with which a particular course of action is followed. In its extreme form this defense mechanism can be seen in the ritualized behavior of obsessive persons, such as the individual who measures every step in an attempt to avoid killing any insects. This is usually an effort to control unconscious sadistic or hostile impulses.

—Michael Rothenberg, *The City College of The City University of New York*
See also Defense Mechanism.

REACTION TIME (RT), the interval between the beginning of a stimulus and the initiating of a response. For example, the length of time it takes to put your foot on the brake is one measure of your RT to a red light. In the usual RT experiment, a subject presses a key (the response) as quickly as possible after a stimulus. *Simple RT* measures one response to one stimulus; *complex* or *Choice RT* a response that depends on which stimulus occurs. The RT experiment was invented by the physiologist Helmhotz more than 100 years ago. He used it to measure the speed of nerve transmission.

REACTIVE DEPRESSION. *See* Depressive Reaction.

READINESS TEST, a test used to determine the entering behavior of an individual before he undertakes learning in some area. It determines the degree to which an individual has the prerequisite skill or knowledge necessary to learn new skills or knowledge. The most widely used readiness tests are those involving reading.

The knowledge obtained from such tests is used to help prepare the person for the new learning as well as to decide which methods of teaching would best fit him in order to promote the most efficient learning. Such tests are especially valuable in the field of education.

—Louis Snellgrove, *Lambuth College*
See also Measurement.
Consult (12) Cronbach, 1970.

READING DISABILITY (also dyslexia, paralexia, specific primary dyslexia, reading retardation, developmental dyslexia). This broad concept encompasses a variety of disorders in which there is retardation or deficiency in reading of two or more years. It is estimated that some 10 to 15 percent of all school-age children have some form of reading disability, even though they have normal intelligence and do not show obvious causes. The most common term used to denote the problem is *dyslexia* (from the Greek, meaning "word difficulty").

The disorder was first described as a clinical entity in 1896, when an English physician observed reading retardation in children who were otherwise intellectually normal. No single overwhelming cause has been identified. The reported variables include deficient or impaired neurological functioning, perceptual (especially visual and hearing) deficiencies, and even hereditary background.

One of the most authoritative reports on reading disabilities identifies three major categories of reading disorders. In *brain injury,* the impairment is the result of neurological deficit. History typically reveals the cause of the insult, common agents being prenatal toxicity, birth trauma or anoxia, encephalitis, and adventitial head injury. In *primary reading retardation,* the impairment is not associated with brain damage either in history or on neurological examination. The defect appears to be in the basic capacity to integrate written material and to associate concepts with symbols. In *secondary reading retardation,* the capacity to learn to read appears to be intact but is utilized insufficiently for the child to achieve a reading level commensurate with his intelligence. These children are deficient as a result of exogenous factors, such as anxiety conditions, negativism, depression, psychosis, and limited or disadvantaged home or school environment. [*Consult* (14) Rabinovitch, *et al.,* 1954.]

Among the most frequently used remedial and therapeutic procedures for reading disabilities are traditional remedial reading instruction, perceptual-motor training and exercises (in which tactile- kinesthetic experiences are used to supplement and reinforce visual-audio perception of symbols), neuromuscular coordination exercises (especially those that emphasize ocular motility skills, eye movements, eye aiming, eye teaming, and the like), and alteration of the child's immediate learning environment (for example, reducing the sources of external sensory stimulation). Drug therapy has been used in some cases that are also diagnosed as hyperactive or hyperkinetic.

—Frank T. Vitro, *University of Maine*
See also Aphasia; Brain Disorders; Hyperkinetic Children.

REALITY PRINCIPLE, in psychoanalytic theory, a response to awareness of the fact that behavior has to be adjusted to demands of the environment. The young child is motivated by the pleasure principle, but he soon learns that forces in the real world outside himself require him to postpone or give up some gratifications. If he finds, for example, that his parents disapprove of certain actions, he will come to feel that avoiding reproof or gaining praise is more important than quick gratification of an impulse. The reality principle becomes part of the structure of the ego.

See also Ego.

REASONING. *See* Problem Solving; Thinking.

RECALL. *See* Memory.

RECEPTORS, the input organs for the nervous system. These fall into two basic classes, general receptors and special receptors. *General receptors* are located over large areas of the body surface and are important for the sensations of touch, heat, cold, pressure, and pain. *Specialized receptors* generally are found in the head region and mediate such functions as hearing, vision, taste, smell, and equilibrium.

See also Sensation *and articles on the various senses.*

RECOGNITION, a method of determining how much learning has been retained by requiring only that the subject identify the correct answer to a question. In a multiple-choice examination or a true-false test, recognition plays a primary role in determining which answer will be chosen. It is generally believed that the recognition of a correct response in a test situation is not as difficult a task as requiring the subject to write the correct answer when no alternatives are presented.

See also Memory.

RECREATIONAL THERAPY, using recreational activities as part of the treatment program for mentally ill patients. A wide range of activities has been tried—sports, games, hobbies, dramatics, movies, music (listening or performing), square dancing, folk dancing, and others. Moreover, the program may offer parties, picnics, and trips outside the hospital. The program is intended to offer each patient activities that fit his personality and the nature of his problems.

Many hospitals now employ recreation specialists, who are qualified for their professional standing by education and experience.

REDUNDANCY IN LANGUAGE. *See* Information Theory.

REFLEX, according to the conventional definitions, the immediate reaction with a stereotyped response to the presentation of a discrete stimulus. A common example is the reaction to placing one's hand in a kettle of hot water. Heat above a certain intensity is the stimulus, and the resulting rapid withdrawal of the hand is the response. But many reflexes are neither machinelike in execution nor beyond modification. There are documented cases of persons who have walked unharmed on hot coals. Indeed, Pavlov established that so-called unconditioned reflexes could be the basis for new reflexes.

Most research on reflexes has occurred in the physiological laboratory, using restrained or drugged animals or those whose nervous systems have been damaged. Such work, which reveals little if anything about behavioral processes in healthy, free-living animals, emphasizes an automatic reflex response correlated with the exact nature and intensity of a transient stimulus. The end result has been a downgrading of the role of reflexes in behavior in recent years. Yet many reflexes are of vital importance, especially such ubiquitous responses as the vestibular reactions of the inner ear that keep us oriented upright and the eye and head movements (nystagmus) that occur whenever either our head or the external visual world moves.

Reflexes, then, are stimulus-response correlations of either a transient or near continuous nature, usually protective or adaptive to the functioning of the organism and stereotyped in form. Although most of them involve only parts of an animal (for example, knee jerk, eye blink), reflexes can also involve the entire animal (startle response). They blend into the fixed-action-pattern relations of ethology, on the one hand, and form the basis of some important learning processes, on the other.

—Gordon M. Burghardt, *University of Tennessee*
See also Pavlovian Conditioning.
Consult (6) Easton, 1972; Kimble, 1967.

REGRESSION, the process by which an individual under great stress reverts to responses and sources of gratification that characterized his behavior at an earlier stage of development.

This occurs quite commonly in young children upon the birth of a younger brother or sister. Perceiving their secure position in the

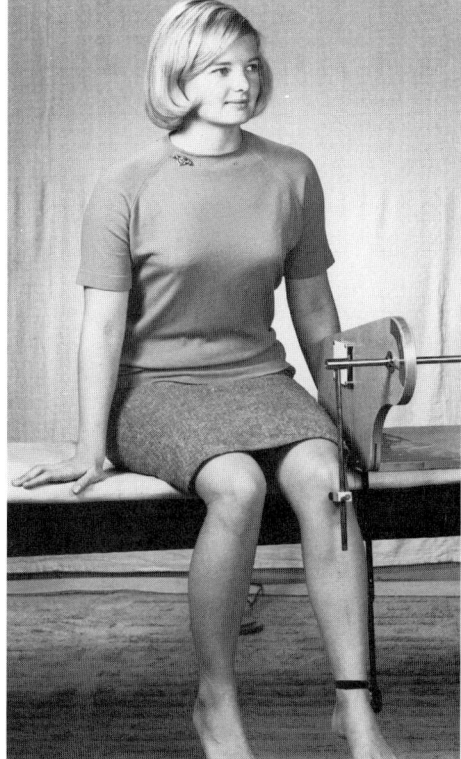

Device used to measure the knee-jerk reflex.

household threatened by the almost totally helpless infant, they are likely to return to more infantile modes of behavior. Thus, a child who has been toilet-trained for months will suddenly lose control of his bladder or bowel. Many children regress to crawling or sucking their thumbs.

In its most extreme forms, regression can be highly destructive and debilitating. Adult psychotic patients may regress to childlike levels of functioning. They are unable to care for themselves even minimally and suffer from profound distortions of reality.

—Michael Rothenberg, *The City College of The City University of New York*
See also Defense Mechanism; Homesickness.

REGULATORY BEHAVIOR. *See* Homeostasis.

REINFORCEMENT. A stimulus that increases the probability that a response will occur is a reinforcer. Such a stimulus may be unconditioned or conditioned. An unconditioned stimulus produces a response immediately without training. An ideal unconditioned stimulus is the presentation of food to a hungry animal, which leads to salivation. An ideal negative reinforcer (stimulus) is electric shock, which invariably produces a withdrawal or escape response. These reinforcers, whether positive, such as food, or negative, such as shock, can be paired with a neutral conditioned stimulus. Hence, if a bell is presented followed by an electric shock to the foot, the bell will come to elicit withdrawal of the leg from the shock source before the shock is turned on. This is an example of a classically (Pavlovian) conditioned avoidance response. The bell could also be paired with food, as in Pavlov's famous experiments, where it will lead to conditioning of the salivation response in anticipation of the food.

In operant (instrumental) conditioning, instead of eliciting a response by presenting a stimulus, one waits until a response naturally occurs. Positive reinforcement of that response will increase the probability that it will occur; negative reinforcement will lead to the elimination of that response. For example, when a small child touches a valuable piece of furniture, a hand slap will lead to inhibition of the operant—touching. If a dog spontaneously sits up and is rewarded with food, the probability of this operant—sitting—will be increased. Operant conditioning is used for teaching circus animals many tricks.

Reinforcement can be achieved in many ways. The most basic is known as *continuous* reinforcement, or *CRF*, where every response made is reinforced. When a piece of food is made available each time a rat presses a lever, the rate of lever pressing is increased. On the other hand, the animal becomes rapidly sati-

ated after a small number of presses have been made. A more efficient method of training employs schedules of *partial* reinforcement.

In one of these, known as the *fixed-ratio schedule,* the animal is reinforced for making a predetermined number of responses. A human parallel to this situation would be offering a factory worker one dollar in payment for each set of fifty nuts and bolts he completes, so that the worker will work as fast as he possibly can. Ratio schedules lead to high outputs.

Another approach, known as the *fixed-interval schedule,* requires that the subject make only one response at the end of a specific time period in order to obtain reinforcement. Pigeons placed on fixed-interval schedules of one minute press a key relatively slowly for the first thirty seconds and then speed up toward the end of the one-minute interval. If the factory worker had to assemble only one nut and bolt every fifteen minutes to receive his dollar, all other things being equal, he would probably turn out only one set in that time period. Interval schedules lead to a low rate of response. There are many schedules of reinforcement, and some are complex. Partial schedules of reinforcement have been extremely useful in devising complex learning tasks for many testing situations.

—Joel F. Lubar, *University of Tennessee*
See also Operant Conditioning; Pavlovian Conditioning.

REJECTION, an attitude of unacceptance directed toward a child by his parents. There are many degrees of rejection, varying from lack of interest in the child to severe physical abuse. Evidence of rejection may be seen in frequent scolding, neglect, ridiculing, disapproval, and denial of affection.

Parental rejection has harmful effects on the child's personality. It is often associated with passivity, submission, distrustfulness, withdrawal, aggressive defiant behavior, and emotional disturbance in children. Maternal coldness has also been found to be related to feeding problems and bed wetting.

—Ragaa Mazen, *Southern Connecticut State College*
Consult (11) Becker, *et al.*, 1962; Kessler, 1966; Sears, *et al.*, 1957.

RELATIVE DEPRIVATION. People compare their outcomes with what they expect to receive. If their expectations are exceeded they experience *relative gratification;* if their expectations are not met they experience *relative deprivation.* For example, a World War II study showed that Air Corps cadets had a very rapid promotion rate compared with military policemen. Yet the policemen were much more satisfied with promotions than were cadets because MPs had a very low expectation for promotion, whereas cadets had an exceedingly

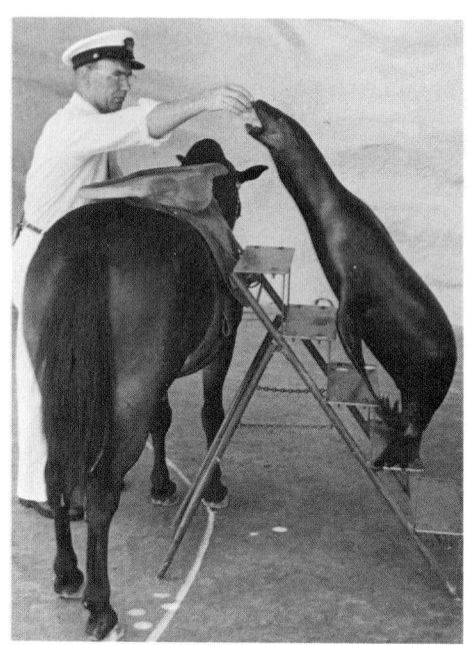
Reinforcement is presented to the sea lion as it completes a step in its circus routine.

high expectation for advancement. This illustrates the major thesis of relative deprivation theory: It is not what one objectively has that matters but rather how this compares with one's expectations.

Relative deprivation may be a factor in political rebellions, and the concept also contributes much to our understanding of the urban riots in America during the last decade. Revolutions generally occur *after* objective improvements have occurred, because the improvements trigger or inflate expectations.

Many of the individual's expectations accrue from his comparison of his experiences with those that he believes individual *referents* or *reference groups* are receiving. For this reason, the relative-deprivation construct may be viewed as a special application of *reference group theory.*

—R. Gary Bridge, *Columbia University Consult* (10) Davis, 1959; Merton, 1957.

RELIABILITY, in measurement, the consistency of a test. The reliability of a test depends on the extent to which it gives approximately the same results if used repeatedly under the same conditions.

REM SLEEP, a stage of sleep during which rapid eye movements can be detected. *See* Sleep and Dreams.

REMEMBERING. *See* Memory.

REPETITION-COMPULSION. *See* Obsessive-Compulsive Reaction.

REPRESSION, the act of pushing out of consciousness ideas and feelings that are painful or disturbing. A person may repress wishes, events, or memories if the recognition of them would seriously disrupt his functioning.

This mechanism results in the elimination of most memories of the first six years of childhood. Indeed, Freud stated that the Oedipal conflict is resolved by the child's repression of his unacceptable sexual desires for the parent of the opposite sex and identification with the parent of the same sex.

Repression is probably the most common of all defenses. It may be the precursor of another defense mechanism, such as displacement, or of the development of various physical or behavioral symptoms, such as headaches or tics. If used excessively, it can lead to an overwhelming feeling of tension and fatigue, because a great deal of an individual's energy is required to accomplish and maintain the expulsion of thoughts and feelings from conscious awareness.

—Michael Rothenberg, *The City College of The City University of New York*
See also Defense Mechanism; Oedipus Complex.

RESEARCH METHODS. *See* Experimental Design; Scientific Method.

RESPONSE, any reaction to a stimulus. The term covers acts from reflexes to complex behavior. For common uses of the word, *see* Pavlovian Conditioning; Stimulus-Response Psychology.

RETARDATION. *See* Mental Retardation.

RETENTION. *See* Memory.

RETRIEVAL. *See* Memory.

RETROACTIVE INTERFERENCE or INHIBITION. *See* Memory.

RETROGRADE AMNESIA. *See* Amnesia.

REWARDS VERSUS PUNISHMENTS. In the laboratory, rewards and punishments are used to motivate animals in learning experiments. Food reinforces a desired response, and electric shocks punish an unwanted action. Similarly, parents and teachers use incentives and penalties to train children. The means employed may not have the immediate impact of food or a shock, but giving or withholding praise and lifting or lowering status can appeal to powerful drives.

Psychologists have made a number of studies of the relative effectiveness of rewards and punishments, and the results favor rewards. E. L. Thorndike found rewards more efficient in training animals; experiments with school children point the same way. Punishment can have damaging effects, for example, by causing confusion and emotional tension. Punishment may change performance without affecting learning. When a child is penalized, he may stop what he is doing but this does not mean he has "unlearned" the undesirable pattern of behavior or learned a new one. Reward has the advantage of strengthening the desirable behavior.

Rewards have disadvantages—for example, competing for prizes can cause anxiety and tension. Punishment may be necessary to check specific bits of behavior. For the long run, however, rewards have a more positive effect.

See also Operant Conditioning; Reinforcement.

RH FACTOR. *See* Mental Retardation.

RHINE, JOSEPH BANKS (1895-   ), American parapsychologist. Born in Waterloo, Pa., he received a Ph.D. in biology from the University of Chicago in 1925. He was founder (1934, with William McDougall) and director of the Parapsychology Laboratory at Duke University and founder (1962) and director of its successor,

Pioneer parapsychologist Joseph Rhine expanded and popularized psychical research.

the Foundation for Research on the Nature of Man, Durham, N. C.

Rhine's contributions to parapsychology are varied. He restructured it by introducing such terms as "parapsychology" (instead of "psychical research"), "extrasensory perception," and "psychokinesis." He revitalized it by emphasis on quantitative research and recruitment of many able workers; and he popularized it by his writings and lectures. With Zener he developed the widely used ESP cards. In 1937 he founded the *Journal of Parapsychology*, where research from his laboratory was published, and in 1957 he arranged the founding of the Parapsychological Association. His own experiments and influence have emphasized preliminary demonstration of ESP and PK, then rigorous confirmatory research with full control of experimental conditions.

His major publications are *Extrasensory Perception* (1935), *Extrasensory Perception after 60 Years* (1940, coauthor), *The Reach of the Mind* (1947), *New World of the Mind* (1953), and *Parapsychology: Frontier Science of the Mind* (1957, coauthor).

Rhine's wife, Dr. Louisa E. Rhine, has been his close associate in research and in editing the *Journal of Parapsychology*. Her own books include *Hidden Channels of the Mind* (1961), *ESP in Life and Lab* (1967), and *Mind Over Matter* (1970).

—Gertrude R. Schmeidler, *The City College of The City University of New York*

See also Parapsychology.

RISKY SHIFT. Group decisions often deviate from the average initial sentiments of the individual group members. This was first observed in decisions involving risk, and it was initially believed that groups take greater chances than individuals—a phenomenon called the risky shift. Subsequent research has shown that groups may be more cautious than individuals in some situations as well as more risk-taking in others. The term "choice shift" is now applied to this phenomenon. This label also reflects the fact that shifts have been found in a variety of settings that do not involve risk.

The direction in which a group will shift depends largely on the initial proclivities of its members. Risky shifts are found when most members are initially attracted toward taking chances, and cautious shifts when their initial biases favor security. Thus, in a sense, people gain the courage of their convictions in group decisions. Further evidence suggests that the shifts are produced by discussion of the issues preliminary to decision rather than the act of decision itself.

A number of theories have been developed to explain choice shifts. It appears that the arguments presented in group discussion tend to be heavily biased in the direction of

shift. There is also some evidence for a *social comparison mechanism*: when group members learn from the discussion that other members are not so moderate as they had thought, they are encouraged to move in the direction of their initial proclivities.

—Dean G. Pruitt, *State University of New York at Buffalo*

Consult (10) Brown, 1965; Pruitt, 1971; Silverthorne, 1971; Wallach, *et al.*, 1962; Wallach and Kogan, 1965.

RNA, ribonucleic acid, is related to DNA, from which it is formed. RNA carries genetic information initially programmed by DNA to sites in the body where this genetic information is implemented. Unlike DNA, which is an extremely stable molecule, RNA is subject to change by environmental influences.

Structurally, RNA contains four kinds of nucleotides, which are composed of sugar and a phosphate group linked to a base. The bases in RNA are adenine, guanine, cytosine, and uracil.

There are three basic classes of RNA, differing in molecular weight and function. One, soluble or transfer RNA, is found in the cytoplasm of cells. Its molecular weight lies between 20,000 and 40,000. A second type of RNA, messenger RNA, is found in the nucleus of the cell and has a molecular weight of between 300,000 and 500,000. A third type of RNA, ribosomal RNA, is found in the ribosomes and has a molecular weight of several million.

Messenger RNA is formed directly from DNA. Its function is to activate ribosomes for the formation of proteins. It is also known that messenger RNA codes the specific sequences of amino acids that form the various types of protein.

Recently there has been considerable evidence to suggest that either RNA or RNA-coded protein molecules might be involved in memory processes. Experiments have shown that during specific types of learning specific changes occur in the amount and in the composition of the RNA in different regions of the brain. In vestibular learning tasks, for example, RNA production is increased in the vestibular nuclei of the brain stem.

—Joel F. Lubar, *University of Tennessee*

See also Brain Storage; DNA.

ROGERS, CARL RANSOM (1902–   ), American psychologist and psychotherapist, born in Oak Park, Ill.

Rogers is known as the founder of the client-centered approach to personality and psychotherapy. He rejected the psychological determinism and instinct theory of psychoanalysis. He found unacceptable a view of man as driven by a series of antisocial impulses that he suppresses only with great effort and sacri-

Carl Rogers, founder of client-centered therapy.

In role playing the individual adopts the role of another person in order to gain new insights into his own behavior and the behavior of others.

fice. In place of instincts, Rogers postulated a drive toward self-actualization, out of which all other motives derive. He contends that every individual has a natural urge to realize his potential and function autonomously. Under conditions of warmth and acceptance by others and similar feelings toward oneself, this tendency will flourish. But when these conditions are not present, the individual is forced to distort his experiences to avoid the discomfort they might cause him.

In client-centered therapy, individuals are helped to remove whatever obstacles exist to the expression of their self-actualization drive. Rogerian therapy focuses on the current feelings and attitudes of the client and does not concern itself with his early childhood experiences and unconscious conflicts.

While Rogers' therapeutic approach has gained some measure of popularity, his primary contribution may be his introduction of genuine humanistic concern for the individual into personality theory.

Rogers was president of the American Psychological Association (1946–1947) and of the American Academy of Psychotherapists (1956–1958). His major publications include *Client Centered Therapy,* 1951, and *On Becoming a Person,* 1961.

—Michael Rothenberg, *The City College of The City University of New York*

ROLE PLAYING.

This procedure, which has a multitude of uses in clinical psychology, is widely used in sensitivity and therapeutic groups. The individual is required to adopt the role of another person and experience the world in a way that is not usual for him. This experience is designed to produce new insights into an individual's perceptions of his own behavior and that of others.

Role playing has been effectively used, for example, in programs to establish better police-community relations. In such cases police play the roles of protestors, while protestors play those of policemen. This use of role playing is thought to increase empathy by providing individuals with some ability to relate to others' experiences. For this reason, role playing has been used in attempts to improve race relations and increase interpersonal sensitivity. Role playing may also increase the likelihood of altruistic and help-giving acts.

Within a therapeutic relationship a patient may play the role of the therapist in an attempt to better understand himself. The therapist may, in turn, play the role of the patient to provide himself greater insight into the patient's personality and needs and also to provide a mirrorlike representation in which the patient can see himself. In specific therapies, such as those for building adequate assertive behavior, role playing may constitute the major proportion of the process. In these cases it is hoped that the client will actually change his behavior to become more similar to the person whose role he has played.

—Brenda B. Bankart and C. Peter Bankart, *Wabash College*

See also Attitude and Attitude Change; Empathy.

Consult (10) Alberti, 1970; Janis and King, 1954; (13) Moreno, 1946.

RORSCHACH TECHNIQUE, a method of personality assessment developed by the Swiss psychiatrist Hermann Rorschach in the early part of the century and first published in 1923. It was further developed in the United States by Bruno Klopfer and Samuel J. Beck. Information was disseminated through a journal first known as the *Rorschach Research Exchange* and now called the *Journal of Personality Assessment.*

The Rorschach test consists of ten cards with inkblots printed upon them: five are black and five are multicolored. The person taking the test is asked to look at each card and tell the examiner what the blot reminds him of, what it resembles, or what it might represent. Interpretations are based upon norms that exist for different ages and different subcultures. Interpreters are interested in various aspects of performance. For example, persons whose approach is global will use the entire blot, whereas those with a more piecemeal approach will use parts. The kinds of persons, animals, and objects cited reveal the content of someone's thinking. Ways of reacting to different colors may reflect the mood of the person taking the test.

The Rorschach technique is the most frequently used personality test in the United States and is second only to the Wechsler Adult Intelligence Scale in overall test usage. Although its validity remains a matter of dispute, most clinical psychologists who engage in human personality assessment include it in their techniques of appraisal.

—Walter G. Klopfer, *Portland State University*

Consult (12) Klopfer, *et al.,* 1954, 1956.

ROSENZWEIG PICTURE FRUSTRATION (P-F) STUDY, a projective technique of personality assessment developed originally for adults by Saul Rosenberg. A children's form was subsequently designed. In both forms, subjects are presented somewhat frustrating situations. Two "speech balloons" appear in each cartoon: one is blank and the other contains antagonists' comments. The subject is required to fill in the protagonists' inquiry to clarify ambiguous responses.

This technique assumes that the testee identifies with the "injured party" and expresses his own mode of reacting to frustration in the response offered. Rosenzweig's scoring

RORSCHACH TECHNIQUE

In the Rorschach Test ten inkblots similar to the one shown are used.

system is based on an involved theory of frustration tolerance and aggression. Responses are classified according to reaction types, direction of aggression, and response conformity (with respect to the standardization sample). However, many examiners analyze results in a more informal, intuitive fashion.

—Randolph S. Kraft, *Federation of the Handicapped, N.Y.*

Consult (12) Rosenzweig, 1944; Rosenzweig, 1947; Rosenzweig and Fleming, 1948.

RUBELLA ("German measles"). *See* Mental Retardation.

RUMORS, an unverified story circulating in a community from person to person, largely by word of mouth. It has been suggested that rumors develop during a period of crisis and when there is lack of information regarding an unclear situation that has importance to the individual.

In laboratory studies conducted by G. Allport and L. Postman, a picture was projected on a screen and one individual was asked to describe it to another subject in detail. That subject was then asked to report it as accurately as he could to still another, and so on, with each subject reporting to the next without seeing the picture. It was concluded that as a rumor travels it becomes shorter and simplified (leveling), certain details are emphasized (sharpening), and its content is assimilated to each transmitter's cultural background and attitudes.

—Ragaa Mazen, *Southern Connecticut State College*

Consult (10) Allport and Postman, 1945; Marlowe, 1971.

RUSH, BENJAMIN (1746–1813), American psychiatrist, surgeon, and politician born in Philadelphia. After studying for his M.D. at the University of Edinburgh, he became professor of chemistry at Dickinson College (1769–1789). He was a signer of the Declaration of Independence.

Regarded as the father of American psychiatry, Rush devoted much of his busy life to the reform of treatment for the mentally ill, particularly at Pennsylvania Hospital. He recognized that insanity was a disease and that the patients should be treated rather than imprisoned, and so he brought mental diseases into the area of medicine. However, some of Rush's methods of treatment could hardly be regarded as an improvement over prison. He believed that insanity was caused by an improper balance of blood in the brain; the result of too much blood was a maniacal state, while too little blood caused a torpid state. Methods Rush used to reduce blood in the brain included bloodletting, purging, intimidation

Benjamin Rush was the first American physician to consider mental diseases part of the province of medicine.

(such as threats of death), and a confining contraption called the "tranquilizer chair." Torpid patients were handled more gently, although a rotating mechanical cage was used to force blood back into the brains of torpid patients.

SADISM, the desire to inflict pain. As in the case of masochism, the pain may be either physical or psychological and is often associated with sexual behavior.

Aggressiveness and force are common correlates of sexual behavior. As is so often the case in defining sexual deviancy, the point at which a special term is needed is unclear. The very rare, bizarrely brutal sex murder is clearly sadism. The typical rapist, who constitutes about 14 percent of institutionalized sex criminals, is not likely to be a sadist. He is often simply a man who grew up in a subculture in which use of force in general is more acceptable than in the middle-class community. One researcher found that the large majority of his "violent men" used force to advance their self-interest in the conventional sense. Less than 6 percent obtained pleasure from terrorizing others.

Individuals with sadistic tendencies usually have accompanying masochistic inclinations and may be termed sadomasochistic. The person who is exclusively sadistic seems to be a rarity.

—Eugene E. Levitt, *Indiana University School of Medicine*

See also Masochism.

Consult (13) Allen, 1962; Gebhard, 1969; Levitt, 1971; Toch, 1969.

SADOMASOCHISM. *See* Masochism; Sadism.

SAMPLING. The units that make up a large population are similar in many ways, and therefore social scientists can learn a great deal about the population by examining only a small portion, or *sample,* of the units in the population. Sampling involves the selection of units to represent a larger population; in contrast, a *census* is a complete enumeration of all of the elements in the population. Sampling is preferred to a complete enumeration because (1) it is less expensive, (2) it is faster because fewer data have to be collected and analyzed, and (3) frequently the examination process itself destroys the unit (as when the average life of a batch of lightbulbs is determined by burning a sample of bulbs). Fortunately, small scientifically selected samples can provide very accurate estimates of the population's characteristics (parameters), and the precision of these estimates improves as the size of the sample increases.

Samples are of two types: *probability* and *nonprobability*. In a probability sample every unit in the population has a known, but not necessarily equal, probability of being included in the sample. For example, in a *simple random sample* (SRS) with equiprobabilities, every element has an equal change of being chosen. The advantage of probability sampling is that the researcher can estimate statistically how well the sample's characteristics represent the population's true characteristics. Nonprobability samples do not permit this estimate of accuracy; however, they are generally much simpler and much cheaper.

—R. Gary Bridge, *Columbia University*
Consult (10) Chein, 1959; Cochran, 1963; Kish, 1965.

SAT. *See* Scholastic Aptitude Tests.

SATYRIASIS, excessive desire for sexual activity in the male—the counterpart of nymphomania.

Medical or psychiatric diagnoses of satyriasis are even more rare than for nymphomania.

As in many areas of sex, culturally based value judgments are heavily involved. Sexual hyperactivity in the male is at least acceptable socially, if not actually desirable. In the female, it is generally frowned upon.

The true "satyromaniac" is either a psychotic person, like the nymphomaniac, or the victim of a rare physiological condition known as *priapism*. Its principal symptom is persistent penile erection. Though the erections of priapism are often not accompanied by sexual desire, the sufferer may nevertheless engage in continual sexual activity in an effort to relieve the condition.

—Eugene E. Levitt, *Indiana Univeristy School of Medicine*
Consult (13) Pumpia-Mindlin, 1967.

SAVINGS, or relearning, the amount of material retained after a subject has mastered a specific task. Of the various measures of savings, one commonly used multiplies by 100 the ratio of the difference between the number of trials or errors obtained in first learning the task and the number of trials and errors necessary for relearning the task after a rest period, divided by the sum of the latter two measures. Thus, if a rat learns a task initially in 100 trials and relearns the task in 50 trials it has shown a 33 percent savings.

Generally whenever a task has been mastered it is retained quite strongly. Cats trained on a avoidance conditioning task where they are required to jump from one compartment of an electrifiable box to another compartment that is not electrified learn this task readily in about forty trials. A conditioned stimulus, a buzzer, is used to signal the forthcoming shock. Retention of this task is usually between 90 and 100 percent. In fact, cats tested as much as two years after initially learning this task have shown better than 90 percent retention.

Measures of retention and savings are extremely useful in the study of drug effects and brain damage. There are many situations in which brain lesions lead to a complete loss in retention but relearning the task occurs more rapidly than initially. For example, removal of the primary auditory cortex in the cat will often produce a total loss in the retention of a previously learned frequency discrimination in which the animal is required to distinguish between tones of 800 and 1,000 hertz. Although retention of this task may be nil, the animal will rapidly relearn the discrimination.

In human studies of learning it has been known since the work of Hermann Ebbinghaus in 1885 that meaningful material is retained much better than meaningless material. Meaningless material in Ebbinghaus' experiments consisted of three-letter nonsense syllables. Retention of material whether meaningful or meaningless drops rapidly after the material has been learned but this loss in retention tends to decelerate after time. For example, in one experiment Ebbinghaus showed that one day after lists of words had been memorized, only about 40 percent was retained, but retesting six days later resulted in a further drop of only about 5 percent in retention scores.

—Joel F. Lubar, *University of Tennessee*
See also Memory.

SCAPEGOATING, blaming another person or a group for one's own troubles, failures, or frustrations. Minority groups often become targets for displaced aggression. *See* Aggression.

SCHACHTER, STANLEY (1922–   ), American social psychologist. Born in New York City, he received a Ph.D. from the University of Michigan (1950) and is currently Nivens Professor of social psychology at Columbia University.

Schachter's research has been concerned with emotion, group behavior, and social influences. As one of the authors of *When Prophecy Fails* (1956), he worked with Leon Festinger on the theory of cognitive dissonance. In the *Psychology of Affiliation* (1959) he examined socially acceptable forms of acting out dependency—one of the first attempts to study such needs experimentally. He then demonstrated experimentally the role of the environment on interpretations of emotion.

Schachter's most recent work, on the problems of obesity, is reported in his *Obesity, Emotion and Crime* (1971).

—Nina Adams, *Yale University*

SCHEDULES OF REINFORCEMENT. *See* Reinforcement.

SCHIZOID PERSONALITY, a personality pattern marked by poor socialization, withdrawal,

Social psychologist Stanley Schachter has studied group behavior, social influence, dependency needs.

and feelings of isolation. The schizoid individual's mood state ranges from oversensitivity and mild depression to emotional coldness. As compared with the cyclothymic personality, the schizoid is not emotionally responsive to his environment or the persons in it. He feels cut off from others and is frequently disliked or ridiculed by them. As a result he tends to be secretive about his thoughts and feelings and generally uncommunicative with others. Often intelligent and ambitious, he may channel much of his energy into intellectual and scholarly activities, sometimes driving himself mercilessly. The schizoid is also prone to applying harsh and unrealistic standards to his own performance, thus undermining his own efforts.

Many schizoids, unable to find expression of their needs in more appropriate ways, resort to an active and extensive fantasy life, which increases their isolation from others. While some schizoid individuals never develop more extreme psychopathology, there is evidence to suggest that many of them eventually exhibit schizophrenic reactions.

—Michael Rothenberg, *The City College of The City University of New York*
        See also Cyclothymic Personality; Personality Disorders.

SCHIZOPHRENIA, a term that describes the commonest and usually the most serious form of functional psychoses or mental diseases. (The only other significant group of functional psychoses are those included in the manic-depressive category.) Functional psychoses are distinguished from organic psychoses in that experts have been unable to discover any anatomical, physical, infectious, or toxic causes for them. Furthermore, on post-mortem examination experts cannot detect any changes in the nervous systems of mentally sick patients that differ from those in mentally healthy individuals.

The term "schizophrenia" was coined in 1911 by the Swiss psychiatrist Eugen Bleuler. Prior to the diffusion and general acceptance of Bleuler's ideas, the schizophrenics were classified under the term "dementia praecox," according to the teachings of the German psychiatrist Emil Kraepelin. Because this term implies a "precocious" (early) onset and progressive intellectual deterioration and because many cases do not show these characteristics, schizophrenia has been preferred by most modern psychiatrists.

The word "schizophrenia" literally means "schism" or "splitting" in the mind between the *functions* of feeling, or emotions, and the *functions* of thinking or mentation. Essentially this means that there exists or develops an inappropriateness or imbalance (inadequacy or excessiveness) of the emotional re-

actions as related to the ideas or thought content associated with these feelings. Schizophrenia means nothing more than this. It does not mean "dual" personalities, Jekyll-Hyde character aberrations, "split personalities," or other rare syndromes that are often alluded to as "schizophrenic" by novelists and journalists.

Despite improved methods of treatment developed in the last two decades, schizophrenia remains the major psychiatric problem. In most mental institutions, over 60 percent of the patients remaining as more or less permanent inmates are schizophrenics. Invariably, those who have improved sufficiently to return to the community still need follow-up treatment, medication, and some supervision. In most instances, they are incapable of earning a livelihood.

Six Subtypes of Schizophrenia

There are six subtypes (or forms) of schizophrenia: simple, hebephrenic, paranoid, catatonic, schizoaffective, and hypochondriacal (pseudoneurotic). Characteristic symptoms of each are described briefly here.

Simple Schizophrenia. The outstanding symptoms are a marked lack of emotional attachment to the ordinary, so-called normal things. There is likely to be a lack of interest in what is going on around the patient or in the world, a lack of affection for near relatives or friends, and an utter lack of ambition or initiative. There is no real sadness, only apathy and indifference. Such patients do not read newspapers, listen to the radio, or watch television; they might be confined to a ward for years without bothering to learn or remember the names of any fellow patients, nurses, or attendants. They show no worry or concern over illness or any other misfortune involving family or friends. They tend to remain inert, although if urged sufficiently, they will usually follow the path of least resistance and occupy themselves in simple tasks. They never complain that anything bothers them and often permit physical illness to become far advanced before calling attention to it. If some privilege is denied them, they do not complain but merely accept the denial listlessly. Nothing seems important enough for them to expend any effort to attain. They lead what is called a "vegetative" existence—eating, sleeping, excreting—and display little enthusiasm in any of these functions.

Hebephrenic. The hebephrenic patients are the most numerous in hospital psychiatry. They characteristically show the bizarre speech, childish mannerisms, and silly behavior often considered the hallmark of insanity. They are likely to wear a continuously silly, insipid expression and to dress in a peculiar fashion. They are often observed grimacing and talking to themselves rapidly and incoherently; on closer observation, they appear to be responding to imaginary voices. It is evident that they are preoccupied with fantasies, and that (as with the simple form) they have lost interest in the real things in their daily lives and in the outside world. As the disease progresses, this lack of interest becomes reflected in an increasing lack of knowledge and loss of what has formerly been learned.

They may exhibit delusions or false ideas of grandeur or of persecution, but they express little concern about these delusions and do not bother to elaborate any logical explanation of their ideas. They often complain of bizarre bodily feelings or sensations, and may imagine they are suffering from fantastic and impossible physical ailments; that some or all of their vital organs are missing, diseased, or dead; or that various kinds of machines, mechanisms, animals, or persons have taken residence in their bodies.

Paranoid. The paranoid forms comprise the second most numerous group of schizophrenic patients. These individuals usually present a rather normal appearance to the uninitiated. They carry themselves well, are careful about their dress, clean in their habits, and generally show a fairly well-preserved intellectual capacity. However, because they believe they are superior persons and that others are jealous of them, they manifest an air of arrogance, haughtiness, or martyrdom. They feel that they are surrounded by jealous enemies who are constantly talking about them, plotting against them, trying to poison them. Often they hear imaginary voices cursing or threatening them, and accusing them of unspeakable thoughts and actions. They usually construct a superficially logical theory to explain why they are the objects or victims of these persecutions. They sometimes react violently against persons in the vicinity, imagining them to be their persecutors.

Catatonic. The catatonic forms are characterized by an extremely bizarre group of symptoms, which depend upon what seems to be a blocking of thought and action, a sort of inertia that causes the patients to persist in definite forms of activity or inactivity. These symptoms include a marked tendency to stuporous states in which the patients will sit, stand, or lie in fixed postures or attitudes for weeks or months on end. In these stupors their eyelids usually are closed (though an extremely rapid nervous flickering is common); they do not speak or respond in any way to questioning, although they are aware of what is going on about them. In the deeper forms of stupor, they may make no effort to feed themselves or to use the toilet. Frequently, they must be force-fed with a stomach tube to prevent starvation.

Often a condition known as *waxy flexibility (cerea flexibilitas)* is shown. Patients remain in whatever constrained or awkward

position they may be placed, as if their bodies were made of some inert wax. They may show *stereotypy,* repeating interminably some meaningless movement or gesture that may have been suggested by others or may be a symbolic expression of their own mental complexes. Similarly, they may repeat interminably specific words, phrases, noises, or figures of speech.

In contrast with these stuporous, automatic, and passive states, patients may have periods in which they are wildly excited, extremely overactive, impulsive, destructive, and assaultive. They may manifest marked tendencies to mutilate or destroy themselves. At such times they may be hallucinating and will rant on noisily against the "voices" they hear berating and threatening them. Strange as it seems, these most dramatic and obviously abnormal types of schizophrenic patients are more likely than others to have periods of definite normality and mental lucidity.

Schizoaffective. The schizoaffective forms of schizophrenia comprise a fairly large number of patients who show an episodic, cyclic course much like that shown by cases of manic-depressive psychosis. However, unlike the pure manic-depressive cases, they are apt to show grandiose, expansive, and/or persecutory delusions with hallucinations corresponding to these delusions, especially during the more active phases of their illness.

Hypochondriacal. The hypochondriacal (pseudoneurotic) forms usually display a multitude of physical symptoms, which convince the patients that they have contracted some dire form of physical illness, either generalized or localized to some organ system. They complain of headaches, dizzy spells, palpitations, difficulties in breathing, and so on. Usually, they have made the rounds of general practitioners and internists and have undergone laboratory and X-ray studies, which have failed to show organic disease. They may have succeeded in persuading some uncritical surgeons to operate on them, or they may have made the rounds of chiropractors, who have put them through prolonged courses of "spinal adjustments." They wind up in a psychiatrist's office, because they are also likely to have brief overtly psychotic episodes with symptoms of anxiety, depression, hallucinations, and delusions. The hypochondriacal schizophrenics also present a variety of typically neurotic characteristics such as diffuse anxiety, phobias, or obsessive symptoms.

By no means do all clinical cases of schizophrenia neatly fall into one of the six main categories. They often contain features characteristic of two or more types. However, it is important to distinguish in which group a particular case belongs, because the ultimate outcome and response to treatment usually

APTITUDE TEST

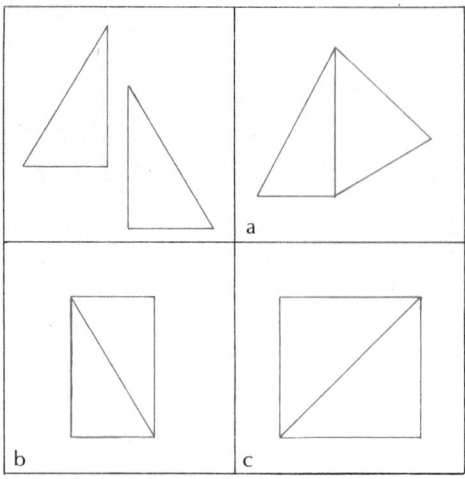

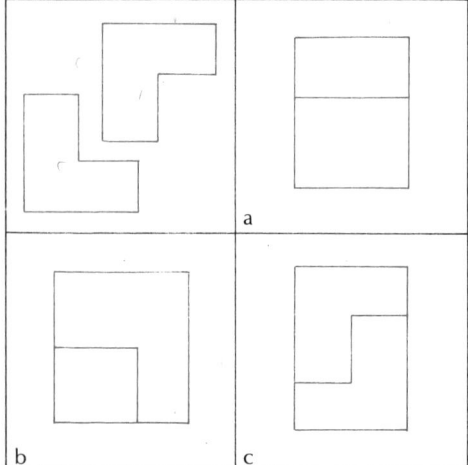

One type of aptitude test designed to measure speed and accuracy in the perception of spatial relations. The forms in the upper left square can be assembled to make forms A, B, or C.

depend on the type. As a rule, a poor prognosis is associated with the hebephrenic and simple forms, and substantial improvement may be obtained with the paranoid, catatonic, and schizoaffective forms.

Case History

The history of a typical case of schizophrenia will help the reader obtain a better idea of an average case. The patient when first seen by the psychiatrist is often in late adolescence. He is usually described by his parents as a "good boy," a diligent, hard-working student, (perhaps too much of a "worrier"), an introvert, a "gentleman," not a roughneck, probably inept and awkward in sports, with a body build described as *asthenic* (poorly muscled, thin, and lanky) or *dyplastic* (dysproportioned, excessively obese or flabby). He probably has been excessively shy and unsophisticated—ill-at-ease with girls and reluctant to participate in social activities. Compared to the others in his peer group, he shows an excessive naivete and inexperience in sexual matters, and exhibits excessive guilt feelings over the usual adolescent sexual activity, masturbation.

The parents bring him to the psychiatrist because they now have noticed a marked change in his behavior patterns and adjustment. Actually, it is more accurate to say that there has occurred a decided increase in the degree of his introversion. He neglects his school work, and his attendance becomes lax. The teachers note that he is inattentive and seems to daydream a lot. His grades decline, and he explains this by saying he cannot concentrate on his studies. Often he does not sleep well, or he sleeps too much. He withdraws more and more from contacts with his friends and spends more time at home, often in his own room. When questioned about the reasons for his withdrawal, he admits that he is "self-conscious"; people "notice" him and look at him significantly even in public places, perhaps because of his mode of dress, his mannerisms, or physical peculiarities. These "ideas of reference" are often followed by his hearing them make contemptuous or derogatory remarks about him—at first in whispers, later in clear voices. As his illness progresses he may hear the "voices" even though there is nobody else around. By this time, he usually has begun to explain his hallucinations, by saying that he has enemies who are plotting against him. Often, the patient's interpretation of others' contemptuous attitudes is connected with his own extremely low self-esteem, as expressed by saying he is becoming "ugly," has skin blemishes that betray his immoral habits, and that his appearance is changing—that is, he has "disturbances of the body image."

Treatment

Unless he responds to treatment and improves, the patient cannot be talked out of his delusions. He stubbornly resists all efforts to give him insight. Fortunately, the newer methods of treatment, if applied early enough, can arrest and sometimes reverse the schizophrenic process. Medications belonging to the phenothiazine and related groups of drugs often dramatically stop hallucinations and delusions in a few days in acute cases. Even in chronic cases the psychiatric symptoms of hallucinations and delusions can often be suppressed, but the emotional changes—shallowness, inappropriateness, loss of interest, lack of ambition—usually persist. Chronic cases usually require that phenothiazine type of medication be continued indefinitely. In acute cases, it is usually advisable to continue medication for at least a year after all significant symptoms have subsided.

Psychosurgery may be tried in very severe cases. Electroshock treatment is often used, and psychotherapy holds promise after drugs have altered a patient's condition.

—Emanuel Messinger, M.D., *U.S. Veterans Hospital, Northport, N.Y.*

See also Constitutional Types; Electroconvulsive Therapy; Manic-Depressive Psychosis; Psychotherapy; Schizoid Personality.

Consult (13) Arieti, 1966; Arieti, 1970.

SCHIZOPHRENIC REACTION. *See* Schizophrenia.

SCHIZOPHRENOGENIC FAMILY. Studies of schizophrenic patients suggest that family patterns can contribute to the development of mental illness. *See* Psychotic Disorders.

SCHOLASTIC APTITUDE TEST (SAT), a specialized type of aptitude test used to predict a student's chances of success if he continues his education. The Scholastic Aptitude Test has been widely used to evaluate applicants for college. The SAT is one of the College Entrance Examination Board tests administered by the Educational Testing Service. The test measures mathematical and verbal abilities, with the average score set at 500. Another measure used to assess college applicants is the American College Testing Program (ACT).

—Louis Snellgrove, *Lambuth College*
See also Measurement.
Consult (12) Cronbach, 1970.

SCHOOL PHOBIA, a form of emotional or behavioral maladjustment characterized by a persistent refusal to attend school, usually accompanied by vague complaints of physical ailments. The condition is observed primarily in elementary school children, especially those who are starting school for the first time. The major cause is the child's fear of separation from his mother and the loss of the security of his home when he must leave for school. The problem typically occurs among overly dependent and immature youngsters whose mothers are particularly overindulgent, overprotective, and anxiety-ridden.

SCHOOL PSYCHOLOGY, field of specialization that focuses upon the development and adjustment of the child in the school situation. *See* Educational Psychology.

SCIENTIFIC METHOD. No universally accepted description adequately defines this kind of thinking and working. Some experts regard it as a specific set of orderly steps used to analyze and solve problems. Others argue that valid scientific procedures must have certain characteristics. Some find the use of complex equipment such as electronic equipment and microscopes essential, but such hardware may or may not be necessary, depending upon the particular problem being studied. In fact, it is possible to use the scientific method with no apparatus whatsoever.

Humans do not ordinarily think in terms of delineated steps. But scientific procedures can be used by individuals in their daily lives, not only to solve problems but quite often to explain solutions to problems in an orderly manner.

The scientific method usually involves more inductive than deductive reasoning. It moves from the observation of many different facts toward relating those facts in a general conclusion rather than deducing specific conclusions from different general principles. The accuracy of a specific deductive conclusion applied to an individual case of prediction depends upon the accuracy of the principles.

Those who believe the scientific method is composed of specific steps usually list five: (1) statement of the problem; (2) formation of the hypothesis; (3) experimentation; (4) interpretation; and (5) drawing conclusions. Implied at each step is a constant review of how it is related to every other step. These procedures have been designed and described for the past several hundred years.

Statement of the Problem. The first step in the scientific method is clear delineation of some problem. For example, an observer may notice, entirely by chance, that when one event occurs, another one also occurs. If he progresses no further than the first step, he may incorrectly assume that one event causes another, which may or may not be true. Let us say that a department store manager begins to have music "piped" into his store over a sound system and notices that receipts grow considerably during the month that the music is first played. But at this point he is careful not to jump to any conclusions.

Forming a Hypothesis. A hypothesis is a belief, statement, or proposition that can be tested in ways that will reveal whether or not it is true and to what degree. If the store manager believes that there is a relationship between music playing and increase in sales, he may form the hypothesis that if he continues playing music in his store, sales will increase.

Experimentation. The scientific method in such areas as chemistry and physics generally does not involve the control of as many relative variables as appear in connection with human and animal behaviors. It is easier to manipulate inanimate objects than humans or animals. For example, even if the store manager continues to have music played during store hours for months, he may realize that other factors can affect an increase in sales. Perhaps the bad weather during the month before the music was played may have been responsible for a decrease in sales. Or perhaps several new employees were hired after the music was played and have been performing better than previous sales clerks.

In order to eliminate or control the possible influence of such factors, the store manager must set up procedures that enable him to compare sales receipts over a longer period of time before and after music was played. Perhaps he will check the sales records of various employees and consider seasonable variations.

Interpreting the Data. After some period of time, enough relevant information has been collected and can be interpreted firmly. The store manager may compare sales receipts on specific days of the week or month, consider whether the weather was good or bad on those days, eliminate sales records of new employees, and note many other factors.

Drawing Conclusions. On the basis of the interpreted data, certain conclusions may be possible. For example, the store manager may decide that music playing does increase sales. However, there may or may not be a relationship between these two variables, depending upon how well other factors have been recognized and controlled or eliminated in some way. The manager cannot be certain that there was a significant relationship between the variables unless he is sure that all relevant factors had been dealt with. Perhaps he has overlooked the fact that he held a sale when the music was playing. The scientific method is aimed at promoting a better understanding of man, his environment, and the relationship between them. Implied in its aim is that the use of data will provide a better world for man to live in. The characteristics usually listed for the scientific method are (1) objectivity; (2) explicitness; (3) interpretation; and (4) reporting.

Objectivity. One of the most important characteristics of the scientific method, objectivity indicates that the person performing the

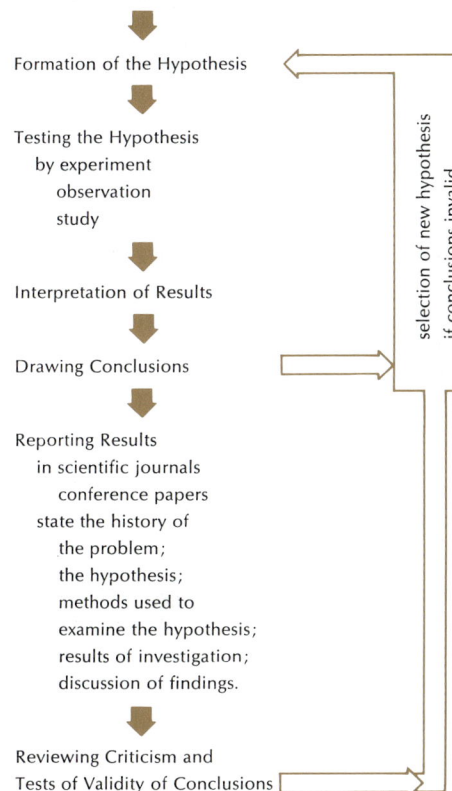

PRINCIPLES OF THE SCIENTIFIC METHOD

Statement of the Problem

Formation of the Hypothesis

Testing the Hypothesis
 by experiment
  observation
  study

Interpretation of Results

Drawing Conclusions

Reporting Results
 in scientific journals
  conference papers
 state the history of
  the problem;
  the hypothesis;
  methods used to
  examine the hypothesis;
  results of investigation;
  discussion of findings.

Reviewing Criticism and
Tests of Validity of Conclusions

selection of new hypothesis if conclusions invalid

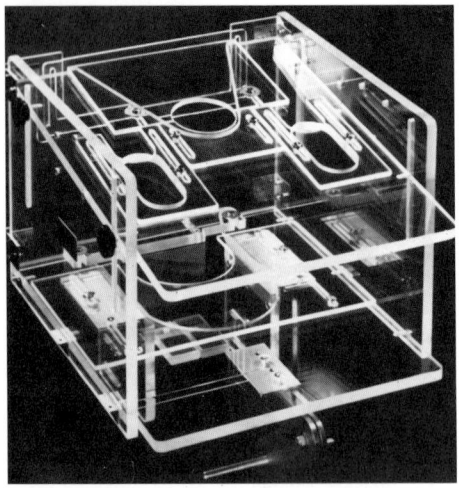

Primate chair, used when a large degree of restraint of the animal's movement or position is desired.

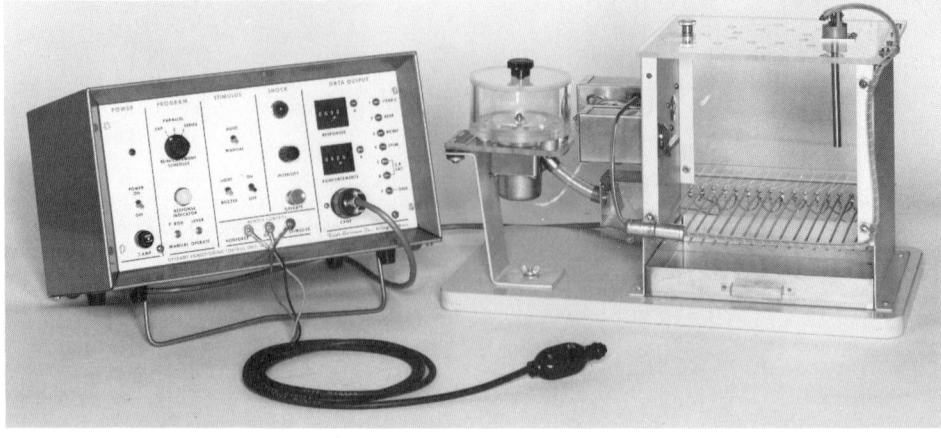

Operant conditioning unit, with rat cage, pellet dispenser, and experimenter's programming console.

Cumulative recorder, a machine that provides a continuous record of the level of responses.

Memory drum, a device used in verbal learning experiments to present items to be memorized at a preset rate.

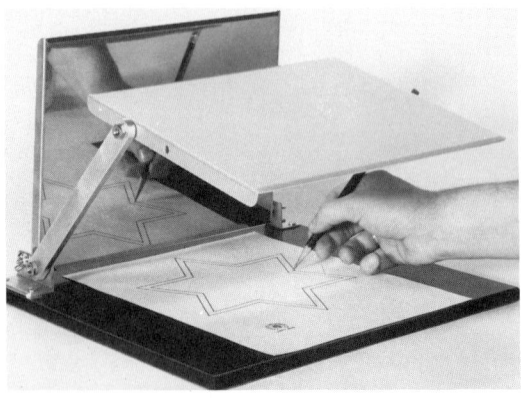

Mirror tracing apparatus, designed to show the effects of a conflict in visual and kinesthetic feedback.

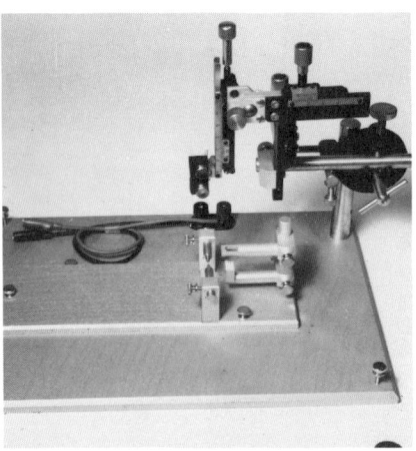

Stereotaxic, a precision positioning device used in studying the brain of small animals.

Color wheel, when rotated, mixes colored angular sectors of two or more colors.

procedures does not allow his own feelings or inclinations to bias results. Even if the outcomes of procedures are contrary to the original beliefs or expectations of a scientist, they will still be made known and available to others.

Explicitness. The procedures are described in such detail that another investigator can duplicate them. The more explicitly the procedures are described, the more objectivity can be obtained.

Interpretation. After compiling his data, the investigator correlates and develops his findings in conjunction with other relevant and factual data. The interpretation is usually tentative and often suggests further problems for future research. The scientific method usually creates many more problems and questions than it solves or answers.

Reporting. A written account of the experiment describes the hypothesis, methods, and results, and contains a discussion of the findings. It also usually includes a history of the problem, which is a summary of the data found by other researchers, perhaps under somewhat different conditions. It may also indicate any limitations of the study, so that future researchers may correct any such deficiencies.

The scientific method not only provides data from which life becomes better and more understandable for man. It also serves as a basic communication system between scientists, whether they are chemists, physicists, biologists, or psychologists.

—Louis Snellgrove, *Lambuth College*
See also Experimental Animals; Experimental Design; Experimental Psychology; Experimenter Bias.
Consult (2) Boring, 1950; Brown and Ghiselli, 1965; Wilson, 1952; Woodworth and Schlosberg, 1954.

SEDATIVE-HYPNOTICS, barbiturates, antianxiety agents, and other drugs such as alcohol and ether. *See* Drugs and Behavior.

SELECTIVE ATTENTION. *See* Attention.

SELF-ACTUALIZATION. This concept assumes that one great force, some kind of genetic blueprint, determines each individual's potential. The theory emphasizes holistic tendencies toward growth and development rather than reductionistic tension reduction, physical-need satisfaction, or self-preservation. Jung's postulation of the "self" archetype stressed the realization and development of all aspects of an individual into harmonious balance. An ideal rather than an attainable goal, its essentials were precursors of later self-actualization theories.

Goldstein, Angyal, Cantril, Lecky, and others emphasized the maintaining, actualizing, and enhancing of the capacities of the experiencing organism. If society does not interfere, a healthy personality results. For Rogers and Maslow, the healthiest personality is that which most fully expresses the self-actualizing tendency. Maslow also assumes *deficiency motivations,* a core tendency pressing toward physical survival. *Growth motivation,* which aims at enhancing rather than merely preserving life, will predominate if society has not had an inhibiting effect and if deficiency motives have been met.

—M. G. Affinito, *Southern Connecticut State College*
Consult (9) Allport, 1960; Rogers, 1961.

SELF-CONCEPT, each person's unique way of perceiving himself. The self-concept begins in infancy as he discovers himself as a distinct individual and continues to develop throughout childhood as he becomes increasingly aware of his physical image and his various abilities. The environment plays such an important role in the formation of the self-image that Sullivan referred to the self-concept as an accumulation of reflected appraisals.

Once the self-concept is formed, the individual chooses goals and behavior that are consistent with his self-concept. Those experiences that are consistent are perceived accurately, but those that are not are likely to be distorted or denied. Understandably, it is easier to accept a self-concept that is flattering than one that is derogatory. Closely associated with a flattering self-image is the discovery by psychologists that people with positive attitudes about themselves are relatively free of conformity and exhibit a greater degree of independence.

—Duane Harmon, *Southern Connecticut State College*

SELF-FULFILLING PROPHECY. *See* Experimenter Bias.

SELF-STIMULATION OF THE BRAIN. *See* Brain.

SELYE, HANS (1907–   ), Austrian physician. Born in Vienna, he received his M.D. (1929) and Ph.D. (1931) from German University, Prague.

Selye is known to psychologists for his studies of stress. He described the body's reaction to stress as the general adaptation syndrome (GAS), which has three distinct stages: an alarm reaction, resistance to stress over time, and exhaustion, perhaps leading to death. He showed that the complicated physiological changes that occur during adaptation may lead to "diseases of adaptation" of the adrenals, thymus, and lymph and to ulcerated stomach. Selye's principal works in this area are *The Stress of Life,* 1956, and *The*

Austrian physician Hans Selye's General Adaptation Syndrome outlines physiological reaction to stress.

SEMANTIC DIFFERENTIAL

"Polite"

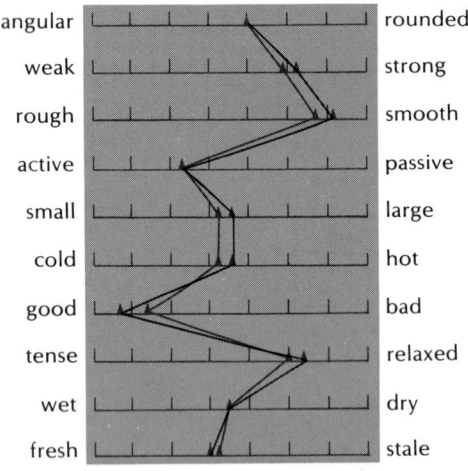

angular	rounded
weak	strong
rough	smooth
active	passive
small	large
cold	hot
good	bad
tense	relaxed
wet	dry
fresh	stale

The plot lines show the ratings given by two groups to the connotative meaning of the word "polite" on ten lines of the Osgood semantic differential scale. The pooled judgment of each group is much like that of the other.

Physiology and Pathology of Exposure to Stress, 1960.

—Nina Adams, *Yale University.*

SEMANTIC DIFFERENTIAL, technique devised by Charles Osgood and his colleagues to assess connotative meanings of words, that is, to "differentiate" between "semantics." It is based on subjects' ratings of the meanings of words along several seven-point scales or polar dimensions. Research has demonstrated that the meanings of most words can be summarized using only three dimensions: activity (active-passive), potency (weak-strong), and evaluative (good-bad). More stable nuances require other dimensions, but these three basic dimensions provide useful ways of comparing connotative meanings between individual persons and between words. Changes of ratings on the semantic differential are sometimes used to measure the effects of some kinds of experimental manipulations (that is, as a dependent variable).

—Roland Siiter, *Montclair State College*
See also Language; Meaning.
Consult (7) Osgood, 1952; Osgood, *et al.,* 1957.

SEMANTICS. *See* Language; Meaning; Semantic Differential.

SENILE PSYCHOSIS. *See* Senility, Mental Disorders of.

SENILITY, MENTAL DISORDERS OF. Several psychotic disorders are associated with old age. They may develop at any time from the sixties into the nineties but a frequent age of appearance is around seventy.

Senile psychosis (senile brain disease, senile dementia) is caused in part by atrophy and deterioration of brain tissue in older people. A number of types have been described, with considerable overlapping in lists of symptoms. Among the frequently observed symptoms are the following: lack of attention, forgetfulness of recent events (though the early life may be recalled in detail), failure to recognize family and friends, disorientation for time and place, narrowing of attention and interests, restlessness, irritability, hostility, and insomnia. Some patients roam around the house at night or wander out of the house. Some become untidy. Some develop paranoid delusions, delirious states, or states of agitation and depression.

A diagnosis of *psychosis with cerebral arteriosclerosis* is made when there is evidence of "hardening" of the arteries in the brain, causing sluggish or blocked circulation. This form of disorder can come on gradually or may begin suddenly with a "stroke"—an attack indicating either a hemorrhage in the brain or the blocking of an artery. Symptoms often resemble those of senile psychosis.

These disorders of old age are caused in part by deterioration or damage in organs, but psychological factors seem to be even more influential. Some men and women remain alert, productive, and creative far longer than others. Some are able to function more or less normally in spite of brain deterioration. Among those who develop psychoses in old age, many have a history of inadequate adjustment or maladaptive behavior in earlier years, and these people seem prone to break down if they suffer brain damage.

The breakdown can also be triggered by psychological stresses. Old people have to face the end of employment, loss of independence, loneliness, decline in sex life, and fear of dying.

The psychoses of old age are responsible for a rising number of admissions to mental hospitals, and the problem is expected to worsen as the older population increases.

See also Aging.
Consult (13) Coleman, 1964.

SENSATION. The senses—vision, hearing, equilibrium, and others—provide organisms with critical information about events outside and within their bodies. The study of sensation is a search for the lawful and consistent correlations between physical events acting as stimuli on living organisms and the behavior or experiences that they evoke. It also tests the physiological capacity of an organism, for sensation only occurs when a stimulus is appropriate and intense enough to activate a receptor.

Studies have explored human sensitivity to wavelengths of light in color vision, to frequencies of sounds in hearing, and to a wide range of taste, odor, and skin stimuli. Four distinct attributes of sensation can be measured: *quality,* the sensory system (vision vs. hearing) or part of a sensory system (sweet vs. bitter) that is being stimulated; *intensity,* which increases with an increase in physical stimulation, but not linearly; *extent,* the area covered (for example, skin area, volume of sound, area of visual field); and *duration.* Although sensation helps describe our environment, we are also affected by things that we cannot sense (we can get headaches from high-pitched sounds, burns from ultraviolet light).

For many years, psychologists made fairly neat distinctions between sensation and perception. They defined sensation as the process of stimulation of a receptor, and perception as the meaning given to that sensation. For example, it might be said that the sensation of light on a bright day consisted in the activity of stimulated rods and cones in the eye. The perception of light resulted in the statement "The sun is bright." However, recent investigations suggest that the processes involved in

SENSATION

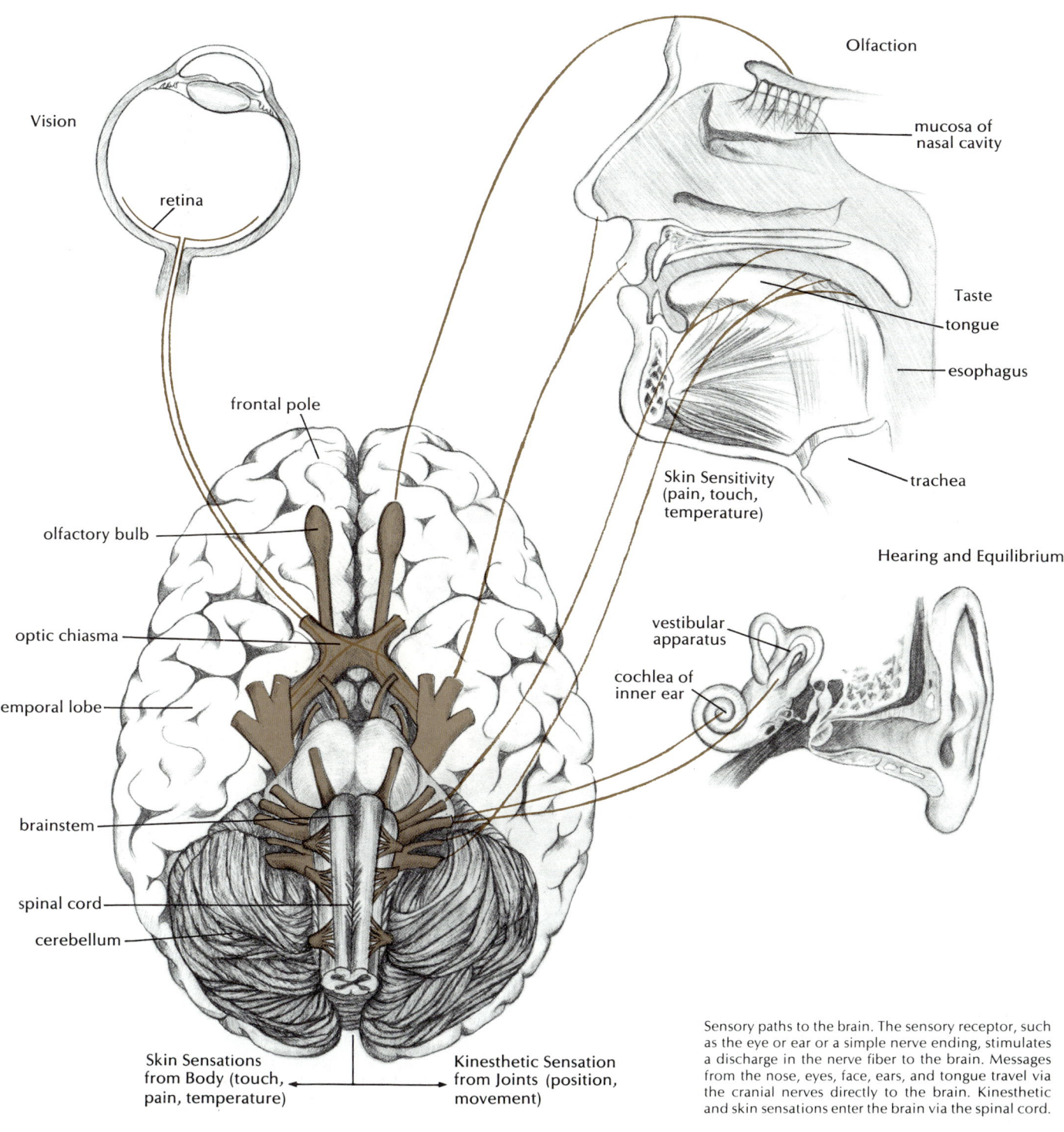

Vision

Olfaction

mucosa of
nasal cavity

retina

Taste

tongue

esophagus

frontal pole

Skin Sensitivity
(pain, touch,
temperature)

trachea

olfactory bulb

Hearing and Equilibrium

vestibular
apparatus

optic chiasma

cochlea of
inner ear

temporal lobe

brainstem

spinal cord

cerebellum

Skin Sensations
from Body (touch,
pain, temperature)

Kinesthetic Sensation
from Joints (position,
movement)

Sensory paths to the brain. The sensory receptor, such
as the eye or ear or a simple nerve ending, stimulates
a discharge in the nerve fiber to the brain. Messages
from the nose, eyes, face, ears, and tongue travel via
the cranial nerves directly to the brain. Kinesthetic
and skin sensations enter the brain via the spinal cord.

SENSATION AND PERCEPTION

The Senses

EQUILIBRIUM SENSE
    static sense
    vestibular sense
VERTIGO

HEARING
    audition
DEAFNESS
NOISE

INTEROCEPTIVE SENSES
    organic senses
    visceral senses

KINESTHETIC SENSE
    muscle sense
    position sense
    proprioception

PAIN

SKIN SENSES

SMELL

TASTE

TEMPERATURE SENSE

TOUCH
    mechanoreception
    pressure sense

VISION
COLOR VISION
COLOR BLINDNESS
AFTERIMAGE
DARK ADAPTATION
LIGHT ADAPTATION

Concepts

SENSATION
PERCEPTION
    perceptual constancy
STIMULUS
RECEPTORS

JUST-NOTICEABLE DIFFERENCE
SUBLIMINAL PERCEPTION
THRESHOLD
SIGNAL DETECTION THEORY

ATTENTION
ATTENTION SPAN
REACTION TIME
SET
SENSORY ADAPTATION
CONTRAST EFFECT
SOCIAL PERCEPTION

Perceptual Problems

ILLUSION

AMES ROOM
APPARENT MOVEMENT
    phi phenomenon
DEPTH PERCEPTION
MOON ILLUSION
VISUAL CLIFF

PARAMNESIA
SENSORY DEPRIVATION
SYNESTHESIA

EXTRASENSORY PERCEPTION

Articles on the physiological structures involved in sensing and perceiving are listed in the Item Guides accompanying the articles on BRAIN and NERVOUS SYSTEM and in the Subject Map on PHYSIOLOGICAL PSYCHOLOGY.

The Subject Maps in the Encyclopedia illustrate the coverage of particular aspects of psychology, showing the interrelationships among the articles in twelve major areas of study. Entries in capital letters are subjects for which there are separate articles in the Encyclopedia. Entries in small letters are cross references.

The Subject Maps appear in the Encyclopedia under the following titles:

Abnormal and Clinical Psychology
Developmental Psychology
Emotion and Motivation
Intelligence
Learning and Memory
Measurement
Personality and Individual Difference
Physiological and Comparative Psychology
Psychology: Divisions and Schools
Sensation and Perception
Social Psychology
Thinking and Language

sensing and perceiving are extremely complex. (*See the discussion in* Perception.)

The various senses are treated in the separate articles listed below.

—Nina Adams, *Yale University*
See also Attention; Equilibrium Sense; Hearing; Interoceptive Senses; Kinesthetic Sense; Pain; Perception; Skin Senses; Smell; Taste; Temperature Sense; Touch; Vision, *Other articles listed in the Item Guide under* Sensation and Perception.
Consult (4) Bertley, 1969; Geldard, 1971.

SENSE RECEPTORS. *See* Receptor; Sensation.

SENSES. *See* Sensation.

SENSITIVITY GROUP. *See* Encounter Group; Sensitivity Training.

SENSITIVITY TRAINING (T-groups), generic term for a variety of (primarily verbal) group-interaction experiences for individuals and organization staffs. The group sessions are intended to help people function more effectively in their jobs by developing an understanding of group dynamics, increasing awareness of their own and other people's feelings, becoming more direct in talking about those feelings, and exchanging "feedback" about other people's style of interacting.

In 1946 Kurt Lewin and Ronald Lippitt were training community workers and recording group interactions. When participants in the project accidentally heard their behavior being described and wanted to participate in the discussion, this idea seemed so exciting that the National Training Laboratories (NTL) developed and expanded the T-group method.

The leaders of the diverse groups now functioning are often inadequately trained and therefore deal poorly with the strong emotional reactions that groups evoke. There is little evidence that changes generated in the group become integrated into the lives of the participants or their organizations.

—Bruce L. Maliver, Author of *The Encounter Game*
See also Encounter Groups; Human Potential Movement.
Consult (13) Bradford, *et al.*, 1964.

SENSORY ADAPTATION, the reduction in sensitivity as stimulation persists, usually because of a decreased output of the sensory receptors. The responses measured with electrodes directly from different receptors in the body have shown that they can be classified as *nonadapting* (deep pressure, pain), *slow-adapting* (pressure), or *fast-adapting* (touch). Examples of adaptation are common in each sensory system. For touch, when you pull on a glove, the strong sense of pressure fades until it is scarcely felt. For temperature, air conditioning on a hot day will feel cool only for a little while. For smell, the initial odor in a newly painted room fades rapidly. For taste, the first bite of ice cream always tastes richest.

—Nina Adams, *Yale University*
See also Dark Adaptation; Light Adaptation.

SENSORY DEPRIVATION. In certain experiments conducted during the 1950s volunteer college students spent three to four days lying in bed, in a tiny, soundproof room that was constantly lit, wearing goggles, gloves, and earphones. At first they slept a great deal; then they began to sing and talk to themselves and became restless. Toward the end, they found it impossible to concentrate or organize ideas and had periods of blanking out and daydreaming, even some hallucinating. These experiments show that normal behavior is extremely dependent upon environmental stimulation.

Animals deprived of visual sensation when young show serious perceptual deficits. In one experiment, the eyes of kittens were sewn shut at birth. Later testing showed that the animals' visual behavior, the anatomical structure of their visual brain cells, and the electrical behavior of those cells were all abnormal.

—Nina Adams, *Yale University*
Consult (4) Solomon, 1961.

SEPTAL REGION. The septum is a region of the telencephalon of the brain lying anterior to the thalamus. It contains several nuclei and is a portion of a larger region known as the limbic system. The septum plays a very important role in the regulation of motor responses, motivational and emotional behavior, and thirst. Destruction of the septal region produces profound deficits in certain types of avoidance conditioning behavior. Also reported are increased water intake and a type of rage behavior related to a hypersensitivity to somesthetic (movement, temperature, touch, pain), auditory, and visual stimulation. The septum is also a site of positive reinforcement for self-stimulation.

—Joel F. Lubar, *University of Tennessee*
See also Brain; Limbic Region.
Consult (3) Isaacson, *et al.*, 1971.

SERIAL LEARNING, a procedure used to study verbal learning and memory in which items (words, nonsense syllables) are presented as an ordered list. Each successive item on the list is the stimulus for the next item as a response.

Serial anticipation refers to serial learning in which a subject must try to announce each item in the series, one at a time, when presented with the item that precedes it. Alternatively, the recall method is sometimes used; here the subject views the whole list for a while

SENSATION

The stimuli and receptors of the human senses

Sense	Stimulus	Sense organ	Receptor	Sensation
Sight	Light waves	Eye	Rods and cones retina	Colors, patterns, textures, etc.
Hearing	Sound waves	Ear	Hair cells of organ of Corti	Noises, tones
Skin sensations	Skin	Skin	Nerve endings in skin	Touch, pain, warmth, cold
Smell	Volatile substances	Nose	Hair cells of olfactory epithelium	Odors (musky, flowery, burnt, minty, etc.)
Taste	Soluble substances	Tongue	Taste buds of tongue	Flavors (sweet, sour, salty, bitter)
Body movement	Mechanical energy	Muscles, joints, tendons	Nerve endings	Position, movement, pressure, pain
Equilibrium	Mechanical and gravitational forces	Inner ear	Hair cells of semicircular canals and vestibule	Spatial movement, gravitational pull
Organic sensitivity	Mechanical energy	Portions of digestive tract	Nerve endings	Pressure, pain

SEPTAL REGION

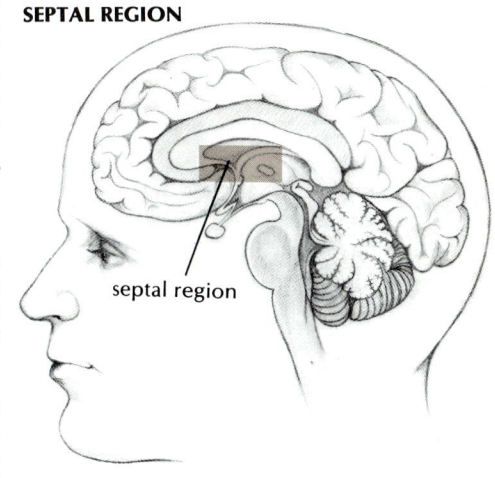

septal region

SEX IDENTITY

To supplement the comprehensive discussion of sexual roles, masculinity-feminity, in SEX IDENTITY, see CHILD DEVELOPMENT and ADOLESCENCE.

Psychoanalytic theories of psychosexual development are discussed in CHARACTER DEVELOPMENT, ANAL CHARACTER, PHALLIC STAGE, OEDIPUS COMPLEX, and other articles. According to Freud, many neuroses arise out of conflicts over sexual roles—see for example CASTRATION ANXIETY.

Views of sex as a primary drive are presented in SEX DRIVE and ID.

Various forms of sexual behavior are called problems anomalies, or deviations. See, for example, SEXUAL DEVIATIONS, AUTOEROTICISM, INCEST, and MASOCHISM.

and then tries to write down or recite all the items in order.

Serial learning was once thought to occur as a very simple "chain" of interitem associations, from A to B, B to C, C to D, and so on. However, modern investigators have revealed that it is much more complex: apparently associations between items and their serial positions on the list are learned, and these are probably more important for serial learning than are interitem associations. In other words, the subject is learning 1–A, 2–B, 3–C, and so on, though he is outwardly responding with A–B, B–C, C–D, and so on. Thus it is often very difficult to specify precisely what the relevant stimulus is in serial learning: is it the last item or the serial position? For this reason, the serial learning task is no longer favored as a productive way to analyze verbal associations.

—Roland Siiter, *Montclair State College*
See also Memory; Memory Drum.

Consult (6) Deese and Hulse, 1967; Smith and Rohrman, 1970; Young, 1962.

SET, a readiness or preparation for a particular kind of action or experience. It may result from instructions or from a habitual tendency to respond in a particular manner. The term "set" need not imply inflexibility. Such readiness can facilitate the responses a person is prepared to make and inhibit competing responses (for example, "On your mark, get set, go" in running). However, a set can induce a persistence that hinders solution. To overcome this problem, one can formulate the assumptions underlying the attempts and consider alternatives or lay the problem aside for awhile.

See also Attention.

SEVERE MENTAL RETARDATION. *See* Mental Retardation.

SEX DIFFERENCES. *See* Adolescence; Character Development; Child Development; Sex Identity.

SEX DRIVE. Like hunger and thirst, sex is considered a primary drive. Sexual drive in lower animals is primarily controlled through hormones. The central brain structure involved in the regulation of this hormonal control is the hypothalamus. In more complex organisms, including man, hormones play a lesser role and psychological factors a greater role in determining sexual drive. However, even in the case of the human female, periods of receptivity are linked with the menstrual cycle, which is under hormonal control. In the human male, the cerebral cortex plays a major role in the development of sexual drive. However, the strength of the sex drive in humans is largely determined through learning and socialization.

—Joel F. Lubar, *University of Tennessee*
See also Id; Sex Identity.

SEX IDENTITY. The concept of sex identity is clearly one of the most basic aspects of self-definition. When people are asked to describe themselves, in contrast to or in agreement with other individuals, in all probability one of the first labels to come to mind will be "male" or "female." The distinction, which is present from birth, is stronger than hair color, eye color, or even skin color. But how does this distinction affect the behavior of human beings, while they are growing up and as adults? This is the problem area that nonscientists have pondered for generations and that scientists have been actively investigating for many years.

Biology. When children are born, it can clearly be stated whether they are boys or girls, either on the basis of apparent genital differences or more exacting chromosome typing. In addition to obvious physical differences, researchers have observed a number of ways in which male and female infants typically differ at birth. For example, male children tend to be larger and heavier but are more susceptible to disease; they also show greater activity than female infants; females display sensitivity to a greater number of stimuli, including tactile and pain sensitivity.

Although it is impossible at this time to determine the exact effects of sex hormones on the behavior of humans, animal research can provide some information that may be partially generalizable. A number of researchers have investigated the effects of injecting animals with hormones of the opposite sex, either prenatally or postnatally, and the evidence suggests that if these are administered during a limited critical period, the effects on behavior may be quite substantial. Either because of direct action of the hormone itself or through its indirect effects on the brain structure, the animals adopt many of the behaviors typically found in the opposite sex. These include not only sexual-reproductive patterns, but also more general activities such as aggression and activity patterns. Such evidence certainly suggests that there are biological differences between the sexes, though these differences are probably not related to all aspects of sex identity. [*Consult* (4) Beach, 1965; Hamburg and Lunde, 1966; Levine, 1966; Young, *et al.,* 1965.]

Learning. In addition to these possible biological differences, a large part of human sex is the result of the praise and punishment that children receive, their acquisition of the cultural norms that express the expected behaviors in which males and females should partake, and their direct experiences with their own sex and the other sex. Considerable research has been conducted to determine how the concept of sexual identity is developed in childhood. Perhaps one of the earliest theories was that of Freud, who discussed the differences between men and women in terms of his general theory of sexuality. [*Consult* (9) Freud, 1927, 1932, 1933.]

Freud suggested that the major basis of sex identity arises during the phallic stage of development, which occurs when the child is approximately five years of age. During this phase the genital organs become of prime importance to the child, and incestuous Oedipal feelings are experienced toward the parents. Male children, according to Freud, experience castration anxiety, fearing that their fathers will castrate them in punishment for desiring their mother. Girls, in contrast, are said to experience penis envy because they lack this organ. According to Freud, these anatomical differences and their psychological consequences lead to quite different sex identities: while males can in general successfully overcome their childhood sexual fantasies, females are affected throughout life by a feeling of inadequacy, which is most nearly resolved by having a baby in later life.

Two cautions are important with regard to the Freudian interpretation. Much of the adult behavior that he used as evidence of his theory can be readily explained on the basis of social learning experiences. Furthermore, Freud himself acknowledged that his understanding of women was less than that of men—and many current writers and researchers would be quick to agree.

More experimentally inclined psychologists in recent years have conducted numerous studies observing the ways in which boys and girls behave in a wide variety of situations. Certain differences appear to be fairly consistent. Girls, for example, develop more personal affiliations, express greater interest in and more positive feelings toward others, and generally show greater anxiety. Boys are in most instances superior to girls in tests of spatial relationships, while girls excel on tests of verbal fluency and articulation. Although it is possible that such differences are biologically influenced, particularly in the case of verbal and perceptual skills, a number of studies have shown the important effects that reinforcement by the parents can and does have. Parents are far more likely to tolerate aggressive behavior from a boy, for example, and to discourage dependent behavior in him than they are with a girl. Other studies have shown that parents expect higher achievement from male children than from females.

It is important to realize that many of these parental practices are begun when the child is only two or three. Thus, it seems likely that much behavior is equally typical of boys and girls when they are still quite young but is systematically encouraged or discouraged as they grow older and are expected to adopt behavior considered appropriate to their sex. [*Consult* (9) Kagan and Moss, 1962; Maccoby, 1966.]

Adolescence. A major stage in the development of sex identity occurs during adolescence. Again, both biological and psychological factors are at work.

Biologically, an activation of the hormonal functions propels the child into sexual adulthood. Boys acquire secondary sex characteristics, such as body and facial hair. For girls, the signs include the development of breasts and the advent of menstruation. The effects of these biological changes on behavior and sex identity is probably substantial for both males and females.

Psychologist Judith Bardwick and her students have begun to study the psychological effects of the menstrual cycle in females, and their results suggest that mood is highly correlated with production of estrogen. [*Consult* (9) Bardwick, 1971.]

Greatest optimism is displayed during the period of ovulation, while more negative feelings of anxiety and hostility are likely to occur during the premenstrual phase. Preliminary evidence suggests that certain birth control pills, however, will flatten out this cyclic pattern. Less is known about the biological cycles of males, if or to what extent they exist.

During this period the increasingly frequent heterosexual contacts provide an equally important basis for sex identity. Successful or unsuccessful encounters with members of the opposite sex tend to affirm or question ideals of what a successful male or female is like.

Adulthood. Much of the behavior learned throughout childhood and adolescence is manifested in the adult male and female, and researchers have demonstrated a number of ways in which males and females typically, though not necessarily, differ. Masculinity-femininity interest scales have been developed to measure how typical a person's interests are of the average male or female (not how masculine or feminine a person is in terms of biological characteristics). There are wide variations in these measures, and they reflect sociocultural factors as much as basic sex differences. College males, for example, frequently score higher on femininity than noncollege males because they more often endorse items dealing with the arts, which are coded as "feminine." Conversely, college females are likely to show a greater interest in science or other "masculine"-coded items than their noncollege counterparts.

Males and females have also been shown to differ on a variety of other measures, though it is important to recognize that these distributions are overlapping in nearly every instance; that is, both males and females display these characteristics, but some are more likely to be shown by one sex than the other. Females tend to be more susceptible to conformity pressures, view themselves as more de-

Dress of three generations ago, emphasizing the differences between men and women, contrasts with the "unisex" look of today. Different learning experiences and expectations have altered the concept of sex identity and will doubtless alter it further in future generations.

pendent, and show stronger needs for affiliation; males show greater ability at mathematical reasoning and more independence in judgment. Frequently the differences are matters of form rather than basic nature. For example, while males generally display more physical aggression than females, females are often found to show more verbal aggression.

One area of recent interest relating to sex differences is achievement motivation. In the past measures of achievement generally showed that males had greater drive to achieve than did females, and in fact research tended to concentrate primarily on males. In part the greater evidence of achievement behavior in males may be due to learned differences in childhood; in part, the tests may tend to measure only those achievement areas where men concentrate, rather than more affiliative and empathetic activities in which women may express their achievement drives.

Another aspect of this problem has recently been investigated by psychologist Matina Horner. Her investigations have shown the existence of a strong motive to avoid success among women, in addition to the more standard tendency to aspire to success. Horner's results suggest that women in particular learn to fear success because of the potentially unpleasant consequences, such as perceived loss of femininity (by deviating from the predominant female role) and difficulties in relating to males (by challenging the dominant-submissive formulation of male-female relationships). [*Consult* (9) Horner, 1970.]

Expectations. Conceptions of appropriate male-female relationships are another important aspect of the development of sex identity. Across cultures, the expectations regarding the roles of husband and wife or mother and father may differ substantially, suggesting again the importance of learning in sex identification. Norms regarding appropriate sexual behavior frequently differ for males and females (the so-called double standard), and in general greater leniency is associated with the male role.

Even within societies, different values are held about what is normal and what is deviate in sexual behavior. The majority of the population of the United States, for example, regards a homosexual preference as deviate. At a less extreme level, various forms of intercourse are considered improper by some segments of the population but are endorsed and freely practiced by others.

For both males and females marriage has also implied different roles. For the man, his success as a male depends not simply on a marriage but, even more importantly, on his career development. For the woman, in contrast, successful sex identity may often be achieved by the single role of wife and mother.

In this sense, the society may expect more of the male than the female.

Challenges. While much of what has been said thus far accurately describes the general knowledge of sex identity and sex role behavior, certain groups are currently challenging the validity of such assumptions. Women's liberation advocates question the basis of many of the distinctions between male and female and argue for less differentiation on the basis of sex. The basic question here is not whether there are differences, but whether they are inevitable and whether they are relevant to many different areas of human performance.

Clear evidence of discrimination against females in employment has been established, and recent court and legislative actions have attempted to eliminate some of the inequities. For both men and women, cultural norms may tend to restrict behavior to those activities considered appropriate to the particular sex role, and deviations by an individual may undermine his or her sex identity. Current research is directed to the question of how men and women are differentially evaluated in a variety of areas and what the consequences of role deviations are.

In terms of the more basic question of the inevitability of differences, it is clear that a substantial portion of the behavior associated with sex roles is, in fact, learned. While there are definite biological differences, the human being is far less dependent on basic genetic programming than are infrahuman animals. Thus different learning experiences and expectations could radically alter the concept of sex identity for both males and females in generations of the future.

—Kay Deaux, *Purdue University*
Consult (9) Bardwick, 1971; Bardwick, 1972; Maccoby, 1966; Rosenberg and Sutton-Smith, 1972; Schoeffer, 1971; Seward and Williamson, 1970.

SEX ROLE. *See* Character Development; Sex Identity.

SEXISM. *See* Prejudice.

SEXUAL DEVIATIONS. Many forms of sexual behavior are called "deviant" because they depart from what is considered normal by a society. Deviations such as exhibitionism and rape are penalized by law. Other behaviors on the list are personal problems—frigidity and impotence, for example.

The line between what society calls "normal" and "abnormal" shifts with time. "Deviation" is a classifying label applied at a given time, and does not imply a condemnation of everything under this heading. Some authorities have suggested that "sexual anomaly" would be a preferable term.

Deviations (problems, anomalies) are discussed in separate articles.

See Autoeroticism; Bestiality; Exhibitionism; Fetishism; Frigidity; Homosexuality; Impotence; Incest; Masochism; Masturbation; Necrophilia; Nymphomania; Onanism; Pedophilia; Rape; Sadism; Satyriasis; Sodomy; Transsexualism; Transvestism; Voyeurism.

Consult (9) Katchadourian and Lunde, 1972; Kinsey, *et al.,* 1948; Kinsey, *et al.,* 1953. (13) Allen, 1962; Gebhard, *et al.,* 1965.

SEXUALITY. *See* Sex Identity.

SHAPING. *See* Operant Conditioning; Successive Approximation.

SHELL SHOCK. *See* Combat Neurosis.

SHERIF, MUZAFER (1906–   ), American social psychologist. Born in Turkey, he received his Ph.D. from Columbia University (1935) and is director of the psychosocial studies program at Pennsylvania State University.

Sherif is known for his research on group behavior, particularly the influences of the group upon judgments. He found that attribution of literary material to prestigious authors affects evaluation of the merits of a work. He studied the mutual influences among two or three people facing an ambiguous but identical situation (such as the "apparent movement" phenomenon).

Sherif's works include *The Psychology of Social Norms* (with H. Cantril), 1936; *The Psychology of Ego-Involvements,* 1947; *An Outline of Social Psychology,* 1948; *Groups in Harmony and Tension* (with C. Sherif), 1953; *Social Psychology* (with C. Sherif), 1969; *Reference Groups, An Exploration into Conformity and Deviation of Adolescents,* 1964.

—Nina Adams, *Yale University*

SHERRINGTON, CHARLES SCOTT (1857–1952), English physiologist who received the Nobel Prize in physiology and medicine in 1932 for his work on the function of nerve cells.

Sherrington's work at Cambridge produced fundamental information on the nature of nerve activity and served as the basis for much subsequent research on the physiology of the nervous system. His experiments with spinal reflex patterns were described in his widely influential book *The Integrative Action of the Nervous System* (1906). Sherrington originated the concept of the nerve synapse. He also conducted extensive studies on the effects of fatigue and drugs on the nervous system. His findings provided psychologists with information on the neural basis of behavior and stimulated research in the area of physiological psychology.

SHOCK THERAPY. This term usually refers to

electroshock treatment for mental disorders. For a time insulin shock was also used; large doses of insulin were administered to induce coma, and this was reported to alleviate symptoms. Insulin treatment has been virtually abandoned, however. *See* Electroconvulsive Therapy.

SHORT-TERM MEMORY. *See* Memory.

SIGNAL-DETECTION THEORY. Sensitivity to a stimulus depends not only upon the stimulus intensity but also upon the experience, expectation, and motivation of the person being tested. Signal detection theory attempts to separate out the nonsensory factors in order to obtain a pure measure of sensory capacity. Experiments have shown that if the stimulus is presented at low intensity on each trial, the subject, influenced by motivation or set, will tend toward detection.

Signal-detection theory has introduced the concept of *catch trials,* in which no signal is presented. If the subject says the signal is present when it has been presented, his response is termed a "hit"; if the subject says the signal is present when it is not, the response is called a "false alarm." The number of catch trials will influence the number of false alarms. The *receiver operating characteristic (ROC) curve* plots how may hits and false alarms occur, depending upon the number of catch trials. This curve then represents the pure sensory capacity of the person tested.

—Nina Adams, *Yale University*

SKELETAL MUSCLES. *See* Effectors.

SKILLS, LEARNING OF. The learning of the skills of everyday life, such as typing, driving a car, walking, and running can all be examined in terms of their segments, which are labeled as responses by psychologists. These segments are dependent upon the particular skill being learned or studied, and they are highly arbitrary in definition. Acquisition of a particular skill is influenced by its simplicity or complexity and the conditions under which it is performed as well as by the part or parts of the anatomy it involves. Thus, playing a piano requires more dexterity than throwing a baseball.

Early studies dealt with the task difficulty, uniqueness of the skill, presentation of the task, practice effects, and knowledge of results. More recent work has been concerned with the incentive for task learning or completion, reinforcement, the results of the task completion, and feedback.

Reinforcement for completion and practice of a skill has led to such applications as piece work in factories. Feedback or servomechanism logic has been central to the development of complex theories concerning task

Group influence on judgment was focus of major psychosocial studies by Turkish-born Muzafer Sherif.

Once a child has reached the appropriate level of maturation, only a small amount of practice is necessary to develop the motor skills consistent with that level.

SKIN SENSES

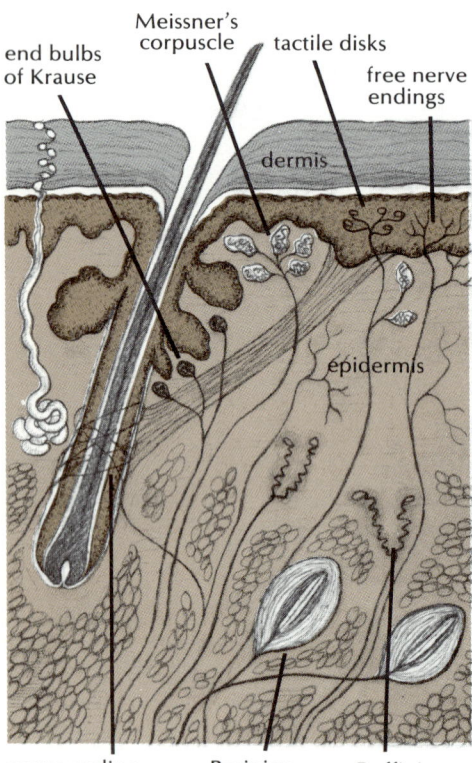

Several types of receptors are found in the skin, but there is no clear correlation between a specific sensation (pain, cold, warmth, touch) and a particular type of receptor.

Students using a Skinner box in a school laboratory.

learning and execution. As a result of these theories of learning, apparatuses are being developed to retrain highly intricate neurological functions, such as muscle coordination, walking, or even speech, following trauma or nervous system disease.

—A. Ronald Seifert, *University of Tennessee*

SKIN DISORDERS, as reactions to psychological stress. *See* Psychosomatic Disorders.

SKIN SENSES. The familiar sensations of the skin can be divided into four distinct categories: touch (pressure), warm, cold, and pain. Other skin sensations, such as itch, tickle, vibration, and burning, are all variations of these four.

The physiology of skin sensation has been studied in terms of the kinds of stimulation necessary for the different sensations, the relationship between the anatomy of the skin and sensation, and the relationship between different size nerves of the skin and sensation. Studies in the late 1800s explored the skin's surface with hairs, needles, and warm and cold probes to locate spots receptive to the four different sensations. Pain spots were most numerous, followed in order by touch, cold, and warm spots. This research led anatomists to look for specialized receptors for each sensation. Several types were found, all of which, through their specialized anatomy, help translate the quality and frequency of stimuli for the sensory nerve. But there is no clear correlation between each sensation and one specific type of receptor. In fact, the cornea of the eye, which senses pain, touch, cold, and warm, has only free nerve endings, with no specialized receptors.

Most recent research indicates that the different skin sensations are due to stimulation of receptive spots whose nerve fibers vary in diameter and terminate in different parts of the central nervous system. Experiments show that when nerves from an area of skin are anesthetized, the smallest nerves block first and the largest last. Thus, the different sensations disappear in specific order: pain first, then cold and warm, and finally touch.

—Nina Adams, *Yale University*
See also Sensation.
Consult (4) Geldard, 1971.

SKINNER BOX, an apparatus designed by B. F. Skinner for animal learning experiments. It is a small box containing, basically, a lever and an automatic food dispenser. When the lever is pressed, a food pellet drops out into a cup. Such boxes are used in studies of operant, or instrumental, conditioning, where the animal's rate of lever pressing is the conditioned response.

SKINNER, BURRHUS FREDERIC (1904-   ), American psychologist. Born in Susquehanna, Pa., he taught at Indiana and Harvard. He was appointed to the William James chair in psychology at Harvard in 1947.

Skinner is most noted for his rigorous adherence to the principles of behaviorism as first elaborated by Watson. He contends that observable behavior is the only appropriate object of study for psychology, whose purpose is to describe the conditions under which behavior is modified (learning), not to explain why this occurs. He studies behavior within the framework of conditioning.

One of Skinner's most important contributions is the distinction between classical Pavlovian conditioning, in which behavior is elicited (for example, reflex), and operant conditioning, in which behavior is emitted. To test his claim that most important behavior is under the control of the organism and therefore operant, he constructed the Skinner box, in which one particular operant response, a rat's bar press, is isolated. His exhaustive studies using this model to determine those factors that influence the learning of this response showed that different schedules of reinforcement produce different rates of learning.

More recently, Skinner's discoveries have been applied in education. The development of the teaching machine, based on his principles of reinforcement, has marked a major technological advance. Moreover, psychologists and psychiatrists have developed techniques of behavior modification, based on operant conditioning, to alleviate symptoms in neurotic and even psychotic patients.

The range of potential application of Skinner's work will probably not be fully understood for many years. His major works are *Behavior of Organisms,* 1938; *Walden Two,* 1948; and *Beyond Freedom and Dignity,* 1971.

—Michael Rothenberg, *The City College of The City University of New York*

SLEEP AND DREAMS. Knowledge about sleep and dreams has been greatly enhanced by the discoveries that sleep (1937) and dreams (1953) could be measured by changes in the electroencephalogram (EEG or Brain Waves—a measure of electrical activity in the brain). These discoveries permitted the continuous and objective measurement of sleep without disturbing the sleeper and without reference to consciousness. Furthermore, since essentially the same criteria could be used across different ages and with animals, individual and species comparisons became possible. The latter fact also gave impetus to neurophysiological research related to sleep.

Stages of Sleep. In human subjects five stages of sleep are identifiable. Four stages (one through four) represent a continuum of the depth of sleep. The fifth stage, identified by a Stage 1 EEG and rapid eye movements (REM) and certain other physiological changes, has been associated with visual dreaming in human subjects.

The young adult, during a night of sleep, will change from stage to stage frequently. There are on the average about thirty such changes a night. In the young adult about 5 percent of the night will be spent in stage 1, 50 percent in stage 2, 5 percent in stage 3, 15 percent in stage 4, and 25 percent in REM sleep. REM sleep is rhythmic in its appearance, appearing in bursts at average intervals of ninety to one hundred minutes. The episodes become longer across the night, hence REM sleep is more abundant in the latter part of the sleep period. In contrast, most of stage 4 or deep sleep occurs in the first third of the night.

Age is a strong determinant of the length of sleep and the number and placement of sleep episodes. The newborn sleeps on the average about sixteen hours, with a range of individual differences from about twelve to twenty-two hours. Sleep of the newborn is also polyphasic, occurring in some six to twelve bursts of sleep and waking during the twenty-four hours, and is distributed in equal amounts during the night and day. The average amount of sleep declines about two hours in the first six months, about two more hours in the first two years, and stabilizes at about seven to eight hours in the late teens. In the elderly the average amount of sleep remains about the same but individual differences in sleep length are greater.

The infant also begins consolidating his periods of sleep, especially during the night, and extending his periods of wakefulness during the day. By three months, only about one-third of a sample of children were awake between midnight and 5 a.m., and less than 10 percent of the children were awakening by one year. Naps are similarly reduced and constitute about 12 percent of the total sleep between one and two years of age and about 5 percent by the age of four.

The intrasleep patterns also change with age. REM sleep constitutes about 50 percent of the newborn's sleep and declines to about 30 percent in the two-year-old and stabilizes at around 25 percent in the ten-year-old. It remains at this level into the sixties. On the other hand, stage 4 or deep sleep begins to decline in the thirties with an associated increase in light sleep and awakening.

Neurophysiological "Circuits." Significant advances have been made in locating the neurophysiological "circuitry" of sleep. Lesion and stimulation procedures indicate that sleep, waking, and REM sleep phenomena center around the brain stem. Waking appears influenced by the ascending reticular (brain stem)

system and the posterior hypothalamus, whereas sleep is influenced by the lower brain stem and the basal forebrain. The cortex is necessary for slow wave sleep, and REM sleep is specifically referent to a particular area in the reticular system, the pontine tegmentum. More recent attention has focused on biochemical aspects of sleep, and it now appears that the answers will lie within actions of the brain monoamines.

Sleep Pathology. Studies of sleep pathology have led to surprising findings. Sleepwalking, nightmares or night terrors (in contrast to bad dreams), enuresis (bed-wetting), and sleeptalking are not, as expected, related to REM sleep. Rather, sleepwalking and night terrors have been shown to be closely associated with stage 4 sleep. On the other hand, narcolepsy, a clinical condition in which persons are intermittently overpowered by sleep, is associated with dysfunction of REM sleep.

Deprivation Studies. Attempts to understand the function of sleep have centered around deprivation studies—total deprivation of sleep and differential deprivation of certain stages of sleep. The total deprivation studies have been characterized by a lack of positive findings. Systematic and extensive studies of deprivation periods of eight to ten days failed to define a major physiological or biochemical system breakdown. Although subjects are indeed sleepy, they can typically accomplish short-term tasks effectively, and their personality remains essentially intact. There are, of course, signs that the subject is sleepy. Prolonged vigilance tasks are affected by as little as one night of deprivation, and very sleepy subjects may show signs of irritability and even confusion.

Subjects have also been deprived of REM or dream sleep experimentally for as many as twelve days. Again, the positive findings have not yet been found impressive. There have been no established cases of highly disorganized personality responses to such deprivation. Effects on memory have been absent or unimpressive. Indeed, there is some evidence of improvements resulting from REM sleep deprivation in depressive cases.

In both total deprivation and in REM deprivation, subjects do show a need for such sleep by increased pressure to enter into the state as deprivation increases and by tendencies to "make up" for losses during recovery periods. The nature or basis of this need has not yet been determined.

Dream Analysis

The content of dreams has evoked a wide range of responses throughout history and across cultures. Among the earliest specimens of writing is an Egyptian papyrus of about 2000 B.C. which is a record of dream interpretations. Hundreds of temples of Aescu-

Behavioral psychologist B. F. Skinner has concentrated on the role of reinforcement in conditioning.

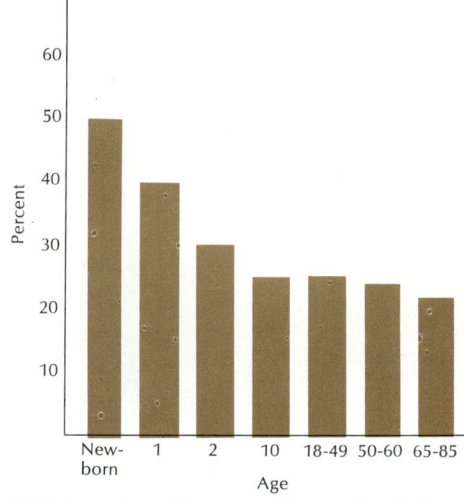

REM TIME AS PERCENT OF TOTAL SLEEP TIME

REM sleep, about 50 percent of the newborn's sleep, stabilizes at about 25 percent by the age of ten.

SLEEP AND DREAMS

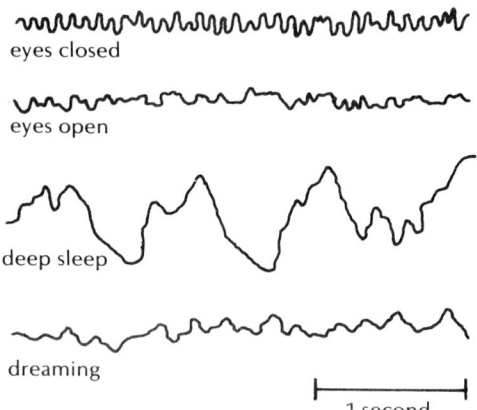

eyes closed

eyes open

deep sleep

dreaming

|← 1 second →|

Brain-wave patterns during stages of sleep and wakefulness.

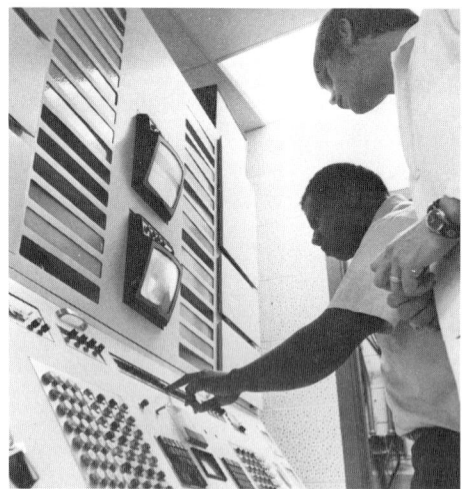

Monitoring a sleep chamber by closed-circuit television.

lapius in early Greece emphasized the curative role of dreams by providing instructions and omens as messages from the gods. The Bible is rife with prophetic dreams. The early American Indians of the Iroquois tribe centered much of their culture around dreams as a form of reality.

There are four dimensions into which we may classify these reactions: dreams as reality, as curative, as omens, or as extensions of the waking state. In a crude way these categories parallel cultural development: the more primitive cultures typically hold that the dreamer enters into a different and real world in dreaming, and the more contemporary views hold dreams to be within a continuum of consciousness and related to the waking state. The attitudes often exist side by side in a given culture. Today we have dream books that interpret dreams as omens on the same newsstand with books on dreams as reflectors of personality.

Freud's Theories. The categories are not mutually exclusive. Sigmund Freud developed an approach to dream content analyses by viewing dreams as meaningfully reflecting the waking state of an individual and by elaborating the curative potential of dreams. In Freud's theory, during sleep the mental functioning becomes more primitive and regressive and repression is reduced. Repressed wishes become partially freed from monitoring (censorship). The particular content of the dream is derived from chance stimuli, recent experiences (day residue), and infantile memories. This forms the *manifest* content while the repressed wishes are expressed as *latent* content. The apparently bizarre nature of dreams comes from "dream work"—the expression of repressed impulses in symbolic and concretized forms, condensation, and displacement of affect. This dream work serves to evade the censor and maintain sleep. There is an implicit curative role of dreams; during sleep the repressed impulses may be discharged and the interpretive dream may serve as "omens" about the crucial unconscious conflicts of the person.

Recent Research. Research on dreams since the 1950s has not solved the mystery of dreams but has made questionable any simplistic solution. We now know that all people spend between one-fourth and one-fifth of their sleep time in dreaming. This neurophysiological condition is a rhythmic one and exists in all mammals as well as birds. There are gross changes with age in the amount of this dream state, which do not seem to closely parallel behavioral changes. There are little differences, at least in amount, of this dream state between radically different personality conditions such as schizophrenics and normals or geniuses and dullards. Deprivation studies have not yet demonstrated a clear and certain effect on

behavior functioning. Within this field the classical problems of the mind-body issue are not resolved.

—Wilse B. Webb, *University of Florida*
See also Brain Waves.

Consult (3) Foulkes, 1966; Kales, 1969; Klietman, 1963; Luce and Segal, 1966.

SLEEP-DREAM CYCLE. *See* Sleep and Dreams.

SLEEP DRIVE. The need to sleep is essential for the survival of organisms and seems to be a basic characteristic of all animals. Even protozoa, flatworms, and mollusks display periods of relative inactivity. In complex organisms sleep is controlled primarily through the role of the reticular formation, a series of tracts and nuclei found in the brain stem.

Sleep comprises at least four distinct stages. These are graded from light sleep, in which the sleeper is to some extent aware of the external events, through the deeper stages, from which arousal is extremely difficult.

One important stage of sleep is called *REM (rapid eye movement) sleep.* During this stage the subject's electroencephalograph is active, whereas in deep sleep it is relatively slow. During this stage there are REMs, and dreaming usually occurs. Of all the stages of sleep, REM appears to be the most important for psychological well-being. Individuals who are specifically deprived of REM become extremely agitated and disoriented. This evidence indicates that dreaming itself may have drive properties.

—Joel F. Lubar, *University of Tennessee*
See also Sleep and Dreams.

SLEEPING SICKNESS. *See* Encephalitis.

SLEEPWALKING. Somnambulism, or sleepwalking, is a relatively rare type of functional nervous disorder that is generally classified under the "dissociative-neurotic reactions" and thus is a form of hysterical reaction. It is more apt to occur in males and is more frequent in childhood.

It was first studied extensively by the famous French psychiatrist Pierre Janet, in the late nineteenth century. He considered sleepwalking episodes to be trancelike states, with "moral causes," having the same type of unconscious roots as hysterical convulsive attacks, fugues, and hysterical amnesias. The sleepwalker is emotionally perturbed or preoccupied. He has suppressed intention, wish, anxiety, or fear and enacts in his somnambulistic ritual the fulfillment or attempt to escape from these thoughts. A classic example of somnambulism in literature is the sleepwalking, hand-washing scene of Lady Macbeth after the murder of King Duncan.

Characteristically, the somnambulist has no recall or memory of the elaborate organized activity and speech he carried on during the trancelike state. Also, characteristically, he never injures himself or bumps into obstacles during his walks. Typically, episodes last from fifteen to thirty minutes.

The best logical treatment for this type of sleepwalking has been some analytic type of psychotherapy, designed to bring to the surface the pertinent subconscious impulses. Hypnotherapy also is useful as a treatment modality.

In a series of papers published in the Archives of General Psychiatry in 1966, a team from the Los Angeles Sleep Study Center, headed by Anthony Kales, uncovered significant new facts about somnambulism. They studied four adult and seven child patients. They recorded continuously and simultaneously the brain-wave activity, the general muscle activity, and the rapid eye movements that are characteristic of dreaming, in ordinary sleep and during sleepwalking episodes. Their work showed that sleepwalking does not occur in association with ordinary dreaming. It also suggested the presence of both organic and functional factors in the sleepwalking process. It was noted that the organic features (abnormal brain waves) were more apt to be associated with periods of nonpurposive wandering, stumbling, and the like—periods when the patients could conceivably injure themselves by falling or bumping into objects. It is reasonable, therefore, to look for organic causes in cases of somnambulism and to treat medicinally (for example, with antiepileptic drugs) those cases where such causes are found.

—Emanuel Messinger, M.D., *U.S. Veterans Hospital, Northport N.Y.*

SLOW LEARNER, the term used to identify children with below-average intelligence who experience learning difficulties in academic tasks. In its broadest use it encompasses even those levels of subnormal intelligence indicating mental retardation; however, its specific diagnostic meaning does not denote mental deficiency. The IQ range typically specified for identification of the slow learner is between 80 and 90, frequently referred to as the dull-normal range of intellectual functioning.

Critical incidence figures vary, but the most widely accepted statistic regarding the prevalence of slow learners seems to be between 15 and 18 percent of the total school-age population. According to G. O. Johnson, "In an average community where the school serves children from all cultural, social and economic levels, a class of 30 unselected children can be expected to contain 4 or 5 slow learners."

In academic work, statistics show that slow learners receive the majority of the grades in the lowest quartile. There also tends to be a high incidence of school dropouts among slow learners as well as a higher incidence of antiso-

cial and deviant behavior and adjustment problems among slow learners as compared to so-called average or normal children. Because of the apparent tendency of the slow learner to come from families of lower socioeconomic status, some researchers suggest that cultural deprivation and environmental disadvantages are primary etiological factors.

From the point of view of educational provisions, the slow-learning child generally does not require placement in a special class for the mentally handicapped (although this is a widely practiced policy). He can usually acquire the same subject matter, although not to the same extent or with the same speed or facility as the normal child. Instructional adaptations should be made for him within the context of the regular class. Ideally, teachers of regular classes can and should differentiate learning activities to adjust to a broader concept of "normality."

—Frank T. Vitro, *University of Maine*
Consult (14) Johnson, 1963; Reger, *et al.*, 1968.

SMELL (olfaction), the nasal detection of certain molecules in the airstream. Sniffing increases the ability to smell because it brings the airborne substances in contact with the millions of sensory receptor cells of the olfactory muscosa, which lies in the upper portion of the nasal cavity. In the olfactory system, the sensory cell is actually a nerve cell. Each such cell is drawn out into a long fiber directly into the central nervous system. (This is extremely unusual; all the other sensory systems involve synapses, or junctions, between the sensory cells and the nerves to the brain.) Each olfactory cell, connected by its own nerve, provides very fine sensitivity. Electrical recordings directly from the receptor nerve cells indicate specific responses to seven different groups of odors: camphor, musk, floral, peppermint, ether, pungent, and putrid. From combinations of these primary odors it is possible to match any other known odor.

One theory of olfaction suggests that molecules, which differ in chemical shape, are absorbed selectively by membranes of the sensory cells. This is called a *lock and key theory*, since the shape of the molecule (the key) fits the shape of the membrane (the lock).

The role of olfaction in human behavior is not clear. Its loss is annoying but not necessarily dangerous. For animals, however, it is often a more important sense than vision.

—Nina Adams, *Yale University*
See also Sensation.
Consult (4) Geldard, 1971.

SMOOTH MUSCLES. *See* Effectors.

SOCIAL BREAKDOWN SYNDROME (or institutional neurosis). A number of investigators

SMELL

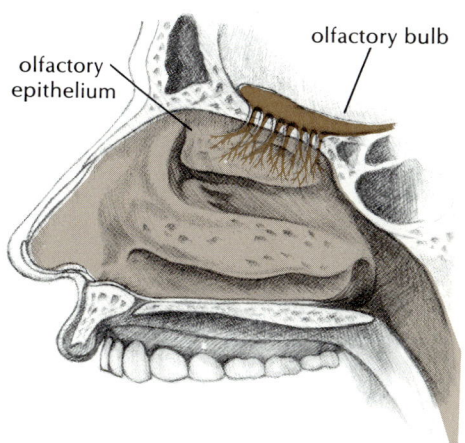

olfactory bulb

olfactory epithelium

Impulses conveying the sense of smell arise from nerve cells embedded in the olfactory epithelium at the top of the nasal passage and travel only a very short distance to the olfactory bulb of the brain.

have concluded that some of the symptoms of chronic mental patients are caused by the depersonalizing and depressing nature of the hospitals in which they are confined. In less enlightened hospitals, patients are locked into barren areas, do not have their own clothes or personal belongings, are cut off from friends and families, have little that is meaningful to do, and are treated as cases rather than as individuals. These factors can aggravate whatever problems the patient had when admitted. The patient is cast in the role of sick person, and in time he learns to play the part.

New methods in hospital design and operation should reduce the tendency to promote social breakdown. Treating patients in the community through clinics and mental health centers is a means to avoid the institutional experience.

See also Mental Hospital.

Consult (13) Barton, 1959; Gruenberg and Zusman, 1964; Zusman, 1966.

SOCIAL CONFLICT. *See* Conflict, Social.

SOCIAL ISOLATION. How would isolation from other people affect development? Hints at an answer have come from reports on children who have grown up in a wild state. *See* Wild Children.

SOCIAL LEARNING THEORY. *See* Imitation.

SOCIAL PERCEPTION. A number of social phenomena (for example, personal interaction, cultural values and beliefs, and socially learned expectations) influences an individual's perception not only of other people but also of inanimate objects and events.

Basic Perceptual Processes. During the late 1940s and early 1950s research and theory emphasized the role of social influences on the basic processes of perception. It was determined that expectancies evolving out of accumulated past experiences or the individual's needs, values, or goals could influence the speed or accuracy with which the person perceived different stimuli. Thus, a hungry individual might, around mealtime, perceive an ambiguous stimulus as food-related, or children might perceive a jar of candy as "bigger" than a similar jar of sawdust.

Three process of selective perception were often cited: *leveling* involves selective inattention to those particular details of an experience that are inconsistent with desires or expectations; *sharpening* involves the selective accentuation of particular details that are consistent with desires or expectations; *assimilation* involves a process whereby even slight ambiguities are distorted in order to maximize consistency with desires or expectations. All of these processes are important in explaining the spread of incorrect rumors about an event and the maintenance of prejudices and stereotypes about various groups despite evidence to the contrary. They were eventually incorporated into the theory of *cognitive dissonance,* which stressed the need for an individual to maintain a state of consonance (balance, consistency) among his perceptions, attitudes, and behavior.

Perceptual selectivity and distortion can operate to reduce dissonance (imbalance, inconsistency) and increase consonance. Basically, most individuals seem to find it easier or more economical to change or distort their perception of a single event than to alter an existing complex of integrated and organized attitudes, concepts, and behavior. For example, a habitual smoker who reads a research report linking smoking and lung cancer may subsequently "perceive" only reviews critical of that research, which convince him he can safely ignore the findings. This process is easier than stopping the smoking habit and accepting the implication that he has been behaving unwisely and dangerously by smoking for so many years.

"Person Perception." During the late 1950s and 1960s, social psychologists increasingly turned their attention to the study of how we come to judge and understand other people with whom we interact socially. It became apparent that, in viewing others, we go beyond their physical attributes and even beyond mere description of their actions. We try to make sense out of their behavior and, in doing so, usually perceive them as causal agents. We infer their intentions and emotional states, and generally we go so far as to develop some idea of their long-term behavior or "personality" traits. But how accurate are our perceptions of other people? What clues or events influence our attempts to understand and judge other people?

Apparently, the ability to judge others accurately varies greatly among people, and it does not seem related to either intelligence or special training. Those who are most inaccurate in judging others seem to be those who attribute their own qualities and characteristics to others (projection) and who tend to be very easygoing or benevolent in judging others. Most people prove to be more accurate in judging those people who behave in some extreme fashion or who conform readily to popular social expectations for their role (for example, the absent-minded professor).

In many cases, our first impressions of strangers persist even though they later behave differently. However, individuals who are closely and frequently associated tend to judge one another more accurately than outsiders. Our ability to perceive others accurately is also stronger when we are dealing with a person in a specific situation that is familiar to us. Thus, we may be accurate in perceiving a person in the classroom but inaccurate in predicting how he will behave on a date or at a party.

—Bruce Muller, *Southern Connecticut State College*

SOCIAL POWER. *See* Power.

SOCIAL PSYCHOLOGY, the study of individuals in their social context and of the interactions of individuals in groups. The scope of interests of social psychologists can be shown by listing some of the topics they investigate: social influences on perception of objects and persons; conformity to group norms; intergroup tensions and prejudice; attitudes and how they are formed and changed; public opinion; communication, propaganda, and coercive persuasion (brainwashing); aggression; group structure and leadership; comparative psychological studies of behavior in various cultures. Social psychologists build theories, and they also try to help with immediate problems, such as the sources of misunderstanding between police and civilians or the causes of riots in city slums.

It is difficult to make a neat separation of social psychology from other areas of psychological study, because there are social aspects to most behavior. Many researchers who do not call themselves social psychologists are interested in social factors—for example, a child psychologist studying family influences on emotional development or a clinical psychologist investigating the influence of staff and other inmates on hospital patients.

It is also difficult to mark off social psychology from sociology and social anthropology. Workers in all three fields study the behavior of people in groups. Kurt Lewin once remarked that, because he was officially a social psychologist, he should apologize to the sociologists when his work on autocratic and democratic groups took him over the boundary of his own field. A sort of boundary can be noted: social psychologists tend to look more at the individual, while sociologists and anthropologists seek theories of group behavior. Nevertheless, there is considerable overlapping.

See the Subject Map on page 262 for lists of articles on social psychology.

Consult (10) Hollander, 1971; Hollander and Hunt, 1971; Hollander and Hunt, 1972; Lindzey and Aronson, 1968; Maccoby, *et al.,* 1958.

SOCIAL WORK, PSYCHIATRIC. *See* Psychiatric Social Worker.

SOCIALIZATION, a process by which a child learns the different patterns of behavior expected from him and accepted by his society. In general, the individual will adopt forms of behavior that are appropriate to his or her own sex and ethnic, religious, and social background. Although heredity may be a contributing factor in personality formation, each person acquires most of his or her characteristics, values, beliefs, and attitudes through socialization.

Since the socialization process begins early in life, parents, through child-rearing practices, serve as models and regulators of behavior. The home climate, size of family, relationship between siblings, and parent-child relations are all important factors in the formation of personality. Parental attitudes and behavior in the areas of feeding, toilet training, aggression, dependency, and sexual behavior seem to have significant psychological impact on the individual. However, studies have not clearly established the exact and lasting effects of the consequences of child-rearing practices on personality characteristics.

—Ragaa Mazen, *Southern Connecticut State College*
See also Child Development.

SOCIOGRAM. *See* Sociometry.

SOCIOMETRY, a method for quantitative study of the structure of small groups and the personalities of individual members. The interactions of members can be plotted on a map or diagram called a *sociogram*. Data for the map are obtained by asking group members such questions as these: Who would you most like to work with on a job? Serve with on a committee? Share a dormitory room with? Sometimes the investigator asks for first, second, and third choices.

On the sociogram, circles represent people and arrows point the direction of preferences. The map shows which individuals are most preferred, least preferred, and so on. The diagram also shows whether the group is closely bound together, who the centers of attraction are, and whether some members are virtually left out. Sociometry was developed by a psychiatrist, J. L. Moreno.

SOCIOPATHIC PERSONALITY DISTURBANCE, a disorder characteristic of chronically antisocial persons who seem unable or unwilling to live within established social and moral frameworks and who do not form stable and intimate interpersonal relationships. The primary concern of such individuals is the immediate gratification of their own needs and desires, and they show no interest in the effect their behavior may have on other persons or groups. Their actions are irresponsible and often destructive, yet they experience no guilt in the face of repeated recriminations. They often

SOCIOGRAM

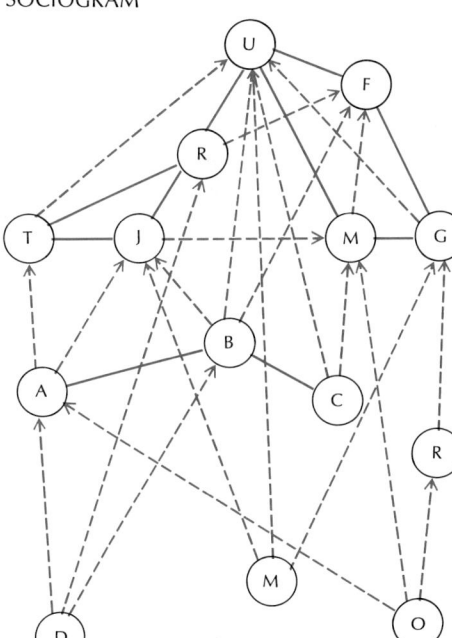

A sociogram representing patterns of friendship in a group. Solid lines show reciprocal friendships; broken arrows indicate one-way relationships.

SOCIAL PSYCHOLOGY

The work of social psychologists is related to studies of personality, environmental psychology, and community psychology. See the Subject Map for PERSONALITY and the article on BEHAVIORAL ECOLOGY, and COMMUNITY PSYCHIATRY.

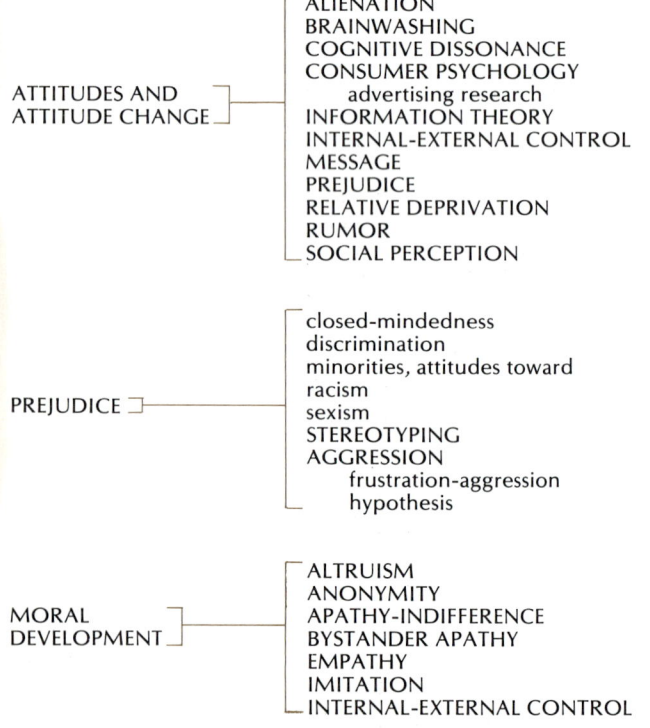

ATTITUDES AND
ATTITUDE CHANGE
- ALIENATION
- BRAINWASHING
- COGNITIVE DISSONANCE
- CONSUMER PSYCHOLOGY
  - advertising research
- INFORMATION THEORY
- INTERNAL-EXTERNAL CONTROL
- MESSAGE
- PREJUDICE
- RELATIVE DEPRIVATION
- RUMOR
- SOCIAL PERCEPTION

GROUP
BEHAVIOR
- ALIENATION
- BARGAINING
- CONFLICT, SOCIAL
- CONFORMITY
- DOMINANCE RELATIONSHIP
- INTERPERSONAL ATTRACTION
- POWER
- RISKY SHIFT
  - choice shift
- SENSITIVITY GROUP
- SOCIOMETRY

PREJUDICE
- closed-mindedness
- discrimination
- minorities, attitudes toward
- racism
- sexism
- STEREOTYPING
- AGGRESSION
  - frustration-aggression
    - hypothesis

MORAL
DEVELOPMENT
- ALTRUISM
- ANONYMITY
- APATHY-INDIFFERENCE
- BYSTANDER APATHY
- EMPATHY
- IMITATION
- INTERNAL-EXTERNAL CONTROL

The Subject Maps in the Encyclopedia illustrate the coverage of particular aspects of psychology, showing the interrelationships among the articles in twelve major areas of study. Entries in capital letters are subjects for which there are separate articles in the Encyclopedia. Entries in small letters are cross references.

The Subject Maps appear in the Encyclopedia under the following titles:

Abnormal and Clinical Psychology
Developmental Psychology
Emotion and Motivation
Intelligence
Learning and Memory
Measurement
Personality and Individual Difference
Physiological and Comparative Psychology
Psychology: Divisions and Schools
Sensation and Perception
Social Psychology
Thinking and Language

construct elaborate rationalizations, which make their behavior seem acceptable and even necessary.

The sociopath suffers from characterological defects related to an inadequately developed superego. In many cases he is the product of a chaotic family background in which he was unwanted as an infant and neglected as a child and where no structure or limits were imposed on his behavior. Because the problem in a sociopathic disturbance involves a basic flaw in the personality structure, the likelihood of significant improvement in therapy is minimal.

—Michael Rothenberg, *The City College of The City University of New York*

SODOMY, anal coitus. Scientifically, the term applies only to insertion of the penis into the rectum of a person of either sex. In the laws of a number of states, however, sodomy includes oral-genital acts and bestiality.

The regular practice of anal coitus among heterosexuals seems to be rare, probably because the painfulness of the initial experience for the female blocks its association with the sex drive. Even among homosexual males, it is practiced only by about one out of five.

—Eugene E. Levitt, *Indiana University School of Medicine*
See also Bestiality.
Consult (13) Allen, 1962.

SOMATIC SENSES. *See* Nervous System.

SOMATOPSYCHOLOGY, the study of the psychological impact of physiological disease or disability. Psychologists are interested in the adjustments people make to having tuberculosis or cancer or to being deaf, blind, disfigured, or crippled. The range of patterns of response is great. Some people lose their self-confidence and become withdrawn, self-pitying, and irritable, yet others face their handicaps without developing severe emotional problems.

Somatopsychology should be distinguished from psychosomatic medicine, which investigates physiological illnesses with psychological causes.

SOMATOTYPE. *See* Constitutional Types.

SOMESTHESIS (somatic senses). *See* Nervous System.

SOMNAMBULISM. *See* Sleepwalking.

SOUND. *See* Hearing.

SPACE PSYCHOLOGY. This term is not commonly recognized as such in psychology. This does not mean that psychologists have not been active in applying their science to space

flight. On the contrary, they were engaged in numerous investigations related to the space effort even before man was put into orbit. [For example, *Consult* (14) Voas, 1961, for a description of early work associated with Project Mercury.]

Research Areas. The main contributions of psychology to space exploration are in the selection and training of astronauts, the measurement of the effects of hostile and exotic environments on human performance; the study of altered work-rest cycles; the human-factors design of space suits, space vehicles, and associated equipment; and the investigation of a variety of operational questions associated with space flight. Only a few of these topics will be elaborated on here.

Much of the early research on *reduced gravity* and *weightlessness* was done in aircraft flying parabolic patterns or Keplerian trajectories. Using different simulation techniques—for example, water immersion, magnetic pads, and other sophisticated devices—such research not only has told us much of practical value for work in space, but also has succeeded, for example, in uncoupling man's gravity senses from his sense of vision. Thus, its findings have been of considerable theoretical value in clarifying the contribution of visual stimuli and gravity to the perception of the vertical. [*Consult* (14) Deutsch, 1969; Simons, 1964.]

The requirement for altered *work-rest cycles* in space has stimulated a great deal of research. Among the findings of more academic and theoretical interest is the revelation of the influence of powerful and persistent circadian periodicities on both physiological and psychological performance. At a more practical level, such studies have shown that markedly altered work-rest cycles are feasible in space flight. [*Consult* (14) Chiles, *et al.,* 1968.]

Research on the *operational problems* of space flight has ranged over a wide spectrum of topics. Examples are the performance of crews in artificially created gravity, the visual capabilities and performance of crews in the operation of manned space systems, and the provision of recreational facilities for space crews on flights of long duration. [*Consult* (14) Ramsey, 1971; Baker, 1963; Karnes, *et al.,* 1971.]

Status. Psychological investigations of space-related problems are difficult and expensive, requiring technical competences, facilities, and funds far beyond the capabilities of the ordinary university department of psychology. Once such studies have been completed, very few of them are published in ordinary psychological journals. The bulk of the voluminous research output appears only in government and industry technical reports, memoranda, and similar documents. Primarily for these reasons, work on problems of space falls outside the mainstream of traditional aca-

Scuba divers assist an astronaut in the Neutral Buoyancy Simulator at Marshall Space Flight Center. He wears a fully pressurized suit while training for extravehicular activity in the Skylab project.

An experimental dry-immersion bed designed to test the effects of weightlessness on sleep processes.

demic psychology. This has the unfortunate result that psychological contributions to space exploration are seldom discussed in psychology textbooks.

—Alphonse Chapanis, *The Johns Hopkins University*
See also Engineering Psychology.

SPEAKING IN TONGUES. *See* Glossolalia.

SPEARMAN, CHARLES EDWARD (1863–1945), English psychologist. Born in London, he received a Ph.D. at Leipzig University and was professor of psychology at the University of London (1928–1931).

Recognized as one of the founders of the factor analysis method in intelligence testing, Spearman did major work in the application of mathematics to testing. His 1904 paper "General Intelligence Objectivity Determined and Measured" set forth his two-factor theory of human capacity, which used statistics to determine how closely pairs of tests correlated with each other. If there was a high degree of correlation, Spearman argued, these tests measured a common factor—general intelligence. Later the existence of such intelligence was disputed; instead, it was claimed that one's general ability could be analyzed into a number of different abilities, or factors. With his 1927 *The Abilities of Man,* Spearman acknowledged the existence of other common factors. His work led to the development of factor analysis in the 1930s by Thurstone, Thomson, and others. Spearman's publications include *The Principles of Cognition,* 1923; *Creative Mind,* 1931; *Psychology Down the Ages,* 1937; and *Human Abilities,* 1950. His autobiography is in C. Murchison, *Psychology in Autobiography,* 1930, I, 299–333.

SPECIES-TYPICAL BEHAVIOR, or species-specific behavior. *See* Instinct.

SPECIFIC HUNGER, the need of an organism to obtain certain dietary substances in order to maintain a state of vigorous physical health. Research has shown that animals as well as humans deprived of rather specific vitamins or minerals tend to seek food containing them. The eating of dirt or grass by children has been described as one example of an attempt to satisfy a specific hunger for a missing food substance.

SPEECH, articulation of sounds, words, and language by the human vocal apparatus. While language emphasizes structure and meaning, speech stresses language as sound, and in this particular sense is studied by *phonetics,* a branch of *acoustics,* the study of physical properties of sounds in general. Physically different speech sounds are called *phones,* and

the range of possible differences in loudness, frequency, and articulation of phones is practically infinite. However, within any one language, only a restricted number of sound classes are used, called the *phonemes* of that language.

Speech perception by the human listener depends on hearing consonants (high frequencies) and perceiving a complex changing pattern among sound wave characteristics. The importance of high frequencies can be illustrated by "peak clipping," where electronic devices eliminate the high-amplitude (loud) sounds and amplify the low-intensity (and high-frequency) sounds in human speech. Since the normally loud vowel sounds contribute little to intelligibility, peak clipping does not affect speech perception (though it does make the speech sound different). With "center clipping," where the low-amplitude (and high-frequency) tones are eliminated, speech becomes unintelligible. Peak clipping is used in hearing aids, radio transmitters, and other communications systems to enhance intelligibility by eliminating most "noisy" sounds.

—Roland Siiter, *Montclair State College*
See also Information Theory; Language.

SPEECH DISORDERS. The general term "speech disorder" usually describes faulty production and patterning of the sounds of the language (vowels, consonants, acoustical features of voice, and temporal patterns). Speech is defective when its qualities differ so markedly from the average speech characteristics of other persons of the same age, sex, and cultural environment that it fails to serve the personal and social needs of the speaker.

Speech Processes. Disordered speech results from a breakdown in one or more of the processes necessary for speech production. The central and peripheral nervous systems serve to innervate, transmit, and modulate motor and sensory information (auditory, tactile, kinesthetic) to and from the physical systems used in speech production. These systems are *respiration* (air flow), *phonation* (voicing), *articulation* (modification of tone into speech sounds within the oral cavity), and resonation (voice-quality characteristics). Breakdown or deviation from average of any of these processes may result from structural and/or physiological impairments (organic disorders) or from the learning of improper speaking habits, which have become perpetuated over time (functional disorders).

Terminology. Many systems have been devised to classify the various forms of disordered speech. Some terms are descriptive in origin, using Greek or Latin roots, while other systems utilize terms that denote the cause of the disorder. The classifications discussed here are those most commonly used within speech pathology today and are based upon the most apparent symptons.

Disorders of articulation include disturbances of speech intelligibility attributable to the distortion, omission, substitution, or inappropriate insertion of the sounds of the language. Articulation disorders may result from neurological and structural impairment, such as brain injury following stroke or cerebral palsy. Such conditions affect temporal and resonance patterns as well as precision of executing speech sounds and are called *dysarthrias.* School-age children who have mislearned certain speech-sound patterns are commonly classified as exhibiting "functional" disorders.

Voice disorders are defects of phonation and/or resonation. These range from the complete absence of phonation to various conditions of pitch, loudness quality, and melody (*prosody*) of the voice. Causes include various structural, neurological, and histological conditions of the larynx and palate as well as emotional problems resulting in vocal symptoms.

Disorders of speech flow include stuttering, the most frequently observed of such speech disturbances. Stuttering is characterized by inappropriate repetition and/or prolongation of sounds or moments of silence. Such behavior usually begins during childhood in the form of relaxed repetitions, and adult forms may develop to include severe tension and struggle with speech production and anxiety levels and avoidance reactions related to the speech attempt. *Cluttering* is a disturbance in the intelligibility and rhythm of speech because of distortion and transposition of sounds in a rapid and dysrhythmic manner. While cluttering is thought to have a neurological basis, stuttering is usually considered to have multiple origins, the behavior being modified through various forms of learning.

Certain physical abnormalities, such as cleft palate, cerebral palsy, and hearing loss, produce speech characteristics in individuals that cannot be ascribed to any single category. These problems usually include abnormalities of articulation—resonance, phonation, prosody, and speech flow—and frequently include language impairment.

Glossary of Speech Disorders

A-—a syllable denoting the absense of a function; for example, *aphonia,* the complete loss of voice.

Acquired speech disorder—a speech disorder appearing after birth, such as *dysarthria* following accidental head injury.

Articulators—those organs that modify the voiced or unvoiced airstream into meaningful sounds; namely, the lower jaw, lips, teeth, tongue, and soft palate.

Cleft palate—congenital fissure of the soft palate, sometimes extending through the hard palate, gum ridge, and upper lip.

Congenital speech disorder—a speech disorder resulting from a condition present at birth, or as a result of a birth injury; for example, speech associated with cerebral palsy.

Dys-—a syllable denoting the partial loss of a function; for example, *dysphonia,* the partial loss of voice, as in the vocal condition of hoarseness.

Larynx—the organ of voice, within which the vocal folds (or cords) function in a vibratory manner to produce sound (phonation).

Lisp—defective production of sibilant sounds (*s, z, sh, ch*), common in childhood.

Palate—the roof of the mouth, including the anterior hard palate and the posterior soft palate.

Resonance—modification of the quality of a laryngeal tone as it passes through the throat, mouth and nasal cavities.

—Irv J. Meitus, *Purdue University*
See also Aphasia.

Consult (7) Berry and Eisenson, 1956; Perkins, 1971; Van Riper, 1972; West and Ansberry, 1968.

SPEED, colloquial name for the stimulant drug methamphetamine. *See* Drugs and Behavior.

SPINAL CORD. *See* Nervous System.

STABILITY OF INTELLIGENCE. *See* Constancy of the IQ.

STAGES OF SLEEP. *See* Sleep and Dreams.

STAMMERING. *See* Speech Disorders.

STANDARD DEVIATION. In a distribution of scores or observations, two descriptive measures are particularly significant: indices of central tendency and variability. Measures of central tendency (mean, median, mode) focus on a typical property or aspect of the distribution. Indices of variability, on the other hand, delineate the extent to which scores in the distribution vary. The standard deviation is the most widely used index of variability. It is used only with numerical data at the interval level of measurement, data for which means can be generated.

Basically, the standard deviation reveals the degree to which scores in a distribution are clustered around the mean. Thus, a distribution with a high standard deviation would consist of scores with a wide "spread" (a heterogeneous distribution) and a low standard deviation would describe scores that are less divergent (homogeneous distribution).

The standard deviation for a particular distribution is computed as follows:
1. A mean is generated: M
2. The difference between each score and that mean is figured: $X_i - M$
3. Each difference is squared: $(X_i - M)^2$
4. The differences are added up for the entire distribution: $\Sigma(X - M)^2$
5. The standard deviation (s) is computed by taking the square root of this value:

$$S = \sqrt{\frac{\sum_i (X_i - M)^2}{N}}$$

—Randolph S. Kraft, *Federation of the Handicapped, N.Y.*

STANDARDIZED TEST. *See* Measurement.

STANFORD-BINET SCALES. The predecessor of the scales currently known as the Stanford-Binet tests was the first individually administered intelligence test.

History. Devised by Alfred Binet and Theodore Simon in 1905, it was known as the Binet-Simon Scales. The French government had become concerned with the large number of failures in school and requested Binet to devise some means for identifying persons who could not adequately profit from school experiences.

To develop the original scale, which measured the individual's ability to name objects, complete sentences, and comprehend questions, Binet and Simon devised a number of items and applied them to children of different chronological ages (age since birth). One method they used was to administer each item to a large number of children. If a larger proportion of older children obtained the correct answers to an item than younger children, this was one of the criteria for placing that item at a particular chronological age level. Another criterion was that a majority of children of a specific grade level passed an item. This was based on the concept of mental growth, so as an individual grew in chronological age, there should also be growth in mental age.

Items on the Binet-Simon Scales were arranged in order of level of difficulty. Therefore, an individual who passed more difficult items than found at his chronological age level would have higher mental ability than the average person of his own chronological age. Conversely, if an individual was unable to pass items found at his age level, his mental ability would be less than that of the average person of that age group.

The original Binet-Simon Scales underwent revisions in 1908 and 1911. Translations of the scale were made in the United States, the most widely known by Lewis M. Terman at Stanford University in 1916. A major revision made in 1937 by Terman and M. A. Merrill and

called the Revised Stanford-Binet, used two forms (L and M). In 1960 the test was again revised, combining the best items from both forms.

Current Methods. The present Stanford-Binet tests measure intelligence from age two years through the adult level. There are basically six items at each age level; these measure, at different age levels, such factors as verbal memory, naming parts of the body, and reading. Each item passed by an individual yields two months of mental-age credit.

The individual's mental age is determined by first establishing a basic age—the lowest age level at which the person passes all items. All items from that age up are given to the person until a ceiling—the highest age level at which all items are failed—is reached. By giving mental age credit for all items passed and those below the basal age, a mental age can be calculated. The mental age of a person is his present level of mental functioning.

The Stanford-Binet test has the weakness that strong and weak areas within overall intelligence cannot be determined because items measuring the same factor are not grouped together.

—Louis Snellgrove, *Lambuth College*
See also Intelligence and Intelligence Testing.
Consult (12) Cronbach, 1970.

STATISTICS, the science concerned primarily with the analysis of empirical data. The work can also refer to the data itself or the characteristics of a sample, such as the sample mean and standard deviation.

Statistics and Scientific Method. The primary goal of statistics is to allow the researcher to proceed from knowledge derived from a sample to a statement concerning the entire population from which the sample was taken. This is the process of inference, drawing conclusions concerning the whole on the basis of a careful examination of the parts. It is basically the scientific method.

Statistics in the Social Sciences. Much of social science relies heavily on statistical techniques and methods. Because of its ability to separate the effects of systematic variation of a variable from the effects of chance variation, statistics allows the scientific method to be controlled in laboratory conditions. Moreover, statistics allows us to make exact statements of confidence concerning the characteristics of the population on the evidence supplied by the sample.

Hypothesis and Belief. We all formulate beliefs concerning the world on the basis of the evidence supplied by our senses. An important branch of statistics is concerned with the testing of these beliefs, called hypotheses, by confrontation with the facts. Suppose we are interested in reducing the crime rate. If we

INTERPRETATION OF STANFORD-BINET IQ	
140 & above	Very superior
120-139	Superior
110-119	High average
90-109	Average
84-89	Low average
68-83	Borderline retardation
52-67	Mild retardation
36-51	Moderate retardation
20-35	Severe retardation
below 20	Profound retardation

believe that increased police protection will reduce crime, we can test the hypothesis by hiring more police in some cities while maintaining existing levels in others. Suppose the mean crime rate in those cities with increased police protection drops by 10 percent in comparison with the other cities. Can this decrease be attributed to the expenditure on police or could it merely due to chance? Statistics has the power to answer such questions, questions that can have profound implications for society.

—Carlisle E. Moody, *College of William and Mary*

See also Correlation; Frequency Distribution; Mean; Median; Mode; Norm; Percentile; Sampling; Standard Deviation.

Consult (2) Blommers and Lindquist, 1960; Hays, 1965; McNemar, 1962.

STATUS, the standing or position of an individual or group of individuals in a social system. Status may be acquired by some fortuitous factor, such as birth or ethnic group, or through special achievement or significant contribution to the group.

The dimensions for the achievement of status vary from group to group, and it is possible to attain high status in one group and medium or low status in other groups within the same society. The individual often measures himself and others by the level of status he has attained. This evaluation may be based upon a society or a group within the society. Status in one group may be used in order to obtain higher status within some other group. A person who is very secure in his status may display reverse status symbols; for example, a very wealthy man may wear old clothes.

—A. Ronald Seifert, *University of Tennessee*

STEALING. *See* Kleptomania.

STEREOPSIS, seeing things in three dimensions. *See* Depth Perception; Vision.

STEREOTYPING, assigning characteristics or attributes to a person mainly on the basis of the group, class, or category to which he belongs. It has been noted that when minimum information is provided about a person, a perceiver tends to judge him according to previous knowledge about his ethnic group, class, or other category. Categorization of people is usually based on age, racial characteristics, religion, social class, profession, or political affiliation.

In each society certain attributes are attached to different groups, for example: professors are said to be idealistic; Americans, hard workers; English people, conventional; women, emotional; or Italians, passionate.

Stereotypes are based on generalization, so the judgment in any particular case may or may not be true. One obvious reason is that not all individuals in a given category necessarily possess all characteristics assigned to their group. Individual differences do exist between people in respect to their potentials, exposure to certain experiences, family structure, and hereditary factors regardless of their membership in any specific group.

—Ragaa Mazen, *Southern Connecticut State College*

See also Prejudice.

STEVENS, S(TANLEY) S(MITH) (1906–1973), American psychophysicist. Born in Ogden, Utah, he received his Ph.D. at Harvard (1933) where he remained as professor of psychology, director of the psychophysics laboratory, and director of the psychoacoustic labaoratory.

Stevens' law is a mathematical description of the relationship between stimulus intensity and sensory experience. Stevens developed techniques for scaling subjective experiences experimentally and used them to measure brightness, shock, visual length perception, cross-modality matching, and, in addition, complex stimulus dimensions, such as attitudes.

Stevens was editor of the *Handbook of Experimental Psychology,* 1951. Other works include *Hearing: Its Psychology and Physiology* (with H. Davis), 1938; *The Varieties of Human Physique* (with others), 1940; and *Sound and Hearing* (with F. Warshofsky), 1965.

—Nina Adams, *Yale University*

STIMULANTS, amphetamines, antidepressants, caffeine, and other drugs. *See* Drugs and Behavior.

STIMULUS, a physical or chemical agent acting on an appropriate sense receptor. Stimuli vary according to the sense stimulated (for example, visual, auditory), in intensity and duration, and in the area stimulated. A stimulus can also be any objectively describable situation or event that is the occasion for a response. Here stimulus acts as a signal, sign, or cue.

See also Conditioning; Sensation; Stimulus-Response Psychology.

STIMULUS-RESPONSE PSYCHOLOGY, a school of psychological thought that contends that specified responses always occur following stimulation. Stimulus-response psychology grew out of early studies of reflexive behavior and is still the primary doctrine of psychological thought in the Soviet Union. It views man basically as an input-output machine. Through learning or genetics, specific predictable responses become linked to specific external events.

STORAGE. *See* Brain Storage; Memory.

STRATEGIES. *See* Concept Learning.

STRATTON, GEORGE MALCOLM (1865–1957), American psychologist. Born in Oakland, Cal., he studied for his Ph.D. at Leipzig (1896).

Stratton is known for his classic study on perception. He fitted himself with lenses that inverted the visual field and reversed right and left, and wore them for several days. His self-observations indicated that the process of adaptation took several days and that readaptation was required after removal of the lenses. Stratton also did research on eye movements, esthetics, and social and political psychology. His major works include *Experimental Psychology and Its Bearing Upon Culture*, 1903; *Psychology of the Religious Life*, 1911; *Social Psychology of International Conduct*, 1929 and *Man, Creator or Destroyer*, 1952.

STRESS. When an individual is placed under great stress, he may find that he cannot continue to function normally. Most frequently the result of prolonged stress is a breakdown in the homeostatic mechanisms that normally keep the system working as a whole.

A variety of factors can produce stress. Infections, nervous strain, excessive heat and cold, and muscular fatigue are all stressors that the individual encounters in varying degrees in everyday life. Stress does not become a matter for concern until either the ability to cope with it is somehow impaired or until there is a sudden change in the amount of stress an individual is exposed to.

As the body tries to adapt to excessive stress, a number of physiological changes take place. These can be as disruptive as the stress itself. For example, the individual who is stressed by excessive worry or anxiety may develop headaches, ulcers, high blood pressure, or muscular ailments. Such ailments, generally referred to as *psychosomatic illnesses,* reflect actual organic disorders that are caused by the body's trying to cope with unusually high quantities of stress.

The relation between stress and psychosomatic disorder is not a simple one, however. A series of experiments by J. V. Brady and his colleagues has shown that when two animals are subjected to identical amounts and kinds of stress, one may develop severe ulceration of the stomach while the other develops no psychosomatic disorders. In Brady's experiments one monkey controlled the exposure of shock to himself and to the control animal, who simply received shocks without any control over the environment. It was the "executive monkey" that developed ulcers. Apparently making responses acted as an additional stressor and was involved with the need to make decisions. It is also interesting to note that the "executive monkeys" developed the most serious ulceration when they were not being

tested; periods of relative nonstress, such as weekends and holidays, were the most dangerous times for these animals.

Research with stress in humans has centered on observations of the autonomic nervous system's responses to the threat of stress. It has been found that individuals can learn to cope by being exposed to stressful stimuli in small doses or repeatedly. Sky divers for example, show evidence of extreme stress when they first learn the sport, but as they gain more experience, their stress reactions continue to decrease in intensity and tend to peak earlier and earlier in the jump sequence.

Research on how individuals differ in their responses to anticipated and actual stress will continue to shed light on how coping mechanisms develop. It may reveal why some people develop severe psychosomatic disorders while others are only minimally affected by stress. There is some evidence to indicate that early experience with stress and with learning to cope with mild stress may be integral to the development of adequate coping mechanisms in later life.

—Brenda B. Bankart and C. Peter Bankart, *Wabash College*

See also Anxiety; Overcrowding; Psychosomatic Disorders.

Consult (13) Brady, 1967; Goldstein and Palmer, 1963; LeShan, 1966; Selye, 1950; Selye, 1956.

STRIPED (STRIATED) MUSCLES. *See* Effectors.

STRUCTURE, surface and deep. *See* Language.

SUBLIMATION, a psychological process in which strongly conflicting unconscious impulses are transformed and expressed as socially desirable activities. Because the most direct form of need satisfaction is unattainable, the resulting frustration is met by obtaining satisfaction through socially acceptable substitutes. In this changed form they are permitted to become conscious without causing undue anxiety. Everyone makes use of sublimation to some extent. It is one of the most constructive of all defense mechanisms and is a central factor in the socialization of children in any culture.

A standard example of sublimation is found in the individual who, beset by hostile impulses, expresses his aggression in the form of literary, social, or intellectual criticism. This concept of sublimation has been attacked on several grounds. It is argued, for example, that the redirection of hostility may reduce tensions but does not remove the basic impulses.

—Michael Rothenberg, *The City College of The City University of New York*
See also Defense Mechanism.

SUBLIMINAL PERCEPTION, the ability to cor-

Stress

Stress

rectly guess at or respond to a stimulus even when one does not realize that it is present.

In experiments on subliminal perception, the stimuli are presented at low intensities and for short durations. Upon questioning, the subjects report that they did not see the stimuli, which are below the threshold of verbal recognition. However, if shock is paired with a subliminally presented nonsense syllable, subjects will show a galvanic skin response (GSR), indicating an emotional response, even without seeing the syllable. Seemingly guessing at random, subjects can distinguish above chance levels between numbers and letters. When presented with sexual versus neutral words at subliminal levels, subjects take longer to recognize the taboo words. Of course, every day we act without being able to verbalize what we have done. We encourage and discourage by means of sounds and movements we are not aware of making and are influenced, in turn, by cues presented to us.

In the mid-fifties a commercial firm claimed that subliminal presentation of the words "Eat Popcorn" and "Drink Coca-Cola" during a movie led to increased sales at the candy counter. This created a furor over commercial possibilities versus the ethics of mind control. Scientifically, this demonstration was never carefully presented or controlled, and the results are difficult to interpret. No demonstration of subliminal perception has yet shown that people can be influenced to do unusual or complicated behavior.

SUBSTITUTION, reacting to frustration or failure by shifting to attainable goals. This may be a constructive way to act—for example, if a young man cannot afford medical school he may scale down his plans and achieve a useful career as a lab technician. Substitution can also be a defense mechanism; for instances, *see* Displacement; Sublimation.

SUBVOCAL SPEECH, or internalized speech. *See* Language.

SUCCESSIVE APPROXIMATION, a form of operant (instrumental) conditioning, also called *shaping.* This technique is used to establish a desired response of specific form, force, or duration that does not exist in the organism's current repertoire.

At first, all responses similar to the desired response are reinforced. As these responses are brought closer together in time, only those essential to the goal are reinforced. Thus, all the nonessential responses are progressively eliminated, leaving only those that, when combined over time, more and more resemble the desired response.

—A. Ronald Seifert, *University of Tennessee*

See also Instrumental Conditioning.

SUGGESTION, the process of inducing someone to believe something or do something without using direct argument, command, or force. Suggestion is a major device of advertisers. Instead of describing the qualities of a product, they say that professional athletes use it—linking the product to the prestige of the pro. Advertisers also use the "everybody's-doing-it" theme, assuming people will conform to what they see as a social norm. Politicans hope that a bandwagon effect will get them elected.

The term suggestion is also used in describing procedures in hypnosis. *Autosuggestion* simply means using suggestion on oneself. The term applies particularly to a system of self-treatment of self-improvement popularized by a Frenchman, Emile Coué (1857–1926), and described in *Self Mastery Through Conscious Autosuggestion* (1922). Coué told his patients to repeat twenty or thirty times daily the sentence "Every day in every way I am getting better and better." A degree of self-hypnosis was involved in this routine.

Self-encouragement can be helpful, but a person with serious problems will probably need the help of a therapist in working to a new adjustment.

SUICIDE. Suicide is the human act of self-inflicted, self-intentioned cessation. Self-killing is one of the ten leading causes of death in the United States. According to official statistics, about 22,000 Americans kill themselves each year. Experts believe that the actual number is greater—perhaps more than 40,000 a year.

Who Commits Suicide? Social scientists have made many studies of suicide statistics, sometimes concluding that certain groups are more suicide-prone than others. Official records show that some countries (Hungary, Austria, West Germany, and Finland, for example) have higher suicide rates than the United States, while many other countries report lower rates (Italy and Ireland, for example). Within the United States, some significant differences in group rates have been noted. More men than women take their own lives (the ratio is three to one). Among United States college students suicide is the third ranking cause of death, following accidents and cancer.

Statistical analyses of suicide, however, have serious limitations. Some countries do not keep as careful death records as others. In any country, distinctions between accidental death and intentional self-killing are often hard to make. For example, one study of automobile killings in the United States concluded that as many as 8,000 "accidental deaths" in a year were, in fact, suicides. The fact seems to be that all kinds of humans—regardless of sex, race, religion, or economic status—are capable of committing suicide.

FACTS AND FABLES ON SUICIDE*

FABLE: People who talk about suicide don't commit suicide.

FACT: Of any ten persons who kill themselves, eight have given definite warnings of their suicidal intentions.

FABLE: Suicide happens without warning.

FACT: Studies reveal that the suicidal person gives many clues and warnings regarding his suicidal intentions.

FABLE: Suicidal people are fully intent on dying.

FACT: Most suicidal people are undecided about living or dying, and they "gamble with death," leaving it to others to save them. Almost no one commits suicide without letting others know how he is feeling.

FABLE: Once a person is suicidal, he is suicidal forever.

FACT: Individuals who wish to kill themselves are "suicidal" for only a limited period of time.

FABLE: Improvement following a suicidal crisis means that the suicidal risk is over.

FACT: Most suicides occur within about three months following the beginning of "improvement," when the individual has the energy to put his morbid thoughts and feelings into effect.

FABLE: Suicide strikes much more often among the rich—or, conversely, it occurs almost exclusively among the poor.

FACT: Suicide is neither the rich man's disease nor the poor man's curse. Suicide is very "democratic" and is represented proportionately among all levels of society.

FABLE: Suicide is inherited or "runs in the family."

FACT: Suicide does not run in families. It is an individual pattern.

FABLE: All suicidal individuals are mentally ill, and suicide always is the act of a psychotic person.

FACT: Studies of hundreds of genuine suicide notes indicate that although the suicidal person is extremely unhappy, he is not necessarily mentally ill.

*From *Some Facts about Suicide* by E. S. Shneidman and N. L. Farberow, Washington, D. C., PHS Publication No. 852, U. S. Government Printing Office, 1961.

A boy threatening suicide.

A related point is that suicide is not really a one-person event. The whole society is affected. A person who kills himself or herself may do so because of some acute problem with another person, such as a spouse or lover. Moreover, despite the argument that "It is *my* business, *my* life to do what I want with," others are deeply involved by a suicide. More important, the survivors may need help ranging from child support to mental health care.

Suicidologists—psychologists and others who specialize in the study of suicide—are interested in statistics but more concerned with why people take their lives (or try to) and with what can be done to prevent their actions.

Why Do People Want to Die? No one has found a neat set of answers to this question, but several important theories have been proposed. The nineteenth-century French sociologist Emile Durkheim believed that the causes of suicide could be found in man's relationships to his society—specifically, in the degree of strength of society's control. Society can demand what Durkheim called the "altruistic" suicide. In Japan, for example, hara-kiri was an honorable death, demanded in certain circumstances by the feudal code. The individual felt he had no choice but to take the proper way out. [*Consult* (13) Durkheim, 1897.]

A second category Durkheim called "egoistic" suicides. In this case, the individual is in trouble because he does not feel bound to his community. Even though the group wants him to live, he does not care. This situation may explain why those who are divorced or widowed or otherwise feel alone kill themselves more often than those who have strong ties to a group such as a family or a church.

Durkheim called a third class of reasons "anomic." Death may seem a way out when a person suddenly loses a job, a lot of money, or a close friend. The abrupt shattering of the familiar relationship with society leads to suicide.

While Durkheim focused on problems between the individual and society, Sigmund Freud sought explanations of suicide within the self. Many psychoanalysts have viewed suicide as an impulse to murder turned against the self. For example, a man who dressed himself in his wife's clothing and hung himself might have been hanging his mother (and wife) in effigy. He may also have been punishing himself for what he considered his own guilts and failures.

Other psychodynamic explanations agree that hostility is a major force behind suicide, but they hold that the general human condition in Western civilization contributes to the problem. People in this society often seem to be unable to cope with hostility, to get close to others, to give and accept love. Feelings of being alone, helpless, and hopeless—driven to run, but not knowing where to run—can push people to suicide. [*Consult* (13) Litman, 1967.]

One important fact about the psychodynamics of suicide is that people are typically ambivalent: at the same time, they want and don't want. A man can say "I am eager to die" and yet be of several minds about actually pulling a trigger, wishing also be be rescued. A woman may take a dangerous dose of sleeping pills and immediately telephone for help. In the United States, 200,000 or more people try suicide each year. There are nearly ten who try for each one who dies, and it is hard in some cases to judge how serious the attempt was. However, suicidologists believe that all attempted self-killings should get serious attention and should never be dismissed as mere bids for sympathy.

Although some may threaten or try suicide and survive, others may in fact commit suicide without consciously planning it. As already noted, hundreds of automobile "accidents" may be suicidal. Such events are called *subintentional* deaths. A *psychological autopsy* is proposed in cases where it is difficult to distinguish an accidental death from a suicidal one. In such an investigation, social and behavioral scientists study the dead person's situation and recent acts for diagnostic clues. Did the person, for example, talk about "going away," act depressed, give away cherished belongings? [*Consult* (13) Litman, *et al.*, 1963; Shneidman, 1969.]

How Can Suicides Be Prevented? Psychologists and other concerned professionals feel that attempted suicides or threats of suicide should be seriously regarded as cries for help. Completed suicides may mean that no one heard or paid attention to the pleas for aid. To help those who feel in danger of being inundated by problems, services have been established throughout the United States. A major focus was provided in 1966 when the federal government established the Center for Studies of Suicide Prevention as part of the National Institute of Mental Health.

The first full-scale, professionally staffed center was established in Los Angeles in 1958. The staff includes psychologists, psychiatrists, and social workers. In addition, lay volunteers respond to telephone calls twenty-four hours a day. A man or woman who is in fear of suicide can call and talk to a trained person, who will ask about the caller's trouble and try to assess how acute the danger is. Often just having someone sympathetic to talk to will get a person through a crisis. Then the center can get the caller to come in for a talk with a psychiatrist, psychologist, or social worker. The staff will also try to see the others involved, friends and family members. If the danger of suicide is judged to be acute, the center may suggest that the caller be referred to a hospital for further evaluation and treatment. By 1970 there were more than 200 centers for "crisis intervention" with people contemplating suicide. [*Consult* (13) Shneidman and Mandelkorn, 1967.]

—Edwin S. Shneidman, *University of California, Los Angeles*

Consult (13) Alvarez, 1971; Choron, 1972; Dublin, 1963; Farberow, 1969; Farberow and Shneidman, 1961; Feifel, 1961; Menninger, 1938; Shneidman and Farberow, 1957; Shneidman, 1967; Shneidman, 1969; Shneidman, *et al.,* 1970; Stengel, 1964; US Department of Health, Education, and Welfare, 1970; World Health Organization, 1968.

SULLIVAN, HARRY STACK (1892–1949), American psychiatrist, born in Norwich, New York.

Sullivan is known for his theory of personality development and his concept of therapy. Using a neoanalytic approach, Sullivan based his theory on the concept that development occurs through a series of interpersonal situations from infancy to adulthood. Satisfying relations produce a secure feeling, anxious ones produce insecurity. Instead of accepting Freud's description of development in biological and psychosexual terms, Sullivan added and emphasized social patterns, particularly the key interpersonal relations with both real and imaginary people (for example, idealized characters such as dream girls). He identified the unit of personality as the "dynamism"—a habitual reaction toward other people; examples are obsessionalism, hypochondria, and paranoid feelings. Dynamisms are needed to protect a person from anxiety when he has not been successful in his interpersonal relationships. Sullivan identified the way people carry on their relationships as self-dynamism; the goal of self-dynamism is self-esteem and security. Mental illness results when misconceptions of both the self and others dominate an individual's life.

Sullivan's theory of interpersonal relations can also apply to his concept of therapy. Once he can identify with the patient's anxiety, he can identify what went wrong during the developmental periods of the patient's life and discuss these findings with the patient.

His publications include *Psychiatry: Introduction to the Study of Interpersonal Relations* (1948).

SUPEREGO, a major feature of the psychoanalytic theory of personality structure—namely, the hypothetical agency responsible for self-imposed standards of conduct and morality and the source of feelings of self-approval or guilt and remorse.

Freud foreshadowed the concept in *Mourning and Melancholia* (1917), where he suggested that a self-critical and punitive part of the personality in depressed patients had been formed by identification with and internalization of former ambivalent love objects.

But it was not until 1923, in the *Ego and the Id,* that Freud clearly proposed the superego as one of the three major elements of his structural model of personality. The superego is the internal representative of the values and ideals of the society, in contrast to the id, which represents instinctual urges, and the ego, which represents realistic adaptation. As the moral aspect of the personality, the superego demands goodness rather than pleasurable gratification and represents the ideal rather than the actual.

Freud held that the superego developed in response to parental punishments and rewards. Transgression of this internalized code is felt, consciously or unconsciously, to require punishment according to a pattern of guilt and atonement. The child thus incorporates or introjects the image and commands of the all-important parents, in both their approving and their punishing aspects, as a powerful and enduring part of his personality.

While Freud's theories emphasized the early childhood years and basic identification with parents in superego formation, many psychologists (for example, Jean Piaget and Lawrence Kohlberg) have also studied the considerable importance of later experience and cognitive growth to the acquisition and modification of conscience and morality.

—Alden E. Wessman, *The City College of The City University of New York*

See also Ego; Id; Psychoanalysis.

Consult (13) Fenichel, 1945; Freud, 1927; Freud, 1949.

SUPPRESSION, a *conscious* attempt to avoid unwanted thoughts or inhibit undesirable actions. The child is taught "not to think about it" or "to check that impulse." If social, familial, or personal restrictions are sufficiently severe, suppression may eventually become *repression,* the *unconscious* rejection of thoughts or actions.

See also Repression.

SYMBOLIZATION, in psychoanalytic theory the disguised representation of unconscious thoughts or feelings. Freud believed that dreams are full of symbols that can give clues to repressed impulses. For example, a boy's dream of walking upstairs to meet his mother could be a symbolic expression of incestuous wishes that he could not express directly. While dreaming and while awake, people interpret many objects as phallic symbols—posts, pipes, and snakes, for example.

Symbolization is also considered a factor in phobias and in disorders, such as kleptomania and pyromania.

Consult (3) Foulkes, 1966. (13) Hall, 1954.

SYMBOLS, in thinking and language. *See* Meaning.

SYNAPSE

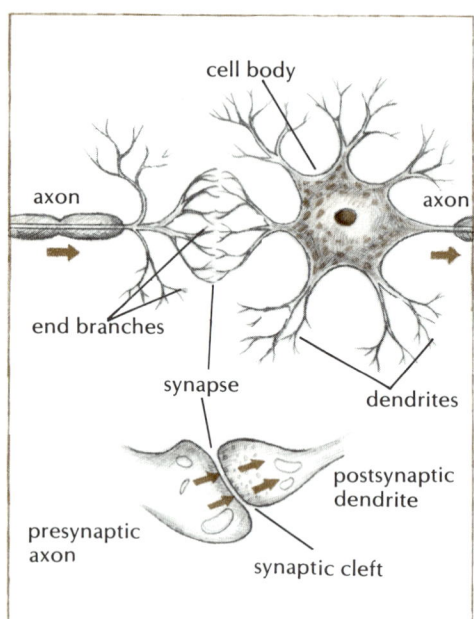

The upper drawing shows the cell body, axon, and dendrites of a typical neuron. Below it is shown the synapse, the junction between the axon of one neuron and the dendrite of another.

TASTE

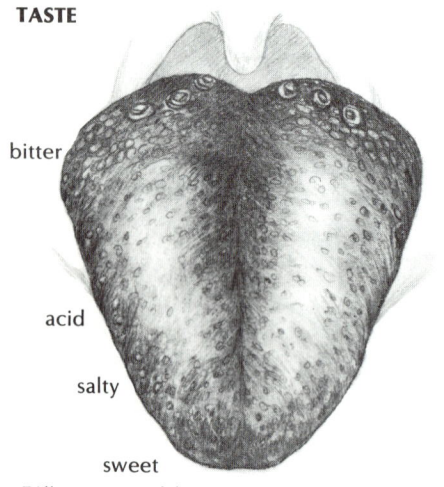

Different parts of the tongue are primarily sensitive to different sensations: sweet, salty, bitter, and sour, or acid.

SYMPATHETIC NERVOUS SYSTEM. *See* Autonomic Nervous System; Nervous System.

SYMPATHY. *See* Empathy.

SYMPTOM, a bit of behavior that indicates the existence of a physical or psychological disorder. Careful diagnosis is based on a pattern of symptoms, or *syndrome,* rather than on a single manifestation. *See the discussion of symptoms in* Psychoneurotic Disorders, Psychotic Disorders, *and related articles.*

SYNAPSE, the electrical or chemical junction between two neurons. Most synapses are chemical: they consist of the termination of axon end buttons upon either dendrites or cell bodies. There is no direct physical contact in the synapse, but a small synaptic cleft of about 200 Angstrom units between the presynaptic axon and the postsynaptic cell body or dendrite. The neurotransmitter is released from the presynaptic side, diffuses across the synaptic cleft, and produces excitation on the postsynaptic side of the membrane. In some cases axo-axonic synapses have been found. These play an important role in inhibition in the nervous system.

In addition to chemical synapses, a few electrical synapses have been found, particularly in the outer layers of the cortex. Here electrical excitation is transmitted directly from cell to cell through a process known as *ephaptic transmission.* Electrical synapses play a more dominant role in the invertebrate nervous system.

—Joel F. Lubar, *University of Tennessee*
See also Neuron.
Consult (3) Isaacson, *et al.,* 1971.

SYNESTHESIA, regular linking of the perception of a certain sensation with images from another sensory modality, producing a subjective sensation of a sense other than the one being stimulated. Some people experience synesthesia regularly. The most common form is "colored hearing" (chromesthesia), where certain sounds evoke images of colors.

SYNTAX. *See* Language.

SYPHILIS, as a cause of brain disorder. *See* General Paresis.

SYSTEMATIC DESENSITIZATION, a method of treatment for mental disorders. *See* Phobia; Psychoneurotic Disorders.

SZASZ, THOMAS STEPHEN, (1920–   ), American psychiatrist. Born in Budapest, Hungary, he studied for his M.D. at the University of Cincinnati (1944). He has been professor of psychiatry at the State University of New York at Syracuse since 1956. Szasz is chairman of the board and founder of the American Association for the Abolition of Involuntary Mental Hospitalization.

Szasz has been concerned with the ethical, political, and social aspects of the practice of psychiatry. He has written about the doctor-patient relationship and about his approach to psychiatric problems as "problems in living"—biological, economic, political and sociological, as well as psychological. His writings include *Pain and Pleasure,* 1957; *The Myth of Mental Illness,* 1961; *Law, Liberty and Psychiatry,* 1963; *The Ethics of Psychoanalysis,* 1965; *Psychiatric Justice,* 1965; *Ideology and Insanity,* 1970; and *The Manufacture of Madness,* 1970.
—Nina Adams, *Yale University*

TACHISTOSCOPE, an instrument used to present words or other visual stimuli for short periods of time by limiting the duration of the exposure. Highly sophisticated electronic devices have been manufactured for the purpose. Often however, a tachistoscope consists merely of a sheet of paper wound around a revolving cylinder with an opening in front through which the words passing by are exposed.

TALENTED. *See* Genius; Gifted Children.

TANTRUM BEHAVIOR. *See* Temper Tantrums.

TASTE, the detection of certain chemical substances, in solution, by the receptors on the tongue, larynx, and pharynx. Experiments have shown that taste is a mixture of four specific responses: to salt, to sweet, to sour, and to bitter. The different parts of the tongue are primarily sensitive to one of the four different sensations: the front of the tongue to salt, the middle-front to sweet, the back to bitter, and the sides to sour. Because the taste buds are replenished every seven days, a burned tongue is only a temporary problem.

Man's tongue contains approximately 10,000 taste buds, with ten to fifteen sensory cells within each bud. These cells send out hairlike projections, through pores, to the tongue's surface. Around the sensory cells are wrapped endings of sensory nerves, which carry information from the sensory cell to the brain.

The taste of a fresh, cold apple, however, is much more than a simple response to salt, sweet, sour, and bitter. It also includes responses to the pressure of the bite, the texture and coolness of the fruit, and, most important, its odor. Anyone whose nose is stuffed up by a cold knows the strong contribution of smell to taste.

Taste can be traced back to primitive organisms. Fish have taste buds all over their bodies. Man's taste buds are confined to to the mouth because they must be kept moist and will only respond to chemicals when they are in solution.

—Nina Adams, *Yale University*

See also Sensation.

Consult (4) Geldard, 1971.

TAXIS, the postural or spatial orientation of organisms with reference to some point source or gradient of stimulation. Orientations directed toward the stimulus are termed positive, while those turned away are negative. Taxes encompass a broad range of behavior. They can be classified by stimulus, including phototaxis (light), thermotaxis (heat), geotaxis (gravity), and rheotaxis (water current, wind). Other classifications are based on the presumed mechanisms used by the species involved— usually invertebrates.

—Gordon M. Burghardt, *University of Tennessee*

Consult (3) Fraenkel and Gunn, 1961; Jander, 1963.

TEACHING MACHINE. *See* Programmed Instruction.

TELEKINESIS, physical changes not caused by normal means. These are usually associated with spiritualistic seances, held in darkness, that are said to produce raps (perhaps spelling messages), movement of tables, ectoplasm, and other phenomena. Careful observation, aided by infrared photography, has uncovered so many frauds among such claims that the technical term used to label them, "telekinesis," is in disrepute.

See also Parapsychology.

TELEPATHY (one form of extrasensory perception, or ESP), a direct response to someone else's mental activity. Anecdotes frequently report it, as when someone "knows" who is calling when the telephone rings or when a mother "knows" of injury to her child or when friends say the same thing at the same time. But such cases cannot prove telepathy: perhaps some word triggered the same association in both friends, or the mother habitually feared accidents.

Even in the laboratory, telepathy is hard to identify. If an "agent" tries to send telepathic messages about random targets, scores higher than chance may be clairvoyant responses to the targets instead of telepathic responses to the messages. However, some experiments circumvented this difficulty by having the agent use a private code to translate random digits into symbols. Subjects guessed the symbols (which existed only in the agent's consciousness). Extrachance results gave good evidence for telepathy.

Other research, which did not exclude clairvoyance, found significantly higher ESP scores when "agent" and subject were engaged or married than when they were strangers and also when they were congenial than when they were reserved or hostile. This is consistent with anecdotal evidence about conditions for successful telepathy.

—Gertrude R. Schmeidler, *The City College of The City University of New York*

See also Extrasensory Perception; Parapsychology.

Consult (14) McMahan, 1946; Rice and Townsend, 1962; Schmeidler, 1961.

TELEVISION EFFECTS ON CHILDREN. Most television research has been focused on violence, partly because American commercial television is saturated with violence. Children's cartoons have an average of twenty-five violent acts per hour. Eighty percent of all prime time programs contain at least one violent incident with about eight per hour. Violent and illegal actions are often presented as approved and highly successful ways of coping with conflicts and frustrations. [*Consult* (11) Gerbner, 1972.]

Research on the effects of observing violence consistently shows increased aggressive behavior among children from preschool through adolescent years. Long-term effects of childhood viewing are suggested by one study in which the aggressive behavior of eighteen-year-olds was predicted by their exposure to television violence at age eight. Other behaviors affected include reduced self-control, lowered tolerance for minor frustrations, and increased anxiety. However, extensive investigations failed to find any effects on dream content or anxiety in dreams. [*Consult* (11) Foulkes, *et al.*, 1972; Lefkowitz, *et al.*, 1972; Siegel, 1956; Stein and Friedrich, 1972.]

The impact of televised violence depends on the context in which it occurs. In experimental studies, imitation of aggression is enhanced when the model is rewarded or when he has laudable motives. In one study of children from four through eighteen, there was an increase with age in understanding the consequences and motives portrayed in actual programs, but aggression increased regardless of motives or consequences. There is some evidence that aggression is more likely if children believe televised violence is real rather than fictional, but cartoons are as effective as other fictional presentations despite their obvious unreality. [*Consult* (11) Feshbach, 1972; Leifer and Roberts, 1972.]

The effects of television violence occur across ages, genders, social classes, ethnic groups, and intelligence levels. Nevertheless, certain types of children are especially likely to react aggressively: those with relatively high

TASTE

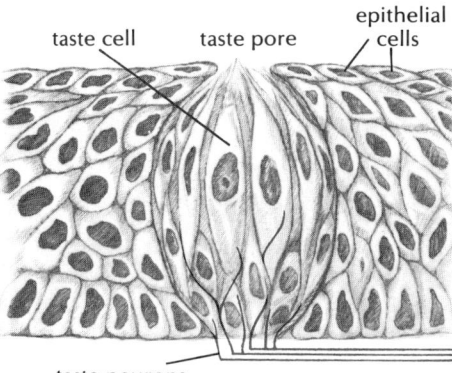

A single taste bud consists of a cluster of ten to fifteen sensory taste cells embedded in the epithelium of the tongue. Sensory nerve endings wrapped around the taste cells carry information to the brain.

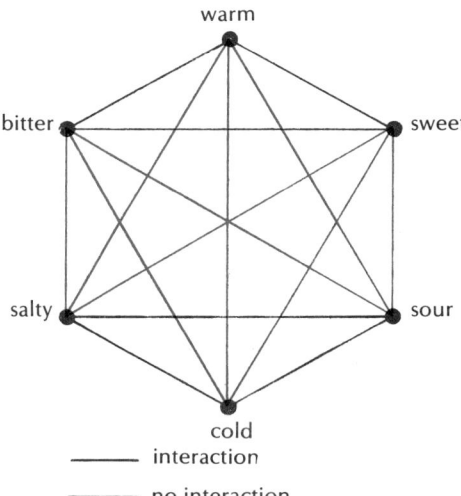

An interesting experiment involves stimulating both sides of the tongue at the same time with different stimuli to determine when two sensations appear to fuse at the middle of the tongue (interaction) and when they remain distinct (no interaction).

Aimed at children between the ages of three and five, "Sesame Street" has demonstrated that appropriate television programming can have positive effects on social and cognitive development.

TEMPORAL LOBE

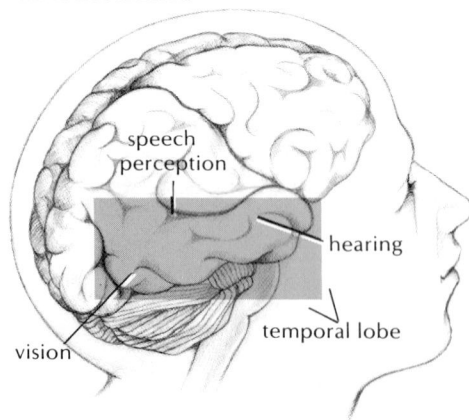

prior levels of aggression and those whose families do not convey strong alternative values.

The effects of advertising on very young children has also been studied. Children below age seven do not understand the purpose of commercials, do not separate commercials from reality, and are confused about the trustworthiness of advertisements. By age nine, children are distrustful of the claims made, they distinguish commercials from reality, and understand their sales purpose. Mothers report frequent pressures from their children to buy the products they see advertised. [*Consult* (11) Ward, 1972.]

Programs designed to promote cognitive and social development also have some effects. Preschool children who watch "Sesame Street" learn such skills as letter recognition and concept formation. Evaluations of "Misterogers' Neighborhood," which emphasizes social and emotional development, have shown improved interpersonal relations among children, improved task persistence, and increased self control. Other research suggests that, with appropriate programming, television has the potential to help children become altruistic, overcome fears, and learn achievement standards. [*Consult* (11) Ball and Bogatz, 1970; Bandura, 1969; Hoffman, 1970; Stein and Freidrich, 1972.]

—Aletha Huston Stein, *Pennsylvania State University*

Consult (11) Rubenstein, *et al.,* 1972; Surgeon General's Scientific Advisory Committee on Television and Social Behavior, 1971.

TEMPER TANTRUMS, short-lived, violent outbursts of behavior displayed by most, if not all, preschool children. The incidence is highest in the second year of life and decreases in frequency and intensity from two to five years of age, but 3 percent of eleven-year-olds still have tantrums once weekly. Tantrums are twice as common in boys and occur more frequently in children who are emotionally disturbed or highly irritable or who have low tolerance for frustration. However, most children with tantrums are psychiatrically normal.

It is important to remember that tantrums may indicate physical illness in the young child. When they are part of a general psychiatric disturbance, their management is part of the treatment of that disturbance. The usual tantrum in psychiatrically normal children is best evaluated by considering severity, frequency, situations where shown, precipitants, and ameliorating factors. Once tantrums are charted in this fashion, behavior modification programs of an operant type can be designed to eliminate them. It is important to protect a child from harming himself or others during a tantrum. However, nothing can usu-

ally be done to eliminate the tantrum while it is occurring.

—Dennis P. Cantwell, M.D., *University of California, Los Angeles*

TEMPERAMENT, an aspect of personality believed to involve genetic predispositions toward certain types of emotional reactions and levels of sensitivity. Research with newborn infants strongly suggests that differences in temperament appear at the earliest stages of development. Thus some infants will cry considerably more than others, some will show a much higher general activity level, and some will be more placid. Other studies have shown consistent differences in such factors as response to loud noises, sensitivity to light, and pain threshhold.

Although these tendencies are rather crude and undifferentiated at birth, they provide the framework within which adult personality develops. The irritable, overreactive baby is more likely to develop into an anxious, troubled adult. However, temperament can be modified somewhat, either positively or negatively, by an individual's experiences as he is maturing.

—Michael Rothenberg, *The City College of The City University of New York*

TEMPERATURE SENSE. Temperature sensibility is composed of two distinct qualities, warm and cold. Spots sensitive to either warm or cold are distributed over the surface of the skin. There are more cold spots than warm spots and many more spots on the hands and face than anywhere else on the body.

The nerve fibers from these receptive spots are very specific. Discharge of a nerve from a cold spot always produces the sensation of cold, whether it is activated by a cold stimulus or an electrical impulse. In fact, if a cold spot is stimulated with a very hot probe (45° C.) the sensation of cold is perceived. This phenomenon, called *paradoxical cold,* is probably due to discharge of cold nerve fibers during injury. The sensation of hot is due to a combined sensation of pain plus cold.

The temperature senses respond to extremely tiny shifts in temperature but not to slow gradual changes, even when they are very large.

—Nina Adams, *Yale University* *See also* Sensation.

TEMPORAL LOBES, prominent structures found in primates, including man, located on the lateral surface of the brain. Each temporal lobe is partially separated from the frontal and parietal lobes by a band of tissue known as the operculum. The lateral surface of the lobe contains important regions for the processing of auditory and visual information. It also contains deep structures, such as the *hippo-campal formation* and underlying *amygdaloid complex*, which play an important role in memory function and emotionality, respectively. Removal of the temporal lobes often results in profound memory deficits.

—Joel F. Lubar, *University of Tennessee*
See also Brain.

TENSION. An extension of the physiological designation of the strain maintained by muscular contraction, this term is often used to refer to an experience of anxiety, discomfort, and restlessness. The relationship is direct, since bodily and emotional changes occur concomitantly.

In psychological theory, "tension" may refer to psychological conflict or to distance between motive and goal.

See also Anxiety; Conflict (within the person).

TERMAN, LEWIS MADISON (1877–1956), American psychologist, born in Johnson County, Indiana. A professor of psychology at Stanford (1910–1942), he published the first widely used individual intelligence test in the United States.

Terman is best known for his work in intelligence testing and his studies of gifted children. In 1916 he revised the Binet-Simon scale for use in the United States, where it gained wide acceptance. He was the first researcher to consistently use an index of brightness (IQ), which was suggested by the German psychologist William Stern. This figure is established by multiplying the ratio of the mental age to the chronological age by 100.

Terman is also well known for his studies of highly intelligent persons. In 1921 he and his associates began their research on 1,500 children with a minimum intelligence quotient of 140, and several later investigations of the group have been made. One of the major contributions of this study has been to disprove many misconceptions about highly intelligent individuals. For example, it was found that the gifted tend to be healthier and better adjusted and to have lower divorce rates than the population in general.

Terman's major publications include *The Measurement of Intelligence,* 1916; *Genetic Studies of Genius,* 1925, (coauthor); and *The Gifted Child Grows Up,* 1947, (coauthor).

—Louis Snellgrove, *Lambuth College*
See also Gifted Children; Stanford-Binet Scales.

TERRITORIALITY. *See* Aggression.

TESTING. *See* Measurement.

T-GROUP. *See* Sensitivity Training.

THALAMUS, a part of the brain located in the diencephalon (interbrain) and consisting of groups of important nuclei and fiber tracts. The thalamus acts to some extent as a huge relay network for conveying sensory information to the appropriate portions of the cortex and for channeling motor information from the motor cortex to the appropriate portions of the spinal cord. The thalamus contains more than thirty thalamic nuclei, including the *lateral geniculate* for visual processing, the *ventrobasal complex* for the somesthetic (movement, temperature, touch, pain) system, and the *medial geniculate body* for audition. Some nuclei relay information to the cerebellum. Other thalamic nuclei lying along the midline are part of the reticular formation of the brain and play an important role in sleep and wakefulness.

—Joel F. Lubar, *University of Tennessee*
See also Brain.
Consult (3) Isaacson, *et al.,* 1971.

THANATOLOGY. Physicians and psychologists have recently taken a new interest in the circumstances surrounding death. They investigate, for example, how the dying feel about what is happening and how doctors, nurses, and family members react. The traditional practice has been to "keep the bad news" from patients who are soon to die. Some may want to cling to the hope that they will miraculously recover, but a mortally ill person is likely to guess that he has not long to live, and the kindest course may be to talk frankly with him about what is going to happen. Many old and ill people reach a stage of resignation—they give up hope and wait for the end. Talking with them may help them to accept the reality of dying and live out their last days more cheerfully.

It has also been a custom to leave aged and dying people pretty much alone. Even if they can no longer talk, however, they may want company and comfort.

Consult (13). Kubler-Ross, 1970.

THANATOS, Freudian theory. *See* Death Instinct.

THEMATIC APPERCEPTION TEST (TAT) a projective technique widely used in personality assessment and as a standard part of diagnostic psychological test batteries. In the words of Henry A. Murray, who developed the test, "Special value resides in its power to expose the underlying inhibited tendencies which the subject, or patient, is not willing to admit, or cannot admit because he is unconscious of them." Furthermore, the TAT has been extensively used and adapted for research purposes.

The TAT consists of nineteen cards showing pictures and one blank card. The subject is required to make up a story about

THALAMUS

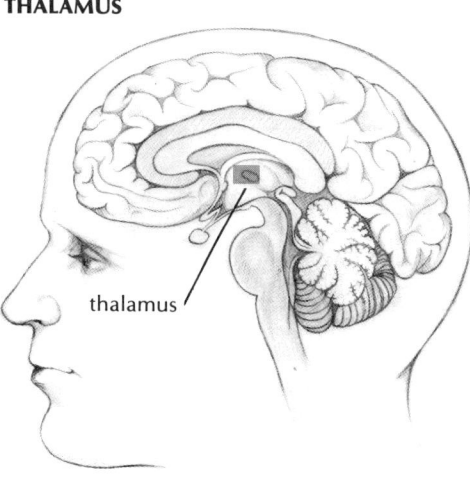

thalamus

American Lewis Terman is noted for developing new intelligence testing and scoring techniques.

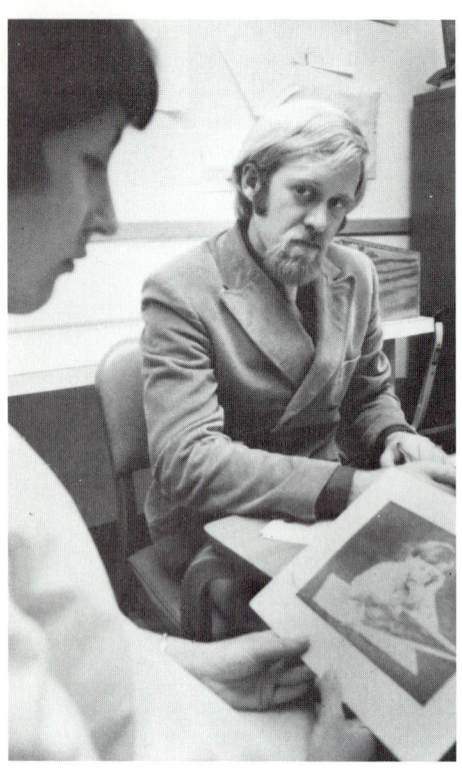

Administering the Thematic Apperception Test (TAT). The card has been altered but is similar to those used.

American psychologist-educator Edward Lee Thorndike's findings on how lab animals select appropriate responses to given stimuli by trial and error became a keystone of subsequent learning theory.

each card, describing what is happening, what led up to the situation, what the outcome will be, and what the characters are thinking and feeling. With the blank card, the subject must first imagine a picture and then make up the story.

As originally proposed by Murray, administration of the complete set of pictures was suggested. However, most examiners currently use an abbreviated selection of about ten cards. These are chosen on the basis of relevance for the subject at hand and recommendations of TAT specialists such as Bellak and Henry.

Interpretive methods vary widely, from fairly subjective analyses of content to more formal systems, such as Bellak's Analysis Sheet. All methods assume that subjects project their own feelings, needs, and problems into the depicted situations. Thus, story themes, roles, and character relationships indirectly reveal key personality dynamics of the testee.

—Randolph S. Kraft, *Federation of the Handicapped, N.Y.*

Consult (12) Atkinson, 1958; Bellak, 1954; Henry, 1956; Murray, 1943.

THERAPY. The treatment of mental disorders is discussed in Psychoneurotic Disorders, Psychotic Disorders, Psychotherapy, and related articles. *See* the Subject Map for Abnormal and Clinical Psychology.

THINKING, behavior from which it can be inferred that an individual is employing symbolic representations of events and objects and manipulating ideas, images, or concepts. Thinking is implicit in that it cannot be observed directly but must be inferred from its products—knowledge, remembering, skills, abilities, intentions, and so on.

The word "thinking" is vague and commonly refers to either of two broad classes of symbolic activity: (1) *Associative or nondirected thinking,* where the flow of symbolic activity is not controlled or manipulated for an explicit purpose, includes daydreaming, free association, autistic thinking, and the like. (2) *Directed thinking,* the phenomenon that most psychologists identify and study as "thinking," includes the following topics, which are discussed in separate articles: Concept Learning; Creativity; Language; Meaning; Problem Solving; Verbal Learning. *Other articles are listed in the Item Guide under* Thinking and Communication.

—Roland Siiter, *Montclair State College*

THIRST DRIVE. The need to satisfy thirst, which is basic to the survival of the organism, is, like hunger, a complex phenomenon. It depends upon dryness or dehydration of tissues, particularly in the oral cavity, the volume of blood circulating through the body, and the tonicity of bodily fluids (that is, the amount of salt and solids concentrated in them).

Brain mechanisms for the control of thirst include the function of regions in the hypothalamus and in particular osmoreceptors that are sensitive to the tonicity of the blood. When an organism becomes dehydrated through sweating or urination, the osmoreceptors send signals to appropriate hypothalamic regions, which release antidiuretic hormone (ADH). ADH acts at the kidney to conserve water through decreased urinary output, so that the body reestablishes normal water balance.

—Joel F. Lubar, *University of Tennessee*

THOMAS, WILLIAM ISAAC (1863-1947), American social scientist, born in Virginia. He was a teacher of sociology at the University of Chicago, 1894-1918.

Thomas was a pioneer in social psychology. One of his contributions was to insist on scientifically oriented research procedures. Many of his studies were concerned with the interrelationships of the individual and his environment. He believed that patterns of behavior can be analyzed into four constituents, called the "four wishes": for security, recognition, new experience, and mastery or response.

His major works are *Source Book of Social Origins,* 1909; *The Polish Peasant in Europe and America* (with Florian Znaniecki), 5 vols., 1918-1921; *The Unadjusted Girl,* 1923; *Primitive Behavior* (revision of *Source Book of Social Origins),* 1937; and *Social Behavior and Personality,* 1951.

THORNDIKE, EDWARD LEE (1874-1949), American psychologist and educator. Born in Williamsburg, Mass. he studied under William James at Harvard and taught psychology at Teachers College, Columbia, for forty years.

Thorndike developed the first integrated learning theory, which has profoundly influenced the course of learning theory throughout the twentieth century. In addition, he pioneered in the application of psychological principles to such fields as teaching reading, language development, and mental testing. He was one of the first researchers to do laboratory experiments with animals and to attempt to generalize his findings into a theory of human learning. On the basis of his work with cats in puzzle boxes, he described trial-and-error as a basic type of learning. Trial-and-error learning involves the association of one or more responses to a particular stimulus complex. No new responses are learned; rather an appropriate response is selected from an already existing repertoire. Many responses are tried and "stamped out" as unsuccessful until the correct response is found. This response will be "stamped in" because it brings about a desired result.

THINKING AND LANGUAGE

THINKING

COGNITIVE PSYCHOLOGY
COGNITIVE DEVELOPMENT THEORY
LEARNING THEORY
ASSOCIATIONISM

Directed Thinking

CONCEPT LEARNING
VERBAL LEARNING
IMAGERY
MEANINGFULNESS
CREATIVITY
LANGUAGE
MEMORY
   encoding
PROBLEM SOLVING
INSIGHT
FUNCTIONAL FIXEDNESS
MEDIATION
COMPUTER SIMULATION
CYBERNETICS

Associative Thinking

AUTISTIC THINKING
DAYDREAMING
FREE ASSOCIATION
DELUSION
HALLUCINATION
PSYCHOTIC DISORDERS

LANGUAGE

grammar
morpheme
psycholinguistics
semantics
transformational-generative grammar

CODABILITY
MEMORY
   encoding
LANGUAGE UNIVERSAL
MEANING
SEMANTIC DIFFERENTIAL
PRESCRIPTIVE LINGUISTICS
INFORMATION THEORY
ATTITUDES AND ATTITUDE CHANGE
MESSAGE
SPEECH

The Subject Maps in the Encyclopedia illustrate the coverage of particular aspects of psychology, showing the interrelationships among the articles in twelve major areas of study. Entries in capital letters are subjects for which there are separate articles in the Encyclopedia. Entries in small letters are cross references.

The Subject Maps appear in the Encyclopedia under the following titles:

Abnormal and Clinical Psychology
Developmental Psychology
Emotion and Motivation
Intelligence
Learning and Memory
Measurement
Personality and Individual Difference
Physiological and Comparative Psychology
Psychology: Divisions and Schools
Sensation and Perception
Social Psychology
Thinking and Language

Founder of the Structuralist school of psychology, British-born E. B. Titchener trained laboratory subjects to analyze their own sensory experience.

THYROID GLAND

thyroid gland

parathyroid glands

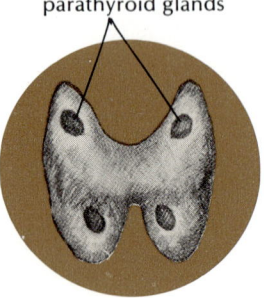

In these findings was the germ of Thorndike's *law of effect,* which stands as a foundation of modern learning theory. In its simplest form, the law states: Of several responses to the same stimulus, the one that is followed by satisfaction to the organism will be more likely to recur, while those that are followed by neutral or unsatisfying experiences will be less likely to recur. To this he added the *law of exercise,* which states: S-R connections can be made stronger by repetition.

Thorndike also made an inventory of words to determine those most frequently used. On the basis of his count, he produced a word book in 1921 and a dictionary in 1935.

Major Works. *Animal Intelligence,* 1898; *The Original Nature of Man, The Psychology of Learning,* and *Mental Work and Fatigue and Individual Differences and Their Causes,* 1913–1914; *The Measurement of Intelligence,* 1926; *The Fundamentals of Learning,* 1932; *A Teacher's Word Book of 20,000 Words,* 1921 (later revised); and *Thorndike-Century Junior Dictionary,* 1935.

—Michael Rothenberg, *The City College of the City University of New York*

THRESHOLD, the amount of stimulus necessary to produce sensation. For example, the number of grams necessary to feel weight on the hand is the pressure threshold. Because it varies slightly from measurement to measurement, the exact threshold is usually defined as the stimulus experienced 50 percent of the time.

THUMB-SUCKING. Whether or not to allow thumb-sucking has been for some time a controversial topic among experts. While some believe that allowing sufficient sucking during feeding will provide an infant with adequate oral gratification and therefore prevent subsequent thumbsucking, others feel that the oral drive will be strengthened by more sucking and as a consequence non-nutritive sucking behavior is likely to occur. In evaluating whether or not thumbsucking is a pathological symptom, factors such as the child's age, the persistence and frequency of the behavior, and the overall personality characteristics should be considered.

THURSTONE, LOUIS LEON (1887–1955), American psychologist born in Chicago. He received his Ph.D. from the University of Chicago (1917) and was professor of psychology there from 1924.

Thurstone is one of the developers of the factor analysis method and of paper-and-pencil tests in intelligence. Thurstone believed that Charles Sperman's postulated "general intelligence" could be analyzed into several different factors. He gave sixty different tests to a

group of children. Each test was to measure a specific type of ability, such as reasoning. He then grouped together the test scores that had high correlations with one another. The result was seven factors that Thurstone called "primary abilities"—numerical ability, word fluency, verbal meaning, memory, reasoning, spatial relations, and perceptual speed. He used these findings to develop the Primary Mental Abilities Test (1938), which seemed as successful as the Binet test in measuring intelligence.

Thurstone also developed the Thurstone Neurotic Inventory and the Thurstone scale for measuring personal attitudes toward such subjects as capital punishment, making it possible to study and survey attitudes on a quantitative basis. Thurstone's many publications include *The Nature of Intelligence,* 1924; *The Measurement of Attitude,* 1929; *Primary Mental Abilities,* 1938; and *Multiple Factor Analysis,* 1947.

See also Intelligence and Intelligence Measurement.

THYROID GLAND. Located in the throat, this endocrine gland is important for control of body metabolism. It releases a substance, thyroxin, which effects the function of many organs. Decreased thyroid function (hypothyroidism) can result in diminished circulation, decreased utilization of food, and (in severe cases) mental retardation. Oversecretion (hyperthyroidism) can cause tension and excitability.

TIC (ticquer), a persistent muscle movement, such as twitching the mouth, licking the lips, blinking the eyes, clearing the throat, "making faces," turning the neck, or shrugging the shoulders. Often the person with a tic is not aware that he has this nervous mannerism. Tics may be a problem in adults but are most common in children aged six to fourteen.

In most cases, tics are caused by psychological factors such as a need to reduce tension. Feelings of inadequacy or uneasiness can create tension. A shy child (or adult) may feel embarrassment about speaking in front of strangers and may repeatedly clear his throat or moisten his lips. The mannerism seems to have some effect as on outlet for tension. If the person is made aware of his tic, his tension is likely to increase, and his tic may become more severe. Psychotherapy may be required to get at the causes of the tic.

TITCHENER, EDWARD BRADFORD (1867–1927), British psychologist and educator, born at Chichester. He studied for his Ph.D. under Wilhelm Wundt at Leipzig, then migrated to the United States, where he taught at Cornell for thirty-five years. He was a charter member of the American Psychological Association.

Titchener was the founder of the structuralist school of psychology. His years with Wundt greatly influenced his thinking, and his own research and theoretical interests centered on the discovery of general psychological principles of human experience. He sought to explain such processes as emotion and thought by means of particular aspects of sensory experience. In order to do this, he developed the method of *introspection,* in which he trained laboratory subjects to analyze their own sensory experience objectively.

Titchener was convinced that he could unravel the secrets of consciousness by understanding the operation of the nervous system. He staunchly opposed the then popular functionalist approach, which favored the consideration of individual differences and the application of psychology to practical problems. The attitude of serious scientific research he brought to psychology in America remains his legacy to this day. His major publication is *Experimental Psychology,* 1901–1905.

—Michael Rothenberg, *The City College of The City University of New York*

TOILET TRAINING. In Western culture, the second year in life seems to be the usual time for teaching a child to acquire control over his elimination. Studies suggest that the most successful training takes place at the latter part of the second year, since the neuromuscular mechanisms must be sufficiently matured before they can be voluntarily controlled. When toilet training starts at that time, it is accomplished faster than when it begins earlier. Success also depends on the mother's general attitude toward the child and the process of training. Control of the bowel is usually accomplished earlier than bladder control, since movements are less frequent and more regular than urination.

Psychoanalytic theory suggests that anal evacuation is pleasurable and gratifying to a child and contends that he experiences a feeling of power as he realizes that he is capable of controlling a part of his own body. Severity in training, according to this theory, may lead to such personality characteristics as perfectionism or stinginess. Although research evidence is not conclusive in this area, most psychologists emphasize the importance of warmth and patience in achieving success in toilet training.

—Ragaa Mazen, *Southern Connecticut State College*
See also Anal Character.

TOKEN ECONOMY. *See* Behavior Therapy.

TOLERANCE, for drugs. *See* Drugs and Behavior.

TOLMAN, EDWARD CHACE (1886–1959), American psychologist, born in West Newton,

Mass. He taught at the University of California for 45 years, and was president of the American Psychological Association, 1937.

Primarily a learning theorist, Tolman called his system "purposive behaviorism." He drew heavily from the work of John B. Watson but felt that Watson's concept of the conditioned reflex as the basic behavioral act was too limited. Tolman believed that all behavior is purposive and that the most meaningful unit of study is the goal-directed act. This is a molar concept including muscular movements, organized around a particular goal and guided by cognitive processes. He saw learning as occurring by means of a system of trial and error from which responses resulting in reward are selected.

One of Tolman's most important contributions is the concept of *latent learning,* learning that occurs unobserved but, under certain changes in conditions, can be revealed in increased efficiency in performance. These findings qualified the contention of other theorists that all learning was based on drive reduction. Tolman's major publication was *Purposive Behavior in Animals and Men* (1932).

—Michael Rothenberg, *The City College of The City University of New York*

TOMKINS-HORN PICTURE ARRANGEMENT TEST (PAT). Originally designed as a means of evaluating work attitudes of industrial employees, this method has been used at all work levels within the business community. Essentially a projective technique, it assumes that the testee identifies with the characters depicted and expresses his own thoughts and feelings in the sentences and picture arrangements called for.

Test administration is simple and readily adaptable to large groups. Subjects are presented with a series of pictures, three to a set, in a haphazard arrangement and are asked to put them in sensible order. Then they are required to write a sentence about each picture, developing a short story.

The test can be machine-scored and extensive quantitative norms are offered in the manual. Operative modes in job-related situations are obviously derived. In addition, tentative conclusions can be reached concerning achievement orientation, self-concept, pronounced defense mechanisms, and other aspects of the subject's personality.

—Randolph S. Kraft, *Federation of the Handicapped, N.Y.*
Consult (12) Tomkins, *et al.,* 1957.

TOPOLOGICAL PSYCHOLOGY, an attempt to represent the structure and dynamics of the human organism and its environment by means of mathematical concepts. Kurt Lewin devised such a system based upon three prin-

TOMKINS-HORN PICTURE ARRANGEMENT TEST

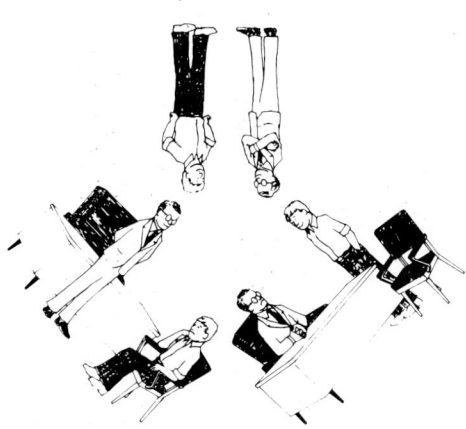

In the Tomkins-Horn Picture Arrangement Test, the subject is asked to arrange three pictures in a sensible order and describe the result.

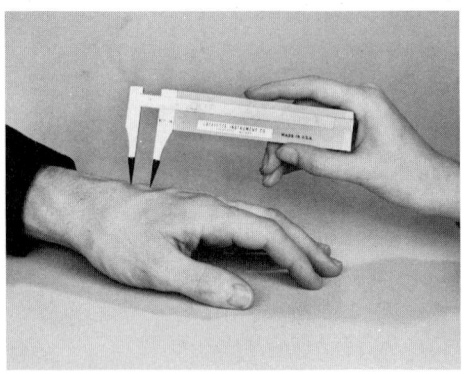

The aesthesiometer is used to study the sensitivity of the skin to touch.

ciples: (1) behavior is a function of the field that exists at the time the behavior occurs, (2) analysis begins with the situation as a whole and then differentiates its parts, and (3) the motives of a person in a given situation can be represented mathematically.

TOUCH. Sometimes called mechanoreception, touch is one of the four basic sensations of the body. The touch receptors respond at very low intensities to a change in the mechanical stimulation of the skin but adapt very rapidly and give very little information about the intensity or duration of the stimulation.

See also Sensation.

TOXIC PSYCHOSES. *See* Brain Disorders.

TRAINABLE MENTALLY RETARDED. *See* Mental Retardation.

TRAIT THEORY. *See* Personality.

TRANQUILIZER, a drug in the sedative-hypnotic classification used as an antianxiety agent. *See* Drugs and Behavior.

TRANSFER OF TRAINING, in general, the influence of past learning on new learning. When such transfer aids new learning, it is labeled "positive"; when it inhibits new learning, it is "negative." Transfer can also be specific or nonspecific. *Specific transfer* occurs when the past and new learning tasks have identifiable elements in common. For example, specific positive transfer is likely to occur from learning arithmetic and mathematics to learning architecture, statistics, or engineering, since all of these topics involve identical elements. *Nonspecific transfer* occurs when new learning involves rules or principles that have been mastered through practice of past tasks of the same general type.

Transfer of training can be defined operationally by the following experimental conditions: Experimental Group (E) learns Task A, then Task B, then is tested on B. Control Group (C) learns nothing, then Task B, then is tested on B. Transfer of training is said to occur if the performance of E on Task B differs from the performance of group C on Task B. If E does better than C, then positive transfer for E has taken place; if C does better, then transfer was negative from Task A to B for group E.

Research. Historically, much of the modern work on transfer of training can be traced to developments in psychology and education near the end of the nineteenth century. At this time the "formal discipline theory," which was popular in education, held that practice in any mental discipline (for example mathematics, Latin) would strengthen all other mental faculties in much the same

way that muscles are strengthened by using them. This broad, nonspecific theory of transfer was disproved by studies of E. L. Thorndike and others that showed that no one school subject transferred very strongly to any other. As a result of this work, psychologists subsequently stressed the importance of specific identical elements between tasks for positive transfer. The measureable degree to which two tasks might be similar and the effects of similarity on transfer were studied in great detail for many tasks. In general, it was found that a strong similarity between tasks or materials to be learned tended to produce positive transfer, while moderate similarity produced negative transfer effects.

However, in modern psychology and education it is recognized that both specific and nonspecific varieties of transfer can occur, depending on the particular circumstances and tasks involved. In education, general positive transfer effects can be encouraged by making materials to be learned as meaningful and as close to the students' own experiences as possible. Arithmetic, for example, will become an everyday matter if it is taught in such a way that methods and principles are related to the student's own life and background. Like generalization, transfer of training is thought to be a basic process that underlies problem-solving performance, thinking, and most other cognitive and verbal functions in humans.

—Roland Siiter, *Montclair State College*

See also Learning Theory; Learning-to-Learn; Problem Solving.

Consult (6) Deese and Hulse, 1967; Smith and Rohrman, 1970; Thorndike and Woodworth, 1901.

TRANSFORMATIONAL-GENERATIVE GRAMMAR. *See* Language.

TRANSSEXUALISM, a powerful desire to be a person of the opposite sex. The drive to change sexual identity is so strong that the transsexualist may sometimes be self-deluded into believing that he or she is, in fact, a legitimate member of the opposite sex who has, through a most incredible mistake, been endowed somehow with incorrect secondary sexual characteristics.

The true transsexualist, in most cases an anatomical male, is distinctly different from the transvestite or the homosexual. Transsexual males tend to be puritanical, with low sex drive. Their interest is primarily in assuming the female sociocultural role. Playing the female role in sexual behavior is seen as necessary, but definitely secondary.

Several thousand males have been surgically and endocrinologically altered to eliminate their maleness and to assume an external female appearance. Adjusting psychologically to the gender change is sometimes stressful. Those transsexualists who adjust most successfully are young and are physically attractive as females.

—Eugene E. Levitt, *Indiana University School of Medicine*
Consult (13) Benjamin, 1966; Green and Money, 1969; Stoller, 1968.

TRANSVESTISM, gratification through wearing the clothing of the opposite sex. The large majority of transvestites are males, probably because clothing fashions have, for several decades, permitted women to wear various types of male attire.

Transvestites fall into a number of categories. A small number are transsexuals who are, in their view, simply wearing the clothing of their own sex. Some are homosexuals who are going "in drag" in order to attract sexual partners. Most transvestites are heterosexual males (many have stable marriages) who have never had homosexual contacts of any kind and who never appear in female attire outside of their own homes. While it seems obvious that the pleasure in transvestism must be basically sexual in nature, most of the transvestites in this category disclaim the connection. They refer to the motivation for cross-dressing in terms of relaxation and comfort rather than sexual arousal.

Clinical investigation suggests that many of the heterosexual transvestites had parents who deliberately prolonged the babyhood period in which males and females are dressed indistinguishably or actually dressed a boy child in feminine fashion up to the age of four, five or longer.

—Eugene E. Levitt, *Indiana University School of Medicine*
Consult (13) Benjamin, 1966; Green and Money, 1969; Stoller, 1968.

TRAUMA, medically, an injury, wound, or shock; psychologically, any life-threatening danger experienced consciously or unconsciously as such by the individual. Psychological trauma can range from the discovery that one is critically ill to less obviously threatening circumstances such as absence of mother for the young child or loss of "face" for the adult. One traumatic experience may make an individual anxious and hypersensitive to the possibility of another.

TRIAL-AND-ERROR LEARNING. When an organism is confronted by a novel situation in which it is required to make some response, environmental cues and previous experience combine to determine which response will be made. In many cases the most dominant response is emitted first and is the appropriate response. In other cases, however, the most

dominant response is not appropriate, and a second response is then emitted. If neither of these responses is successful in obtaining a reinforcement, a third, fourth, or fifth response may be required.

This process of plugging old responses into new situations has been called trial-and-error learning. The organism may be required to emit a large number of responses before he finally emits an appropriate response. Usually a rough approximation to the correct response will result in some small reinforcement. At this point the trial-and-error process will be terminated and the response will be further refined and specialized through the process of shaping.

—Brenda B. Bankart and C. Peter Bankart, *Wabash College*
See also Operant Conditioning.

TROPISM, a directed growth process in stationary organisms. For example, plants often bend toward a light source as they grow (phototropism). The most renowned research in this area was conducted by Jacques Loeb, who attempted to extend tropisms to much animal and even human behavior.

See also Taxis.
Consult (3) Loeb, 1918.

ULCERS. Peptic ulcers are believed to be caused by emotional stress. See Psychosomatic Disorders.

UNCONDITIONED RESPONSE. See Pavlovian Conditioning.

UNCONDITIONED STIMULUS. See Pavolovian Conditioning.

UNCONSCIOUS. Lack of conscious awareness of one's behavior or surrounding events has long been recognized by the term "unconscious." Behaviorists describe the phenomenon as inability to verbalize.

Most often, the term means an aspect of Sigmund Freud's psychoanalytic theory. A concept, not a place, the unconscious encompasses some impulses, present at birth, that never do achieve consciousness, as well as wishes and memories, unacceptable and frightening to the individual, that have been repressed. Dynamic, uncontrolled, unconscious content is forever striving to attain consciousness, involving tremendous energy in keeping it repressed. Others may sometimes recognize the unconscious motivation behind accidents, slips of the tongue, aggressive behavior, sexual interest, symptom formation, and the like, where the repressing individual does not.

In his theory, Carl Jung distinguished between the personal and the collective un-

Phototropism is the response of a plant to light. The bending toward the light (positive phototropism) is caused by unequal growth of the stem.

TRIAL-AND-ERROR LEARNING

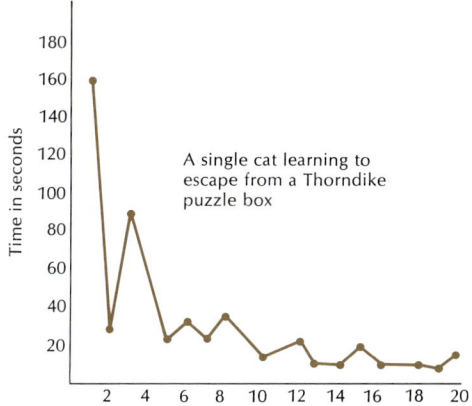

A single cat learning to escape from a Thorndike puzzle box

The graph shows that with successive trials the cat requires less and less time to escape from the puzzle box.

VISION

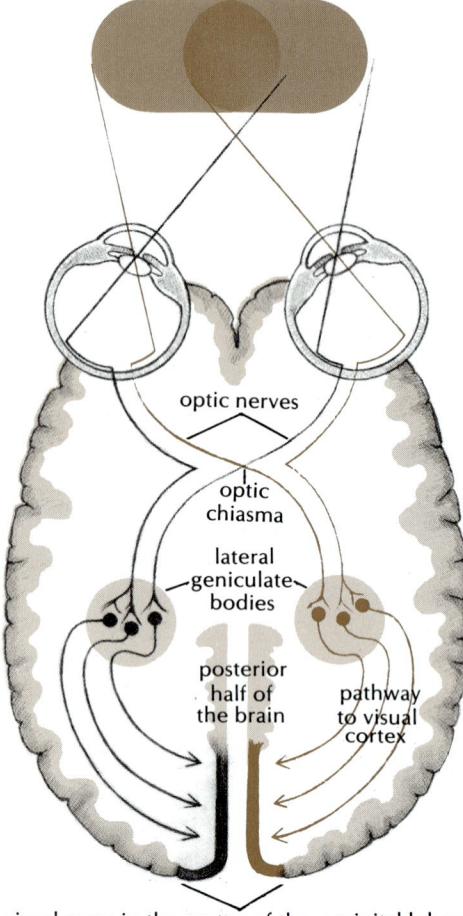

visual areas in the cortex of the occipital lobes

When the eyes converge on the same object each eye sees a slightly different image. Light from a point on the right side of the visual field falls on the left side of both retinas. The path of the optic nerve is such (note the crossing over at the optic chiasma) that impulses from the left side of both retinas activate areas only in the left visual cortex at the back of the brain. The pathway is mirrored for the right side of the retinas. Each side of the brain, therefore, receives slightly different signals from the same half of the visual field, but somehow we are able to assemble a meaningful image.

conscious and described positive as well as negative aspects.

—M. G. Affinito, *Southern Connecticut State College*

See also Consciousness; Preconscious; Psychoneurotic Disorders; Repression; Unconscious, Collective.

Consult (13) Hall, 1954.

UNCONSCIOUS, COLLECTIVE, concept developed by Carl Jung. In Freudian theory, each individual has a personal unconscious. In this portion of the mind are found, first, infantile wishes and impulses that have never reached the conscious level and, second, ideas, memories, and impulses that were in consciousness but have been repressed because they are threatening. Jung proposed that, in addition to the personal unconscious, there is another division: the collective. He called this division also the racial unconscious, and stated that it held ideas, symbols, images, and myths common to societies, peoples, or mankind as a whole. These collective ideas or general concepts are not acquired by each individual from his experience but are fundamental aspects of all human experience.

Consult (13) Jung, 1928.

UNDERACHIEVER, a term applied to the student whose academic performance is significantly lower than his measured ability. While the problem can start at any time, it most frequently has its origin in the elementary grades. Incidence figures show a higher frequency of underachievers among boys than girls, and the tendency appears to be most common among very bright children. Frequently mentioned causal factors include problems in motivation and interest in school work, excessive pressure to achieve, personality and emotional problems, family relationship problems, and general hostility toward school.

—Frank T. Vitro, *University of Maine*
See also Overachiever.

VALENCE, the personal value attached to a goal or an object. Whatever the individual seeks to attain is said to have a positive valence; whatever he seeks to avoid is said to have negative valence. The term is usually associated with the system known as field theory, proposed by Kurt Lewin.

VALIDITY, in educational and psychological measurement, the extent to which a test measures what it is designed to measure. Suppose questions on a history test were filled with foreign phrases and literary allusions. The test might be a better measure of knowledge of languages and letters than of history.

Validity can be measured by comparing test scores with a criterion of what the test is

supposed to assess. If a test is designed to predict success in studying a language, scores on the test can be compared with results of another test given at the completion of the course.

Consult (12) Cronbach, 1970.

VARIABLE, dependent and independent. *See* Experimental Design.

VERBAL LEARNING, traditional area of experimental psychology concerned with studying how verbal associations are learned and remembered in specific experimental situations, namely paired-associate learning, serial learning, free-recall learning, and transfer. Verbal learning should not be confused with the study of how words and language are originally acquired during early childhood. This is discussed in the article on language.

See also Associationism; Ebbinghaus; Free-Recall Learning; Paired-Associate Learning; Serial Learning.

VERTIGO, a state of confusion or uneasiness about spatial position or movement, which may be accompanied by intense dizziness. Vertigo is often described as a sense of turning or rotating or as the sensation that stationary objects appear to be moving. It is usually due to unusual or intense stimulation of the inner ear.

See also Equilibrium Sense.

VESTIBULAR SENSE. *See* Equilibrium Sense.

VISCERAL LEARNING. *See* Biofeedback.

VISCERAL SENSES. *See* Interoceptive Senses.

VISION, like the other sensory modalities, is a process by which a form of physical energy is ultimately transformed into a perceptual experience. Yet it is only in this generalized way that visual perception corresponds to other senses. Visual processes are unique in terms of a number of descriptive criteria.

The Physical Stimulus. The external stimulation that initiates the visual process, light, is employed by this sensory channel alone. Thus, it differs from mechanical stimulation, for example, which is involved in some way in several senses, including touch and hearing. In fact, vision is so specialized that only a tiny portion of the electromagnetic energy spectrum, of which visible light is merely one phenomenon, is utilized as an adequate stimulus. Other electromagnetic phenomena, such as radio waves, X-rays, and ultraviolet light, are not detected visually.

The Anatomical Process. When light strikes the clear protuberant front surface of the eye, it is bent, or "refracted," by this structure, the *cornea,* and then passes through a small aperture, the *pupil.* When the eye is viewed from the front, the pupil appears as a black dot, and its size is regulated by the surrounding structure, the *iris,* which is the circular colored portion surrounding the pupil. Immediately behind the iris is the *lens* of the eye, which continues the refraction and causes an image to be formed on the inner layer of the eyeball, the *retina.*

It should be noted that the organism does not actually see an object directly; that is, the object itself does not in some way enter the nervous system. Instead, an image of the object is made available to the nervous system in the form of a pattern of light falling upon the retina. The retina, in turn, is composed of many millions of nervous system receptors (called *rods* and *cones*), which trigger a chain of electrochemical changes in the neurons leading from the retina to the brain. Therefore, a second unique characteristic of vision is that the receptor organ (the eye), the pathways in the nervous system, and even the ultimate destinations of this information in the brain are anatomically specialized for vision alone.

The Perceptual Experience. Perhaps most importantly, vision is distinguished from the other senses because it gives rise to a unique experience, whether it is called "seeing" or "vision" or "visual perception." It is impossible, for example, to attempt to explain what seeing is like to someone who has been blind since birth; if he has had no visual experience, then there is no way he can come to understand what seeing is like, either in words or in terms of analogies to other senses.

Scientists find the study of vision intriguing in part because so many categories of information are processed within a single sensory modality. At its simplest level, vision conveys information about the presence or absence of light in the external environment (*brightness detection*). It also enables organisms to determine whether an object exists (*form perception*) and to make further judgments about its *movement, color,* and *distance* from them and from other objects. The question of how so much about the external world can be understood from a single sensory modality is but one mystery for perceptual psychologists and others to unravel.

Research. In order to understand how visual perception functions, scientists have come to recognize that they must understand the entire visual process. The physics of light, the physiology of the visual nervous system, and the psychology of perceptual experience must all be clarified. Psychologists are particularly anxious to know which aspects of visual perception are innate and which are learned, for there is increasing evidence that both phenomena occur, sometimes within a single visual function. The ultimate goal may be to comprehend the complex interactions be-

tween different stages in visual processing; for example, how do changes in the nervous system give rise to the experience of an object? In order to understand and identify the physiological changes, we must understand their psychological counterparts, and vice versa.

—Mark B. Fineman, *Southern Connecticut State College*
See also Blindness; Color Vision; Depth Perception; Illusion.
Other entries listed in the Item Guide under Sensation *and* Perception.
Consult (4) Geldard, 1972; Kenshalo, 1971; Pirenne, 1970.

VISUAL CLIFF, an apparatus employed to test for the presence of depth perception in animals or infants. The subject is placed on a narrow glass-topped platform at a height. To one side of the platform he can see, through the glass, a surface that is well below it; to the other side he sees a surface directly against the glass. Thus the only difference is that *visually* there is a severe drop on one side but not on the other.

Assuming that most animals will innately fear height, they should avoid going off the central platform to the "deep" side and prefer the "shallow" side *if* they can perceive depth. Thus, the apparatus makes it possible to test for depth perception in newborn animals or those deprived of vision until the time of testing.

Research has now established that most animals do perceive distance at or shortly after birth, that is, that the perception of the third dimension is innately determined. Research with this apparatus has also been aimed at the question of which cues to distance are operative in the infant subjects.

—Irvin Rock, *Rutgers University*
See also Depth Perception.
Consult (4) Gibson and Walk, 1960.

VOCATIONAL APTITUDE TESTS, scales designed to determine the ability or abilities of an individual to learn tasks or skills in some occupation. Whereas in scholastic aptitude testing a small number of abilities are measured, vocational aptitude tests measure a larger number of different factors. Therefore, a multifactor aptitude test battery is more appropriate.

One of the most widely used multifactor vocational aptitude tests at the precollege level is the *Differential Aptitude Test.* This consists of seven subtests: verbal reasoning, numerical reasoning, abstract reasoning, spatial relations, mechanical reasoning, clerical speed and accuracy, and language usage. A large amount of research data has been collected by the publishers of the test, and follow-up studies have calculated correlations to show the relationships between scores and success in college,

VISION

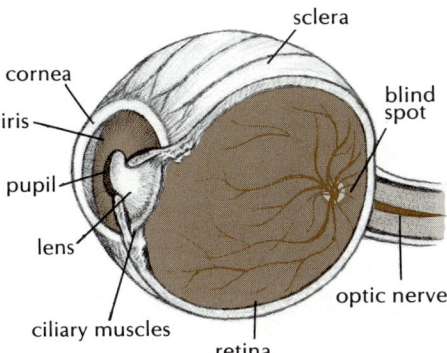

The anatomy of the eyeball.

Locating the Blind Spot

The blind spot of the eye is a point on the retina where there are no retinal cells; this is the location of the optic nerve. To locate this spot in your own eye, close the left eye and look at the plus sign from a distance of six to seven inches; the round spot will disappear. Reverse the procedure for the left eye. Some individuals may have to rotate the page slightly.

A child encouraged by his mother to cross over the visual cliff shows innate caution.

In the Small Parts Dexterity Test, a vocational aptitude test, the subject inserts small pins in close-fitting holes then places small rings over the pins.

school grades, and patterns of aptitude in terms of occupations.

Two primary uses of such tests are vocational guidance and vocational selection. For guidance one learns what aptitudes are most highly related to a particular occupation and then determines the degree to which a given individual has these aptitudes. In vocational selection an employer who knows which aptitudes are necessary or required for a particular job tests applicants so that the person with the highest probability of success can be hired. In other words, vocational guidance helps to guide an individual into the occupation in which he has the highest aptitude, and vocational selection is a screening process used by employers.

Vocational aptitude tests are used in education, governmental agencies, the armed forces, and industries.

—Louis Snellgrove, *Lambuth College*
See also Measurement.
Consult (12) Cronbach, 1970.

VOCATIONAL COUNSELING. Psychologists use their professional skills and knowledge to match people with vocations. Personnel work developed in the early part of the twentieth century as one of the first branches of applied psychology. Counseling about jobs has grown more important and more complex as the world of work has expanded and varieties of jobs have multiplied.

Counselors try to find out all they can about a person who asks for advice. They consider his school grades, intelligence test scores, and whatever they can determine from questionnaires and interviews, about his personality traits, interests, and aptitudes. Past experience is one guide; they may also have a candidate take tests of aptitudes and interests and personality measures such as projective techniques. In matching an individual with a vocation, it is important to consider not only the obvious factors of pay, hours, and skills but also the psychological dimensions. For example, will the individual find a job so devoid of challenge that he will soon be unhappy?

Psychologists have made a number of studies of the traits of people in various career fields, but no definitive picture of the "right person" for a job has yet been drawn.
See also Vocational Aptitude Test.
Consult (14) Roe, 1952; Roe, 1956; Thorndike and Hagen, 1959.

VOYEURISM, in its broadest sense, gratification from watching sexual objects or acts. At one time voyeurism was restricted to looking at bodies, while observing sexual acts was called *scoptophilia* or *scotophilia*. This distinction is no longer made.

The characteristic problem of defining the deviant in sexual behavior occurs here as in other areas. The man who becomes sexually aroused watching his wife undress as a coital preliminary or who is excited by "girlie" shows or magazines and the woman who is stimulated by the sight of hairy chests or broad shoulders are both voyeurs if the term is loosely defined. A substantial proportion, if not a clear majority, of American adults have been sexually stimulated at one time or another by viewing objects or occurrences. In this sense, voyeurism, like sadism and masochism, is fairly common in its milder form. H. A. Katchadourian and D. T. Lunde suggest that voyeurism is abnormal "when it is preferred to coitus or indulged in at serious risk."

The Institute for Sex Research investigators have defined as a *peeper* the voyeur "who has no legal right to be at the location from whence be observes," probably a dark or otherwise unobserved place from which he can look into some area or room in the hope of seeing a partially nude or nude female. Like most institutionalized sex criminals, peepers are invariably male. The majority of institutionalized "voyeurs" have had inadequate heterosexual lives. Like the exhibitionist and pedophile, the voyeur tends to be an unaggressive, socially maladroit individual.

—Eugene E. Levitt, *Indiana University School of Medicine*
Consult (13) Gebhard, *et al.* 1965; Katchadourian and Lunde, 1972.

WATSON, JOHN BROADUS (1878–1958), American psychologist. Born in Greenville, S.C., he received his Ph.D (1903) under Dewey and Angell at the University of Chicago. He taught at Johns Hopkins (1908–1920), then pursued a career in advertising.

Watson fathered what has come to be known as the "behaviorist revolt." He rejected the then popular trend of studying such matters as mental activity and conscious experience, arguing that concepts of that sort belong in the realm of philosophy. They have no place in an objective science because there is no way of directly observing or objectively measuring them. He declared that psychology should be limited to the study of behavior and should concern itself especially with stimulus-response connections, which he called habit formation. Given the stimulus connections, the psychologist should be able to predict the response. It was Watson who claimed that if given full charge of twelve healthy infants, he could, by means of behavioral conditioning, produce any type of person he desired—doctor, lawyer, or even criminal.

Watson's theory freed him from concern with mentalistic concepts and subjective methods of measurement. His was an objective and pragmatic theory that he favored the application of psychology to practical problems. His own interests in this regard included child

"Behaviorist revolt" fathered by American psychologist John B. Watson stressed a pragmatic approach to behavior study and emphasized habit formation by S-R conditioning.

rearing, advertising, and industry. His impact on psychology is most prominent today in the work of B. F. Skinner, who has expanded and popularized Watson's behaviorist theories. His major works are *Psychology from the Standpoint of a Behaviorist,* 1919; *Behaviorism,* 1927; and *Psychological Care of the Infant and Child,* 1928.

—Michael Rothenberg, *The City College of The City University of New York*

WAXY FLEXIBILITY, a condition observed in patients with the catatonic type of schizophrenia; also called by the Latin name *cerea flexibilitas. See* Schizophrenia.

WEBER, ERNST (1795–1878), German physiologist. Born in Wittenberg, he taught anatomy and physiology at Leipzig for forty years. He was cofounder of the German Polytechnic Society.

Weber was one of the first scientists to adapt the laboratory methods of physiology to the investigation of psychological variables. This arose out of his work with the sense of touch and kinesthetics. It was during this research that Weber discovered and described the first quantitative psychological principle. While investigating the way in which the kinesthetic sense is used to discriminate between objects of similar size but different weights, he discovered that the *just noticeable difference* (minimum difference necessary for discrimination) between the two weights was in a constant ratio to the weight of the one used as a standard: the greater the weight of the standard, the greater must be the difference between it and the comparison stimulus in order for them to be experienced as different in weight.

Although Weber expanded his investigations to include visual brightness discrimination and other sensory modalities, he never formulated his findings into one general law. However, reports of his work stimulated Gustav Fechner to conduct the research that culminated in the general law about stimulus difference discrimination which bears both of their names. This law states $S = K \log R$ where S is sensation, R is the magnitude of the standard stimulus, and K is a constant. Weber's work anticipated the development of psychophysics and created an atmosphere in which Fechner could make the first steps toward a science of experimental psychology.

—Michael Rothenberg, *The City College of The City University of New York*

WECHSLER, DAVID (1896–   ), American psychologist, born in Lespede, Rumania. He received a Ph.D. from Columbia (1925) and was clinical professor of psychology, NYU College of Medicine, from 1942.

Wechsler developed scales of intelli-

gence and is the author of the *Wechsler Intelligence Scale for Children* (1949) and the *Wechsler Adult Intelligence Scale Manual* (1955). Wechsler's intelligence tests have two separate measures—a verbal scale and a performance scale. Wechsler is also the author of: *The Range of Human Capacities,* 1935; *Wechsler-Bellevue Intelligence Scale,* 1939; *The Measurements of Adult Intelligence,* 1944; and *Wechsler Preschool and Primary Scale of Intelligence,* 1967.

WECHSLER INTELLIGENCE SCALES. An American psychologist, David Wechsler, originated a series of intelligence tests, the first of which was known as the Wechsler-Bellevue. Although this is no longer widely used, later issues of the Wechsler series are based on the original principles used to develop it.

The Wechsler Adult Intelligence Scale (WAIS) consists of eleven subtests: six are primarily verbal, and five measure performance or nonverbal aspects of intelligence. The six verbal subtests are information, comprehension, arithmetic, similarities, digit span, and vocabulary. The performance subtests include digit symbol, picture completion, block design, picture arrangement, and object assembly. The WAIS is usually given to individuals fifteen years of age or older.

The Wechsler Intelligence Scale for Children (WISC) is similar to the WAIS except that it is designed to cover the age range from five to fifteen years. The major difference is that items on the WISC were designed to be more appropriate to these age levels.

The latest in the series of the Wechsler tests is the Wechsler Preschool and Primary Scale of Intelligence (WPPSI) and was published in 1963. This test was developed for children between the ages of four to six and one-half years of age. Although very similar to the WAIS and WISC, the WPPSI has three substituted subtests: sentences, animal house, and geometric design.

The Wechsler series group similar items together and all items within a subtest are arranged in order of difficulty from the easiest to the most difficult item. This gives the Wechsler tests the advantage of determining the strong and weak areas in intellectual development for a person.

—Louis Snellgrove, *Lambuth College*
See also Intelligence and Intelligence Testing.
Consult (12) Cronbach, 1970.

WERTHEIMER, MAX (1880–1943), German psychologist and philosopher. Born in Prague, Czechoslovakia, he took his Ph.D. at Wurzburg, where he studied under Oswald Kulpe, founder of act psychology. He emigrated to the United States in 1934 and taught at the New School for Social Research.

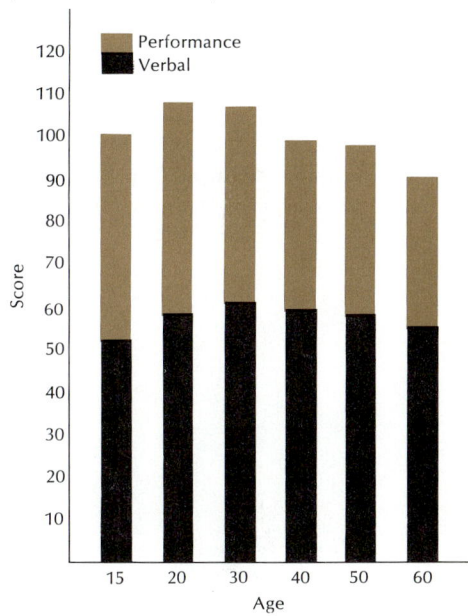

WECHSLER ADULT INTELLIGENCE SCALE

Showing typical scores at different ages for the performance and verbal parts of the test

A pioneer in American psychiatric training and research, William A. White helped gain acceptance for psychoanalytic methods.

Lightner Witmer was a pioneer in the development of psychological clinics.

Wertheimer was one of the three founders of Gestalt psychology. It was Wertheimer's work with the "phi phenomenon" that marked the beginning of the Gestalt school. He discovered that if two straight lines are flashed on a screen in close succession there is the illusion of one line moving through space. Movement is experienced by the perceiver although no movement has occurred. He contended that no amount of introspection, as advanced by the structuralists, could account for this phenomenon. This led to the conclusion that in perception the whole is indeed greater than the sum of its parts.

Among the first subjects in his perceptual research were Wolfgang Köhler and Kurt Koffka. Together they opposed traditional psychologists' attempts to analyze experience into component parts, claiming they must be considered in their totality, as organized wholes. While most of their early work was in the area of perception, Wertheimer attempted to extend Gestalt principles to thinking and education. In one study he demonstrated that more learning occurred when classroom exercises were organized into meaningful related wholes than during rote drills. *Productive Thinking,* 1945, is his major work.

—Michael Rothenberg, *The City College of The City University of New York*

WHITE, WILLIAM ALANSON (1870–1937), American psychiatrist, born in Brooklyn, N.Y. He was superintendent of the Government Hospital for the Insane (St. Elizabeth's), Washington, D.C., from 1903 until 1937.

An influential leader in the development of American psychology, White organized one of the first psychology laboratories in a mental hospital, established St. Elizabeth's as a center for psychiatric training, and fostered the psychoanalytic movement in the United States. His goal was to establish the mental hospital as a scientific community where research, training, and total medical treatment of the mental patient would replace the merely custodial care goals of most mental institutions.

White's early studies in the unconscious led him to the works of Freud, and in 1913, with S. E. Jelliffe, he founded the *Psychoanalytic Review.* He helped psychoanalysis become accepted in America by defending this approach, especially before the American Psychiatric Association. He later served as president of this organization, as well as of other psychiatric organizations.

White was a prolific writer on psychiatry. One of his special interests—forensic psychiatry—was the subject of *Insanity and the Criminal Law,* 1923, and *Crimes and Criminals,* 1933. Among his other books are *Outlines of Psychiatry,* 1907; *Diseases of the Nervous Sys-*

tem (with Jelliffe), 1915; and *Essays on Psychopathology,* 1925.

The William Alanson White Foundation and the William Alanson White Institute, both organized in honor of White, have been responsible for an extensive range of psychiatric research.

WHORFIAN HYPOTHESIS, which states that human thinking is highly dependent on the language spoken by the individual thinker, is also called the *linguistic-relativity hypothesis.* It was advocated by the anthropologist and linguist Benjamin Lee Whorf.

See also Codability; Language.

WILD CHILDREN, or feral children, term applied to abandoned or lost youngsters who allegedly were "adopted" by animals and thereby survived. Legends of the Romulus and Remus variety have abounded for centuries, prompting Linnaeus in 1758 to coin the term feral (or wolf) men.

Very few such cases have been authenticated. The first involved a boy found by a French physician, Itard, in 1799. His attempts to socialize the boy and teach him language were largely unsuccessful. In contrast, however, is the case of a five-year-old boy captured in Salvador in 1932 who thrived under proper care and within three years had recovered fully from the effects of his earlier experiences.

Such cases are potentially useful in assessing the effects of extreme social isolation in early life. Their value is severely limited, however, by lack of crucial data regarding the child's age and mental and emotional condition prior to abandonment and the length of time spent in isolation.

—Cynthia MacRitchie, *Southern Connecticut State College*
Consult (11) Singh and Zingg, 1942.

WITHDRAWAL, a physical or psychological removal of oneself from a frustrating, anxious situation. Withdrawal can be the best solution to an immediate problem, as when one leaves the scene of a riot. Or it may be the end result of a long series of attempts to overcome frustration through problem solving, aggressive action, and perhaps overt hostility. A final defeated withdrawal into apathy—an apparent "I don't care" attitude that really means "There's no sense trying"—may be seen in the defeated ghetto dweller who is no longer even hunting for a job. Often the attention withdrawn from the environment is focused on one's own needs and wishes, leading to autistic thinking, as in daydreaming or, in the extreme, to schizophrenia.

—M. G. Affinito, *Southern Connecticut State College*
See also Defense Mechanism.

WITMER, LIGHTNER (1867–1956), American psychologist. Born in Philadelphia, he studied for his Ph.D. (1892) at Leipzig under Wilhelm Wundt. He was professor of psychology (1904–1937) and director, psychological laboratory and clinic, University of Pennsylvania.

The founder of the first psychological clinic in the United States, Witmer was largely responsible for creating the profession of clinical psychology. He applied psychological techniques to child guidance and developed many psychological tests for diagnosing speech and educational disorders. In 1907 Witmer founded the *Journal of Clinical Psychology*. He also helped establish psychological clinics throughout the country.

WOLF CHILDREN. *See* Wild Children.

WOLPE, JOSEPH (1915–   ), psychiatrist. Born in Johannesburg, South Africa, he took his M.D. at Witwatersrand University (1948) and is professor, Department of Behavior Science, Temple University Medical School. Wolpe is one of the founders of behavior therapy, a therapeutic technique based on modification of the behavior of the patient through learning rather than developing insights or resolving unconscious conflicts.

Wolpe is the author of several works including *Psychotherapy by Reciprocal Inhibition* (with others), 1958, and *Behavior Therapy Techniques* (with A. A. Lazarus), 1966.

WOODWORTH, ROBERT SESSIONS (1869–1962), American psychologist. Born in Belchertown, Mass., he studied for his A.B. (1895) and A.M. (1897) under Royce and James at Harvard, and for his Ph.D. (1899) under Cattell at Columbia. He was professor of Psychology at Columbia, from 1909 until 1942.

As an experimental psychologist, Woodworth is credited with helping to establish functional psychology—a study of causes, or the "why," of mental processes, rather than the "what" or "how" of structuralism. He described his psychology as dynamic and wanted to understand both the mechanisms of human thought and action and the stimuli that determined "the specificity of the drives." He summed up this goal with the statement that "the mechanism becomes a drive," and he believed that mechanism and drive could account for all human activity. This functional approach was in direct contrast to the psychology being supported by such major psychologists as E. B. Titchener and Hugo Munsterberg. Among Woodworth's publications are *Elements of Physiological Psychology* (with G. T. Ladd), 1911; *Dynamic Psychology*, 1917; the popular and classic textbook *Psychology*, 1921, 5th ed. 1947; and *Experimental Psychology*, 1938.

WORD ASSOCIATION TEST (also called free association test), a projective technique used in assessing personality and diagnosing behavior abnormalities. The basic technique is simple. The tester reads a prepared list of words. The subject, who is made as comfortable and relaxed as possible, is told to respond to each stimulus word with the first word that comes to mind. The examiner writes down the response word and notes the time required for each response and any special inflections or other reactions that can be detected. To help with the interpretation of the results, lists of common and uncommon responses to standard lists have been compiled.

The test was first used by Sir Francis Galton as a personality measure. Carl Jung used it as a help in psychoanalysis on the theory that repressed feelings would be revealed in reactions to emotionally charged words. The technique has also been tried for other purposes such as trapping a person suspected of crime, but studies have raised questions about the validity of word associations for revealing guilt.

Joseph Wolpe, a founder of behavior therapy.

WORK, STUDIES OF. Engineers as well as psychologists and other social scientists have made many studies of patterns of work. For example, laboratory experiments and observations of men on the job have produced *work curves* or work graphs. Frequently a worker's output climbs during a warming-up period to reach a peak, after which a slow decline begins. There may be an end spurt when the workman realizes he has only a short while to go before quitting time. Graphs vary, of course, according to the kind of task and the individuality of the worker.

Time-and-motion studies have had a great influence on production methods and personnel policies in American industry. These studies were first made by a mechanical engineer, Frederic Winslow Taylor, in the 1880s. By analyzing the motions of workers in a steel plant, he was able to propose principles of scientific management that increased production. Another famous efficiency expert was Frank Gilbreth, who with his wife made more elaborate work-time studies, using such means as photographs and movies. He and others drew up rules for "motion economy" in industrial production jobs and other tasks including bricklaying.

Taylor and others investigated such factors as motivating workers by various systems of pay. More recently, industrial psychologists have studied such topics as lighting, ventilation, accident prevention and safety, the value of rest breaks, management-employee relations, and morale. As jobs have become more and more technical, the design of man-machine systems has become increasingly important. Engineering psychologists make elaborate

Robert Woodworth helped divert the thrust of American psychology from structuralism to the functional search for cause and effect in mental process.

efforts to design equipment for efficiency, safety, and comfort.

Since the 1950s social scientists have begun to look at work as a part of a man's whole life and to examine the satisfactions a worker gets—or fails to get—from his occupation. People need food, shelter, and security, but they also want self-esteem, recognition from others, and a chance to do something well—to feel creative and productive. Many men and women complain that, despite their economic security, their jobs are deindividualized and monotonous. This monotony has resulted from efficiency studies that recommended breaking work down into small components, as on assembly lines. Many employees, in offices as well as industrial plants, feel that they lack knowledge or control of what the company is doing; they have nothing to take personal pride in. Some observers believe that dissatisfaction with work leads to serious amounts of absenteeism and inefficiency on the job and also contributes to personal emotional disturbances and feelings of alienation and rebelliousness.

See also Engineering Psychology; Space Psychology.

Consult (14) Gilbreth and Gilbreth, 1917; Taylor, 1911; *Work in America* 1972.

WUNDT, WILHELM (1832–1920) German psychologist. Born in Baden, he studied and taught at Heidelberg and Zurich. He established the first psychology laboratory at Leipzig, where he remained until his death.

Wundt was the first scientist to devote himself almost exclusively to psychological research. He believed that the object of study for psychology was human conscious experience and that the means to accomplish this was introspection or self-observation. In his laboratory, Wundt attempted to train his subjects to analyze their own sensory experiences into more basic elements. He was convinced that once these basic elements were identified, the process by which they became related and integrated could be made explicit. He applied his laboratory methods to the study of perception, auditory sensation, touch, taste, attention, time-sense, and feeling. To all of these problems, which had previously been in the realm of philosophy and physiology, he brought the same systematic methodological approach.

Wundt's influence extended to the United States through the work of E. B. Titchener, the founder of structuralism. While many of his research investigations now appear outdated, Wundt is remembered for helping to establish psychology as a legitimate scientific discipline. His major publication is *Physiological Psychology* 1880.

—Michael Rothenberg, *The City College of The City University of New York*

Through his extensive, methodical research on a wide range of sensory experience, German Wilhelm Wundt helped gain acceptance of psychology as a science.

WÜRZBURG SCHOOL. Würzburg University in Germany, circa 1880, formed the cradle from which modern experimental psychology was developed. Wilhelm Wundt, Oswald Külpe, and E. B. Titchener, the mentors associated with this school, held that science is empirical and that observation is the method of science. If one wanted to know about thought, one watched people and asked them to describe their thinking (introspection).

XENOPHOBIA, morbid fear of strange persons or places. *See* Phobia.

YERKES, ROBERT MEARNS (1876–1956), American biologist. Born in Breadysville, Pa., he received his Ph.D. from Harvard and became director of the Yale Laboratories of Primate Biology in 1919 (renamed Yerkes Laboratories at his retirement in 1941).

Well-known for his systematic studies of the anthropoid apes, Yerkes is considered the leader in the development of American comparative psychology. He concentrated on the study of learning experiences to refute the instinct theories used at the time to explain animal behavior. He succeeded, for example, in showing that kittens kill mice as a result of learning experiences, not by instinct.

In 1911, Yerkes developed a multiple-choice test that could be used for testing abstraction in animals. In this test, a row of nine or fewer boxes, both open and closed, was set before the animal; the animal had to determine which open box had food in it and then remember that box in subsequent testings. Yerkes' findings on the mental processes of apes include a demonstration that chimpanzees will imitate each other and also humans and that an orangutan can stack boxes to reach food after a demonstration and then transfer this learning to other problems.

Yerkes helped develop the Point Scale for measuring human ability for the U.S. Army during 1915, and he worked on the Yerkes-Dodson law—strong motivation will interfere with the learning of a difficult discrimination problem but helps with learning simpler tasks. Yerkes' many publications include *The Mental Life of Monkeys and Apes*, 1916; *The Mind of a Gorilla*, 1927; and *Chimpanzees: A Laboratory Colony*, 1943.

YOGA, a Sanskrit word meaning "union," used as a general designation for a Hindu religious school whose objective is union with Brahma, the Absolute. Diverse branches of Yoga seek, through centuries-old disciplines, to strengthen the physical, mental, spiritual, and moral aspects of man until he attains Samadhi, the state of knowledge of the Divine that is the indweller of all beings and the source of all life.

The *Hatha Yoga* branch of yogic practice

emphasizes disciplined breath control and asanas (bodily postures), which are thought to cure illness and restore the vital energy of the body. Advocates believe that proper diet and the practice of Hatha Yoga strengthen the body for further progress in mental and spiritual development.

Karma Yoga is concerned with the law of action and reaction, selfless service for others performed for its own sake without thought of reward. Its practitioners believe that these purify the mind and that the sense of personal identity merges with the Cosmic Consciousness.

Bhakti Yoga is the path of love and devotion to God or a divine incarnation. Its precepts are echoed in the Judeo-Christian tradition, "Thou shalt love the Lord thy God with all thy might, mind and strength."

Jana Yoga advocates knowledge attained through self-analysis and awareness, identifying with the Divinity within. It is for aspirants who choose the intellectual and philosophical path to God.

Japa Yoga is the practice of repeating a mantra, or the name of God. Constant reiteration of this sound structure, representing an aspect of the Divine, is believed to produce the vibrations of the mantra within the individual's entire system, bringing great peace and ultimately the goal of divine consciousness.

Raja Yoga, the "royal road," is for individuals who are scientific by inclination. It is the way to enlightenment through psychological experimentation with oneself. The practice of mental exercises and observation of their effects cuts through the deeper layers of consciousness into the awareness of Being itself.

Yogic practices offer Western psychology functionally efficient, personally appropriate, multidimensional courses of action. Each of these aims toward development of the physical, mental, spiritual, and moral being and the ideal integration of the inner self.

—Barbara B. Brown, *Veterans Administration Hospital, Sepulveda, California Consult* (14) Eliade, 1958; Eliot, 1921; Govinda, 1960; Kitagawa, 1960; Murti, 1955; Radhakrishnan and Moore, 1957.

ZEN, word derived from the Chinese Ch'an (from the Sanskrit *Dyana*), translated as "meditation." It defines the meditative school of Chinese and Japanese Buddhism. The goal of Zen meditation is to so still the mind that consciousness disappears. Its ultimate aim is *Satori*, or enlightenment, an awareness of the reality beyond the limits of individual consciousness. Through flashes of such awareness, and after long and arduous periods of training, the mind is freed from its habitual ways of perceiving, and the walls between self and reality dissolve.

The *Rinzai school* of Zen practice uses the *koan*, a puzzle without a logical solution, as a device for breaking the restrictions of the conscious mind and developing intuition. Guided by a master, the student tries to attain with the conscious mind that which can come only from something outside of consciousness, beyond the duality of the knower and the known. Part of this almost inexplicable experience is the Rinzai tradition of irrelevant or baffling statements, especially in answer to the student's questions. Perhaps the most famous koan is "What is the sound of one hand clapping?"

In the *Soto sect* of Zen the emphasis is on *zazen*, or "just sitting," with the mind intensely involved in a state of concentrated awareness. Experiencing true reality must be repeated and reinforced until the practitioner perceives the essence of mind, which is No-Mind, seeing into things as they are, into their "suchness." There must be a true alteration of consciousness, a perception of that which lies behind all differentiation.

The emphasis in Zen is on simplicity: to eat when hungry, drink when thirsty, to reduce living and perceiving to essentials. Like early Christian Gnosticism, Zen leads away from rigid dogma to make each person learn from within, although guidance of a teacher is necessary. Zen is a path for man to see into his own nature, to experience rather than to desire. It lends itself readily to Western psychological research, since it is not only a profound experience for the individual but adheres to a strict discipline for exploring altered states of consciousness and nonordinary levels of awareness and perception.

—Barbara B. Brown, *Veterans Administration Hospital, Sepulveda, California Consult* (14) Benoit, 1959; Humphreys, 1971; Kapleau, 1965; Miura and Sasaki, 1965; Moore, 1967; Suzuki, 1949.

ZOOPHOBIA, morbid fear of animals. *See* Phobia.

Students of Hatha Yoga.

This comprehensive bibliography lists all of the books and articles that are cited in the encyclopedia. Titles are grouped in fourteen sections according to divisions of the whole field of psychology.

In the body of the encyclopedia, the reader will find two kinds of references to the bibliography. At the end of most articles there are *Consult* references—for example, *Consult* (2) Boring, 1950. This directs the reader to the book by Edwin Boring listed in Section 2 of the bibliography. Within the text of many articles there are similar citations, inserted to support a point made in the text or to refer to a source that amplifies that particular statement.

The reader can find the book or article by turning to the bibliography, then to the numbered section, and then finding the author. If more than one book by that author is listed, the publication date identifies the title referred to.

Journals for reference in specific areas of psychology are noted at the end of a number of the bibliographic sections.

1. INTRODUCTORY TEXTBOOKS AND READINGS

Abrams, A. M., and Stanley, J. C., "Preparation of High School Psychology Teachers by Colleges," *American Psychologist,* 1967, 22, 166–69.

Allen, G. W., *William James: A Biography* (New York: 1967).

American Psychological Association, *A Career in Psychology* (Washington, D.C.: American Psychological Association, 1970).

American Psychological Association, *Directory* (Washington, D.C.: Published at frequent yearly intervals).

Annual Editions, *Readings in Psychology '72–'73* (Guilford, Conn.: The Dushkin Publishing Group, 1972).

Astin, Helen S., "Employment and Career Status of Women Psychologists," *American Psychologist,* 1972, 27, 371–381.

Bardon, J. I., and Bennett, Virginia, "Preparation for Professional Psychology: An Example from a School Psychology Training Program," *American Psychologist,* 1967, 22, 652–656.

Bardon, J. I., and Walker, N. W., "Characteristics of Graduate Training Programs in School Psychology," *American Psychologist,* 1972, 27, 652–656.

Bayton, J. A., Roberts, S. O., and Williams, K., "Minority Groups and Careers in Psychology," *American Psychologist,* 1970, 25, 504–510.

Brickman, W. W., and Lehrer, S. (eds.), *John Dewey: Master Educator,* 2d ed. (1965).

Campbell, D. P., and Soliman, A. M., "The Vocational Interests of Women in Psychology, 1942–1966," *American Psychologist,* 1968, 23, 158–163.

Candland, D. K., and Campbell, J. F., *Exploring Behavior* (New York: Basic Books, 1961).

Cates, Judith, and Dawson, W., "Master's in Psychology," *American Psychologist,* 1971, 26, 928–930.

Daniel, Robert S., (ed.), *Contemporary Readings in General Psychology,* 2d ed. (Boston: Houghton Mifflin, 1965).

Engle, T. L., "Objectives for and Subject Matter Stressed in High School Courses in Psychology," *American Psychologist,* 1967, 22, 162–166.

Engle, T. L., "Teaching Psychology at the Secondary School Level: Past, Present, Possible Future," *Journal of School Psychology,* 1967, 5, 168–178.

Engle, T. L., and Snellgrove, Louis, *Psychology: Its Principles and Applications,* 6th ed. (New York: Harcourt Brace Jovanovich, 1973).

English, H. B., and English, H. C., *A Comprehensive Dictionary of Psychological and Psychoanalytical Terms* (New York: David McKay Co., 1958).

"Ethical Standards of Psychologists," *American Psychologist,* 1968, 23, 357–361.

Eysenck, Hans J., *Uses and Abuses of Psychology* (Baltimore: Penguin Books, 1953).

Finger, F. W., " 'Professional Problems': Preparation for a Career in College Teaching," *American Psychologist,* 1969, 24, 1044–1049.

Goldenson, Robert M., *The Encyclopedia of Human Behavior* (Garden City: Doubleday, 1970).

Harriman, Philip L., *Handbook of Psychological Terms* (Totowa, N.J.: Littlefield, Adams, 1965).

Hebb, Donald O., *A Textbook of Psychology,* 2d ed. (Philadelphia: W. B. Saunders, 1966).

Heidbreder, Edna, *Seven Psychologies* (New York: Appleton-Century-Crofts, 1933).

Hilgard, Ernest R., and Atkinson, Richard C., *Introduction to Psychology,* 5th ed. (New York: Harcourt Brace Jovanovich, 1971).

Hill, L. K., "Some Observations on the Selection of 'Psychology Technicians'," *American Psychologist,* 1964, 19, 687–689.

Howell, R. J., and Murdock, M. L., "The Questionable Value of a Master's Degree for a Ph.D. Pursuing Student," *American Psychologist,* 1972, 27, 647–651.

Kalish, Richard A., *Psychology of Human Behavior* (Belmont, Calif.: Wadsworth Publishing Co., 1969).

Kimble, Gregory A., and Garmezy, N., *Principles of General Pyschology* (New York: Ronald Press, 1963).

Koffka, K., *Principles of Gestalt Psychology* (New York: Harcourt Brace, 1935).

Köhler, W., *Gestalt Psychology* (New York: Liveright, 1929, 1947).

Köhler, W., *The Task of Gestalt Psychology* (Princeton: Princeton University Press, 1969).

Leuba, Clarence, *Man: A General Psychology* (New York: Holt, Rinehart and Winston, 1961).

Lewin, K., *Principles of Topological Psychology* (New York: McGraw-Hill, 1936).

Lindgren, Henry C., Byrne, Donn, and Petrinovich, L. F., *Psychology: An Introduction to a Behavioral Science,* 2d ed. (New York: John Wiley, 1971).

Little, K. B., "Epilogue: Academic Marketplace 1984," *American Psychologist,* 1972, 27, 504–506.

Long, Barbara E., "A Model for Elementary School Behavioral Science as an Agent of Primary Prevention," *American Psychologist,* 1970, 25, 571–574.

Love, R. E., "Getting Your First Job: A View from the Bottom," *American Psychologist,* 1972, 27, 425–430.

Lunneborg, Patricia W., "Where Have All the Baccalaureates Gone?" *American Psychologist,* 1968, 23, 826–827.

McCollom, I. N., "Psychological Thrillers: Psychology Books Students Read When Given Freedom of Choice," *American Psychologist,* 1972, 26, 921–927.

McKeachie, Wilbert J., and Doyle, Charlotte L., *Psychology,* 2d. ed. (Reading, Mass: Addison-Wesley, 1970).

MacLeod, R. B., "The Teaching of Psychology," *American Psychologist,* 1971, 26, 245–249.

Manning, T. T., and Cates, Judith, "Specialization Within Psychology," *American Psychologist,* 1972, 27, 462–467.

Meyer, H. H., "The Future for Industrial and Organizational Psychology: Oblivion or Millennium?" *American Psychologist,* 1972, 27, 608–614.

Miller, G., "Psychology as a Means of Promoting Human Welfare," *American Psychologist,* 1969, 24, 1063–1075.

Morgan, Clifford T., and King, Richard A., *Introduction to Psychology,* 3d ed. (New York: McGraw-Hill, 1966).

Mosher, R. L., and Sprinthall, N. A., "Psychological Education in Secondary Schools: A Program to Promote Individual and Human Development," *American Psychologist,* 1970, 25, 911–924.

Munn, Norman L., *Psychology,* 5th ed. (Boston: Houghton Mifflin, 1966).

Murphy, Gardner, *Historical Introduction to Modern Psychology,* rev. ed. (New York: Harcourt Brace Jovanovich, 1949).

Noland, R. L., "School Psychologists and Counselors View the Role of the High School Psychology Course," *Journal of School Psychology,* 1967, 5, 177–184.

Norton, Fay-Tyler M., "Two-Year College Instruction: Opportunities for Psychology," *American Psychologist,* 1972, 27, 445–450.

Peck, R. F., "Why Should We Teach Elementary School Children About the Principles of Human Behavior?" *Journal of School Psychology,* 1967, 5, 235–236.

Roen, S. R., "Teaching the Behavioral Sciences in Elementary Grades," *Journal of School Psychology,* 1967, 5, 205–216.

Bibliography

Rubinstein, Joseph, *Psychology '73-'74 (Guilford, Conn.: The Dushkin Publishing Group, Inc., 1973)*.

Ruch, Floyd L., *Psychology and Life*, 8th ed. (Chicago: Scott, Foresman, 1971).

Sanford, Fillmore H., *Psychology: A Scientific Study of Man*, 2d ed. (Belmont, Calif.: Wadsworth Publishing Co., 1970).

Sargent, Stephen S., and Stafford, Kenneth, *Basic Teachings of the Great Psychologists* (Garden City: Doubleday, 1965).

Schein, Virginia E., "The Woman Industrial Psychologist: Illusion or Reality?" *American Psychologist,* 1971, 26, 704-712.

Sills, D. L., (ed.), *International Encyclopedia of the Social Sciences* (New York: Crowell Collier and Macmillan, 1968).

Task Force on the Practice of Psychology in Industry, "Effective Practice of Psychology in Industry," *American Psychologist,* 1971, 26, 974-991.

Thornton, B. M., "A Survey of the Teaching of Psychology in the High Schools," *American Psychologist,* 1967, 22, 677-678.

Thornton, B. M., and Colver, R. M., "The Psychology Course in Secondary Schools," *Journal of School Psychology,* 1967, 5, 185-190.

Traxler, A. J., "State Certification of School Psychologists: Recent Trends," *American Psychologist,* 1967, 22, 660-666.

Trow, W. C., "Psychology and the Behavioral Sciences in the Schools," *Journal of School Psychology,* 1967, 5, 241-249.

Viteles, M. S., "Psychology Today: Fact and Foible," *American Psychologist,* 1972, 27, 601-607.

Whittaker, James O., *et al., Introduction to Psychology* (Philadelphia: W. B. Saunders, 1970).

Woodworth, R. S., *Contemporary Schools of Psychology,* rev. ed. (New York: Roland Press, 1948).

Woods, P. J., "A History of APA's Concern with the Master's Degree: Or, Discharged with Thanks," *American Psychologist,* 1971, 26, 696-707.

Wrenn, Robert L., *Basic Contribution to Psychology: Readings* (Belmont, Calif.: Wadsworth Publishing Co., 1966).

Journals giving general coverage of psychology

American Psychologist, published monthly by American Psychological Association.

Contemporary Psychology, published monthly by American Psychological Association.

Psychological Abstracts, published monthly by American Psychological Association.

Psychology Today, published monthly by Communications/Research/Machines, Inc.

Behavior Today, weekly newsletter by Communications/Research/Machines, Inc.

Human Behavior, published by Western Psychological Services.

2. EXPERIMENTAL PRINCIPLES AND PROCEDURES

Blommers, P., and Lindquist, E. F., *Elementary Statistical Methods in Psychology and Education* (Boston: Houghton Mifflin, 1960).

Boring, Edwin G., *A History of Experimental Psychology,* 2d ed. (New York: Appleton-Century-Crofts, 1950).

Brown, C. W., and Ghiselli, E. E., *The Experimental Method in Psychology* (New York: McGraw-Hill, 1965).

Candland, Douglas K., *Psychology: The Experimental Approach* (New York: McGraw-Hill, 1968).

Garrett, H. E., *Great Experiments in Psychology* (New York: Appleton-Century-Crofts, 1930).

Hays, W. L., *Statistics for Psychologists* (New York: Holt, Rinehart and Winston, 1965).

Kling, J. W., and Riggs, L. A., *Woodworth and Schlosberg's Experimental Psychology* (New York: Holt, Rinehart and Winston, 1971).

McNemar, Q., *Psychological Statistics* (New York: John Wiley, 1962).

Marquis, Donald G., "Research Planning at the Frontier of Science," *American Psychologist,* 1948, 3, 432-435.

Postman, Leo, and Egan, J. P., *Experimental Psychology: An Introduction* (New York: Harper & Row, 1949).

Postman, Leo, and Egan, J. P., *Experiments and Demonstrations* (New York: McGraw-Hill, 1967).

Rosenthal, Robert A., *Experimenter Effects on Behavioral Research* (New York: Appleton-Century-Crofts, 1966).

Snellgrove, Louis, *Psychological Experiments and Demonstrations* (New York: McGraw-Hill, 1967).

Stevens, S. S. (ed.), *Handbook of Experimental Psychology* (New York: John Wiley, 1951).

Underwood, Benton J., *Experimental Psychology* (New York: Appleton-Century-Crofts, 1966).

Willems, E. P., and Raush, H. L., *Naturalistic Viewpoints in Psychological Research* (New York: Holt, Rinehart, and Winston, 1969).

Wilson, E. B., Jr., *An Introduction to Scientific Research* (New York: McGraw-Hill, 1952).

Woodworth, Robert S., and Schlosberg, H., *Experimental Psychology,* rev. ed. (New York: Holt, Rinehart and Winston, 1954).

Journal covering experimental principles and procedures

Journal of Experimental Psychology, published monthly by American Psychological Association. Note that periodicals in general psychology and in the various specialized fields frequently report and discuss experiments.

3. PHYSIOLOGICAL AND COMPARATIVE PSYCHOLOGY

Ardrey, R., *The Social Contract* (New York: Atheneum, 1970).

Ardrey, R., *The Territorial Imperative: A Personal Inquiry into the Animal Origins of Property and Nations* (New York: Atheneum, 1966).

Ax, A. F., "The Physiological Differentiation Between Fear and Anger in Humans," *Psychosomatic Medicine,* 1953, 14, 433-442.

Beach, F. A., *Hormones and Behavior* (New York: Holden, 1948).

Bernard, L. L., *Instinct, A Study in Social Psychology* (New York: Henry Holt, 1924).

Black, P. (ed.), *Physiological Correlates of Emotion* (New York: Academic Press, 1970).

Blurton Jones, N. (ed.), *Ethological Studies of Child Behavior* (New York: Cambridge University Press, 1972).

Bowlby, J., *Attachment and Loss:* Vol. 1, *Attachment* (New York: Basic Books, 1969).

Burghardt, G. M., and Hess, E. H., "Food Imprinting in Turtles," *Science,* 1966, 151, 108-109.

Caldwell, B. M., "Usefulness of the Critical Period Hypothesis in the Study of Filiative Behavior," *Merrill-Palmer Quarterly of Behavior and Development,* 1962, 8, 229-242.

Cannon, W. B., *The Wisdom of the Body* (New York: W. W. Norton, 1932).

Darwin, Charles, *The Origin of Species* (New York: Collier, 1900; original 1859).

Deutsch, J. A., and Deutsch, D., *Physiological Psychology.* (Homewood, Ill.: Dorsey, 1966).

Eibl-Eibesfeldt, I., *Ethology: The Biology of Behavior* (New York: Holt, Rinehart, & Winston, 1970).

Eysenck, H. J., *The IQ Argument: Race, Intelligence, and Education* (New York: Library Press, 1971).

Fletcher, R., *Instinct in Man* (New York: International Universities Press, 1957).

Foulkes, D., *The Psychology of Sleep* (New York: Charles Scribner's Sons, 1966).

Fraenkel, G. S., and Gunn, D. L., *The Orientation of Animals* (New York: Dover, 1961).

Freud, S., "Instincts and Their Vicissitudes" (1915), in E. Jones (ed.), *The Collected Papers of Sigmund Freud,* Vol. 4. (New York: Basic Books, 1959).

Gardner, Ernest, *Fundamentals of Neurology* (Philadelphia, Penn.: W. B. Saunders Co., 1968).

Gellhorn, E., *Autonomic Regulations: Their Significance for Physiology, Psychology, and Neuropsychiatry* (New York: Interscience Publishers, 1943).

Glass, D. C. (ed.), *Neurophysiology and Emotion* (New York: Rockefeller University Press, 1967).

Hasler, A. D., *Underwater Guideposts: Homing of Salmon* (Madison: University of Wisconsin Press, 1966).

Hess, E. H., "Imprinting: An Effect of Early Experience," *Science,* 1959, 130, 133–141.

Hess, E. H., "Imprinting in Nature," *Scientific American,* 1972.

Hinde, R., *Animal Behaviour,* 2d ed. (New York: McGraw-Hill, 1970).

Hyden, H., and Egyhazi, E., "Glial RNA Changes during a Learning Experiment in Rats," *Proceedings, National Academy of Science,* 1963, 49, 618–624.

Isaacson, R. L., *et al., A Primer of Physiological Psychology* (New York: Harper & Row, 1971).

Jacob, S. W., and Francone, C. A., *Structure and Function in Man* (Philadelphia: W. B. Saunders, 1970).

Jander, R., "Insect Orientation," *Annual Review of Entomology,* 8, 1963, pp. 95–109.

Jensen, A. R., *et al., Environment, Heredity, and Intelligence.* Harvard Reprint Series, No. 2 (Cambridge: Harvard University Press, 1969).

Kales, A. (ed.), *Sleep: Physiology and Pathology* (Philadelphia: J. B. Lippincott, 1969).

Kallmann, F. J., "Genetic Aspects of Psychoses," *The Biology of Mental Health and Disease* (New York: Harper, 1952).

Kallmann, F. J., *Heredity in Health and Mental Disorder* (New York: W. W. Norton, 1953).

Kallmann, F. J., "The Use of Genetics in Psychiatry," *Journal of Mental Science,* 1958, 104, 542–549.

Karczmer, A. G., and Eccles, J. C., *The Brain and Human Behavior* (New York: Springer, 1972).

Kleitman, N., *Sleep and Wakefulness* (Chicago: University of Chicago Press, 1963).

Leukel, F., *Introduction to Physiological Psychology* (St. Louis: C. V. Mosby, 1972).

Lenneberg, E. H., *Biological Foundations of Language* (New York: John Wiley, 1967).

Levine, R. P., *Genetics,* Modern Biology Series (New York: Holt, Rinehart & Winston, 1962).

Loeb, J., *Forced Movements, Tropisms, and Animal Conduct* (Philadelphia: Lippincott, 1918).

Lorenz, K., *King Solomon's Ring* (New York: T. Y. Crowell, 1952).

Lorenz, K., *Evolution and Modification of Behavior* (Chicago: University of Chicago Press, 1965).

Lorenz, K., "Companions as Factors in the Bird's Environment," in *Studies in Animal and Human Behavior,* Vol. 1 (Cambridge: Harvard University Press, 1970; original 1935).

Lorenz, K., *Studies in Animal and Human Behavior* (Cambridge: Harvard University Press, Vol. 1, 1970, Vol. 2, 1971).

Luce, G., and Segal, S., *Sleep* (New York: Coward-McCann, 1966).

Marler, P. R., and Hamilton, W. J., *Mechanisms of Animal Behavior* (New York: John Wiley, 1966).

Morris, D., *The Naked Ape* (New York: McGraw-Hill, 1967).

Olds, J., and Milner, P., "Positive Reinforcement Produced by Electrical Stimulation of Septal Area and Other Regions," *Journal of Comparative and Physiological Psychology,* 1954, 47, 419–427.

Richter, C. P., "The Self-Selection of Diets" in *Essays in Biology* (Berkeley: University of California Press, 1943).

Richter, C. P., "Total Self-regulating Functions in Animals and Human Beings," *Harvey Lectures,* 1942–1943, 38, 63–103.

Robinson, D. N. (ed.), *Heredity and Achievement, A Book of Readings* (London: Oxford University Press, 1970).

Sluckin, W., *Imprinting and Early Learning* (Chicago: Aldine, 1965).

Scott, J. P., "Critical Periods in Behavioral Development," *Science,* 1962, 138, 949–958.

Stasko, A. B., and Sullivan, C. M., "Responses of Planarians to Light—an Examination of Klino-Kinesis," *Animal Behavior Monographs,* 1971, 4, 47–124.

Stellar, E., and Sprague, J. M. (eds.), *Progress in Physiological Psychology* (New York: Academic Press, 1966).

Teitelbaum, Philip, *Physiological Psychology: Fundamental Principles* (Englewood Cliffs, N.J.: Prentice-Hall, 1967).

Thiessen, D. D., *Gene Organization and Behavior* (New York: Random House, 1972).

Thompson, Richard F., *Foundations of Physiological Psychology* (New York: Harper & Row, 1967).

Tinbergen, N., "On Aims and Methods of Ethology," *Zeitschrift für Tierpsychologie,* 1963, 20, 410–433.

Tinbergen, N. *The Study of Instinct* (Oxford: Clarendon Press, 1951).

Warren, J. M., "Primate Learning in Comparative Perspective," in A. M. Schrier, H. F. Harlow, and F. Stollnitz (eds.), *Behavior of Nonhuman Primates,* Vol. 1 (New York: Academic Press, 1965).

Wooldridge, D. E., *The Machinery of the Brain* (New York: McGraw-Hill, 1963).

Zuckerman, S., *The Social Life of Monkeys and Apes* (London: Kegan Paul, 1932).

Journal for reference on comparative and physiological psychology

Journal of Comparative and Physiological Psychology, published monthly by the American Psychological Association

4. SENSATION AND PERCEPTION

Alpiner, J. G., "Audiologic Problems of the Aged," *Geriatrics,* Jan. 1963, 18.

Alpiner, J. G., "The Audiologist Views Vocational Programs for Hearing-Impaired Adolescents and Adults," *Journal of the Rehabilitation of the Deaf,* April 1969.

Alpiner, J. G., *Speech and Hearing Disorders in Children* (Boston: Houghton Mifflin, 1970).

Alpiner, J. G., "Teacher of the Deaf and Audiology Training Programs: Limitations and Goals," *Proceedings of the 44th Meeting of the Convention of American Instructors of the Deaf,* March 1970.

Alpiner, J. G., "Planning a Strategy of Aural Rehabilitation for the Adult," *Hearing and Speech News,* Sept.-Oct. 1971.

Ames, A., "Biocular Vision as Affected by Relations Between Uniocular Stimulus Patterns in Commonplace Environments," *American Journal of Psychology,* 1946, 59, 333–357.

Bartley, H. S., *Principles of Perception* (New York: Harper & Row, 1969).

Boring, E. G., "The Moon Illusion," *American Journal of Physics,* 1943, 11, 55–60.

Broadbent, D. E., and Little, E. A. J., "Effects of Noise Reduction in a Work Situation," *Occupational Psychology,* 1960, 34, 133–140.

Bibliography

Carroll, T. J., *Blindness* (Boston: Little, Brown, 1961).

Davis, H., and Silverman, S. R. (eds.), *Hearing and Deafness* (New York: Holt, Rinehart & Winston, 1970).

Fletcher, H., *Speech and Hearing in Communication* (New York: Van Nostrand, 1953).

Fraser, G. R., *The Causes of Blindness in Childhood* (Baltimore: Johns Hopkins, 1967).

Geldard, F. A., *The Human Senses,* 2d ed. (New York: John Wiley, 1972).

Gibson, E. J., "The Development of Perception as an Adaptive Process," *American Scientist,* 1970, 58, 98–107.

Gibson, E. J. and Walk, R. D., "The Visual Cliff," *Scientific American,* 1960, 202, 64–71.

Gibson, J. J., *The Perception of the Visual World* (Boston: Houghton Mifflin, 1950).

Graunke, W. L., "Comment on Sociological and Psychological Factors Associated with Hearing Loss," *Journal of Speech and Hearing Rehabilitation,* June 1970.

Gregory, R. L., *Eye and Brain* (New York: McGraw-Hill, 1966).

Gregory, R. L., "Visual Illusions," *Scientific American,* 1968, 219, 66–76.

Held, R., and Richards, W., *Perception: Mechanism and Models* (San Francisco: Freeman, 1972).

Hirsh, I. J., *The Measurement of Hearing* (New York: McGraw-Hill, 1952).

Hochberg, J. E., *Perception* (Prentice-Hall, 1964).

Jerison, H. J., "Effects of Noise on Human Performance," *Journal of Applied Psychology,* 1959, 43, 96–101.

Kaufman, L., and Rock, I., "The Moon Illusion," *Scientific American,* 1962.

Kenshalo, D. R., "Basic Mechanisms of Neural Function," in Kling, J. W., and Riggs, L. A., *Woodworth and Schlosberg's Experimental Psychology* (New York: Holt, Rinehart & Winston, 1971).

Koffka, K., *Principles of Gestalt Psychology* (New York: Harcourt Brace, 1935).

Köhler, W., *Gestalt Psychology* (New York: Liveright, 1947).

Kolers, P., "The Illusion of Movement," *Scientific American,* 1964.

Luckiesh, M., *Visual Illusions* (New York: Dover, 1965).

McConnell, J. V., *et al.,* "Subliminal Stimulation: An Overview," *American Psychologist,* 1958, 13, 229–242.

Morkovin, B., *Through the Barriers of Deafness and Isolation* (New York: Macmillan, 1960).

Pirenne, M. H., *Optics, Painting, and Photography* (New York: Cambridge University Press, 1970).

Rainer, J. D., *et al.,* (eds.), *Family and Mental Health Problems in a Deaf Population* (New York: New York State Psychiatric Institute, 1963).

Rock, I., *et al.,* "Perception of Stroboscopic Movement: Evidence for Its Innate Basis," *Science,* 1965, 147, 1050–1052.

Rose, D. E., *Audiologic Assessment* (Englewood Cliffs, N.J.: Prentice-Hall, 1971).

Rushton, W. A. H., "Visual Pigments in Man," *Scientific American,* Nov. 1962.

Segall, M. H., *et al.,* The Influence of Culture on Visual Perception (New York: Bobbs-Merrill, 1966).

Senden, M. von, *Space and Sight,* trans. by P. Heath (Glencoe, Ill.: Free Press, 1960).

Solomon, P., *et al.* (eds.), *Sensory Deprivation* (Cambridge: Harvard University Press, 1961).

Subcommittee on Sensory Aids, Committee on Prosthetics Research and Development, Division of Engineering, National Research Council, "Evaluation of Sensory Aids for the Visually Handicapped" (Washington, D.C.: National Academy of Sciences, 1972).

U. S. Department of Health, Education and Welfare, Public Health Service, National Institute of Neurological Diseases and Blindness. *Annual Tabulations of the Model Reporting Area for Blindness Statistics: 1964 Statistical Report.* PHS Publication No. 1419 (Washington, D.C.: U. S. Government Printing Office, 1966).

Vernon, M., "Fifty Years of Research on the Intelligence of the Deaf and Hard of Hearing: A Survey of the Literature and Discussion of Implications," *Journal of Rehabilitation of the Deaf,* 1968.

Vernon, M., "Sociological and Psychological Factors Associated with Hearing Loss," *Journal of Speech and Hearing Rehabilitation,* Sept. 1969.

Vernon, M. D., *Perception Through Experience* (London: Methuen & Co., 1970).

World Health Organization, "Blindness: Information Collected from Various Sources," *Epidemiologic and Vital Statistics Reports,* 1966, 19, 437–511.

Zahl, P. E., *Blindness: Modern Approaches to the Unseen Environment* (Princeton: Princeton University Press, 1962).

5. INTELLIGENCE

Cronbach, L. J., *Educational Psychology,* 2d ed. (New York: Harcourt Brace).

Eysenck, H. J., *The IQ Argument: Race, Intelligence, and Education* (New York: Library Press, 1971).

Guilford, J. P., *The Nature of Human Intelligence* (New York: McGraw-Hill, 1967).

Heim, Alice, *Intelligence and Personality: Their Assessment and Relationship* (Middlesex, England: Penguin Books, 1970).

Jensen, A. R., *et al., Environment, Heredity, and Intelligence,* Harvard Reprint Series, No. 2 (Cambridge: Harvard University Press, 1969).

Justman, J., "Assessing the Intelligence of Disadvantaged Children," *Education,* 1967, 87, 354–362.

Lennon, R. T., *Testing and the Culturally Disadvantaged Child* (New York: Test Department, Harcourt Brace Jovanovich, 1964).

Peterson, J., *Early Conceptions and Tests of Intelligence* (Yonkers, N.Y.: World Book Company, 1925).

Robinson, D. N. (ed.), *Heredity and Achievement: A Book of Readings* (London: Oxford University Press, 1970).

Terman, L. M., *et al., Genetic Studies of Genius: The Mental and Physical Traits of a Thousand Gifted Children,* Vol. 1 (Stanford, Calif.: Stanford University Press, 1925).

Terman, L. M., and Oden, M. H., *The Gifted Child Grows Up; Genetic Studies of Genius,* Vol. 4 (Stanford, Calif.: Stanford University Press, 1947).

Terman, L. M., and Oden, M. H., *The Gifted Group at Midlife* (Stanford, Calif.: Stanford University Press, 1959).

Wechsler, D., *The Measurement and Appraisal of Adult Intelligence,* 4th ed. (Baltimore: Williams & Wilkins, 1958).

6. LEARNING AND MEMORY

Adams, J. A., *Human Memory* (New York: McGraw-Hill, 1967).

Bandura, A. H., "Vicarious Processes: A Case of No-trial Learning," in L. Berkowitz (ed.), *Advances in Experimental Social Psychology,* Vol II (New York: Academic Press, 1965).

Bandura, H., and Walters, R. H., *Social Learning and Personality Development* (New York; Holt, Rinehart, & Winston, 1963).

Black, A. H., "Direct Control of Neural Processes by Reward and Punishment," *American Scientist,* 1971, 59.

Bourne, L. E., Jr., *et. al., The Psychology of Thinking* (Englewood Cliffs, N.J.: Prentice-Hall, 1971).

Bousfield, W. A., "The Occurrence of Clustering in the Recall of Randomly Arranged Associates," *Journal of General Psychology,* 1953, 49, 229–240.

Bower, G. H., "Analysis of a Mnemonic Device" *American Scientist,* 1970, 58, 496–510.

Bruner, J. S., *et al., A Study of Thinking* (New York: John Wiley, 1956).

Bruner, J. S., "The Course of Cognitive Growth," *American Psychologist,* 1964, 19, 1–15.

Bruner, J. S., *et al., Studies in Cognitive Growth* (New York: John Wiley, 1966).

Cermak, L. S., *Human Memory: Research and Theory* (New York: Ronald Press, 1972).

Deese, J., and Hulse, S. H., *The Psychology of Learning* (New York: McGraw-Hill, 1967).

Harlow, H. F., "The Formation of Learning Sets," *Psychological Review,* 1949, 56, 51–65.

Harper, R. J. C., *et al.* (eds.), *The Cognitive Processes* (Englewood Cliffs, N.J.: Prentice-Hall, 1964).

Hilgard, E. R., and Bower, G. H., *Theories of Learning,* 3d ed. (New York: Appleton-Century-Crofts, 1966).

Hill, W. F., *Learning: A Survey of Psychological Interpretations,* rev. ed. (Scranton: Chandler, 1971).

Kimble, G. A., *Hilgard and Marquis' Conditioning and Learning,* 2d ed. (New York: Appleton-Century-Crofts, 1961).

Kimble, G. A. (ed.), *Foundations of Conditioning and Learning* (New York: Appleton- Century-Crofts, 1967).

Kimble, G. A., and Garmezy, N., *Principles of General Psychology* (New York: Ronald, 1968).

Köhler, W., *The Mentality of Apes* (New York: Harcourt, Brace, 1925).

Mancuso, J. C. (ed.), *Readings for a Cognitive Theory of Personality* (New York: Holt, Rinehart & Winston, 1970).

Marx, M. H. (ed.), *Learning: Theories* (New York: Macmillan, 1970).

Miller, N. E., "Alpha Waves, Artifacts," *Psychological Bulletin,* 1968, 69.

Miller, N. E., and Dollard, J., *Social Learning and Imitation* (New Haven: Yale University Press, 1941).

Neisser, U., *Cognitive Psychology* (New York: Appleton-Century-Crofts, 1967).

Norman, D. A., *Memory and Attention* (New York: John Wiley, 1969).

Nutt, R. H., *How to Develop a Good Memory* (New York: Simon & Schuster, 1941).

Part, C. (ed.), *Altered States of Consciousness* (New York: John Wiley, 1969).

Smith, W. I., and Rohrman, N. L., *Human Learning* (New York: McGraw-Hill, 1970).

Thorndike, E. L., "Animal Intelligence," *Psychological Monographs,* 1898.

Thorndike, E. L., and Woodworth, R. S., "The Influence of Improvement in One Mental Function Upon the Efficiency of Other Functions," *Psychological Review,* 1901, 8, 247–261, 384–395, 553–564.

Tulving, E., "Subjective Organization in Free Recall of Unrelated Words," *Psychological Review,* 1962, 69, 344–354.

Underwood, B. J., *et al.,* "Response Learning in Paired-Associate Lists as a Function of Intralist Similarity," *Journal of Experimental Psychology,* 1959, 58, 70–78.

Yates, F. A., *The Art of Memory* (Chicago: University of Chicago Press, 1966).

Young, R. K., "Tests of Three Hypotheses About the Effective Stimulus in Serial Learning, *Journal of Experimental Psychology,* 1962, 63, 307–313.

7. THINKING AND COMMUNICATION

Archer, E. J., "Re-evaluation of the Meaningfulness of All Possible CVC Trigrams," *Psychological Monographs,* 1960.

Berry, M. F., and Eisenson, J., *Speech Disorders* (New York: Appleton-Century-Crofts, 1956).

Bourne, L. E., Jr., *et al., The Psychology of Thinking* (Englewood Cliffs, N.J.: Prentice-Hall, 1971).

Brown, R. W., and Lenneberg, E. H., "A Study in Language and Cognition," *Journal of Abnormal and Social Psychology,* 1954, 49, 454–462.

Bruner, J. S., *et al., A Study of Thinking* (New York: John Wiley, 1956).

Bruner, J. S., *The Process of Education* (Cambridge, Mass.: Harvard University Press, 1960).

Chomsky, N., "A Review of B. F. Skinner's 'Verbal Behavior.'" *Language,* 1959, 35, 26–58.

Chomsky, N., *Language and Mind* (New York: Harcourt Brace Jovanovich, 1968).

Deese, J., and Hulse, S. H., *The Psychology of Learning* (New York: McGraw-Hill, 1967).

Duncker, K., "On Problem-Solving," *Psychological Monographs,* 1945, 58, No. 270.

Fletcher, H., *Speech and Hearing in Communication* (New York: Van Nostrand, 1953).

Glucksberg, S., and Weisberg, R. W., "Verbal Behavior and Problem Solving: Some Effects of Labeling in a Functional Fixedness Problem, *Journal of Experimental Psychology,* 1966, 71, 659–664.

Guilford, J. P., *The Nature of Human Intelligence* (New York: McGraw-Hill, 1967).

Halpern, H., *Adult Aphasia* (Indianapolis: Bobbs-Merrill, 1972).

Harper, R. J. C., *et al., The Cognitive Processes* (Englewood Cliffs, N.J.: Prentice-Hall, 1964).

Hovland, C. I., and Hunt, D. E., "Computer Simulation of Concept Attainment," *Behavioral Science,* 1960, 5, 265–267.

Langacker, R. W., *Language and its Structure* (New York: Harcourt, Brace, 1967, 1968).

Lashley, K. S., "Persistent Problems in the Evolution of Mind," *Quarterly Review of Biology,* 1949, 24, 28–42.

Lenneberg, E. H., *Biological Foundations of Language* (New York: John Wiley, 1967).

Luchins, A. S., "Mechanization in Problem Solving: the Effect of Einstellung," *Psychological Monographs,* 1942, 54, No. 248.

Luria, A. R., *The Mind of a Mnemonist* (New York: Basic Books, 1968).

McGuire, W. J., "Theory of the Structure of Human Thought," in R. P. Abelson, *et al., Theories of Cognitive Consistency: A Sourcebook* (Chicago: Rand-McNally, 1968).

McLuhan, M., and Fiore, Q., *The Medium Is the Message* (New York: Bantam, 1967).

Maier, N. R. F., "Reasoning in Humans, I, On Direction," *Journal of Comparative Psychology,* 1930, 10, 115–143.

Mancuso, J. C. (ed.), *Readings for a Cognitive Theory of Personality* (New York: Holt, Rinehart & Winston, 1970).

Miller, G. A., "The Magic Number Seven, Plus or Minus Two: Some Limits on Our Capacity for Processing Information," *Psychological Review,* 1956, 63, 81–97.

Miller, G. A., *et al., Plans and the Structure of Behavior* (New York: Holt, 1960).

Miller, G. A., and McNeill, D., "Psycholinguistics," in Aronson, E., & Lindzey, G. (eds.), *The Handbook of Social Psychology,* Vol III, 2d ed. (Reading, Mass.: Addison-Wesley, 1969).

Neisser, U., *Cognitive Psychology* (New York: Appleton-Century-Crofts, 1967).

Bibliography

Newell, A., and Simon, H. A., "Computer Simulation of Human Thinking," *Science,* 1961, 134, 2011–2017.

Noble, C. E., "An Analysis of Meaning," *Psychological Review,* 1952.

Osgood, C. E., "The Nature and Measurement of Meaning," *Psychological Bulletin,* 1952, 49, 197–237.

Osgood, C. E., *et al., The Measurement of Meaning* (Urbana: University of Illinois Press, 1957).

Paivio, A., *Imagery and Verbal Processes* (New York: Holt, Rinehart & Winston, 1971).

Perkins, W. H., *Speech Pathology* (St. Louis: C. V. Mosby, 1971).

Phillips, J. L., Jr., *The Origins of Intellect: Piaget's Theory* (San Francisco: W. H. Freeman, 1969).

Piaget, J., "The Stages of the Intellectual Development of the Child," *Bulletin of the Menninger Clinic,* 1962, 26, 120–145.

Schuell, H., *et al., Aphasia in Adults* (New York: Harper & Row, 1964).

Shannon, C. E., "A Mathematical Theory of Communication," *Bell Systems Technical Journal,* 1948, 27, 379–423, 623–656.

Shannon, C. E., and Weaver, W., *A Mathematical Theory of Communication* (Urbana: University of Illinois Press, 1949).

Slobin, D. I., *Psycholinguistics,* (Glenview, Ill.: Scott-Foresman, 1971).

Smith, W. I., and Rohrman, N. L., *Human Learning* (New York: McGraw-Hill, 1970).

Van Riper, C., *Speech Correction: Principles and Methods* (Englewood Cliffs, N.J.: Prentice-Hall, 1972).

Vygotsky, L. S., *Thought and Language* (Cambridge: MIT Press, 1962).

Wallas, G., *The Art of Thought* (New York: Harcourt, Brace, 1926).

Warr, P. B. (ed.), *Thought and Personality* (Baltimore: Penguin Books, 1970).

West, W., and Ansberry, M., *The Rehabilitation of Speech* (New York: Harper & Row, 1968).

Wiener, Norbert, *Cybernetics, or Control and Communication in the Animal and the Machine,* 2d ed. (Cambridge: MIT Press, 1961).

Wiener, Norbert, and Schadé, J. P., *Nerve, Brain, and Memory Models* (New York: American Elsevier, 1963).

Wiener, Norbert, and Schadé, J. P., *Cybernetics of the Nervous System* (New York: American Elsevier, 1965).

8. EMOTIONS, DRIVES, MOTIVES

Arnold, M. B., *Emotion and Personality,* 2 vols. (New York: Columbia University Press, 1960).

Arnold, M. B. (ed.), *Feelings and Emotion* (New York: Academic Press, 1970).

Atkinson, J. W. (ed.), *Motives in Fantasy, Action, and Society* (Princeton, N.J.: Van Nostrand, 1958).

Ax, A. F., "The Physiological Differentiation between Fear and Anger in Humans," *Psychosomatic Medicine,* 1953, 14, 433–442.

Bard, P., "On Emotional Expression after Decortication with Some Remarks on Certain Theoretical Views," Parts I and II, *Psychological Review,* 1934, 41, 309-329, 424–449.

Berlyne, D. E., *Conflict, Arousal, and Curiosity* (New York: McGraw-Hill, 1960).

Black, P. (ed.), *Physiological Correlates of Emotion* (New York: Academic Press, 1970).

Brady, J. V., "Emotion and the Sensitivity of Psychoendocrine Systems," in D. C. Glass (ed.), *Neurophysiology and Emotion* (New York: Rockefeller University Press, 1967).

Bridges, K. M. B., "A Genetic Theory of Emotions," *Journal of Genetic Psychology,* 1930, 37, 514–527.

Bridges, K. M. B., "Emotional Development in Early Infancy," *Child Development,* 1932, 3, 324–341.

Callum, M., *Body Talk* (New York: Bantam, 1971).

Cannon, W. B., "The James-Lange Theory of Emotion: A Critical Examination and an Alternative Theory," *American Journal of Psychology,* 1927, 39, 106–124.

Cannon, W. B., "Again the James-Lange and the Thalamic Theories of Emotion," *Psychological Review,* 1931, 38, 281–295.

Dittmann, A. T., *Interpersonal Messages of Emotion* (New York: Springer, 1972).

Fast, Julius, *Body Language* (New York: Pocket Books, 1971).

Frijda, N. H., "Emotion and Recognition of Emotion," in Arnold, M. B. (ed.), *Feelings and Emotion* (New York: Academic Press, 1970).

Gates, G. S., "An Observational Study of Anger," *Journal of Experimental Psychology,* 1926, 9, 325–336.

Geen, R. G., "Effects of Frustration, Attack, and Prior Training in Aggressiveness upon Aggressive Behavior," *Journal of Personality and Social Psychology,* 1968, 9, 316–321.

Gellhorn, E., *Autonomic Regulations; Their Significance for Physiology, Psychology, and Neuropsychiatry* (New York: Interscience Publishers 1943).

Glass, D. C. (ed.), *Neurophysiology and Emotion* (New York: Rockefeller University Press, 1967).

James, W., "What Is an Emotion?" *Mind,* 1884, 9, 188–205.

James, W., *The Principles of Psychology* (New York: Holt, 1890).

Lacey, J. I., "Somatic Response Patterning and Stress: Some Revisions of Activation Theory," in Appley, M. H., and Trumbull, R. (eds.), *Psychological Stress: Issues in Research* (New York: Appleton-Century-Crofts, 1967).

Lacey, J. I., and Lacey, B. C., "Some Autonomic-Central Nervous System Interrelationships," in Black, P. (ed.), *Physiological Correlates of Emotions* (New York: Academic Press, 1970).

Lewin, Kurt, *Field Theory in Social Science* (New York: Harper, 1951).

Lindsley, D. B., "Emotion," in Stevens, S. S. (ed.), *Handbook of Experimental Psychology* (New York: John Wiley, 1951).

Lindsley, D. B., "The Role of Nonspecific Reticulthalamo-cortical Systems in Emotion," in Black, P. (ed.), *Physiological Correlates of Emotions* (New York: Academic Press, 1970).

McClelland, D., *The Achieving Society* (Princeton, N.J.: Van Nostrand, 1961).

Mandler, G., "Emotion," in Newcomb, T. M. (ed.), *New Directions in Psychology* (New York: Holt, Rinehart & Winston, 1962).

Maslow, A. H., *Motivation and Personality* (New York: Harper, 1954).

Murray, H. A., *et al., Explorations in Personality* (New York: Oxford University Press, 1938).

Olds, J., "Self Stimulation of the Brain," *Science,* 1958, 127, 315–323.

Olds, J., and Milner, P., "Positive Reinforcement Produced by Electrical Stimulation of the Septal Area and Other Regions of the Rat Brain," *Journal of Comparative and Physiological Psychology,* 1954, 47, 411–427.

Schachter, S., and Singer, J. E., "Cognitive, Social and Physiological Determinants of Emotional State," *Psychological Review,* 1962, 69, 379–399.

Schlosberg, H., "The Description of Facial Expression in Terms of Two Dimensions," *Journal of Experimental Psychology,* 1952, 44, 229–237.

Selye, H., "The General-Adaptation-Syndrome in Its Relationship to Neurology, Psychology, and Psychopathology," in Weider, A. (ed.), *Contributions Toward Medical Psychology,* Vol. 1 (New York: Ronald, 1953).

Selye, H., *The Stress of Life* (New York: McGraw-Hill, 1956).

Thomas, W. I., *The Unadjusted Girl* (Boston: Little, Brown, 1923).

Watson, J. B., and Rayner, R., "Conditioned Emotional Reactions," *Journal of Experimental Psychology*, 1920, 3, 1–14.

Young, P. T., *Motivation and Emotion* (New York: John Wiley, 1961).

9. PERSONALITY

Adorno, T. W., *et al., The Authoritarian Personality* (New York: Harper, 1950).

Allport, G. W., *Becoming* (New Haven: Yale Paperbound, 1960).

Allport, G. W., *Pattern and Growth in Personality* (New York: Holt, Rinehart & Winston, 1961).

Allport, G. W., and Vernon, G. E., *Studies in Expressive Movement* (New York: Macmillan, 1933).

Anastasi, A., *Differential Psychology* (New York: Macmillan, 1965).

Aronfreed, J., *Conduct and Conscience* (New York: Academic Press, 1968).

Bandura, A. H., and Walters, R. H., *Social Learning and Personality Development* (New York: Holt, Rinehart & Winston, 1963).

Bardwick, J. M., *Psychology of Women: A Study of Bio-cultural Conflicts* (New York: Harper & Row, 1971).

Bardwick, J. M. (ed.), *Readings on the Psychology of Women* (New York: Harper & Row, 1972).

Beach, F. (ed.), *Sex and Behavior* (New York: John Wiley, 1965).

Beauvoir, Simone de, *The Second Sex* (New York: Knopf, 1957).

Coleman, J. C., *Personality Dynamics and Effective Behavior* (1960).

Dollard, J., and Miller, N. E., *Personality and Psychotherapy* (New York: McGraw-Hill, 1950).

Ellis, A., and Abarbanel, A. (eds.), *Encyclopedia of Sexual Behavior*, 2d ed. (New York: Hawthorn Books, 1967).

Erikson, E., "Growth and Crises of the Healthy Personality," *Psychological Issues*, 1959, 1, 50–100.

Fast, Julius, *Body Language* (New York: Pocket Books, 1971).

Festinger, L., *A Theory of Cognitive Dissonance* (New York: Harper & Row, 1957).

Freud, Anna, *The Ego and the Mechanisms of Defense* (London: Hogarth Press, 1937).

Freud, Sigmund, *A General Introduction to Psychoanalysis* (New York: Doubleday, 1920).

Freud, Sigmund, "Some Psychological Consequences of the Anatomical Distinction Between the Sexes," *International Journal of Psychoanalysis*, 1927, 8, 133–297.

Freud, Sigmund, "Female Sexuality," *International Journal of Psychoanalysis*, 1932, 13, 281–297.

Freud, Sigmund, "The Psychology of Women," in *New Introductory Lectures on Psychoanalysis* (New York: W. W. Norton, 1933).

Goldman, G. D., and Milman, D. S., *Modern Woman: Her Psychology and Sexuality* (Springfield, Ill.: C. C. Thomas, 1969).

Goldstein, J. H., and McGhee, P. E. (eds.), *The Psychology of Humor* (New York: Academic Press, 1972).

Guilford, J. P., *Personality* (New York: McGraw-Hill, 1959).

Hamburg, D. A., and Lunde, D. T., "Sex Hormones in the Development of Sex Differences in Human Behavior," in E. E. Maccoby (ed.), *The Development of Sex Differences* (Stanford, Calif.: Stanford University Press, 1966).

Henry, W. E., *The Analysis of Fantasy: The Thematic Apperception Technique in the Study of Personality* (New York: John Wiley, 1956).

Hoffman, M. L., "Moral Development," in P. Mussen (ed.), *Carmichael's Manual of Child Psychology,* (3d ed.) Vol. 2 (New York: John Wiley, 1970).

Holt, A. G., *Handwriting in Psychological Interpretation* (Springfield, Ill.: C. Thomas, 1965).

Horner, M. S., "Femininity and Successful Achievement: A Basic Inconsistency," in J. M. Bardwick *et al., Feminine Personality and Conflict,* (Belmont Calif.: Wadsworth, 1970).

Kagan, J., and Moss, H. A., *Birth to Maturity* (New York: John Wiley, 1962).

Katchadourian, H. A., and Lunde, D. T., *Fundamentals of Human Sexuality* (New York: Holt, Rinehart & Winston, 1972).

Kohlberg, L., "The Development of Children's Orientation Toward a Moral Order, I, Sequence in the Development of Moral Thought," *Vita Humana*, 1963, 6, 11–33.

Kohlberg, L., "Development of Moral Character and Moral Ideology," in M. L. Hoffman and L. W. Hoffmann, *Review of Child Development Research*, Vol. 1 (New York: Russell Sage Foundation, 1964, 383–431).

Kretschmer, E., *Physique and Character* (New York: Harcourt Brace, 1925).

Levine, Jacob (ed.), *Motivation in Humor* (New York: Atherton Press, 1969).

Levine, S. N., "Sex Differences in the Brain," *Scientific American*, April 1966.

Lewinson, T. S., and Zubin, J., *Handwriting Analysis* (New York: Kings Crown Press, 1942).

Maccoby, E., *The Development of Sex Differences* (Stanford, Calif.: Stanford University Press, 1966).

Maddi, S. R., *Personality Theories: A Comparative Analysis* (Homewood, Ill.: Dorsey Press, 1968).

Mancuso, J. C. (ed.), *Readings for a Cognitive Theory of Personality* (New York: Holt, Rinehart & Winston, 1970).

Mindess, Harvey, *Laughter and Liberation* (Los Angeles: Nash Publications, 1971).

Munroe, R. L., *Schools of Psychoanalytic Thought* (New York: Dryden Press, 1955).

Murray, H. A., *et al., Explorations in Personality* (New York: Oxford University Press, 1938).

Rogers, C. R., *On Becoming a Person: A Therapist's View of Psychotherapy* (Boston: Houghton Mifflin, 1961).

Rosenberg, B. G., and Sutton-Smith, B., *Sex and Identity,* (New York: Holt, Rinehart & Winston, 1972).

Schoeffer, D. L. (ed.), *Sex Differences in Personality: Readings* (Belmont, Calif.: Wadsworth, 1971).

Seward, G., and Williamson, R. E., *Sex Roles in a Changing Society* (New York: Random House, 1970).

Sheldon, W. H., *et al., The Varieties of Human Physique: An Introduction to Constitutional Psychology* (New York: Harper, 1940).

Sheldon, W. H., *et al., Atlas of Men: A Guide for Somatotyping the Adult Male at All Ages* (New York: Harper, 1954).

Symonds, P. M., *The Ego and the Self* (New York: Appleton-Century-Crofts, 1951).

Wolpe, J., and Lazarus, A. A., *Behavior Therapy Techniques: A Guide to the Treatment of Neuroses* (London: Pergamon Press, 1966).

Young, W. C., *et al.,* "Phoenix, Hormones and Sexual Behavior," in J. Money (ed.), *Sex Research: New Developments* (New York: Holt, Rinehart & Winston, 1965).

Journal for Reference on Personality

Journal of Personality and Social Psychology, published monthly by The American Psychological Association.

10. SOCIAL BEHAVIOR

Adams, J. S., "Inequity in Social Exchange," in Leonard Berkowitz (ed.), *Advances in Experimental Social Psychology*, Vol. 2 (New York: Academic Press, 1965).

Adorno, T. W., *et al., The Authoritarian Personality* (New York: Harper, 1950).

Bibliography

Alberti, R. E., *Your Perfect Right* (California: Impact Press, 1970).

Allport, G. W., *The Nature of Prejudice* (Reading, Mass.: Addison-Wesley, 1954).

Allport, G. W., and Postman, L., *The Basic Psychology of Rumor* (New York Academy of Science, Series II, 8, 1945).

Altman, D., *et al.*, in Stanley Milgram, "The Experience of Living in Cities," *Science*, 1970, 1461-68.

Ardrey, R., *The Territorial Imperative* (New York: Atheneum, 1966).

Ardrey, R., *The Social Contract* (New York: Atheneum, 1970).

Aronson, E., "Some Antecedents of Interpersonal Attraction," in W. J. Arnold and D. Levine (eds.), *Nebraska Symposium on Motivation, 1969* (Lincoln: University of Nebraska Press, 1969).

Asch, S. E., *Social Psychology* (Englewood Cliffs, N.J.: Prentice-Hall, 1952).

Asch, S. E., "Opinions and Social Pressures," *Scientific American*, 1955, 193, 31-35.

Asch, S. E., "Studies of Independence and Submission to Group Pressure; I. A. Minority of One Against a Unanimous Majority." *Psychological Monographs*, 1956, 70, No. 416.

Ashmore, R. D., "Prejudice: Causes and Cures," in B. E. Collins (ed.), *Social Psychology* (Reading, Mass.: Addison-Wesley, 1970).

Atkinson, J. W., "Motivational Determinants of Risk-Taking Behaviour," *Psychological Review*, 1957, 64, 359-372.

Bandura, A. H., and Walters, R. H., *Social Learning and Personality Development* (New York: Holt, Rinehart & Winston, 1963).

Bandura, A. H., "Vicarious Processes: A Case of No-Trial Learning," in L. Berkowitz (ed.), *Advances in Experimental Social Psychology*, Vol II (New York: Academic Press, 1965).

Bandura, A. H., *Principles of Behavior Modification* (New York: Holt, Rinehart & Winston, 1969).

Bandura, A. H., and Walters, R. H., *Adolescent Aggression* (New York: Ronald Press, 1959).

Beach, F. A., *Hormones and Behavior* (New York: Holden, 1948).

Bergler, E., *The Psychology of Gambling* (New York: International Universities Press, 1970).

Berkowitz, L., *Aggression: A Social Psychological Analysis* (New York: McGraw-Hill, 1962).

Berkowitz, L. (ed.), *Advances in Experimental Social Psychology* (New York: Academic Press, 1965).

Berkowitz, L., *The Roots of Aggression* (New York: Atherton Press, 1969).

Berlyne, D. E., *Conflict, Arousal, and Curiosity* (New York: McGraw-Hill, 1960).

Bernard, L. L., *Instinct, A Study in Social Psychology* (New York: Holt, 1924).

Bersheid, Ellen, and Walster, Elaine, *Interpersonal Attraction* (Reading, Mass.: Addison-Wesley, 1969).

Boyd, W. H., and Bolen, D. W., "The Compulsive Gambler and Spouse in Group Psychotherapy," in I. Kusyszyn (ed.), *Studies in the Psychology of Gambling* (Toronto: York University, 1972).

Brehm, J. W., and Cohen, A. R., *Explorations in Cognitive Dissonance* (New York: John Wiley, 1962).

Brown, R., *Social Psychology* (New York: Free Press, 1965).

Byrne, Donn, "Attitudes and Attraction" in L. Berkowitz (ed.), *Advances in Experimental Social Psychology*, Vol. 4 (New York: Academic Press, 1969).

Calhoun, J. B., "A Behavioral Sink," in E. L. Bliss (ed.), *Roots of Behavior* (New York: Harper & Row, 1962).

Carsmith, J. M., *et al.*, "Studies in Forced Compliance: The Effect of Pressure for Compliance on Attitude Change Produced by Face-to-face Role Playing and Anonymous Essay Writing," *Journal of Personality and Social Psychology*, 1966, 4, 1-13.

Chein, I., "An Introduction to Sampling," in Sellitz Claire, *et al.*, *Research Methods in Social Relations*, rev. ed. (New York: Holt, Rinehart & Winston, 1959).

Cochran, S., *Sampling Techniques* (New York: John Wiley, 1963).

Cohen, J., "The Nature of Gambling," in I. Kusyszyn (ed.), *Studies in the Psychology of Gambling* (Toronto: York University, 1972).

Cohen, J., *Psychological Probability* (London: Allen & Unwin, 1972).

Cook, S. W., and Sellitz, C., "A Multiple Indicator Approach to Attitude Measurement," *Psychological Bulletin*, 1964, 62, 36-55.

Darley, J. M., and Latane, B., "Bystander Intervention in Emergencies: Diffusion of Responsibilities," *Journal of Personality and Social Psychology*, 1968, 8, 377-383.

Davies, J. C., "Toward a Theory of Revolution," *American Sociological Review*, 1962, 27, 5-19.

Davis, J. A., "A Formal Interpretation of the Theory of Relative Deprivation," *Sociometry*, 1959, 22, 280-296.

Deutsch, M., "Trust and Suspicion," *Journal of Conflict Resolution*, 1958, 2, 265-279.

Dollard, J., *et al.*, *Frustration and Aggression* (New Haven: Yale University Press, 1939).

Edwards, W., "Probability Preferences Among Bets with Differing Expected Values," *American Journal of Psychology*, 1954, 67, 56-67.

Farber, I. E., *et al.*, "Brainwashing, Conditioning, and DDD (Debility, Dependency, and Dread)," *Sociometry*, 1957, 20, 271-285.

Festinger, L., *A Theory of Cognitive Dissonance* (Palo Alto: Stanford University Press, 1957).

Festinger, L., *et al.*, *Social Pressures in Informal Groups: A Study of Human Factors in Housing* (New York: Harper, 1950).

Festinger, L., and Carlsmith, J. M., "Cognitive Consequences of Forced Compliance," *Journal of Abnormal and Social Psychology*, 1959, 58, 203-210.

Fishbein, M., *Readings in Attitude Theory and Measurement* (New York: John Wiley, 1967).

Fishbein, M. and Ajzen, I., "Attitudes," in P. Mussen and M. Rosenzweig (eds.), *Annual Review of Psychology*, 1972, 23, 487-544.

Freedman, J., and Sears, D. O., "Selective Exposure," in L. Berkowitz (ed.), *Advances in Experimental Social Psychology*, Vol. 2 (New York: Academic Press, 1965).

Gamson, W. A., *Power and Discontent* (Homewood, Ill.: Dorsey Press, 1968).

Geen, R. G., "Effects of Frustration, Attack, and Prior Training in Aggressiveness upon Aggressive Behavior," *Journal of Personality and Social Psychology*, 1968, 9, 316-321.

Goodnow, J. J., "Determinants of Choice Distribution in Two-Choice Situations," *American Journal of Psychology*, 1955, 68, 106-116.

Gouldner, A. W., "The Norm of Reciprocity: A Preliminary Statement," *American Sociological Review*, 1960, 25, 161-178.

Gurin, P. *et al.*, "Internal-external Control in the Motivational Dynamics of Negro Youth," *Journal of Social Issues*, 1969, 25, 29-33.

Gurr, T., *Why Men Rebel* (Princeton, N.J.: Princeton University Press, 1970).

Hacker, H., "Women as a Minority Group," *Social Forces*, 1951, 30, 60-69.

Harding, J., *et al.*, "Prejudice and Ethnic Relations," in G. Lindzey and E. Aronson, (eds.), *Handbook of Social Psychology*, Vol. 5, 2d ed. (Reading, Mass.: Addison-Wesley, 1969).

Heider, F., *The Psychology of Interpersonal Relations* (New York: John Wiley, 1958).

Hollander, E. P., *Principles and Methods of Social Psychology*, 2d ed. (New York: Oxford University Press, 1971).

Hollander, E. P., and Hunt, R. G., *Current Perspectives in Social Psychology: Readings with Commentary*, 3d ed. (New York: Oxford University Press, 1971).

Hollander, E. P., and Hunt, R. G., *Classic Contributions to Social Psychology: Readings with Commentary* (New York: Oxford University Press, 1972).

Homans, G. C., *Social Behavior: Its Elementary Forms* (New York: Harcourt Brace, 1961).

Hovland, C. I., *et al., Experiments on Mass Communications* (Princeton: Princeton University Press, 1949).

Hovland, C. I., *et al., Communication and Persuasion* (New Haven: Yale University Press, 1953).

Inbau, F. E., and Reid, J. E., *Criminal Interrogation and Confessions*, 2d ed. (Baltimore: Williams and Wilkins, 1967).

Janis, I. L., "Effects of Fear Arousal on Attitude Change: Recent Developments in Theory and Experimental Research," in L. Berkowitz (ed.), *Advances in Experimental Social Psychology*, Vol. 3 (New York: Academic Press, 1967).

Janis, I. L., and King, B. T., "The Influence of Role-Playing on Opinion Change," *Journal of Abnormal and Social Psychology*, 1954, 49, 211–218.

Janis, I. L., *et al., Personality and Persuasibility* (New Haven: Yale University Press, 1959).

Jones, E. E., *Ingratiation: A Social Psychological Analysis* (New York: Appleton-Century-Crofts, 1964).

Jones, E. E., and Gerard, H. B., *Foundations of Social Psychology* (New York: John Wiley, 1967).

Jones, J., *Prejudice and Racism* (Reading, Mass.: Addison-Wesley, 1972).

Katz, D., "The Functional Approach to the Study of Attitudes," *Public Opinion Quarterly*, 1960, 24, 163–204.

Kelley, H. H., *et al.,* "Negotiating the Division of a Reward Under Incomplete Information," *Journal of Experimental Social Psychology*, 1967, 3, 361–398.

Kelley, H. H., and Stahelski, A. J., "Social Interaction Basis of Cooperators' and Competitors' Beliefs about Others," *Journal of Personality and Social Psychology*, 1970, 16, 92–109.

Kelman, H. C., "Compliance, Identification, and Internalization: Three Processes of Attitude Change," *Journal of Conflict Resolution*, 1958, 2, 51–60.

Kelman, H. C., and Baron, R. M., "Inconsistency as a Psychological Signal," in R. P. Abelson, *et al.* (ed.), *Theories of Cognitive Consistency: a Sourcebook* (Chicago: Rand-McNally, 1968).

Kish, L., *Survey Sampling* (New York: John Wiley, 1965).

Knowles, E. S., *et al.,* "Risk-Taking as a Personality Trait," *Social Behaviour and Personality*, 1972.

Knox, R. E., and Inskster, J. A., "Postdecision Dissonance at Post Time," in I. Kusyszyn (ed.), *Studies in the Psychology of Gambling* (Toronto: York University, 1972).

Kogan, N., and Wallach, M. A., *Risk Taking: A Study in Cognition and Personality* (New York: Holt, Rinehart & Winston, 1964).

Kogan, N., and Wallach, M. A., "Risk Taking as a Function of the Situation, the Person and the Group," in *New Directions in Psychology III* (New York: Holt, Rinehart & Winston, 1967).

Krech, D., *et al., Individual in Society* (New York: McGraw-Hill, 1962).

Kusyszyn, I., "The Gambling Addict Versus the Gambling Professional: A Difference in Character?" in I. Kusyszyn (ed.) *Studies in Psychology of Gambling* (Toronto: York University, 1972).

Lasswell, H. D., "The Structure and Function of Communication in Society," in L. Bryson (ed.), *Communication of Ideas* (New York: Harper & Row, 1948).

Latane, B., and Darley, J. M., *The Unresponsive Bystander: Why Doesn't He Help?* (New York: Appleton-Century-Crofts, 1970).

Lee, D. H. K., "The Role of Attitudes in Responses to Environmental Stress," *Journal of Social Issues*, 1966, 4, 83.

Lefkowitz, M. M., *et al.,* "Television Violence and Child Aggression: A Follow-up Study," in *Television and Social Behavior*, Vol. 3 (Washington, D. C.: U. S. Government Printing Office, 1972).

Levinger, G. and Snoek, D., *Attraction in Relationship: A New Look at Interpersonal Attraction* (Morristown, N.J.: General Learning Press, 1972).

Lewin, K., *Field Theory in Social Science* (New York: Harper, 1951).

Lewis, A. J., "Problems of Obsessional Illness," *Proceedings of the Royal Society of Medicine*, 1936, 29, 325.

Lewis, S. A. and Pruitt, D. G., "Orientation, Aspiration Level and Communication Freedom in Integrative Bargaining," *Proceedings*, 79th Annual Convention, American Psychological Association, 1971.

Liebert, R. M., *et al.,* "The Effects of Information and Magnitude of Initial Offer on Interpersonal Negotiation," *Journal of Experimental Social Psychology*, 1968, 4, 431–441.

Lindzey, Gardner, and Aronson, E. (eds.), *Handbook of Social Psychology*, 5 vols. (Reading, Mass.: Addison-Wesley, 1968).

Liverant, S., and Scodel, A., "Internal and External Control as Determinants of Decision Making Under Conditions of Risk," *Psychological Reports*, 1960, 1, 59–67.

Lorenz, K., *On Aggression* (New York: Harcourt Brace Jovanovich, 1966).

Lupfer, M., "The Effects of Risk-Taking Tendencies and Incentive Conditions on the Performance of Investment Groups," *Journal of Social Psychology*, 1970, 82, 135–136.

McClelland, D., *The Achieving Society* (Princeton, N. J.: Van Nostrand, 1961).

Maccoby, E., *et al., Readings in Social Psychology*, 3d ed. (New York: Holt, Rinehart & Winston, 1958).

McGlothlin, W., "A Psychometric Study of Gambling," *Journal of Consulting Psychology*, 1954, 18, 145–149.

McGuire, W. J., "Nature of Attitudes and Attitude Change," in G. Lindzey and E. Aronson (eds.), *The Handbook of Social Psychology*, Vol. 3 (Reading, Mass.: Addison-Wesley, 1968).

McGuire, W. J., "Theory of the Structure of Human Thought," in R. P. Abelson, *et al., Theories of Cognitive Consistency: a Sourcebook* (Chicago: Rand-McNally, 1968).

McGuire, W. J., "Attitude Change: The Information Processing Paradigm," in C. G. McClintock (ed.), *Experimental Social Psychology* (New York: Holt, Rinehart & Winston, 1972).

McLuhan, M., and Fiore, Q., *The Medium is the Message* (New York: Bantam, 1967).

Marlowe, Leigh, *Social Psychology* (Rockleigh, N.J.: Holbrook Press, 1971).

Merton, R. K., *Social Theory and Social Structure*, rev. ed. (Glencoe, Ill.: Free Press, 1957).

Mogy, R. B., and Pruitt, D. G., "The Effects of a Threatener's Enforcement Costs on Threat Credibility and Compliance," *Journal of Personality and Social Psychology*.

Moran, E., "Gambling as a Form of Dependence," *British Journal of Addictions*, 1970, 64, 419–428.

Moran, E., "Pathological Gambling," in I. Kusyszyn (ed.), *Studies in the Psychology of Gambling* (Toronto: York University, 1972).

Munson, R. F., "Decision-Making in an Actual Gambling Situation," *American Journal of Psychology*, 1962, 75, 640–643.

Bibliography

Nemeth, Charlan, "A Critical Analysis of Research Utilizing the Prisoner's Dilemma Paradigm for the Study of Bargaining," in Leonard Berkowitz (ed.), *Advances in Experimental Social Psychology,* Vol. 6 (New York: Academic Press, 1972).

Osgood, C. E., *An Alternative to War or Surrender* (Urbana, Ill.: University of Illinois Press, 1962).

Osgood, C. E., and Tannenbaum, P. H., "The Principle of Congruity in the Prediction of Attitude Change," *Psychological Review,* 1955, 62, 42–55.

Peck, D. F., and Ashcroft, J. B., "The Use of Stimulus Satiation in the Modification of Habitual Gambling," *Proceedings of the Second BEA Conference on Behaviour Modification* (Kilkenny, Ireland: 1970).

Pettigrew, T., "Social Evaluation Theory: Convergences and Applications," in D. Levine (ed.), *Nebraska Symposium on Motivation, 1967* (Lincoln: University of Nebraska Press, 1967).

Pruitt, D. G., "Definition of the Situation as a Determinant of International Action," in H. C. Kelman (ed.), *International Behavior* (New York: Holt, Rinehart & Winston, 1965).

Pruitt, D. G., "Choice Shift in Group Discussion, An Introductory Review," *Journal of Personality and Social Psychology,* 1971, 20, 339360.

Pruitt, D. G., "Indirect Communication and the Search for Agreement in Negotiation," *Journal of Applied Social Psychology,* 1971, 1, 205–239.

Rapoport, A., and Chammah, A. M., *Prisoner's Dilemma* (Ann Arbor: University of Michigan Press, 1965).

Raven, B., and Kruglanski, A. W., "Conflict and Power," in Paul Swingle (ed.), *The Structure of Conflict* (New York: Academic Press, 1970).

Rhine, R. J., "Some Problems in Dissonance Theory Research on Information Selectivity," *Psychological Bulletin,* 1967.

Rokeach, M., and Mezei, L., "Race and Shared Belief as Factors in Social Choice," *Science,* 1966, 151, 167–172.

Roston, R. A., "Some Personality Characteristics of Male Compulsive Gamblers," *Proceedings of the American Psychological Association,* 1965.

Rotter, J. B., "Generalized Expectancies for Internal Versus External Control of Reinforcement," *Psychological Monographs,* 1966, 80, No. 1.

Rubenstein, E. A., *et al., Television and Social Behavior,* 5 vols. (Washington, D.C.: U. S. Government Printing Office, 1972).

Rule, B. G., and Fischer, D. G., "Impulsivity, Subjective Probability, Cardiac Response, and Risk-Taking: Correlates and Factors," *Personality,* 1970, 1, 251–260.

Rule, B. G., *et al.,* "The Effect of Arousal on Risk Taking, *Personality,* 1971, 2, 239–247.

Seager, C. P., "Treatment of Compulsive Gamblers Using Electrical Aversion," in I. Kusyszyn (ed.), *Studies in the Psychology of Gambling* (Toronto: York University, 1972).

Sears, D. O., and Abeles, R., "Attitudes," in P. Mussen and Rosenzweig (eds.), *Annual Review of Psychology,* 1969, 21.

Sears, D. O., and McConahay, J. B., "Racial Socialization, Comparison Levels and the Watts Riot," *Journal of Social Issues,* 1969, 26, 121–140.

Schelling, T. C., *The Strategy of Conflict* (Cambridge, Mass.: Harvard University Press, 1960).

Secord, P. F., and Backman, C. W., *Social Psychology* (New York: McGraw-Hill, 1964).

Seeman, Melvin, "On the Meaning of Alienation," *American Sociological Review,* 1959, 24, 782–791.

Sherif, M., and Hovland, C. I., *Social Judgments: Assimilation and Contrast Effects in Communication and Attitude Change* (New Haven: Yale University Press, 1961).

Sherif, M., and Sherif, C. W., *Social Psychology* (New York: Harper & Row, 1969).

Siegel, S., and Fouraker, L. E., *Bargaining and Group Decision Making* (New York: McGraw-Hill, 1960).

Siegel, S., and Goldstein, D. A., "Decision-Making Behavior in a Two-Choice Uncertain-Outcome Situation," *Journal of Experimental Psychology,* 1959, 57, 37–42.

Silverthorne, C. P., "Information Input and the Group Shift Phenomenon in Risk-Taking," *Journal of Personality and Social Psychology,* 1971, 20, 456–461.

Smith, M. B., "Attitude Change," in D. Sills (ed.), *Encyclopedia of the Social Sciences* (New York: Crowell Collier and Macmillan, 1969).

Stouffer, S. A., *et al., The American Soldier. Vol I: Adjustment During Army Life,* and *Vol. II: Combat and Its Aftermath* (Princeton, N.J.: Princeton University Press, 1949).

Swingle, Paul (ed.), *The Structure of Conflict* (New York: Academic Press, 1970).

Tec, N., *Gambling in Sweden* (Totowa, N.J.: Bedminster, 1964).

Tedeschi, J. T., "Threats and Promises," in Paul Swingle (ed.), *The Structure of Conflict* (New York: Academic Press, 1970).

Thibaut, J. W., and Kelley, H. H., *The Social Psychology of Groups,* (New York: John Wiley, 1959).

Throop, W. F., and MacDonald, A. P., Jr., "Internal-external Locus of Control: A Bibliography," *Psychological Reports,* 1971.

Toch, H., *Violent Men: An Inquiry into the Psychology of Violence* (Chicago: Aldine, 1969).

Triandis, H. C., "A Note on Rokeach's Theory of Prejudice," *Journal of Abnormal and Social Psychology,* 1961, 62, 184–186.

U.S. Army, *Psychological Operations,* Army Field Manual FM33-5, 1962.

U. S. Commission on Civil Rights, *Racism in America and How to Combat It* (Washington, D.C.: U.S. Government Printing Office).

Victor, R. G., and Krug, C. M., "Paradoxical Intention in the Treatment of Compulsive Gambling," *American Journal of Psychotherapy,* 1967, 21, 808–814.

Von Neumann, J., and Morgenstern, O., *Theory of Games and Economic Behavior* (Princeton, N.J.: Princeton University Press, 1947).

Wallach, M. A., *et al.,* "Group Influence on Individual Risk Taking," *Journal of Abnormal and Social Psychology,* 1962, 65, 75–86.

Wallach, M. A., and Kogan, N., "The Roles of Information, Discussion, and Consensus in Group Risk Taking," *Journal of Experimental Social Psychology,* 1965, 1, 1–19.

Walton, R. E., and McKersie, R. B., *A Behavioral Theory of Labor Negotiations* (New York: McGraw-Hill, 1965).

Waly, P., and Cook, S. W., "Effect of Attitude on Judgments of Plausibility," *Journal of Personality and Social Psychology,* 1965, 2, 395–402.

Weinstein, M. S., "Achievement Motivation and Risk Preference," *Journal of Personality and Social Psychology,* 1969, 13, 153–172.

White, R. K., *Nobody Wanted War* (Garden City, N.Y.: Doubleday, 1970).

Winch, R., *et al.,* "The Theory of Complementary Needs in Mate Selection: An Analytic and Descriptive Study," *American Sociological Review,* 1954, 19, 241–249.

Wrightsman, L., *et al., Cooperation and Competition: Readings on Mixed-Motive Games* (Belmont, Calif.: Brooks/Cole, 1972).

Ziller, R. C., "Individuation and Socialization," *Human Relations,* 1964, 17, 341–360.

Zimbardo, P. G., "The Human Choice: Individuation, Reason, and Order versus Deindividuation, Impulse, and Chaos," in W. J. Arnold and D. Levine (eds.), *Nebraska Symposium on Motivation* (Lincoln: University of Nebraska Press, 1969).

Zuckerman, S., *The Social Life of Monkeys and Apes* (London: Kegan Paul, 1932).

Journal for reference on Social Behavior

Journal of Personality and Social Psychology, published monthly by the American Psychological Association.

11. DEVELOPMENTAL PSYCHOLOGY

Ames, L., and Ilg, F., "The Developmental Point of View with Special Reference to the Principle of Reciprocal Neuromotor Interweaving," *Journal of Genetic Psychology,* 1964, 105, 195–209.

Ball, S., and Bogatz, G. A., *The First Year of Sesame Street: an Evaluation* (Princeton: Educational Testing Service, 1970).

Bandura, A., *Principles of Behavior Modification* (New York: Holt, Rinehart & Winston, 1969).

Becker, W. C., *et al.,* "Relations of Factors Derived from Parent-interview Ratings to Behavior Problems of Five-year-olds," *Child Development,* 1962, 33, 509–535.

Belmont, L., and Birch, H., "Lateral Dominance and Right-Left Awareness in Normal Children," *Child Development,* 1963, 34, 257–270.

Birren, J. E., *The Psychology of Aging* (Englewood Cliffs, N.J.: Prentice-Hall, 1964).

Blos, P., "The Second Individuation Process of Adolescence," *The Psycho-analytic Study of the Child,* 1967, 221, 162–186.

Bossard, J. H. S., and Ball, E. S., "Personality Roles in the Large Family," *Child Development,* 1955, 26, 71–78.

Bowlby, J., "Maternal Care and Mental Health," *Monograph* (Geneva: World Health Organization, 1951).

Bridges, K. M. B., "Emotional Development in Early Infancy," *Child Development,* 1932, 3, 324–341.

Bronfenbrenner, U., *Two Worlds of Childhood: U.S. and U.S.S.R.* (New York: Russell Sage Foundation, 1970).

Brown, J., "Differential Hand Usage in Three-Year Old Children," *Journal of Genetic Psychology,* 1962, 100, 167–175.

Bruner, J. S., *The Process of Education* (Cambridge: Harvard University Press, 1960).

Caldwell, B. M., "Usefulness of the Critical Period Hypothesis in the Study of Filiative Behavior," *Merrill-Palmer Quarterly of Behavior and Development,* 1962, 8, 229–242.

Clarke, A. D. B., and Clarke, A., "Some Recent Advances in the Study of Early Deprivation," *Child Psychology and Psychiatry,* 1960, 1, 26–36.

Cohen, A., "Hand Preference and Developmental Status in Infants," *Journal of Genetic Psychology,* 1966, 108, 337–345.

Cumming, E., and Henry, W. E., *Growing Old* (New York: Basic Books, 1961).

De Lys, Claudia, *A Treasury of American Superstitions* (New York: Philosophical Library, 1948).

Denenberg, V. H., and Rosenberg, Kin, "Nongenetic Transmission of Information," *Nature,* 1967, 216, 549–550.

Denenberg, V. H., and Whimby, A. E., "Behavior of Adult Rats is Modified by the Experiences Their Mothers Had as Infants," *Science,* 1963, 142, 1192–1193.

Dennis, W., "Creative Productivity Between the Ages of Twenty and Eighty Years," in B. L. Neugarten (ed.), *Middle Age and Aging* (Chicago: University of Chicago Press, 1968).

Dinkmeyer, D. C., *Child Development: The Emerging Self* (Englewood Cliffs, N.J.: Prentice-Hall, 1965).

Eisdorfer, C., and Lawton, M. P. (eds.), *Psychology and the Process of Aging* (Washington: American Psychological Association, 1972).

Erikson, E. H., *Childhood and Society* (New York: W. W. Norton, 1950; 2d ed. 1963).

Falkner, F., and Reaser, G. P., (eds.), *Child Health and Development: Progress 1963–1970* (Washington, D.C.: U. S. Government Printing Office, 1970).

Feshback, S., "Reality and Fantasy in Filmed Violence," in *Television and Social Behavior,* Vol. 2 (Washington, D.C.: U. S. Government Printing Office, 1972).

Foulkes, D., *et al.,* "Televised Violence and Dream Content," in *Television and Social Behavior,* Vol. 5 (Washington, D.C.: U. S. Government Printing Office, 1972).

Frank, L. K., *On the Importance of Infancy* (New York: Random House, 1966).

Freud, Sigmund, *A General Introduction to Psychoanalysis* (New York: Doubleday, 1920).

Gerbner, G., "Violence in Television Drama: Trends and Symbolic Functions," in *Television and Social Behavior,* Vol. 1 (Washington, D.C.: U. S. Government Printing Office, 1972).

Ginsburg, H., and Opper S., *Piaget's Theory of Intellectual Development: An Introduction* (Englewood Cliffs, N.J.: Prentice-Hall, 1969).

Glass, H., and Kase, N. G., *Woman's Choice* (New York: Basic Books, 1970).

Gray, Madeline, *The Normal Woman* (New York: Charles Scribner's Sons, 1967).

Harrell, R. F., *et al., The Effects of Mothers' Diet on the Intelligence of Offspring* (New York: Bureau of Publications, Teachers College, Columbia, 1955).

Heim, A., *Intelligence and Personality, Their Assessment and Relationship* (Middlesex, England: Penguin Books, 1970).

Hoffman, M. L., "Moral Development," in P. Mussen (ed.), *Carmichael's Manual of Child Psychology,* 3d ed. (New York: John Wiley, 1970).

Inhelder, B., and Piaget, J., *The Growth of Logical Thinking from Childhood Through Adolescence* (New York: Basic Books, 1958).

Jersild, A., *Child Psychology,* 6th ed. (Englewood Cliffs, N.J.: Prentice-Hall, 1968).

Joffe, J. M., "Genotype and Prenatal and Premating Stress Interact to Affect Adult Behavior in Rats," *Science,* 1956, 150, 1844–1845.

Joffe, J. M., *Prenatal Determinants of Behavior* (London: Pergamon Press, 1969).

Kagan, J., and Moss, H. A., *Birth to Maturity* (New York: John Wiley, 1962).

Kessen, W., *The Child* (New York: John Wiley, 1965).

Kessler, Jane, *Psychopathology of Childhood* (Englewood Cliffs, N.J.: Prentice-Hall, 1966).

Kohlberg, L., "The Development of Children's Orientation Toward a Moral Order: I. Sequence in the Development of Moral Thought," *Vita Humana,* 1963, 6, 11–33.

Kohlberg, L., "Development of Moral Character and Moral Ideology," in M. L. Hoffman and L. W. Hoffman (eds.), *Review of Child Development Research,* Vol. 1 (New York: Russell Sage Foundation, 1964).

Lambert, B. *et al., Adolescence, Transition from Childhood to Maturity* (Brooks/Cole, 1972).

Larson, O. N. (ed.), *Violence and Mass Media* (New York: Harper & Row, 1968).

Lefkowitz, M. M., *et al.,* "Television Violence and Child Aggression: a Follow-up Study," *Television and Social Behavior,* Vol. 3 (Washington, D.C.: U. S. Government Printing Office, 1972).

Leifer, A. D., and Roberts, D. F., "Children's Responses to Television Violence," in *Television and Social Behavior,* Vol. 2 (Washington, D.C.: U. S. Government Printing Office, 1972).

Maddi, S. R., *Personality Theories: A Comparative Analysis* (Homewood, Ill.: Dorsey Press, 1968).

Montagu, M. F. A., *Prenatal Influences* (Springfield: Charles C. Thomas, 1962).

Bibliography

Muss, Rolf, *Theories of Adolescence* (New York: Random House, 1968).

Neugarten, B. L., *et al.*, *Personality in Middle and Late Life* (New York: Atherton, 1964).

Neugarten, B. L., (ed.), *Middle Age and Aging* (Chicago: University of Chicago Press, 1968).

Olson, W. C., *Child Development*, 2d ed., (Boston: D. C. Heath, 1959).

Palmer, R., "Development of a Differential Handedness," *Psychological Bulletin*, 1964, 62, 257–272.

Paschke, R. E., *The Maternal Environment and Behavior* (doctoral dissertation, Purdue University, 1969).

Phillips, J. L., Jr., *The Origins of Intellect: Piaget's Theory* (San Francisco: W. H. Freeman, 1969).

Piaget, J., "The Stages of the Intellectual Development of the Child, *Bulletin of the Menninger Clinic*, 1962, 26, 120–145.

Riley, M. W., and Foner, A., *Aging and Society, Vol. 1: An inventory of research findings* (New York: Russell Sage Foundation, 1968).

Rubenstein, E. A., *et al.* (eds.), *Television and Social Behavior*, 5 vols. (Washington, D.C.: U. S. Government Printing Office, 1972).

Scott, J. P., "Critical Periods in Behavioral Development," *Science*, 1962, 138, 949–958.

Sears, R. R., *et al.*, *Patterns of Child Rearing* (New York: Harper & Row, 1957).

Siegel, A. E., "Film-Mediated Fantasy Aggression and Strength of Aggressive Drive," *Child Development*, 1956, 27, 365–378.

Singh, J., and Zingg, R., *Wolf-Children and Feral Man* (New York: Harper, 1942).

Skipper, J. K., and Nass, G., "Dating Behavior: A Framework for Analysis and an Illustration," *Journal of Marriage and the Family*, 1966, 28, 412–420.

Spock, B., *Baby and Child Care*, rev. ed. (New York: Pocket Books, 1968).

Stein, A. H., "Mass Media and Young Children's Development," *Yearbook of the National Society for the Study of Education*, 1972, 71, Part II, 181–202.

Stein, A. H., and Friedrich, L. K., "Television Content and Young Children's Behavior," *Television and Social Behavior*, Vol. 2 (Washington, D.C.: U. S. Government Printing Office, 1972).

Stone, L. J., and Church, J., *Childhood and Adolescence*, 2d ed. (New York: Random House, 1968).

Surgeon General's Scientific Advisory Committee on Television and Social Behavior. *Television and Growing Up: the Impact of Televised Violence* (Washington, D.C.: U. S. Government Printing Office, 1971).

Thompson, W. R., "Influence of Prenatal Material Anxiety on Emotionality in Young Rats," *Science* 1957, 125, 693–699.

Volpe, E. P., *Human Heredity and Birth Defects* (New York: Bobbs-Merrill, 1971).

Ward, S., "Effects of Television Advertising on Children and Adolescents," *Television and Social Behavior*, Vol. 4 (Washington, D.C.: U. S. Government Printing Office, 1972).

Watson, J. B., *Psychological Care of Infant and Child* (New York: W. W. Norton, 1928).

Watson, R. I., *Psychology of the Child*, 2d ed. (New York: John Wiley, 1965).

Weiner, I. B., and Elkind, D., *Child Development: A Core Approach* (New York: John Wiley, 1972).

Winter, G., and Nuss, E., *The Young Adult* (Chicago: Scott Foresman, 1969).

Wolstenholme, G. E. W., and O'Connor, M., *Foetal Autonomy*, (London: J. & A. Churchill Ltd., 1969).

Journals for reference on developmental psychology

Developmental Psychology, published bimonthly by the American Psychological Association.

Child Development, published quarterly for the Society for Research in Child Development by the University of Chicago Press.

12. MEASUREMENT

Adams, G. S., and Torgerson, T. L., *Measurement and Evaluation in Education, Psychology, and Guidance* (New York: Holt, Rinehart & Winston, 1964).

Allport, G. W., *et al.*, *Study of Values*, 3d ed. (Boston: Houghton Mifflin, 1960).

Atkinson, J. W., (ed.), *Motives in Fantasy, Action and Society* (Princeton, N.J.: Van Nostrand, 1958).

Bellak, L., *The Thematic Apperception Test and the Children's Apperception Test in Clinical Use* (New York: Grune & Stratton, 1954).

Bender, Lauretta, "A Visual Motor Gestalt Test and Its Clinical Use," *American Orthopsychiatric Association, Research Monograph*, 1938, No. 3.

Bender, Lauretta, *Instructions for the Use of the Visual Motor Gestalt Test* (New York: American Orthopsychiatric Association, 1946).

Blommers, P., and Lindquist, E. F., *Elementary Statistical Methods in Psychology and Education* (Boston: Houghton Mifflin, 1960).

Buck, J. N., "The H-T-P technique: A Quantitative and Qualitative Scoring Manual," *Journal of Clinical Psychology Monograph Supplement*, 1948, 5.

Buck, J. N., and Jolles, I., *H-T-P: House-Tree-Person Projective Technique* (Los Angeles: Western Psychological Service, 1956).

Chein, I., "An Introduction to Sampling," in Sellitz, C., *et al.*, *Research Methods in Social Relations* (New York: Holt, Rinehart & Winston, 1959).

Cleary, T. A., "Test Bias: Prediction of Grades of Negro and White Students in Integrated Colleges," *Journal of Education Measurement*, 1968, 5 (2), 115–124.

Cochran, S., *Sampling Techniques* (New York: John Wiley, 1963).

Cook, S. W., and Sellitz, C., "A Multiple Indicator Approach to Attitude Measurement," *Psychological Bulletin*, 1964, 62, 36–55.

Cronbach, L. J., *Essentials of Psychological Testing*, 3d ed. (New York: Harper & Row, 1970).

Dahlstrom, W. G., and Welsh, G. S., *An MMPI Handbook: A Guide to Use in Clinical Practice and Research* (Minneapolis: University of Minnesota Press, 1960).

Downie, N. M., *The Fundamentals of Measurement: Techniques and Practices*, 2d ed. (Fair Lawn, N.J.: Oxford University Press, 1967).

Edwards, A. L., *Techniques of Attitude Scale Construction* (New York: Appleton-Century-Crofts, 1957).

Fine, R., "A Scoring Scheme for the T.A.T. and Other Verbal Projective Techniques," *Journal of Projective Techniques*, 1955, 19, 306–309.

Fishbein, M., *Readings in Attitude Theory and Measurement* (New York: John Wiley, 1967).

Goodenough, F. L., *Measurement of Intelligence by Drawings* (Yonkers, N.Y.: World Book Co., 1926).

Hammer, E. F., "The House-Tree-Person (H-T-P) Drawings as a Projective Technique with Children," in Rabin, A. T., and Haworth, M. R. (eds.), *Projective Techniques with Children* (New York: Grune & Stratton, 1960).

Hathaway, S. R., and Meehl, P. F., *An Atlas for the Clinical Use of the Minnesota Multiphasic Personality Inventory* (Minneapolis: University of Minnesota Press, 1951).

Hays, W. L., *Statistics for Psychologists* (New York: Holt, Rinehart & Winston, 1965).

Henry, W. E., *The Analysis of Fantasy: The Thematic Apperception Technique in the Study of Personality* (New York: John Wiley, 1956).

Justman, J., "Assessing the Intelligence of Disadvantaged Children," *Education*, 1967, 87, 354–362.

Kish, L., *Survey Sampling* (New York: John Wiley, 1965).

Klopfer, B., *et al., Developments in the Rorschach Technique,* 2 vols. (New York: Harcourt Brace, 1954, 1956).

Koppitz, E. M., *The Bender Gestalt Test for Young Children* (New York: Grune & Stratton, 1964).

Lennon, R. T., *Testing and the Culturally Disadvantaged Child* (New York: Test Department, Harcourt Brace Jovanovich, 1964).

Levy, S., "Figure Drawing as a Projective Test," in Abt, L. E., and Bellak, L. (eds.), *Projective Psychology: Clinical Approaches to the Total Personality* (New York: Grove Press, 1959).

Machover, Karen, *Personality Projection in the Drawing of the Human Figure* (Springfield, Ill.: C. C. Thomas, 1949).

McNemar, Q., *Psychological Statistics* (New York: John Wiley, 1962).

Mitchell, B. C., "Predictive Validity of the Metropolitan Readiness Tests and the Murphy-Durrell Reading Readiness Analysis for White and for Negro Pupils," *Educational and Psychological Measurement,* 1967, 27, 1047–1054.

Murray, H. A., *Thematic Apperception Test Manual* (Cambridge, Mass.: Harvard University Press, 1943).

Noll, V. H., *Introduction to Educational Measurement,* 2d ed. (Boston: Houghton Mifflin, 1965).

Oppenheim, A. N., *Questionnaire Design and Attitude Measurement* (New York: Basic Books, 1966).

Pascal, G. R., and Suttell, B. J., *The Bender-Gestalt Test: Quantification and Validity for Adults* (New York: Grune & Stratton, 1951).

Peterson, J., *Early Conceptions and Tests of Intelligence* (Yonkers, N.Y.: World Book Co., 1925).

Robertson, G. L., "Innovation in the Assessment of Individual Differences: Development of the First Group Mental Ability Test," *Test Service Notebook,* No. 30 (New York: Harcourt Brace Jovanovich, 1970).

Rosenzweig, S., "An outline of Frustration Theory," in Hunt, J. McV. (ed.), *Personality and the Behavior Disorders,* Vol. I (New York: Ronald Press, 1944).

Rosenzweig, S., *Rosenzweig Picture-Frustration Study* (St. Louis, Mo.: Author, 1947).

Rosenzweig, S., *et al., The Children's Form of the Rosenzweig Picture-Frustration Study* (St. Louis, Mo.: Author, 1948).

Shneidman, E. S., *The Make a Picture Story Test* (New York: Psychological Corporation, 1949).

Stanley, J. C., and Porter, A. C., "Correlation of Scholastic Aptitude Test Score with College Grades for Negroes Versus Whites," *Journal of Educational Measurement,* 1967, 4, 199–218.

Summers, G., *Attitude Measurement* (Chicago: Rand McNally, 1970).

Thorndike, R. L., and Hagen, E. P., *Measurement and Evaluation in Psychology and Education,* 2d ed. (New York: John Wiley, 1961).

Tomkins, S. S., *et al., The Tomkins-Horn Picture Arrangement Test* (New York: Springer, 1957).

Webb, E.; Campbell, D. T.; Schwartz, R. D.; and Sechrest, L., *Unobtrusive Measures: Nonreactive Measures for the Social Sciences* (Chicago: Rand-McNally, 1966).

Wechsler, D., *The Measurement and Appraisal of Adult Intelligence,* 4th ed. (Baltimore: Williams & Wilkins, 1958).

13. ABNORMAL AND CLINICAL PSYCHOLOGY

Abey-Wickrama, I., *et al.,* "Mental Hospital Admissions and Aircraft Noise," *Lancet,* 1969, 2, 1275–1277.

Abraham, K., *Selected Papers on Psychoanalysis,* 1968.

Ackerman, N., "Toward an Integrative Therapy of the Family," *American Journal of Psychiatry,* 1958, 114, 727–733.

Ackerman, N., "Family Therapy," in S. Arieti (ed.), *American Handbook of Psychiatry* (New York: Basic Books, 1966).

Adelson, D., and Kalis, B. L. (eds.), *Community Psychology and Mental Health: Perspectives and Challenges* (Scranton, Pa.: Chandler, 1970).

Alberti, R. E., *Your Perfect Right* (Los Angeles: Impact Press, 1970).

Alcoholics Anonymous, *AA Comes of Age* (New York: Harper & Row, 1957).

Alexander, F., and Selesnick, S., *The History of Psychiatry* (New York: Harper & Row, 1966).

Allen, C., *A Textbook of Psychosexual Disorders* (London: Oxford University Press, 1962).

Almond, R., "The Therapeutic Community," *Scientific American,* 1971, 224, 34–42.

Alvarez, A., *The Savage God: A Study of Suicide* (New York: Random House, 1971).

American Medical Association, "Report on Medical Uses of Hypnosis," *Journal of the American Medical Association,* 1958, 168, 186–189.

American Medical Association, "Training in Medical Hypnosis," *Journal of the American Medical Association,* 1962, 180, 693–698.

American Psychiatric Association, *Diagnostic and Statistical Manual of Mental Disorders* (DSM-I), 1952.

American Psychiatric Association, *Diagnostic and Statistical Manual of Mental Disorders,* 2d ed. (DSM-II), 1968.

Ansbacher, H., and Rowena, R. (eds.), *The Individual Psychology of Alfred Adler* (New York: Basic Books, 1956).

Arieti, S., "Special Logic of Schizophrenia and Other Types of Autistic Thought," *Psychiatry,* 1948, 11, 325–338.

Arieti, S. (ed.), *American Handbook of Psychiatry* (New York: Basic Books, 3 vols., 1959–1966).

Arieti, S. (ed.), *The World Biennial of Psychiatry and Psychotherapy* (New York: Basic Books, 1970).

Atthowe, J. M., Jr., and Krasner, L., "The Systematic Application of Contingent Reinforcement Procedures (Token Economy) in a Large Social Setting: A Psychiatric Ward," Paper presented at the annual meeting of the American Psychological Association, 1965.

Ax, A. F., "The Physiological Differentiation Between Fear and Anger in Humans," *Psychosomatic Medicine,* 1953, 14, 433–442.

Bandura, Albert, *Principles of Behavior Modification* (New York: Holt, Rinehart & Winston, 1969).

Barker, P., *Basic Child Psychiatry* (London: Staples Press, 1971).

Bartemeir, L. H., *et al.,* "Combat Exhaustion," *Journal of Nervous and Mental Disease,* 1946, 104.

Barton, Russell, *Institutional Neurosis* (Bristol: John Wright, 1959).

Bateson, G., "Minimal Requirements for a Theory of Schizophrenia," *Archives of General Psychiatry,* 1960, 2, 477–491.

Beauvoir, Simone de, *The Second Sex* (New York: Knopf, 1957).

Beck, A. T., *Depression: Clinical, Experimental, and Theoretical Aspects* (New York: Harper & Row, 1967).

Benjamin, H., *The Transsexual Phenomenon* (New York: Julian Press, 1966).

Bennett, C. C., *et al., Community Psychology: A Report of the Boston Conference on the Education of Psychologists for Community Mental Health,* May, 1965 (Boston: Boston University Press, 1966).

Berne, E., *Group Treatment* (New York: Grove Press, 1966).

Berry, M. F., and Eisenson, John, *Speech Disorders* (New York: Appleton-Century-Crofts, 1956).

Bier, W. C. (ed.), *Problems in Addiction: Alcohol and Drug Addiction,* Pastoral Psychology Series, No. 2 (New York: Fordham University Press, 1962).

Bibliography

Birnbaum, M., "The Right to Treatment," *American Bar Association Journal*, 1960, 46, 499.

Bowlby, J., *Attachment and Loss*, Vol. 1 *Attachment* (New York: Basic Books, 1969).

Boyd, W. H., and Bolen, D. W., "The Compulsive Gambler and Spouse in Group Psychotherapy," in I. Kusyszyn (ed.), *Studies in the Psychology of Gambling* (Toronto: York University, 1972).

Bradford, L. P., et al., *T-Group Theory and the Laboratory Method* (New York: John Wiley, 1964).

Bradley, C., "Characteristics and Management of Children with Behavior Problems Associated with Brain Damage," *Pediatric Clinics of North America*, 1957.

Brady, J. V., "Ulcers in 'Executive Monkeys'," *Scientific American*, 1958, 199, 95–98, 100.

Brady, J. V., "Emotion and the Sensitivity of Psychoendocrine Systems," in D. C. Glass (ed.), *Neurophysiology and Emotion* (New York: Rockefeller University Press, 1967).

Breuer, J., and Freud, S., *Studies in Hysteria* (New York: Avon, 1966).

Brown, N. O., *Life Against Death: The Psychoanalytic Meaning of History* (Middletown, Conn.: Wesleyan University Press, 1959).

Cahn, S., *The Treatment of Alcoholism: An Evaluative Study* (New York: Oxford University Press, 1962).

Cantwell, D. P., "Psychiatric Illness in the Families of Hyperactive Children," *Archives of General Psychiatry*, 1972, 27, 414–418.

Caplan, R. B., *Psychiatry and Community in Nineteenth-Century America* (New York: Basic Books, 1969).

Cavanagh, J. R., *Fundamentals of Pastoral Counseling* (1962).

Chafetz, M. E., *Liquor: The Servant of Man* (Boston: Little, Brown, 1965).

Chafetz, M. E., and Denmore, H. W., Jr., *Alcoholism and Society* (New York: Oxford University Press, 1962).

Chess, Stella, *An Introduction to Child Psychiatry* (New York: Grune & Stratton, 1969).

Choron, J., *Suicide* (New York: Crowell Collier & Macmillan, 1972).

Chu, F., and Trotter, S., *Community Mental Health Centers* (Washington, D.C.: Center for the Study of Responsive Law, 1972).

Clausen, J. A., "Values, Norms, and the Health called 'Mental': Purposes and Feasibility of Assessment," in Sells, S. B. (ed.), *The Definition and Measurement of Mental Health* (Washington, D.C.: National Center for Health Statistics, 1968).

Clinebell, H. J., *Understanding and Counseling the Alcoholic Through Religion and Psychology* (Nashville, Tenn.: Abingdon Press, 1968).

Coleman, J. C., *Abnormal Psychology and Modern Life*, 3d ed. (Glenview, Ill.: Scott, Foresman, 1964).

Conners, C. K., and Eisenberg, L., "The Effects of Methylphenidate on Symptomology and Learning in Disturbed Children," *American Journal of Psychiatry*, 1963, 120, 1458.

Consumers Union, *Licit and Illicit Drugs* (Boston: Little, Brown, 1972).

Cook, P. E., *Introductory Readings in Community Psychology and Community Mental Health: Book of Readings* (San Francisco: Holden-Day, 1970).

Cooper, J. R., et al., *The Biochemical Basis of Neuropharmacology* (New York: Oxford University Press, 1970).

Dearborn, L. W., "Autoerotism," in A. Ellis and A. Abarbanel (eds.), *Encyclopedia of Sexual Behavior*, 2d ed. (New York: Hawthorn Books, 1967).

Dershowitz, A., "The Psychiatrists's Power in Civil Commitment: A Knife That Cuts Both Ways," *Psychology Today*, 1969.

Dohrenwend, B. P., and Dohrenwend, B. S., *Social Status and Psychological Disorder* (New York: John Wiley, 1969).

Dollard, J., and Miller, N. E., *Personality and Psychotherapy: An Analysis in Terms of Learning, Thinking and Culture* (New York: McGraw-Hill, 1950).

Dublin, L., *Suicide: A Sociological and Statistical Study* (New York: Ronald Press, 1963).

Dubos, R., "Foreword," in Williams, J. S., Jr., et al. (eds.), *Pollution: Its Impact on Mental Health* (Rockville, Md.: National Clearinghouse for Mental Health Information, 1972).

Durkheim, E., *Suicide* (1897), trans. by J. A. Spaulding and G. Simpson (Glencoe, Ill.: Free Press, 1951).

Ellis, A., and Abarbanel, A. (eds.), *Encyclopedia of Sexual Behavior*, 2d ed. (New York: Hawthorn Books, 1967).

Ellis, E., and Sagarin, E., *Nymphomania: A Study of the Oversexed Woman* (New York: McFadden-Bartel, 1965).

Ellis, N., *International Review of Research in Mental Retardation* (New York: Academic Press, 1968).

Encyclopedia of Mental Health (New York: Franklin Watts, 1963).

Erikson, E., "Growth and Crises of the Healthy Personality," *Psychological Issues*, 1959, 1, 50–100.

Eysenck, H. J., "Behavior Therapy, Spontaneous Remission, and Transference in Neurotics," *American Journal of Psychiatry*, 1963, 119, 869–871.

Farber, B., *Mental Retardation* (Boston: Houghton Mifflin, 1968).

Farberow, N. L., *Bibliography on Suicide and Suicide Prevention, 1897–1967*, PHS Publication No. 1479 (Washington, D.C.: U. S. Government Printing Office, 1969).

Faberow, N. L., and Shneidman, E. S. (eds.), *The Cry for Help* (New York: McGraw-Hill, 1961).

Faris, R. E. L., and Dunham, H. W., *Mental Disorders in Urban Areas: An Ecological Study of Schizophrenia and Other Psychoses* (Chicago: University of Chicago Press, 1965; original 1939).

Feifel, H., (ed.), *The Meaning of Death* (New York: McGraw-Hill, 1961).

Fenichel, Otto, *The Psychoanalytic Theory of Neurosis* (New York: W. W. Norton, 1945).

Freedman, A. M., and Kaplan, H. I. (eds.), *Comprehensive Textbook of Psychiatry* (Baltimore: Williams and Wilkins, 1967).

Freeman, W., and Watts, J. W., *Psychosurgery in the Treatment of Mental Disorders and Intractable Pain*, 2d ed. (Springfield, Ill.: Charles C. Thomas, 1950).

Freud, Anna, *The Ego and the Mechanisms of Defense* (London: Hogarth Press, 1937).

Freud, Sigmund, *A General Introduction to Psychoanalysis* (New York: Doubleday, 1920).

Freud, Sigmund, "Formulations Regarding the Two Principles in Mental Functioning (1911)," *Collected Papers*, Vol. IV (London: Hogarth Press, 1925).

Freud, Sigmund, *The Ego and the Id* (London: Hogarth Press, 1927).

Freud, Sigmund, "Some Psychological Consequences of the Anatomical Distinction Between the Sexes," *International Journal of Psychoanalysis*, 1927, 8, 133–297.

Freud, Sigmund, "Female Sexuality," *International Journal of Psychoanalysis*, 1932, 13, 281–297.

Freud, Sigmund, "The Psychology of Women," in *New Introductory Lectures of Psychoanalysis* (New York: W. W. Norton, 1933).

Freud, Sigmund, *The Basic Writings of Sigmund Freud*, A. A. Brill (ed.) (New York: Modern Library, 1938).

Freud, Sigmund, *Beyond the Pleasure Principle* (New York: Liveright Publishing Co., 1950; original 1920).

Freud, Sigmund, *A General Introduction to Psychoanalysis* (New York: Liveright, 1953; original 1920).

Freud, Sigmund, *The Standard Edition of the Complete Works of Sigmund Freud,* J. Strachey, (ed.), 24 vols. (London: Hogarth Press and the Institute of Psycho-Analysis, 1953-1964).

Freud, Sigmund, "Instincts and Their Vicissitudes," in E. Jones (ed.), *The Collected Papers of Sigmund Freud,* Vol. 4 (New York: Basic Books, 1959).

Freud, Sigmund, *An Outline of Psycho-Analysis* (New York: W. W. Norton, 1964).

Freud, Sigmund, *New Introductory Lectures on Psychoanalysis* (New York: W. W. Norton, 1965).

Gagnon, J. H., and Simon, W. (eds.), *Sexual Deviance,* parts III and IV (New York: Harper & Row, 1967).

Galle, O. R., *et al.,* "Population Density and Pathology: What Are the Relations for Man?" *Science,* 1972, 176, 23-30.

Gardner, E. A., *et al.,* "A Cumulative Register of Psychiatric Services in a Community," *American Journal of Public Health,* 1963, 53, 1269-1277.

Gazda, G. M., *Basic Approaches to Group Psychotherapy and Group Counseling* (Springfield, Ill.: C. C. Thomas, 1968).

Gebhard, P. H., "Fetishism and Sadomasochism," *Science and Psychoanalysis,* 1969, 5, 71-80.

Gebhard, P. H., *et al., Sex Offenders* (New York: Harper & Row, 1965).

Giesler, R., *et al., Survey of General Hospitals Admitting Psychiatric Patients* (Washington, D.C.: U. S. Public Health Service Publication 1462, 1966).

Gill, M., and Brenman, M., *Hypnosis and Related States* (New York: International Universities Press, 1959).

Glidewell, J., "Priorities of Psychologists in Community Mental Health," in G. Rosenblum, *Issues in Community Psychology and Preventive Mental Health* (New York: Behavioral Publications, 1971).

Goffman, E., *Asylums* (New York: Doubleday, 1961).

Golann, S., and Eisdorfer, C., *Handbook of Community Psychology and Mental Health* (New York: Appleton-Century-Crofts, 1973).

Goldhammer, H., and Marshall, A. W., *Psychosis and Civilization* (Glencoe, Ill.: Free Press, 1953).

Goldstein, A., *The Insanity Defense* (New Haven: Yale University Press, 1967).

Goldstein, M. J., and Palmer, J. O., *The Experience of Anxiety* (New York: Oxford University Press, 1963).

Goth, A., *Medical Pharmacology,* 6th ed. (St. Louis: Mosby, 1972).

Green, R., and Money, J. (eds.), *Transsexualism and Sex Reassignment* (Baltimore: Johns Hopkins, 1969).

Greenblatt, M., "Psychosurgery," in *Comprehensive Textbook of Psychiatry,* ed. by Freedman, A. M., and Kaplan, H. I. (Baltimore: Williams & Wilkins, 1967).

Grinker, R. R., and Spiegel, J. P., *War Neuroses* (Philadelphia: Blakiston, 1945).

Gruenberg, E. M., and Zusman, J., "The Natural History of Schizophrenia," *International Psychiatry Clinics,* 1964, 1, 699.

Gurin, G., *et al., Americans View Their Mental Health* (New York: Basic Books, 1960).

Hagnell, O., *A Prospective Study of the Incidence of Mental Disorders* (Stockholm: Bonniers, 1966).

Haley, J., "An Interactional Description of Schizophrenia," *Psychiatry,* 1959, 22, 321-332.

Hall, C. S., *A Primer of Freudian Psychology* (New York: New American Library, 1954).

Halpern, *et al., Proposal for a National Council on the Rights of the Mentally Impaired* (Washington, D.C.: Center for Law and Social Policy, 1972).

Halpern, H., *Adult Aphasia* (Indianapolis: Bobbs-Merrill, 1972).

Hammer, M., "An Analysis of Social Networks as Factors Influencing the Hospitalization of Mental Patients," Ph.D. Thesis, Columbia University, 1961.

Haywood, C., *Social-Cultural Aspects of Mental Retardation* (New York: Appleton-Century-Crofts, 1970).

Heath, *et al.,* "Effect on the Behavior in Humans with the Administration of Taraxein," *American Journal of Psychiatry,* 1957, 114, 14-24.

Hendin, David, *Death as a Fact of Life* (New York: W. W. Norton, 1973).

Hilgard, E. R., *Hypnotic Susceptibility* (New York: Harcourt Brace, 1965).

Hinsie, L. E., and Campbell, R. J., *Psychiatric Dictionary,* 4th ed. (New York: Oxford University Press, 1970).

Hollingshead, A. B., and Redlich, F. C., *Social Class and Mental Illness: A Community Study* (New York: John Wiley, 1958).

Hooker, E., "Sexual Behavior, Part 5: Homosexuality," in D. L. Sills (ed.), *International Encyclopedia of the Social Sciences* (New York: Macmillan & Free Press, 1968).

Horney, K., *New Ways in Psychoanalysis* (New York: W. W. Norton, 1939).

Howells, J. G., (ed.), *Modern Perspectives in Child Psychiatry* (Edinburgh: Oliver and Boyd, 1965).

Howells, J. G. (ed.), *Modern Perspectives in International Child Psychiatry* (Edinburgh: Oliver and Boyd, 1969).

Hume, P. B., "General Principles of Community Psychiatry," in S. Arieti (ed.), *American Handbook of Psychiatry* (New York: Basic Books, 1966).

"Interim Report of the Commission of Inquiry into the Non-medical Use of Drugs," *Information Canada* (Ottawa, 1970).

Jacobi, J., *The Psychology of C. G. Jung* (New Haven: Yale University Press, 1962).

Jahoda, M., *Current Concepts of Positive Mental Health* (New York: Basic Books, 1958).

Joint Commission on Mental Illness and Health, *Action for Mental Health* (New York: Basic Books, 1961).

Jones, Ernest, *The Life and Works of Sigmund Freud,* 3 vols. (New York: Basic Books, 1953, 1957).

Jung, C. G., *Contributions to Analytical Psychology* (London: Kegan Paul, 1928).

Kalinowsky, L. and Hoch, P. H., *Shock Treatment, Psychosurgery and Other Somatic Treatments in Psychiatry,* 2d ed. (New York: Grune & Stratton, 1952).

Kalinowsky, L. B., "The Convulsive Therapies," in *Comprehensive Textbook of Psychiatry,* Freedman, A. M., and Kaplan, H. I. (eds.) (Baltimore: Williams & Wilkins, 1967).

Kalinowsky, L. B., and Hippius, H., *Pharmacological Convulsive, and Other Somatic Treatments in Psychiatry* (New York: Grune & Stratton, 1969).

Kallmann, F. J., "Genetic Aspects of Psychoses," *The Biology of Mental Health and Disease* (New York: Harper, 1952).

Kallmann, F. J., *Heredity in Health and Mental Disorder* (New York: W. W. Norton, 1953).

Kallmann, F. J., "The Use of Genetics in Psychiatry," *Journal of Mental Science,* 1958, 104, 542-549.

Kanfer, F. H., and Phillips, J. S., *Learning Foundations of Behavior Therapy* (New York: John Wiley, 1970).

Kanner, L., "Early Infantile Autism," *Journal of Pediatrics,* 1944, 25, 211-217.

Kanner, L., *Child Psychiatry,* 4th ed. (Springfield, Ill.: C. C. Thomas, 1972); 3d ed. 1957.

Karczmer, A. G., and Eccles, J. C., *The Brain and Human Behavior* (New York: Springer, 1972).

Kardiner, A., "The Neuroses of War," *War Medicine,* 1941, 1, 219-226.

Karon, B. P., and VandenBos, G. R., "The Consequences of Psychotherapy for Schizophrenic Patients," *Psychotherapy,* 1972, 9, 111-119.

Bibliography

Katchadourian, H. A., and Lunde, D. T., *Fundamentals of Human Sexuality* (New York: Holt, Rinehart & Winston, 1972).

Katz, S., "My Twelve Hours as a Madman," *Maclean's Magazine,* Oct. 1, 1953.

Kelly, J. G., "Towards an Ecological Conception of Preventive Interventions," in D. W. Adelson and B. Kales (eds.), *Community Psychology and Mental Health* (San Francisco: Chandler, 1970).

Kesey, K., *One Flew Over the Cuckoo's Nest* (New York: Viking Press, 1962).

Kessler, Jane, *Psychopathology of Childhood* (Englewood Cliffs, N.J.: Prentice-Hall, 1966).

Kety, S. S., *et al.,* "Mental Illness in the Biological and Adoptive Families of Adopted Schizophrenics," *American Journal of Psychiatry,* 1971, 128.

Kinsey, A. C., *et al., Sexual Behavior in the Human Male* (Philadelphia: W. B. Saunders, 1948).

Kinsey, A. C., *et al., Sexual Behavior in the Human Female.* (Philadelphia: W. B. Saunders, 1953).

Kisker, G. W., *The Disorganized Personality* (New York: McGraw-Hill, 1964, 1972).

Koegler, R. E., and Brill, N. Q., *Treatment of Psychiatric Outpatients* (New York: Appleton-Century-Crofts, 1967).

Kolstoe, O., *Teaching Educable Mentally Retarded Children* (New York: Holt, Rinehart & Winston, 1970).

Kolvin, I., "Enuresis," *Proceedings of the Newcastle Colloquium on Enuresis. Clinics in Developmental Medicine* (Philadelphia: J. B. Lippincott, 1972).

Kramer, M., "Statistics of Mental Disorders in the United States," *Journal of the Royal Statistical Society,* 1969, 132, 353–407.

Kubler-Ross, E., *On Death and Dying* (New York: Macmillan, 1970).

Laing, R. D., and Esterson, A. *Sanity, Madness and the Family* (London: Tavistock, 1964).

Laufer, M. S., and Denhoff, E., "Hyperkinetic Behavior Syndrome in Children," *Journal of Pediatrics,* 1957, 50, 463–474.

Laufer, M. W., *et al.,* "Hyperkinetic Impulse Disorders in Children's Behavior Problems," *Psychosomatic Medicine,* 1957, XIX, No. 1.

Laufer, M. W., "Cerebral Dysfunction and Behavior Disorders of Adolescents," *American Journal of Orthopsychiatry,* 1962, 32, 501.

Lee, D. H. K., "The Role of Attitudes in Response to Environmental Stress," *Journal of Social Issues,* 1966, 4, 83.

Lehmann, H. E., "Epidemiology of Depressive Disorders," in Fieve, R. (ed.), *Depression in the 1970's* (New York: Excerpta Medica, 1970).

Leighton, D. C., *et al., The Character of Danger* (New York: Basic Books, 1963).

Lennard, H. L., *et al., Mystification and Drug Misuse* (San Francisco: Jossey-Bass, 1971).

Lennox, W., *Science and Seizures* (New York: Harper & Row, 1941).

LeShan, L., "An Emotional Life-History Pattern Associated with Neoplastic Disease," *Annals of the New York Academy of Sciences,* 1966, 125, 780–793.

Levine, M., and Levine, A., *A Social History of Helping Services* (New York: Appleton-Century-Crofts, 1970).

Levinson, D. J., and Gallagher, E. B., *Patienthood in the Mental Hospital* (Boston: Houghton Mifflin, 1964).

Levitt, E. E., "Sadomasochism," *Sexual Behavior,* 1971, Vol. 1, No. 6.

Levitt, E. E., "Nymphomania," *Sexual Behavior,* 1973, Vol. 3, No. 3.

Lewis, A. J., "Problems of Obsessional Illness," *Proceedings of the Royal Society of Medicine,* 1936, 29, 325.

Lewis, H. B., *Shame and Guilt in Neurosis* (New York: International Universities Press, 1971).

Liddell, H. S., "Experimental Neuroses in Animals," in J. M. Tanner (ed.), *Stress and Psychiatric Disorders* (Oxford: Blackwell Scientific Publications, 1960).

Litman, R. E., "Sigmund Freud on Suicide," in E. S. Shneidman (ed.), *Essays in Self-Destruction* (New York: Science House, 1967).

Litman, R. E., *et al.,* Investigations of Equivocal Suicide," *Journal of the American Medical Association,* 1963, 184, 924–929.

Livermore, J., *et al.,* "On the Justifications for Civil Commitment," 117 *University of Pennsylvania Law Review,* 1968, 75, 88.

Louria, D. B., "Cool Talk about Hot Drugs," *New York Times Magazine,* Aug. 6, 1972.

McClelland, D. C., *et al., The Drinking Man* (New York: Free Press, 1972).

McKinney, F., *Psychology of Personal Adjustment,* 3d ed. (New York: John Wiley, 1960).

Maliver, B. L., *The Encounter Game* (New York: Stein and Day, 1972).

Malzberg, B., *Social and Biological Aspects of Mental Disease* (Utica, N.Y.: State Hospitals Press, 1940).

Mann, M., *Marty Mann Answers Your Questions about Drinking and Alcoholism* (New York: Holt, Rinehart & Winston, 1970).

Marmor, J. (ed.), *Sexual Inversion* (New York: Basic Books, 1965).

Masserman, J. H., *Principles of Dynamic Psychiatry* (Philadelphia: W. B. Saunders, 1961).

Masserman, J. H., "The Neurotic Cat," *Psychology Today,* 1967, 1, 36–39, 56–57.

Masters, W. H., and Johnson, V. E., *Human Sexual Inadequacy* (Boston: Little, Brown, 1970).

Meehl, P., *Clinical Versus Statistical Prediction* (Minneapolis: University of Minnesota Press, 1954).

Meltzoff, Julian, and Kornreich, Melvin, *Research in Psychotherapy* (New York: Atherton, 1970).

Mendelson, W., *et al.,* "Hyperactive Children as Teenagers: A Follow-up Study," *Journal of Nervous and Mental Disorders,* 1971, 153, 273–278.

Mendlewicz, J., *et al.,* "Manic Depressive Illness: A Comparative Study of Patients with and without a Family History," *British Journal of Psychiatry,* 1972, 120, 558.

Menkes, M. M. *et al.,* "A Twenty-Five Year Follow-up Study on the Hyperkinetic Child with Minimal Brain Dysfunction," *Pediatrics,* 1967, 39, 3.

Menninger, K., *Man Against Himself* (New York: Harcourt, Brace, 1938).

Menninger, K., "Toward a Unitary Concept of Mental Illness," in *A Psychiatrist's World: The Selective Papers of Karl Menninger* (New York: Viking, 1958).

Miller, E. (ed.), *The Neuroses in War* (New York: Macmillan, 1943).

Miller, E. (ed.), *Foundations of Child Psychiatry* (Oxford: Pergamon Press, 1966).

Millichap, J. G., and Fowler, G. W., "Treatment of Minimal Brain Dysfunction Syndromes," *Pediatric Clinics of North America,* 1967, 14, 767.

Millichap, J. G., *et al.,* Hyperkinetic Behavior and Learning Disorders III, Battery of Neuropsychological Tests in Controlled Trial of Methylphenidate," *American Journal of Disabled Children,* 1968, 116, 235.

Millichap, J. G., "Drugs in Management of Hyperkinetic and Perceptually Handicapped Children," *Journal of the American Medical Association,* 1968, 206, 1527.

Minde, K., *et al.,* "The Hyperactive Child in Elementary School: A Five Year Controlled Follow-up," *Exceptional Children,* November 1971, 215–221.

Mohr, J. W., *et al.*, *Pedophilia and Exhibitionism: a Handbook* (Toronto: University of Toronto Press, 1964).

Moran, E., "Gambling as a Form of Dependence," *British Journal of Addictions*, 1970, 64, 419–428.

Moran, E., "Pathological Gambling," in I. Kusyszyn (ed.), *Studies in the Psychology of Gambling* (Toronto: York University, 1972).

Moreno, J. L. (ed.), *Psychodrama and Group Psychotherapy*. Monograph No. 18 (New York: Beacon House, 1946).

Moreno, J. L., *The Theater of Spontaneity: An Introduction to Psychodrama* (New York: Beacon House, 1947).

Moreno, J. L., "Psychodrama," in S. Arieti (ed.), *American Handbook of Psychiatry* (New York: Basic Books, 1966).

Morrison, J. R., and Steward, M. A., "A Family Study of the Hyperkinetic Child Syndrome," *Biological Psychiatry*, 1971, 3, 189–195.

Mullahy, Patrick, *Oedipus-Myth and Complex* (New York: Hermitage House, 1948).

Munroe, Ruth L., *Schools of Psychoanalytic Thought* (New York: Dryden Press, 1955).

National Association for Mental Health, *The Clergy and Mental Health.*

Neier, A., and Fabricant, N., "New York Civil Liberties Union Legislative Memorandum #1," December 1969.

Neubardt, S., *A Concept of Contraception* (New York: Trident Press, 1967).

Newbrough, J. R., "Comment on S. Lehmann's Article: Community, Psychology, and Community Psychology," *American Psychologist*, 1972, 27, 770–772.

Noyes, A. P., and Kolb, L. C., *Modern Clinical Psychiatry* (Philadelphia: W. B. Saunders, 1958).

Oates, W. E., *An Introduction to Pastoral Counseling* (Nashville, Tenn.: 1959).

Peck, D. F., and Ashcroft, J. B., "The Use of Stimulus Satiation in the Modification of Habitual Gambling," *Proceedings of the Second BEA Conference on Behaviour Modification*, Kilkenny, Ireland, 1970.

Perkins, W. H., *Speech Pathology* (St. Louis: C. V. Mosby, 1971).

Perls, F. S., *Gestalt Therapy Verbatim* (Lafayette, Calif.: Real People Press, 1968).

Pokorny, A. D., *et al.*, "Vehicular Suicides," *Life-Threatening Behavior*, 1972, 2, 105–120.

Proshansky, H. M., *et al.* (eds.), *Environment Psychology: Man and His Physical Setting* (New York: Holt, Rinehart and Winston, 1970).

Pumpian-Mindlin, E., "Nymphomania and Satyriasis," in C. W. Wahl, (ed.), *Sexual Problems: Diagnosis and Treatment in Medical Practice* (New York: Free Press, 1967).

Quay, H., and Werry, J., (eds.), *The Psychopathology of Childhood* (New York: McGraw-Hill, 1972).

Rabinovitch, R. D., *et al.*, "A Research Approach to Reading Retardation," *Publication of the Association for Nervous and Mental Diseases*, 1954, 34, 363–396.

Rachman, S., and Teasdale, J. D., "Aversion Therapy: An Appraisal," pp. 279–320 in: Franks, C. M. (ed.), *Behavior Therapy: Appraisal and Status* (New York: McGraw-Hill, 1969).

Rainer, J. D., *et al.*, (eds.), *Family and Mental Health Problems in a Deaf Population* (New York State Psychiatric Institute, 1963).

Raker, J. W., *et al.*, *Emergency Medical Care in Disasters: A Summary of Recorded Experiences*. Disaster Study No. 6, National Academy of Sciences, National Research Council, Publication No. 457, 1956.

Rech, R. H., and Moore, K. E., *An Introduction to Psychopharmacology* (New York: Raven Press, 1971).

Robinson, H., and Robinson, N., *The Mentally Retarded Child* (New York: McGraw-Hill, 1965).

Rogers, C. R., *Counseling and Psychotherapy* (New York: Grune & Stratton, 1942).

Rogers, C. R., *Client Centered Therapy* (Boston: Houghton Mifflin, 1951).

Rogers, C. R., *On Becoming a Person: A Therapist's View of Psychotherapy* (Boston: Houghton Mifflin, 1961).

Rogers, C. R., and Dymond, R. F. (eds.), *Psychotherapy and Personality Change* (Chicago: University of Chicago Press, 1954).

Rokeach, M., *The Three Christs of Ypsilanti* (New York: Vintage Books, 1967).

Rosen, E., and Gregory, I., *Abnormal Psychology* (Philadelphia: W. B. Saunders, 1965).

Rosen, H., *Hypnotherapy in Clinical Psychiatry* (New York: Julian Press, 1953).

Rothstein, J., *Mental Retardation* (New York: Holt, Rinehart & Winston, 1971).

Rutter, M. (ed.), *Infantile Autism: Concepts, Characteristics and Treatment* (Edinburgh and London: Churchill and Livingstone, 1972).

Saper, B. "What To Tell the Architect," *Community Mental Health*, 1968, 4, 17–25.

Sargent, W., and Slater, E., *An Introduction to Physical Methods of Treatment in Psychiatry* (London: E. & S. Livingston, 1963).

Satterfield, J. H., and Dawson, M. E., "Electrodermal Correlates of Hyperactivity in Children," *Psychophysiology*, 1971, 8, 191.

Satterfield, J. H., *et al.*, "EEG Aspects in the Diagnosis and Treatment of Minimal Brain Dysfunction," *Annals of the New York Academy of Sciences*, 1972.

Satterfield, J. H., "EEG Issues in Children with Minimal Brain Dysfunction," *Seminars in Psychiatry*, Jan. 1973.

Schaefer, L. C., "Frigidity," in G. D. Goldman and D. S. Milman, *Modern Woman: Her Psychology and Sexuality* (Springfield, Ill.: C. C. Thomas, 1969).

Schwab, J. J., *et al.*, "Sociocultural Aspects of Depression in Medical Inpatients," *Archives of General Psychiatry*, 1967, 17, 533–543.

Seager, C. P., "Treatment of Compulsive Gamblers Using Electrical Aversion," in I. Kusyszyn (ed.), *Studies in the Psychology of Gambling* (Toronto: York University, 1972).

Sells, S. B. (ed.), *The Definition and Measurement of Mental Health* (Washington, D.C.: National Center for Health Statistics, 1968).

Selye, H., *The Physiology and Pathology of Exposure to Stress* (Montreal: Acta, 1950).

Selye, H., "The General Adaptation Syndrome in Its Relationship to Neurology, Psychology, and Psychopathology," in Weider, A. (ed.), *Contributions Toward Medical Psychology*, Vol. 1 (New York: Ronald Press, 1953).

Selye, H., *The Stress of Life* (New York: McGraw-Hill, 1956).

Shaw, C. R., *The Psychiatric Disorders of Childhood* (New York: Appleton-Century-Crofts, 1971).

Shetty, T., "Alpha Rhythms in the Hyperkinetic Child," *Nature*, Dec. 24, 1971.

Shneidman, E. S. (ed.), *Essays in Self-Destruction* (New York: Science House, 1967).

Shneidman, E. S. (ed.), *On the Nature of Suicide* (San Francisco: Jossey-Bass, 1969).

Shneidmen, E. S., "Suicide, Lethality and the Psychological Autopsy," in E. S. Shneidmen and M. Ortego (eds.), *Aspects of Depression* (Boston: Little, Brown, 1969).

Shneidman, E. S., and Farberow, N. L. (eds.), *Clues to Suicide* (New York: McGraw-Hill, 1957).

Shneidman, E. S., and Mandelknorn, P., *How to Prevent Suicide*. Public Affairs Pamphlet No. 406, 1967.

Shneidman, E. S., *et al.*, *The Psychology of Suicide* (New York: Science House, 1970).

Slavson, S. R., *An Introduction to Group Therapy* (New York: The Commonwealth Fund, 1943).

Bibliography

Slavson, S. R., *Analytic Group Psychotherapy* (New York: Columbia University Press, 1950).

Smith, M. B., "Competence and Mental Health: Problems in Conceptualizing Human Effectiveness," in Sells, S. B. (ed.), *The Definition and Measurement of Mental Health* (Washington, D.C.: National Center for Health Statistics, 1968).

Special Issue: "The Role of Medication in the Treatment of Learning Disabilities and Related Behavior Disorders," *Journal of Learning Disabilities,* November 1971.

Spielberger, C. D., *Anxiety and Behavior* (New York: Academic Press, 1966).

Spivack, M., "Sensory Distortions in Tunnels and Corridors," *Hospital and Community Psychiatry,* Jan. 1967, 24–30.

Srole, L., *et al., Mental Health in the Metropolis: The Midtown Manhattan Study* (New York: McGraw-Hill, 1962).

Stengel, E., *Suicide and Attempted Suicide* (Baltimore: Penguin Books, 1964).

Stern, Edith, *Mental Illness: A Guide for the Family,* 5th ed. (New York: Harper & Row, 1968).

Stern, M., and Robbins, E. S., "Physical Treatment in Psychiatry," in *Traumatic Medicine and Surgery for the Attorney* (New York: Matthew Bender).

Stevens, H., and Heber, R., *Mental Retardation* (Chicago: University of Chicago Press, 1964).

Stewart, M. A., *et al.,* "The Hyperactive Child Syndrome," *American Journal of Orthopsychiatry,* 1966, 36, 861–867.

Stewart, M. A., "Hyperactive Children," *Scientific American,* 1970, 222.

Stoller, R. J., *Sex and Gender* (New York: Science House, 1968).

Strupp, H. H., *Psychotherapy and the Modification of Abnormal Behavior* (New York: McGraw-Hill, 1971).

Strupp, H. H., *et al., Patients View Their Psychotherapy* (Baltimore: Johns Hopkins, 1969).

Symonds, P. M., *The Ego and the Self* (New York: Appleton-Century-Crofts, 1951).

Szasz, T., "Psychiatry, Ethics and Criminal Law," *Columbia University Law Review,* 1958, 58, 182–198.

Szasz, T., "The Myth of Mental Illness," *American Psychologist,* 1960, 15, 113–118.

Szasz, T., *The Myth of Mental Illness* (New York: Hoeber-Harper, 1961).

Szasz, T., *Law, Liberty, and Psychiatry* (New York: Macmillan, 1963).

Szasz, T., *The Ethics of Psychoanalysis* (New York: Basic Books, 1965).

Szasz, T., *The Myth of Mental Illness* (New York: Dell, 1967).

Szasz, T., "Science and Public Policy: The Crime of Involuntary Mental Hospitalization," *Medical Opinion and Review,* 1968, 4, 24–35.

Thigpen, C. H., and Cleckley, H. M., *Three Faces of Eve* (New York: McGraw-Hill, 1957).

Thomas, A., *et al., Temperament and Behavior Disorders in Children* (New York: New York University Press, 1968).

Tolchin, G., *et al.,* "The Mental Patient and Civil Rights: Some Moral, Legal and Ethical Considerations," *Professional Psychology,* 1970, 212–216.

Tolchin, G., "Notes on the Social Functions of a Mental Hospital," Paper presented at the Eastern Psychological Association Meeting, April 1972.

Ullmann, L. P., *Institution and Outcome* (London: Pergamon Press, 1967).

Ullmann, L. P., and Krasner, L. A., *A Psychological Approach to Abnormal Behavior* (Englewood Cliffs, N.J.: Prentice-Hall, 1969).

U. S. Department of Health, Education, and Welfare, *The Facts of Life and Death* (Washington, D.C.: U. S. Government Printing Office, 1970).

Victor, R. G., and Krug, C. M., "Paradoxical Intention in the Treatment of Compulsive Gambling," *American Journal of Psychotherapy,* 1967, 21, 808–814.

Weinberg, S. K., *Incest Behavior* (New York: Citadel Press, 1955).

Weiss, G., *et al.,* "A Comparison of the Effects of Chlorpromazine, Dextroamphetamine, and Methylphenidate on the Behavior and Intellectual Functioning of the Hyperkinetic Child," *Canadian Psychiatric Association Journal,* 1971, 104, 20–25.

Weiss, G., *et al.,* "The Hyperactive Child VIII: Five year Follow-up," *Archives of General Psychiatry,* May 1971.

Weitzenhoffer, A. M., *Hypnotism: An Objective Study in Susceptibility* (New York: John Wiley, 1953).

Werry, J. S., "Studies on the Hyperactive Child: IV: An Empirical Analysis of the Minimal Brain Dysfunction Syndrome," *Archives of General Psychiatry,* July 1968, 19, 9–16.

Werry, J. S., "The Effect of Methylphenidate and Thioridazine on Classroom Behavior in a Single Subject Design," unpublished paper, University of Illinois.

West, D. J., *Homosexuality* (Chicago: Aldine, 1967).

Wheelis, A., *The Quest for Identity* (New York: W. W. Norton, 1958).

Williams, J. S., Jr., *et al.* (eds.), *Pollution: Its Impact on Mental Health* (Rockville, Md.: National Clearinghouse for Mental Health Information, 1972).

Wilner, D. M., *et al., The Housing Environment and Family Life: A Longitudinal Study of the Effects of Housing on Morbidity and Mental Health* (Baltimore: Johns Hopkins, 1962).

Wing, J. (ed.), *Early Childhood Autism* (Oxford: Pergamon Press, 1966).

Wolpe, J. *Psychotherapy by Reciprocal Inhibition* (Stanford: Stanford University Press, 1958).

Wolpe, J., and Lazarus, A. A., *Behavior Therapy Techniques: A Guide to the Treatment of Neuroses* (Oxford: Pergamon Press, 1966).

Wolpe, J., *The Practice of Behavior Therapy* (New York: Pergamon Press, 1969).

World Health Organization, *The Prevention of Suicide* (Geneva: World Health Organization, 1968).

Wright, G. N., *et al.,* (eds.), *Total Rehabilitation of Epileptics* (U. S. Department of Health, Education, and Welfare, 1962).

Zusman, J., "Development of the Social Breakdown Syndrome Concept," *The Millbank Memorial Fund Quarterly,* 1966, 44, 1, Part 2.

Journals for reference on clinical psychology

Journal of Abnormal Psychology, published bi-monthly by the American Psychological Association.

American Journal of Psychiatry, published monthly by the American Psychiatric Association.

American Journal of Orthopsychiatry, published by the American Orthopsychiatric Association.

Journal of the American Academy of Child Psychiatry, published quarterly for the American Academy of Child Psychiatry by International Universities Press.

14. OTHER FIELDS OF RESEARCH AND APPLICATION

Adelson, D., and Kalis, B. L., *Community Psychology and Mental Health: Perspectives and Challenges* (Scranton, Pa.: Chandler, 1970).

American Medical Association, "Report on Medical Uses of Hypnosis," *Journal of the American Medical Association,* 1958, 168, 186–189.

American Medical Association, "Training in Medical Hypnosis," *Journal of the American Medical Association,* 1962, 180, 693–698.

American Psychological Association, Division of Community Psychology, *Newsletter,* Dec. 1971.

Baker, C. A. (ed.), "Visual Capabilities in the Operation of Manned Space Systems," *Human Factors*, 1963, 5.

Barker, R. G. (ed.), *The Stream of Behavior* (New York: Appleton-Century-Crofts, 1963).

Barker, R. G., *Ecological Psychology* (Stanford, Calif.: Stanford University Press, 1968).

Barker, R. G., "Wanted: An Eco-Behavioral Science," In E. P. Willems & H. L. Raush (eds.), *Naturalistic Viewpoints in Psychological Research* (New York: Holt, Rinehart & Winston, 1969).

Barker, R. G., and Gump, R. V., *Big School, Small School* (Stanford: Stanford University Press, 1964).

Barker, R., and Wright, H. F., *Midwest and Its Children* (Evanston, Ill.: Row Peterson, 1955).

Bennett, C. C., *et al., Community Psychology: A Report of the Boston Conference on the Education of Psychologists for Community Mental Health*, May 1965 (Boston: Boston University Press, 1966).

Benoit, Herbert, *The Supreme Doctrine* (New York: Viking, 1959).

Bier, W. C., (ed.), *Problems in Addiction: Alcohol and Drug Addiction*, Pastoral Psychology Series, No. 2 (New York: Fordham University Press, 1962).

Birnbaum, M., "The Right to Treatment," *American Bar Association Journal*, 1960, 46, 499.

Bowman, H. A., *Marriage for Moderns*, 6th ed. (New York: McGraw-Hill, 1970).

Britt, S. H., *Consumer Behavior and the Behavioral Sciences* (New York: John Wiley, 1966).

Broadbent, D. E., and Little, E. A. J., "Effects of Noise Reduction in a Work Situation," *Occupational Psychology*, 1960, 34, 133–140.

Carter, H., and Glick, P. C., *Marriage and Divorce: A Social and Economic Study* (Cambridge, Mass.: Harvard University Press, 1970).

Cavanagh, J. R., *Fundamentals of Pastoral Counseling, (1962).*

Chapanis, A., *Man-Machine Engineering* (Belmont, Calif.: Wadsworth Publishing, 1965).

Chiles, W. D., *et al.*, "Work Schedules and Performance During Confinement," *Human Factors*, 1968, 10, 143–196.

Clinebell, H. J., *Understanding and Counseling the Alcoholic through Religion and Psychology* (Nashville, Tenn.: Abingdon Press, 1968).

Cook, P. E., *Introductory Readings in Community Psychology and Community Mental Health: Book of Readings* (San Francisco: Holden-Day, 1970).

Cronbach, L. J., *Educational Psychology*, 2d ed. (New York: Harcourt Brace).

DeCecco, J., *The Psychology of Learning and Instruction* (Englewood Cliffs, N.J.: Prentice-Hall, 1968).

De Greene, K. B. (ed.), *Systems Psychology* (New York: McGraw-Hill, 1970).

Dershowitz, A., "The Psychiatrist's Power in Civil Commitment: A Knife That Cuts Both Ways," *Psychology Today*, 1969.

Deutsch, S. (ed.), "Record-Gravity Simulation," *Human Factors*, 1969, 11.

Dubos, R., *Man Adapting* (New Haven: Yale University Press, 1965).

Ebon, M., *Prophecy in Our Time* (New York: New American Library, 1968).

Eliade, Mircea, *Yoga: Immortality and Freedom* (Princeton: Princeton University Press, 1958).

Eliot, Sir C., *Hinduism and Buddhism* (London: Arnold, 1921).

Engel, J. F., *et al., Consumer Behavior* (New York: Holt, Rinehart & Winston, 1968).

Faris, R., and Dunham, H., *Mental Disorders in Urban Areas: An Ecological Study of Schizophrenia and Other Psychoses* (Chicago: University of Chicago Press, 1965; original 1939).

Gilbreth, F. B., and Gilbreth, L. M., *Applied Motion Study* (New York: Sturgis and Walter, 1917).

Glidewell, J., "Priorities of Psychologists in Community Mental Health," in G. Rosenblum, *Issues in Community Psychology and Preventive Mental Health* (New York: Behavioral Publications, 1971).

Golann, S., and Eisdorfer, C., *Handbook of Community Psychology and Mental Health* (New York: Appleton-Century-Crofts, 1973).

Govinda, Lama, *The Foundations of Tibetan Mysticism* (New York: E. P. Dutton, 1960).

Gard, B., "Some Biological Effects of the Laying on of Hands," *Journal of the American Society for Psychical Research*, 1965, 59, 95–127.

Gump, P. V., and Kounin, J. S., "Issues Raised by Ecological and Classical Research Efforts," *Merrill-Palmer Quarterly*, 1960, 6, 145–152.

Gump, P. V., *et al.*, "The Behavior of the Same Child in Different Milieus," in R. G. Barker (ed.) *The Stream of Behavior* (New York: Appleton-Century-Crofts, 1963).

Gurney, E., *et al., Phantasms of the Living* (London: Trubner, 1886).

Hart, H., *The Enigma of Survival* (Springfield, Ill.: Thomas, 1959).

Hilgard, E. F., *Hypnotic Susceptibility* (New York: Harcourt, Brace, 1965).

Honorton, C., *et al.*, "Feedback Augmented EEG Alpha, Shifts in Subjective State, and ESP Card-guessing Performance," *Journal of the American Society for Psychical Research*, 1971, 65, 308–323.

Humphreys, Christmas, *The Way of Action* (Baltimore: Penguin Books, 1971).

Iscoe, I., and Spielberger, C. (eds.), *Community Psychology: Perspectives in Training and Research* (New York: Appleton-Century-Crofts, 1970).

Jerison, H. J., "Effects of Noise on Human Performance," *Journal of Applied Psychology*, 1959, 43, 96–101.

Johnson, G. O., *Education for the Slow Learner* (Englewood Cliffs, N.J.: Prentice-Hall, 1963).

Kapleau, Philip, *The Three Pillars of Zen* (Boston: Beacon, 1965).

Karnes, E. W., *et al.*, "Recreational Preferences in Potential Space Crew Populations," *Human Factors*, 1971, 13, 51–58.

Kassarjian, H. H., and Robertson, T. S., *Perspectives in Consumer Behavior* (Chicago: Scott, Foresman, 1968).

Kelly, J. G., "Toward an Ecological Conception of Preventive Interventions," in D. E. Adelson and B. Kales (eds.), *Community Psychology and Mental Health* (San Francisco: Chandler, 1970).

Kitagawa, J., *Religions of the East* (Philadelphia: Westminster, 1960).

Klausmier, H. J., and Ripple, R. E., *Learning and Human Abilities*, 2d ed. (New York: Harper & Row, 1971).

Kohn, J., and Kursten, J., *Unwillingly to School* (New York: Macmillan, 1964).

Lange, P. E., (ed.), *Programmed Instruction*, National Society for the Study of Education, 66th Yearbook, Part 2 (Chicago, 1967).

McDonald, F. J., *Educational Psychology*, 2d ed. (Belmont, Calif.: Wadsworth, 1965).

McMahan, E., "An Experiment in Pure Telepathy," *Journal of Para-Psychology*, 1946, 10, 273–288.

McNeal, James U., *Dimensions of Consumer Behavior*, 2d ed. (New York: Appleton-Century-Crofts, 1969).

Miura, I., and Sasaki, R. F., *The Zen Koan* (New York: Harcourt Brace, 1965).

Moore, C. A., *The Japanese Mind,* (Honolulu: East-West Center Press, University of Hawaii Press, 1967).

Morgan, C. T., *et al., Human Engineering Guide to Equipment Design* (New York: McGraw-Hill, 1963).

Murphy, G., *Challenge of Psychical Research* (New York: Harper, 1961).

Murti, T. R. V., *The Central Philosophy of Buddhism* (New York: Macmillan, 1955).

National Association for Mental Health, *The Clergy and Mental Health*.

Oates, W. E., *An Introduction to Pastoral Counseling* (Nashville, Tenn.: Broadman, 1959).

Owen, A. R. G., *Can We Explain the Poltergeist?* (New York: Garrett, 1964).

Palmer, J., "Scoring in ESP Tests as a Function of Belief in ESP," *Journal of the American Society for Psychical Research,* 1971, 65, 373–408.

Pratt, J. G., "The Case for Psychokinesis," *Journal of Parapsychology,* 1960, 24, 171–188.

Pratt, J. G., "On the Evaluation of Verbal Material in Parapsychology," *Parapsychological Monographs,* No. 10, 1969.

Proshansky, H. M., *et al.,* (eds.), *Environmental Psychology: Man and His Physical Setting* (New York: Holt, Rinehart & Winston, 1970).

Rabinovitch, R. D., *et al.,* "A Research Approach to Reading Retardation," *Publication of the Association for Nervous and Mental Diseases,* 1954, 34, 363–396.

Radhakrishnan, Sarvepalli, and Moore, C.A. (eds.), *Indian Philosophy* (Princeton: Princeton University Press, 1957).

Ramsey, H. R., "Human Factors and Artificial Gravity: A Review.," *Human Factors,* 1971, 13, 533–542.

Rao, K. R., *Experimental Parapsychology* (Springfield, Ill.: C. C. Thomas, 1957).

Rao, K. R., "The Bidirectionality of PSI," *Journal of Parapsychology,* 1965, 29, 230–250.

Raush, H. L., *et al.,* "The Interpersonal Behavior of Children in Residential Treatment," *Journal of Abnormal and Social Psychology,* 1959, 58, 9–27.

Raush, H. L., "Naturalistic Method and the Clinical Approach," in E. P. Willems and H. L. Raush (eds.), *Naturalistic Viewpoints in Psychological Research* (New York: Holt, Rinehart & Winston, 1969).

Reger, R., *et al., Special Education: Children with Learning Problems* (New York: Oxford University Press, 1968).

Rhine, L. E., *ESP in Life and Lab* (New York: Macmillan, 1967).

Rhine, L. E., *Mind over Matter: The Story of PK Research* (New York: Macmillan, 1970).

Rhine, J. B., & Pratt, J. G., *Parapsychology* (Springfield, Ill.: C. C. Thomas, 1957).

Rhodes, W. C., "A Community Participation Analysis of Emotional Disturbance," *Exceptional Children,* 1970, 36, 309–314.

Rice, G. E., and Townsend, J., "Agent-Percipient Relationship and GESP Performance," *Journal of Parapsychology,* 1962, 26, 211–217.

Roe, A., *The Making of a Scientist* (New York: Dodd, Mead, 1952).

Roe, A., *The Psychology of Occupations* (New York: John Wiley, 1956).

Rogers, C. R., *Becoming Partners: Marriage and Its Alternatives* (New York: Delacorte, 1972).

Rosen, H., *Hypnotherapy in Clinical Psychiatry* (New York: Julian Press, 1953).

Sangharakshita, *The Three Jewels* (Garden City, N.Y.: Doubleday Anchor, 1970).

Schmeidler, G. R., "Evidence for Two Kinds of Telepathy," *International Journal of Parapsychology,* 1961, 3, 5–48.

Schmeidler, G. R., *Extrasensory Perception* (Chicago: Aldine-Atherton, 1969).

Schmeidler, G. R., "Mood and Attitude on a Pretest as Predictors of Retest ESP Performance," *Journal of the American Society for Psychical Research,* 1971, 65, 324–335.

Schmeidler, G. R., "PK Changes in Recordings of Temperature," *Proceedings of the Parapsychological Association,* 1972.

Schmidt, H., "Clairvoyance Test with a Machine," *Journal of Parapsychology,* 1969, 33, 300–307.

Schulzinger, M. S., "Accident Syndrome." *Archives of Industrial Hygiene and Occupational Medicine,* 1954, 10, 426–433.

Sells, S. B., "Ecology and The Science of Psychology," *Multivariant Behavioral Research,* 1966, 1, 131–143.

Sidgwick, Mrs. Henry, "An Examination of Book Tests Obtained in Sittings With Mrs. Leonard," *Proceedings of the Society for Psychical Research,* 1921, 31, 241–400.

Simons, J. C., "An Introduction to Surface-Free Behavior," *Ergonomics,* 1964, 7, 23–36.

Sommer, R., "Small Group Ecology," *Psychological Bulletin,* 1967, 67, 145–152.

Srole, L., *et al., Mental Health in the Metropolis: The Midtown Manhattan Study* (New York: McGraw-Hill, 1962).

Suzuki, D., *An Introduction to Zen Buddhism* (New York: Harper & Row, 1949).

Szasz, T., *Law, Liberty and Psychiatry* (New York: Macmillan, 1963).

Task Force on the Practice of Psychology in Industry, "Effective Practice of Psychology in Industry," *American Psychologist,* 1917, 26, 974–991.

Taylor, F. W., *The Principles of Scientific Management* (New York: Harper, 1911).

Theory and Practice of the Mandala (London: Rider, 1961).

Thomas, A., *et al., Temperament and Behavior Disorders in Children* (New York: New York University Press, 1968).

Thorndike, R. L., and Hagen E., *Ten Thousand Careers* (New York: John Wiley, 1959).

Thouless, R. H., *From Anecdote to Experiment in Psychical Research* (London: Routledge & Kegan Paul, 1971).

Trickett, E. J., *et al., The Social Environment of the High School: Guidelines for Individual Change and Organizational Redevelopment,* Unpublished Paper, 1970.

Trickett, E. J., and Todd, D. M., "The High School Culture: An Ecological Perspective," *Theory into Practice 11* (1), 1972, 28–37.

Tyrrell, G. N. M., *Apparitions* (London: Duckworth, 1953).

Voas, R. B., "A Description of the Astronaut's Task in Project Mercury," *Human Factors,* 1961, 3, 149–165.

Walkins, G. K., and Watkins, A. M., "Resuscitation of Anesthetized Mice," *Journal of Parapsychology,* 1971, 35, 257–272.

Weitzenhoffer, A. M., *Hypnotism: An Objective Study in Susceptibility* (New York: John Wiley, 1953).

Willems, E. P., "Planning a Rationale for Naturalistic Research," in E. P. Willems and H. L. Raush (eds.), *Naturalistic Viewpoint in Psychological Research* (New York: Holt, Rinehart & Winston, 1969).

Willems, E. P., and Raush, H. L., *Naturalistic Viewpoints in Psychological Research* (New York: Holt, Rinehart & Winston, 1969).

Work in America: Report of a Special Task Force to the Secretary of Health, Education, and Welfare (Cambridge, Mass.: MIT Press, 1972).

Zimmer, Heinrich, *Philosophies of India* (New York: Bolingen, 1951).

3. Louise Van Der Meid; Van Bucher, Courtesy of Wagner College, Dept. of Psychology/Photo Researchers, Inc.
4. The Bettmann Archive
6. Donald Wright Patterson, Jr.; Stephen J. Potter/Stock, Boston
7. Ian Cleghorn
8. B. B. Vidibor
9. Stephanie Jungmann
10. Magnum Photos; Ann Zane Shanks
11. Patricia Hollander Gross/Stock, Boston; American Psychological Association
13. "From THE PSYCHOLOGY OF CONSCIOUSNESS by Robert E. Ornstein. W. H. Freeman and Company. Copyright © 1972."
15. American Psychological Association, FPG Photographs
16. Collection, The Museum of Modern Art, New York
18. S. E. Asch
23. Allan Grant
26. Dept. of Psychology, Stanford University; Theodore Barber
27. Brown Brothers
29. University of Wisconsin
30. The Bettmann Archive
32. The Bettmann Archive; Donald Wright Patterson, Jr./Stock, Boston; Harvard University
38. Ted Polumbaum; Culver Pictures
39. Owen Franken/Stock, Boston (top and center); The Bettmann Archive
40. Brown Brothers; Raymond B. Cattell, University of Illinois
42. The Bettmann Archive
43. Anne Zane Shanks
44. Michael Heron/Monkmeyer Press Photo Service; Daniel S. Brody/Stock, Boston; Stock, Boston
45. James J. Shields, Jr.; Allan Grant
46. Ivan Massar/Black Star; Dept. of Pathology, Charleston Area Medical Center, Peter P. Ladewig, M.D.
47. David B. Eisendrath, Jr.
48. Dianne Smith
52. Magnum Photos
53. Olin Pettingill, Jr. from National Audubon Society
56. Dianne Smith
57. Monkmeyer Press Photo Service; The Bettmann Archive
61. George Zimbel/Monkmeyer Press Photo Service
63. The Bettmann Archive
64. Magnum Photos
65. The New York Times
69. The Bettmann Archive
71. Pictorial Parade
72. The Bettmann Archive
73. Photo Researchers, Inc.; Monkmeyer Press Photo Service
74. Michael Weisbrot/Black Star
76. Mimi Forsyth/Monkmeyer Press Photo Service
78. Rogers/Monkmeyer Press Photo Service
80. Black Star
81. Van Bucher, Courtesy of NYU Research Center for Mental Health/Photo Researchers, Inc.

83. Bill Stanton/Magnum Photos
85. Ian Berry
87. NASA
88. Clemens Kalischer
90. The Bettmann Archive
91. Thomas McAvoy, Life Magazine 1972, Time Inc.
92. Charles River Breeding Laboratories
93. Van Bucher, Courtesy of University of Florida Clinical Psychology; Sponholz/Monkmeyer Press Photo Service; Hugh Rogers/Monkmeyer Press Photo Service
94. Van Bucher, Stanford University Medical Center/Photo Researchers, Inc.
95. Van Bucher, Stanford University Medical Center/Photo Researchers, Inc.
96. J. B. Rhine; H. J. Eysenck
97. The Bettmann Archive
98. Leon Festinger, New School for Social Research
101. Dr. N. Gidal/Black Star
102. Pictorial Parade
104. The Bettmann Archive; Elliott Erwitt/Magnum Photos
105. Jim Cron/Monkmeyer Press Photo Service; Inge Morath/Magnum Photos
109. Brown Brothers
111. Dianne Smith
112. Clark University
114. The Bettmann Archive
116. Culver Pictures
120. The Bettmann Archive
121. PARIS MATCH/Pictorial Parade
124. Lafayette Instrument Co.
125. Dianne Smith
126. Nina Leen, Life Magazine, Time, Inc.
128. University Extension, University of Wisconsin
129. Mary Alice McAlpin
132. Hugh Rogers/Monkmeyer Press Photo Service
135. Russ Kinne/Photo Researchers, Inc.
138. Harvard University; The Bettmann Archive
139. Patrick Taylor, Saturday Evening Post; Dr. Georg Gerster/Black Star
140. University of Michigan; University of Chicago
141. Harvard University
142. Culver Pictures; The Bettmann Archive
147. MIT
149. The Bettmann Archive
150. University of Michigan
154. Sponholz/Monkmeyer Press Photo Service
156. Brown Brothers; Ken Heyman
161. Ralph Gerbrands Company; Culver Pictures
163. The Bettmann Archive
165. Stanton/Magnum Photos
166. William Carter 1972/Photo Researchers, Inc.; Chris Maynard/Magnum Photos
169. Culver Pictures
170. Elliott Erwitt/Magnum Photos
172. Dickey Chapelle/Nancy Palmer Photo Agency; Eugene H. Kone/Rockefeller University
173. Bettye Lane/Photo Researchers, Inc.
174. J. L. Moreno
175. University of Wisconsin; Culver Pictures
176. Brown Brothers

179. Dr. E. R. Lewis/University of California
180. University of Michigan; Mimi Forsyth/Monkmeyer Press Photo Service
182. Museum of Modern Art, Film Stills Archive
183. University of Michigan
187. University of Illinois
188. Guy Gillette/Photo Researchers, Inc.
189. Dianne Smith
193. Culver Pictures, Inc.
195. Montreal Neurological Institute
202. The Bettmann Archive, Inc.
204. Yves DeBraine/Black Star
205. Hays/Monkmeyer; Tania D'Avignon; Hugh Rogers/Monkmeyer Photo Press Service
206. J. B. Rhine
207. Steve Eagle/Nancy Palmer Photo Agency
211. George Zimbel/Photo Researchers, Inc.
213. Clark University
214. J. B. Rhine
231. Bill Stanton/Magnum Photos
235. Lafayette Instrument Company
236. Robert J. Smith/Black Star
237. J. B. Rhine
238. Center for Studies of the Person, La Jolla; Marion Faller/Monkmeyer Press Photo Service
239. Van Bucher/Photo Researchers, Inc.
240. Culver Pictures
241. Columbia University
246. Pallace Inc. (top left); Ralph Gerbrands (top center and top right); Tech Serv, Inc. (bottom center and bottom left)
247. Pictorial Parade
253. The Bettmann Archive
255. The Pennsylvania State University; Raimondo Borea ASMP/Photo Researchers, Inc.
256. Hugh Rogers/Monkmeyer Press Photo Service
257. The New York Times
258. Van Bucher, Courtesy of University of Florida Dept. of Clinical Psychology/Photo Researchers, Inc.
263. NASA; Van Bucher, Courtesy of University of Florida Dept. of Clinical Psychology
268. Maude Dorr/Photo Researchers, Inc.; Jerry Irwin
270. Nancy Hays/Monkmeyer Press Photo Service
274. Carl Byoir & Associates, Inc.
276. Van Bucher 1971/Photo Researchers, Inc.; Teachers College, Columbia University
278. Brown Brothers
280. Lafayette Instrument Co.
281. Russ Kinne/Photo Researchers, Inc.
283. Monkmeyer Press Photo Service
284. Lafayette Instrument Company; Johns Hopkins University
286. Brown Brothers
287. Joseph Wolpe, Temple University; Columbia University
288. The Bettmann Archive
289. Nancy Hays/Monkmeyer Press Photo Service

Contributing Artists: Marion Needham Krupp of Craven and Evans Creative Graphics; Craven and Evans Creative Graphics Studio; Louise Emmons Merriman; Rae Avena; and Nathalie VanBuren

Psychology
Encyclopedia Staff

Consulting Editor	**Loring Batten**
Editor	**Anne Storz**
Assistant Publisher	**Gayle Johnson**
Designer	**Louise Emmons Merriman**
Photo Researcher	**Dianne Smith**
Production Supervisor	**Carol Dudley**

This book was set in Optima on the Fototronic CRT by Rocappi/Lehigh, Pennsauken, New Jersey.

The text was printed in web offset lithography and bound by Kingsport Press, Inc., Kingsport, Tennessee.

Text paper is Finch Title '94,' furnished by Pratt Paper Company, Boston, Massachusetts.

The cover material is Lexotone, furnished by The Holliston Mills, Inc., Norwood, Massachusetts.

Covers were printed in offset lithography by The Lehigh Press/Lithographers, Pennsauken, New Jersey.